Redefining the Roles of Educators and Students in the AI Era

Harish Chandra Chandan
https://orcid.org/0000-0003-1035-426X
Independent Researcher, USA

Supriya Srivastava
https://orcid.org/0000-0002-5440-4364
Shoolini University, India

IGI Global
Scientific Publishing
Publishing Tomorrow's Research Today

Vice President of Editorial Melissa Wagner
Director of Acquisitions Mikaela Felty
Director of Book Development Jocelynn Hessler
Production Manager Mike Brehm
Cover Design Jose Rosado

Published in the United States of America by
IGI Global Scientific Publishing
701 East Chocolate Avenue
Hershey, PA, 17033, USA
Tel: 717-533-8845 | Fax: 717-533-7115
Website: https://www.igi-global.com E-mail: cust@igi-global.com

Library of Congress Cataloging-in-Publication Data

LCCN: 2026002157 (CIP Data Pending)
ISBN13: 9798337380278
Isbn13Softcover: 9798337380285
EISBN13: 9798337380292
British Cataloguing in Publication Data
A Cataloguing in Publication record for this book is available from the British Library.

Table of Contents

Detailed Table of Contents

prepare learners for future work environments. Ultimately, it argues for responsible, human-centered AI integration to ensure that technological advancement aligns with the core values of education.

This chapter considers the impact of Artificial Intelligence on teachers' and students' roles within Cambodia's higher education system and makes the case for pedagogy-led, ethics-first integration of AI tools within the education system. It posits that educators will need to shift from being content repositories to becoming learning architects and facilitators. Students will also need to shift from being passive consumers of AI tools to being active collaborators who use and engage with AI tools responsibly and reflectively. This chapter makes the case for institutions to incorporate ethical, AI education, and digital equity frameworks to balance and align with available national policies to ensure the sustainable use of AI. This will help ensure that system strengthen the human capacity for self-governance and cultural ingenuity in the presence of AI toward operationalization the human judgment first, AI second notion to foster responsible innovation.

This study examines how generative artificial intelligence (AI) reshapes the process of becoming a mathematics teacher through a reflective autoethnographic lens. Drawing on personal journals, field notes, and memory-based vignettes from classroom observations and teaching assistantship experiences in a public high school in the southern Philippines, the study explores how encounters with AI-mediated student learning transformed my emerging professional identity. Thematic analysis revealed three interrelated moments of sense-making: disruption, adaptation, and redefinition. Disruption captures the pedagogical and emotional tensions arising from students' use of AI tools. Adaptation reflects reframing AI as a collaborative pedagogical resource, while redefinition signifies a deeper reconceptualization of mathematics teaching as a human, ethical, and relational practice. Rather than positioning AI as a threat, the findings highlight teaching as an evolving process of humanization in algorithmically mediated classrooms.

This study explored how science pre-service teachers use AI tools during practice teaching. The result of the survey and interview with 32 science pre-service teachers showed AI tools are used in lesson planning, understanding content, creating instructional materials, and constructing assessments. Popular and useful AI tools include ChatGPT, Cici, Quillbot, Grammarly, and Gemini because of their diverse capabilities. The findings reflect a growing recognition of AI as a valuable teaching aid that enhances efficiency, content delivery, and teacher confidence. However, the findings highlight the imperative for teacher education programs to adapt to the emerging significance of AI technology as a valuable tool in instructional practice.

The relationships between teachers and students are essential to quality education. As A.I. is more and more woven into educational practice, these relationships are being configured in ways that go beyond efficiency of instruction. Examine how AI-mediated educational environments influence the trust, dialogue, and human bonding targets of teacher-student relationships in the AI era. Through the lens of relational and ethical theories of education, AI is conceptualized as a sociotechnical mediator rather than a neutral/moral agent. The examination illustrates that algorithmic authority can destroy relational trust while the simulated interaction obscures the ethical grounding of pedagogical dialogue and over-automation threatens the loss of emotional presence and care. In response, the research forwards a human-centered relational framework that situates AI as an augmentative aid supporting rather than supplanting human judgment, dialogic engagement, and human bonding, and outlines implications for practice, teacher education, and policy.

Artificial intelligence (AI) has become an argumentative concern in educational contexts. This phenomenon offers personalization, adaptive tutoring, and real-time feedback for learners. However, its widespread use has triggered deep ethical and privacy concerns. This chapter reports these concerns by tracing how AI reshapes pedagogy, governance, and integrity in education. Taking the stance of community-wide ethical frameworks (Holmes et al., 2022) and bibliometric mappings of philosophical and practical principles of Yu & Yu (2023), it situates AI ethics within deontological, utilitarian, and virtue-ethical orientations that emphasize transparency, fairness, accountability, and non-maleficence. Particular attention is given to privacy as a pedagogical and policy issue. The datafication of learning, surveillance-based analytics, and the opacity of commercial EdTech infrastructures challenge both institutional trust and learners' autonomy (Ryan et al., 2021; Kousa & Niemi, 2023). In response, the chapter advances the notion of privacy literacy, the capacity of teachers and students to understand, question, and ethically manage data practices embedded in AI-mediated learning (Neff et al., 2024; Aljabr & Al-Ahdal, 2024). Parallel to privacy risks, the expansion of generative systems such as ChatGPT has destabilized conventional understandings of authorship and academic honesty. Emerging concepts like AI-giarism expose new grey zones between assistance and misconduct (Cotton et al., 2023; Chan, 2025; Goddiksen et al., 2024). The chapter

Preface

The rapid advancement of artificial intelligence (AI) is transforming nearly every domain of human activity, and education stands at the forefront of this profound shift. Once defined by structured classrooms, standardized curricula, and teacher-centered instruction, education is now evolving into a dynamic, data-informed, and highly personalized ecosystem. In this new landscape, the roles of educators and students are being fundamentally redefined, not replaced, but reimagined.

This volume, *Redefining the Roles of Educators and Students in the AI Era*, brings together diverse scholarly perspectives that examine how human intelligence and artificial intelligence can coexist in meaningful, ethical, and transformative ways. Rather than positioning AI as a disruptive force that diminishes human agency, the chapters in this book collectively argue for a collaborative paradigm, one in which AI augments human potential while educators and learners retain central roles as decision-makers, designers, and ethical agents.

A recurring theme throughout this work is the shift from transmission-based education to design-oriented and relationship-centered learning. Educators are increasingly called upon to act as facilitators, mentors, learning architects, and ethical guides, while students are emerging as active participants, critical thinkers, and co-creators of knowledge. At the same time, this transformation brings complex challenges, including concerns related to data privacy, algorithmic bias, digital inequality, and the erosion of human connection in technologically mediated environments.

This book addresses these opportunities and tensions by integrating theoretical insights, empirical studies, reflective narratives, and global perspectives. It emphasizes that the successful integration of AI in education depends not only on technological innovation but also on pedagogical wisdom, ethical responsibility, and a sustained commitment to human-centered values.

By exploring the evolving identities of teachers and learners, this volume aims to contribute to ongoing conversations about the future of education and to provide educators, researchers, policymakers, and practitioners with a comprehensive understanding of how to navigate and shape AI-enhanced learning environments.

CHAPTER OVERVIEW

Chapter 1 introduces the concept of human–AI collaboration in education, highlighting how AI serves as an enabling partner rather than a replacement for educators. It explores the transformation of teachers into facilitators and ethical stewards while addressing key challenges such as bias, privacy, and governance.

Chapter 2 examines the AI-enabled classroom as a space of pedagogical innovation. It discusses how AI enhances personalized learning, improves institutional efficiency, and supports inclusive education, while also raising critical ethical considerations.

Chapter 3 provides a contextual perspective from Cambodia, emphasizing the importance of AI literacy, ethical integration, and culturally grounded pedagogy. It advocates for a "human judgment first, AI second" approach in educational systems.

Chapter 4 offers a reflective autoethnographic account of becoming a mathematics teacher in the age of AI. It traces a journey of disruption, adaptation, and redefinition, ultimately framing teaching as a deeply human and relational practice.

Chapter 5 explores how pre-service science teachers use AI tools in practice teaching. It highlights the growing reliance on AI for lesson planning, content understanding, and assessment design, while underscoring the need for teacher education reform.

Chapter 6 reconceptualizes pre-service teachers as learning experience designers. It outlines essential competencies required in AI-enhanced classrooms, including critical evaluation of AI outputs and the creation of supportive learning environments.

Chapter 7 further elaborates on the evolving identity of educators as learning architects, ethical guides, and data-driven mentors. It emphasizes the increasing importance of ethical responsibility alongside technological proficiency.

Chapter 8 shifts focus to students, positioning them as "prompt engineers." It explores how learners develop precision, creativity, and metacognitive awareness when interacting with AI systems, reframing learning as an active and reflective process.

Chapter 9 provides a sociological analysis of how AI reshapes student identity, learning practices, and inequality. It examines issues such as digital capital and hybrid cognition, particularly in the context of the Global South.

Chapter 10 centers on teacher–student relationships in AI-mediated environments. It highlights the importance of trust, dialogue, and emotional connection, while warning against the risks of over-automation and diminished human presence.

Chapter 11 addresses ethical and privacy concerns in AI-mediated education, advocating for transparency, accountability, and privacy literacy as essential components of responsible AI integration.

Chapter 12 expands on ethical frameworks and governance mechanisms, offering strategies for balancing innovation with equity, human agency, and institutional responsibility.

Chapter 13 further examines ethical and privacy challenges, with attention to the evolving role of educational technology and policy-driven developments in AI adoption.

Chapter 14 concludes the volume by synthesizing key themes and exploring practical applications of AI in teaching and learning. It reflects on future directions while reaffirming the importance of preserving human-centered educational values.

Harish C. Chandan
Independent Researcher, USA

Supriya Srivastav
Shoolini University, India

Chapter 1
Human–AI Collaboration in Education:
Evolving Roles of Educators and Learners

Amrik Singh
http://orcid.org/0000-0003-3598-8787
Lovely Professional University, India

ABSTRACT

Human–AI collaboration in education marks a significant paradigm shift in how teaching, learning, and knowledge creation are designed and experienced. Rather than replacing educators or diminishing human agency, artificial intelligence increasingly functions as an enabling partner that augments human capabilities. This collaboration reshapes the traditional roles of educators from information transmitters to learning designers, facilitators, mentors, and ethical stewards who guide the responsible use of AI-driven tools. AI applications such as adaptive learning platforms, learning analytics, intelligent tutoring systems, and generative technologies enable customized feedback, inclusive learning environments, and competency-based progression. However, the effectiveness of human–AI collaboration depends not merely on technological sophistication but on thoughtful pedagogical integration grounded in equity, transparency, and academic integrity. Critical challenges including algorithmic bias, data privacy, digital divides, and overreliance on automation, necessitate robust governance.

DOI: 10.4018/979-8-3373-8027-8.ch001

1. INTRODUCTION

The high-speed development of Artificial Intelligence (AI) is changing societies, economies, and institutions worldwide, and education is at the frontier of this change. Since intelligent tutoring software and adaptive learning environment became a reality, and automated assessment instruments, learning analytics, and generative AI applications have become a part of modern educational ecosystems (Alam & Mohanty, 2023). Schools of all levels are becoming more and more open to AI-based solutions to enhance efficiency, personalize learning, and address the increasing diversity of the needs of learners. Nonetheless, the greatest change can be found not in the substitution of human actors, but in the beginning of the human-AI collaboration the synergistic partnership between educators and learners and intelligent systems to improve pedagogy, education, and the development of knowledge.

Human-AI-collaboration

Human-AI-collaboration in education is a serious paradigm shift of considering technology as a passive teaching tool to active cognitive partner, AI. Contrasting the previous technologies of education that served only content delivery purposes or administrative ones, AI systems now perform more complicated tasks like identifying learning gaps, providing specific feedback, simulating real-life situations, or decision support (Agboola & Yassin, 2025; Suhag & Singh, 2026). The given evolution casts crucial concerns regarding the transforming character of pedagogy, the balance of power between humans and machines and the redesigning of positions in educational settings. With increased ability and autonomy of AI systems, there is a need to renegotiate the distribution of responsibility, agency and expertise between educators and learners. The issue of AI implementation is the threat to the long-held belief of educators as the primary source of knowledge. As AI is able to offer immediate explanations, personalized materials, and automated testing, the role of an educator becomes more and more similar to that of a learning designer, facilitator, mentor, and moral compass. Teachers are now expected to design valuable learning experiences, decipher AI generated insights, and nurture students cognitively and emotionally- where human judgment and situational understanding cannot be substituted. Simultaneously, the new competencies to be taught to educators will be AI literacy, the ability to interpret data, and ethical consciousness so that they could effectively cooperate with intelligent systems instead of just monitoring them. Equally, the role of the learners is also in a dramatic change (Chiu & Rospigliosi, 2025). Learners in the AI-enabled settings will be enabled to gain even more control over their learning experiences in the individualized learning trajectories, by using adaptive feedback and self-paced learning opportunities. Students no longer receive standardized instruction as passive receivers, but they are active participants and key contributors to knowledge. By communicating with AI tools, learners will be able to experiment, attempt to discover intricate problems, and participate in the reflective learning process. Nonetheless, the learners are also burdened with new responsibilities and must have greater self-regulation, critical thinking, and digital literacy. Along with learning together with AI, learners need to learn about AI, its capabilities, limitations, and possible bias. Although AI integration has the potential to transform the education sector, there are some challenges associated with this integration. Although AI has the potential to make education more efficient, scalable, and personalized, it does not imply that education is not a very human experience founded on values, emotions, social interaction, and ethical reasoning. The dependency on automated systems may lead to the decline in the learning to quantifiable results, the disregard of creativity, the moral growth, and the social learning. In addition, data privacy, algorithmic bias, transparency, and the digital divide are among the issues with problematic ethical and equity implications. AI can unwillingly contribute to the perceptions of inequality and exclusion without a detailed design and governance, because it tends to concentrate on the current disparities, or isolate students who do not have access to technology or digital literacy. Thus, AI integration in education is not the main question, but it is how education can be adapted to human-centered educational objectives (Dadhich et al., 2025; Nuong Deri et al., 2024). The collaboration of humans and AI has to be based on pedagogical will as opposed to technological determinism. AI must complement rather than substitute human abilities, and ought to be integrated into systems that are more focused on inclusiveness, equity, and student welfare. The valuable working collaboration needs to be designed deliberately, educators to be professionally developed continuously, the institutional policy supportive, and strong ethical standards that put humans on the definite loop. Human-AI collaboration within education and ways in which AI is revising the roles of the educator as well as the learner in modern learning contexts. It examines the major pedagogical changes, the opportunities which arise and the most important issues related to the adoption of AI. Besides this, it also touches on the ethical, social and equity issues that should feature prominently in any discussion of AI in education. The chapter claims that the future of education is not the human intelligence or the artificial intelligence, but the collaboration of the two in a responsible and thoughtful manner, by focusing on the relevance of purposeful design, assistance of the policy, and the desire to be inclusive.

2. Theoretical Principles of Human-AI Work.

The concept of the human-AI cooperation in the educational field needs a robust conceptual framework explaining what collaboration is and what theoretical viewpoints can be applied to support the idea of introducing it into the process of teaching and learning (Edwards et al., 2025). Instead of looking at AI as a replacement of human intellect, the modern discourse in education focuses on collaboration, cohesion, and joint responsibility between humans and intelligent systems. To define Human-AI Collaboration, it is necessary to first identify what is meant by a human and what is meant by an AI. Human-AI collaboration can be explained as a dynamic and two-way interaction where human and AI systems co-compete in the decision-making, problem-solving, and learning process. The idea is entirely different to that of automation where machines are used to substitute human labor to enhance efficiency or minimize labor. Within a collaborative paradigm, AI systems are created to complement human abilities as opposed to destroying human intervention. The focus is on complementarity - using the unique capabilities of the human intellect and artificial intelligence to produce results that neither can achieve on its own.Human intelligence introduces such qualities as creativity, empathy, contextual awareness, ethical thinking, and reflectivity. These qualities are imperative in the learning institutions, where motivation, social interaction, cultural setting, and moral values play a vital role in the learning process (Garg et al., 2024). Artificial intelligence, on the other hand, is more efficient in data processing, recognizing trends, providing quick responses, and expanding individualised services to different groups of learners. The collaboration of humans with AI occurs on the crossroads of these strengths, and it ensures more responsive, inclusive, and efficient educational practices. In education, this collaboration can be achieved in various ways. AI-assisted instruction relies upon adaptive algorithms to customize the content, pace, and difficulty to a single learner, and teachers use these insights and offer valuable feedback. Shared learning trajectories enable learners, educators, and AI systems to co-create educational trajectories in accordance with goals, performance, and interests. The feedback systems feed directly on the actions of learners, which is promptly accompanied by human feedback to cover the emotional, motivational, and ethical aspects. Equally, smart content generation tools can support educators and learners to generate learning materials, tests, and simulations, whereas humans will remain in charge of accuracy, relevance, and pedagogical orientation.

Human–AI Collaboration in Education: Beyond Automation-Driven Models

Human–AI collaboration represents a pedagogical paradigm in which artificial intelligence functions as a supportive partner to human cognition rather than a substitute for it. This approach contrasts sharply with automation-driven models that prioritize efficiency, standardization, and task replacement. In educational contexts—particularly in management and professional learning—this distinction is critical for preserving judgment, creativity, and ethical reasoning.

Automation-driven models typically deploy AI to execute tasks with minimal human intervention, such as automated grading, content generation, or prescriptive learning pathways. While these systems can reduce administrative burden and scale instruction, they risk diminishing learner agency and oversimplifying complex cognitive processes. When students passively accept AI-generated outputs or feedback, learning may become transactional, reinforcing compliance rather than critical engagement. In contrast, human–AI collaboration emphasizes co-action and mutual complementarity. AI contributes computational power, pattern recognition, and rapid feedback, while humans retain responsibility for interpretation, decision-making, and value judgments. In collaborative classrooms, AI tools support brainstorming, scenario analysis, and formative feedback, but students are required to explain, critique, and adapt AI suggestions. This process strengthens metacognition by making thinking visible and intentional. From a conceptual standpoint, human–AI collaboration aligns with constructivist and experiential learning theories. Rather than automating learning outcomes, AI scaffolds inquiry, enabling learners to explore multiple perspectives and test assumptions. In management education, for example, AI-driven simulations can generate alternative market scenarios, but strategic choices remain human-led, grounded in contextual understanding and ethical considerations. Importantly, collaborative models also mitigate risks associated with psychological dependence and academic integrity. By positioning AI as an advisor rather than an authority, students are encouraged to challenge outputs and disclose AI use transparently. This reinforces accountability and preserves academic ownership. In summary, human–AI collaboration offers a conceptually robust alternative to automation-driven education. It re-centers human judgment, promotes learner agency, and ensures that AI enhances rather than replaces the intellectual and ethical dimensions of learning.

REVIEW OF LITERATURE

The general idea of the human-AI collaboration is not to create AI-led education, where machines determine how people learn, but to foster AI-enhanced education that will maximize the potential in human beings. This model has AI as a partner in cognition, which improves the efficiency of teaching and learner interaction without eliminating the human-focused objective of education.

Theoretical Perspectives

A number of the educational and technological theories lay a strong ground on which human-AI collaboration can be understood and implemented. Sociocultural theory considers the process of learning to be socially mediated and is influenced by the interaction between the learner and the other people, as well as the cultural tools. In this view, AI can also act as a mediating tool that assists learners in their zones of proximal development by providing support in the form of scaffolding, prompts and adaptive support (Järvelä et al., 2023). Nevertheless, the human interaction is still at the center of attention, meaning that the meaning-making process, as well as social learning, cannot be completely automated. Constructivism and connectivism also give more significance to learner agency and active knowledge construction in networks and through experience. The AI-based personalization fits well into both of these theories because it allows learners to discovery-learn, to connect and to study at their own pace in digitally networked settings. AI does not control, but facilitates the process of knowledge building in the learner. Lastly, HITL models highlight the importance of human supervision of AI systems. The models are accountable, transparent, and ethical in their decision-making by maintaining human participation in the process of monitoring, interpreting, and intervening in AI-mediated processes. These two viewpoints have placed AI as an equal partner and not a substitute, affirms the continuing critical role of human judgment, interaction and responsibility in education (Ji et al., 2023; Singh, 2022). The introduction of AI into the academic systems has radically changed the professional identity and role of teachers. Instead of degrading the role of the teachers, AI has added and transformed the role, with the focus no longer on delivery but on higher-level pedagogical, analytical, and ethical tasks. In AI-enhanced education, teachers no longer serve in the role of knowledge relayers, but as creators of the learning experience, information-based decision-makers, and moral guardians who position education as grounded in human values.

3. Knowledge Transmitters to Learning Designers

Conventionally, teachers were perceived as being the main point in the classroom, where they pass knowledge on the subject of learning to students by lectures and standardized resources. The restrictions in information access and the need to have teachers as content gatekeepers influenced this model. The large number of digital resources and AI-based tools, however, have significantly changed this dynamic. Currently, intelligent tutoring systems and conversational AI, as well as adaptive learning platforms enable learners to get instant access to explanations, tutorials, and examples. Consequently, teacher educators are becoming more of learning designers and facilitators. They do not concentrate on providing static content since they organize meaningful learning processes that foster inquiry, critical thinking, and knowledge application. Educators pose complex, real-world problems, develop interdisciplinary projects, and create learning environments that allow the student to go through the concepts and not read passively (Katsenou et al., 2025; Nuong Deri et al., 2024). Their professional knowledge is in organizing the learning pathways, consistency of activities with the learning outcomes, and the technology application that is pedagogic. The platforms are supported by AI to facilitate this transition through the possibility of designing flexible curricula to address the needs of individual learners. These systems are able to analyze data on learners and recommend content, change difficulty levels, and give targeted practice. This will enable teachers to leave behind the one-size-fits-all approach in their teaching, and work on mentoring, coaching and development of reflective learning. When routine clarifications and practice are left to the AI systems, teachers have more time and thinking room to handle the learning of higher order, socializing, and the formation of critical and ethical reasoning.

Teachers as Knowledge-based Decision Makers

The other major change in the role of educators in AI-enhanced education is the fact that now educators are becoming data-informed decision makers. Analytics in learning and AI-based dashboards offer real-time data on the engagement of students, the trends in their performance, the zones of learning, and patterns of their behavior. These tools can help teachers to see struggling students early before the situation worsens, tailor-program interventions, and better analyze the success of teaching methods. Data-informed instruction can help teachers to shift their intuition or possible hindsight to proactive and evidence-based teaching. To mention a few, analytics may be used to point out what is most difficult or what activity is the most engaging to learners or which students are vulnerable to losing engagement (Katsenou et al., 2025). Teachers can subsequently modify teaching methods, redesign learning tasks or give specific attention using these insights. Nonetheless, this change also brings in new obligations and issues. Teachers need to acquire data literacy skills, such as the capacity to comprehend visualizations, the characteristics of algorithmic advice, and the correlation and causation. There is a necessity to interpret critically since the AI systems can mirror the biases in the training data or assumptions. Teachers should therefore background and deepen meaning to the AI-generated insights and not blindly take them at face value. The role of human judgment in making the decisions of the data guiding the pedagogical decisions will always be needed to ensure that the analytics support and do not limit the educational practice.

Teachers as Moral Citizens and Human Placeholders

With the AI systems becoming more and more involved in the process of assessment, feedback, and progression of the learners, educators begin to play an important role of an ethical steward. It is their duty to guarantee the fairness, transparency, and accountability in using AI technologies. This involves the safeguarding of the privacy of student data, informed consent, circumventing abuses of surveillance technology and concerns with with the bias of algorithms which might favor some groups of learners more than others (Kayyali, 2024). Teaching staff also have a key role in ensuring the integrity of academics in AI enhanced settings. Authorship, originality, and ethical application of technology have become more complicated with the advent of the generative AI.

DISCUSSION AND INTERPRETATION

Educators have to instruct learners on responsible use of AI, build concrete rules and expectations, and reinvent forms of assessment to focus on critical thinking, reflection, and real practice. In addition to ethical control, teachers also act as human connectors in an overly technologicalized learning process. Although AI is capable of faking conversation and feedback, it cannot possibly mimic empathy, morality, and real human connection. Teachers offer emotional assistance, mentoring, and social connectedness- factors that learners need to be motivated and healthy. In this regard, AI adds the technical aspects to education, and the human aspect is maintained by the educators.

4. Transformation of Learners' Roles in Human–AI Collaboration

The role of educators is changing so is the one of learners in AI-enhanced learning, which is experiencing a paradigm shift. The collaboration between humans and AI and puts learners in active roles by interacting with smart systems to build knowledge, manage their learning process, and be critical of technological assistance. The tools with the help of AI enable the learners to shift their mindset off of passive information consumption and onto active co-creation of knowledge (Kayyali, 2025). With the help of generative AI applications, simulations, virtual laboratories, and design tools, learners can work with complex situations, experiment, and generate original artifacts (reports, models, and creative works). The process of learning becomes discoverative and investigative where AI assists in trial and error. Such a change boosts the learner agency, creativity, and control over the learning process.

Students are to ask questions, choose and consider the results which is more or less consistent with competency-based and experience-based learning models. AI serves as a partner which increases the ability of learners to explore and innovate, whereas human teachers offer direction, feedback, and perspective.

Individualized and Self-managed learning

Personalization can be considered one of the most important contributions of AI to education. Adaptive Systems present behavior and performance of the learner and preferences to tailor the content, pacing and feedback. This individualization aids in a variety of learning requirements and helps the learner to learn at his or her speed thereby being more engaged and confident. Consequently, learners become more and more active in self-regulated learning where they acquire metacognitive skills, including setting goals, monitoring progress, and reflection in the learning strategies (Kayyali, 2025). Nevertheless, this self-regulation cannot be developed as an automatic process. The most productive collaboration between humans and AI involves educators scaffolding the learners' interactions with AI and make them interpret feedback, create realistic goals, and not rely on automated support too much.

Transforming AI Literacy and Critical Awareness

Learners in AI-enhanced educational settings also need to acquire AI literacy, or knowledge of the functioning of AI systems, their shortcomings, and their social consequences in general. Students should be able to critically assess the products of AI implementation, doubt the suggestions offered by algorithms, and understand possible bias or inaccuracy. By being guided, the learners become critical users and evaluators of AI, instead of being automated assistance consumers (Wong & Looi, 2024). This self-consciousness is required to equip learners to engage in an AI-driven society in a responsible manner, which supports the need to educate learners to become informed, ethical, and reflective citizens.

Instructional Paradigms

The adoption of Artificial Intelligence in education requires not only the technological capacity but also the professional model that makes the use of AI functions meaningful regarding human teaching and learning. Pedagogical frameworks facilitating human-AI collaboration focus on balance, i.e. taking advantage of AI to enhance efficiency, personalization and scalability whilst maintaining the human aspects of interaction, judgment, and moral direction. Blended/hybrid learning, intelligent tutoring and mentoring system, project based and experiential learning has become a model that has been found to be very effective in promoting a healthy cooperation between intelligent systems and human beings.

5.Blended and Hybrid Learning Models

Blended and hybrid models of learning entail collaboration of face-to-face education and online, AI-based elements of education. The use of AI systems in these settings is characterized by typical routine, repetitive, or data-intensive operations, e.g. quizzes, practice exercises, content recommendations, and progress tracking (Kim, 2024). This enables teachers to direct their face-to-face or synchronous work to more valuable processes, such as discussion, concept insight, group problem-solving, and individual help. Blended learning is a true example of human-AI collaboration, which is efficient in terms of technology and at the same time, it is meaningful in terms of human experiences. The content of AI-powered platforms is adjusted to the level and learning styles of individual learners so that the basic knowledge is obtained at a reasonable pace. Meanwhile, classroom time is used by educators as a means of deepening the knowledge, misconcepts clearing, and critical thinking development. Such division of labor is beneficial in that it gives each of the actors, a human and a machine, the opportunity to do what they can do best. Hybrid models are also more flexible and more accessible, which allows them to support different needs and contexts of learners. Students will appreciate the fact that they receive constant AI-based feedback even when they are not in the classroom, and teachers will maintain pedagogical control of learning goals and evaluation criteria. Notably, blended learning alters the role of a teacher as a content presenter and turns him into a facilitator and a mentor, which confirms the humanistic education even in the technological environment.

Intelligent tutoring and Mentoring Systems

One of the best-known uses of AI in the field of education is intelligent tutoring systems (ITS). Such systems offer personalized learning through the diagnosis of the performance of the learner, modification of the difficulty, and instant and focused feedback. ITS can provide the simulation of one-on-one tutoring, where the learner is provided with guidance through the practice of skills, problems and moving through the material at their own pace (Kim et al., 2022). Intelligent tutoring systems combined with human mentoring form a dual-support system that is effective in improving the learning results. The AI tutors are assigned with the routine instructional work and unlimited, personalized guidance, whereas the human education teachers are concentrated on the conceptual knowledge, motivation, and the socio-emotional progress. This mix is especially useful in either big or heterogeneous classrooms, where one-on-one guidance by the teacher can be a challenge. Human mentors are important in contextualizing AI feedback, overcoming struggles of the learners and fostering perseverance. They also keep track of AI performance, which makes sure that suggestions are correct, just and they are in tandem with curricular aims. Instead of substituting the teachers, smart tutoring systems make them reach wider, realizing more inclusive and responsive education (Kim et al., 2022). The concept of project-based and experiential learning is based on four key principles that explain its application within the instructional process. Project-based and experiential learning has four main principles on which its application in the instructional process is founded. The models of project-based and experiential learning focus on solving real-life problems, teamwork, and use of knowledge. Artificial intelligence can be used to facilitate these strategies by providing simulations, data analysis possibilities, predictive modeling, and the generation of scenarios. Through AI, learners are able to learn more about complex systems, hypotheses, and possible solutions in real-world situations (Kim et al., 2025). In project-based learning, AI becomes a thinking partner, which increases inquiry and imagination. As an example, students can apply AI to process datasets, model the environment or economy, or come up with design options. Teachers will help students to frame problems, interpret AI generated knowledge and think about the ethical and practical ramifications. This partnership supports experiential and competency-based learning through linking theory and practice and fostering reflective learning.

Notably, teachers make sure that the projects are learner-centered and not AI-centered. They also focus on critical analysis of AI products, moral thinking, collaboration, and make sure that technology improves but does not subjugate the learning process. Human-AI cooperation facilitates deep learning, innovation, and applicability using this model.

6. Assessment and Feedback in Human–AI Collaboration

Effective learning involves assessment and feedback, which AI has offered new opportunities to make more timely, personalized and informative. Nevertheless, there must exist a delicate balance between human judgment and automated efficiency in meaningful assessment in human-AI collaboration.

AI-Assisted Assessment

A wide variety of learning activities can be assessed using AI-assisted assessment to provide automated grading, formative assessment and real-time feedback. Objective tests like quizzes, short answers and practice tasks can easily be graded within a short period of time and this gives the learners immediate feedback on their performance. This helps lessen the administrative burden of educators and enables it to conduct more assessments (Kovari, 2025). Access to the continuous assessment data helps to identify the learning gaps in time and provide intervention. Teachers can apply AI-generated insights to make modifications to instruction, offer specific assistance, and measure the efficiency of teaching methods. By so doing, AI-assisted assessment becomes more responsive and helps individualize the learning processes. Nonetheless, excessive dependence on automated evaluation is dangerous. AI systems are likely to focus on quantifiable results, which can limit the extent of learning and underestimate creativity, moral thinking, and the ability to solve complicated problems. As such, human judgment will be crucial in assessing higher-order learning outcomes, interpretative responses, and in being fair. AI is not to substitute professional expertise of educators in assessment, but it should assist them.

Feedback as a Participatory Process

When human and AI work on collaboration, the feedback becomes a multi-layered and collaborative process. AI gives immediate and data-based feedback to learners in order to detect errors, monitor progress, and modify strategies in real time. This immediate feedback facilitates self-directed learning and decelerates anxiety that comes with delayed assessment. Teachers are able to supplement AI feedback with contextual, empathetic, and motivational feedback (Kyambade et al., 2025). Human feedback takes care of social and emotional aspects of learning and assists the learners in making sense of the information produced by AI and fosters thought and development. Combining AI and human feedback, a more holistic feedback ecosystem is formed which facilitates cognitive growth and well-being of learners. Through the combination of technological effectiveness and human intuition, the pedagogical framework of human-AI cooperation promotes the quality of learning and strives to retain the essentially human intention of education.

Ethical, Social, and Equity Perceptions

The development of AI in education is associated with great possibilities of personalization, efficiency, and innovation. Nonetheless, it also comes with intricate ethical, social, and equity-based issues that should be thought over to make sure that the cooperation between humans and AI can have a positive impact on the quality of education and social justice (Luckin, 2025). Having no explicit protective measures, AI systems can be used to reinforce existing inequalities, undermine privacy, and marginalize vulnerable groups of learners. The inclusion of ethics in the governance and the design of AI is, thus, at the core of responsible AI implementation in education.

Cross-Country Variations in AI Adoption Policies: Implications for Learner Autonomy, Psychological Dependence, and Academic Integrity

Artificial Intelligence (AI) has become a transformative force in education worldwide, yet its adoption is shaped by significant cross-country variations in policy frameworks, ethical norms, institutional readiness, and cultural attitudes toward technology. These variations influence how AI tools are deployed in teaching and learning, particularly within management education, where data-driven decision-making, analytics, and automation skills are increasingly central. Understanding these policy differences is critical to assessing their implications for learner autonomy, psychological dependence on AI, and mechanisms safeguarding academic integrity. At the policy level, countries in the Global North, such as the United States, the United Kingdom, and members of the European Union, tend to adopt structured yet distinct regulatory approaches. The European Union's AI Act emphasizes risk-based regulation, transparency, and human oversight, positioning AI as an assistive tool rather than a replacement for human judgment. In educational contexts, this approach encourages learner autonomy by mandating explainable AI systems that allow students to understand how recommendations or feedback are generated. Conversely, the United States follows a more decentralized and innovation-driven model, where federal guidelines coexist with institutional autonomy. This flexibility has enabled rapid experimentation with AI tutors, learning analytics dashboards, and generative AI tools in business schools, but it also places greater responsibility on institutions to manage ethical and academic risks. In contrast, several Asian countries, including China, Singapore, and South Korea, have adopted state-led AI strategies that integrate education as a national priority. These policies often emphasize efficiency, scalability, and workforce readiness. For example, China's AI education policies promote intelligent tutoring systems and adaptive platforms to personalize learning at scale. While such systems can enhance learner autonomy by tailoring content to individual progress, they also raise concerns about over-reliance on algorithmic guidance. When AI systems dominate learning pathways, students may become passive recipients of recommendations rather than active agents in setting goals and evaluating their own learning strategies. Learner autonomy is a central consideration across these policy environments. In countries with strong traditions of academic freedom and learner-centered pedagogy, AI is increasingly framed as a "co-pilot" rather than a decision-maker. Management institutions in the United Kingdom, for instance, encourage students to use AI tools for brainstorming, market analysis, and scenario modeling while requiring reflective justification of decisions. This approach reinforces metacognitive skills and ensures that autonomy is preserved even as AI augments cognitive capacity. By contrast, in systems where performance metrics and standardized outcomes dominate, AI may unintentionally constrain autonomy by nudging learners toward predefined "optimal" solutions. Another emerging concern is the potential psychological dependence on AI tools. Cross-country policy differences shape how this risk is addressed. Scandinavian countries, known for their strong emphasis on digital well-being, have begun incorporating AI literacy and "critical AI use" into curricula. Students are explicitly trained to question AI outputs, recognize limitations, and maintain confidence in their own analytical abilities. In contrast, in rapidly digitizing educational systems with limited regulatory guidance, students may come to view AI as an authoritative source, leading to reduced self-efficacy and overdependence. In management education, this is particularly problematic, as leadership and strategic decision-making require judgment under uncertainty skills that cannot be fully outsourced to algorithms. Academic integrity mechanisms further highlight cross-country variation. Institutions in Australia and Canada, for example, have revised academic integrity policies to explicitly address generative AI. Rather than banning AI outright, they distinguish between acceptable assistance (e.g., data analysis, language refinement) and misconduct (e.g., unacknowledged AI-generated submissions). Business schools in these countries increasingly use AI-resilient assessment designs, such as live case analyses, oral defenses, and project-based evaluations, to ensure authenticity. In contrast, regions with less developed policy frameworks often rely on traditional plagiarism detection tools, which are ill-equipped to identify AI-generated content, creating enforcement gaps. Real-world examples from management institutions illustrate how policy contexts translate into practice. At leading business schools in the United States, AI tools like predictive analytics platforms and simulation-based decision environments are embedded into MBA curricula to enhance experiential learning. Faculty oversight and honor codes serve as primary integrity safeguards. In Singapore, management institutes leverage AI-driven career advising and adaptive learning systems aligned with national AI strategies, while simultaneously embedding ethics modules to mitigate dependence and promote responsible use. Meanwhile, European business schools increasingly require transparency statements in assignments, where students disclose how AI tools were used, reinforcing accountability and ethical awareness. In conclusion, cross-country variations in AI adoption policies significantly shape the educational experience, influencing learner autonomy, psychological dependence, and academic integrity. While advanced AI systems offer powerful opportunities to personalize and enrich management education, their impact depends on thoughtful policy design and institutional implementation. A balanced approach—one that combines innovation with ethical safeguards, critical AI literacy, and robust assessment mechanisms is essential to ensure that AI enhances, rather than undermines, the human capacities at the core of education.

Real Classroom Implementation Cases, Quick-Reference Frameworks, and Student-Agency Perspectives in AI-Enabled Learning

The practical integration of Artificial Intelligence (AI) into classroom settings has moved beyond pilot experimentation toward structured, real-world implementation, particularly within management and professional education. Documented classroom cases demonstrate that the effectiveness of AI is not determined solely by technological sophistication, but by how thoughtfully it is embedded into pedagogy, assessment, and learner agency. Real classroom implementation cases from management institutions highlight diverse and pragmatic applications. In business analytics courses, AI-powered dashboards are increasingly used to support data interpretation and scenario modeling. For example, students analyze simulated market data using AI-based forecasting tools, while instructors require written or oral justifications of final decisions. This hybrid approach ensures that AI augments analytical capacity without replacing human judgment. Similarly, in strategy and entrepreneurship classrooms, generative AI tools are employed for ideation, competitor scanning, and risk assessment, but outputs must be critically evaluated against real-world constraints. Faculty feedback emphasizes reasoning quality rather than AI-generated accuracy, reinforcing higher-order thinking skills.

Another notable classroom practice involves AI-assisted formative feedback. Adaptive learning systems provide instant feedback on quizzes or case reflections, allowing students to identify learning gaps early. Instructors retain control over summative evaluation, ensuring that AI supports learning progression rather than becoming the primary evaluator. These cases illustrate a clear pattern: successful implementation treats AI as an instructional scaffold, not an authoritative decision-maker. To support such practices, quick-reference framework visuals are increasingly used by institutions to guide faculty and students. While these frameworks are often presented as infographics, they can be conceptually summarized into three interlinked layers:

1. Purpose Layer (Why AI is used): Clarifies whether AI supports ideation, feedback, practice, or simulation.
2. Process Layer (How AI is used): Specifies acceptable tools, stages of use (pre-task, during task, post-task), and required human input.
3. Accountability Layer (How learning is validated): Includes disclosure requirements, reflective justification, and integrity checks.

This quick-reference structure enables instructors to rapidly design AI-aligned activities while providing students with clear boundaries. Its visual simplicity supports consistency across courses and reduces ambiguity, particularly in interdisciplinary programs where AI use varies widely. From a student-agency perspective, learners consistently express appreciation for AI when it enhances control over pacing, feedback, and exploration. Students report feeling more confident when AI tools allow them to test ideas privately before engaging in peer or instructor discussions. This autonomy is particularly valuable for diverse classrooms, where differences in language proficiency or prior knowledge may otherwise limit participation. However, students also voice concerns about over-dependence and reduced originality. When AI outputs are perceived as "optimal answers," learners may hesitate to challenge or deviate from them. Classrooms that actively address this issue encourage students to critique AI responses, compare multiple outputs, and reflect on discrepancies. Such practices restore agency by positioning students as evaluators rather than consumers of AI-generated content. Overall, real classroom cases demonstrate that AI can meaningfully enhance learning when guided by clear frameworks and agency-centered pedagogy. Quick-reference visuals provide operational clarity, while deliberate attention to student perspectives ensures that AI adoption strengthens autonomy, confidence, and critical engagement. Together, these elements create an educational environment where AI functions as a partner in learning supportive, transparent, and firmly subordinate to human judgment.

7. Fairness, Bias and Transparency

Among the most pressing ethical issues in AI-enhanced education, the possibility of bias and unfair results can be mentioned. The AI systems are taught using historical and live data, and these data can be based on the current social, cultural, or institutional inequalities. In the event that these data are biased, recommendations based on assessment, placement, and learner support that are offered under the jurisdiction of AI can unintentionally underrepresent certain groups due to socioeconomic status, gender, language, disability or cultural background (Mariyono & Nur Alif, 2025). When applied to education, discriminative algorithms may impact grading, predictive analytics and student profiling to affect access to and career pathways of learners. A case in point is predictive systems that identify students as at risk: without attention, this will support assumptions based on deficit. Educators and institutions should, therefore, take a closer look at the manner in which AI systems are trained, the information they take, and the opinions they represent. These risks can be solved through transparency in algorithmic decision-making. At least on a conceptual level, educators and learners should know how AI systems come up with recommendations or evaluations. Open communication, explainable AI methods, and documentation contribute to the development of trust and allow people to have a level of informed supervision. Teachers are instrumental in doubting AI results, putting them into context, and interfering with them in cases where results seem to be unjust or inaccurate (Suhag & Singh, 2026; Tran, 2024). A proactive approach to bias includes constant assessment, a variety of data, and representative designing, including teachers, students, and the marginalized groups. The fairness in human-AI cooperation is not a technical solution that can be provided once, but an ongoing ethical devotion to the culture and practice of the institutions.

Data privacy and surveillance issues

Educational AI usage entails the analysis of a large volume of data, such as academic achievement and behavioral trends, engagement rates, and occasionally biometric or emotional data. Although such data provide possibilities to personalize and gain learning analytics, it also brings a lot of serious concerns about privacy, monitoring, and consent. The students might have a sense of being supervised at all times, and this can interfere with autonomy, trust, and psychology. Maintaining privacy of students is an essential ethical duty. The institutions should develop a strong data governance structure that spells out what data is gathered, where it is stored and accessed as well as the duration of retention. Informed consent must not be symbolic but both meaningful and make sure that learners and their families do know how data are used and what rights they have towards access, correction or deletion. Teachers are also very crucial in the mediation of data use. They have to strike a balance between the advantages of learning analytics and dignity and autonomy of the learner (Muthukrishna et al., 2025; Nuong Deri et al., 2024). Open information on information handling practices, defining the extent of surveillance technology, and ethical oversight measures can ensure that trust in AI-enhanced learning systems is preserved. In addition, institutions are obligated to abide by applicable legal and regulatory standards of data protection as well as promote ethical behaviors beyond the confines of the minimum standards of compliance. Human-AI collaboration needs to be responsible, which means that the data about the learners should not be regarded as a resource but be a trust that is placed in educational institutions. Digital Divide and Inclusion Digital Divide and Inclusion Digital divide refer to variations among groups of people across various cultures and societies concerning access to digital information devices and technologies.

Digital Divide and Inclusion

Digital Divide and Inclusion Digital divide is the differences between groups of people in different cultures and societies with regard to the access of digital information information devices and technology. The cooperation of humans and AI should also respond to the continued inequalities in technology, connection, and computer literacy. Digital divide has been a major obstacle to fair education, especially to the learners in the low-income, rural, or marginalized strata. Assuming that educational innovations based on AI will involve universal access to devices, high-speed internet, and high levels of digital literacy, it is likely that they will increase rather than decrease the existing inequalities (Nuong Deri et al., 2024; Padovano & Cardamone, 2024). The idea of inclusive AI integration needs deliberate plans that would make all learners have access and participate. These involve availing low-priced or shared equipment, developing platforms that will operate with low-bandwidth conditions, and preserving low-tech or offline options as needed. Inclusive human-AI collaboration also entails accessibility characteristics of learners with disabilities, multilingual interface, and culturally responsive design. Capacity-building programs are very important in inclusion. Educators and learners should be assisted in becoming digital and AI literate to interact successfully with the intelligent systems. In the absence of this, technological innovation can help only those who are already privileged, and education will no longer serve as a social mobility and equity driver.

Implications in Institutional and Policy

Policymakers and institutions have a determinative determination in the way human-AI collaboration is played out in education. The work of individual educators and learners cannot help to solve ethical, social, and equity issues; they require systemic assistance, clear guidelines, and long-term investment. Learning institutions should develop clear policies on the use of AI that define pedagogical, ethical and legal principles. Such guidelines ought to formulate acceptable AI applications, transparency and accountability guidelines, and procedures to address ethical issues. The institutional leadership should also invest in the infrastructure that will facilitate secure, inclusive, and scalable AI integration. It is especially the professional development. Teachers should get continuous training on how to use AI tools as well as on deciphering their implications, limitations, and the ethical aspects (Padovano & Cardamone, 2024). The field of education together with technological, ethical, and policy makers should work together interdisciplinarity to embrace a more integrated and responsible attitude towards the use of AI. Governments and regulatory bodies should strike the right balance between regulation and innovation at the policy level. Too strict policies can be a drag on experimentation and advancement, and lack of strictness may put learners in danger. Good policy frameworks facilitate ethical practices, safeguard rights and responsible innovation by offering funding, supporting research and collaborations between government and commercial. Finally, moral, communal and equity are never marginal to human-AI collaboration in education, on the contrary, they are core to its validity and sustainability. With the help of inclusive principles, open governance, common accountability, AI can help in having a more equitable, more human, and future-oriented educational system.

FUTURE PERSPECTIVES OF EDUCATION

Co-evolution has become the future of education, where humans and Artificial Intelligence systems keep adapting to each other according to their capabilities and limitations and roles. Instead of a linear process where the world becomes more and more automated, this vision of the future would represent a form of a dynamic collaboration between educators, learners, institutions, and AI technologies, which would jointly define educational practices. With more advanced AI systems, the way they are used in the education field will venture beyond efficiency and personalization to more advanced models of interaction, creativity, and social influence. The creation of emotionally responsive AI is also one of the emerging trends that are the most important (Pahi et al., 2024). The development of the field of affective computing allows AI to recognize the emotional indicators of frustration, confusion, or disengagement based on the pattern of learner behavior, language, or interaction. Emotionally aware AI in education can be used to modify feedback, learning rate, or teaching methods to more effectively enhance student motivation and well-being. This is conceived, as an example, of an AI tutor feeling encouraged when a learner is having a hard time or recommending a break in the case of cognitive overload. Nevertheless, the emotional AI is not to substitute the human empathy; it supplements it by notifying educators about learners that might require further assistance. The teacher will still have a moral duty of making sense of emotional information and acting in a caring and situational way (Agboola & Yassin, 2025; Suhag & Singh, 2026; Tran, 2024; Wong & Looi, 2024).

AI-assisted immersive learning

The introduction of AI-assisted immersive learning environments is another direction that is important. Mixed reality, along with virtual reality (VR) and augmented reality (AR) technologies, provides learners with the opportunity to conduct a rich and experience-based learning with the help of intelligent systems. The skills of the learners in the science, healthcare, engineering, and hospitality sector can be practiced, decisions made, and consequences experienced with AI-based simulations, which can mimic the complex real-world situations in a safe environment. Teachers led the reflection, moral thinking, and application of learning in simulated situations to the real one (Wong & Looi, 2024). Such immersive facilitate experiential and competence-based learning, which is the strengthening of the symbiotic relationship between human mentorship and AI-driven exploration. The lifelong learning ecosystems also become part of the future of human-AI collaboration. Due to the changes in the labor markets and the needs of society, the education does not last just until people finish their formal schooling but it goes through the life span. With AI-based learning systems, continuous upskilling and reskilling can be maintained, personalized learning plans can be proposed, previous learning is identified, and learning content can be adjusted to evolving objectives. Teachers, coaches and schools can make the difference in helping the learners across careers and life levels so that the lifelong learning process is significant, inclusive and aligned with the personal interests. AI has a role to play as an adaptive guide in this ecosystem with purpose, motivation and ethical direction being offered by humans (Katsenou et al., 2025; Wong & Looi, 2024).

Human-AI co-creativity

The next possible future direction is the growing importance of human-AI co-creativity. Generative AIs allow students and teachers to work together to develop content, designs and solutions. This is in line with innovation, interdisciplinary learning, and creative expression in the education field. Teachers are able to teach students how to set the problems, analyze the results and speculate about the creative process so that AI can contribute to the originality and not passive reliance (Garg et al., 2024; Nuong Deri et al., 2024). Co-creativity supports the notion of learning as an activity of human imagination and machine ability working together in interaction. Even with such optimistic changes, the future of human-AI collaboration will rely on the ability to have a human-centered vision of education. Technology should also be used to support educational values, and not to define them. Human values like ethical reasoning, social responsibility, cultural understanding and whole person development should be kept at the core. Teachers will remain very significant in the expression of values, community and emotional and moral development of learners. The AI systems no matter how sophisticated they are do not possess inherent values and thus they should be controlled and directed by humans.

Equity and inclusion

This will continue being influential factors when designing future directions. With the spread of AI-driven innovations, institutions and policymakers should guarantee that the benefits are evenly spread across and that the vulnerable groups are not left behind. The new type of educational inequality could be prevented by including design, accessible infrastructure, and capacity-building measures. The cooperation between human and AI is not supposed to be a tool of centralizing the learning opportunities but it should be the tool of democratizing the learning opportunities (Agboola & Yassin, 2025; Suhag & Singh, 2026; Tran, 2024). Lastly, the continuation of the process would rely on reflection, research and constant conversation between the educator, technologists, learners and policymakers. Human-AI collaboration is not a definitive stage but a changing process which should be flexible and ethically mindful. Through the adoption of co-evolution based on human values, the transitional capabilities of AI can be used to improve education systems without neglecting the social, moral and developmental functions of education. It is in this medium that education as we know it in the future is not a war between humans and machines, but a shared endeavour towards more responsive, inclusive and meaningful education. The collaboration between human and AI in education is a transformative but subtle change in the digitalized teaching and learning conceptualization and practice. The integration of Artificial Intelligence can transform and enhance the duties and roles of educators and learners, instead of decreasing them by spreading out tasks, increasing abilities, and providing new avenues of valuable interaction. The main point that comes out of this discussion is that AI is not as useful in education as it can be substitutive of human intelligence but rather as a complementary entity that enhances human capabilities (Padovano & Cardamone, 2024; Singh, 2022). To educators, AI-powered environments are indicating the shift of the traditional role of passing the content to more complicated and influential role of learning designers, mentors and ethical guardians.

CONCLUSION

AI can enable teachers by simplifying routine instructional and administrative processes and responsibilities to concentrate on higher-order pedagogical functions and activities, including facilitating inquiry, facilitating critical thinking, and fostering social and emotional development, in students. Simultaneously, teachers are going to play a crucial role of the mediator of the AI systems- understanding data, challenging algorithm outputs, and making sure the use of technology does not contradict the educational objectives, ethical practices, and the well-being of learners. The professional judgment, empathy, and contextual understanding cannot be replaced by them in the context of keeping the human core of education alive. The learners also go through a huge change in the human-AI cooperation. Personalization and adaptive learning systems run by AI allow learners to be more in control of their learning processes, which stimulates self-regulated learning, creativity, and engagement. Students are more and more involved as knowledge creators, making use of smart tools to investigate issues, refute and/or come up with novel work.

This empowerment however comes with responsibility. To succeed in assessing the generated information by AI and identify limitations, biases, and act ethically, learners need to acquire AI literacy, critical thinking, and moral awareness to be able to use technology responsibly. Through this, education is prepared to ensure that learners are trained on how to not only use AI, but to live and work intelligently in an AI-shaped society. The degree to which human-AI cooperation works depends on technological maturity and refined thinking, but this integration should be based on prudent pedagogy, morals and justice. In the absence of educational intent, AI will just be a kind of efficiency machine that will reduce learning to quantifiable results and ignore creativity and moral thinking and social interaction. On the other hand, AI could positively influence the quality of learning, accommodate the needs of various learners, and increase access to learning and education under the conditions of proper pedagogical constructs and inclusive values. All phases of AI adoption should keep ethical aspects to the agenda and be fair, transparent, protect information, and inclusive to become trusted and legitimate. On an institutional and policy level, long-term funding on educator training, defined structures of governance and interdisciplinary cooperation is crucial in facilitating responsible human-AI cooperation. The education systems should be flexible, thoughtful, and sensitive towards changes in the AI technologies so that the innovation can be beneficial to the human and societal interests in the long term. Finally, education in the future is not human or artificial, it is collaborative. It is formed under the influence of common intelligence of humans and machines in agreement with each other on common educational intentions. The transformation that AI has the potential to bring to education can be used in a way that preserves the core values of education of human growth, social responsibility, and lifelong learning, by adopting this collaborative vision.

REFERENCES

Agboola, O. P., & Yassin, Y. N. H. M. (2025, July). AI applications in education: Enhancing human creativity through collaborative design. In *International Conference on Knowledge Management in Organizations* (pp. 45-69). Cham: Springer Nature Switzerland. DOI: 10.1007/978-3-031-95901-1_4

Alam, A., & Mohanty, A. (2023). Educational technology: Exploring the convergence of technology and pedagogy through mobility, interactivity, AI, and learning tools. *Cogent Engineering*, *10*(2), 2283282. DOI: 10.1080/23311916.2023.2283282

Chiu, T. K., & Rospigliosi, P. A. (2025). Encouraging human-AI collaboration in interactive learning environments. *Interactive Learning Environments*, *33*(2), 921–924. DOI: 10.1080/10494820.2025.2471199

Dadhich, A., Yadav, R., Yadav, M., Huzooree, G., & Dewasiri, N. J. (2025). Teacher-AI Collaboration and the Future of the Educator's Role. In *Transformative AI Practices for Personalized Learning Strategies* (pp. 355–378). IGI Global Scientific Publishing. DOI: 10.4018/979-8-3693-8744-3.ch013

Edwards, J., Nguyen, A., Lämsä, J., Sobocinski, M., Whitehead, R., Dang, B., Roberts, A.-S., & Järvelä, S. (2025). Human-AI collaboration: Designing artificial agents to facilitate socially shared regulation among learners. *British Journal of Educational Technology*, *56*(2), 712–733. DOI: 10.1111/bjet.13534

Garg, A., Singh, A., & Yanan, J. (2024). Exploring the Impact of Digital Detoxification on Higher Education Students' Learning. In *Business drivers in promoting digital detoxification* (pp. 111-126). IGI Global Scientific Publishing.

Järvelä, S., Nguyen, A., & Hadwin, A. (2023). Human and artificial intelligence collaboration for socially shared regulation in learning. *British Journal of Educational Technology*, *54*(5), 1057–1076. DOI: 10.1111/bjet.13325

Ji, H., Han, I., & Ko, Y. (2023). A systematic review of conversational AI in language education: Focusing on the collaboration with human teachers. *Journal of Research on Technology in Education*, *55*(1), 48–63. DOI: 10.1080/15391523.2022.2142873

Katsenou, R., Kotsidis, K., Papadopoulou, A., Anastasiadis, P., & Deliyannis, I. (2025). Beyond Assistance: Embracing AI as a Collaborative Co-Agent in Education. *Education Sciences*, *15*(8), 1006. DOI: 10.3390/educsci15081006

Kayyali, M. (2024). Future possibilities and challenges of AI in education. In *Transforming education with generative AI: Prompt engineering and synthetic content creation* (pp. 118–137). IGI Global Scientific Publishing. DOI: 10.4018/979-8-3693-1351-0.ch006

Kayyali, M. (2025). The Evolution of AI in Education From Concept to Classroom. In *Navigating Barriers to AI Implementation in the Classroom* (pp. 325–368). IGI Global Scientific Publishing. DOI: 10.4018/979-8-3373-1827-1.ch013

Kim, J. (2024). Leading teachers' perspective on teacher-AI collaboration in education. *Education and Information Technologies*, *29*(7), 8693–8724. DOI: 10.1007/s10639-023-12109-5

Kim, J., Lee, H., & Cho, Y. H. (2022). Learning design to support student-AI collaboration: Perspectives of leading teachers for AI in education. *Education and Information Technologies*, *27*(5), 6069–6104. DOI: 10.1007/s10639-021-10831-6

Kim, J., Yu, S., Detrick, R., Lin, X., & Li, N. (2025). Designing AI-powered learning: Adult learners' expectations for curriculum and human-AI interaction. *Educational Technology Research and Development*, *73*(6), 1–25. DOI: 10.1007/s11423-025-10549-z

Kovari, A. (2025). A systematic review of AI-powered collaborative learning in higher education: Trends and outcomes from the last decade. *Social Sciences & Humanities Open*, *11*, 101335. DOI: 10.1016/j.ssaho.2025.101335

Kyambade, M., Namatovu, A., & Male Ssentumbwe, A. (2025). Exploring the evolution of artificial intelligence in education: From AI-guided learning to learner-personalized paradigms. *Cogent Education*, *12*(1), 2505297. DOI: 10.1080/2331186X.2025.2505297

Luckin, R. (2025). Nurturing human intelligence in the age of AI: Rethinking education for the future. *Development and Learning in Organizations*, *39*(1), 1–4. DOI: 10.1108/DLO-04-2024-0108

Mariyono, D., & Nur Alif Hd, A. (2025). AI's role in transforming learning environments: A review of collaborative approaches and innovations. *Quality Education for All*, *2*(1), 265–288. DOI: 10.1108/QEA-08-2024-0071

Muthukrishna, M., Dai, J., Panizo Madrid, D., Sabherwal, R., Vanoppen, K., & Yao, H. (2025). AI Can Revolutionise Education but Technology Is Not Enough: Human Development Meets Cultural Evolution. *Journal of Human Development and Capabilities*, *26*(3), 1–11. DOI: 10.1080/19452829.2025.2517740

Nuong Deri, M., Singh, A., Zaazie, P., & Anandene, D. (2024). Leveraging Artificial Intelligence in Higher Educational Institutions: A Comprehensive Overview. *Education and Law Review*, (30). Advance online publication. DOI: 10.1344/REYD2024.30.45777

Padovano, A., & Cardamone, M. (2024). Towards human-AI collaboration in the competency-based curriculum development process: The case of industrial engineering and management education. *Computers and Education: Artificial Intelligence*, *7*, 100256. DOI: 10.1016/j.caeai.2024.100256

Pahi, K., Hawlader, S., Hicks, E., Zaman, A., & Phan, V. (2024). Enhancing active learning through collaboration between human teachers and generative AI. *Computers and Education Open*, *6*, 100183. DOI: 10.1016/j.caeo.2024.100183

Singh, A. (2022). Conceptual framework on Smart Learning Environment- An Indian perspective. *Education and Law Review*, (25). Advance online publication. DOI: 10.1344/REYD2022.25.36706

Suhag, N., & Singh, A. (2026). Blended Learning in the Age of Artificial Intelligence: Transforming Education Through Innovation. In Ul Rehman, S. (Ed.), *Reshaping Blended Learning Environments With AI* (pp. 29–52). IGI Global Scientific Publishing., DOI: 10.4018/979-8-3373-3815-6.ch002

Tran, M. T. (2024). A systematic literature review on the human-AI partnership roles in higher education. *Enhancing and Predicting Digital Consumer Behavior with AI*, 28-38.

Wong, L. H., & Looi, C. K. (2024). Advancing the generative AI in education research agenda: Insights from the Asia-Pacific region. *Asia Pacific Journal of Education*, *44*(1), 1–7. DOI: 10.1080/02188791.2024.2315704

Chapter 2

Reimagining Learning With the AI-Enabled Classroom:

The Transformative Power of Artificial Intelligence in Education

Seema Yadav
http://orcid.org/0000-0002-8477-5895
Bhopal School of Social Sciences, Bhopal, India

ABSTRACT

Artificial Intelligence (AI) is reshaping the landscape of education by transforming how learning is designed, delivered, and experienced. This chapter examines the evolving role of AI as a catalyst for pedagogical innovation, institutional efficiency, and inclusive learning. It explores key AI applications such as personalized learning systems, intelligent tutoring models, automated assessments, and AI-driven analytics that enhance both teaching and student engagement. The chapter highlights how AI supports educators by reducing administrative burdens, enabling data-informed decision-making, and enriching professional development. It also addresses the ethical considerations surrounding AI deployment, including issues of privacy, bias, transparency, and digital well-being. Through global examples and emerging trends, the chapter underscores AI's potential to strengthen educational equity and prepare learners for future work environments. Ultimately, it argues for responsible, human-centered AI integration to ensure that technological advancement aligns with the core values of education.

DOI: 10.4018/979-8-3373-8027-8.ch002

INTRODUCTION

Artificial Intelligence (AI) has emerged as a defining force in the 21st-century education landscape, reshaping long-established assumptions about teaching, learning, and institutional functioning. The rapid expansion of digital technologies, coupled with increasing access to data and computational power, has positioned AI as a central component of contemporary educational reform (Soliha & Fadila, 2025). Its applications—ranging from adaptive learning systems and automated assessment to learning analytics and intelligent tutoring—demonstrate a shift toward more personalized, efficient, and data-informed educational environments. At the same time, AI introduces new pedagogical possibilities by supporting differentiated instruction, enhancing learner engagement, and assisting educators with complex decision-making (Chowdhury et al., 2025). Understanding AI within this broader socio-technological context is essential, as it reflects not only a technological advancement but also a transformation in how educational institutions conceptualize their roles and responsibilities in preparing learners for evolving global demands. Artificial Intelligence (AI) has caused significant changes in a number of sectors, including education (Bulathwela et al., 2024) (Chima Abimbola Edeni et al., 2024). Due to these advancements, AI must be taught in K–12 classrooms. However, the necessity for students to study AI necessitates that instructors focus more on it, think it's important, and plan to spread awareness of it among their peers and students (Temitayo et al., 2024).

Similar to the introduction of digital technologies in earlier decades, the incorporation of artificial intelligence (AI) into education offers a substantial possibility to improve teaching and learning. AI technology has been used in many aspects of engineering education, such as personalized learning, where AI tools have made it simpler to monitor student progress and customize instructional materials to each student's needs (Ravi, 2025). Artificial intelligence (AI) has become a disruptive force in many industries, changing how decisions are made, procedures are optimized, and results are attained. AI has brought cutting-edge tools and systems to education that meet the various needs of teachers and students. Adaptive learning systems allow students to advance at their own speed by providing personalized lessons based on real-time performance analysis. Teachers can now concentrate on more important facets of education, such as mentoring and encouraging creativity, thanks to automated grading software. By providing students with round-the-clock assistance and lowering reliance on conventional classroom boundaries, virtual teaching assistants have further improved accessibility. When taken as a whole, these AI-driven developments are creating a new paradigm in education by improving accessibility, efficiency, and personalization (M. Jeyakumaran et al., 2025). Research on artificial intelligence in education, or AIEd, is expanding quickly (BAI et al., 2024). As education systems adapt to the demands of a knowledge-based and digitally networked society, the integration of AI also prompts a re-examination of pedagogical priorities and institutional capacities. Schools and universities are increasingly expected to cultivate digital literacy, critical thinking, and problem-solving skills that align with AI-mediated environments. This shift requires educators to not only understand AI tools but also to critically evaluate their implications for curriculum design, assessment practices, and learner autonomy. Moreover, the growing presence of AI highlights disparities in access, infrastructure, and digital competence, underscoring the need for equitable policies that prevent the deepening of educational inequalities. Thus, contextualizing AI within the 21st-century education landscape involves recognizing both its transformative potential and the systemic challenges that accompany its adoption, calling for thoughtful, inclusive, and ethically grounded implementation strategies. By increasing student engagement, knowledge retention, and employability, the rapid development of smart classrooms and e-learning technology is transforming business education (Inamdar et al., 2024). Given that advanced artificial intelligence (AI) technology can customize instruction by supporting immediate instructional intervention, facilitating teachers' decision-making processes, and tailoring educational materials and feedback to individual student needs, it offers significant opportunities for enhancing teachers' pedagogical innovation (Shi et al., 2024).

UNDERSTANDING ARTIFICIAL INTELLIGENCE IN EDUCATION (AIED)

Understanding Artificial Intelligence in Education (AIED) requires an appreciation of how computational techniques are being used to interpret learning behaviours, support instructional decisions, and create responsive educational environments. AIED encompasses a wide range of approaches that analyse patterns in student data, identify learning needs, and provide timely guidance or resources. These systems do not replace the professional judgement of teachers; rather, they function as supportive tools that help educators manage diverse classrooms and offer more personalised pathways for learners. By drawing on principles from computer science, cognitive theory, and educational research, AIED attempts to design learning experiences that are adaptive, meaningful, and evidence-informed. As the field expands, it encourages educators and institutions to reconsider traditional methods and explore how intelligent digital systems can contribute to more effective and equitable learning opportunities (BAI et al., 2024).

AI AS A CATALYST FOR PEDAGOGICAL INNOVATION

Artificial Intelligence is emerging as a powerful catalyst for pedagogical innovation by enabling educators to rethink how learning is designed, facilitated, and assessed. Rather than simply automating routine tasks, AI introduces new possibilities for creating dynamic, learner-centred environments that respond to individual needs and preferences (Wei et al., 2024). Adaptive learning platforms, for instance, adjust the level and sequence of content based on a learner's progress, while intelligent tutoring systems offer targeted feedback that mirrors aspects of one-on-one instruction. AI-driven analytics provide educators with deeper insights into student engagement, misconceptions, and learning patterns, supporting more informed instructional decisions. These innovations encourage a shift from traditional, teacher-directed models toward more flexible, interactive, and inquiry-based approaches. As AI continues to evolve, it challenges educators to explore novel pedagogical strategies that blend human judgement with computational intelligence, ultimately enriching the learning experience and expanding opportunities for meaningful, personalised education. It is crucial to equip teachers for this changing environment since the development and spread of artificial intelligence (AI) technologies are changing STEM fields and pedagogical approaches. AI was acknowledged by STEM educators as a socio-affective tool that can improve teacher-student relationships and as a cognitive scaffold that can help students comprehend complicated content (Avci et al., 2025). Artificial intelligence (AI) in education has opened up new avenues for improving language learning, but its quick development presents problems if it is not balanced with psychological and cognitive preparedness (Hanifansyah, 2025).

The innovative potential of AI in pedagogy also lies in its ability to support richer forms of experiential and inquiry-based learning. By analysing how students interact with content, AI systems can recommend alternative pathways, resources, or activities that align with a learner's style, pace, or interests (Rahiman & Kodikal, 2024). This creates opportunities for deeper engagement and sustained curiosity. Furthermore, AI facilitates collaborative learning by connecting students with peers, mentors, or digital agents who can extend discussions and promote higher-order thinking. These developments are not meant to replace the teacher; rather, they empower educators to design more personalised and diverse learning experiences. When implemented thoughtfully, AI becomes a partner in expanding the pedagogical repertoire, allowing teachers to focus on facilitation, creativity, and the relational aspects of teaching that technology cannot replicate (Feng et al., 2025).

Artificial Intelligence (AI) has emerged as a transformative force in education, reshaping pedagogical practices and enabling more responsive, inclusive, and learner-centred instructional models. One of the most significant contributions of AI is its ability to generate personalized learning pathways, wherein students receive content, activities, and support tailored to their individual learning needs, pace, and preferences (Murakami et al., 2024). Adaptive learning platforms use real-time data analytics to continuously diagnose learner performance and automatically adjust the difficulty level, sequencing, and type of instructional materials. This data-driven approach empowers teachers to make informed decisions, identify learning gaps at an early stage, and optimize instructional time for targeted interventions.

AI further enhances pedagogy through the integration of Intelligent Tutoring Systems (ITS), which simulate one-to-one tutoring by offering immediate guidance, hints, and explanations. These systems support mastery learning and provide students with ample opportunities to practice concepts in safe, low-pressure environments. Additionally, AI-driven assessment and feedback mechanisms streamline both formative and summative evaluation by automating scoring, detecting patterns in student responses, and delivering timely, actionable feedback. Beyond assessment, AI enriches engagement through gamification, simulations, and immersive learning experiences, such as virtual labs, scenario-based learning, and AI-supported AR/VR environments. These innovations make complex concepts more accessible and cultivate higher-order thinking, problem-solving, and experiential learning. Collectively, AI technologies are redefining contemporary pedagogy by promoting flexibility, efficiency, and deeper learning outcomes. The importance of smart classrooms in contemporary educational settings has been greatly emphasized by the rapid advancement of artificial intelligence (AI) technologies. Even with this advancement, there are still significant obstacles in the way of automatically evaluating students' participation in smart classroom settings (Wei et al., 2024). ChatGPT is an innovative AI chatbot that has had a big impact on academia. Numerous research have examined the impact of AI on education, but there hasn't been much attention paid to the reasons why students use it (Chowdhury et al., 2024).

ENHANCING STUDENT LEARNING AND ENGAGEMENT THROUGH AI

Artificial intelligence has emerged as a powerful enabler for enhancing student learning and engagement by fostering more personalized, inclusive, and interactive educational experiences. AI-driven systems can analyze learners' progress, preferences, and learning patterns to tailor content, pacing, and instructional strategies, thereby supporting individualized learning trajectories and improving academic outcomes (Mena-Guacas et al., 2024). Such customization helps address diverse learning needs, including those of students who require additional support or advanced challenges. Moreover, AI-based tools facilitate active engagement by promoting inquiry, collaboration, and creativity through intelligent feedback, adaptive tasks, and interactive learning environments. By supporting self-regulated learning, these technologies encourage students to set goals, monitor their progress, and reflect on their learning processes. AI also expands opportunities for research, problem-solving, and collaborative knowledge construction by enabling access to intelligent search, data analysis, and co-creation tools. When thoughtfully integrated within pedagogically sound frameworks, AI can enhance learner motivation and engagement while maintaining the central role of human guidance and meaningful educational interactions.

AI FOR TEACHERS: SUPPORT, EFFICIENCY, AND PROFESSIONAL DEVELOPMENT

Artificial Intelligence offers substantial support to teachers by streamlining tasks, enhancing instructional quality, and strengthening professional growth (Alam et al., 2024). By automating administrative tasks such as attendance, grading, documentation, and scheduling, AI reduces teachers' workload and frees valuable time for instructional and mentoring activities. Additionally, AI-powered lesson planning and content creation tools assist educators in designing pedagogically sound and contextually relevant materials (Zhang et al., 2024). These tools can suggest learning objectives, curate resources, develop assessments, and generate differentiated tasks aligned with curriculum standards, enabling teachers to respond more effectively to diverse classroom needs. AI-driven classroom analytics further empower educators by providing real-time insights into learner performance, engagement patterns, and conceptual difficulties. Such evidence-based data support informed instructional decisions, allowing teachers to adjust pacing, identify struggling learners early, and personalise learning interventions (Wafik et al., 2024).

Alongside these instructional supports, AI also contributes to strengthening teachers' professional capacities. Platforms designed for digital pedagogy and continuous professional development offer adaptive learning modules, micro-credentialing, practice simulations, and reflective tools that help educators stay updated with emerging trends. These resources promote digital competence and enhance teachers' confidence in integrating technology meaningfully into their pedagogy (Shi et al., 2024). As AI becomes more embedded in classroom ecosystems, teachers' roles increasingly shift from information deliverers to facilitators of learning, guiding students in critical thinking, problem-solving, and responsible technology use. In this evolving landscape, teachers remain central to the learning process, using AI not as a replacement but as a collaborative partner to enrich instructional practice and strengthen learner outcomes (BAI et al., 2024).

Artificial Intelligence has become a valuable ally for teachers by easing administrative burdens, enhancing instructional planning, and creating new pathways for ongoing professional growth (Hurlburt & Reisman, 2024). AI-powered tools streamline time-consuming tasks such as grading objective assessments, organising attendance records, generating lesson plans, and analysing student performance data (Essien et al., 2024). By automating routine responsibilities, teachers gain more time to focus on higher-order tasks, including designing meaningful learning experiences and engaging with students individually. AI-based systems also assist in lesson preparation by suggesting resources, identifying common misconceptions, and aligning content with curriculum standards. In addition, intelligent platforms support professional development by offering personalised learning modules, instructional recommendations, and real-time feedback on teaching practices. These innovations do not aim to replace the teacher; rather, they strengthen the teacher's capacity to make informed decisions, respond to diverse learner needs, and continuously refine their professional competencies in a rapidly evolving educational landscape (Gofman & Jin, 2024).

The growing presence of AI in teachers' professional lives also encourages a shift toward more data-informed and reflective teaching practices. With access to detailed analytics on student engagement, learning progress, and common areas of difficulty, teachers can make more precise instructional adjustments and provide targeted interventions (Memarian & Doleck, 2024). These insights help educators differentiate instruction more effectively and anticipate learning challenges before they escalate. Moreover, AI-driven platforms facilitate collaborative professional development by enabling teachers to share resources, analyse classroom data collectively, and engage in virtual learning communities. Such environments promote continuous learning and foster a culture of innovation within schools. However, the effective use of AI in professional development requires thoughtful integration, adequate training, and an emphasis on ethical considerations to ensure that data-driven insights enhance rather than constrain teacher autonomy. When these conditions are met, AI becomes a meaningful partner in strengthening teacher expertise and advancing educational quality (Murakami et al., 2024).

AI FOR INCLUSIVE AND ACCESSIBLE EDUCATION

Artificial Intelligence has emerged as a powerful enabler of inclusive and accessible education by offering tools that address diverse learning needs and reduce structural inequities. A wide range of AI-supported tools for students with disabilities—including text-to-speech readers, predictive text applications, speech-to-text converters, and visual recognition systems—enhance learners' ability to access, interpret, and engage with educational content. These assistive technologies provide essential support for students with visual, auditory, cognitive, or motor impairments, ensuring greater autonomy and participation in classroom activities (Su & Yang, 2024). Additionally, AI-driven multilingual learning and translation tools facilitate comprehension for learners from varied linguistic backgrounds by offering real-time translation, language scaffolding, and adaptive vocabulary support. Such systems promote linguistic inclusion and help multilingual classrooms function more smoothly. Beyond addressing individual needs, AI contributes to reducing educational inequities through targeted interventions, using data analytics to identify learning gaps, recommend personalised support, and allocate resources where they are most needed. By offering timely feedback, differentiated instruction, and context-sensitive accommodations, AI helps create equitable learning environments where all students can thrive.

AI-enabled tools play a crucial role in supporting students with disabilities by providing accessible pathways to participate fully in learning. These technologies address a range of needs, including visual, auditory, cognitive, and motor impairments, through features that enhance information access and communication. For example, screen readers and text-to-speech systems help learners with visual impairments engage with written content, while speech-to-text tools assist students with hearing or motor challenges in expressing their ideas more easily. Cognitive support tools, such as guided reading platforms, simplified text generators, and task-management applications, offer structured assistance for learners who require additional processing support. Together, these tools promote greater independence, reduce barriers to participation, and create learning environments where students with disabilities can engage meaningfully and confidently with academic tasks.

AI-driven assistive technologies such as text-to-speech, predictive text, and visual recognition systems significantly enhance accessibility for learners with diverse disabilities. Text-to-speech tools convert written content into natural-sounding audio, enabling students with visual impairments, dyslexia, or reading difficulties to access information with greater ease. Predictive text applications support learners with motor challenges, language impairments, or writing difficulties by suggesting words and phrases, reducing the physical and cognitive load involved in producing written responses. Visual recognition technologies further extend accessibility by identifying objects, reading printed text aloud, and interpreting visual information—features particularly valuable for students with low vision or blindness. Together, these AI-assisted tools not only remove barriers to learning but also foster independence, confidence, and active participation in educational settings. The industry for artificial intelligence in educational tools and applications has grown quickly and garnered a lot of attention—not all of it constructive (Boulay, 2024).

AI has significantly strengthened multilingual learning by providing real-time language support and translation services that enhance comprehension and communication in diverse classrooms (J. Ou et al., 2025). AI-powered translation tools assist learners who are non-native speakers by offering instant translation of text, audio, and visual content, thereby reducing language barriers that often hinder participation and understanding. Adaptive language platforms personalise vocabulary development, grammar practice, and pronunciation feedback, helping students progress at their own pace while receiving targeted linguistic support. Additionally, AI-enabled captioning and subtitling tools make lectures and digital resources more accessible to multilingual learners, ensuring equitable access to instructional materials. By facilitating smoother interaction between teachers and students from different linguistic backgrounds, AI contributes to more inclusive, culturally responsive, and effective learning environments (Jamshed et al., 2025).

DATA, ETHICS, AND RESPONSIBLE USE OF AI IN EDUCATION

The increasing integration of AI into educational environments demands a careful examination of data governance, ethical considerations, and responsible use. One of the most pressing concerns relates to privacy, surveillance, and student data protection, as AI systems rely extensively on student information to generate insights and personalise learning. Without strict protocols and transparent data management practices, sensitive information may be misused or exposed to security breaches. Excessive monitoring through AI analytics can also contribute to a culture of surveillance, potentially affecting students' sense of autonomy, freedom, and trust. Ensuring compliance with data protection regulations, defining clear consent mechanisms, and maintaining robust cybersecurity measures are essential to safeguard students' digital rights.

Closely linked to privacy concerns are issues of bias, fairness, and algorithmic discrimination. AI tools trained on skewed or non-representative datasets may reinforce existing inequities by misclassifying learners, favouring dominant cultural or linguistic groups, or perpetuating stereotypes. Such biases threaten the inclusivity and equity that education seeks to uphold. Addressing this challenge requires regular auditing of algorithms, incorporating diverse datasets, and ensuring transparent mechanisms for reviewing AI-generated decisions. This vigilance helps create fairer systems that treat all learners with equal consideration.

To guide ethical and responsible AI deployment, international frameworks and guidelines have been developed by organisations such as UNESCO, OECD, and the European Union. These frameworks emphasise transparency, accountability, inclusiveness, human oversight, and respect for human dignity. Their principles help institutions and policymakers make informed decisions about adopting AI in a manner that is pedagogically meaningful and ethically sound. Embedding these guidelines into institutional policies ensures that AI supports, rather than undermines, the core goals of education.

Another important dimension of responsible AI use is digital well-being and safeguarding. While AI tools can enhance engagement and efficiency, they may also contribute to increased screen time, digital fatigue, or exposure to harmful online interactions. Students may experience stress due to continuous monitoring or automated assessments. Therefore, AI systems should be designed to promote healthy digital habits, encourage positive online behaviour, and provide protective measures against cyberbullying and inappropriate content. Supporting learners' emotional and psychological safety is essential for maintaining a balanced, holistic educational experience.

AI IN EDUCATIONAL ADMINISTRATION AND MANAGEMENT

AI has become an essential component of modern educational administration by enabling data-driven planning, operational efficiency, and proactive management. One of its most influential applications is the use of predictive analytics for enrollment, retention, and performance, where AI models analyse historical and real-time data to forecast admission trends, identify students at risk of dropout, and anticipate academic outcomes. These insights help institutions allocate resources strategically, design targeted support systems, and implement timely interventions that improve student success and institutional effectiveness. Institutions of higher learning are confronted with increasing difficulties. More effective resource management and administrative decision-making are required due to growing enrollment, tight budgets, and sustainability objectives. The AI wireless framework represents a significant advancement in the management and optimization of educational resources (Koukaras et al., 2025). A transition from reactive, siloed management to collaborative, predictive governance is made possible by bridging high-speed networks, robust IoT infrastructure, and sophisticated AI algorithms. The framework's modular design and forward-thinking mentality offer an appealing roadmap for institutions of various sizes, even while obstacles like infrastructure upgrades, data integration, and stakeholder approval must be overcome. This strategy will probably keep developing as technology continues to converge, providing educational leadership with a robust, effective, and essentially more intelligent way forward (Koukaras et al., 2025).

Beyond operational forecasting, AI also plays a transformative role in policy planning and institutional decision-making. By synthesising vast datasets related to student demographics, programme effectiveness, financial management, and institutional performance, AI tools support leaders in making evidence-based decisions. These systems can simulate policy scenarios, evaluate the potential impact of reforms, and identify areas requiring improvement, thereby strengthening strategic planning and governance. AI-driven dashboards offer administrators real-time visibility into institutional operations, promoting transparency and informed leadership.

In addition, the emergence of smart campuses and intelligent resource management has further enhanced institutional efficiency. AI-enabled systems automate functions such as energy optimisation, security management, classroom scheduling, and maintenance operations. Smart sensors and analytics support sustainable campus practices by monitoring resource consumption and optimising infrastructure usage. Integrated platforms streamline communication, improve accessibility of services, and enhance the overall campus experience for students, faculty, and staff. Through these innovations, AI contributes to more responsive, sustainable, and intelligent educational environments that align with the evolving needs of contemporary learners (Gunder et al., 2025).

CHALLENGES AND BARRIERS TO AI ADOPTION IN EDUCATION

The adoption of AI in education faces multiple challenges that limit its effective implementation and long-term sustainability. One of the most significant barriers stems from technological limitations and infrastructural gaps, particularly in regions where internet connectivity, digital devices, and technical support remain inadequate for AI-enabled learning environments. These disparities are closely connected to the digital divide and affordability issues, which restrict access to AI tools for underserved schools and marginalised learners, risking the widening of existing educational inequities. Additionally, a major obstacle lies in the lack of teacher readiness and training, as many educators feel unprepared to integrate AI into their pedagogy due to insufficient professional development, limited digital confidence, or unfamiliarity with emerging technologies. Beyond practical constraints, schools and communities often encounter cultural resistance and misconceptions, with concerns about job displacement, loss of teacher autonomy, and fears surrounding automation leading to hesitation or opposition. The situation is further complicated by governance and regulatory constraints, including unclear policy frameworks, gaps in accountability structures, and data management challenges, all of which hinder the responsible and transparent use of AI. Collectively, these barriers demonstrate that meaningful AI adoption in education requires not only technological investment but also strategic planning, capacity building, and ethical policy development to ensure equitable and sustainable transformation. University students frequently utilize AI-powered language tools (AILTs), but little is known about how they use and view these tools in regular academic communication practice (A. W. Ou et al., 2024).

Despite its transformative potential, the integration of AI in education faces several challenges and structural barriers that limit its widespread adoption. Technological limitations and infrastructural gaps remain among the most significant hurdles, especially in regions with inadequate internet connectivity, outdated hardware, or insufficient technical support. Many educational institutions lack the robust digital ecosystems required to implement AI-driven tools effectively, resulting in inconsistent access and limited functionality.

Closely related are concerns surrounding the digital divide and affordability issues, which disproportionately affect learners and institutions in under-resourced communities. The high cost of devices, software, and maintenance restricts opportunities for equitable participation, leading to uneven implementation across socio-economic groups. This disparity risks widening existing inequalities rather than fostering inclusion, particularly when AI tools become integral to academic support and assessment.

Another critical barrier is the lack of teacher readiness and training. Many educators feel unprepared to integrate AI meaningfully into their pedagogy due to limited exposure, inadequate professional development, or unfamiliarity with emerging technologies. Without sustained capacity-building initiatives, teachers may struggle to harness AI effectively, reducing its potential impact on learning and instructional quality.

In addition to technical and pedagogical challenges, cultural resistance and misconceptions can impede AI adoption. Concerns about job displacement, fears regarding excessive automation, and misunderstandings about the role of AI in education may create reluctance among educators, parents, and policymakers. These perceptions often stem from limited awareness of AI's collaborative and supportive capabilities.

Finally, effective AI integration is often constrained by governance and regulatory limitations. Many educational systems lack clear policies, ethical guidelines, or regulatory frameworks to ensure safe, transparent, and responsible AI use. Issues related to data privacy, accountability, and cross-border data governance further complicate adoption efforts. Establishing strong regulatory structures, ethical oversight, and institutional governance mechanisms is therefore essential to ensure that AI deployment aligns with educational values and protects the rights of all stakeholders.

FUTURE DIRECTIONS OF AI IN EDUCATION

The future of AI in education is poised to transform learning and teaching through innovative collaborations between humans and intelligent systems. AI-human collaboration models will increasingly define classrooms, where AI augments educators' capabilities rather than replacing them. Such models enable teachers to focus on critical thinking, creativity, and socio-emotional support while AI handles data-driven insights, adaptive instruction, and personalised learning pathways. The synergy between human expertise and AI efficiency is expected to enhance decision-making, instructional quality, and learner engagement. Through an engaging, flexible, and adaptable learning environment, technology-enabled education benefits business education. Digital literacy, ethics, and faculty acclimation are issues that require answers. Investing in faculty work, integrating AI-enabled data to enable individual learning, and expanding infrastructure to make it inclusive are all advised (Inamdar et al., 2024).

Generative AI is anticipated to play a central role in the next decade, supporting content creation, tutoring, assessment, and interactive learning experiences (Rahiman & Kodikal, 2024). From generating adaptive learning materials and simulations to providing tailored feedback on student work, generative AI will expand the possibilities of personalised education. Its capacity to produce creative and context-specific educational resources will allow educators to design richer, more flexible learning experiences that respond dynamically to student needs (Boscardin et al., 2024).

The integration of AI with AR/VR, robotics, and metaverse learning offers another frontier for transformative education. Immersive environments powered by AI will enable experiential, project-based, and simulation-driven learning, allowing students to interact with complex scenarios in safe, engaging, and highly interactive ways. Robotics combined with AI will enhance practical skill development, collaborative problem-solving, and hands-on experimentation across disciplines. Metaverse learning ecosystems will provide virtual campuses where learners can collaborate globally, explore simulated environments, and participate in innovative pedagogical models.

Looking forward, AI is expected to influence educational reforms by driving data-informed policy decisions, curriculum innovation, and equitable access initiatives. Institutions may adopt AI-powered assessment systems, predictive analytics for student success, and intelligent learning platforms that personalise education at scale. Collectively, these developments suggest a future where AI supports not only operational efficiency but also deeper, more meaningful learning, enabling education systems to evolve in alignment with the demands of the 21st-century knowledge society.

CASE STUDIES AND BEST PRACTICES

Examining real-world implementations of AI in education provides valuable insights into both the potential and challenges of integrating intelligent technologies. Global examples of successful AI deployment illustrate how diverse educational contexts leverage AI to enhance learning outcomes and operational efficiency. For instance, universities in the United States and Europe use predictive analytics to improve student retention and personalise academic advising, while schools in Asia and Africa implement AI-powered adaptive learning platforms to support individualized instruction and bridge learning gaps. Governments in several countries have introduced AI-driven policy tools to monitor educational progress, optimise resource allocation, and inform curriculum reforms.

Lessons learned from schools, universities, and governments highlight key factors for successful AI adoption. Effective implementation often depends on robust teacher training, transparent data governance, culturally responsive design, and alignment with pedagogical goals. Pilot projects demonstrate the importance of iterative testing, stakeholder engagement, and continuous monitoring to ensure AI tools deliver meaningful outcomes without reinforcing inequities or bias. These case studies also reveal that a collaborative approach, combining the expertise of educators, technologists, and policymakers, is critical for sustainable impact.

Finally, scalable and sustainable models of AI integration emphasise strategies that can be adapted across different educational contexts. Successful models typically combine adaptive learning systems, AI-assisted assessment, and data-driven decision-making with professional development for educators and strong institutional support (Sun & Sun, 2025). Sustainability is achieved through ongoing evaluation, policy frameworks, and ethical oversight, ensuring that AI contributes to long-term improvements in teaching and learning. These best practices provide actionable guidance for institutions seeking to implement AI in a responsible, effective, and scalable manner.

PREPARING TEACHERS FOR AI-DRIVEN EDUCATIONAL TRANSFORMATION

Teacher professional development in artificial intelligence has become a critical priority as educational systems adapt to rapidly evolving digital and societal demands. Effective AI-focused professional development goes beyond technical training and emphasises pedagogical understanding, ethical awareness, and reflective practice, enabling teachers to integrate AI meaningfully into teaching and learning processes (Tan et al., 2025). It supports educators in understanding how AI-driven tools can enhance lesson design, personalise learning pathways, and provide timely feedback while maintaining the central role of human judgment, empathy, and professional autonomy. Continuous and practice-oriented development models—such as mentoring, collaborative learning communities, and classroom-based experimentation—help teachers build confidence and reduce apprehension toward emerging technologies (Sun & Sun, 2025). Equally important is the cultivation of AI literacy, which empowers teachers to critically evaluate algorithmic decision-making, address issues of data privacy and bias, and guide students in responsible and informed use of AI (Huynh et al., 2025). Inclusive professional development frameworks also recognise disparities in access and readiness, ensuring that teachers from diverse institutional and socio-economic contexts receive equitable opportunities for capacity building. When aligned with institutional support and policy vision, teacher professional development in AI becomes a transformative process that strengthens instructional quality, promotes innovation, and prepares educators to lead learners in an increasingly intelligent and interconnected educational landscape (Somabut et al., 2025).

AN EXPLICIT CONCEPTUAL FRAMEWORK FOR AI-ENABLED CLASSROOMS TRANSFORM PEDAGOGY, ROLES, AND INSTITUTIONAL PRACTICES

An explicit conceptual framework for AI-enabled classrooms positions artificial intelligence as an integrative layer that reshapes pedagogical processes, redefines professional roles, and reorients institutional practices within the education system. At the pedagogical level, AI functions as a mediating tool that supports personalized, adaptive, and data-informed instruction, enabling learning designs that are responsive to individual learner needs while maintaining alignment with curricular goals. Teaching strategies shift from standardized content delivery toward facilitation, mentoring, and formative support, as real-time insights from learning analytics inform instructional decisions. In this framework, the role of teachers evolves from being primary transmitters of information to designers of learning experiences and ethical stewards of technology use, while students assume more active roles as self-directed learners who engage in inquiry, reflection, and collaborative knowledge construction. At the institutional level, AI influences assessment practices, academic support systems, and administrative decision-making by enabling predictive insights, streamlined processes, and evidence-based planning. Governance structures and professional development mechanisms are embedded within the framework to ensure responsible data use, transparency, and continuous capacity building. Collectively, this conceptual framework illustrates how AI-enabled classrooms do not merely introduce new tools but foster a systemic transformation in pedagogy, professional identity, and organizational culture, aligning technological innovation with educational values, equity, and human-centered learning.

RECOMMENDATIONS

Based on the preceding discussion, several recommendations are proposed to support the responsible and effective integration of artificial intelligence in education. First, educational institutions and policymakers should invest in robust digital infrastructure to ensure reliable access to AI-enabled tools across diverse educational contexts, particularly in underserved and rural areas. Second, systematic and continuous professional development programs should be designed to enhance teachers' digital competencies, ethical awareness, and pedagogical skills for integrating AI meaningfully into teaching and learning processes. Third, clear institutional policies and regulatory frameworks must be established to safeguard data privacy, ensure transparency, and mitigate algorithmic bias, thereby promoting trust and accountability in the use of AI systems. Fourth, curriculum frameworks should be revised to incorporate AI literacy, critical thinking, and ethical reasoning, enabling learners to engage with AI technologies as informed and responsible users. Fifth, inclusive design principles should guide the development and deployment of AI tools to address the needs of diverse learners, including students with disabilities and those from linguistically and socioeconomically diverse backgrounds. Finally, collaborative partnerships among educators, researchers, technologists, and policymakers should be encouraged to share best practices, evaluate impact, and develop scalable and context-sensitive models of AI integration. Collectively, these recommendations emphasize a balanced approach that aligns technological innovation with pedagogical purpose, equity, and ethical responsibility in education.

CONCLUSION

The integration of artificial intelligence into education represents a transformative opportunity to enhance teaching, learning, and institutional effectiveness, while also posing complex challenges that demand careful consideration. As discussed, AI has the potential to personalize learning, support diverse learners, empower teachers, and improve educational administration through data-informed decision-making and innovative pedagogical practices. At the same time, its adoption is constrained by technological and infrastructural limitations, persistent digital divides, gaps in teacher preparedness, cultural apprehensions, and evolving governance and regulatory frameworks. These challenges underscore the need for a balanced and context-sensitive approach that prioritizes ethical responsibility, inclusivity, and human-centered design. Effective implementation of AI in education must therefore move beyond mere technological deployment to encompass sustained professional development, equitable access, transparent data practices, and collaborative policy formulation. When guided by strong ethical principles and aligned with educational values, AI can function not as a replacement for human agency but as a complementary tool that strengthens the role of educators and enriches student learning experiences. Ultimately, the future of AI in education depends on thoughtful integration that harmonizes innovation with equity, accountability, and pedagogical integrity, ensuring that technological advancement contributes meaningfully to the broader goals of educational development and social progress.

REFERENCES

Alam, S., Hameed, A., Madej, M., & Kobylarek, A. (2024). Perception and practice of using Artificial Intelligence in education: An opinion based study. *XLinguae, 17*(1), 216–233. DOI: 10.18355/XL.2024.17.01.15

Avci, H., Lunn, S. J., & Hazari, Z. (2025). Exploring STEM educators ' perspectives on the integration of AI-enabled technologies in teaching and learning. *Computers and Education Open, 9*, 1–12. DOI: 10.1016/j.caeo.2025.100304

Bai, J. Y. H., Zawacki-Richter, O., & Muskens, W.BAI. (2024). RE-EXAMINING THE FUTURE PROSPECTS OF ARTIFICIAL INTELLIGENCE IN EDUCATION IN LIGHT OF THE GDPR AND ChatGPT. *Turkish Online Journal of Distance Education, 25*(1), 20–32. DOI: 10.17718/tojde.1248901

Boscardin, C. K., Gin, B., Golde, P. B., & Hauer, K. E. (2024). ChatGPT and Generative Artificial Intelligence for Medical Education: Potential Impact and Opportunity. *Academic Medicine, 99*(1), 22–27. DOI: 10.1097/ACM.0000000000005439 PMID: 37651677

Boulay, B. (2024). Pedagogy, Cognition, Human Rights, and Social Justice. *International Journal of Artificial Intelligence in Education, 34*(1), 116–121. DOI: 10.1007/s40593-023-00355-0

Bulathwela, S., Pérez-Ortiz, M., Holloway, C., Cukurova, M., & Shawe-Taylor, J. (2024). Artificial Intelligence Alone Will Not Democratise Education: On Educational Inequality, Techno-Solutionism and Inclusive Tools. *Sustainability (Basel), 16*(2), 1–20. DOI: 10.3390/su16020781

Chowdhury, A., Akter, S., Sultana, J., & Rahman, A. (2025). Computers and Education : Artificial Intelligence Can generative AI Be an effective Co-Teacher? An experiment. *Computers and Education: Artificial Intelligence, 8*(May), 1–15. DOI: 10.1016/j.caeai.2025.100418

Chowdhury, A., Bari, A., Sultana, J., Chowdhury, R., Meem, F., Islam, A., Mahmud, S., Jahan, I., & Sarkar, M. (2024). Computers and Education : Artificial Intelligence Why do students use ChatGPT? Answering through a triangulation approach. *Computers and Education: Artificial Intelligence, 6*(January), 1–13. DOI: 10.1016/j.caeai.2024.100208

Edeni, C. A., Adeleye, O. O., & Adeniyi, I. S.Chima Abimbola EdeniOlabisi Oluwakemi AdeleyeIdowu Sulaimon Adeniyi. (2024). The role of AI-enhanced tools in overcoming socioeconomic barriers in education: A conceptual analysis. *World Journal of Advanced Research and Reviews*, *21*(3), 944–951. DOI: 10.30574/wjarr.2024.21.3.0780

Essien, A., Bukoye, O. T., O'Dea, X., & Kremantzis, M. (2024). The influence of AI text generators on critical thinking skills in UK business schools. *Studies in Higher Education*, *49*(5), 865–882. DOI: 10.1080/03075079.2024.2316881

Feng, T., Xu, J., & Wu, K. (2025). Design of Multimedia Education and Teaching Management System based on Artificial Intelligence and Computational Technology. *Scalable Computing: Practice and Experience*, *26*(4), 1653–1670. DOI: 10.12694/scpe.v26i4.4531

Gofman, M., & Jin, Z. (2024). Artificial Intelligence, Education, and Entrepreneurship. *The Journal of Finance*, *79*(1), 631–667. DOI: 10.1111/jofi.13302

Gunder, A., Vito, M., Ramirez, M., & Arcolin, C. (2025). Bridging Borders: Global Faculty Learning Communities on AI for Transforming Teaching and Learning. *Ubiquity Proceedings*, *6*(1), 1–8. DOI: 10.5334/uproc.185

Hanifansyah, N. (2025). Reviving the Arabic Language Instinct: A Psycholinguistic and AI Synergy. *Al-Wazan: Journal of Arabic Education*, *3*(1), 32–47. DOI: 10.58223/al-wazan.v3i1.338

Hurlburt, G., & Reisman, S. (2024). Intelligence in Education : First of Two Roundtables. *Computer*, *57*(January), 21–26. DOI: 10.1109/MC.2023.3327648

Huynh, L., Le, T. H., Dang, B., An, B. T., Vu, C. T., & Nguyen, A. (2025). Mindset matters : Fostering teachers ' responsible AI use through professional development. *Journal of New Approaches in Educational Research*, *14*(23), 1–24. DOI: 10.1007/s44322-025-00043-y

Inamdar, V., Jadhav, P., & Singh, S. (2024). SMART CLASSROOMS AND E-LEARNING : THE FUTURE OF BUSINESS EDUCATION. *ShodhKosh: Journal of Visual and Performing Arts*, *5*(6), 2940–2950. DOI: 10.29121/shodhkosh.v5.i6.2024.6062

Jamshed, M., Fatimah Albedah, , & Sameena Banu, Mohd Sajid Ansari. (2025). Assessing the Efficacy of AI-Driven Corrective Feedback via WhatsApp Application to Improve ESL Learners' Writing Skills. [IJIM]. *International Journal of Interactive Mobile Technologies*, *19*(07), 190–205. DOI: 10.3991/ijim.v19i07.52709

Jeyakumaran, M., D., P. Saravanan, D., & K. Sundararajan, P. (. (2025). Revolutionizing Education: The Impact of Artificial Intelligence on Personalized Learning and Teacher Roles in India. [IJSMS]. *International Journal of Science and Management Studies*, *8*(1), 5–14. DOI: 10.51386/25815946/ijsms-v8i1p102

Koukaras, C., Hatzikraniotis, E., Mitsiaki, M., Koukaras, P., Tjortjis, C., & Stavrinides, S. G. (2025). Revolutionising Educational Management with AI and Wireless Networks: A Framework for Smart Resource Allocation and Decision-Making. *Applied Sciences (Basel, Switzerland)*, *15*(10), 1–30. DOI: 10.3390/app15105293

Memarian, B., & Doleck, T. (2024). Computers in Human Behavior : Artificial Humans Human-in-the-loop in artificial intelligence in education : A review and entity-relationship (ER) analysis. *Computers in Human Behavior: Artificial Humans*, *2*(1), 1–11. DOI: 10.1016/j.chbah.2024.100053

Mena-Guacas, A. F., Vázquez-Cano, E., Fernández-Márquez, E., & López-Meneses, E. (2024). Artificial intelligence and its scientific production in the area of education | La inteligencia artificial y su producción científica en el campo de la educación. *Formación Universitaria*, *17*(1), 155–164. DOI: 10.4067/S0718-50062024000100155

Murakami, Y., Sho, Y., & Inagaki, T. (2024). Improving Motivation in Learning AI for Undergraduate Students by Case Study. *Journal of Information Processing*, *32*(0), 175–181. DOI: 10.2197/ipsjjip.32.175

Ou, A. W., Stöhr, C., & Malmström, H. (2024). Academic communication with AI-powered language tools in higher education: From a post-humanist perspective. *System*, *121*(January), 1–14. DOI: 10.1016/j.system.2024.103225

Ou, J., Nogueira, J., & Qin, C. (2025). Exploring the impact of AI-assisted practice applications on music learners' performance, self-efficacy, and self-regulated learning. *Frontiers in Psychology*, *16*(October), 1–15. DOI: 10.3389/fpsyg.2025.1675762 PMID: 41159183

Rahiman, H. U., & Kodikal, R. (2024). Revolutionizing education : Artificial intelligence empowered learning in higher education Revolutionizing education : Artificial intelligence empowered learning in higher education. *Cogent Education*, *11*(1), 1–25. DOI: 10.1080/2331186X.2023.2293431

Ravi, M. (2025). Using the TPACK Framework for Gen-AI Enabled Learning Activities: Design, Delivery and Evaluation. *Journal of Engineering Education Transformations, 38*(Special Issue 2), 175–181. DOI: 10.16920/jeet/2025/v38is2/25021

Shi, L., Ding, A. E., & Choi, I. (2024). Investigating Teachers' Use of an AI-Enabled System and Their Perceptions of AI Integration in Science Classrooms: A Case Study. *Education Sciences*, *14*(11), 1–19. DOI: 10.3390/educsci14111187

Soliha, I. A., & Fadila, Y. (2025). Implementation of an Interactive Chatbot System Using ChatGPT and Leonardo AI to Support Islamic Studies Teaching for MI Teachers. *GUYUB: Journal of Community Engagement*, *6*(2), 439–459. DOI: 10.33650/guyub.v6i2.10587

Somabut, A., Tuamsuk, K., Lowatcharin, G., Traiyarach, S., & Kwangmuang, P. (2025). Social Sciences & Humanities Open Preparing for the AI era : Science teachers ' readiness and professional development needs for generative AI integration in secondary education. *Social Sciences & Humanities Open*, *12*(November), 1–14. DOI: 10.1016/j.ssaho.2025.102259

Su, J., & Yang, W. (2024). AI literacy curriculum and its relation to children's perceptions of robots and attitudes towards engineering and science: An intervention study in early childhood education. *Journal of Computer Assisted Learning*, *40*(1), 241–253. DOI: 10.1111/jcal.12867

Sun, N., & Sun, Y. (2025). Acta Psychologica The role of artificial intelligence (AI) tools in EFL teachers ' passion for self-directed professional development. *Acta Psychologica*, *260*(June), 1–7. DOI: 10.1016/j.actpsy.2025.105546 PMID: 40945144

Tan, X., Cheng, G., & Ling, M. H. (2025). Computers and Education : Artificial Intelligence Artificial intelligence in teaching and teacher professional development : A systematic review. *Computers and Education: Artificial Intelligence, 8*(October 2024), 1–19. DOI: 10.1016/j.caeai.2024.100355

Temitayo, I., Musa, S., & Ayanwale, A. (2024). Investigating the moderating effects of social good and confidence on teachers' intention to prepare school students for artificial intelligence education. *Education and Information Technologies*, *29*(1), 273–295. DOI: 10.1007/s10639-023-12250-1

Wafik, H. M. A., Mahbub, S., Arif, Z., Prince, S. K. A., & Huda, M. N. (2024). Academicians' Perspectives on AI Integration in Bangladesh's Education: Balancing Promise and Ethical Realities. *Cognizance Journal of Multidisciplinary Studies*, *4*(2), 139–158. DOI: 10.47760/cognizance.2024.v04i02.014

Wei, L., Wang, F., & Wan, L. (2024). AI-Enabled Learning Engagement Assessment for Smart Classrooms : Applications, Trends and Opportunities. *Journal of Intelligence and Knowledge Engineering*, *2*(4), 64–73. http://www.stemmpress.com. DOI: 10.62517/jike.202404411

Zhang, C., Liu, Z., Aravind, B. R., & Hariharasudan, A. (2024). Synergizing language learning: SmallTalk AI In industry 4.0 and Education 4.0. *PeerJ. Computer Science*, *10*, 1–26. DOI: 10.7717/peerj-cs.1843 PMID: 38435575

KEY TERMS AND DEFINITIONS

Adaptive Learning Systems: Digital platforms that use data and algorithms to modify instructional content in response to learners' performance and progress.

AI Literacy: The knowledge and skills required to understand, use, and critically evaluate AI technologies in educational and social contexts.

Algorithmic Bias: Systematic errors in AI systems that result in unfair or discriminatory outcomes due to biased data or design processes.

Artificial Intelligence (AI): Computer-based systems designed to perform tasks that typically require human intelligence, such as learning, reasoning, and decision-making.

Assistive Technology: Technological tools designed to support learners with disabilities by enhancing accessibility and participation in learning activities.

Digital Divide: The gap between individuals or groups in terms of access to digital technologies, internet connectivity, and digital skills.

Ethical AI: The development and use of AI systems in ways that are transparent, fair, accountable, and respectful of human rights and privacy.

Intelligent Tutoring Systems (ITS): AI-driven tools that provide individualized guidance, feedback, and support to learners without continuous human intervention.

Learning Analytics: The collection and analysis of learner data to understand and improve learning processes and educational outcomes.

Personalized Learning: An instructional approach in which learning content, pace, and strategies are adapted to meet individual learners' needs and abilities.

Chapter 3

Redefining Teachers and Learners in Cambodia:

Building AI-Literate Educators and Critical Student Thinkers in the New Classroom Ecology

Sovanna Huot
http://orcid.org/0009-0006-8335-442X
Department of Education, National Institute of Education, Phnom Penh, Cambodia

Sovanna Loch
http://orcid.org/0000-0002-1211-1248
Department of English, Nava Nalanda Mahavihara University, Bihar, India

Chheangkhy Hok
http://orcid.org/0009-0000-6431-527X
Department of Khmer Literature, University of Heng Samrin Thbongkhmum, Cambodia

Sovannaroth Chheang
http://orcid.org/0009-0007-3382-7169
Department of English, Sovanna Elton Foreign Language School, Phnom Penh, Cambodia

Kimyut Phin
http://orcid.org/0009-0009-5667-7313
Department of English, University of Delhi, New Delhi, India

DOI: 10.4018/979-8-3373-8027-8.ch003

ABSTRACT

This chapter considers the impact of Artificial Intelligence on teachers' and students' roles within Cambodia's higher education system and makes the case for pedagogy-led, ethics-first integration of AI tools within the education system. It posits that educators will need to shift from being content repositories to becoming learning architects and facilitators. Students will also need to shift from being passive consumers of AI tools to being active collaborators who use and engage with AI tools responsibly and reflectively. This chapter makes the case for institutions to incorporate ethical, AI education, and digital equity frameworks to balance and align with available national policies to ensure the sustainable use of AI. This will help ensure that system strengthen the human capacity for self-governance and cultural ingenuity in the presence of AI toward operationalization the human judgment first, AI second notion to foster responsible innovation.

I. INTRODUCTION

The higher education system in Cambodia is experiencing rapid changes owing to technological advancements, new priorities in national development, and demands for modernization on a global level. For the past decade, the Royal Government of Cambodia has been implementing Digital Education as part of closing the gaps in the Cambodian education sector with global and regional frameworks of the Fourth Industrial Revolution. In the Cambodian context, digital literacy, and the reforms that accompany it, is an agenda of national and academic competitiveness. Thus, the MoEYS (2018) visions and policies on education reforms cannot sidestep digital literacy, and so too, the education sector in Cambodia (Un & Sok, 2022). For Cambodia to be able to engage with the ASEAN Knowledge Economy, the education sector must undergo digital transformation (Sen, 2019).

Cambodian university students have begun using AI in class as they gain access to tools such as ChatGPT, Google Gemini, Khanmigo, GrammarlyGO and the like (Huot & Loch, 2025). Students, as per the initial classroom observation and report by the institution, have been employing AI to assist their writing, translating, generating ideas, and summarizing, as well as providing and preparing exam questions (Huot & Tep, 2025). Holmes et al. (2019) have observed the most recent global changes whereby AI fundamentally changes the way students learn, the type of feedback they receive, and the way they perform tasks. This is particularly true for Cambodia, but there is also a large disparity in the access and preparedness for teaching digitally. While many AIs are being integrated into campus life at urban universities, rural universities remain constrained by poor connectivity, outdated infrastructure, and a broad range of inequities in technological literacy and competencies among students and educators (Huot & Em, 2025). Integrating AI into Cambodia's higher education will mean more than just technological adoption. It will necessitate a fundamental change in teaching and learning mechanisms. Selwyn (2019) says educational technologies do not just refine systems; they disrupt and transform whole new systems of pedagogy.

To understand the reasons for the perception of novelty and importance of AI in Cambodian higher education, the historical context of the teacher-student relationship must be reviewed. Education in Cambodia has historically been a one-way street of instruction without dialogue. The teacher has consistently occupied the dominant position in classroom, holding primary authority and being regarded as the principal source of knowledge. This hierarchy has dominated learning activities and has prioritized information transmission rather than interaction. This has had a significant impact on the reception and interpretation of new pedagogical technologies such as AI in higher education. The students will sit and be quiet, listen, memorize, and regurgitate what is told.

Lim and Keuk (2017) have shown us that the sociocultural framework of a classroom mirrors the classroom setting of Cambodia, stemming from the classroom setting of Cambodia, stemming from a sociocultural framework of authority, and a framework of socio-cultural relationships that emphasize the importance of hierarchical relationships. Zhang et al. (2010) also state that students do not have the freedom to ask questions to teachers. The result of all of this has been students being the inactive sponges of the class. Davies (1994) has shown us that the neglect of traditional education gives way to the dependence that education is rote, and that the plan of education is predetermined. Learning inequalities limit higher-order thinking skills, which are increasingly important for all knowledge-based societies, to only one of the societies. Huot and Loch (2025) argue that all other societies will leave Cambodians behind unless they learn how to analyse, synthesize, and create knowledge rather than just memorize and regurgitate. The continuing predominance of teacher-cantered paradigms of instruction makes this essential transition even more difficult. The development of AI technologies must therefore be aligned with, and will greatly amplify, the calls for an abandonment of transmission-based teaching in universities in Cambodia.

AI's effect on teachers' and students' roles has never been this drastic. According to Williamson and Piattoeva (2020), and mediation of AI systems' cognitive decision making shifts the pedagogical interaction balance of teaching and learning. AI will let the flow of information in the classes of Cambodian teachers who control the flow of information and technology, and pedagogical AI tools will destabilize the belief that teachers must control the instructional pacing and be the primary knowledge source. One primary stimulus of this transformation is the AI systems' automation of administrative and instructional purposes. AI systems of pedagogy will lessen the grading workload, lesson planning, data tracking, and feedback to students' automation. According to Luckin (2018), the removal of routine work that has no instructional value will result in heightened complexity of primary instructional work, eliminating the need for teachers to facilitate, mentor, redesign learning activities and to use inquiry of students as the primary focus. The combination of automation and personalized instructions from various computer programs has started to challenge the old ideas about teaching an entire class as one unit. For example, pivot table assignments take much less time and effort for teachers to create, adjust, and present using technology. This enables teachers to tailor their teaching to the unique needs and mental profiles of each student. According to Popenici and Kerr (2017), this completely shifts the learning paradigm from instructor-led to student-centered.

Moreover, in many instances, AI stands as the only example of a content creator, which is both unique and quite interesting. Generative language algorithms can produce human-level texts, including essays, decontextualized explanations, and datasets. While there is a range of advantages to using these systems for learning, there is also a plethora of risks. For example, Buolamwini and Gebru (2018) note that, given the lack of culture and diversity to the training data, AI systems serve a primary imprecise, biased, and culturally insensitive to the western world. Critical literacy to examine, question, and assess the context of AI systems is an absolute necessity for Cambodians. You may also have to deal with a different kind of risk with AI systems.

In the presence of AI systems, one might experience erosion of critical thinking, cognitive effort, and increase chances of academic dishonesty. Klugman (2021) refers to these systems as "black boxes" that could be used to steer human actions in an unethical, unaccountable, and systematic way. This chapter seeks to assist Cambodia in managing the challenges and opportunities brought by the incorporation of AI within the existing higher education systems. Most importantly, the chapter aims to explore the transformations in the roles of teachers and students as AI becomes integrated in the teaching and learning processes. Educators will have to view themselves as learning designers, mentors, ethical gatekeepers, and evaluators of AI. Students will have to take on the position of active co-creators, and responsible, critical, and ethical users of AI. The second contribution of the chapter will be the formulation of an AI literacy framework for Cambodia, which will involve the localization and contextualization of global AI concepts and AI literacy to the cultural and institutional context of Cambodia.

II. CHANGING ROLE OF TEACHERS IN THE AI ERA

2.1 From Content Deliverer to Learning Architect

Cambodian teachers, for many generations, have been and still are culturally and professionally positioned as authoritative chroniclers due to the influence of the country's Buddhist customs and hierarchical social order. According to Zhang et al. (2010), in Southeast Asia, teacher centeredness is not a pedagogical preference, but a cultural one as it embodies and manifests the ideals of respect, order, and harmony. However, the application of AI in higher education classrooms makes this approach to teaching and learning unsustainable. With Luckin (2018), it is AI that redistributes the burden of expertise as information delivery becomes the domain of the machine. Human instructors, however, are still relevant as ChatGPT, Gemini, and other adaptive learning resources summarize information, generate explanations, and provide examples at a speed that far outstrips them. This shift also does not remove teachers' authority but transfers it to a different location in the learning space.

Cambodian teachers now must look at education from a different perspective. They now need to understand the importance of shifting from being mere knowledge transmitters to being creators of learning journeys that inspire. Charlton et al. (2012) argue that such mentoring in the digital era involves creating a clear learning path that encourages students to move through a particular cycle of a learning process that involves questioning, reflecting, providing feedback, and adjusting. This design-focused approach encourages teachers to collect and organize materials around a particular problem, and then guide students through exploration around this problem, integrating pedagogically purposeful AI. A teacher guide may do the same in social science class, ask students to generate ai tool prompts to discuss a contemporary social issue in Cambodia and to cross check the AI-generated response against academic literature, government publications, or the local media (Huot et al., 2026). Students may discuss the AI-generated responses and identify the accurate and oversimplified AI-generated content, and which gap perspectives were not included. This type of activity demonstrates teachers as thoughtful mentors and guide the students to make sophisticated judgements and engage in reflective analysis supported by evidence and reasoning. A teachers guide for example very well might make students in his Cambodian university writing class use chat GPT to get sample essay introductions about environmental sustainability (Huot & Tep, 2025).

With the aid of the AI-generated content, students sample what they would get to analyze counter arguments, identify persuasive weak arguments, or write about vague arguments revisions using the class standards. This will make the teacher not be the only content provider but make the teacher a guide for the students in an activity where they use AI as a helpful resource to provide answers or make content more sophisticated. This approach sees AI as a tool teachers use and not a substitute for teachers. Holmes et al. (2019) maintain that the best AI tools in education focus on enhancing the abilities teachers already have. AI allows teachers to support students in a more personalized way and spend more time on feedback and dialogue with students.

2.2 From Instructor to Mentor and Critical Thinking Facilitator

Teachers facilitating AI-mentored classrooms must also go beyond learning environment design and be scanners of learning and critical thinking. As AI continues to assist with procedural and information tasks, it is human educators who foster judgment, interpretation, and, more importantly, ethical reasoning, the elements Nussbaum (2011) highlights as necessary for democratically engaged citizenship and human thriving. The Cambodian students' strong memorization and reproduction skills beg for scaffolding with a more complex layers of analysis, argumentative and evaluative thinking. It is for these higher-order thinking skills that teachers must focus on and assist students in learning to examine and critique an assumption, an AI- produced text, and its information against a multiplicity of sources.

While AI tools can be provocateurs of inquiry learning, their outputs must be thoroughly interrogated. As noted by Bender et al. (2021), large language models unmapped text and their erroneous and biased content. Students trained in critical evaluation, however, are more likely to surround un-critically accepted text. The onus becomes Cambodian educators to develop students' critical interpretation and analytical skills to detach from AI text. This is achieved by students regulating their metacognition as they confront AI tasks or content, by constructing and explaining their reasoning rather than absorbing what is, and by evaluating from their ethics altitudes to AI spawn response. Additionally, instructors must learn how to assist students with the ethical challenges posed by AI. Klugman (2021) states that there are ways algorithmic systems control knowledge, and that might affect ways of thinking, and there's no clear way of knowing how.

2.3 Teachers as Ethical Gatekeepers

While the advantages of generative AI in education are unquestionable, as the technology is integrated into education, the potential issues concerning bias, misinformation, privacy, surveillance, and academic dishonesty, among others, will need to be addressed. Accordingly, Cambodian teachers as ethical gatekeepers will need to defend and guide the responsible and transparent use of AI. Floridi (2019) interprets this responsibility as vital in defining the moral perimeter of the digital realm, asserting that the digital divide is no longer an issue of technology alone, but of ethics. Educators need to teach students the fact that AI can and will introduce cultural and linguistic bias, particularly when it is the product of a tool that draws from a Western dataset and will be used in a Cambodian context.

In Cambodia, where students use AI for translation, writing, and research tasks, teachers explain not how AI works, but how it does not work. Buolamwini and Gebru (2018) have shown that algorithmic bias either intentionally or unintentionally excludes certain language and demographic groups, demonstrating that AI is not a uniform entity without biases. Educators, therefore, must teach students how to spot biases embedded in AI outputs to cultivate a culture of critique that stems from curiosity rather than a culture of critique that stems from apathy. An illustration can be described with translation activities in classrooms, where learners attempt to use AI to translate values of Cambodian culture to English. Teachers can direct students to see if the AI-generated text distorts, overlooks, or captures, local meaning, cultural subtleties, or presuppositions of an alien context, especially if the context is not Cambodian (Huot & Loch, 2025). Students learn to criticize AI-generated responses through these activities instead of treating them as neutral or contextually valid. Issues of privacy and data security must also be addressed.

As Zuboff (2019), states, digital systems increasingly capture and store data to monetize it, often without the user's knowledge or consent. Educators in Cambodia are therefore expected to teach students digital footprint management, informed consent regarding data use, and responsible practices regarding data. On the institutional side, universities could further this ethical stance by formulating rules at the classroom level, encouraging students to refrain from inputting personal, sensitive, unpublished, or proprietary information, or research into AI systems with public access (Hok et al., 2026; Huot & Such, 2025). Therefore, it is within these rules that teachers can base discussion on privacy, consent, and responsible behavior in the digital space, to build ethical conduct on practice.

2.4 AI Skills Required for Modern Cambodian Educators

An AI-centred classroom in Cambodian schools means teachers need to develop and expand their digital pedagogy and classroom management skills within and beyond the standard ICT frameworks. New challenges and skills emerge such as prompt literacy, which entails the writing of specific prompts that guide AI on what type of response to generate for it to be accurate and relevant to the pedagogy. As noted by Brown and Cariveau (2024), prompt engineering, as the most basic layer of AI, describes the scope and usefulness of the output of the AI for the user. This means that prompt engineering is the first step in the process of managing and engaging with the content produced by AI in a constructive way.

Cambodian educators should be trained on how to design prompts that guide student questioning, assist students in language acquisition, or produce materials for differentiated instruction. Interpreting and unscrambling AI system data is yet another. Educators need to know how AI systems predict, analyse, and generate data as patterns. To this point, Williamson (2017) argues that educational systems are, more than ever, reliant on algorithms, and it thus remains the case that educators need to understand how data, and the systems that work with it, control learning environments. Hence, Cambodian educators need to understand AI analytics and predictive data outputs and work within the data guiding student learning. Another aspect worth considering is the integration of digital tools. AI tools such as adaptive learning platforms, systems with capabilities to detect plagiarism, and generative writing assistants should also be part of the technological tools that educators use. According to Koehler et al. (2017), understanding the interplay of technology, pedagogy, and the subject content is crucial to the successful integration of technology. This what is called TPACK (Technological Pedagogical Content Knowledge). This is the framework that educators in Cambodia will need to ensure that the use of AI tools is supportive of rather than at odds with the pedagogical aims.

Professional development focusing on AI literacy is crucial to the understanding and execution of the new AI roles and competencies. Considering the complexity of these new roles and competencies, Voogt and Knezek (2016) suggested that professional development on technology is most effective using a stepwise approach, focusing on building teacher confidence, and active strategies that incorporate direct engagement with the technology, and a close alignment with the instructional strategies being used. Cambodia's teachers for the future mentioned in *Table 1*, the human sides of teaching and the use of technology in the teaching and learning relationship are more important and will be more important than ever.

Table 1.

Core Theme	Short Summary
Cognitive & Metacognitive Processes	Reading involves executive functions and self-regulated learning; skilled readers monitor, evaluate, and repair understanding.
Motivation & Affective Foundations	Intrinsic motivation and emotional engagement sustain reading effort and deepen comprehension.
Mindfulness in Reading	Present-moment awareness enhances focus, emotional regulation, and cognitive flexibility during reading.
Mindful Reading Framework (MRF)	Integrates monitoring, motivation, affective balance, and reflective meaning-making into a unified literacy model.

III. CHANGING ROLES OF STUDENTS IN AI ERA

3.1 The Arrival of AI

The traditional pedagogy of Cambodia has encouraged behaviours of passive learning. For years, students have mindlessly listened within the classroom, recorded information, and later regurgitated information on exams. In this line, Lim and Keuk (2017) argue that this type of passivity is not only cognitive but is culturally embedding through the values of deference, authority, and social harmony. However, the arrival of AI tools disrupts this dynamic. Large language models (LLMs) such as ChatGPT or Gemini produce ideas, explanations, outlines, and arguments in seconds. If students are still being passive, they are outsourcing their thought processes to a machine, undermining their cognitive development. Thus, a shift is needed toward the more active, collaborative creation of knowledge. Popenici and Kerr (2017) explain that in an ideal setting, tools of AI are not to be thought of as replacing a collaborator and human mind, but as assisting one. Students can shift LLMs to use as a brainstorming technique to formulate ideas, draw arguments, or simulate and defend from multiple positions. However, the responsibility of idea refining and evaluation remain to the students. This shift is an example of Vygotsky (1978), Sociocultural Theory which posits that learning occurs through social interaction and constructive meaning rather than passive reception.

In Cambodia, education has placed external demands on students' internal learning processes, such that it is now critical for students to analyze and critique the reasoning and answers provided by AI to foster engagement and intellectual autonomy. This active engagement shifts students from being passive consumers of knowledge to becoming collaborators in the creation of new knowledge. Students create knowledge when they merge AI-generated text with their own insights, personal experiences, and knowledge of the relevant discipline. This collaborative knowledge creation is necessary because of AI's inability to consider contextual nuances. Bender et al. (2021) explain that the text generation of AI models is a pattern recognition function of statistical models, which is not true comprehension. Therefore, Cambodian students AI's contextual, cultural and ethical reasoning cannot be provided. In this way, AI becomes a cognitive support tool for thinking and formulating ideas, but not for reasoning and concluding.

3.2 From Recitation to Critical Evaluation

Cambodian higher education has focused on rote learning and recitation for many years. Davies (1994) notes how students have been conditioned to repeat information instead of critiquing it, and this has been paired with an examination-based education system. However, the role of AI in education removes recitation's value. AI tools can generate answers to questions and provide summaries, definitions, and explanations. They are even better than students at tasks requiring factual recall. This requires students to rethink cognitive priorities in the direction of higher-order critical evaluation from the simple memorization.

One of the most important things that students need to learn Is that the benefits of AI are not unlimited. According to scholars Floridi (2019) and Klugman (2021), the output of AI is not conclusive information but only probabilistic patterns. Additionally, the AI systems that are trained can fabricate things, which means they can give false information while sounding confident. Furthermore, the AI systems that are trained to produce information can contain errors that stem from their bias toward unequal accuracy and fairness. Cambodian students need to learn how to recognize errors. This means that They need to learn how to note discrepancies, evaluate the reliability of information, and check information against other sources. This change is in accordance with the framework of Paul and Elder (2014) constitute that the essence of critical thinking, and which consists of value, questioning, and interpretation. In most cases, thinking critically involves the use of metacognition which is the level of thinking in which a person can consider his or her thinking. According to Flavell (1979), awareness of the metacognitive process means that learners will understand when they do not understand. This awareness means that learners will change their thinking strategies and will control how much thinking they do.

3.3 Students as Self-Regulated Learners

The adoption of AI tools in post-secondary education is paradigm shifting, making available for the first time fully tailored individual learning experiences. Technologies of the kind of adaptive learning, such as AI tutors, and technologies which provide intelligent feedback and adjust content to the learner's needs in terms of granularity, pace and modality, can provide individualized learning. As Luckin (2018) observed, such learning environments can foster self-regulated learning because students can assume full autonomy in the planning, monitoring, and evaluating of their learning.

That said, personalized learning technologies only lead to enhanced learning in environments where learners have adopted self-autonomy. If students use AI to bypass cognitive effort, they are unwilling themselves to their own problem solving, and even conceptual understanding. Self-regulated learning, as described by Zimmerman (2002), also involves the learner, as to form goals, track progress, and reflect on the outcomes. AI is capable of a portion of these steps, such as providing instant feedback, but not the portion where the learner needs to show their metacognitive capacity. Given the reliance on teacher-centred pedagogy in Cambodia, the shift towards self-regulated learning will require efforts in the development of self-regulation learning skills through various means. Students first and foremost will have to learn to use AI in the context of learning, as opposed to simple task completion. They will also have to learn to manage their focus, stay on task, and maintain motivation in the face of distraction, which digital environments are rife with. Winne and Hadwin (2013) have shown that the academic performance of self-regulated students is of a higher Caliber, as well as being more resilient, as they adapt better to the demands of complex learning environments.

In addition, the use of customized AI is an immense resource that provides the opportunity for students to learn and re-learn the content at their own pace, which ultimately benefits the learners who are slower. That said, more advanced learners will also benefit from the tailored approach. However, with such autonomy comes the need for a greater sense of responsibility. Students will have to make decisions regarding the appropriateness of AI assistance, the need for solo problem solving, and the benefits of collaboration with peers and the teacher to enhance their understanding of a particular concept. It is therefore from this that the self-regulation of learning using AI needs to be disciplined cognitively and emotionally.

3.4. Ethical and Responsible AI Use

With the increasing prevalence of AI tools in academic contexts, students' ethical responsibilities also increase. Perhaps the greatest of these challenges is the risk of plagiarism and achieving assignments without doing the academic work. Zuboff

(2019) states that the digital world skews the balance between true authorship and automated production. In the case of Cambodia, which has a stark and varying degree of transparency in academic misconduct policies, students may unwittingly and academically inappropriately submit work generated by AI as though it is their own.

Students therefore need to assume an ethical pivot in the adoption of AI, with a clear focus on transparency, academic integrity, and responsible choice. This would mean AI use is acknowledged and citations are provided to the AI outputs, and the situation is recognized where AI use is seen as a reduction of learning. Sivasubramaniam (2025) points out that there is a need for ethical literacy, which goes hand in hand with digital literacy, where algorithmic tools in writing and research are employed. Learning to reduce overreliance, which is another ethical concern, also must be taught. Overreliance on AI for brainstorming, writing, and problem-solving reduces one's cognitive faculty. Carr (2010) contends that the use of digital tools, especially the ones that promote effortless and uncritical use of the digital environment, results in a reduction of deep thinking and a superficial encounter. It is therefore critical for Cambodian students to balance AI-enabled tools with their own rationality, where tools amplify their thinking and do not replace it.

Bias or dangerous AI output also means students need to respond to more socio-technical risk. Buolamwini and Gebru (2018) illustrate the conjecture that model's misrepresentation or the maligning of non-Western cultures that misrepresentation and maligning of non-Western cultures are the products of training deficient datasets of the Western world. AI outputs need Cambodian students to contextualize the AI outputs. Such competencies go beyond the basic levels of ICT literacy and require a more sophisticated grasp of the inner workings of AI systems, and comprehension of their outputs, as well as an appreciation of means to interact with them productively (MoEYS, 2018). One of the most critical is AI navigation; the skill to commandeer a suite of AI tools productively, understand the relevance of their functionalities, and make appropriate selections for learning tasks. Strategic use of tools is a digital competency threshold outlined by Shute and Becker (2010), to differentiate tool use from tool mastery. Students need to make decisions on whether to draw on text generators, translation tools, adaptive learning platforms, or use data for analytics, based on the context of their academic tasks.

Developing the Skill of Prompt Engineering. According to Brown and Cariveau (2024), the effectiveness of AI systems is largely determined by the user's input. Learning to write contextually rich prompts and adjusting them to get the desired output is a critical skill for students, especially the ability to use prompts to develop analytical thinking rather than simply request answers. Brown and Cariveau (2024) also explains that in Cambodia where English is a second language, the ability to engineer prompts requires a special understanding of relevant multilingual complexities. Information verification is also important. AI systems can fabricate quotes, have incorrect information, or biased reasoning. Students need to develop verification habits by cross-referencing with reliable sources, tracing the information back to the original document, and discussing with a teacher or colleague. As Metzger and Flanagin (2013) argue, digital literacy is increasingly dependent on one's ability to evaluate the credibility of information, therefore in the era of AI, verification is a must have. Thus, in the Cambodian context, the educational systems in Higher Learning Institutions will need to cultivate a disposition that is characterized by inquiry, critical and ethical thinking to enhance artificial intelligence literacy, as *Table 2* demonstrates.

Table 2.

Core Theme	Short Summary
Executive Function & Comprehension	Metacognitive awareness directs attention, strategy use, and comprehension control.
Motivation as Emotional Fuel	Reward systems and perceived relevance encourage deeper engagement with text.
Interdependence of Metacognition & Motivation	Motivated learners monitor comprehension more effectively; metacognitive training strengthens motivation.

IV. RISKS, CHALLENGES, AND ETHICAL CONCERNS

Perhaps among the first of the countless subjects AI scholarship became concerned with, and which has documented the most for bias, is algorithmic bias. Numerous authors, AI scholars such as Buolamwini and Gebru (2018) argue that AI systems developed using datasets predominately comprising the West, English speaking, and majority-group as in, the more powerful and economically developed people groups, content in datasets universally deny the existence of those in the periphery (*ethnic, small state, and impoverished l ands*) due to the gaping void of AI systems in those under-developed areas. The AI systems operate from models that extrapolate from existing data, the wrongfulness of which is incorporated through training information from skewed, exclusionary, or cultural void training datasets. Cambodian students and educators experience this bias on many fronts, namely: through the erasure of the Khmer culture, the above mistreatment of Southeast Asian contexts or the incapacity of the language model to languages of the majority world, the English language.

Bender et al. (2021) argue that the large language models encode the values, beliefs, and biases that are vested in the training data, and such data is usually in this, most AI systems, the Western data. In Cambodian classrooms, this is demonstrated when AI generated content does not take into consideration the prevailing local worldviews, religious beliefs and practices, or sociohistorical reality. When such outputs are, people (*students*) are most often the intended end users of such outputs, and such people (*students*) highly depend on the outputs in the AI generated content, therefore they are the ones absorbing the most in the distorted information.

Several studies, like Carr (2010), highlight the potential risks of losing critical thinking when the use of sophisticated AI tools in education and other sectors or fields of study, becomes systemic. In the case of Cambodian higher education, Huot and Loch (2025) indicate where critical thinking in teaching and learning has always been neglected the most, the risk of losing critical thinking becomes even more vital in learning AI ChatGPT. In accordance with, Huot and Tep (2025) contend that students can get AI to formulate logical arguments, summarize content, and even solve multipart problems. While learning material can increase the pace and extent of learning, at the same time, it might tempt students to avoid engaging in the struggle to learn cognitive offloading, which is necessary to obtain deep understanding of the content to be learned (Kirschner & Van Merriënboer, 2013). To the extent that students create no original analysis, no evaluation, and no creativity, the other higher-order thinking becomes weaker because that thinking is needed for analysis, evaluation and creativity.

Cambodia's history of education makes this risk particularly troubling. As Huot and Loch (2025) point out, Cambodian learners are used to a system of rote memorization, and an inflexible system of education. Incorporating AI into such a system without proper safeguards will likely make passive learning even worse. Instead of argumentation, learners will likely accept pre-built AI responses and never critique them for relevance or logical coherence. Rather than struggle with higher order thinking, many will simply accept AI responses to questions or problems which have an illusion of certainty. There are many writers such as Knox (2020) and Selwyn (2019) suggest that AI should serve as a tool for higher order thinking rather than a replacement for it. Thought intentional pedagogical design, education should make sure that AI assists rather than takes over synthesis, higher order reflection and evaluation. There is a strong need for Cambodian universities to create metacognitive awareness and design for learning environments that protect AI resistance where technology will enhance rather than impede higher order thinking.

The integration of AI technology in education practices raises ethical questions of privacy, data security, and surveillance. Zuboff (2019) explains that contemporary technologies work in a surveillance capitalism manner where users' data is continually harvested and profited from. Most AI technologies employed in education, especially those that are free or for-profit, convert users' educational requests and writing samples, along with the collection of their sensitive information and digital behavioural patterns. This is especially problematic for countries such as Cambodia, where the digital governance policies are in their infancy and where institutions have little awareness about data ethical matters. These AI technologies could easily and unintentionally archive sensitive data concerning a student's identity, education, or emotional state. There are AI and data analytics-driven Learning Management Systems (LMS) that provide surveillance to students. Universities in Cambodia, especially rural ones that lack IT facilities, may not have sufficient student data security. Also, there are privacy issues regarding abuse of government and corporate power. If AI services distribute student data, students may be subjected to surveillance that violates their privacy and autonomy. As Zeide (2019) points out, there is a need for transparency and regulation around educational AI and the black box data practices surrounding it.

Urban and rural locations in Cambodia and the country's digital infrastructure are widening. The divide also extends to the ability to integrate AI into education. Higher education institutions in Cambodia, even in rural areas, have limited to no digital tools and infrastructure. As a result, AI educational tools are out of their reach. The ability to AI educational tools also varies quite a bit even among universities in urban areas. For example, students in some of the over-privileged universities in Phnom Penh have high-speed internet, high-end computers, and up-to-date digital tools. In contrast, students in rural universities struggle with slow internet, weak computers, and a considerable digital divide. Digital inequity is also defined in terms of the ability to use the tools. For example, students in rural universities may not have the digital literacy skills to use AI tools. These inequities increase the danger of stratifying society through these inequities. Students with better access to technology will likely develop more refined AI competencies and be better able to engage with the global knowledge economy. Students with little to no access will likely continue to be disadvantaged, thereby countering the national objectives of promoting inclusive digital transformation. Additionally, gaps in technology infrastructure are likely to create gaps in the pedagogical approaches of educators.

Some educators, for instance, those at urban universities, might incorporate AI-powered exercises and digital collaboration tools, while their counterparts at rural universities might employ no technology or low-tech pedagogical approaches. As Selwyn and Jandrić (2020) point out, inequitable diffusion of technology results in the digital pedagogical divides that leave many resource-poor students on the margins of the education system. Equally worthy of attention as the emotional and psychological impacts on students, is the potential cognitive and ethical risks of AI adoption. There are many scholars that point out the impacts on motivation and identity and cognitive effort in ways that can be considerably harmful if not properly moderated. Ryan and Deci (2000) have postulated theories on self-determination and stated that internal motivation flourishes when one experiences autonomy, competence, and engagement at a meaningful level. With the assistance of AI tools that write, summarize, or solve problems, the sense of achievement students feels when completing tasks on their own may be lessened. Extensive academic reliance on AI may result in more significant disengagement, frustration, and lowered self-confidence.

Heffernan and Heffernan (2014) argue that adaptive learning systems designed without sufficient attention to the degree of autonomy students possess may unintentionally minimize motivation by simplifying the tasks too much or encouraging a more passive form of engagement. There is also the risk that students will perceive the information generated by AI tools to be authoritative. Broussard (2018) discusses the predominate cultural narrative of algorithmic objectivity and how that leads users to believe that the outputs of the machine are neutral, accurate, and scientifically valid. Students that consider AI outputs as truthful may be left with a huge gap in their intellectual thinking, because of a failure to critically question, contrast, and validate information. Also, students may be overwhelmed by the AI outputs due to their vastness, which is information overload. Kirsh (2009) points out that digital environments, in fact, tend to increase cognitive overload, thereby making it increasingly difficult for learners to filter the information that is relevant, or to create coherent mental models. Cambodian students, particularly those who are inexperienced in digital filtering or evaluation, may be left feeling disoriented or discouraged when AI tools provide complex or illogical outputs.

Lastly, AI tools can affect students' perception of their academic self. Pajares (2006) states that self-efficacy, or belief in one's capability to achieve a task successively, is a strong predictor of one's academic performance. Students may unjustifiably view themselves as inferior by comparing their own thoughts and writings with the outputs of the AI, which in turn, decreases their self-efficacy and results in academic disengagement. Only by effectively managing these challenges, can educators and policymakers in Cambodia achieve the prospect of AI in education that strengthens critical awareness and ethics, rather than undermining them, as illustrated in *Table 3*.

Table 3.

Core Theme	Short Summary
Metacognitive Classroom Practices	Strategies like think-alouds and reflective journals build awareness of reading processes.
Fostering Intrinsic Motivation	Choice, culturally relevant texts, and growth-oriented climates strengthen student identity as readers.
Mindfulness in Literacy Instruction	Focused breathing and visualization reduce anxiety and support concentration.
Teacher as Reflective Model	Educators demonstrate mindful reading and guide students in connecting text to self and society.

V. AN AI LITERATE EDUCATOR AND STUDENT FRAMEWORK FOR CAMBODIA

The foremost part in this framework, and vital part, is the belief that pedagogy needs to come before technology. Using the TPACK model, Koehler et al. (2017) suggest that educators can integrate technology in a meaningful way only when they understand the digital tools, the instruction and the learning processes involved, and the content to be taught. Like many educational systems around the world, Cambodia has experienced the adoption of technology in the classroom due to the novelty of the tools available, or by the influence of policy regarding technology use in the classroom, as opposed to a change in pedagogy. Selwyn (2019) argues that such situations are technology-first approaches, and they characteristically fail because they disregard the teachers, their professional expertise, and the dilemmas they encounter in their practice. The pedagogy-first model of education rethinks the role of artificial intelligence (AI) as not just a fact-checking tool or as a provider of answer to questions, but as a facilitator of the learning process that enables self-directed inquiry, classroom reflection, and deep conceptual engagement. Luckin (2018) points out that the potential of AI in education does not lie in content delivery, but in content sparking learner questioning, and scaffolding individualized learning.

With the pressure to rapidly cover content, Cambodian teachers can shift their use of AI as a content delivery tool to a learning design partner that fosters inquiry as opposed to passive content absorption. Charlton et al. (2012) speak to this process of learning as the achievement of a pedagogically defined theory, wherein learning occurs through iterative cycles of construction, feedback, and refinement of the abstract ideas. For Cambodian teachers to be AI literate, they need to have conceptual knowledge, critical consciousness, and practical knowledge to guide the ethical and effective use of AI in the classroom. Holmes et al. (2019) suggest that teachers' AI literacy should go beyond the procedural level to include knowledge of algorithms, bias, and AI's socio-political place. Existing Cambodian teachers, most of whom have also not been trained in digital pedagogy, will need some scaffolding to build these competencies.

An important skill is creating AI-enhanced learning activities. Based on Puentedura's (2014) SAMR model, technology integration should progress from substitution to other levels, modification and redefinition. Thus, Cambodian lecturers need to understand how AI works and how it shifts learning tasks. Pairing with AI text generators, students can collaborate in brainstorming activities. Also, AI language models can aid in writing development for students who are bilingual. Simultaneously, teachers need to develop the ability to critique AI outputs, to assess the accuracy, culture relevance, and biases present. AI outputs reflect the social inequities of the datasets being analysed by the AI, as demonstrated by the studies of Buolamwini and Gebru (2018). In that sense, Cambodian educators need to deal with issues of factual inaccuracies, stereotypes, and Western epistemic dominance present within AI generated outputs, as they may include linguistic biases that may be detrimental to students who speak Khmer. Another major area is educators' ethical competence. Joyce et al. (2023) states that educators are ethical gatekeepers in technology-mediated settings and must demonstrate transparency, equity, and accountability. Digital tools also require educators' confidence. As Warschauer and Liaw (2011) argue, effective technology use occurs when educators can use different instructional tools to provide feedback, collaboration, and construct knowledge.

In addition, as AI begins to be embedded in evaluation systems, assessment competency becomes more important. AI has the potential to provide automated feedback and track student learning, but as Williamson et al. (2023) suggest, an excessive reliance on algorithms for assessment may result in a loss of subtlety or other forms of undesirable bias. Therefore, Cambodian educators must interpret AI analytics to create assessments where algorithms can assist but should not make evaluative decisions. Finally, sustained teacher professional development is required. Darling-Hammond et al. (2017) stress that effective teacher professional development should be iterative, collaborative, and situated in teacher's context. The shift in students from passive consumers to autonomous thinkers necessitates a new set of skills around the critical, ethical, and reflective use of AI. Digital literacy, as argued by Ng (2012), spans the technical, cognitive, and socio-emotional, which in the case of Cambodia higher education context is particularly salient due to the aurati pedagogy which students have virtually always experienced. The most critical aspect of students' literacy in AI tools is the ability to engage with the tools critically. Wineburg and McGrew (2019) contend that students need to learn lateral reading as a strategy for verifying information and credibility of the digital sources.

Cambodian students' tendency to trust texts that appear to have authority necessitates that they learn to interrogate AI responses, verify claims, identify hallucinations, and flag the culturally biased perspectives. Students should also be given instruction covering the ethical implications of using AI technology. According to Floridi et al. (2018), ethical digital citizenship requires practicing transparency, fairness, and accountability. In the case of Cambodia, students must learn proper citation of AI-generated texts, the distinction of effective assistance from academic misconduct, the avoidance of plagiarism, and the societal implications of the misuse of AI systems. This type of instruction supports academic integrity and helps students learn how to participate ethically in future AI-facilitated workplaces. Along with these initiatives, students must learn the use of AI and how to create AI prompts. Huot et al. (2024) considers prompt engineering an emerging literacy skill. Formulating a prompt entails an understanding of the topic, a command of the language, and an awareness of the context. Thus, Cambodian students, especially in bilingual contexts, need to master the use of iterative, language-diverse, and output-diverse querying. They also need to learn information verification and synthesis. Kahne and Bowyer (2017) emphasize the ability to verify and reason critically; without these, one cannot fully participate in a democracy.

The fourth pillar of the Applied AI ethics framework views AI as a collaborator that extends human reasoning while retaining autonomy and decision-making. Crawford (2021) and Williams (2014) challenge the deterministic perspectives of technologically driven automation that attribute intelligence to machines, and propose a relational perspective that views AI and human thinking as a system, closely coupled and mutually dependent. In this instance, AI is viewed as a cognitive partner, not a cognitive overlord. In this case, AI is a collaborative partner, not a domineering one Sutton et al. (2019) posit that AI is what they call a heuristic generator, a machine that produces ideas, examples, and outlines that assist the user in thinking. The participants, Cambodian students, and educators, can engage AI in an iterative process of questioning, critique, refinement, and synthesis. Rather than losing critical thinking, this process strengthens it, as users must continually evaluate the relevance, quality, and ethical aspects of AI-generated output. The model of human & AI collaboration shows how to balance the different types of cognitive work to be done. Humans excel at understanding social situations, exercising moral reasoning, recognizing context, and thinking creatively. Reliability, on the other hand, excels at recognizing patterns, producing written content, and analyzing large amounts of information.

UNESCO (2023) claims that educational decisions should always be based on the humans involved, and this is particularly relevant for the philosophy of education in Cambodia. Sticking to this hierarchy prevents AI from becoming the default decision maker and preserves the importance of human decisions. In Cambodian classrooms, collaborative use of AI will mean that both students and teachers will have to work with AI in a cyclic manner through a process of prompting, evaluation, and revision. The dialogue will be iterative and will allow both students and teachers to deepen their reflective and analytical skills. Still, educators will have to be on the lookout for the risk of cognitive dependence. Carr (2010) cautions that losing focus will lead to a decline in creativity and problem solving from a system reliant on technology. No institution can remain captive to the silo thinking that supports the training of siloed AI literacy. Institutional coherence, appropriate resources, and ethical frameworks must be in place. Cuban (2020) asserts that any innovations in education will be futile without the appropriate policies, infrastructure, and leadership, and indeed, Cambodian higher education institutions ought to develop systemic support structures based on the principles of equity, ethics, and pedagogy.

Drafting school policies is a critical first step. Universities should establish policies concerning the responsible use of AI, including expectations, transparency concerning the use of AI in the completed work, guidelines regarding the citation of AI, and the use of AI in the context of academic dishonesty. The principles of the OECD (2022) advocate for fairness, privacy, and accountability, and should be incorporated into Cambodia's national and institutional policies. Policy ambiguity is, however, a policy of permission. Darling-Hammond et al. (2017) argue that professional learning should be sustained if the aim is to bring about transformative change in practice. Digital infrastructure is a foundational concern. Education institutions in Cambodia require a digital ecosystem that supports AI and the digital devices for learning, as illustrated in *Table 4*.

Table 4.

Core Theme	**Short Summary**
Pedagogy-First Approach	AI use must serve instructional purpose, not technological novelty.
Teacher AI Competencies	Educators need skills in design, evaluation, ethical governance, and digital integration.
Student AI Competencies	Learners require critical consumption, ethical use, metacognition, and verification skills.
Human–AI Collaboration	AI complements human reasoning: judgment, ethics, and creativity remain human-led.
Institutional Support	Policies, infrastructure, training, and integrity guidelines sustain responsible AI integration.

VI. CONCLUSION AND RECOMMENDATIONS

The rapid proliferation of Artificial Intelligence in global education context places Cambodia's higher education currently in a crucial determining position. The increasing integration of AI tools among universities, lecturers, and students establishes a context where the relevant questions are not based on whether institutions will pedagogically incorporate AI, but rather how institutions will ethically and equitably steer this influence. The adoption of AI is not fundamentally a technological innovation, but rather a redefinition of the roles, expectations, and capacity of all participants in the education system. As presented in this chapter, the future of Cambodia is dependent on how its higher education system prepares the AI-literate educators, the students, and the frameworks that preserve the higher and the cultural integrity.

The most efficient way to use AI technology in education is to first develop a high-quality learning experience design/ pedagogy and then develop learning AI's tools to adapt to it. It is also essential to incorporate deep design, reflective practice, and a genuine appreciation for human agency, as technology is not a panacea for learning. This means that Cambodian educators also need to move away from merely rote learning as passive content transcripts towards becoming learning experience designers who will effectively leverage AI as a learning partner while also safeguarding human reasoning, creativity, and moral agency. This will require a major shift in the educators' professional identities from traditional pedagogues to guidance counsellors, ethical and critical thinking mentors, and cultural surrogates, as AI will become ever more present in learning environments.

Students must also undergo a fundamental reshaping of their role as well. The traditional model of passive memorization must hang when AI can produce summaries, translations, explanations, and argumentative structures. Students must be active co-creators of knowledge: those who scrutinize, examine, and synthesize and refine information, rather than regurgitate it. The capacity to appraise the output of AI, to identify bias or errors, and to exercise personal judgment in digital inquiries is fundamental to scholarship. In this new ecology, self-direction, self-management, self-governance, and ethical awareness are fundamental, alongside knowledge of the subject. Students must understand that AI is a tool, not a replacement, and that a genuine engagement with the material is required, as learning is not a spectator sport.

Cambodian universities will need to be as agile as their students in assuming new roles, especially at the level of institutional leadership and policy design. Higher education institutions need to be able to outline and communicate clear ethical parameters on acceptable AI use, and on the required disclosure of its use, to ensure academic integrity. As AI becomes more embedded in research, assessment, teaching and administration, institutions need to ensure transparency, custody of data, and ethical use of data. Additionally, the integration of AI into teaching and learning methods is essential for universities to ensure that all students, even those outside the STEM fields, can use AI responsibly for problem solving. Digital infrastructure, device access, and faculty training investments to close urban-rural divides and promote equitable collaboration are all essential.

Transformational change hinges on national authorities as well. The Ministry of Education oversees the formulation of an all-encompassing AI education policy that incorporates ethics, data protection, capacity building, and institutional responsibilities. This policy should be culturally and linguistically Cambodian, preventing the adoption of AI from weakening the local identity. Moreover, accreditation frameworks should expand to encompass the effective, balanced integration of AI, equity, and academic rigour. National training efforts, through collaborative arrangements with universities, NGOs, tech companies, and bilateral multilateral agencies, should enable sustained sector-wide training to equip teachers with the skills to use AI for education.

At all levels of the system, be it classroom, institution, or national policymakers, the bottom line should be clear: AI should supplement, and not substitute, human judgment. Education is an activity that is fundamentally human and fundamentally about understanding, feeling, creating, and grappling with ethics. AI can enhance the education system by providing information quickly, offering different viewpoints, and customizing the learning experience. Nevertheless, it will never be able to substitute the richly textured education that comes from lived experience and moral and cultural grounding. AI use in education must be governed by the principle, "Human Judgment First, AI Second." This speaks to the guiding philosophy that will determine policy directions in the future AI-integrated education systems in Cambodia.

Partially Freedom chapter ended with a vision and call for action. Cambodia has the potential for a participatory, culturally reflective, and future-oriented AI-enabled higher education system. Revising normative traditions, commitment to advancing professionally, and ethical principle-compliant innovation will be the necessary cornerstones of such a system. Cambodia will have an educational ai-empowered system that allows for deep, critical, and democratized inquiry if the learners, the educators, the educational entities, and the decision makers collaborate. By placing human agency first and integrating culture, Cambodia can show the world that technological progress can result in educational values being upheld and not eroded in the system, which is the goal of AI integration. Technology is not just a means of modernization and will lead to a more enlightened, equitable, and reflective future for higher education in Cambodia.

REFERENCES

Bender, E. M., Gebru, T., McMillan-Major, A., & Shmitchell, S. (2021). On the dangers of stochastic parrots: Can language models be too big? In Irani, L., Kannan, S., Mitchell, M., & Robinson, D. (Eds.), *Proceedings of the 2021 ACM conference on fairness, accountability, and transparency* (pp. 610–623). Association for Computing Machinery, New York, NY, United States. DOI: 10.1145/3442188.3445922

Broussard, M. (2018). *Artificial unintelligence: How computers misunderstand the world*. Mit Press. DOI: 10.7551/mitpress/11022.001.0001

Brown, A., & Cariveau, T. (2024). A systematic review of simultaneous prompting and prompt delay procedures. *Journal of Behavioral Education, 33*(1), 1–22. DOI: 10.1007/s10864-022-09481-6

Buolamwini, J., & Gebru, T. (2018). Gender shades: Intersectional accuracy disparities in commercial gender classification. *Conference on fairness, accountability and transparency, 81*, 1–15. http://proceedings.mlr.press/v81/buolamwini18a.html

Carr, N. (2010). *The shallows: How the internet is changing the way we think, read and remember*. Atlantic Books Ltd.

Charlton, P., Magoulas, G., & Laurillard, D. (2012). Enabling creative learning design through semantic technologies. *Technology, Pedagogy and Education, 21*(2), 231–253. DOI: 10.1080/1475939X.2012.698165

Crawford, K. (2021). *The atlas of AI: Power, politics, and the planetary costs of artificial intelligence*. Yale University Press.

Cuban, L. (2020). Reforming the grammar of schooling again and again. *American Journal of Education, 126*(4), 665–671. DOI: 10.1086/709959

Darling-Hammond, L., Hyler, M. E., & Gardner, M. (2017). *Effective teacher professional development*. Learning Policy Institute. DOI: 10.54300/122.311

Davies, B. (1994). On the neglect of pedagogy in educational studies and its consequences. *Journal of In-service Education, 20*(1), 17–34. DOI: 10.1080/0305763940200103

Flavell, J. H. (1979). Metacognition and cognitive monitoring: A new area of cognitive–developmental inquiry. *The American Psychologist, 34*(10), 906–911. DOI: 10.1037/0003-066X.34.10.906

Floridi, L. (2019). Translating principles into practices of digital ethics: Five risks of being unethical. *Philosophy & Technology, 32*(2), 185–193. DOI: 10.1007/s13347-019-00354-x

Floridi, L., Cowls, J., Beltrametti, M., Chatila, R., Chazerand, P., Dignum, V., Luetge, C., Madelin, R., Pagallo, U., Rossi, F., Schafer, B., Valcke, P., & Vayena, E. (2018). AI4People—An ethical framework for a good AI society: Opportunities, risks, principles, and recommendations. *Minds and Machines*, *28*(4), 689–707. DOI: 10.1007/s11023-018-9482-5 PMID: 30930541

Heffernan, N. T., & Heffernan, C. L. (2014). The ASSISTments ecosystem: Building a platform that brings scientists and teachers together for minimally invasive research on human learning and teaching. *International Journal of Artificial Intelligence in Education*, *24*(4), 470–497. DOI: 10.1007/s40593-014-0024-x

Hok, C., Phin, K., Saroth, C., Sakhorn, S., Chheang, S., & Huot, S. (2026). Advancing ELT in Cambodia: Sustainability, digital inclusion, and culturally responsive pedagogy. *The Rubrics*, *8*(8), 79–99. DOI: 10.5281/zenodo.18149324

Holmes, W., Bialik, M., & Fadel, C. (2019). *Artificial intelligence in education promises and implications for teaching and learning*. Center for Curriculum Redesign.

Huot, S., & Em, S. (2025). Integrating English language teaching with environmental sustainability: A comprehensive review of pedagogical strategies and global impacts. [CJESS]. *Cambodian Journal of Educational and Social Sciences*, *1*(2), 83–95. DOI: 10.69496/cjess.v2i2.68

Huot, S., & Loch, S. (2025). From rote to reflective: Integrating ChatGPT to transform learning outcomes in Cambodian education. *International Journal of Language and Literary Studies*, *7*(4), 1–15. DOI: 10.36892/ijlls.v7i4.2188

Huot, S., Loch, S., Rin, R., Hok, C., Phin, K., Tep, P., Chay, C., Chheang, S., & Huot, S. (2026). Internationalization and competitive growth in Cambodian higher education: Pathways to positive developmental progress and global visibility. In Salendab, F. A. (Ed.), *Competition in higher education and the role of internationalization in university rankings* (pp. 381–412). IGI Global Scientific Publishing., DOI: 10.4018/979-8-3373-6856-6.ch014

Huot, S., Sam, R., & Nguon, T. (2024). Influencing factors in teaching career choices in Cambodia in teacher education colleges: A conceptual framework. *European Journal of Arts. Humanities and Social Sciences*, *1*(6), 97–108. DOI: 10.59324/ejahss.2024.1(6).11

Huot, S., & Such, C. (2025). Leveraging social media for language learning: Opportunities and challenges. [JEILT]. *Journal of Education Innovation and Language Teaching*, *1*(2), 10–29. DOI: 10.63381/jeilt.v1i2.56

Huot, S., & Tep, P. (2025). Advancing ChatGPT for pedagogical innovation in Cambodia: Insight from global evidence and local implications. *The Context: Journal of English Studies*, *12*(4), 115–135. DOI: 10.5281/zenodo.15806972

Joyce, S., Umney, C., Whittaker, X., & Stuart, M. (2023). New social relations of digital technology and the future of work: Beyond technological determinism. *New Technology, Work and Employment*, *38*(2), 145–161. DOI: 10.1111/ntwe.12276

Kahne, J., & Bowyer, B. (2017). Educating for democracy in a partisan age: Confronting the challenges of motivated reasoning and misinformation. *American Educational Research Journal*, *54*(1), 3–34. DOI: 10.3102/0002831216679817

Kirschner, P. A., & Van Merriënboer, J. J. (2013). Do learners really know best? Urban legends in education. *Educational Psychologist*, *48*(3), 169–183. DOI: 10.1080/00461520.2013.804395

Kirsh, S. J. (2009). *Media and youth: A developmental perspective*. John Wiley & Sons. DOI: 10.1002/9781444317435

Klugman, C. M. (2021). Black boxes and bias in AI challenge autonomy. *The American Journal of Bioethics*, *21*(7), 33–35. DOI: 10.1080/15265161.2021.1926587 PMID: 34152901

Knox, J. (2020). Artificial intelligence and education in China. *Learning, Media and Technology*, *45*(3), 298–311. DOI: 10.1080/17439884.2020.1754236

Koehler, M. J., Mishra, P., & Cain, W. (2017). What is technological pedagogical content (TPACK)? In M. J. Koehler, P. Mishra, & W. Cain (Eds.), *Journal of Education: Pedagogical content knowledge* (Vol. 193, pp. 13–20). Boston University School of Education. https://www.researchgate.net/publication/260281100

Lim, S., & Keuk, C. N. (2017). A sociocultural analysis of Cambodian teachers' cognitions about cultural contents in an 'internationally imported' textbook in a tertiary English learning context. In Widodo, H. P., Perfecto, M. R., Canh, L. V., & Buripakdi, A. (Eds.), *Situating moral and cultural values in ELT materials: The Southeast Asian context* (pp. 87–110). Springer., DOI: 10.1007/978-3-319-63677-1_6

Luckin, R. (2018). *Enhancing learning and teaching with technology: What the research says*. ERIC.

Metzger, M. J., & Flanagin, A. J. (2013). Credibility and trust of information in online environments: The use of cognitive heuristics. *Journal of Pragmatics*, *59*, 210–220. DOI: 10.1016/j.pragma.2013.07.012

MoEYS. (2018). *Policy and strategy on information and communication technology in education.* Ministry of Education, Youth and Sport.

Ng, W. (2012). Can we teach digital natives digital literacy? *Computers & Education, 59*(3), 1065–1078. DOI: 10.1016/j.compedu.2012.04.016

Nussbaum, M. C. (2011). *Creating capabilities: The human development approach.* Harvard University Press. DOI: 10.4159/harvard.9780674061200

OECD. (2022). *Digital transformation and quality in higher education.* OECD Publishing., DOI: 10.1787/f622f257-

Pajares, F. (2006). Self-efficacy during childhood and adolescence. In Urdan, T., & Frank, P. (Eds.), *Self-efficacy beliefs of adolescents* (Vol. 5, pp. 339–367). IAP. DOI: 10.1108/978-1-60752-837-720251016

Paul, R., & Elder, L. (2014). Critical thinking: Intellectual standards essential to reasoning well within every domain of human thought, Part 4. *Journal of Developmental Education, 37*(3), 34–35. https://www.proquest.com/openview/534c73e3bddaeb5be21c4fbcd69596e4/1?cbl=47765&pq-origsite=gscholar

Popenici, S. A., & Kerr, S. (2017). Exploring the impact of artificial intelligence on teaching and learning in higher education. *Research and Practice in Technology Enhanced Learning, 12*(1), 1–13. DOI: 10.1186/s41039-017-0062-8 PMID: 30595727

Puentedura, R. R. (2014). *SAMR and TPCK: A hands-on approach to classroom practice.* https://www.hippasus.com/rrpweblog/archives/2014/12/11/SAMRandTPCK_HandsOnApproachClassroomPractice.pdf

Ryan, R. M., & Deci, E. L. (2000). Self-determination theory and the facilitation of intrinsic motivation, social development, and well-being. *The American Psychologist, 55*(1), 68–78. DOI: 10.1037/0003-066X.55.1.68 PMID: 11392867

Selwyn, N. (2019). *Should robots replace teachers?: AI and the future of education.* John Wiley & Sons.

Selwyn, N., & Jandrić, P. (2020). Postdigital living in the age of Covid-19: Unsettling what we see as possible. *Postdigital Science and Education, 2*(3), 989–1005. DOI: 10.1007/s42438-020-00166-9 PMID: 40477067

Sen, V. (2019). Hybrid governmentality: Higher education policymaking in post-conflict Cambodia. *Studies in Higher Education, 44*(3), 513–525. DOI: 10.1080/03075079.2017.1379985

Shute, V. J., & Becker, B. J. (2010). *Innovative assessment for the 21st century.* Springer. DOI: 10.1007/978-1-4419-6530-1

Sivasubramaniam, S. (2025). Deterring Academic Integrity Breaches: The Roles of Institutions, Academics, and Support Services. *Journal of Scholarly Publishing*, *56*(2), 240–268. DOI: 10.3138/jsp-2024-1115

Sutton, A., Clowes, M., Preston, L., & Booth, A. (2019). Meeting the review family: Exploring review types and associated information retrieval requirements. *Health Information and Libraries Journal*, *36*(3), 202–222. DOI: 10.1111/hir.12276 PMID: 31541534

Un, L., & Sok, S. (2022). (Higher) Education policy and project intervention in Cambodia: Its development discourse. In McNamara, V., & Hayden, M. (Eds.), *Education in Cambodia: From year zero towards international standards* (pp. 215–239). Springer., DOI: 10.1007/978-981-16-8213-1_12

UNESCO. (2023). *Technology integration of Cambodian higher education: Emerging changes since covid-19 and notable challenges*. Global Education Monitoring Report. https://www.unesco.org/gem-report/sites/default/files/medias/fichiers/2023/09/SopheakandPhyrom.pdf

Voogt, J., & Knezek, G. (2016). Guest editorial: Technology enhanced quality education for all–outcomes from EDUsummIT 2015. *Journal of Educational Technology & Society*, *19*(3), 1–4. https://www.jstor.org/stable/10.2307/jeductechsoci.19.3.1

Vygotsky, L. S. (1978). *Mind in society: The development of higher psychological processes*. Harvard University Press.

Warschauer, M., & Liaw, M.-L. (2011). Emerging technologies for autonomous language learning. *Studies in Self-Access Learning Journal*, *2*(3), 107–118. DOI: 10.37237/020302

Williams, J. J. (2014). Internationalizing legal education: A cooperative tool in a globalized world. *Indonesian Journal of International Law*, *12*, 457–473. https://heinonline.org/HOL/Page?handle=hein.journals/indjil12&id=496

Williamson, B. (2017). *Big data in education: The digital future of learning, policy and practice*. SAGE Publications Ltd., DOI: 10.4135/9781529714920

Williamson, B., Komljenovic, J., & Gulson, K. N. (2023). Introduction: Digitalisation of education in the era of algorithms, automation and artificial intelligence. In Williamson, B., Komljenovic, J., & Gulson, K. N. (Eds.), *World yearbook of education 2024* (pp. 1–19). Routledge., DOI: 10.4324/9781003359722

Williamson, B., & Piattoeva, N. (2020). Objectivity as standardization in data-scientific education policy, technology and governance. In Jarke, J., & Breiter, A. (Eds.), *The Datafication of Education* (pp. 81–93). Routledge., DOI: 10.4324/9780429341359-7

Wineburg, S., & McGrew, S. (2019). Lateral reading: Reading less and learning more when evaluating digital information. *Teachers College Record*, *121*(11), 1–56. DOI: 10.1177/016146811912101102

Winne, P. H., & Hadwin, A. F. (2013). Study: Tracing and supporting self-regulated learning in the Internet. In Azevedo, R., & Aleven, V. (Eds.), *International handbook of metacognition and learning technologies* (pp. 293–308). Springer., DOI: 10.1007/978-1-4419-5546-3_20

Zeide, E. (2019). Artificial intelligence in higher education: Applications, promise and perils, and ethical questions. *EDUCAUSE Review*, *54*(3), 1–11. https://ssrn.com/abstract=4320049

Zhang, D., Landmark, L., Reber, A., Hsu, H., Kwok, O., & Benz, M. (2010). University faculty knowledge, beliefs, and practices in providing reasonable accommodations to students with disabilities. *Remedial and Special Education*, *31*(4), 276–286. DOI: 10.1177/0741932509338348

Zimmerman, B. J. (2002). Becoming a self-regulated learner: An overview. *Theory into Practice*, *41*(2), 64–70. DOI: 10.1207/s15430421tip4102_2

Zuboff, S. (2019). Surveillance capitalism and the challenge of collective action. *New Labor Forum*, *28*(1), 10–29. DOI: 10.1177/1095796018819461

Chapter 4
Redefining Teaching in the Age of AI:
A Reflective Autoethnography of Becoming a Mathematics Teacher

Hana An Llenos Alvarado
http://orcid.org/0009-0006-6550-616X
Mindanao State University-Tawi-Tawi College of Technology and Oceanography, Philippines

ABSTRACT

This study examines how generative artificial intelligence (AI) reshapes the process of becoming a mathematics teacher through a reflective autoethnographic lens. Drawing on personal journals, field notes, and memory-based vignettes from classroom observations and teaching assistantship experiences in a public high school in the southern Philippines, the study explores how encounters with AI-mediated student learning transformed my emerging professional identity. Thematic analysis revealed three interrelated moments of sense-making: disruption, adaptation, and redefinition. Disruption captures the pedagogical and emotional tensions arising from students' use of AI tools. Adaptation reflects reframing AI as a collaborative pedagogical resource, while redefinition signifies a deeper reconceptualization of mathematics teaching as a human, ethical, and relational practice. Rather than positioning AI as a threat, the findings highlight teaching as an evolving process of humanization in algorithmically mediated classrooms.

DOI: 10.4018/979-8-3373-8027-8.ch004

INTRODUCTION

When I first stepped into a high school mathematics class as a pre-service teacher, I carried with me my preconceived image of what a math classroom should be and look like. This notion of mathematics teaching and learning was shaped by my own experiences when I was in high school. In this class, I expect to see students working together, competing for the right answer, and discussing complex mathematical equations, challenges, and problems. Instead, I encountered a different reality. It is far from what I expected I would observe inside the mathematics classroom. When the teacher presented the mathematical tasks to the students, I immediately saw some of the students reach out for their mobile phones. The students started typing prompts in one of the generative Artificial Intelligence (AI) tools that can produce immediate and complete solutions. What unfolded before me was not outright disengagement, but somehow a profound transformation of mathematical participation. At that moment, I was startled, unsettled, and dumbfounded seeing the students using Artificial Intelligence (AI). However, I started to realize that what was once a space of discovery, curiosity, and dialogue is slowly turning into an instance of collaboration between the students and the AI algorithm. This realization made me think deeply as an emerging educator in this era, where my students have access to artificial intelligence tools. And it was at this moment that I asked myself: *Now, what does it mean to teach mathematics in the age of Artificial Intelligence (AI)?*

The rapid integration of Artificial Intelligence (AI) into education has fundamentally altered how knowledge is accessed, produced, and legitimized. Recent scholarship has documented the growing presence of generative Artificial Intelligence (AI) tools in classrooms. AI tools are used in class for their capacity to generate solutions, explanations, and representations at unprecedented speed (Kasneci et al., 2023; Zawacki-Richter et al., 2019). In mathematics education, this shift is particularly consequential. Mathematics has long been associated with procedural fluency and correctness of the solutions; the Artificial Intelligence systems perform many of these functions with ease. As a result, long-standing assumptions about the mathematical competence, assessment, and even instruction are being destabilized (Holmes et al., 2019). While there is existing literature focusing on student performance, ethical concerns, or instructional efficiency of Artificial Intelligence (AI), less attention has been given to understand lived experiences of teachers, especially pre-service teachers. The pre-service teachers are navigating to teach with Artificial Intelligence while simultaneously forming their identity in the teaching profession. Highlighting the view and experience of the pre-service teachers also provides an additional vantage point in teacher preparation, as they will be handling classes in the future where students are adept with AI tools and classrooms are AI-infused.

Hence, this chapter is born out of this gap and personal realization as a pre-service mathematics teacher. It mirrors my journey of becoming a mathematics teacher in the era of Artificial Intelligence (AI). An era where knowledge is no longer confined to textbooks or directly taught by teachers to learners. Instead, mathematical understanding is now increasingly co-constructed through complex interactions among students, teachers, and algorithmic AI systems. Through this reflective autoethnography, I narrate and examine how my professional identity, pedagogical beliefs, and instructional practices as an emerging math educator have been reshaped by the presence of Artificial Intelligence (AI) in classrooms. The choice of autoethnography as a qualitative methodology allows for the systemic analysis of my personal experience to illuminate broader cultural, institutional, and educational phenomena (Ellis et al., 2011). In this case, the emergence of artificial intelligence. In like manner, autoethnography has been recognized as a rigorous and reflexive approach for understanding teacher identity, professional becoming, and moments of pedagogical rupture (Adams & Herrmann, 2020), appropriate for this paper.

Framed with this methodological lens, the mathematics classroom is no longer like before. The new reality in the classroom is no longer a fixed environment. It has become an ecosystem where the students' curiosity is enhanced with aided computation from technology, and more importantly, the teacher's role must be reimagined. Within this new ecosystem, the role of the teacher is neither erased nor diminished but profoundly transformed. Some scholars on teacher identity argued that becoming a teacher is not a linear acquisition of skills, but an ongoing negotiation of beliefs, emotions, and professional purpose shaped by the sociocultural contexts (Beauchamp & Thomas, 2009; Lasky, 2005). The prevalence of Artificial Intelligence (AI), a technology with entirely different capabilities, intensifies this negotiation and will surely influence teachers' identity. Now, as a pre-service teacher, I find myself questioning the reality of my chosen profession. Particularly, I began to question my role as a teacher. I then began to wonder: "*Is teaching mathematics still about the procedural fluency and correct answer production?* Or *is it now about cultivating the mathematical consciousness that emphasizes reasoning and sense-making?*"

Indeed, the rapid emergence of Generative Artificial Intelligence (GenAI) tools necessitates *a* redefinition of our pedagogical roles as educators—shifting from mere transmitters of knowledge to curators of curiosity, and moving beyond being assessors of correct answers toward facilitators of students' meaning-making and critical engagement. In the era of GenAI, traditional notions of teacher authority and expertise in mathematics education are being challenged, as these systems can instantly produce correct solutions. Consequently, a teacher's value no longer rests solely on providing answers; rather, it increasingly lies in guiding students to ask better questions, evaluate the outputs of AI critically, and deepen their conceptual understanding. As GenAI reshapes classroom dynamics, teachers must support learners in navigating complex information environments, fostering reflective inquiry, and co-constructing knowledge with both students and intelligent technologies (Creely & Carabott, 2025). Such a shift positions the teacher not as an obsolete dispenser of facts but as an essential mediator of learning experiences, helping to re-humanize education amid rapidly accelerating automation.

Existing literature in Artificial Intelligence (AI) and education often oscillates between technological optimism and moral panic. Some researchers framed Artificial Intelligence (AI) as either a revolutionary solution or an existential threat (Williamson & Eynon, 2020). This paper resists such binaries. Rather, it explores the tensions, possibilities, and ethical questions that arise when a future mathematics teacher learns to teach together with Artificial Intelligence (AI), through Artificial Intelligence (AI), and at times despite Artificial Intelligence (AI). By foregrounding my personal experience with critical reflection, this autoethnography contributes to the teacher-centered perspective that remains underrepresented in high-impact Artificial Intelligence (AI) in education research.

Hence, the novelty of this paper lies in its positioning. While the prior studies have examined and unveiled the Artificial Intelligence (AI) tools as it relates to learning outcomes and student attitudes, few have explored and investigated how Artificial Intelligence (AI) reshapes the pedagogical becoming of mathematics teachers at the pre-service training stage. By situating individual experience within the broader theoretical conversations on teacher identity, mathematics pedagogy, and human-AI interaction, this chapter offers insights that extend beyond a single classroom or context. It argues that teaching mathematics in the age of Artificial Intelligence (AI) is not about competing with the algorithms, but also about reasserting that the distinctly human dimensions, such as judgment, care, creativity, and ethical responsibility.

In sharing this narrative, I invite readers to see the mathematics classroom not as a site of obsolescence, but as a space of becoming. It is a space where both teachers and learners redefine what it indeed means to know, to teach, and ultimately, to be human in an age increasingly shaped by artificial intelligence.

METHODOLOGY

This section discusses the research design, research participants, data sources, data analysis, and positionality and reflexivity of this study.

Research Design. This study utilizes a qualitative, reflective autoethnographic design to examine my experience of becoming a mathematics teacher in the age of Artificial Intelligence (AI). Rather than seeking to measure any variables, the methodology is oriented toward understanding meaning, identity formation, and pedagogical sense-making as they unfold within the lived experience. It positions my personal journey as both the site and source of inquiry. The autoethnography allows the researcher to link herself to the culture. It draws upon the lived experiences to illuminate larger social as well as educational realities (Ellis et al., 2011). By utilizing this approach, I narrate my process of becoming a mathematics teacher amid the pervasive influence of artificial intelligence in the classroom. This research design was deliberately chosen since it captures the complex, emotional, and intellectual dimensions of learning to teach in a rapidly evolving educational landscape.

The research design situates my personal journey as both the site and source of inquiry. As a pre-service mathematics teacher, I occupy a dual role as researcher and participant, engaging reflexively with my experiences in AI-mediated classroom contexts. Autoethnography enables the linking of the individual self to the cultural, institutional, and technological forces that shape teaching and learning. In this paper, my encounters with students' use of generative Artificial Intelligence (AI) tools, my evolving pedagogical responses, and my internal negotiations regarding professional identity form the empirical grounding of the analysis. These experiences are not presented as isolated anecdotes, but as situated moments through which larger questions about mathematics education, teacher authority, and human-AI interaction are explored.

The utilization of the reflective autoethnography in this study was intentional. The learning to teach in a rapidly evolving educational landscape is a purely technical process. And also deeply emotional, ethical, and intellectual. Thus, the autoethnography allows for sustained attention to uncertainty, tension, and transformation. These elements are central and vital to understanding how AI reshapes the work and meaning of teaching. By foregrounding reflection alongside critical interpretation, the methodology acknowledges that becoming a teacher is an ongoing process rather than a fixed outcome.

Throughout the narrative, I engaged as an active participant and reflective practitioner, systematically documenting my observations, reflections, and pedagogical dilemmas as they emerged in classroom contexts. The reflexive writing served as both a data source and an analytic practice, enabling iterative engagement with experience over time. These reflections were examined through the continuous cycles of writing, revisiting, and theorizing, allowing patterns, contradictions, and shifts in belief to surface.

The rigor in this study is established through the transparency of positionality, sustained reflexivity, and theoretical grounding. Rather than aiming for generalizability in a statistical sense, this research seeks analytic depth and conceptual resonance. The value of the methodology lies in its capacity to offer transferable insights into how pre-service teachers experience, negotiate, and reimagine their roles in AI-influenced educational environments. By making the process of becoming visible, this methodological approach contributes to a more nuanced understanding of teaching as a human, relational, and ethical practice in an increasingly algorithmic world.

Data Sources. The primary data sources of this study consist of personal journals, reflective field notes, and memory-based vignettes generated throughout my experiences as a pre-service mathematics teacher. These sources were produced during my classroom observations, teaching assistantship, and practice teaching in a public high school in Tawi-Tawi, Southern Philippines. The writing of these sources was undertaken contemporaneously and retrospectively. It allowed both immediate impressions and later sense-making to inform the analysis. Together, these sources document critical moments in which students engaged with generative AI tools, classroom conversations surrounding the ethical use of AI, and my own internal negotiations as a future teacher grappling with questions of authority, authenticity, and pedagogical purpose.

In addition, the reflective journals and field notes captured the affective and relational dimensions of classroom life, including moments of uncertainty, disruption, and insight that emerged as AI became embedded in mathematical activity. Also, the data were the critical moments of the students utilizing the AI tools, the conversations about the ethical use of AI in classrooms, and my own inner struggles as a future teacher in negotiating authority, authenticity, and most importantly, pedagogy.

Memory-based vignettes were constructed to revisit experiences that were particularly formative or unsettling. It enabled deeper reflection on events that continued to shape my understanding of teaching and learning. In autoethnographic research, these sources are recognized as legitimate data sources that foreground meaning, emotion, and temporality. It allowed the researchers to trace how experiences evolve and are reinterpreted over time (Ellis et al., 2011).

Hence, there is additional contextual depth provided through informal dialogues with mentor teachers and colleagues. While these exchanges of dialogue were not treated as formal interviews, they played an important role in shaping interpretation by offering alternative viewpoints, affirmations, and tensions that extended beyond my individual perspective. These conversations helped situate my reflections within the broader professional, institutional, and cultural realities, particularly within the local educational context of Tawi-Tawi. Rather than being analysed as discrete data sets, these dialogues functioned as interpretive resources that informed reflexive thinking and supported the co-construction of meaning.

Data Analysis. The data analysis was done as an ongoing and reflective journey. It focused more on understanding the meaning than on measuring outcomes. I went through several cycles of reading, coding, and, of course, writing. Also, pausing often to think about what my experiences really meant. In addition, following Hatton and Smith's framework, I began to write a simple descriptive reflection. I simply wrote down what happened in the classroom. Its atmosphere, emotions, and small moments that stood out. After that, I started to do an analytical reflection. I started to see how these experiences were shaping the way I understood teaching mathematics in spaces shared with AI. Thus, I also did a critical reflection, which helped me to connect all of my realizations to larger ideas about what it means to be a teacher today. It is a question of identity, ethics, and the evolving relationship between humans and technology.

Hence, through this multiple layer of my reflections, it moved from my personal experience to a deeper pedagogical insight and eventually to a broader understanding of how AI is reshaping the very heart and purpose of mathematics education.

Positionality and Reflexivity. My positionality as a pre-service mathematics teacher is central to this inquiry and inseparable from the knowledge it produces. I write not as an expert, but as a teacher in the becoming teacher. Becoming a teacher, one who is still navigating the uncertainties, tensions, and contradictions of learning to teach mathematics in a world where artificial intelligence is increasingly mediating knowledge. This in-between position, situated between being a student and teacher, theory and practice, confidence and doubt, provides a very peculiar epistemic standpoint from which to examine how AI reshapes pedagogical meaning, professional identity, and classroom authority.

Before this study began, my relationship with artificial intelligence had already started to take shape in quiet, personal ways. I did not encounter AI as an abstract concept in a textbook. I first came across generative tools like ChatGPT, Dola *(formerly CiCi)*, and Gemini through conversations with classmates. At first, I was simply curious. I wanted to see and explore what it could do. And that curiosity slowly turned into regular use. And then, I began experimenting with AI. I utilized it when drafting lesson plans, refining my essay, and answering practice problems on my subjects, particularly in geometry and calculus. Also, there were moments when I used it for drafting new research papers as well as brainstorming with a partner. Yet, my experience was not purely enthusiastic. There were also moments of hesitation and discomfort. I sometimes questioned whether the AI-generated contents were fully accurate or pedagogically sound. I worried about becoming too dependent on it. I also found myself asking deeper questions: If AI can instantly produce solutions and explanations, what then distinguishes the role of the teacher? What does it mean to genuinely understand mathematics in an era where answers are always within reach? These questions unsettled me.

Over time, I realized that my engagement with AI was shaping not only how I worked, but how I thought about teaching. I experienced AI as both empowering and destabilizing. It made certain tasks more efficient and expanded my instructional imagination, yet it also disrupted my assumptions about authority, originality, and ownership of ideas. I became more aware of the delicate balance between using AI as support and preserving intellectual agency.

With these prior experiences, I do not approach this study as a neutral observer of artificial intelligence. My openness to its possibilities, my caution about its risks, and my critical reflections about its place in mathematics education are all informed by lived encounters. Acknowledging this is important, for these experiences inevitably shaped how I interpreted AI-mediated classroom interactions and how I continue to negotiate my own becoming as a mathematics teacher in the age of AI.

In qualitative and autoethnographic research, positionality is not a bias to be eliminated, but a condition of knowing that must be made visible and critically examined (Creswell & Poth, 2016; Ellis et al., 2011). My experiences as a pre-service mathematics teacher, shaped by my own schooling, teacher education, and early classroom encounters with AI is inevitably influenced how I interpreted students' practices, classroom interactions, and my evolving sense of professional purpose. Acknowledging this positioning allows the reader to understand not only what is being narrated but also from where the narrative emerges.

Moreover, the reflexivity was not treated as a methodological add-on or a retrospective exercise. It functioned as an ongoing, recursive dialogue within myself throughout the writing process. I continuously interrogated my emotions. It ranges from uncertainty and anxiety to curiosity and cautious optimism. It shaped the meanings I assigned to artificial intelligence and to my role as a future mathematics teacher. This reflexive stance required sustained questioning of my assumptions about the mathematical learning and what constitutes "good" teaching in AI-mediated environments now. By attending to these internal negotiations, reflexivity became a means of tracing how my beliefs about teaching and learning were being unsettled, reconstructed, and rearticulated over time.

Thus, critical self-awareness is essential in autoethnographic inquiry, where the self is both the site of investigation and the analytic lens (Adams et al., 2015). Aside from producing purely introspective accounts, reflexivity in this study served an ethical and intellectual function. It ensured that the personal narratives were analytically grounded, theoretically informed, and accountable to broader scholarly conversations. By situating my reflections within the existing literature on teacher identity, mathematics pedagogy, and AI in education, I sought to move beyond the individual experience toward the interpretive insight that resonates with wider educational contexts.

Throughout the process of this study, lived experience is transformed into scholarly knowledge. The integration of personal reflection with the critical interpretation allows this autoethnography to capture becoming, not as a fixed professional identity. But as a dynamic and ongoing process of negotiation. Becoming a mathematics teacher in the age of AI emerges here as a continual redefinition of purpose, agency, and responsibility. It is one shaped by the interplay between human judgment and algorithmic intelligence. This reflexive positioning does not claim generalizability. Instead, it offers analytic depth and conceptual transferability through illuminating how broader transformations in education are experienced, resisted, and reimagined from within the everyday realities of teacher identity formation.

RESULTS AND DISCUSSION

This study's reflective analysis generated three interrelated themes that illuminate my transformation as a pre-service mathematics teacher navigating AI-mediated classroom spaces. These themes are disruption, adaptation, and redefinition. These themes emerged from my sustained engagement with reflective journals, field notes, and memory-based vignettes developed during classroom observations and teaching assistantship experiences. Together, they capture a progressive yet recursive process of sense-making. Through which my understandings of teaching, learning, and professional identity were unsettled and reconstituted in response to the students' use of generative AI tools.

Figure 1. A Reflective Model of Becoming a Mathematics Teacher in AI-Mediated Classrooms

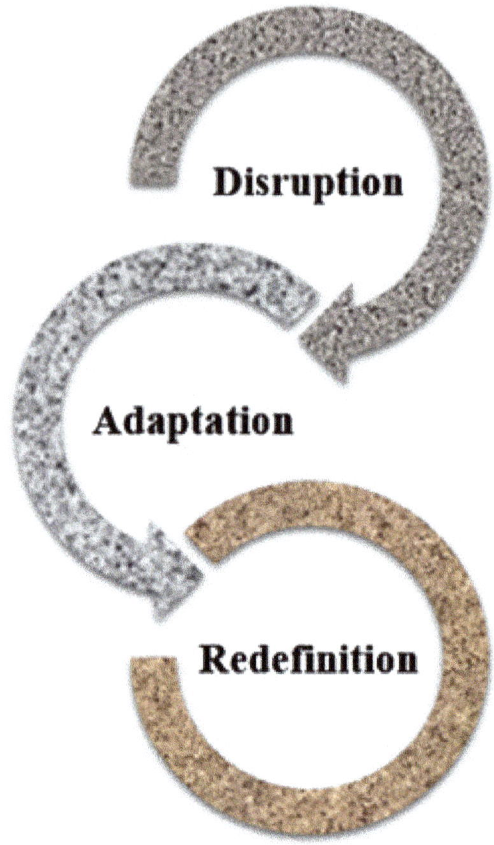

Figure 1 presents the thematic structure of the study. It illustrates the interconnected relationship among the disruption, adaptation, and redefinition as key moments in the process of becoming a mathematics teacher in the age of artificial intelligence.

The first theme is disruption. It represents the initial pedagogical and emotional rupture experienced when AI tools entered the mathematics classroom. It challenged the established assumptions about teaching, learning, and authority. While the adaptation captures the subsequent phase of my journey. The disruption became a pedagogical recalibration. It leads to the reframing of artificial intelligence as a learning partner that extends human reasoning. And the redefinition signifies a deeper professional shift. It is where the teaching of mathematics is reimagined as a fundamentally human practice centered on judgment, ethical responsibility, and mathematical sense-making in AI-rich environments.

This visualization shows the three themes as interconnected and sequential. The figure emphasizes that becoming a teacher in the presence of AI is an ongoing process and not a fixed endpoint. The movement across the themes reflects the continual negotiation between uncertainty and understanding, resistance and acceptance, and automation and human agency. As such, the figure serves as an analytic lens through which the results and discussion are organized. It highlighted how the reflective engagement with AI reshapes both my pedagogical practices and teacher identity.

Phase 1: **Disruption: Encountering Artificial Intelligence (AI) in the Classroom**

This paper is rooted in a deeply transformative moment during my final year as an undergraduate student in the Bachelor of Secondary Education major in Mathematics program. As a part of my academic preparation, I was enrolled in Experiential Learning Courses (ELC 101 and ELC 102). The ELC is designed to immerse the pre-service teachers in authentic classroom settings through structured observations and teaching assistantships. These courses positioned the pre-service teachers within the real classrooms, alongside cooperating teachers and students. These courses required classroom observations and assistantships, allowing me to witness the teaching and learning process first-hand as they unfolded in real time within the institutional constraints, curricular demands, and the lived realities of the learners.

For me, this journey was simultaneously exciting, exhausting, and profoundly unsettling. It was filled with moments that challenged my previous pedagogical assumptions and helped build my emerging identity as a future mathematics teacher in times of Artificial Intelligence. While the teacher education literature has long emphasized the importance of experiential learning in shaping professional identity, Beauchamp and Thomas' (2009) framework on fluid teacher identity and Lasky's 2005 sociocultural perspective on professional learning, my experience unfolded in a context that those earlier frameworks did not fully anticipate: a classroom where the generative AI had already become part of the students' everyday mathematical practice. This highlights the tension between the prior assumptions about teaching and emergent realities, reflecting Flores and Day's (2006) notion of identity dissonance during the pre-service teaching.

The disruption occurred almost immediately. Entering my cooperating teacher's mathematics class, I thought I was going to witness a familiar scene where students copied solutions from the board, whispering and talking to their seatmates or occasionally sneaking a glance at their phones to scroll through social media. Instead, I witnessed something entirely the opposite, which made me dumbfounded. The very moment I stepped into one of my cooperating teacher's mathematics classrooms, I saw students reaching out for their mobile phones. Initially, I thought that they were just going to chat or scroll on social media, but I was wrong. Rather, I saw the students directly reach for their phones opened AI tools such as Gemini, ChatGPT, or Dola. They used these AI tools to solve mathematical problems, do assignments, and at times, even answer quizzes prepared by their mathematics teacher. At a glance, I saw complete and well-structured solutions appear on their screens within seconds.

I was stunned and felt uneasy. As a future mathematics teacher, for a moment, I was afraid. The speed with which AI-generated solutions emerged unsettled my deeply held beliefs about mathematics learning. I unconsciously realized that as though the traditional landscape and way of teaching-one grounded in rigid explanation, struggle, and gradual sense-making- had been changed in an instant. This moment echoed what recent studies describe as a pedagogical rupture. It is where generative AI destabilizes traditional classroom norms surrounding effort, authorship, and mathematical authority (Kasneci et al., 2023). Yet for me, the disruption was not merely instructional. It was existential.

The classroom, which serves as a space where I thought once a room for innovation, curiosity, and guided discovery, felt altered, almost unfamiliar. This reality shocked me in a way that shakes my confidence to teach and face my students in the future. It was as if the classroom I had been preparing to teach and imagine since I chose a teacher education program no longer existed. The image of teaching I had carefully constructed throughout my teacher education has significantly changed. One that is grounded in explanation, scaffolding, and procedural fluency has faded, and I felt a quiet fear. I fear that the role I was preparing for might already be obsolete, and I fear that machines could outperform me in terms of speed, accuracy, and procedural execution. This exemplifies Flores and Day's (2006) "identity dissonance," where professional self-concepts are fragile and actively forming during the pre-service phase. Encountering AI in this way shook my confidence and belief. It challenges the version of teaching I had imagined and formed during the past three years of my teacher preparation.

This disruption was not merely technological. It was deeply personal, too. I found myself suspended in the tension between fear and fascination while experiencing this reality first-hand. I was deeply torn. On one hand, I feared that the erosion of my role as a teacher in a world where answers could be generated faster, cleaner, and sometimes more accurately by machines. On the other hand, I was undeniably fascinated by the power of the secondary students now at their fingertips. I was deeply torn between holding on to the teacher I thought I was becoming and confronting the teacher I needed to be. This tension reflects broader discourse in AI and education, where the generative technologies are simultaneously framed as threats to academic integrity and as catalysts for pedagogical transformation (Williamson & Eynon, 2020).

And now, I began to question myself relentlessly. In an era where knowledge is instantly accessible, and solutions can be produced at the tap of a screen, I constantly ask myself reflective questions such as "*What does it truly mean to teach mathematics? Or who am I as a mathematics teacher when the artificial intelligence can outperform me in speed and procedural accuracy? More importantly, what is left for the human teacher to do?*"

These questions unsettled me. But they also compelled me to reflect more deeply. Gradually, my pedagogical assumptions began to shift. Instead of viewing students' use of AI as a threat, I started seeing it as a useful assistant. This realization reflects the limitations of the traditional teaching approaches that prioritize answers over thinking and procedures over understanding. The presence of AI in the classroom forced me to reconsider my relationship with my students, not as passive recipients of knowledge. But as active meaning-makers navigating a rapidly changing intellectual landscape.

I began to imagine the classroom not as a space where AI must be resisted, banned, or feared but as a space of inquiry where AI becomes a tool for dialogue, critiquing, and reflection. Instead of asking whether students used AI, the more important questions I should ask are: "*How are the students using it? Why do they trust its outputs? Can they evaluate its reasoning, identify its errors, and build upon its solutions?*"

Through this reframing, I came to envision a pedagogical strategy in which human intelligence and artificial intelligence coexist in my math classroom. In this classroom, AI supports but does not replace teachers' guidance. Rather, AI enhances learning by enabling richer mathematical discussions, deeper conceptual exploration, and more meaningful engagement with ideas. My role as a math teacher shifts from being the sole source of answers to becoming a facilitator of thinking, sense-making, and ethical use of technology.

Hence, this first real-life experience with AI in a classroom was a moment of confusion, doubt, and awakening. It revealed that being a mathematics teacher in this age emphasized that it is not about restraining our students from using these AI tools. But, cultivating spaces where the students can learn to think critically, question deeply, and explore creatively with the presence of AI as their partners.

Ultimately, I came to realize that the disruption brought by these AI tools did not diminish my role as a future mathematics teacher. Rather, it redefined mathematics teaching. This experience taught me that teaching in this era is fundamentally an act of humanizing knowledge. This foreshadows the critical pedagogy frameworks, emphasizing the human, reflective, and ethical dimensions of teaching, which AI cannot replicate. What I initially felt like a threat has become an invitation-an invitation to reimagine teaching, learning, and what it truly means to be human in mathematics classrooms.

Phase 2: Adaptation: Embracing Artificial Intelligence (AI) as a Collaborative Partner

After the initial disruption and days of processing and reflections, adaptation emerged not as passive acceptance of artificial intelligence, but as an active pedagogical reorientation. My observations marked a shift in how knowledge, authority, and participation were negotiated in the mathematics classroom. Rather than resisting the advancement brought by the technology, I began to navigate my role as a pre-service mathematics teacher in this reality. I began to recognize that AI had already changed the landscape of learning. Now, it is one where answers are no longer scarce and procedural knowledge is no longer owned solely by the teacher. Through the sustained classroom observations and assistantship experiences, I found myself exploring how AI could be utilized, complemented, and complement and extend my emerging pedagogical practice. This gave me a new pathway to renew my sense of possibility.

And with the new classroom setting I've witnessed, I was inspired to explore these AI tools at home. Later in our classes, I started experimenting with AI tools and thinking about how I am able to integrate these transformative tools into my teaching practice in the future. I tried using AI to generate problem sets, rich mathematics tasks, and asked these tools to provide different strategies to discuss and represent certain mathematical concepts. This reflects Hoyles et al.'s (2020) view that technology acts as a mediating tool in mathematics education, supporting discussion, conceptual understanding, and metacognitive reflection. I used AI tools as my brainstorming partner. A partner that is also a source of stimuli and provocations, igniting my creative, critical, and deeper thinking. At this moment, I came to appreciate AI not as a threat, but as a useful collaborator. My perception of the role as a future teacher began to shift from being primarily an information provider to a facilitator of sense-making, critique, and ethical reasoning.

This personal transformation that happened to me aligns with the emerging research on artificial intelligence in education. For instance, Holmes et al. (2019) argue that generative AI can function as an augmentative tool. It extended human creativity and enabled more reflective engagement, rather than merely automating routine tasks. Similarly, Luckin et al. (2016) emphasize the potential of AI to personalize learning, scaffold reasoning, and free educators to focus on the higher-order thinking and relational aspects of teaching. There is also research in mathematics education that further highlights the importance of viewing technology as a mediating tool. It is when used critically that digital tools can stimulate discussion, support conceptual understanding, and promote metacognition (Hoyles, 2010). My experience aligns with these findings. For me, AI did not diminish my agency. But instead, amplified it. It creates a space for pedagogical experimentation and reflective practice.

My adaptation of artificial intelligence transformed how I allocated my time, tasks, and attention. During my practice teaching, the tasks that previously consumed hours can be done in a shorter period. The time I used it in drafting, checking, or refining mathematical problem sets can now be used for reflection, asking deeper questions, scaffolding student thinking, and designing richer, more engaging mathematical tasks. I can now focus on planning tasks that demand sense-making, creativity, critical thinking skills, and most importantly, mathematical reasoning. I used Artificial Intelligence (AI) as a scaffold and assistant, but not as a substitute.

However, I remain vigilant when utilizing the AI in my teaching. In my class, I encouraged students not to accept the AI outputs directly without analysing and critiquing. I oftentimes ask my students a few questions to guide them on how to utilize AI outputs. Questions like "*Why does this answer make sense? Can you verify it? Can you explain it in your own words or show another method?*" This scenario mirrors the research of Zawacki-Richter et al. (2019), which highlights the ethical and pedagogical responsibilities of teachers in AI-mediated learning.

During this phase, I came to realize that adaptation requires a big shift, not just technological l. Rather, AI adaptation is deeply pedagogical, ethical, and humanizing. It transformed the classroom from a site of output-driven tasks into a space of inquiry, negotiation, and co-construction of knowledge. In doing so, I somehow formed a new professional identity- a new teacher who is not afraid of AI. A new pre-service teacher who embraces AI as a partner and collaborator in this sense, the adaptation during my pre-service mathematics journey becomes a radical act of change. I now believe that AI presence in my classroom amplifies my teacher agency instead of diminishing my creativity. AI in the classroom does not mean the obsolescence of the teacher, but rather the rebirth of what teaching can be. In a world where information can be computed, mathematics teaching should focus more on cultivating curiosity, guiding sense-making, and fostering mathematical consciousness. Embracing AI as a collaborative partner is not surrendering to automation; it is reclaiming what it means to teach, learn, and be human in the age of algorithms.

Phase 3: Redefinition: Transforming the Teacher's Role

After seeing the AI tools as a disruption and then learning to adapt these tools, I unconsciously found myself entering a new phase of redefinition. The redefinition of the teacher's role in this AI era. The presence of these AI tools in the classroom did more than just disrupt. It invited me to envision a different kind of mathematics teacher. An educator whose role is not anchored in providing answers to math questions but in cultivating my students' potential beyond calculations.

During this journey, I came to realize that the teacher I once imagined as a sage on the stage, disseminating mathematical truths, checking problem sets, and grading papers, is now no longer fully relevant in a world where AI can handle much of the mechanical and computational work. With AI capable of generating content, solving procedural problems, and even offering multiple solution paths, the traditional model of teaching becomes inadequate. This aligns with Beauchamp and Thomas' (2009) view of other identity as fluid and socially negotiated, and Flores and Day's (2006) notion of identity dissonance, highlighting that professional roles are actively reconstructed when faced with the new technological realities. The teacher's role must shift toward what I now consider the core of meaningful education. That is facilitation, moral and intellectual mentorship, designing of learning experiences, and providing ethical stewardship. Luckin et al. (2016) on AI as an augmentative tool that allows teachers to focus on higher-order thinking.

As a teacher, artificial intelligence freed me from many repetitive and routine tasks. I could now design richer mathematical activities that foreground exploration, multiple solution pathways, collaboration, and sense-making. Moreover, this transformation has shifted my pedagogical focus. The redefinition also entailed embracing new responsibilities. As students increasingly rely on AI, the teachers must guide them in digital literacy, AI literacy, ethical use, and critical evaluation of the algorithmic outputs (Holmes et al., 2019). In practice teaching, this means teaching the students not only mathematical reasoning but also when, how, and why to trust or question AI-generated solutions. My role as a math teacher thus extends beyond the procedural correctness to nurturing human capacities. Rather, I should inculcate critical judgment, curiosity, and creativity among my students- skills that cannot be replicated by machines.

The redefinition is not without challenges. It requires that I, as the teacher, develop new competencies. These include AI literacy, prompting, and critical evaluation of AI-generated output, ethical sensitivity, and pedagogical creativity. My experience with AI at this phase demands humility. I need to acknowledge that the solutions or insights may emerge from the students or artificial intelligence in ways the teacher had not anticipated. Yet it is precisely this openness that renders the redefined role powerful, relevant, and profoundly human.

Ultimately, my journey through the disruption, adaptation, and redefinition led to a transformed professional identity. I am now convinced that the essence of a math teacher is not serving as a guardian of procedural accuracy, but as a cultivator of mathematical consciousness, ethical reasoning, creative thinking, and human flourishing. This experience made me realize that teaching mathematics in the age of AI is not about competing with these machines. Rather, it is more about taking advantage of their capabilities and reclaiming what these AI tools cannot emulate. That is to allow the students to wonder, create new meaning, and practice empathy.

Together, these three interrelated themes form a coherent narrative of my professional transformation as a mathematics teacher in training. My experiences with

AI highlight how artificial intelligence reshapes not only instructional practices but also my identity. By situating personal experience within the broader theoretical and empirical conversations, the findings contribute to the growing literature on AI in education. It foregrounds the often-overlooked perspective of the pre-service teachers. The study underscores that preparing educators for AI-rich classrooms requires more than technical proficiency. It demands reflective spaces, ethical dialogue, and opportunities for identity work. Thus, this chapter positions mathematics education not as a diminishing field caused by artificial intelligence, but as a new, reinvigorated field re-centered on creativity, problem-solving, and other human values.

CONCLUSION

What started from a simple classroom observation, somehow, led me to a far more consequential realization. Artificial intelligence has irrevocably altered not only how students learn mathematics, but also how to teach math. The introduction of Artificial Intelligence into the math classroom highlighted the need to go beyond providing answers and doing calculations. Rather, education was always about the cultivation of understanding, critical judgment, and the development of human values.

Through the author's experience with the disruption brought by AI, to learning to adapt and finally redefining identity, this paper highlighted that the greatest challenge posed by AI is not technological in nature, but pedagogical and ethical as well. Today, machines can instantly generate mathematically correct solutions with speed and efficiency. Hence, the math teachers' role should refocus on guiding the learners to think critically. Learners should be encouraged to question the reasoning of intelligent systems and to assume responsibility for how mathematical knowledge is used and understood.

This study contributes a critical insight grounded in the lived experience of mathematics pre-service teachers in the age of AI. Traditional teaching practices in the mathematics classroom privilege speed, procedural mastery, and individual performance. However, in AI-mediated classrooms, learning should be manifested in students' ability to interpret, challenge, and humanize machine-generated answers. Teaching in the age of AI, therefore, is redefined not as the transmission of knowledge but as a cultivation of students' agency for learning.

Finally, this inquiry asserts that mathematics teaching in the age of AI must refocus on the cultivation of human cognition and values. While artificial intelligence can compute, explain, and optimize solutions, it cannot show care, doubt, or act ethically. These capacities remain uniquely human, and it is precisely these qualities that the education must be grounded in. With this, the mathematics classroom can become a space where students learn not just how to solve problems, but how to utilize AI as a supplementary tool for learning. Contrary to some teachers' fears, my encounter with the artificial intelligence did not signal the end of the math teacher's relevance. Rather, AI can enhance teachers' expertise. At this time, when the algorithms increasingly shape how learners build their knowledge Teachers can now focus on teaching learners to not merely accept AI outputs, but train learners to question, refine, and situate in their own context.

In doing so, the artificial intelligence does not diminish the role of the teacher. Instead, it reveals the urgency of the shifting teachers' role. The future of mathematics education lies not in competing with machines, but in educating humans who can think beyond them.

LIMITATIONS OF THE STUDY

While this reflective autoethnography provides in-depth insights into the becoming of a pre-service mathematics teacher in AI-mediated classrooms, several limitations must be acknowledged to situate the findings appropriately.

First, this study is grounded in a single autoethnographic account. And as the sole participant and researcher, the narratives, interpretations, and thematic constructions are shaped by my personal experiences, emotions, and positionality as a pre-service mathematics teacher in Tawi-Tawi. Although the reflexivity and theoretical grounding were employed to enhance the rigor, the findings remain context-specific and cannot be generalized to all pre-service teachers, mathematics classrooms, or educational settings. The study offers analytic transferability rather than statistical generalizability. Second, the data sources relied primarily on the reflective journals, field notes, and memory-based vignettes. While these are legitimate forms of data in autoethnographic research, they are inherently subjective and may be influenced by selective recall, emotional intensity, or retrospective reinterpretation. Third, the study was conducted within a specific institutional and cultural context, which was a public high school in Tawi-Tawi, Southern Philippines. The technological infrastructure, student familiarity with generative AI tools, classroom norms, and mentor influences within this context may differ significantly from those in urban, international, or differently resourced educational settings. As such, the dynamics of disruption, adaptation, and redefinition identified in this paper may manifest differently in other contexts. Fourth, the paper does not empirically evaluate the effectiveness of AI integration on student learning outcomes, mathematical achievement, or long-term pedagogical impact. Its purpose is conceptual and reflective rather than evaluative. Therefore, the claims regarding the transformative potential of AI in mathematics education are grounded in lived experience and theoretical dialogue, not in quantitative measurement or experimental comparison. Ultimately, as this research captures a particular moment in time during the rapid emergence of generative AI, the technological landscape continues to evolve. Tools, policies, and classroom practices related to AI are developing rapidly.

Hence, the insights presented here reflect an early-stage engagement with the AI in mathematics education and may require re-examination as technologies and pedagogical norms continue to shift. Despite these limitations, the study contributes meaningful insight into the identity formation of pre-service mathematics teachers navigating AI-rich environments. By making visible the tensions, uncertainties, and redefinitions that accompany this transition, the research offers conceptual depth and a reflective foundation for future empirical and multi-voiced investigations into artificial intelligence in mathematics education.

IMPLICATIONS

The findings of this reflective inquiry suggested many pivotal implications for mathematics education, teacher preparation, and classroom practice in an era increasingly shaped by artificial intelligence. Rather than positioning AI as an external add-on to existing teaching practices, this study suggests that the emergence of AI necessitates a fundamental reconsideration of how mathematical knowledge is taught, learned, and valued.

Foremost, mathematics teaching and learning need to change. The ever-present presence of AI in the mathematics classroom calls for a shift away from traditional looking-for-the-right-answer instruction to the learning environments that prioritize reasoning, interpretation, and critical engagement. When the students can easily access correct solutions through the AI tools, coming up with correct answers alone can no longer serve as a reliable indicator of understanding. Hence, mathematics instruction must emphasize students' higher-order thinking, including justification, comparison of the solution strategies, and reasoning. Math teachers should then design tasks where students are required to critique AI outputs, identify errors or limitations, and explain why certain solutions are valid or invalid within a given context. Moreover, AI-mediated classrooms invite a reconceptualization of mathematical struggle. Struggle is no longer solely about arriving at an answer, but about navigating uncertainty, ambiguity, and making judgments about solutions provided by AI. With solutions to math problems that can now be generated in one click, math teachers are now challenged to think of mathematical tasks that allow students to practice higher-order thinking processes such as sense-making, solution validation, and making ethical judgments.

The findings also suggest the need to incorporate AI into teacher education programs and pre-service teacher preparation. This study underscores the urgency of equipping future mathematics teachers. Pre-service teachers need not only to be familiar with AI tools, but to critically and responsibly use them. Pre-service teachers must be prepared on how AI has reshaped classroom authority, student agency, and the nature of mathematical knowledge itself. This may include engaging future teachers in reflective experiences that surface tensions between traditional teaching identities and emerging AI-mediated practices. Teacher preparation must move beyond the technical training toward ethical and pedagogical formation. The pre-service teachers should be trained to reflect on how AI supports learning or hinders it. Pre-service teachers should be trained to guide students in responsible and reflective engagement with the intelligent systems. Such preparation positions future teachers to adapt AI and use it to design learning environments that positively blend AI and human judgment and values.

In addition, the papers call for a change in the assessment practices in mathematics classrooms. The findings suggest that the conventional approaches to assessment in mathematics, where the goal is to arrive at the correct answers, may not work. In the Artificial Intelligence era, assessments that prioritize procedural accuracy and isolated problem-solving risk becoming obsolete or misleading. Instead, assessment practices should capture students' reasoning processes, their ability to explain and justify solutions, and their capacity to critically evaluate AI-generated responses. This further suggests the need for greater emphasis on open-ended tasks, reflective explanations, and dialogic assessments that value thinking over speed.

Lastly, at a broader level, this study highlights the need for appropriate educational policies that guide teachers in the ethical practice of integrating AI in the classroom. This policy should underscore the need to address the deeper pedagogical shifts required in contemporary classrooms. The policies should support ethical integration frameworks that recognize AI as a permanent feature of students' learning environments and emphasize critical literacy, responsibility, and equity, ensuring all students benefit from AI use.

Ultimately, these implications point toward a more human-centered vision of mathematics education. As artificial intelligence continues to evolve, the role of education is not to shield students from the intelligent technologies but to equip them with the capacity to engage with such technologies thoughtfully, meaningfully, and ethically. Thus, the mathematics classrooms become crucial spaces for cultivating discernment, agency, and moral responsibility-capacities that remain uniquely human.

ACKNOWLEDGEMENT

This work is deeply shaped by the people who talked with me throughout my academic, research, and practice teaching journey. I extend my heartfelt gratitude to my best mentor as well as supervising instructor, *Mr. Potchong M. Jackaria*, whose guidance has been both selfless and transformative. His listening, openness, valuing, and endurance in addressing my numerous inquiries, his willingness to engage in thoughtful discussion and meaningful argument and debate, and his commitment, in which I could grow intellectually and professionally. For his guidance, trust, and mentorship, I will be forever grateful. I realized that some forms of guidance change what we know, but others change who we are allowed to become.

I also wish to acknowledge my cooperating teachers during my practice teaching. Their guidance, feedback, and encouragement helped me navigate the realities of the classroom and deepen my understanding of teaching as both a craft and a responsibility. Their mentorship grounded my academic learning in lived pedagogical practice and affirmed the value of reflective teaching. Ultimately, my sincere appreciation extends to my students, classmates, and peers who shared their ideas, questions, and encouragement throughout this journey. Their presence reminded me that learning and research are always relational and never undertaken alone.

REFERENCES

Adams, T. E., & Herrmann, A. F. (2020). Expanding our autoethnographic future. *Journal of Autoethnography*, *1*(1), 1–8. DOI: 10.1525/joae.2020.1.1.1

Adams, T. E., Jones, S. H., & Ellis, C. (2015). Autoethnography: Understanding qualitative research.

Beauchamp, C., & Thomas, L. (2009). Understanding teacher identity: An overview of issues in the literature and implications for teacher education. *Cambridge Journal of Education*, *39*(2), 175–189. DOI: 10.1080/03057640902902252

Creely, E., & Carabott, K. (2025). Teaching and learning with AI: An Integrated AI-Oriented Pedagogical Model. *Australian Educational Researcher*, *52*(6), 4633–4654. DOI: 10.1007/s13384-025-00913-6

Creswell, J. W., & Poth, C. N. (2016). *Qualitative inquiry and research design: Choosing among five approaches*. Sage Publications. Sage Publications. https://www.sagepub.com/

Ellis, C., Adams, T. E., & Bochner, A. P. (2011). Autoethnography: An overview. *Historical social research. Historische Sozialforschung*, •••, 273–290. https://www.jstor.org/stable/23032294

Flores, M. A., & Day, C. (2006). Contexts which shape and reshape new teachers' identities: A multi-perspective study. *Teaching and Teacher Education*, *22*(2), 219–232. DOI: 10.1016/j.tate.2005.09.002

Holmes, W., Bialik, M., & Fadel, C. (2019). *Artificial intelligence in education promises and implications for teaching and learning*. Center for Curriculum Redesign. https://discovery.ucl.ac.uk/id/eprint/10139722

Hoyles, C. (2010). *Mathematics education and technology: Rethinking the terrain* (Lagrange, J. B., Ed.). Springer., DOI: 10.1007/978-1-4419-0146-0

Hoyles, C., Kieran, C., Rojano, T., Sacristán, A. I., & Trigueros, M. (2020). Reflections on digital technologies in mathematics education across cultures. In *Mathematics Education Across Cultures: Proceedings of the 42nd meeting of PME-NA* (pp. 69-92). DOI: 10.51272/pmena.42.2020-1

Kasneci, E., Seßler, K., Küchemann, S., Bannert, M., Dementieva, D., Fischer, F., Gasser, U., Groh, G., Günnemann, S., Hüllermeier, E., Krusche, S., Kutyniok, G., Michaeli, T., Nerdel, C., Pfeffer, J., Poquet, O., Sailer, M., Schmidt, A., Seidel, T., & Kasneci, G. (2023). ChatGPT for good? On opportunities and challenges of large language models for education. *Learning and Individual Differences*, *103*, 102274. DOI: 10.1016/j.lindif.2023.102274

Lasky, S. (2005). A sociocultural approach to understanding teacher identity, agency and professional vulnerability in a context of secondary school reform. *Teaching and Teacher Education*, *21*(8), 899–916. DOI: 10.1016/j.tate.2005.06.003

Williamson, B., & Eynon, R. (2020). Historical threads, missing links, and future directions in AI in education. *Learning, Media and Technology*, *45*(3), 223–235. DOI: 10.1080/17439884.2020.1798995

Zawacki-Richter, O., Marín, V. I., Bond, M., & Gouverneur, F. (2019). Systematic review of research on artificial intelligence applications in higher education–where are the educators? *International Journal of Educational Technology in Higher Education*, *16*(1), 1–27. DOI: 10.1186/s41239-019-0171-0

Chapter 5
Leveraging the Use of AI Tools in Practice Teaching:
Insights from Science Pre-Service Teachers

Potchong M. Jackaria
http://orcid.org/0009-0006-1678-4841
Mindanao State University Tawi-Tawi College of Technology and Oceanography, Philippines

Monica Mae R. Pon
http://orcid.org/0009-0004-5767-9760
Mindanao State University Tawi-Tawi College of Technology and Oceanography, Philippines

Nurul-Ainie S. Eldani
http://orcid.org/0000-0003-3862-9501
Mindanao State University Tawi-Tawi College of Technology and Oceanography, Philippines

Hana An L. Alvarado
http://orcid.org/0009-0006-6550-616X
Mindanao State University Tawi-Tawi College of Technology and Oceanography, Philippines

Sherlyn A. Iralan
http://orcid.org/0009-0001-4288-6079
Mindanao State University Tawi-Tawi College of Technology and Oceanography, Philippines

DOI: 10.4018/979-8-3373-8027-8.ch005

ABSTRACT

This study explored how science pre-service teachers use AI tools during practice teaching. The result of the survey and interview with 32 science pre-service teachers showed AI tools are used in lesson planning, understanding content, creating instructional materials, and constructing assessments. Popular and useful AI tools include ChatGPT, Cici, Quillbot, Grammarly, and Gemini because of their diverse capabilities. The findings reflect a growing recognition of AI as a valuable teaching aid that enhances efficiency, content delivery, and teacher confidence. However, the findings highlight the imperative for teacher education programs to adapt to the emerging significance of AI technology as a valuable tool in instructional practice.

INTRODUCTION

The proliferation of Artificial intelligence (AI) tools has undoubtedly transformed education. It offered many new possibilities and opportunities for both teachers and students as these tools have the potential to improve teaching process, enhance students' learning experiences, and provide personalized instruction (Aleven et al., 2023). Systematic review of research revealed that AI-supported platforms, such as intelligent tutoring systems and adaptive learning technologies, are now being widely utilized to enhance instructional delivery and student engagement in some schools (Su et al., 2023).

However, alongside these benefits, valid concerns have been raised regarding misuse in school settings. Particularly, AI tools can be used for plagiarism, spread misinformation, and may lead to students' overreliance on AI-generated content (Liyberber, 2023; Xu, 2025). Despite these concerns, AI utilization continues to gain traction in education. Many studies have shown that students are already integrating AI tools into their academic work, using them for research, writing, and problem-solving (Jackaria et al., 2024; Nagaraj et al., 2023; Xu, 2025). A recent report from the World Economic Forum, echoed by reviews in educational research, highlights the urgent need for AI literacy. The report emphasized that students must be taught to develop critical thinking and ethical awareness to help them navigate AI-driven workplaces of the future (Biagini, 2025; Gu & Ericson, 2025).

Given this shift, educators being at the forefront of education, must not only understand AI but also leverage its capabilities to enhance teaching and learning. AI can support educators in various ways, from crafting personalized lessons to generating quizzes, suggesting feedback, and automating grading (Jackaria et al., 2024; Ogunleye et al., 2024). These applications of artificial intelligent tools are not only increasing in scope but are also being integrated into teacher education programs globally (Ogunleye et al., 2024; Xu, 2025). Additionally, AI helps manage teacher workload while also improving instructional effectiveness.

Despite the many advantages of AI tools, many educators readily adopt artificial intelligence, many remain hesitant due to concerns about reliability, ethical implications, and their own lack of familiarity with emerging technologies (Chen & She, 2023). Some teachers are resistant to use AI tools in their classrooms because it can be misused such as increasing plagiarism by the students, and the security issue it entails of student privacy (Thomas, 2024). Teachers lack of familiarly and preparation to used artificial intelligence may also contribute to teacher's negative perception of AI use (Aghaziarati et al., 2023; Mehdaoui, 2024).

However, with artificial intelligence presence in all aspect of life, teachers, must develop AI literacy to effectively teach students who are already adept with AI tools. Pre-service teachers, in particular, because of their role in the future classroom should be guided in positively integrate AI tools in teaching. Research has emphasized the importance of including AI integration in teacher preparation programs to better equip pre-service teachers for AI-driven classrooms (Gu & Ericson, 2025; Su et al., 2023). Developing a foundational understanding of AI not only improves instructional design but also promotes responsible and critical use of technology in the classroom (George, 2023; Daher, 2025).

This chapter explores how science pre-service teachers learn about and utilize AI tools during their practice teaching. It will explore how AI tools are applied in various aspects of practice teaching, such as lesson planning, instructional delivery, assessment, and reflection. Additionally, it captures pre-service teachers' experiences, the challenges they encounter, and the strategies they employ when integrating AI into their teaching practice. Through this lens, the chapter contributes to understanding AI integration in teacher education and the preparedness of future educators in an AI-enhanced learning environment.

PREVIOUS STUDIES ON AI ADOPTION, USAGE, ISSUES AND CONCERN IN PRACTICE TEACHING

Theories on AI Adoption

There are theories that explain the adoption of new technology. The most widely used theoretical perspectives to explain AI adoption are the Technology Acceptance Model (TAM) and the Unified Theory of Acceptance and Use of Technology (UTAUT) (Lee at al., 2025). The technology acceptance model (TAM) postulates that the acceptance of new technology such as AI is predicted by the users' behavioural intention, which in turn, determined by the perception of technology usefulness in performing the task and perceived ease of its use (Marikyan & Papagiannidis, 2024).

Previous study by Hoya et al. (2024) concluded that positive perceptions of AI's professional relevance can strengthen PSTs' intentions to use it in the classroom. Supporting this, Algerafi et al., (2023) identify factors like perceived usefulness, ease of use, and social influence as pivotal in AI adoption among students in higher education. This growing use is further contextualized by Runge et al. (2025), who point out that the perceived usefulness of AI can positively influence PSTs' intention to incorporate it in their future teaching aligning with the TAM model.

On the other hand, UTAUT is a predominant model extensively employed in understanding technology adoption in the educational context, especially in the realm of higher education (Xue et al., 2024). UTAUT expanded the TAM model to include social pressure and infrastructure as factors in AI adoption. Menon and Shilpa's study (2023) demonstrated that the four factors of UTAUT, along with two extended constructs such as perceived interactivity and privacy concerns, can explain users' interaction and engagement with AI particularly ChatGPT.

AI Usage for Practice Teaching

Integrating AI into education introduces new opportunities for both teachers and students. This requires a significant shift in educational practices, driven by AI's expanding role in the classroom. AI-powered tools made it possible for the creation of sophisticated educational environments where instruction becomes more flexible, personalized, and classroom management more inclusive (Pokrivcakova, 2019). AI tool's roles are not merely add-ons but are reshaping how educators design and deliver instruction, responding more precisely to individual student needs. Moreover, Mahana et al. (2012) discuss AI's impact on teachers' assessment practices noting how tools like Turnitin can efficiently detect plagiarism. Other tools can be used to automate grading through integrated rubrics and criteria. As AI becomes increasingly embedded in the virtual world, its growing influence on both general and higher education is undeniable (Al-zahrani & Alasmari, 2024; Zouhaier, 2023). Similarly, Fitria (2021) underscores that AI's presence in education facilitates learning and fosters student independence, as it assists in managing day-to-day teaching and learning tasks. Such functions demonstrate AI's potential to streamline instructional responsibilities, allowing teachers to focus more on student engagement and individualized support. Streilkowski et al., (2025) noted about AI's ability to make learning more interactive and adaptive, supporting varied student needs through diverse content types.

This development on AI utilization reflects a broader transformation in the educational landscape. Digital fluency and technological adaptability are becoming essential competencies for both learners and educators. Hence, the readiness of pre-service teachers (PSTs) in the context of an AI-infused educational landscape should be a pressing concern. As artificial intelligence continues to influence teachers' instructional tools and practices, there is a need to ensure that future educators are prepared to navigate this shift. Bautista et al. (2024) emphasize the timeliness and relevance of exploring this area, especially in terms of identifying the specific competencies needed for effectively integrating AI into educational practices. For the PSTs, it is necessary for them not only to develop technical skills but also cultivate pedagogical awareness in the use of AI.

Complementing this, Hsu et al. (2024) report that most pre-service teachers have begun using AI for both academic purposes, ranging from writing assistance to lesson planning and instructional material development. This indicates the PSTs' proactive engagement with emerging technologies, suggesting that many PSTs are already exploring how AI can enhance their teaching practice. However, usage patterns among pre-service teachers can differ based on context. For instance, according to Satapathy et al. (2025), rural PSTs primarily use AI for concept clarification and assignments, while their urban counterparts lean more toward exam preparation and communication. These variations reflect how access, exposure, and educational environments may shape the ways in which AI tools are adopted. Both groups, however, report minimal usage of AI for content creation and mentoring, suggesting untapped potential in these areas. This limited engagement indicates that while AI is being utilized for basic academic support, many of its broader capabilities such as fostering creativity and facilitating pedagogical mentorships are still underexplored. The study also highlights a general underutilization of AI in creative and social domains, despite a strong reliance on AI for academic tasks. Such findings point to the need for more comprehensive training that could expand PSTs' understanding of the diverse functions AI can serve in educational contexts.

Attitudes toward AI use in the academic context also vary in depth. While many individuals may hold favorable views about AI, the extent and complexity of their understanding can differ significantly. Lumanlan et al. (2025) noted that while pre-service teachers generally express positive attitudes toward AI, their level of AI literacy remains moderate. This discrepancy between enthusiasm and actual competence underlines the importance of aligning attitudes with practical skills and informed use. This gap raises important considerations and opportunities for teacher education curricula revision in the age of AI. Addressing this disconnect requires not only raising awareness but also integrating meaningful AI experiences into pre-service training. Falebita (2024) added that these varied perceptions of AI tools may be influenced by its perceived relevance to students' academic specialization, suggesting that discipline-specific approaches to AI training may be necessary. This implies that a one-size-fits-all model may be insufficient, and targeted training must be employed to better prepare pre-service teachers for integrating AI in contextually appropriate and meaningful ways.

In line with this, Coşgun (2025) recommended embedding AI literacy lessons into curriculum and teacher certification standards. Ethical considerations such as privacy, bias, and technological over-reliance should be addressed through discussion among PSTs for responsible use. Ashoori Tootkabini & Maghsoudi (2025) findings that PSTs are open to AI but tend to rely on it for immediate needs rather than integrating it into core teaching practices.

Additionally, Ko et al. (2025) elaborated on how pre-service teachers value AI for enhancing engagement, creativity, and problem-solving, particularly in academic writing. Their findings pointed to a need for structured guidance in utilizing AI not just for basic tasks but as a robust pedagogical aid. Similarly, Uwosomah and Dooly (2025) report that while PSTs appreciate AI's potential for fostering inclusion and differentiated instruction, they are also cautious about the risks. PSTs are concerned with over-dependence and AI's negative impact on students' creativity and critical thinking. Their study underlines a dual awareness: AI's potential to empower, and its limitations if misused.

The broader educational landscape echoes these findings. Garcia-Velez et al. (2021) highlight the global utility of AI tools for tasks ranging from information filtering to content generation through platforms like YouTube and other digital libraries. Chin (2018) also argues that AI has the potential to radically reshape not only how we learn and teach but how we live and make decisions.

Concerns and Existing Barriers to AI Adoption

The widespread adoption of AI tools is not without consequence. Karataş and Yüce (2024) further reveal that while pre-service teachers recognize the benefits of AI in enhancing and personalizing education, they also express concerns about its implications for academic integrity and information reliability. Foremost concern among educators is the potential misuse of artificial intelligence for Plagiarism due to its ability to generate answers. For instance, students may submit AI-generated work as their own without doing the necessary effort and critical thinking (Jackaria et al., 2024). Educators are also concerned about the potential for AI-assisted cheating for assignments and exams (Aust & Caukin, 2024). While AI-driven plagiarism detection tools have improved in identifying traditional and AI-generated plagiarism, they often lag behind the rapidly advancing development of the field of AI technologies (Mpolomoka et al., 2025).

There is also a concern of artificial intelligence posing risk to students by leaking personal information. This includes the disclosure of personal information due to the exploitation of students' private data and use in data trafficking of student personal information (Huang, 2023). With this, Rauf et al. (2024) emphasized the need for educational institutions and AI developers to establish clear guidelines and protocols for data handling to comply with privacy regulations.

According to Bulawan et al. (2023), students' increasing dependence on AI has led to both enhanced learning efficiency and signs of potential addiction. This concern is echoed by Mohebbi (2025) and Chang et al., (2023), who emphasize the role of AI in promoting learner autonomy through personalized feedback and progress tracking, while also cautioning about the need for balanced use.

Sukarno et al. 's (2026) study showed that some students are already forming personal attachment with AI instead of humans. They expressed concerns and suggested the need for privacy policies including clear consent mechanisms and transparent data usage policies must be present as AI interactions may involve sensitive emotional data. On a similar note, Tyson and Sauers (2021) concluded that many raised concerns about the potential for human interactions to become more limited with the rise of AI leading to users unable to make meaningful relationships with actual humans. It was suggested that this is an issue school leaders must consider.

All these concerns may lead to students being overreliant on AI technologies where students and teachers uncritically accept AI results (Zhai et al., 2024). Studies have revealed that students' overreliance on artificial intelligence tools negatively affects language skill development, classroom engagement, academic integrity, contextual understanding, and collaborative learning. This requires the need to have policies determining the specific boundaries for using AI (Avsheniuk et al., 2025; Nguyen et al., 2024). Even more serious, this overreliance will lead to the problem of reduced critical thinking and creativity among students (Abarzosa & Balaba, 2025; Melisa et al., 2025)

There are also barriers that prevent the adoption of artificial intelligence tools. Woodruff at al., (2023) notes that disparities exist in access to technology and comfort levels among different regions, genders, and age groups. This disparity can impede adoption of AI. In addition, they also pointed out the need for necessary infrastructure, such as reliable internet access, hardware, and software, to support AI adoption. The absence of basic technological infrastructure needed for AI adoption, may lead to the risk of widening technological, economic, and social divides particularly in the least developed countries and regions (Sharma et al., 2022; Vela & Mursi, 2026).

Teacher Readiness also poses a challenge to AI adoption since teachers are at the forefront of education. Herviana, (2025) highlighted that teacher training inadequacy impacts educational institution's ability to integrate AI emphasizing the critical need for comprehensive professional development programs for successful AI adoption. Similarly, Rauf et al., (2024) concluded that there is a need for comprehensive professional development programs to equip educators with the skills required to interpret AI-generated insights and effectively utilize AI tools. How the curriculum copes with AI integration can also be a barrier. Challenges related to curriculum structure, such as the lack of a well-structured and organized curriculum that incorporates state-of-the-art content on emerging technologies like AI (Deriba & Sanusi, 2025).

Across the reviewed literature, there is a shared recognition of AI's transformative potential in education, particularly in enhancing personalization, fostering learner independence, and streamlining instructional and assessment tasks. Pre-service teachers generally hold positive attitudes toward AI and acknowledge its value for academic and professional tasks. However, concerns regarding ethical use, over-reliance, and varying levels of AI literacy persist. The literature highlights that while AI use is growing among PSTs, it remains largely utilitarian, focused on immediate academic needs rather than integrated pedagogical strategies.

Despite the wealth of studies exploring usage, perceptions, and readiness, a notable gap remains in understanding how pre-service teachers develop long-term, pedagogically informed teaching approaches to AI integration particularly in diverse and under-resourced educational contexts. The current study addresses this gap by investigating not just what tools are used, but how future educators critically engage with AI in shaping their evolving teaching identities and practices.

METHODOLOGY

This chapter is exploratory in nature. To fully understand the topic, the study drew findings from both quantitative and qualitative data. Specifically, investigates how Artificial Intelligence (AI) tools are utilized by science pre-service teachers as teaching tools during their practice teaching.

The participants were science pre-service teachers from one state university in the Southern Philippines. Specifically, the study involved 32 practice teachers who are nearing the completion of their practice teaching. While 15 pre-service teachers were selected for an in-depth interview to gain deeper insights of the issue. The respondents were purposively selected as they have had substantial exposure to actual classroom scenarios and may have already used AI during their practice teaching.

The data were collected through surveys and one-on-one interviews using a structured interview questionnaire. The questions centered on the respondents' experiences with AI tools in practice teaching. Prior consents were secured as part of the research ethical consideration and anonymity of the personal details of the respondent is observed. The survey was conducted using paper-and-pencil strategy at the respondents' convenient time. While the follow-up interview was conducted a few days after. Each interview lasted for around 10 - 15 minutes and were tape-recorded. The interview explored the usage, challenges, and strategies employed by the pre-service teachers in utilizing AI.

Collected data from the interview were transcribed, translated, subjected to an appropriate statistical analysis. Specifically, the data were analyzed using both quantitative and qualitative data analysis. Qualitative analyses include frequency and percentage and were visually illustrated using Microsoft Excel.

The qualitative data from the pre-service teachers' responses are presented. It provides triangulation to the quantitative results. The qualitative data were subjected to thematic analysis following the processes outlined by Clarke and Braun (2017).

DISCUSSION OF RESULTS

The collected data was analyzed using both quantitative and qualitative approaches. Quantitative data is presented in tabular or graphical form, while qualitative responses were thematically analyzed to identify recurring patterns and insights.

Science Pre-service Teachers Use of AI Tools During Practice Teaching

The findings reveal that a significant majority of science pre-service teachers (80%) reported using AI tools during their practice teaching (Figure 1). This high percentage of AI use highlights the increasing integration of AI in classroom practice and reflects the growing positive perception among pre-service teachers that AI tools are useful teaching aids. This trend mirrors the observations of Hsu et al. (2024), who noted that pre-service teachers are already using AI for both academic and professional purposes.

Figure 1. Number of Science Pre-service Teachers Using AI (left) and Different AI Tools Used (right)

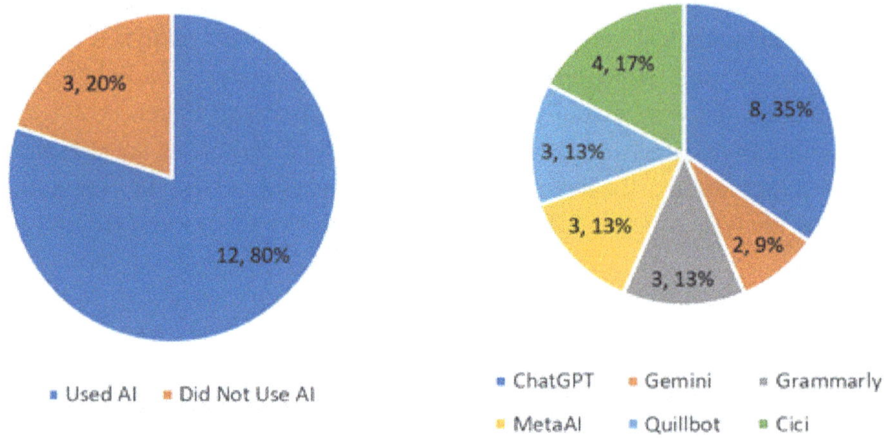

The result shows the most commonly used AI tools include ChatGPT (35%) and Cici (17%), followed by Quillbot, MetaAI, Grammarly, and Gemini. The predominance of ChatGPT and similar large language models suggests that pre-service teachers are utilizing these tools primarily for content generation, clarification of complex concepts, and enhancement of instructional materials. This pattern is consistent with the findings of Karataş and Yüce (2024), who emphasized that PSTs acknowledge AI's benefits for enhancing and personalizing instruction.

The diversity of tools employed further reflects the flexibility and adaptability of PSTs in selecting AI platforms that meet specific instructional needs. For example, PSTs use specific tool for grammar correction (e.g., Grammarly), paraphrasing (e.g., Quillbot), or synthesizing information (e.g., Gemini). This behavior aligns with the observations of Runge et al. (2025), who found that the perceived usefulness of AI positively influences pre-service teachers' intentions to incorporate it into their teaching practice. Moreover, it supports the claim made by Pokrivcakova (2019) that AI-powered environments are fostering more personalized and flexible modes of teaching and learning.

The findings also resonate with those of Maggo and Maggo (2025) who reported that while the specific purposes for using AI may vary between rural and urban contexts, academic support remains the primary function. In the present study, the range of tools cited indicates that science pre-service teachers are primarily engaging with AI for instructional preparation and delivery, rather than for mentoring or fostering creativity which remains underutilized. This underuse aligns with existing literature suggesting that while AI is increasingly relied upon for academic tasks, its potential for supporting creative and socio-pedagogical functions is yet to be fully explored (Uwosomah & Dooly, 2025).

Overall, given that most pre-service teachers did not receive formal training on the use of these AI tools in their classroom, the results reinforce the need for teacher education programs to provide structured guidance and targeted training in AI use, not only to enhance technical competence but also to foster critical and ethical engagement with these tools (Coşgun, 2025; Bautista et al., 2024). Without such support, there is a risk that PSTs will continue to use AI primarily for immediate academic needs rather than integrating it into more transformative pedagogical strategies.

Instructional Uses of AI Tools

As illustrated in Figure 2, pre-service teachers used AI tools for various teaching-related tasks. Foremost, the science pre-service teachers use AI tools for lesson planning (30%) and content understanding (30%). The PSTs employed AI to generate lesson plan drafts, explore creative suggestions for classroom activities such as motivation, and gain clearer understanding of complex science concepts. This finding aligns with Hsu et al. (2024), who observed that pre-service teachers increasingly use AI tools for academic and professional tasks, including lesson planning and material development. It also supports Karataş and Yüce's (2024) view that pre-service teachers recognize AI's role in enhancing instruction, especially in terms of personalization and content clarity. These results support the notion that AI tools are evolving beyond passive assistance to become strategic partners in instructional design.

In like manner, some of the pre-service teachers utilized AI tools for the creation of instructional materials (18%). They reported developing visual aids, worksheets, and multimedia slide presentations with AI support, reflecting integration of these technologies into daily instructional preparation. Ko et al. (2025) similarly found that AI enhances engagement, creativity, and problem-solving in academic settings, suggesting that such tools can strengthen the delivery of science content when thoughtfully applied.

Meanwhile, some participants used AI to improve their writing (15%) and create assessments (7%). These tools helped refine grammar, organize ideas, and even generate quizzes or formative evaluation tasks. This supports the findings of Uwosomah and Dooly (2025), who noted that AI is appreciated for aiding differentiation and communication, though they cautioned against overdependence. Likewise, Mahana et al. (2012) discussed how AI streamlines assessment by enabling automatic generation of quizzes and feedback, echoing the evolving instructional support AI provides.

Overall, the findings suggest that pre-service teachers are not only using AI for efficiency but also for improving instructional quality and pedagogical clarity. This indicates a behavioral shift from viewing AI as a potential threat to embracing it as a collaborative partner in planning and executing lessons. As Runge et al. (2025) highlighted, the perceived usefulness of AI significantly influences pre-service teachers' willingness to adopt it. Hence, such usage patterns reflect not just convenience but a growing readiness to integrate AI meaningfully into science instruction.

Figure 2. Uses of AI During Practice Teaching Among Science Pre-Service Teachers

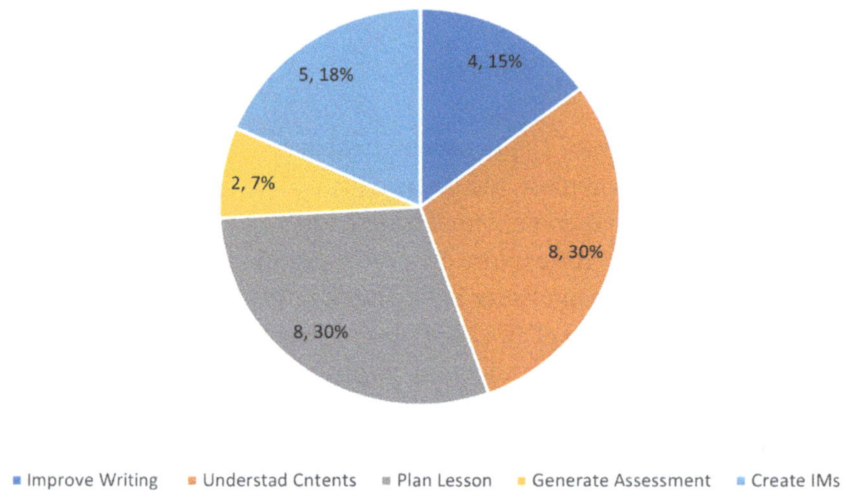

Pre-service Teachers Awareness About AI Tools

Figure 3 shows that most of the pre-service teachers learned to use AI tools through informal learning such as online platforms and social media (36%), followed by peer recommendations (32%) and self-exploration (25%). Alarmingly, only 7% said that AI tools were introduced through their professional education classes. This finding reflects a growing trend where digital tools, rather than formal instruction, serve as the primary means through which pre-service teachers acquire technological competencies.

Further, this result has critical implications to teacher preparation. It suggests that formal teacher education programs have yet to integrate AI literacy as part of the curriculum, leaving students to independently explore these technologies. Although such can mean independence, initiative and digital fluency of the PSTs, it also raised concern that without guidance, the teacher-in-training may develop a fragmented or ethically shallow understanding of AI's broader implications (Chen and She, 2023).

In addition, the lack of proper training on AI use exposes the PST's to potential misinformation or superficial understanding of AI's strengths and limitations.

Similarly, the result also indicates that teacher education institutions must begin integrating well-planned and structured AI training. This can be integrated in courses such as Educational Technology, Curriculum Development, and Assessment. Nagaraj et al. (2023) underscored the urgent need for teacher education programs to offer intentional AI integration, arguing that future educators must be equipped with discipline-specific skills to meaningfully implement AI tools. Doing so will not only legitimize AI as a pedagogical tool but also ensure that pre-service teachers understand how to use it ethically, effectively, and responsibly. As Falebita (2024) also emphasizes, perceptions of AI's relevance are often shaped by academic specialization, suggesting that embedding AI instruction within subject-specific pedagogy is relevant and deepens both engagement and application into PST's later teaching practice.

Figure 3. How Did the Science Pre-service Teachers Learn to Used the AI tools

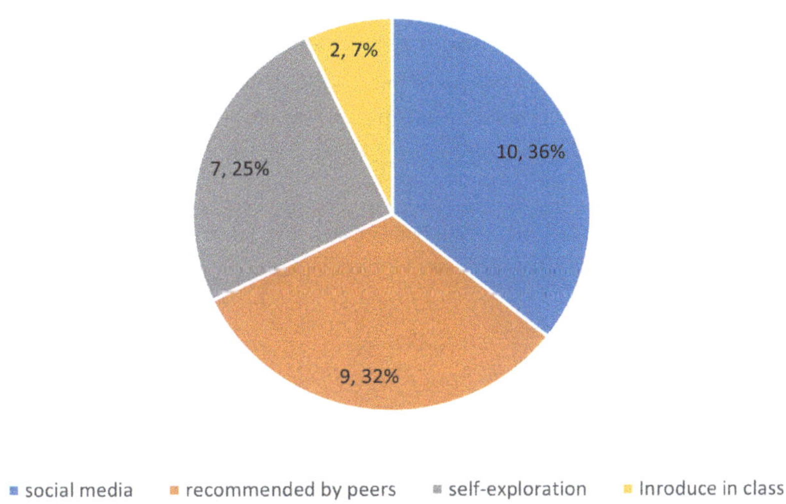

Perceived Benefits of AI Tools in Science Teaching

Responses from the open-ended questions reveal that pre-service teachers found AI tools highly beneficial. When the pre-service teachers were asked about how AI has helped them during the practice teaching, the responses showed that AI tools were helpful to the pre-service teachers. Its wide ranges of application show the AI tools versatility as an aid to teaching. This is reflected in the selected response below:

"Using AI tools in practice teaching was a big help in my journey during the practice teaching. Which provided class it served as my guide and helped accomplishing my tasks" Participant 12

"I found AI to be very helpful during my practice teaching. I am using them for many purposes such as creating ideas for my lesson, construct assessment, and make motivation activities. Participant 1

"Cici AI is very versatile and very accessible with just a phone. It is very useful both for my personal life and my teaching practice... It can provide motivation and help with lesson planning." Participant 5

Some of the pre-service teachers mentioned the specific use of AI tools that were useful to them such as enhancing their grammar and organizing ideas. The sample response from one of the participants is shown below:

"The advantages I experienced of using AI tools during my practice teaching were essentially to enhance my grammar as well as organize the sequence of ideas". Participant 11

"I have been using Grammarly and sometimes Quillbot to check my work. I also use ChatGPT if I am not sure about the organization of my ideas. Participant 8

Others have found AI tools useful during teaching by making the lesson easier such as assisting in providing better examples. The responses showed that the PSTs turn to AI to provide more and clearer examples in addition to those provided in textbooks.

"Yes, I think AI tools helped improve my teaching performance. They gave me ideas for lessons and made it easier to explain topics. I was able to prepare faster and find better examples for my students. It also helped me feel more ready and confident when teaching." Participant 10

"Sometimes, there are science concepts which are not clear for me and how to teach them. So, I use ChatGPT to explain the concepts for me in the simplest terms." Participant 4

The results align with global trends showing that AI can be a catalyst for teacher preparedness, especially in content-heavy subjects like science.

Cautions and Responsible Use of AI

While the overall sentiment was positive, some pre-service teachers expressed caution regarding over-reliance on AI. They recognized the importance of pre-service teachers practicing critical thinking and human judgment when using AI-generated content:

"AI tools are very helpful, but teachers should not depend on them too much. It's important to still use your own ideas and check if the information is right. AI should be used as a support, not the only way to teach." Participant 8

Highlighting the importance of teachers' creativity in teaching, others cautioned the use of AI tools. The response below highlights the central role of teachers while utilizing AI for teaching.

"Use it appropriately. Use AI just to improve your teaching, not to replace your own creativity and your role as a teacher." Participant 3

"There are students who use AI by just copy-and-pasting the results. They do not think and they do not learn. I think this is not good." Participant 6

Since AI is used to help in simplifying the contents taught, the participants emphasized the need of re-checking the results provided by the AI tools. This is also the result of AI tools sometimes providing unverified or inappropriate information. The following is one sample response:

"Yes, I would recommend AI tools to other pre-service teachers because they can help in making lesson plans, finding teaching ideas, and understanding topics better. AI can save time and make teaching easier, especially for beginners. But they should still be careful and check the information before using it." Participant 4

This awareness demonstrates that even with informal exposure to AI, many students understand the need to balance technology with human insight and pedagogical integrity.

DISCUSSION

This study illustrates how artificial intelligence (AI) has become embedded in pre-service teachers' instructional practice. AI is a largely informal component of the science pre-service teachers' experiences. There is recent research that confirms that pre-service educators increasingly accept and use AI applications in education, demonstrating that AI integration is no longer a future prospect but a present classroom reality (Alejandro et al., 2024; Zhang et al., 2023). In addition, there's an undeniably widespread utilization of AI tools even with the absence of structured training within teacher education programs. (Alejandro et al., 2024). This suggests that AI integration is no longer a future possibility. This is a present classroom reality around the world.

Artificial Intelligence (AI) is being introduced not through institutional channels. It usually appears organically through peer networks and suggestions, online platforms, and self-exploration. This reflects how the digital practices often precede formal pedagogical frameworks. This is consistent with findings that pre-service teachers develop technological fluency primarily through self-directed exploration rather than institutional training (Alejandro et al., 2024). Also, this pattern highlights a shift in how pre-service teachers acquire professional competencies. Before the technological fluency was usually developed through traditional coursework, but now, it is also shaped by immediate instructional demands.

The prevalent usage of AI by the PSTs for lesson planning, content understanding, and instructional material development underscores the role of AI as a form of cognitive and pedagogical support during the demanding phase of practice teaching. For most of the science pre-service teachers, AI tools can serve as scaffolds aiding them in clarifying complex scientific concepts, providing suggestions on pedagogy thereby improving their instructional preparedness. Previous studies have shown that many pre-service teachers view AI as a valuable instructional aid that supports lesson design and enhances content knowledge, facilitating efficiency in planning and organization (Espino, 2025). Consonant with this research finding, previous studies also suggests that AI technological tools can serve as scaffolds, helping novice teachers manage workload and clarify complex subject matter, aligning with broader discussions on cognitive support and technological assistance in educational settings (Espino, 2025; Ramnarain et al., 2024). It can be noted that the participants in this study did not frame AI as a substitute for teaching expertise. Rather, it just serves as their guide, improving efficiency and supporting confidence, especially for novice teachers who are still developing their pedagogical identity. The findings can be aligned with research indicating that pre-service teachers' attitudes toward AI are shaped by perceived usefulness and intentions to use the Technology Acceptance Model (Alejandro et al., 2024; Zhang et al., 2023).

While AI tools were valued and utilized by the participants for their ability to generate ideas, refine grammar, and organize content. However, its potential for deeper pedagogical practices such as fostering creativity, inquiry, or student-centered learning remains unexplored. The result suggests that in the absence of explicit pedagogical modelling, pre-service teachers initially utilized AI in ways that only mirror existing teaching practices rather than use it to be more innovative and transform them. This supports findings from research on ethical readiness, which shows that responsible AI integration is linked to both technological competence and ethical consciousness among teacher candidates (Bautista et al., 2024). These findings resonate with the broader research on educational technology adoption in education. It shows that new technological tools are often first used to improve efficiency before enabling pedagogical innovation. The science pre-service teachers demonstrated a notable level of ethical awareness and professional responsibility, even with the largely informal and self-directed nature of AI engagement. It is emphasized by the participants' importance of not overly relying on AI-generated content, highlighting the vital steps which are verifying the AI-generated information. This shows that the pre-service teachers still maintain the central role of human judgment and creativity in their teaching. This underscores that the participants have the capacity for reflective practice, even without formal guidance. The overwhelming positive perception and benefits of AI in practice teaching explains AI prevalent adoption among the pre-service teachers. This aligned with the Technology Acceptance Model particularly on the aspect of perceived usefulness.

Moreover, the absence of formal AI instruction within teacher education programs provides a spotlight to existing critical issues on science teacher preparation. The pre-service teachers resulting in self-exploration reflects initiative and adaptability. However, this unguided exploratory risk pre-service teachers to fragmented knowledge and uneven practices. And without institutional mediation, AI risks being positioned as a productivity tool rather than just as a pedagogical resource grounded in ethical, disciplinary, and instructional considerations. Similar conclusions have been drawn in other studies highlighting that the lack of structured AI training for educators lead to variations in competence and practice (Alejandro et al., 2024). This gap underscores the need for the teacher education institutions to intentionally integrate AI literacy into professional education subjects not merely as a technical skill but as part of professional formation. By embedding the AI tools within courses on science pedagogy, educational technology and assessment could help science pre-service teachers move toward more reflective and transformative applications of artificial intelligence. Despite the pre-service teachers lack of actual training, the prevalence of AI use among the pre-service in can be attributed to recent accessibility of many generative AIs and its many practical applications.

Overall, the results contribute to the growing discussions on the evolving role of the teachers in AI-mediated educational contexts. The AI appears to reinforce the importance of professional judgment, creativity, and ethical responsibility rather than as replacement. When used critically, AI can act as a collaborative partner that supports instructional planning and enhances pedagogical effectiveness. The result aligned with research that emphasizes both the opportunities and limitations of AI in teacher preparation. The result suggests that AI, when utilized critically, can be a collaborative partner that supports instructional planning. The study result highlights the urgency of aligning teacher education with the contemporary classroom realities as well as provide an empirical grounding for reimagining how the future educators are trained and prepared to teach in an increasingly AI-generated world.

CONCLUSION

This study demonstrates that Artificial Intelligence (AI) is no longer a peripheral innovation in teacher preparation. It is also an emergent and self-directed practice of the science pre-service teacher. It shows how they use the AI in lesson planning, content comprehension, instructional material development, assessment construction, and most importantly, teaching during their practicum. These findings reflect an important shift in teacher preparation, where professional learning increasingly occurs at the intersection of three components such as personal agency, digital ecosystems, and classroom realities. The AI tools in this study serve not just experienced as an abstract technological innovation. It also serves as a practical and cognitive companion that aids pre-service teachers in navigating the complex reality of teaching science in secondary level.

This study further reveals a significant misalignment between teacher education structures, the lived experiences of the science pre-service teachers, and the realities of the current classroom. Although the participants actively utilized AI tools in enhancing efficiency, clarity, and confidence, PSTs learning on how to positively use AI for teaching were mostly informal and unguided. This underscores that the science pre-service teachers' reliance on self-exploration and peer-mediated learning reflects both of the adaptability as well as the absence of institutional support. This gap is consequential as it risks narrowing the AI use to surface-level academic assistance rather than fostering deeper pedagogical engagement. Thus, without the intentional integration into teacher education curriculum, the AI's potential to support future educators' enhancement on their teaching practices remains underdeveloped.

Importantly, the findings reveal that the experiences of science pre-service teachers in this study highlight the centrality of human judgment, creativity, and ultimately ethical responsibility in AI-mediated teaching practices. The participants showcased awareness of the need to verify AI-generated content. Another is avoiding overreliance on the provided answers or suggestions of the AI tools. This only suggests that the pre-service teachers are also capable of engaging critically with AI, even though there's a lack of formal training on how to utilize it in their teaching practices in the classroom.

While the small number of the respondents and the context where this study was conducted may limit the application of the finding, the paper opens new insights into current and future AI used for teachers. Through the science pre-service teachers' voices and practices, this paper contributes to the empirical evidence to the ongoing discussion on the role of AI in teacher education as well as professional formation. It underscores the need to redefine that AI literacy is not just a technical skill. It is an integral component of pedagogical knowledge and professional identity development. Thus, this paper positions AI not as a replacement for teaching expertise. It serves as a catalyst for rethinking how these future educators are prepared and trained for a rapidly changing and technologically mediated educational landscape in the 21st century.

IMPLICATIONS

The results of this study have several practical implications for teacher preparations. First, there is a clear need to integrate AI literacy into the curriculum of pre-service teachers. Courses on educational technology, pedagogy, and assessment should include components that train future teachers in using AI tools responsibly and effectively. This incorporation of AI ensures that the future teachers are not only familiar with the range of AI applications but have a deeper understanding of its ethical, pedagogical, and practical implications.

Second, the PSTs current reliance on informal learning sources such as social media and peer recommendations highlights a missed opportunity and gap for institutions to provide directed and research-based guidance. Without this, students may misuse AI tools or rely on inaccurate content. Hence, institutions must take a proactive role in providing training that promotes critical thinking, reflective teaching, and academic integrity.

Faculty development is equally important. Teacher educators must be equipped to model effective and ethical AI use so they can better support their students. Workshops, seminars, and collaborative learning sessions can help bridge the knowledge gap and encourage innovation in the integration of AI into teaching and learning.

Finally, a clear policy on AI use in Teacher Education Institutions is needed to guide teacher-educators, pre-service teachers, and students on how to ethically integrate AI into teaching. The policy should also cover the dos and the don'ts of using artificial intelligence for practice teachers. The policy should be comprehensive and consider both the pros and cons of artificial intelligence.

ACKNOWLEDGMENT

The authors acknowledge the Mindanao State University- Tawi- Tawi College of Technology and Oceanography for its encouragement and support in the successful conduct of this study. In like manner, the researchers also wish to thank the 32 science pre- service teachers of the College of Education for their valuable insights that formed the basis for the analysis of this study. Their cooperation and honesty were valuable for the completion of this study.

REFERENCES

Abarzosa, V. J., & Balaba, E. I. (2025). The Negative Effects of Over-Reliance on AI Tools in IT Student Learning. *Wisdom Journal of Humanities and Social Sciences, 2*(5 (May)), 20-29. https://so19.tci-thaijo.org/index.php/WJHS/article/view/1789

Aghaziarati, A., Nejatifar, S., & Abedi, A. (2023). Artificial intelligence in education: Investigating teacher attitudes. https://www.researchgate.net/profile/Sara-Nejatifar/publication/379042121_Artificial_Intelligence_in_Education_Investigating_Teacher_Attitudes/links/66c794bfc2eaa500230fbcc4/Artificial-Intelligence-in-Education-Investigating-Teacher-Attitudes.pdf

Al-Zahrani, A. M., & Alasmari, T. M. (2024). Exploring the impact of artificial intelligence on higher education: The dynamics of ethical, social, and educational implications. *Humanities & Social Sciences Communications*, *11*(1), 1–12. DOI: 10.1057/s41599-024-03432-4

Alejandro, I. M. V., Sanchez, J. M. P., Sumalinog, G. G., Mananay, J. A., Goles, C. E., & Fernandez, C. B. (2024). Pre-service teachers' technology acceptance of artificial intelligence (AI) applications in education. *STEM Education*, *4*(4), 445–465. DOI: 10.3934/steme.2024024

Aleven, V., Baraniuk, R., Brunskill, E., Crossley, S., Demszky, D., Fancsali, S., & Xing, W. (2023, June). Towards the Future of AI-Augmented Human Tutoring in Math Learning. In International Conference on Artificial Intelligence in Education (pp. 26 – 31). Springer Nature Switzerland. https://link.springer.com/chapter/10.1007/978-3-031-36336-8_310.1007/978-3-031-36336-8_3

Algerafi, M. A., Zhou, Y., Alfadda, H., & Wijaya, T. T. (2023). Understanding the factors influencing higher education students' intention to adopt artificial intelligence-based robots. *IEEE Access : Practical Innovations, Open Solutions, 11*, 99752–99764. https://ieeexplore.ieee.org/abstract/document/10247529. DOI: 10.1109/ACCESS.2023.3314499

Ashoori Tootkaboni, A., & Maghsoudi, M. (2025). Exploring Pre-service EFL Teachers' Readiness to Integrate AI: A UTAUT2 Model Analysis. *Journal of Education, 00220574251379029*, 00220574251379029. Advance online publication. DOI: 10.1177/00220574251379029

Aust, A., & Caukin, N. (2024). AI and academic integrity: Guiding educators through the evolving challenge of student plagiarism. *International Journal of the Whole Child, 9*(2), 73–78. https://libjournals.mtsu.edu/index.php/ijwc/article/view/2560/1518

Avsheniuk, N., Seminikhyna, N., Ruban, L., & Sviatiuk, Y. (2025). Exploring overreliance on AI tools in English for specific purposes courses: challenges and implications for learning and academic integrity. https://papers.ssrn.com/sol3/papers.cfm?abstract_id=5238641

Bautista, A., Estrada, C., Jaravata, A. M., Mangaser, L. M., Narag, F., Soquila, R., & Asuncion, R. J. (2024). Preservice Teachers' Readiness towards Integrating AI-Based Tools in Education: A TPACK Approach. *Educational Process: International Journal, 13*(3), 40–68. DOI: 10.22521/edupij.2024.133.3

Biagini, G. (2025). Towards an AI-Literate Future: A systematic literature review exploring education, ethics, and applications. *International Journal of Artificial Intelligence in Education, 35*(4), 1–51. DOI: 10.1007/s40593-025-00466-w

Bulawan, A. A., Tilos, F. G., Bulawan, A., Samonte, J., Alejo, K., & Carasicas, M. (2023). The lived experiences of students in learning with technology in Noveleta senior high school: A descriptive phenomenological research study. *International Journal of Advanced Multidisciplinary Research and Studies, 3*(4), 438–441. https://www.multiresearchjournal.com/admin/uploads/archives/archive-1690182667.pdf

Chang, D. H., Lin, M. P. C., Hajian, S., & Wang, Q. Q. (2023). Educational design principles of using AI chatbot that supports self-regulated learning in education: Goal setting, feedback, and personalization. *Sustainability (Basel), 15*(17), 12921. DOI: 10.3390/su151712921

Chen, S., & She, W. (2023) Values and Ethics- How artificial intelligence will better serve humanity. B. Majoul et al. (Eds.): ICLAHD 2022, ASSEHR 726, pp. 296 – 300, 2023. DOI: 10.2991/978-2-494069-97-8_37

Chin, R. T. (2018). Education in the Artificial Intelligence Era - QS WOWNEWS. https://qswownews.com/education-in-the-artificial-intelligence-era/

Clarke, V., & Braun, V. (2017). Thematic analysis. *The Journal of Positive Psychology, 12*(3), 297–298. DOI: 10.1080/17439760.2016.1262613

Coşgun, G. E. (2025). Artificial intelligence literacy in assessment: Empowering pre-service teachers to design effective exam questions for language learning. *British Educational Research Journal, 51*(5), 2340–2357. Advance online publication. DOI: 10.1002/berj.4177

Daher, R. (2025). Integrating AI literacy into teacher education: A critical perspective paper. *Discover Artificial Intelligence, 5*(1), 217. DOI: 10.1007/s44163-025-00475-7

Deriba, F. G., & Sanusi, I. T. (2025). Artificial intelligence in Ethiopian school curriculum: Educators' practices, challenges, and recommendations. *Computers and Education Open, 8*, 100251. DOI: 10.1016/j.caeo.2025.100251

Espino, C. (2025). Pre-service teachers' perspectives on generative AI: Insights, applications, and challenges in the classroom. *International Journal on Studies in Education, 7*(3), 732–747. DOI: 10.46328/ijonse.1930

Falebita, O. (2024). Evaluating Artificial Intelligence Anxiety Among Pre-Service Teachers in University Teacher Education Programs. Journal of Mathematics Instruction. *Social Research and Opinion, 4*(1), 1–16. DOI: 10.58421/misro.v4i1.309

Fitria, T. N. (2021). Artificial intelligence (AI) in education: Using AI tools for teaching and learning process. In *Prosiding Seminar Nasional & Call for Paper STIE AAS* (pp. 134 - 147). https://www.researchgate.net/profile/Tira-Nur-Fitria/publication/357447234_Artificial_Intelligence_AI_In_Education_Using_AI_Tools_for_Teaching_and_Learning_Process/links/61ce7029e669ee0f5c76b2ba/Artificial-Intelligence-AI-In-Education-Using-AI-Tools-for-Teaching-and-Learning-Process.pdf

García-Vélez, R., Moreno, B. V., Ruiz-Ichazu, A., Rivera, D. M., & Rosero-Perez, E. (2021). Automating the Generation of Study Teams through Genetic Algorithms Based on Learning Styles in Higher Education. In *Advances in Intelligent Systems and Computing* (Vol. 1213). AISC., DOI: 10.1007/978-3-030-51328-3_38

George, A. S. (2023). Preparing students for an AI-driven world: Rethinking curriculum and pedagogy in the age of artificial intelligence. *Partners Universal Innovative Research Publication, 1*(2), 112–136. DOI: 10.5281/zenodo.10245675

Gu, X., & Ericson, B. J. (2025). AI literacy in K–12 and higher education in the wake of generative AI: An integrative review [Preprint]. arXiv. https://arxiv.org/abs/2503.00079 DOI: 10.1145/3702652.3744217

Herviana, A. (2025). Artificial intelligence in education: Opportunities and challenges of AI integration in Indonesian classrooms. *Journal of Smart Pedagogy and Education*, *1*(1), 33–45. DOI: 10.65101/spedu.v1i1.22

Hoya, F., Mah, D., Prilop, C. N., Jacobsen, L. J., & Weber, K. E. (2024). Pre-service teachers' AI usage: The effects of perceived usefulness, subjective norm, behavioral intention, and self-efficacy. DOI: 10.31219/osf.io/284gk

Hsu, H.-P., Mak, J., Werner, J., White-Taylor, J., Geiselhofer, M., Gorman, A., & Capurro, C. T. (2024). Preliminary Study on pre-service teachers' applications and perceptions of generative artificial intelligence for lesson planning. *Journal of Technology and Teacher Education*, *32*(3), 409–437. DOI: 10.70725/869859beoezu

Huang, L. (2023). Ethics of artificial intelligence in education: Student privacy and data protection. Science insights education frontiers, 16(2), 2577-2587. DOI: 10.15354/sief.23.re202

Jackaria, P. M., Hajan, B. H., & Mastul, A. R. H. (2024). A Comparative Analysis of the Rating of College Students' Essays by ChatGPT versus Human Raters. International Journal of Learning. *Teaching and Educational Research*, *23*(2), 478–492. Advance online publication. DOI: 10.26803/ijlter.23.2.23

Jackaria, P. M., Hajan, B. H., Mastul, A. R. H., & Sali, F. Z. (2024). Generation AI in a reimagined classroom: challenges, opportunities and implications to education. *Exploring youth studies in the age of AI*, 181-192. DOI: 10.4018/979-8-3693-3350-1.ch009

Karataş, F., & Yüce, E. (2024). AI and the Future of Teaching: Preservice Teachers' Reflections on the Use of Artificial Intelligence in Open and Distributed Learning. *International Review of Research in Open and Distance Learning*, *25*(3), 304–325. DOI: 10.19173/irrodl.v25i3.7785

Ko, U., Hartley, K., & Hayak, M. (2025). Exploring AI in education: Preservice teacher perspectives, usage, and considerations. *Journal of Information Technology Education*, *24*, 21. Advance online publication. DOI: 10.28945/5592

Lee, A. T., Ramasamy, R. K., & Subbarao, A. (2025, January). Understanding psychosocial barriers to healthcare technology adoption: a review of TAM technology acceptance model and unified theory of acceptance and use of technology and UTAUT frameworks. In *Healthcare* (Vol. 13, No. 3, p. 250). MDPI. DOI: 10.3390/healthcare13030250

Lumanlan, J., Ayson, M. R., Bautista, M. J., Dizon, J., & Ylarde, C. M. (2025). AI Literacy among Preservice Teachers: Inputs Towards a Relevant Teacher Education Curriculum. *International Journal of Multidisciplinary Educational Research and Innovation*, *3*(1), 242–253. https://philpapers.org/rec/LUMALA

Maggo, J., & Maggo, T. (2025). Disparities in educational opportunities between urban and rural regions across the globe and the potential of AI to bridge the divide. *International Journal of Business Analytics and Intelligence*, *13*(1), 44–54. https://www.proquest.com/docview/3233263880?pq-origsite=gscholar&fromopenview=true. DOI: 10.21863/ijbai/2025.13.1.005

Mahana, M., Johns, M., & Apte, A. (2012). Automated Essay Grading Using Machine Learning. Machine Learning Session Stanford University, 3–7. https://cs229.stanford.edu/proj2012/MahanaJohnsApte-AutomatedEssayGradingUsingMachineLearning.pdf

Marikyan, D., & Papagiannidis, S. (2024). Technology acceptance model: A review. *TheoryHub book*. https://eprints.ncl.ac.uk/302879

Mehdaoui, A. (2024). Unveiling Barriers and Challenges of AI Technology Integration in Education: Assessing Teachers' Perceptions, Readiness and Anticipated Resistance. *Futurity Education*, *4*(4), 95–108. DOI: 10.57125/FED.2024.12.25.06

Melisa, R., Ashadi, A., Triastuti, A., Hidayati, S., Salido, A., Ero, P. E. L., . . . Al Fuad, Z. (2025). Critical Thinking in the Age of AI: A Systematic Review of AI's Effects on Higher Education. Educational Process: International Journal, 14. https://www.ceeol.com/search/article-detail?id=1338520

Menon, D., & Shilpa, K. (2023). "Chatting with ChatGPT": Analyzing the factors influencing users' intention to Use the Open AI's ChatGPT using the UTAUT model. *Heliyon*, *9*(11), e20962. Advance online publication. DOI: 10.1016/j.heliyon.2023.e20962 PMID: 37928033

Mohebbi, A. (2025). Enabling learner independence and self-regulation in language education using AI tools: A systematic review. *Cogent Education*, *12*(1), 2433814. DOI: 10.1080/2331186X.2024.2433814

Mpolomoka, D. L., Luchembe, M., Mushibwe, C., Muvombo, M., Changala, M., Sampa, R. L., & Banda, S. (2025). Artificial intelligence-related plagiarism in education: A systematic review. *European Journal of Education Studies, 12*(4). Advance online publication. DOI: 10.46827/ejes.v12i4.6029

Nagaraj, B. K., Kalaivani, A., Begum, S., Akila, S., & Sachdev, H. K. (2023). The emerging role of artificial intelligence in stem higher education: A critical review. *International Research Journal of Multidisciplinary Technovation, 5*(5), 1–19. DOI: 10.54392/irjmt2351

Nguyen, T. N. T., Van Lai, N., & Nguyen, Q. T. (2024). Artificial Intelligence (AI) in Education: A Case Study on ChatGPT's Influence on Student Learning Behaviors. Educational Process: International Journal, 13(2), 105-121. https://www.ceeol.com/search/article-detail?id=1256337

Ogunleye, B., Zakariyyah, K. I., Ajao, O., Olayinka, O., & Sharma, H. (2024). A systematic review of generative AI for teaching and learning practice [Preprint]. arXiv. https://arxiv.org/abs/2406.09520

Pokrivcakova, S. (2019). Preparing teachers for the application of AI-powered technologies in foreign language education. *Journal of language and cultural education, 7* (3), 135 - 153. DOI: 10.2478/jolace-2019-0025

Ramnarain, U., Ogegbo, A. A., Penn, M., Ojetunde, S., & Mdlalose, N. (2024). Pre-service science teachers' intention to use generative artificial intelligence in inquiry-based teaching. *Journal of Science Education and Technology*, 1 - 14. DOI: 10.1007/s10956-024-10159-z

Rauf, A., Nadeem, S., & Tahir, L. (2024). Integrating artificial intelligence into curriculum design. Multidisciplinary Journal of Emerging Needs of Curriculum, 1(2), 10-19. https://researchcorridor.org/index.php/MJENC/article/view/17

Runge, I., Hebibi, F., & Lazarides, R. (2025). Acceptance of Pre-Service Teachers Towards Artificial Intelligence (AI): The Role of AI-Related Teacher Training Courses and AI-TPACK Within the Technology Acceptance Model. *Education Sciences, 15*(2), 167. DOI: 10.3390/educsci15020167

Satapathy, D., Parida, D., & Pradhan, D. (2025). Pre-Service Teachers' Uses of AI Tools In Teaching-Learning Process. International Journal for Innovative Research In Multidisciplinary Field, 11. https://www.researchgate.net/profile/Deepak-Kumar-Pradhan-3/publication/393097124_Pre-Service_Teachers'_Uses_of_AI_Tools_In_Teaching-_Learning_Process/links/685ef76f39c35835120524c3/Pre-Service-Teachers-Uses-of-AI-Tools-In-Teaching-Learning-Process.pdf

Sharma, H., Soetan, T., Farinloye, T., Mogaji, E., & Noite, M. D. F. (2022). AI adoption in universities in emerging economies: Prospects, challenges and recommendations. In *Re-imagining educational futures in developing countries: Lessons from Global Health crises* (pp. 159–174). Springer International Publishing., DOI: 10.1007/978-3-030-88234-1_9

Su, J., Guo, K., Chen, X., & Chu, S. K. W. (2023). Teaching artificial intelligence in K–12 classrooms: A scoping review. *Interactive Learning Environments*. Advance online publication. DOI: 10.1080/10494820.2023.2212706

Sukarno, A. A., Al-adzkhan, N. A., Bulkia, W. S. M., & Jackaria, P. M. (2026). Students Building Emotional Connections With AI: Insights Into the Future AI-Infused Classroom. In Generators, Bots, and Tutors: Creative Approaches to Human-AI Synergy in Classroom Instruction (pp. 161-184). IGI Global Scientific Publishing. DOI: 10.4018/979-8-3373-0847-0.ch006

Thomas, A. P. (2024). Balancing Innovation and Integrity: Addressing Concerns of AI in Classroom Environments. https://scholarworks.gvsu.edu/gradprojects/451/

Tyson, M. M., & Sauers, N. J. (2021). School leaders' adoption and implementation of artificial intelligence. *Journal of Educational Administration*, *59*(3), 271–285. DOI: 10.1108/JEA-10-2020-0221

Uwosomah, E. E., & Dooly, M. (2025). It Is Not the Huge Enemy: Preservice Teachers' Evolving Perspectives on AI. *Education Sciences*, *15*(2), 152. DOI: 10.3390/educsci15020152

Vela, J. V., & Mursi, J. K. A. (2026). The Next Frontier: AI and Global Trends Shaping Higher Education-A Systematic Review. Consumer Decision-Making Processes in Higher Education, 279-316. DOI: 10.4018/979-8-3373-1499-0.ch011

Woodruff, K., Hutson, J., & Arnone, K. (2023). Perceptions and barriers to adopting artificial intelligence in K-12 education: A survey of educators in fifty states. DOI: 10.5772/intechopen.1002741

Xu, Z. (2025). Patterns and purposes: A cross-journal analysis of AI tool usage in academic writing [Preprint]. arXiv. https://arxiv.org/abs/2502.00632

Xue, L., Rashid, A. M., & Ouyang, S. (2024). The Unified Theory of Acceptance and Use of Technology (UTAUT) in Higher Education: A Systematic Review. *SAGE Open*, *14*(1), 21582440241229570. Advance online publication. DOI: 10.1177/21582440241229570

Zhai, C., Wibowo, S., & Li, L. D. (2024). The effects of over-reliance on AI dialogue systems on students' cognitive abilities: a systematic review. Smart learning environments, 11(1), 28. DOI: 10.1186/s40561-024-00316-7

Zhang, C., Schießl, J., Plößl, L., Hofmann, F., & Gläser-Zikuda, M. (2023). Acceptance of artificial intelligence among pre-service teachers: A multigroup analysis. *International Journal of Educational Technology in Higher Education*, *20*(1), 49. DOI: 10.1186/s41239-023-00420-7 PMID: 36743849

Zouhaier, S. (2023). The impact of artificial intelligence on higher education: An empirical study. *European Journal of Educational Sciences*, *10*(1), 17–33. https://www.ceeol.com/search/article-detail?id=1111750

Chapter 6

Reconstructing the Role of Pre-Service Teachers in the Age of Artificial Intelligence:

From Knowledge Transmitters to Learning Experience Designers

Longfa Yuan
http://orcid.org/0009-0008-7577-5915
Institute for Advanced Studies, Universiti Malaya, Malaysia

Rafiza Abdul Razak
http://orcid.org/0000-0002-1604-7781
Faculty of Education, Universiti Malaya, Malaysia

Amirrudin Kamsin
http://orcid.org/0000-0003-2796-3459
Faculty of Computer Science and Information Technology, Universiti Malaya, Malaysia

Lulian Chen
Faculty of Humanities and Arts, Chongqing University of Mechanical and Electrical Technology, China

Xiaoyuan Xu
Institute for Advanced Studies, Universiti Malaya, Malaysia

DOI: 10.4018/979-8-3373-8027-8.ch006

ABSTRACT

Rapid advances in artificial intelligence (AI), including generative AI, learning analytics, and intelligent tutoring systems, are reshaping educational environments and challenging traditional conceptions of teachers' professional roles. Rather than replacing teachers, AI redistributes instructional functions and intensifies the need for human judgment, ethical reasoning, and learning design expertise. This chapter examines how AI-driven changes transform teacher roles and explores their implications for pre-service teacher education. It conceptualizes teachers as learning experience designers who orchestrate human–AI collaboration, critically evaluate AI outputs, and design cognitively, socially, and emotionally supportive learning environments. Drawing on insights from educational technology, learning sciences, and teacher professional development, the chapter proposes key competency domains and discusses strategies for reforming teacher education to prepare future teachers for AI-enhanced classrooms.

1. INTRODUCTION: AI AND THE TRANSFORMATION OF THE EDUCATIONAL LANDSCAPE

The rapid advancement of artificial intelligence (AI) technologies has begun to profoundly reshape the educational landscape. From early computer-assisted instruction to intelligent recommendation systems, learning analytics platforms, and more recently, generative AI tools, AI has evolved from a peripheral technological aid to an intelligent partner deeply embedded across the entire educational process (Castillo-Martínez et al., 2024; UNESCO, 2023). Whether in instructional content generation, learning path design, adaptive feedback, classroom management, or learner behavior analytics, AI is redefining the relationships among teacher, learner, and learning environment. Against this backdrop of transformation, the role of teachers is undergoing structural shifts, and pre-service teachers, who are still in the process of professional formation, constitute one of the groups most directly exposed to the rapidly changing demands of future educational environments (Guan et al., 2025).

The integration of AI in education is not a linear development; rather, it exhibits a pattern of leapfrogging disruption. Its impact extends far beyond the simple substitution of certain instructional tasks with digital tools. Traditionally, teachers were responsible for the core functions of knowledge transmission, classroom management, and assessment design. However, as AI increasingly automates routine instructional functions and provides large-scale access to information and explanations, the long-standing identity of teachers as knowledge transmitters is becoming insufficient for contemporary classrooms. Today, AI can rapidly generate instructional materials, create personalized learning pathways, analyze learning behaviors, and offer automated feedback (Sajja et al., 2024). This shifting distribution of functions transforms teaching from a task solely executed by human teachers into a form of human-AI collaboration (Molenaar, 2025). At the same time, research in the learning sciences and educational neuroscience continues to highlight teachers' crucial roles in guiding attention, supporting emotion, fostering motivation, and enabling social interaction, domains in which AI remains significantly limited (Gómez-Chacón & Marbán, 2024). These uniquely human contributions signal a necessary role transition—from delivering knowledge to designing learning experiences that integrate cognitive, emotional, and social dimensions. Therefore, in the age of AI, teachers can no longer be adequately merely as transmitters of knowledge. They are increasingly being reconceptualized as learning experience designers who orchestrate human–AI interaction, curate meaningful learning pathways, and ensure the ethical and pedagogical integrity of AI-supported instruction (Bosch et al., 2025).

For pre-service teachers, the challenges brought about by AI are even more pronounced. Beyond mastering subject knowledge and pedagogical theories, they need to acquire the additional competencies necessary to navigate AI-enhanced classrooms. These include understanding the underlying mechanisms of AI tools, evaluating the accuracy of AI-generated outputs, recognizing the potential biases embedded in automated systems, and making informed, data-based professional decisions. More importantly, pre-service teachers must learn how to construct human–AI collaborative learning environments that enhance educational quality without diminishing students' creativity, critical thinking, or socio-emotional development. Because their professional identities are still forming, pre-service teachers are at a pivotal stage where adopting the mindset and competencies of learning experience designers is especially critical. This requires a nuanced understanding of the opportunities and risks associated with AI, as well as the ability to balance technological affordances with human-centered pedagogical principles.

Given these emerging challenges and opportunities, it is essential to systematically examine the trajectory of AI development in education, analyze how AI reshapes learning environments, and explore the new competencies and responsibilities that pre-service teachers must acquire (Kuzu, 2025). Situating these changes within the broader shift from knowledge transmission to learning experience design helps clarify why teacher education must evolve accordingly. By establishing the conceptual foundation for understanding AI's integration into education, this chapter provides the basis for subsequent discussions on the structural transformation of teacher roles (RQ1), the AI-related competencies required of pre-service teachers (RQ2), and strategies for reforming teacher education systems to prepare future educators for AI-driven learning environments (RQ3).

However, this transformation does not occur in a vacuum; it is mediated by institutional regulations, accountability frameworks, and unequal access to AI infrastructures.

1.1 Evolution of AI in Education

The integration of artificial intelligence into education has unfolded across several distinct developmental stages. The first stage can be characterized as the era of rule-based and programmed instruction, exemplified by early Intelligent Tutoring Systems (ITS) (Zawacki-Richter et al., 2019). These systems relied on predefined rules to deliver tiered exercises and immediate feedback, enabling a limited form of individualized learning support. The second stage emerged with the rise of data-driven adaptive learning systems. Learning analytics and big data technologies made it possible to visualize, track, and predict learning processes, thereby allowing instruction to be tailored based on learner behavior and performance patterns (Ahmad et al., 2024). The current stage represents a shift toward intelligent collaboration, powered by generative AI and deep learning models. In this phase, AI systems can independently generate instructional content, explain conceptual knowledge, and engage in interactive learning dialogues (Ng et al., 2023).

The advent of generative AI, in particular, has accelerated the transition from technology-assisted teaching to intelligent co-teaching. AI is now capable of producing course outlines, instructional examples, audio explanations, and formative assessment suggestions. It can also simulate student responses for the purpose of teacher training (Kasneci et al., 2023). This paradigm shift indicates that teaching is no longer understood solely as the domain of the human teacher; rather, it is increasingly situated within a multi-agent instructional ecosystem in which human teachers and intelligent systems co-participate. Such developments not only enhance instructional efficiency but also expand the modalities, spaces, and possibilities of learning.

Despite these advancements, AI's powerful capabilities introduce new challenges, including algorithmic bias, content hallucination, and a general lack of transparency in system decision-making (UNESCO, 2023). Consequently, teachers need to develop the ability to critically evaluate, regulate, and contextualize AI use, ensuring that the technology aligns with legal, ethical, and pedagogical imperatives. The evolution of AI is thus propelling education into an era of human-AI partnership, one that places increasing pressure on teachers to transition from tool operators to critical evaluators, informed selectors, and integrators of intelligent technologies (Molenaar, 2025).

1.2 New Learning Environments Faced by Pre-Service Teachers

As AI becomes increasingly embedded in educational systems, the learning environments encountered by pre-service teachers have are undergoing significant transformation (Wang & Dai, 2025; Zhang & Zhang, 2024). These changes manifest in three major dimensions.

First, new learning environments are characterized by a high degree of intelligence and data-driven operation. Learning analytics systems can capture real-time behavioral data, generate diagnostic reports, and provide personalized feedback (Prestigiacomo et al., 2020). Pre-service teachers increasingly need to develop the capacity to interpret these data, understand their pedagogical implications, and adjust teaching strategies accordingly. Whereas traditional classrooms relied heavily on teachers' intuitive judgments, AI-enhanced classrooms make it important for teachers to make informed decisions grounded in data interpretation, ongoing monitoring, and professional reasoning.

Second, learning environments have become multimodal and hybrid (Álvarez Guayara & Espinosa Sarmiento, 2025). AI-supported online learning platforms, virtual simulation tools, and immersive learning technologies are creating integrated virtual-physical learning spaces (Ishizawa, 2025). The future classroom is increasingly described as extending beyond a single physical location; instead, it consists of interconnected learning modalities mediated by diverse digital tools (Raes et al., 2019). This shift places new demands on pre-service teachers' ability to design learning experiences that bridge online and offline contexts, integrate multiple media formats, and orchestrate multimodal instructional activities.

Third, contemporary learning environments exhibit heightened interactivity and collaboration. Intelligent chatbots, AI learning companions, and group-based analytics tools are reshaping interaction patterns among students, between students and AI, and between teachers and AI (Shikun et al., 2024). Pre-service teachers need to learn how to facilitate such interactions, maintain the humanistic dimension of classroom relationships, and promote students' socio-emotional development in technology-mediated environments (Vistorte et al., 2024). They should also understand how to guide collaboration within human-AI networks while ensuring that AI participation enhances rather than diminishes meaningful learning.

Taken together, AI is transforming the structure, interactional dynamics, and cognitive demands of learning environments, positioning pre-service teachers at a pivotal moment in the evolution of future classrooms. The subsequent sections of this chapter further explore how AI-driven changes are reshaping teacher roles and outline the new competency frameworks and educational reforms required to prepare pre-service teachers for the instructional challenges of the AI era.

2. STRUCTURAL CHANGES IN TEACHER ROLES IN THE AI ERA (RQ1)

The rapid adoption of AI in educational settings is transforming the traditional responsibilities of teachers and reshaping professional expectations in profound ways. As AI tools increasingly support instructional planning, content delivery, assessment, and feedback, teachers are no longer positioned solely as transmitters of knowledge or managers of classroom routines. Instead, the emergence of AI-enabled learning environments requires teachers to occupy more complex, multidimensional roles that integrate human judgment, design expertise, and data-driven decision-making. This chapter examines how AI technologies produce structural changes in teacher roles, moving from traditional expectations toward new responsibilities associated with learning experience design, collaborative problem solving, and professional interpretation of machine-generated insights. The analysis highlights why pre-service teachers must be prepared for this transition and how the nature of teaching itself is being redefined in AI-enhanced classrooms (Tan et al., 2025).

2.1 Limitations of Traditional Teacher Roles

For decades, the dominant model of schooling has been built upon teacher-centered pedagogy, in which the teacher serves as the primary authority, the central source of knowledge, and the main controller of classroom processes. In this traditional paradigm, the teacher is expected to function simultaneously as a content expert, an organizer of classroom activities, and a regulator of student behavior. Instructional materials typically follow a fixed sequence, and teaching decisions rely heavily on the teacher's personal experience, intuition, and established textbooks. This model assumes that learning flows in one direction, from teacher to students, through explanation, demonstration, and repetition.

Although this structure once provided stability and clarity, it is increasingly unable to meet the demands of contemporary classrooms. Traditional teacher-centered approaches struggle to accommodate diverse learner needs, as the uniform pacing and standardized materials limit opportunities for differentiation. Without technological support, teachers must rely solely on informal observations to diagnose student challenges, often leading to delays in identifying misconceptions or learning gaps. Furthermore, this model offers limited flexibility; it is poorly suited for addressing individual variations in learning progress, motivation, or prior knowledge. As classrooms grow more diverse and expectations for personalization rise, these constraints have become more pronounced.

Modern learning sciences further expose the inadequacy of traditional teacher roles. Contemporary research demonstrates that learning is a multidimensional process shaped by cognitive, emotional, social, and motivational factors (Wang et al., 2020). A one-size-fits-all, teacher-centered model cannot adequately respond to these complex dimensions. Insights from educational neuroscience underscore that attention, motivation, and emotion must be dynamically regulated for learning to occur effectively. Neural systems responsible for social connection, empathy, and shared attention play crucial roles in classroom engagement, yet these factors are entirely absent from traditional instructional designs, where students are passive recipients rather than active participants.

Given these limitations, it is evident that the traditional teacher role is no longer sufficient for the complexities of modern classrooms. Moreover, as educational environments become increasingly shaped by large-scale data, digital platforms, and intelligent technologies, teacher-centered instruction is unable to respond to the speed, scale, and diversity of new learning conditions. These shortcomings create a compelling rationale for redefining the teacher's role, one that shifts away from routine content delivery toward higher-level responsibilities involving design, interpretation, coordination, and professional judgment. This establishes the foundation for the transformation required in the AI era.

2.2 AI's Influence on Planning, Teaching, Assessment, and Feedback

AI tools can automatically generate lesson outlines, instructional materials, examples, and practice activities aligned with curriculum standards. Intelligent systems analyze student performance data to propose personalized learning paths and anticipate potential learning difficulties. As a result, teachers shift from being task executors who manually produce lesson materials to evaluators who critically assess AI-generated suggestions. Their work becomes more strategic and judgment-based: interpreting AI recommendations, deciding what to adopt or modify, and ensuring alignment with educational goals. Planning is no longer purely mechanical preparation but a process requiring pedagogical insight and professional discretion.

AI systems influence classroom instruction through adaptive learning technologies, intelligent tutoring systems, and AI-based conversational agents. Adaptive platforms can assign different tasks to different students in real time, based on their learning data (Zawacki-Richter et al., 2019). AI chatbots can provide alternative explanations, generate examples, or support struggling learners. Virtual student simulations offer new opportunities for teacher training and microteaching practice. Despite these developments, human teachers continue to play an indispensable role. They serve as facilitators who guide students' emotional engagement, orchestrate collaborative learning, and cultivate supportive interpersonal relationships, tasks

AI current AI systems are not equipped to perform due to the absence of social cognition and emotional intelligence.

AI is reshaping assessment by automating scoring, providing instant feedback, and conducting real-time analytics (Hernández León & Rodríguez-Conde, 2024). Automated marking systems evaluate short answers, essays, or patterns of student responses, while learning analytics dashboards visualize performance trends and misconceptions. This automation shifts teachers from being graders to being data interpreters. Their responsibility is to verify AI-generated results, contextualize data, and make informed instructional decisions. Assessment evolves from an episodic activity to a continuous, dynamic process supported by analytics.

With AI, students can receive immediate, personalized feedback at any time. AI systems highlight errors, offer hints, and recommend next steps, thereby accelerating learning cycles (Reddig et al., 2025). Yet AI feedback lacks emotional nuance, contextual depth, and motivational support. Teachers must therefore complement AI feedback with human-centered guidance, encouragement, strategic advising, and socio-emotional support. Together, teacher and AI form a hybrid feedback loop, creating more comprehensive support for learners.

Across planning, instruction, assessment, and feedback, AI increasingly handles repetitive and procedural tasks. Consequently, teachers are freed to engage in higher-order responsibilities requiring creativity, empathy, ethical reasoning, and professional judgment. The teacher's role shifts structurally from a task executor to a designer, coordinator, and evaluator in AI-supported learning environments. In theory, this redistribution allows teachers to focus on higher-order work, although in practice institutional and workload constraints may complicate this shift (see Section 5.5)

2.3 The Emergence of the "Learning Experience Designer"

Automation of instructional content displaces what is taught from human control but amplifies the importance of *how* learning is organized, sequenced, and experienced. As AI systems take over content generation and routine instructional functions, teachers are increasingly expected to act as learning experience designers, professionals who orchestrate the entire learning environment rather than merely deliver subject matter (Phommanee et al., 2024). Instead of being knowledge transmitters, teachers design learning sequences, plan collaborative activities, shape classroom culture, and integrate tools to create meaningful learning experiences.

This role is particularly appropriate for the AI era because AI, despite its computational power, is not able to independently create pedagogically meaningful contexts. AI can provide information, but it does not construct social interactions, cultivate curiosity, or design inquiry environments. Teachers must still guide collaborative learning, stimulate deeper thinking, and regulate classroom emotions, tasks that involve interpersonal awareness and contextual understanding. Thus, the designer role reflects responsibilities that AI is unlikely to replace (Zhang et al., 2025).

Neuroscience evidence establishes the limits of AI in education, but it is learning design that determines how those human capacities are pedagogically mobilized. AI systems lack these neural mechanisms and are not capable of directly participating in shared emotional or social experiences (Wu et al., 2021). Therefore, teachers remain essential for designing emotionally supportive environments and orchestrating social interactions that deepen learning.

In this capacity, teachers design instructional variations, develop inquiry-based and project-based tasks, integrate multimodal learning resources, and balance cognitive challenge with emotional support. They coordinate AI tools, interpret learning analytics, and monitor students' emotional states to ensure that learning experiences promote deep understanding rather than superficial memorization. Ultimately, teachers orchestrate dynamic learning ecosystems in which AI amplifies is best positioned to amplify rather than replace their human expertise.

2.4 New Tasks for Pre-Service Teachers: Learning Path Design, Collaborative Problem Solving, Data-Driven Decision-Making

As AI becomes increasingly embedded in teaching and learning processes, pre-service teachers are increasingly expected to take on several new forms of professional work (Vartiainen & Tedre, 2023). One emerging responsibility involves designing learning paths that make pedagogical sense within AI-supported environments. Although AI systems can offer diagnostic information and generate personalized recommendations, it is the teacher who determines their appropriateness and coherence. Pre-service teachers therefore need to learn how to construct meaningful learning trajectories, integrate diverse resources, and adjust pacing and scaffolding in response to students' evolving needs.

Another area requiring new competence is collaborative problem solving. AI tools now participate in classroom interactions as sources of information, feedback, or modeling, which reshapes the dynamics of student collaboration. Teachers are expected to facilitate not only student–student collaboration but also interactions that involve students and AI systems. This work includes managing new patterns of participation, guiding teamwork, and addressing the socio-emotional issues that arise when technology mediates communication and joint activity. Designing collaboration structures that genuinely support communication, creativity, and mutual engagement becomes essential.

A further responsibility lies in data-driven decision-making. AI-powered dashboards increasingly provide continuous streams of information about learners' behavior, attention, and performance. Rather than relying solely on intuition, teachers must interpret these analytics, identify emerging difficulties, and make informed pedagogical decisions. This process requires them to integrate quantitative indicators with contextual knowledge and exercise professional judgment, ensuring that data are used to meaningfully inform instruction rather than dictate it.

Taken together, these developments illustrate that AI does not diminish the complexity of teaching; instead, it elevates the profession. As routine tasks become automated, teachers must engage in higher-level forms of design, coordination, interpretation, and decision-making. For pre-service teachers, this shift underscores the need for expanded knowledge frameworks and more sophisticated skill sets to navigate AI-enhanced learning environments effectively.

2.5 Institutional Redistribution of Authority

The AI-driven transformation of teaching involves not only changes in what teachers do, but also in where pedagogical authority is located. Traditionally, teachers exercised professional autonomy over curriculum design, instructional strategies, assessment, and classroom decisions. As AI systems become embedded in planning, content generation, analytics, and feedback, however, many of these decisions are increasingly shaped by platform-based algorithms and institutional data systems rather than by teachers alone. Adaptive learning platforms may suggest learning paths, pacing, or instructional priorities, while analytics dashboards highlight specific performance indicators, subtly guiding how teaching is organized and evaluated. Authority shifts not because AI gives recommendations, but because institutions increasingly embed those recommendations into accountability, pacing, and evaluation systems. In this context, teachers are no longer the sole authors of instructional decisions; they increasingly operate as interpreters, mediators, and regulators of algorithmic recommendations.

This redistribution of authority is not merely a technical shift but a structural and institutional one. Schools and education systems adopt AI tools within broader frameworks of accountability, standardization, and efficiency, which can constrain teachers' professional discretion. As a result, the move toward learning experience design does not occur entirely through teachers' individual choice, but through externally defined systems that reshape how teaching is planned, monitored, and judged. While AI can support more informed and responsive instruction, it also raises important questions about professional autonomy and responsibility. Teachers must navigate a learning environment in which decisions are co-produced by human judgment and algorithmic systems, making the ability to critically evaluate, override, and contextualize AI outputs an essential dimension of contemporary teacher professionalism.

The expanding use of AI in education has generated an important tension between automation and teacher agency. While AI is often presented as a tool that enhances teaching through personalization, feedback, and efficiency, critical perspectives warn that algorithmic systems may reduce opportunities for teachers to exercise professional judgment by shifting decisions about content, pacing, and assessment away from professional judgment and toward data-driven platforms. The increasing datafication of learning further intensifies this risk, as what is measured and optimized by algorithms may not fully capture learners' emotional, cultural, or motivational realities. The learning experience designer framework proposed in this chapter responds to these concerns by positioning teachers not as passive users of AI, but as active designers and regulators of AI-mediated learning environments. In this model, AI becomes an object of professional judgment rather than its replacement, allowing teachers to preserve pedagogical autonomy while drawing on the analytical and generative capacities of intelligent systems.

As summarized in Table 1, different AI functions generate distinct changes in learning environments, which in turn lead to specific shifts in teacher roles and competency demands for pre-service teachers.

Table 1. Synthesis of AI functions, learning changes, teacher roles, and required competencies

AI functions	Changes in learning environments	Shifts in teacher roles	Required competencies of pre-service teachers
Generative AI	AI tools generate lesson content and examples on demand, enabling more dynamic and personalized learning resources.	From sole content provider to curator and co-designer of AI-generated content; the teacher ensures its pedagogical alignment and quality.	Requires critical evaluation of AI outputs, effective AI prompt design, alignment of AI content with learning objectives, and ethical AI use.
Learning analytics	Real-time analytics dashboards provide continuous data on student performance, enabling evidence-based personalization and timely interventions.	From relying on intuition to acting as a data-informed decision maker; the teacher interprets analytics to identify learning gaps and plans targeted interventions.	Requires strong data literacy, skills in interpreting and contextualizing analytics, ability to translate data insights into instructional decisions, and commitment to data privacy and ethics.
Intelligent tutoring systems	Adaptive AI-driven tutoring platforms deliver individualized practice and feedback, creating self-paced and interactive learning pathways.	From one-size-fits-all instructor to facilitator and mentor orchestrating personalized learning; the teacher oversees AI-student interactions, addresses gaps current AI systems are not yet able to, and provides socio-emotional support.	Requires proficiency in integrating AI tutoring systems into instruction, monitoring and interpreting AI-driven student progress, providing timely human interventions, and maintaining student engagement and motivation.

continued on following page

Table 1. Continued

AI functions	Changes in learning environments	Shifts in teacher roles	Required competencies of pre-service teachers
Automated feedback and assessment	AI-based tools automate grading and deliver instant feedback, enabling continuous formative assessment with real-time insights.	From primary grader to quality controller of assessments and feedback; the teacher verifies AI-generated scores, contextualizes results, and provides complementary human feedback.	Requires proficiency with AI-driven assessment tools, ability to interpret and verify AI-generated results for validity and fairness, and skill in integrating automated feedback with human guidance.
Multimodal / immersive learning platforms	Immersive technologies (e.g., AR/VR) and simulations create integrated virtual–physical spaces, allowing learning across multiple modalities beyond the traditional classroom.	From single-mode content deliverer to hybrid learning designer; the teacher integrates in-person and virtual activities, manages multiple media formats, and ensures coherence across modalities.	Requires ability to design technology-enhanced learning experiences, proficiency with AR/VR and simulations, skill in integrating multimedia content, and classroom management across virtual and physical settings.

3. AI COMPETENCIES AND PROFESSIONAL JUDGMENT FOR PRE-SERVICE TEACHERS (RQ2)

While Table 1 maps competencies to specific AI-enabled teaching scenarios, the following section reorganizes these requirements into a cross-cutting competency framework. The rapid expansion of artificial intelligence in education has placed unprecedented demands on pre-service teachers, requiring them not only to acquire technical knowledge but also to cultivate sophisticated pedagogical, cognitive, and ethical capacities. As AI systems increasingly support lesson planning, content generation, assessment, and personalized learning pathways, future teachers must navigate a dual responsibility: leveraging AI to enhance learning while simultaneously exercising human-centered professional judgment. This chapter argues that pre-service teachers need a comprehensive and integrated competency framework that equips them to work effectively with AI as collaborators, evaluators, and designers of learning experiences. These competencies extend beyond basic tool operation to include AI literacy, critical evaluation of algorithmic outputs, ethical reasoning, and advanced learning design abilities. Together, these dimensions form the foundation for effective human–AI collaboration in contemporary classrooms.

3.1 AI Literacy

AI literacy is increasingly regarded as an important foundation for developing broader AI-related teaching competencies (Sperling et al., 2024; UNESCO, 2023). For pre-service teachers, it encompasses three interrelated dimensions: understanding how AI systems operate, using AI tools effectively, and recognizing the limitations and risks associated with intelligent technologies (Kalniņa et al., 2024). Understanding these elements does not require expertise in computer science or algorithm engineering; rather, it involves developing conceptual clarity about how AI generates predictions, recommendations, and content. Pre-service teachers must be aware that AI systems rely on probabilistic models trained on large datasets, meaning that their outputs reflect patterns in data rather than deep comprehension or contextual understanding. Such awareness may help teachers form more realistic expectations about what AI can and cannot do in educational contexts.

In addition to conceptual understanding, pre-service teachers must cultivate practical competence in using AI tools in pedagogically meaningful ways. This includes generating lesson materials, designing learning prompts, organizing differentiated activities, and supporting students' inquiry. Effective use of AI often involves developing prompting strategies that shape the quality of AI-generated outputs. For instance, a teacher who provides precise instructional parameters, learning goals, grade levels, cognitive demands, or curriculum standards, will obtain more accurate and useful content than one who simply requests a lesson plan. Through iterative prompting, teachers can refine results, correct misunderstandings, and guide AI systems toward more contextually aligned outputs.

However, AI literacy also requires the ability to recognize risks and limitations. Because AI outputs may contain biased patterns, fabricated references, or inaccurate information, pre-service teachers must be vigilant in identifying potential harms associated with the misuse of AI. Furthermore, teachers must understand that AI-generated suggestions are not neutral, objective truths; they reflect the structure of their training data and may reproduce stereotypes or reinforce existing inequities. Developing this awareness ensures that teachers do not adopt AI outputs uncritically but instead engage with them as provisional suggestions requiring human verification. AI literacy can be understood as an integration of conceptual understanding, operational skill, and critical awareness, an increasingly important starting point for navigating AI-enhanced educational environments (Runge et al., 2025).

3.2 Critical Evaluation of AI Outputs

As AI systems increasingly generate educational content, feedback, and assessments, pre-service teachers need to develop the ability to critically evaluate

AI outputs. This competency is essential because AI-generated information often appears coherent and authoritative even when it contains errors (Nguyen et al., 2024). Teachers therefore play a central role as quality gatekeepers, ensuring that what AI produces aligns with factual accuracy, curriculum standards, and pedagogical appropriateness.

Critical evaluation begins with the ability to identify different types of AI inaccuracies. One common issue is bias, which occurs when AI systems reproduce stereotypes present in their training data. In educational contexts, such bias might manifest in examples that disproportionately depict certain groups or in recommendations that reflect cultural assumptions not applicable to all learners. Another issue is hallucination, in which AI systems generate fabricated facts, inaccurate references, or logically inconsistent explanations. Teachers must also evaluate AI outputs for partial accuracy, where information may be generally correct but oversimplified, outdated, or not fully aligned with disciplinary standards. Finally, teachers must assess the relevance and alignment of AI-generated suggestions with specific learning objectives, grade-level requirements, and pedagogical strategies.

Beyond identifying inaccuracies, pre-service teachers must engage in verification and triangulation strategies. This includes cross-checking AI-generated content against authoritative sources, consulting multiple AI tools, and using professional knowledge to interpret complex or ambiguous information. Teachers must also consider the pedagogical implications of AI suggestions: whether the content fosters deep learning, whether it supports diverse learners, and whether it aligns with developmental appropriateness. In this sense, critical evaluation is not merely technical fact-checking but a form of pedagogical reasoning that integrates subject expertise, curriculum knowledge, and instructional judgment. By applying these evaluative skills, pre-service teachers ensure that AI serves as a supportive resource rather than an unquestioned authority in the classroom.

3.3 Professional Judgment: the Human Dimension AI Cannot Replace

Although AI offers powerful computational capabilities, it cannot replicate the social, emotional, and moral dimensions of teaching. Professional judgment, teachers' ability to interpret student behavior, respond to emotional cues, make ethical decisions, and create supportive learning environments, remains a distinctly human domain (Zhang et al., 2024). Pre-service teachers must therefore develop strong professional judgment to complement AI-driven analytics and automated recommendations.

Professional judgment involves interpreting complex learning situations that current AI systems are not yet able to fully capture or interpret. For example, a learning analytics dashboard may indicate that a student's engagement is declining, but only a teacher can determine whether the cause is confusion, anxiety, lack of motivation, or external factors unrelated to the lesson. Likewise, AI currently cannot directly perceive subtle emotional signals such as frustration, boredom, or excitement, nor can it respond empathetically to students' personal challenges. Human teachers draw upon emotional intelligence, cultural understanding, and interpersonal sensitivity to make sense of learners' needs, dimensions of cognition deeply rooted in human social and neural systems.

Furthermore, professional judgment enables teachers to determine when and how to use AI appropriately. Teachers must decide whether AI-generated suggestions are suitable for particular learners, whether AI should be used for specific tasks, and how to balance AI support with human interaction. In many instances, effective teaching depends not on the availability of AI tools but on a teacher's ability to choose the right tool, adapt it to learners' needs, and override automated outputs when necessary. This flexible, context-sensitive decision-making goes beyond the current capabilities of AI. Therefore, professional judgment represents not only the irreplaceable human dimension of teaching but also the central mechanism through which teachers maintain pedagogical integrity in AI-enhanced classrooms.

3.4 Ethical Competence

With AI becoming increasingly embedded in educational processes, ethical competence is emerging as a critical requirement for pre-service teachers. This competence includes understanding the ethical risks associated with AI, applying ethical principles in instructional decisions, and protecting student rights and well-being in AI-supported environments. Ethical competence is especially important because teachers often serve as the first line of defense against potential AI misuse (Gümüş et al., 2023).

One core ethical responsibility is protecting student privacy. AI-powered learning tools frequently collect behavioral, cognitive, and performance data, raising concerns about data storage, consent, and third-party access. Pre-service teachers must understand how student data are used and must ensure that AI tools comply with legal and institutional requirements. They should also communicate transparently with students and families about data collection practices.

Fairness represents another key dimension of ethical competence. Because AI systems may contain algorithmic biases, teachers must monitor whether AI-generated assessments or recommendations disadvantage certain student groups. Ethical competence also includes academic integrity: teachers must explicitly guide students in the responsible use of AI, preventing overdependence, plagiarism, or misuse of AI-generated content. Additionally, teachers must understand the limits of AI transparency. Since many AI algorithms lack interpretability, teachers must exercise caution when relying on automated decisions that cannot be fully explained.

Collectively, these ethical considerations highlight the importance of equipping pre-service teachers with the knowledge and sensitivity required to implement AI responsibly. Ethical competence ensures that AI enhances rather than undermines equity, autonomy, and trust within the educational environment.

3.5 Learning Design Ability

As AI increasingly automates routine teaching tasks, learning design ability is increasingly recognized as a central competency for pre-service teachers. This capability involves creating meaningful, engaging, and adaptive learning experiences that integrate human insight with AI support. Learning design ability extends beyond selecting instructional resources; it encompasses designing learning pathways, structuring multimodal content, and supporting inquiry-based and collaborative learning.

One crucial component of learning design is differentiated instruction. AI tools can help identify individual learners' needs by analyzing learning behaviors and performance patterns, but teachers must design differentiated tasks that respond to these diverse needs. Effective differentiation requires teachers to design tasks at varying levels of complexity, to provide multiple pathways for understanding concepts, and to adapt instruction dynamically based on real-time data. This level of intentional design is unlikely to be fully automated; it relies on teacher expertise in curriculum goals and student development.

A second component is the creation of multimodal learning environments. AI enables teachers to generate diverse instructional materials. However, AR/VR, simulations, and multimodal content require a learning experience design (LXD) perspective (Czerkawski & Berti, 2021). Importantly, the pedagogical effectiveness of multimodal content depends on how well it is aligned with learning outcomes. Pre-service teachers must therefore learn to select, sequence, and integrate these resources in ways that support conceptual understanding rather than overwhelming learners.

Finally, inquiry-based and project-based learning represent critical areas in which AI can augment but not replace teachers' design expertise. AI tools can support inquiry by helping students search for information, test hypotheses, or model complex processes, but teachers must design open-ended problems, guide students' inquiry strategies, and facilitate collaboration. Teachers must balance AI-supported exploration with human-facilitated reflection and discussion, ensuring that students develop higher-order thinking skills rather than simply relying on automated answers.

Learning design ability therefore represents a synthesis of creativity, pedagogical knowledge, and technological fluency. It empowers teachers to transform AI tools into meaningful learning experiences and positions them as architects of intellectually rich, human-centered learning environments.

AI competency and professional judgment together form the core of pre-service teachers' preparedness for AI-enhanced educational environments. These dimensions resonate with emerging AI competency frameworks for teachers that conceptualise AI literacy as an integrated set of knowledge, skills, and attitudes (UNESCO, 2024). AI literacy equips teachers with foundational understanding and operational skills; critical evaluation ensures that AI outputs are used responsibly; professional judgment preserves the human dimension of teaching; ethical competence safeguards fairness and student rights; and learning design ability reshapes teachers as creators of dynamic learning experiences. These competencies represent not isolated skills but an integrated framework that enables future teachers to thrive in human-AI collaborative classrooms.

The competency framework proposed in this chapter builds on established international models such as TPACK and DigCompEdu, which have long guided how teachers integrate technology, pedagogy, and content knowledge and develop digital competence for teaching and learning. While these frameworks remain foundational, they were largely developed before the widespread adoption of generative AI, learning analytics, and algorithmic decision-making in education, and thus tend to treat technology primarily as a set of tools rather than as intelligent systems that actively shape content, feedback, assessment, and learning pathways. By conceptualizing teachers as learning experience designers who orchestrate human-AI collaboration, exercise data-informed professional judgment, and govern the ethical use of algorithmic systems, the framework advanced in this chapter extends these existing models to address the distinctive challenges of AI-mediated education, positioning technological competence not merely as tool use but as the design, evaluation, and regulation of complex AI-supported learning environments.

4. PREPARING LEARNING EXPERIENCE DESIGNERS: STRATEGIES FOR TEACHER EDUCATION REFORM (RQ3)

As artificial intelligence becomes increasingly embedded in teaching and learning environments, teacher education programs will need to undergo substantial reform to prepare pre-service teachers for their evolving professional identity as learning experience designers (Carrillo et al., 2025). This chapter outlines key strategies for reimagining teacher preparation in the AI era, addressing how programs can cultivate AI literacy, enhance practice-based experiences, integrate AI-enabled pedagogical tools, establish comprehensive competency frameworks, and leverage authentic case examples. Together, these strategies aim to equip future teachers with the knowledge, skills, and dispositions necessary to design, implement, and reflect upon high-quality learning experiences in AI-supported classrooms.

4.1 Curriculum Reforms (AI Literacy Courses, Prompt Engineering, Critical AI Evaluation Modules)

Teacher education programs are increasingly required to reconsider their curricular structures in light of the changing expectations placed on future educators. As digital and data-driven technologies become embedded in everyday instructional practice, pre-service teachers need systematic preparation that helps them understand how such technologies influence teaching, learning, and professional decision-making (Bilbao-Eraña & Arroyo-Sagasta, 2025). One important area of development involves building a conceptual foundation that enables future teachers to make sense of how contemporary technologies operate, the assumptions they embed, and the pedagogical implications that follow. Courses introducing key ideas, such as the nature of computational models, the role of data in shaping outputs, and the limitations inherent in automated systems, provide this essential groundwork. The goal is not technical specialization but the cultivation of educators who can engage thoughtfully with technologically mediated learning environments.

A second area of curricular innovation concerns the changing nature of instructional design. As digital tools become more involved in lesson preparation and content development, teachers must learn to articulate instructional intentions clearly, anticipate learner needs, and frame requests in ways that yield pedagogically meaningful materials. Practice with generating and refining instructional inputs, whether for planning, explanation, or assessment, helps pre-service teachers recognize how different forms of wording and contextual detail shape the usefulness of the resulting materials. This work ultimately strengthens their broader capacity for designing coherent learning experiences.

Equally important is the development of a critical stance toward technology-generated information. Automated outputs can appear polished yet still be inaccurate, incomplete, or biased. Teacher education programs therefore need to prepare future educators to examine information carefully, verify claims against trustworthy sources, and evaluate whether proposed explanations or examples align with curricular goals and learners' developmental needs. Cultivating this evaluative judgment reinforces teachers' professional agency and prevents overreliance on digital tools.

Ethical considerations must also figure prominently within contemporary teacher preparation. Questions concerning data privacy, transparency, equity, and the responsible use of student information arise frequently in technologically enriched classrooms. Engaging pre-service teachers in case discussions and scenario analyses can support their ability to navigate these dilemmas and to make decisions that protect students' interests and promote fairness.

Together, these curricular emphases can help reduce the likelihood that future teachers are not merely passive users of educational technologies but reflective practitioners who can integrate new tools responsibly, interpret them critically, and align them with broader educational purposes.

4.2 Practice-Based Reforms (AI-Supported Simulated Teaching, Virtual Practicum)

Developing competence in AI-supported teaching requires more than conceptual understanding; it necessitates continuous engagement with practice-based experiences that allow pre-service teachers to experiment, reflect, and refine their instructional approaches. Embedding authentic, practice-oriented activities within teacher education programs ensures that future teachers learn to work productively with emerging technologies while maintaining pedagogical intentionality.

One promising approach involves the use of simulation-based teaching environments in which pre-service teachers interact with digitally generated student representations. These environments replicate common classroom scenarios, such as managing differing levels of engagement, addressing misconceptions, or responding to variations in emotional states, while allowing teacher candidates to rehearse instructional moves without the risks associated with live classrooms. Because simulations can be repeated, paused, or reconfigured, they create structured opportunities for deliberate practice and guided reflection, enabling candidates to examine how particular decisions influence the unfolding of classroom interactions.

Practice-based preparation can also be expanded through virtual practicum experiences that complement or extend conventional school placements (Wilson et al., 2025). In these settings, pre-service teachers work with the digital tools commonly used in contemporary classrooms, including adaptive learning platforms, writing support systems, and learning analytics dashboards. Engaging with these tools in authentic instructional tasks allows teacher candidates to consider how technological affordances shape pacing, differentiation, and assessment. Virtual practica are particularly valuable in helping to promote more equitable access to field experiences for students who may face geographical or institutional limitations in securing placements.

Microteaching, long recognized as an effective method for developing foundational teaching skills, likewise benefits from technology-enhanced refinements. When microteaching sessions are supplemented with analytic feedback, such as indicators of questioning patterns, distribution of teacher talk, or student engagement cues, pre-service teachers gain clearer insights into aspects of their practice that are often difficult to recognize in real time. This form of augmented microteaching strengthens the connection between pedagogical theory and classroom application by providing candidates with concrete, data-informed evidence of their instructional strengths and areas for growth.

Collectively, these practice-based reforms cultivate a preparation model in which pre-service teachers develop adaptable, reflective, and context-sensitive professional habits. By engaging with diverse forms of simulated, virtual, and feedback-rich practice, teacher candidates acquire the practical experience necessary to navigate the complexities of AI-supported learning environments (Wilson et al., 2025).

4.3 Pedagogical Tool Integration (Generative AI, Learning Analytics Dashboards)

As AI-enabled technologies become increasingly embedded in classroom practice, teacher education programs must equip pre-service teachers with the capacity to integrate these tools in ways that strengthen, not replace, pedagogical decision-making. Rather than treating AI applications as isolated add-ons, preparation programs need to help future teachers understand how different forms of digital support can contribute to instructional design, learner engagement, and differentiated guidance. Three categories of tools have become especially prominent in recent educational contexts: generative content systems, learning analytics platforms, and adaptive tutoring environments (P.T et al., 2025). Each requires distinct forms of pedagogical reasoning and professional competence.

Generative technologies now play an influential role in the production of instructional materials, offering possibilities for the creation of examples, explanations, scaffolds, and multimodal resources. Within teacher education, however, the focus must extend beyond learning how to operate such tools. Pre-service teachers benefit from examining how generative outputs can be aligned with curricular aims, modified to address learner diversity, and used to support deeper forms of inquiry or problem solving (Kohnke et al., 2025). Through guided practice, they learn to treat generative systems not as automatic solution providers but as resources whose effectiveness depends on careful judgment, adaptation, and evaluation.

Learning analytics dashboards represent a second category of tools shaping contemporary classrooms. These platforms present teachers with real-time information about student engagement patterns, progression, and performance trends. For pre-service teachers, the central challenge lies not in accessing the data but in interpreting it responsibly. Teacher education programs therefore need to cultivate the analytical dispositions required to distinguish between meaningful patterns and superficial fluctuations, understand the limitations of algorithmically generated indicators, and integrate data with contextual knowledge about learners' motivations, backgrounds, and needs. This analytical competence enables future teachers to shift from intuition-driven practice to more evidence-sensitive instructional reasoning.

A third type of tool increasingly present in schools is the intelligent tutoring system, designed to deliver adaptive guidance and individualized support. Pre-service teachers must develop an understanding of how such systems structure learning pathways, what forms of knowledge they are best suited to address, and where their limits lie. Training should encourage candidates to consider how automated guidance interacts with broader learning goals, how students respond to adaptive prompts, and when teacher intervention becomes essential for ensuring conceptual understanding, emotional support, or collaborative engagement.

Across these different tool categories, the overarching goal is to help pre-service teachers develop an integrative perspective on technology use, one that positions digital systems as part of a broader pedagogical ecology. When teachers learn to interpret, adapt, and coordinate these tools with deliberate intent, AI-enhanced environments become opportunities to enrich learning rather than merely automate instructional tasks.

4.4 Comprehensive Competency Model for Pre-Service Teachers

As teacher education systems confront rapidly evolving digital learning environments, it becomes increasingly important to articulate a coherent set of professional competencies that can guide curriculum planning and program reform. Rather than focusing narrowly on tool operation or procedural tasks, contemporary competency frameworks emphasize a broader constellation of knowledge, pedagogical reasoning, and reflective dispositions that enable future teachers to navigate complex instructional contexts. A comprehensive model typically integrates several interrelated dimensions that together shape teachers' professional formation.

A foundational dimension concerns teachers' understanding of the technological systems that influence classroom learning. This includes familiarity with the underlying principles that govern digital tools, awareness of their pedagogical possibilities and constraints, and an informed appreciation of how technology interacts with broader educational processes. Such literacy provides a conceptual grounding that allows teachers to engage critically with new tools rather than adopt them unreflectively.

A second-dimension centers on teachers' capacity to design instruction that supports diverse learners. Contemporary pedagogical practice requires attention to multimodal learning resources, differentiated pathways, and inquiry-oriented designs that foster student autonomy and deeper engagement. The ability to integrate varied forms of representation, structure meaningful learning sequences, and anticipate learner needs remains central to effective teaching across digital and non-digital contexts.

Closely connected is the capacity to interpret information generated during the learning process. As classrooms become more data-rich, teachers must learn to make sense of patterns in student performance, engagement, or progression and to draw on this evidence in making instructional decisions (Kim, 2023). This form of data literacy is less about technical manipulation than about integrating quantitative indicators with contextual understanding and pedagogical judgment.

Professional responsibility also requires teachers to exercise discernment in complex or ambiguous situations. Ethical considerations, sensitivity to learner diversity, and the ability to mediate social and emotional dimensions of classroom life remain integral to teaching, even as technological systems take on expanded roles. Professional judgment thus acts as a counterbalance to overreliance on automated recommendations.

Finally, effective teaching in contemporary environments calls for an openness to exploring emerging tools, evaluating their suitability, and adapting one's practice accordingly. Such adaptability reflects not only technical confidence but also a disposition toward continuous learning and reflective engagement with innovation.

Taken together, these domains form a competency model that can inform the design of teacher preparation programs and provide a basis for evaluating pre-service teachers' readiness for contemporary instructional settings (Setiyawan et al., 2025). The model underscores that technological sophistication alone is insufficient; effective teaching requires a synthesis of conceptual understanding, pedagogical expertise, analytical capacity, and reflective professionalism.

4.5 Case Examples of AI-Enhanced Learning Design

Concrete case examples help pre-service teachers understand how AI can be meaningfully incorporated into instructional design. Three illustrative cases demonstrate the diverse possibilities of AI-enhanced learning.

Case 1: Differentiated Reading Instruction Using AI Suggestion Engines

In a primary literacy class, a teacher uses an AI platform that analyzes reading fluency, vocabulary knowledge, and comprehension patterns. The system recommends texts at varied difficulty levels, along with targeted exercises. The teacher then designs differentiated small-group activities based on these insights, integrating human-led discussions with AI-supported practice. Students receive personalized reading pathways, while the teacher focuses on guiding comprehension strategies

(Wagner, 2024). This case illustrates how learning analytics–driven recommendations require teachers to exercise professional judgment in aligning AI suggestions with literacy goals and differentiated instructional strategies.

Case 2: AI-Supported Scientific Inquiry in Middle School

A middle school science teacher uses generative AI to model hypotheses, simulate experiments, and visualize scientific phenomena. Students use AI tools to test variables, compare outcomes, and reflect on findings. The teacher designs an inquiry sequence that balances AI-enabled exploration with group collaboration, ensuring that students articulate reasoning rather than accepting AI outputs uncritically (Aleven et al., 2022). The example highlights the teacher's role as a learning experience designer who structures inquiry processes, ensuring that generative AI supports scientific reasoning rather than substituting for it.

Case 3: Data-Informed Mathematics Instruction in High School

An AI-powered learning analytics dashboard aggregates student performance data across algebra units. The teacher identifies patterns of misconception and reorganizes instruction accordingly. Small-group interventions are designed based on analytics, while AI provides targeted practice exercises. The teacher uses the dashboard to track progress and adjust instructional strategies in real time (Aleven et al., 2022). This case demonstrates how data-informed instruction depends on teachers' capacity to interpret analytics meaningfully and translate insights into pedagogically sound interventions.

These cases illustrate how AI can support, but not replace, teacher expertise. They provide pre-service teachers with models of effective learning design that integrate human judgment and machine intelligence.

Preparing pre-service teachers as learning experience designers requires comprehensive reform spanning curriculum, practice, tools, competencies, and case-based understanding. AI-era teachers must think critically, design creatively, interpret data wisely, and act ethically. This chapter emphasizes that teacher education reform is not merely about adding new technologies to old structures, it is about cultivating a new professional identity equipped to thrive in AI-enhanced learning environments.

4.6 Implications for student learning

The reconceptualization of teachers as learning experience designers has direct implications for how students learn in AI-enhanced environments. When teachers actively shape how AI is used in instruction, students are more likely to experience learning that is adaptive, meaningful, and responsive to their individual needs rather than narrowly driven by algorithmic optimization. Thoughtfully designed human-AI learning experiences can support timely feedback, diverse representations of knowledge, and opportunities for reflection and self-regulation, enabling learners to engage more deeply with both content and process. At the same time, teacher judgment plays a critical role in protecting learner agency and equity, ensuring that AI-generated guidance does not limit students' autonomy or reinforce bias. In this sense, the professional capacity of teachers to design and govern AI-mediated learning environments becomes a key determinant of whether AI contributes to richer, more inclusive, and more empowering student learning experiences.

4.7 How these competencies can be assessed

For AI-related competencies to become meaningful components of teacher professionalism, they must be embedded in transparent and credible assessment practices. Evaluation cannot rely solely on written examinations or self-reported confidence in using AI tools; instead, it should focus on how pre-service teachers apply professional judgment in authentic, AI-supported teaching situations. One promising approach is performance-based assessment, in which teacher candidates design, implement, and reflect on learning activities that integrate AI tools, learning analytics, and ethical decision-making. Digital portfolios can document how pre-service teachers select, adapt, and critique AI-generated materials, providing evidence of their learning design ability and critical evaluation skills.

Simulation-based and microteaching environments also offer valuable opportunities for assessing competence. In AI-supported simulations, pre-service teachers can be observed as they respond to automated feedback, interpret learner data, and manage pedagogical and ethical dilemmas in real time. Such environments make it possible to evaluate not only technical fluency but also the quality of teachers' professional judgment, including how they balance algorithmic recommendations with contextual and human-centered considerations. By aligning assessment with authentic teaching tasks, teacher education programs can ensure that AI-related competencies are evaluated as integral elements of professional practice rather than as isolated technical skills.

4.8 Alignment with accreditation and policy

For the role of learning experience designer to be sustainably embedded in teacher education, AI-related competencies must be aligned with existing accreditation and certification frameworks. Teacher standards in many systems already emphasize pedagogical knowledge, professional judgment, and ethical responsibility; AI-related competencies should be integrated into these domains rather than treated as an additional or optional layer. This means that expectations regarding data-informed decision-making, ethical governance of digital tools, and the design of AI-supported learning environments need to be reflected in program accreditation criteria and teacher licensing requirements.

Such alignment helps ensure that teacher education institutions have a strong incentive to incorporate AI-related learning outcomes into their curricula and practicum experiences. When accreditation bodies and professional regulators recognize these competencies as core aspects of teaching, they become part of what it means to be a qualified teacher, rather than a specialized skill held by a few innovators. In this way, institutional and regulatory alignment plays a crucial role in translating the conceptual shift toward learning experience design into durable and system-wide change within teacher education.

5. CHALLENGES AND RISKS IN TEACHER ROLE TRANSFORMATION

The transformation of teacher roles in the AI era brings not only opportunities but also a series of challenges and risks that must be critically addressed. While AI-powered tools can enhance instructional efficiency, support personalized learning, and generate rich data insights, they also reshape teacher identity, ethical responsibility, and professional boundaries. This chapter identifies four major areas of concern, over-reliance on AI, identity anxiety, data ethics and privacy, and inequity in AI access, highlighting the complex landscape that teacher education programs must navigate as they prepare future educators for AI-enhanced environments.

5.1 Over-Reliance on AI

One of the central risks in AI-enabled classrooms is the potential for teachers to become overly dependent on automated systems. As AI increasingly handles routine tasks such as content generation, assessment, and feedback, teachers may unconsciously delegate too much cognitive authority to machines. Over-reliance can lead to diminished professional judgment, reduced pedagogical creativity, and a weakening of teacher agency (Zhai et al., 2024).

This risk is compounded by the persuasive fluency of AI-generated text, which often appears accurate and coherent even when it contains errors or biases. Teachers who lack strong AI literacy may accept AI outputs uncritically, resulting in inappropriate instructional decisions or the perpetuation of flawed information. Furthermore, excessive dependence may discourage reflective practice, as teachers rely on technological suggestions rather than engaging deeply with student needs, curriculum goals, and contextual nuances. If left unaddressed, over-reliance threatens to shift teaching from a profession rooted in expertise and judgment to one centered on passive technology management.

5.2 Identity Anxiety and Blurred Professional Boundaries

The integration of AI into core teaching functions raises important questions about teacher identity. As AI systems begin to generate lesson plans, model solutions, or provide feedback to students, teachers may question their role: What remains uniquely human about teaching? What aspects of expertise are still valued?

Such uncertainties can produce identity anxiety, particularly among pre-service teachers who are still forming their professional self-concept. The traditional markers of teacher expertise, mastery of content, ability to plan instruction, and capacity to evaluate student work, now appear to overlap with machine capabilities. This overlap blurs professional boundaries, making it difficult for teachers to determine where AI ends and where human responsibility begins.

Beyond psychological concerns, blurred boundaries create practical challenges. Teachers may struggle to define their ethical obligations when AI participates in decision-making or influences student learning outcomes. If teachers perceive AI as a co-teacher rather than a tool, confusion about accountability may arise, especially in cases involving errors, bias, or student complaints. Clear frameworks are therefore essential to help teachers maintain a strong sense of professional identity grounded in empathy, relational work, ethical reasoning, and human-centered judgment (Jeon & Lee, 2023).

5.3 Data Ethics and Privacy Issues

AI-supported learning environments rely heavily on data, introducing complex ethical and privacy challenges. Many AI systems collect granular information about students' performance, behavioral patterns, attention levels, and even emotional states. Without robust safeguards, such data collection can infringe on privacy, create opportunities for misuse, or expose students to security risks.

Teachers play a key role in mediating these risks but often lack formal training in data ethics. They may not fully understand what data are being collected, how long they are stored, or who has access to them. Moreover, teachers must make informed decisions about when data collection is pedagogically necessary and when it may be intrusive. Students and families may be unaware of the extent of data collection and monitoring in AI-supported classrooms, raising questions about transparency and consent (Chan, 2023).

Another concern is algorithmic bias embedded within AI systems. When decisions about assessment, feedback, or learning opportunities are influenced by biased algorithms, vulnerable student groups may experience unequal treatment. Teachers must remain vigilant in identifying bias, advocating for fairness, and ensuring that algorithmic decisions do not replace human ethical judgment. Data ethics is therefore not a peripheral issue but a central responsibility in AI-mediated education.

5.4 Inequity in AI Access and Educational Opportunities

Although AI holds great promise for enhancing learning, its benefits are not evenly distributed. Schools and communities differ significantly in their access to technology, bandwidth, infrastructure, and technical support. As a result, AI integration can widen existing educational inequalities rather than reduce them.

Students in under-resourced schools may receive limited exposure to AI tools, reducing their opportunities to develop digital competencies essential for future careers. Meanwhile, students in well-funded schools may have access to advanced adaptive learning systems, AI tutors, and data-informed interventions. This inequitable landscape creates a digital privilege gap that reinforces socioeconomic disparities.

For teachers, inequitable access to AI means unequal preparation and professional development opportunities. Pre-service teachers placed in low-resource schools may have fewer chances to practice integrating AI tools, putting them at a disadvantage compared with peers who train in better-equipped environments. If teacher education programs do not address these disparities intentionally, inequity will persist across generations of educators and learners (Zipf et al., 2025).

Teacher role transformation in the AI era involves navigating significant risks alongside potential benefits. Over-reliance on AI threatens teacher agency; identity anxiety challenges teachers' sense of purpose; data ethics raise questions of fairness and privacy; and inequitable access risks deepening social disparities. To prepare competent, confident educators, teacher education programs must address these challenges explicitly, cultivating critical awareness, ethical responsibility, and a commitment to equity. These efforts can help teachers harness AI's potential while safeguarding the human-centered values at the heart of education.

5.5 Institutional and Workload Constraints

Although AI is often presented as a means of reducing teachers' workload, in practice it can introduce new forms of institutional and cognitive burden. Teachers are expected not only to use AI systems but also to monitor their outputs, verify their accuracy, and manage the ethical and pedagogical implications of algorithmic recommendations. These additional responsibilities emerge in a context where teachers already face heavy workloads, rigid curricula, and increasing accountability pressures. Moreover, many educational systems lack the infrastructure, technical support, and professional development necessary to integrate AI meaningfully into everyday practice. As a result, the role of the teacher as a learning experience designer may be constrained by institutional realities such as limited time, insufficient training, and policy mandates that prioritize standardization over pedagogical flexibility. Without addressing these structural conditions, AI-driven role transformation risks becoming an added layer of expectation rather than a genuine professional enhancement. These effects vary by system maturity, platform design, and institutional support.

6. CONCLUSION AND FUTURE DIRECTIONS

The rapid integration of artificial intelligence into educational systems has initiated a profound transformation in teacher roles that is increasingly difficult to reverse in many education systems in the near term. As demonstrated throughout this chapter, current AI systems are not yet simply an instructional tool but a structural force that reshape the nature of teaching, learning, and professional practice. Teachers are shifting from knowledge transmitters to learning experience designers who must orchestrate human-AI collaboration, interpret data-driven insights, and exercise ethical, pedagogically grounded judgment. This transformation is better understood as a long-term reconfiguration of educational work, driven by technological progress and validated by research in learning sciences and educational neuroscience.

6.1 The Irreversible Trend of Teacher Role Transformation

The transformation of teacher roles reflects long-term, systemic shifts rather than temporary disruptions. AI now supports core instructional processes, including planning, assessment, feedback, and behavioral monitoring, making routine tasks increasingly automated. Consequently, the value of human teachers lies in higher-order functions: designing rich learning experiences, fostering socio-emotional connections, guiding inquiry, and interpreting the complexities that current AI systems are not yet able to understand. Evidence from neuroscience further reinforces that human relational work, empathy, and emotional attunement remain irreplaceable. As AI capabilities continue to advance, teacher roles will increasingly emphasize creativity, criticality, and relational expertise, suggesting that the learning experience designer identity is likely to become increasingly central.

6.2 Implications for Teacher Education Institutions and Policymakers

Teacher education programs will likely undergo intentional, structural reform to support this role transformation. Institutions will need to expand curricula to include AI literacy, ethical reasoning, professional judgment, and data-informed pedagogical design. Practice-based learning opportunities, such as AI-supported simulations, virtual practicums, and analytics-augmented microteaching, are well positioned to become core components of teacher preparation. Policymakers are well positioned to establish guidelines for responsible AI integration, ensuring data privacy, algorithmic transparency, and equitable access across schools. Furthermore, accreditation and certification frameworks will need to evolve to assess teachers' competencies in human-AI collaboration, not merely technical tool operation. Without these systemic reforms, pre-service teachers will remain underprepared for the realities of AI-enhanced classrooms.

At the policy level, the shift toward teachers as learning experience designers requires more than curricular innovation; it demands structural alignment across accreditation, governance, and institutional support systems. If AI-related competencies such as data-informed judgment, ethical decision-making, and human–AI learning design are not embedded in teacher certification standards and program evaluation frameworks, they risk remaining aspirational rather than professionally binding. At the same time, schools and universities must be provided with the resources, infrastructure, and regulatory clarity needed to support responsible AI use, including safeguards for data privacy, transparency, and teacher autonomy. Without such policy and institutional coordination, the promise of AI-enhanced teacher professionalism is unlikely to be realized in sustainable and equitable ways.

6.3 Future Research Directions (AI Co-Teaching Models, AI-Assisted Assessment of Teacher Competencies)

Future research should further explore emerging models of human-AI collaboration in teaching. AI co-teaching models, where AI systems dynamically assist with feedback, adaptive instruction, or formative assessment, require investigation into optimal role division, trust calibration, and shared decision-making (Edwards et al., 2024). Additionally, AI-assisted assessment of teacher competencies represents a promising yet underexplored area. Intelligent systems may support teacher evaluation through analysis of discourse patterns, feedback quality, or student engagement signals, but such applications require careful study to ensure validity, fairness, and ethical soundness. Research should also examine how AI influences teacher identity development, emotional labor, and long-term professional well-being.

Collectively, these future directions highlight the importance of continued interdisciplinary inquiry. As AI reshapes the educational landscape, teacher education must remain responsive, evidence-driven, and ethically grounded. Ultimately, the goal is not to replace teachers with machines but to empower teachers to thrive in classrooms where human expertise and artificial intelligence complement one another in service of deeper, more equitable learning.

COMPETING INTERESTS

The authors of this publication declare there are no competing interests.

FUNDING

This research received no specific grant from any funding agency in the public, commercial, or not-for-profit sectors. Funding for this research was covered by the author(s) of the article.

SCHOLARLY SIGNIFICANCE AND EXPECTED CONTRIBUTIONS

This chapter contributes to the literature on artificial intelligence and teacher education by offering an integrative perspective on how teaching is being reconfigured in AI-enhanced learning environments. Rather than examining isolated instructional functions or individual technologies, the chapter conceptualizes teacher role transformation as a structural shift spanning instructional planning, assessment, feedback, and learning support. By articulating these interrelated changes within a single theoretical model, it provides a coherent framework for understanding how professional teaching practice evolves in response to the increasing presence of AI in educational settings.

Building on this role-based perspective, the chapter develops a core competency framework for pre-service teachers that addresses the demands of human-AI collaborative teaching. Moving beyond narrowly defined technical skills, the framework integrates AI literacy, professional judgment, ethical competence, and learning design ability as mutually reinforcing dimensions of professional practice. This approach responds to a persistent gap in the literature, where AI-related competencies are often treated in fragmented or tool-specific ways, and foregrounds professional judgment as a central human capacity that mediates the educational use of AI.

In addition to its theoretical contributions, the chapter offers practice-oriented implications for teacher education reform. By explicitly connecting role transformation and competency development with strategies such as curriculum redesign, practice-based learning, and pedagogical tool integration, it establishes a conceptual bridge between theory and implementation. These pathways support teacher education programs in preparing pre-service teachers to assume the emerging professional identity of learning experience designers, capable of orchestrating AI-enhanced learning environments while maintaining pedagogical coherence and human-centered educational values.

REFERENCES

Ahmad, K., Iqbal, W., El-Hassan, A., Qadir, J., Benhaddou, D., Ayyash, M., & Al-Fuqaha, A. (2024). Data-Driven Artificial Intelligence in Education: A Comprehensive Review. *IEEE Transactions on Learning Technologies*, *17*, 12–31. DOI: 10.1109/TLT.2023.3314610

Aleven, V., Blankestijn, J., Lawrence, L., Nagashima, T., & Taatgen, N. (2022). A dashboard to support teachers during students' self-paced AI-supported problem-solving practice. In I. Hilliger, P. J. Muñoz-Merino, T. De Laet, A. Ortega-Arranz, & T. Farrell, *Educating for a New Future: Making Sense of Technology-Enhanced Learning Adoption Cham*. https://doi.org/10.1007/978-3-031-16290-9_2

Álvarez Guayara, , D. LEspinosa Sarmiento, , D. M. (2025). Ambiente de aprendizaje híbrido para el fortalecimiento de las competencias investigativas de estudiantes de ingeniería. *Academia y Virtualidad, 18*(2), 117-133. DOI: 10.18359/ravi.7621

Bilbao-Eraña, A., & Arroyo-Sagasta, A. (2025). Fostering AI literacy in pre-service teachers: Impact of a training intervention on awareness, attitude and trust in AI. *Frontiers in Education, 10*, 1668078. Advance online publication. DOI: 10.3389/feduc.2025.1668078

Bosch, N., Härkki, T., & Seitamaa-Hakkarainen, P. (2025). Teachers as reflective learning experience designers: Bringing design thinking into school-based design and maker education. *International Journal of Child-Computer Interaction, 43*, 100695. Advance online publication. DOI: 10.1016/j.ijcci.2024.100695

Carrillo, C., Flores, M. A., & Mena, J. (2025). Artificial intelligence in the context of teacher education: Emerging themes and critical issues. *European Journal of Teacher Education, 48*(5), 1143–1162. DOI: 10.1080/02619768.2025.2584283

Castillo-Martínez, I. M., Flores-Bueno, D., Gómez-Puente, S. M., & Vite-León, V. O. (2024). AI in higher education: A systematic literature review. *Frontiers in Education, 9*, 1391485. Advance online publication. DOI: 10.3389/feduc.2024.1391485

Chan, C. K. Y. (2023). A comprehensive AI policy education framework for university teaching and learning. *International Journal of Educational Technology in Higher Education, 20*(1), 38. DOI: 10.1186/s41239-023-00408-3

Czerkawski, B., & Berti, M. (2021). Learning experience design for augmented reality. *Research in Learning Technology, 29*. Advance online publication. DOI: 10.25304/rlt.v29.2429

Edwards, J., Nguyen, A., Lämsä, J., Sobocinski, M., Whitehead, R., Dang, B., Roberts, A. S., & Järvelä, S. (2024). Human-AI collaboration: Designing artificial agents to facilitate socially shared regulation among learners. *British Journal of Educational Technology, 56*(2), 712–733. DOI: 10.1111/bjet.13534

Gómez-Chacón, I. M., & Marbán, J. M. (2024). Epistemic emotions and pre-service mathematics teachers' knowledge for teaching. *ZDM Mathematics Education, 56*(6), 1223–1237. DOI: 10.1007/s11858-024-01624-5

Guan, L., Zhang, Y., & Gu, M. M. (2025). Pre-service teachers preparedness for AI-integrated education: An investigation from perceptions, capabilities, and teachers' identity changes. *Computers and Education: Artificial Intelligence*, *8*, 100341. Advance online publication. DOI: 10.1016/j.caeai.2024.100341

Gümüş, M. M., Çakır, R., & Korkmaz, Ö. (2023). Investigation of pre-service teachers' sensitivity to cyberbullying, perceptions of digital ethics and awareness of digital data security. *Education and Information Technologies*, *28*(11), 14399–14421. DOI: 10.1007/s10639-023-11785-7

Hernández León, N., & Rodríguez-Conde, M.-J. (2024). Inteligencia artificial aplicada a la educación y la evaluación educativa en la Universidad: Introducción de sistemas de tutorización inteligentes, sistemas de reconocimiento y otras tendencias futuras. [RED]. *Revista de Educación a Distancia*, *24*(78). Advance online publication. DOI: 10.6018/red.594651

Ishizawa, T. (2025). Architectural informatics self-hackathon workshop — Reassessing professional essence through generic and generative artificial intelligence. *International Journal of Architectural Computing*, 14780771251335108. Advance online publication. DOI: 10.1177/14780771251335108

Jeon, J., & Lee, S. (2023). Large language models in education: A focus on the complementary relationship between human teachers and ChatGPT. *Education and Information Technologies*, *28*(12), 15873–15892. DOI: 10.1007/s10639-023-11834-1

Kalniņa, D., Nīmante, D., & Baranova, S. (2024). Artificial intelligence for higher education: Benefits and challenges for pre-service teachers. *Frontiers in Education*, *9*, 1501819. Advance online publication. DOI: 10.3389/feduc.2024.1501819

Kasneci, E., Sessler, K., Küchemann, S., Bannert, M., Dementieva, D., Fischer, F., Gasser, U., Groh, G., Günnemann, S., Hüllermeier, E., Krusche, S., Kutyniok, G., Michaeli, T., Nerdel, C., Pfeffer, J., Poquet, O., Sailer, M., Schmidt, A., Seidel, T., & Kasneci, G. (2023). ChatGPT for good? On opportunities and challenges of large language models for education. *Learning and Individual Differences*, *103*, 102274. Advance online publication. DOI: 10.1016/j.lindif.2023.102274

Kim, J. (2023). Leading teachers' perspective on teacher-AI collaboration in education. *Education and Information Technologies*, *29*(7), 8693–8724. DOI: 10.1007/s10639-023-12109-5

Kohnke, L., Zou, D., & Xie, H. (2025). Microlearning and generative AI for pre-service teacher education: A qualitative case study. *Education and Information Technologies*, *30*(15), 21221–21248. DOI: 10.1007/s10639-025-13606-5

Kuzu, S. (2025). Artificial intelligence in pre-service teacher education: Bibliometrics analysis. *Pedagogical Research, 10*(4), em0249. Advance online publication. DOI: 10.29333/pr/17402

Molenaar, I. (2025). Human-AI Collaboration in Education: The Hybrid Future *Proceedings of the 30th ACM Conference on Innovation and Technology in Computer Science Education* V. 1, Nijmegen, Netherlands. DOI: 10.1145/3724363.3729083

Ng, D. T. K., Su, J., Leung, J. K. L., & Chu, S. K. W. (2023). Artificial intelligence (AI) literacy education in secondary schools: A review. *Interactive Learning Environments, 32*(10), 6204–6224. DOI: 10.1080/10494820.2023.2255228

Nguyen, A., Hong, Y., Dang, B., & Huang, X. (2024). Human-AI collaboration patterns in AI-assisted academic writing. *Studies in Higher Education, 49*(5), 847–864. DOI: 10.1080/03075079.2024.2323593

Phommanee, W., Plangsorn, B., & Siripipattanakul, S. (2024). An exploratory study of current competency for learning experience designer: Job announcement analysis. *Journal of Computers in Education, 12*(2), 391–419. DOI: 10.1007/s40692-024-00315-0

Prestigiacomo, R., Hunter, J., Knight, S., Martinez-Maldonado, R., & Lockyer, L. (2020). Data in practice: A participatory approach to understanding pre-service teachers' perspectives. *Australasian Journal of Educational Technology, 36*(6), 107–119. DOI: 10.14742/ajet.6388

P.T, S., Chacko, A. M., & Kumar, S. D. M. (2025). Beyond the One-Size-Fits-All: A Systematic Review of Personalized and Gamified e-Learning for Neurodivergent Learners. *Electronic Journal of E-Learning, 23*(3), 101-119. DOI: 10.34190/ejel.23.3.4051

Raes, A., Detienne, L., Windey, I., & Depaepe, F. (2019). A systematic literature review on synchronous hybrid learning: Gaps identified. *Learning Environments Research, 23*(3), 269–290. DOI: 10.1007/s10984-019-09303-z

Reddig, J. M., Arora, A., & MacLellan, C. J. (2025). Generating In-Context, Personalized Feedback for Intelligent Tutors with Large Language Models. *International Journal of Artificial Intelligence in Education, 35*(6), 3459–3500. Advance online publication. DOI: 10.1007/s40593-025-00505-6

Runge, I., Hebibi, F., & Lazarides, R. (2025). Acceptance of Pre-Service Teachers Towards Artificial Intelligence (AI): The Role of AI-Related Teacher Training Courses and AI-TPACK Within the Technology Acceptance Model. *Education Sciences, 15*(2), 167. Advance online publication. DOI: 10.3390/educsci15020167

Sajja, R., Sermet, Y., Cikmaz, M., Cwiertny, D., & Demir, I. (2024). Artificial Intelligence-Enabled Intelligent Assistant for Personalized and Adaptive Learning in Higher Education. *Information (Basel), 15*(10), 596. Advance online publication. DOI: 10.3390/info15100596

Setiyawan, A., Soeharto, S., Wijaya, T. T., Korenova, L., & Lavicza, Z. (2025). Measuring Teachers' competencies for AI integration: Development and validation of the AI-TPACK in vocational education. *Computers and Education Open, 9*, 100319. Advance online publication. DOI: 10.1016/j.caeo.2025.100319

Shikun, S., Grigoryan, G., Huichun, N., & Harutyunyan, H. (2024). AI Chatbots: Developing English Language Proficiency in EFL Classroom. *Arab World English Journal, 1*(1), 292–305. DOI: 10.24093/awej/ChatGPT.20

Sperling, K., Stenberg, C.-J., McGrath, C., Åkerfeldt, A., Heintz, F., & Stenliden, L. (2024). In search of artificial intelligence (AI) literacy in teacher education: A scoping review. *Computers and Education Open, 6*, 100169. Advance online publication. DOI: 10.1016/j.caeo.2024.100169

Tan, X., Cheng, G., & Ling, M. H. (2025). Artificial intelligence in teaching and teacher professional development: A systematic review. *Computers and Education: Artificial Intelligence, 8*, 100355. Advance online publication. DOI: 10.1016/j.caeai.2024.100355

UNESCO. (2023). *Guidance for generative AI in education and research.* https://unesdoc.unesco.org/ark:/48223/pf0000386693

UNESCO. (2024). *AI competency framework for teachers.* https://doi.org/10.54675/ZJTE2084

Vartiainen, H., & Tedre, M. (2023). Using artificial intelligence in craft education: Crafting with text-to-image generative models. *Digital Creativity (Exeter), 34*(1), 1–21. DOI: 10.1080/14626268.2023.2174557

Vistorte, A. O. R., Deroncele-Acosta, A., Ayala, J. L. M., Barrasa, A., Lopez-Granero, C., & Marti-Gonzalez, M. (2024). Integrating artificial intelligence to assess emotions in learning environments: A systematic literature review. *Frontiers in Psychology, 15*, 1387089. DOI: 10.3389/fpsyg.2024.1387089 PMID: 38966729

Wagner, C. J. (2024). Differentiating Children's Reading Materials with Artificial Intelligence: Exploring Possibilities for Personalized Learning. *The Reading Teacher, 78*(3), 191–194. DOI: 10.1002/trtr.2361

Wang, L., & Dai, J. (2025). Understanding Chinese EFL Teachers' Actual Experiences With AI-Mediated Instruction Through the Lens of Expectancy Value Theory. *European Journal of Education*, *60*(4), e70279. Advance online publication. DOI: 10.1111/ejed.70279

Wang, M.-T., Henry, D. A., & Degol, J. L. (2020). Chapter Four - A development-in-sociocultural-context perspective on the multiple pathways to youth's engagement in learning. In Elliot, A. J. (Ed.), Vol. 7, pp. 113–160). Advances in Motivation Science. Elsevier., https://doi.org/10.1016/bs.adms.2019.11.001

Wilson, K., Cohen, J., & Erickson, S. (2025). Teacher Candidates' Perceptions of Mixed Reality Simulations: Variations by Task, Support, and Mode of Delivery. *AERA Open*, *11*, 23328584251375064. Advance online publication. DOI: 10.1177/23328584251375064

Wu, J.-Y., Yang, C. C., Liao, C.-H., & Nian, M.-W. (2021). Analytics 2.0 for precision education. *Journal of Educational Technology & Society*, *24*(1), 267–279.

Zawacki-Richter, O., Marín, V. I., Bond, M., & Gouverneur, F. (2019). Systematic review of research on artificial intelligence applications in higher education – where are the educators? *International Journal of Educational Technology in Higher Education*, *16*(1), 39. Advance online publication. DOI: 10.1186/s41239-019-0171-0

Zhai, C., Wibowo, S., & Li, L. D. (2024). The effects of over-reliance on AI dialogue systems on students' cognitive abilities: A systematic review. *Smart Learning Environments*, *11*(1), 28. Advance online publication. DOI: 10.1186/s40561-024-00316-7

Zhang, J., & Zhang, Z. (2024). AI in teacher education: Unlocking new dimensions in teaching support, inclusive learning, and digital literacy. *Journal of Computer Assisted Learning*, *40*(4), 1871–1885. DOI: 10.1111/jcal.12988

Zhang, J. J., Wang, Y. W., Ruan, Q., & Yang, Y. (2024). Digital tourism interpretation content quality: A comparison between AI-generated content and professional-generated content. *Tourism Management Perspectives*, *53*, 101279. Advance online publication. DOI: 10.1016/j.tmp.2024.101279

Zhang, S., Ganapathy Prasad, P., & Schroeder, N. L. (2025). Learning About AI: A Systematic Review of Reviews on AI Literacy. *Journal of Educational Computing Research*, *63*(5), 1292–1322. DOI: 10.1177/07356331251342081

Zipf, S., Wu, C., & Petricini, T. (2025). Using the information inequity framework to study GenAI equity: analysis of educational perspectives. *Information Research an international electronic journal, 30*(iConf), 533-547. DOI: 10.47989/ir30iConf47284

Chapter 7
AI-Enhanced Teaching Redefining Educators as Learning Architects, Ethical Guides, and Data-Driven Mentors in the AI Era

Rocky Kumar
http://orcid.org/0009-0002-6995-2037
Poornima University, Jaipur, India

Jameel Ahmad Qurashi
http://orcid.org/0000-0003-0763-595X
Cluster University of Srinagar, India

ABSTRACT

The field of education is changing by the presence of artificial intelligence since the focus is changing into individualized, data-driven, and morally oriented learning systems. With the automation of administrative functions, the creation of learning materials, assessment of the student and adaptive feedback through the application of AI technology, the role of an educator is experiencing a fundamental change. Teachers are no longer expected to be content deliverers but are being more and more placed in the role of learning architects, expected to design learning experiences that are meaningful and student-centred. Meanwhile, the development of AI brings a new and urgent problem of bias, transparency, fairness, academic integrity and proper use, which makes the educator an ethical guide more than ever. This chapter

DOI: 10.4018/979-8-3373-8027-8.ch007

investigates how AI changes the professional identity of teachers interested in their new roles as mentors, facilitators of learning, curators of the content and decoders of knowledge driven by AI.

1. INTRODUCTION

Artificial Intelligence (AI) has been quickly moving from a side-kick technological innovation to a game-changer that is transforming the ecosystems of education in the world. Over the past decade, accelerated developments in machine learning, natural language processing (NLP), generative AI, learning analytics and intelligent tutoring systems (ITS) have dramatically increased the capabilities of educational technologies (Holmes et al., 2022). As various institutions in our world are opting for the AI-powered tools, the role of educators is undergoing a paradigm shift - from the traditional knowledge transmitters to learning architects, ethical guides and data-driven mentors. This chapter focuses on the complex change of the roles of teachers during the AI revolution, in which we propose a conceptual framework to understand the ways educators can navigate and harness AI for improving student learning outcomes. The increasing penetration of systems with artificial intelligence (AI) in instructional design, assessment, classroom management and individualised learning marks a new era in which human-AI partnership should be at the centre of educational practice (Zawacki-Richter et al., 2019). This evolution requires new competencies to be learned on the part of the teachers, along with a rethinking of pedagogical approaches and a dynamic role that is adequate to the demands of twenty-first century learning. Thus, aim of this chapter is to provide an in-depth discussion on how AI is redefining roles of teachers, what challenges face educators and how pedagogical, ethical and data driven strategies can enable them to effectively integrate AI in teaching. While the transformative potential of artificial intelligence in education to personalize teaching, reduce costs, and inform data-driven decisions can be great, the integration of artificial intelligence in education also poses important ethical, social and professional challenges. Issues such as algorithmic bias, data privacy, unequal access to AI technologies and issues surrounding teacher autonomy require responsible human oversight. Therefore, the effective adoption of AI in education calls for a standard of balance to integrate technological innovation with human factors like ethical responsibility, pedagogical judgment and human-centered values.

1.1 Overview Of Ai Transformation In Education

The entry of AI in the field of education has been marked by deep technological, pedagogical and systemic changes. Intelligent tutoring systems, automated feedback systems, conversational AI systems such as ChatGPT and GPT-5, adaptive learning systems and predictive analytics systems have paved the way for new forms of personalized learning and instructional automation (Chen et al., 2023). As such, these systems allow for students to benefit from individualized learning pathways, real-time recommendations, automated formative feedback, and individualized content (Ifenthaler & Yau, 2020).

At the institutional level, AI-driven analytics plays the role of assisting factors to administrators and educators in the decision-making process such as the identification of students at risk, optimization of curriculum, and increased retention rates. The advent of generative AI has further increased the possibilities for teaching as teachers and students can start building content, simulations, create assessments, and problem-solving with human-AI collaboration. (Luckin, 2021).

Moreover, AI has come to the core of the educational reform of the world. National AI strategies launched by countries such as the United States of America, China, India, Singapore, and the United Kingdom have identified the field of education as an important area for the deployment of AI. UNESCO (2023) stresses that AI has the potential to democratize access to quality education, minimize achievement gaps, and achieve personalization. However, it also raises the concern regarding risks on data privacy, algorithmic bias, and ethical misuse. The transformation brought about by AI is not confined to the adoption of technology, but changes fundamentally the pedagogical relationships, the learning environment and the nature of the teacher's responsibilities. As AI can take care of the routine administrative tasks and provide intelligent feedback to the learners, this leaves the educators with the opportunities to work on higher-order tasks such as mentoring, motivation, creativity, and socio-emotional support (Holstein et al., 2020).

1.2 Shifting Roles Of Educators In The AI-Driven Ecosystem

Traditionally, teachers have been mostly content experts and instructional leaders. However, the new focus of education with artificial intelligence is not about direct teaching but the design and orchestration as well as the facilitation of complex learning environments. In the AI era, educators have the role of multiple identities:

1.2.1 Teachers As Learning Architects

Educators increasingly plan artificial intelligence (AI)-supported learning paths, incorporate intelligent systems in curriculum planning, and personalize the learning process from AI-generated insights (Chou & Chan, 2021). This means that teachers have to know how algorithms classify behaviour, recommend content, and detect misconceptions by students.

1.2.2 Teachers As Ethical Guides

As students interact with AI tools, educators are then responsible for ensuring responsible AI use, data consent, transparency and algorithmic fairness (Williamson & Eynon, 2020). They must instruct learners in building digital citizenship, critical AI literacy and ethical awareness.

1.2.3 Teachers As Data-Driven Mentors

With the increase of learning analytics dashboards and predictive modelling systems, educators now mentor their students using evidence-based insights (Slade & Prinsloo, 2019). They interpret patterns in data, identify the gaps in learning and make specific interventions.

1.2.4 Teachers As Human–AI Collaborators

Educators co-operate with AI systems instead of replacing them as facilitators. They retain emotional presence, creativity, empathy, and cultural responsiveness - all the things that AI cannot.

1.2.5 Teachers As Innovators And Change Leaders

Educators therefore need to constantly adapt to new technologies, revamp pedagogies, and work with technology developers, researchers and policymakers (Koehler & Mishra, 2020). These enlarging roles reflect the transition from teacher centered teaching to learner centered AI assisted education. These shifts require new competencies, ongoing professional development and institutional support and these become the basis for this chapter.

2.1 Evolution Of Teaching Roles In The Digital Era

The development of teaching roles during the digital age is indicative of a deeper change in the professional identity of educators throughout the world. Prior to the integration of technology across widely used levels, teachers had the primary role of conveying knowledge, which was based on textbook-centered pedagogy and standardized pedagogies. As digital technologies emerged, starting with computers, projectors, and the internet, teachers were able to become facilitators as they guided their learners through multimedia resources, online discussions, and virtual collaboration (Means et al., 2020). The advent of learning management systems and digital classrooms also broadened the role of the educator and changed them into instructional designers that had to also curate digital content, manage online systems for Learning in addition to facilitating student engagement outside of the brick-and-mortar walls. The development of big data and analytics in the 2010s changed the teacher into data-interpreters who now had the opportunity to analyse dashboards and call out the gaps in learning and make informed data-driven decisions about instruction (Slade & Prinsloo, 2019). Today, in the age of artificial intelligence, educators are facing a complex situation in which automation, adaptive systems and intelligent agents redefine their job as professionals. They are no longer instructors, but architects of learning, ethical supervisors and data-driven mentors who are responsible for the design of AI integrated learning paths and making sure that AI is used responsibly. Thus, digital era has changed the role of teaching from being content delivery to technology-rich learning orchestration.

Figure 1. Evolution of Teaching Roles from Traditional to AI-Enhanced Education

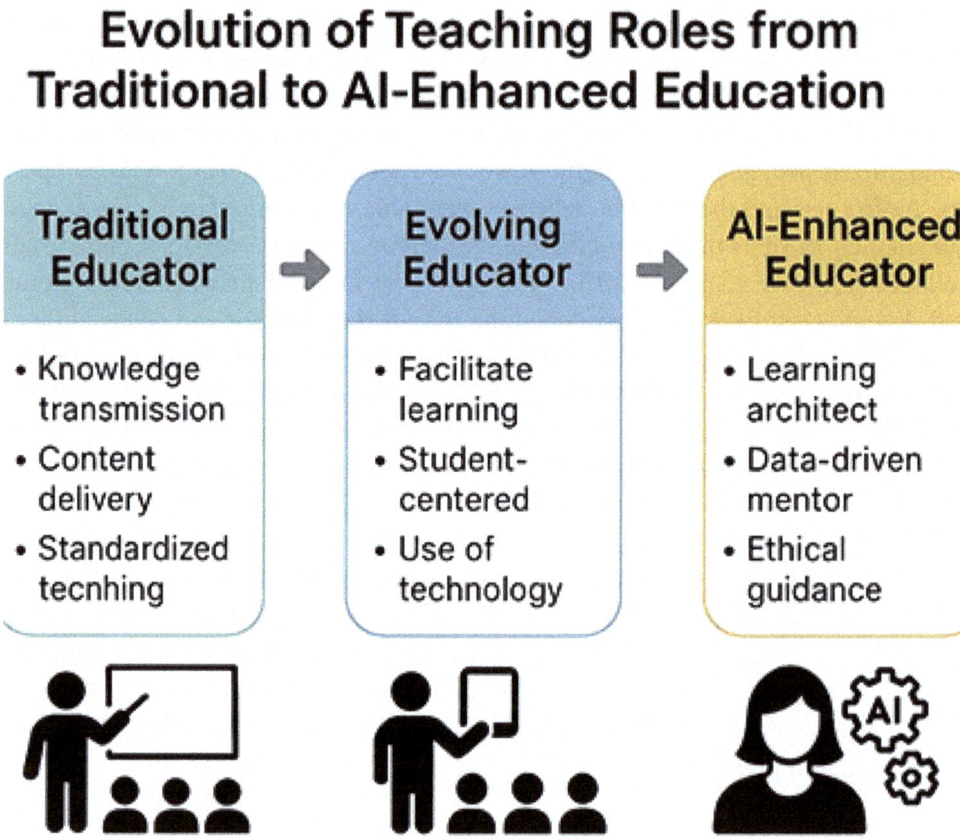

2.2 Rise Of AI-Powered Learning Systems And Pedagogical Innovation

The advent of artificial intelligence (AI) powered learning systems has enabled transformational pedagogical innovations that are reaping the nature of learning delivery, assessment and experience to a whole new level. Adaptive learning technologies now provide personalized instructional content based on learner performance, cognitive behaviours and engagement patterns, thus providing customized learning pathways to support diverse learning needs (Chassignol et al., 2018). Intelligent tutoring systems try to imitate the individualized attention given by a human tutor by providing step-by-step scaffolding and automated feedback and error-specific hints that help the learner to enhance his or her conceptual understanding and problem-solving capabilities (VanLehn, 2020). Learning analytics platforms enable educators to monitor real-time student activity and identify at-risk students and use timely interventions to boost academic success. (Ifenthaler & Yau, 2020).

Generative AI tools - including ChatGPT, DeepSeek, Gemini and Claude - have further increased the instructional possibilities by automating the process of assessing instruction, creating creative content, supporting writing activities, and conversational tutoring. Automated grading systems and essay scorers help lessen the workload of teachers and make feedback much more efficient, while affective computing systems use the speech, facial expressions and behavioural cues of the students to understand the socio-emotional needs of the students (D'Mello & Graesser, 2021). Collectively, these innovations are a step towards more customized, efficient and interactive learning environments, which means that AI is a key driver of pedagogical shift.

Figure 2. AI-Powered Learning Ecosystem in Modern Education

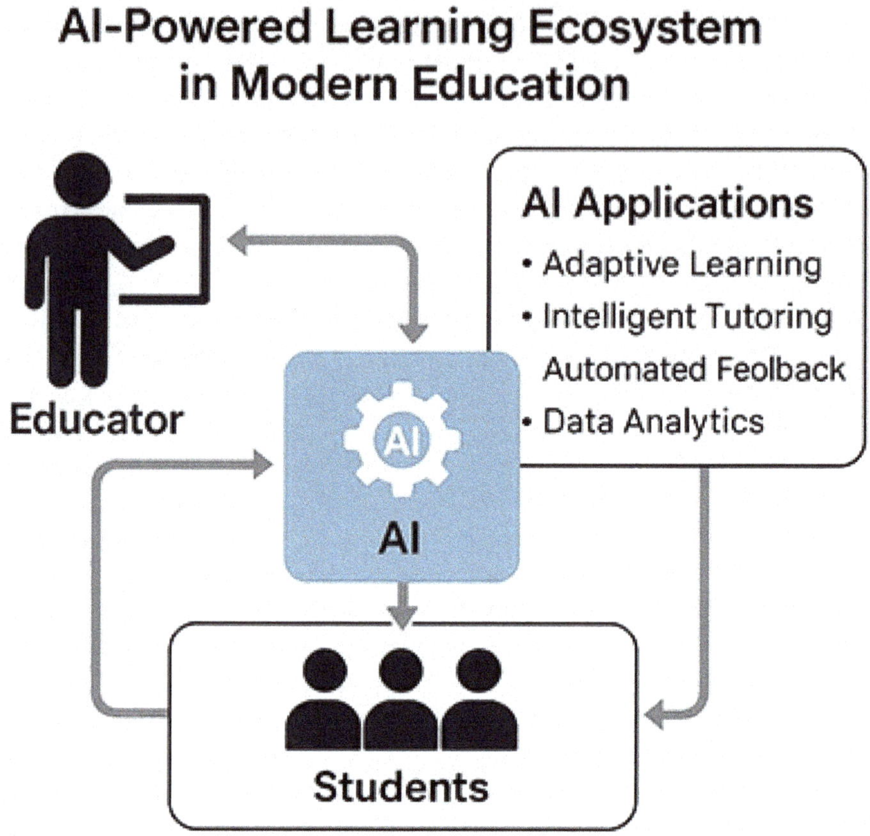

2.3 Theoretical Foundations Supporting AI-Enhanced Teaching

The integration of artificial intelligence with an education is deeply rooted in basic theories of learning which gives information about the construction of knowledge, network formation and collaboration with intelligent agents by the students. Constructivism lays emphasis on the value in the active learning and the construction of individual knowledge, the concept being reflected in the adaptive learning systems that are AI technology driven and can tailor content and provide personalized feedback (Jonassen, 2018). Connectivism extends beyond this, however, and it is concerned with the effect that digital networks, distributed knowledge and algorithmic systems are having on the learning experience in the modern era (Siemens, 2018). In addition, a new frame of human-AI collaborative pedagogy has teachers, learners, and AI tools in the learning process as co-participants as they have complementary strengths and common responsibilities (Holstein et al., 2020). Together, these theoretical perspectives form the basis for the explosion of adoption of AI for classroom setting, as well as the ability for educators to create meaningful and effective educational and technological learning environments. While many scholars highlight the potential of AI to improve teaching through use of personalization, adaptive feedback, and learning analytics, among others, critical perspectives focus on possible unintended consequences, such as teacher deskilling, excessive prioritization of automation, and more classroom surveillance. Some studies state that in the absence of appropriate governance and pedagogical mediation AI systems can move the power of the decision-making process away from educators. This chapter sets educators as central agents in bridging over these perspectives by implementing AI as an augmentation, rather than a substitute, which will continue to preserve professional autonomy, while making data-driven findings.

2.3.1 Constructivism

Constructivism helps to understand, Learners construct knowledge through meaningful engagement, exploration and reflective thinking. AI technologies are very much compatible with this philosophy from the perspectives of self-paced learning, inquiry-driven exploration and individual scaffolding. Intelligent tutoring systems, for example, allow learners to try things out and get specific prompts about enhancing their conceptual understanding (Holmes et al., 2022). Adaptivity--the cornerstone of AI systems--is antithetical to the idea of "one size fits all" learning. 2 The concept of adaptability is not new; it has a long history in constructivist beliefs. 3 Adaptive learning is a process where instructional pathways are continually conditioned based on learner performance, needs, and cognitive processes. Generative AI is another way of enhancing the constructivist way of learning with possibilities for creativity, such as story generation, simulations, models, or explanations that learners can assess, refine, and use. Thus, the AI operationalization of constructivist principles is the transformation of students into active creators of knowledge rather than recipients.

2.3.2 Connectivism

Connectivism sets learning as a process of making connections between digital platforms, resources, individuals and algorithmic systems. AI enhances this theoretical basis as a powerful node in the knowledge networks of learners and makes recommendations of personalised resources, curricular content and supports collaboration across disciplines and communities (Downes, 2022). Through semantic search tools, recommendation engines, and generative models, AI helps learners efficiently navigate through enormous information ecosystems, which in turn increases digital fluency and network literacy. Connectivism also focuses on the dynamic nature of knowledge, which is in line with AI's capacity to update, refine, and produce new insights based on changing patterns of data. By promoting constant learning and individual exploration, AI promotes connectivism ideas in contemporary educational practice.

2.3.3 Human–AI Collaborative Pedagogy

Human-AI collaborative pedagogy is the modern model of the concept of learning as a cooperative dynamic among teachers, students and AI systems. This way, it is acknowledged that while AI can perform well in terms of patterns, automation and data processing, human educators can offer valuable insights into emotions, ethics and context that cannot be replicated by AI (Holstein et al., 2020). In this model, AI is responsible for tasks such as AI-generated feedback generation and efficiency, performance prediction, content generation, etc. Teachers interpret the outputs of AI's, provide socio-emotional support, and make equitable access available. The pedagogy here puts focus on augmentation of each other with both humans and AI bringing their respective unique strengths to deliver improved learning outcomes. This framework holds to the importance of transparency, critical AI literacy, ethical oversight in AI-created recommendations, and thus, teachers become the mediators in helping students responsibly navigate the AI-created recommendations.

Figure 3. Human–AI Collaborative Pedagogy Model

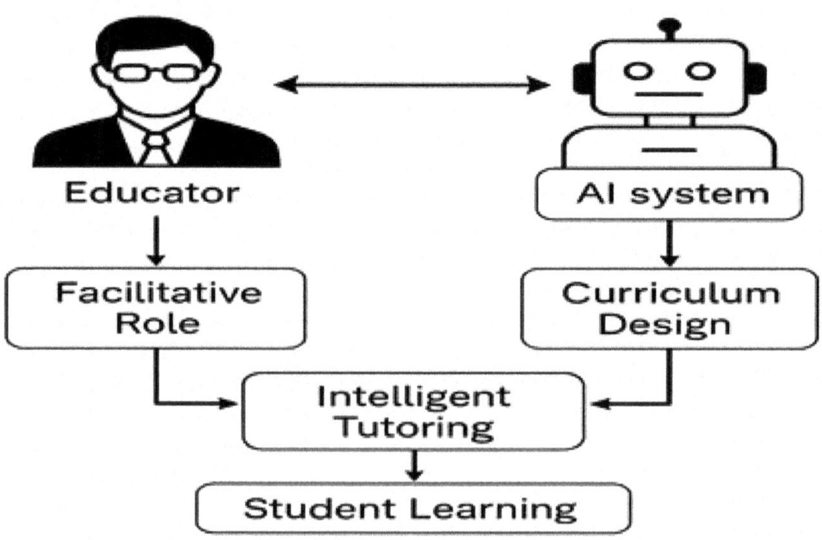

2.4 Global Trends In AI Adoption In Education

Globally the adoption of AI in education has been witnessed at an exponential pace with governments adopting national policies to support the technology, investing in technology development and institution-level reforms to prioritize digital transformations. Countries like China, Singapore, South Korea, India and members of the European Union have included AI literacy, digital competency training and AI aided instruction in their national education strategies (UNESCO, 2023). The global EdTech industry has witnessed unprecedented growth with AI powered startups to come up with various solutions in personalized learning, predictive analytics, automated assessment and generative content. Universities around the globe are launching AI research labs and interdisciplinary programs with the goal of creating the pedagogical, ethical and societal implications surrounding the use of AI technologies in teaching and learning. Time period of 2023 to 2025 sees an exponential adoption of generative AI tools which has changed the way of curriculum design, academic integrity policy and classroom practices. Despite these advancements, concerns revolving around algorithmic bias and data privacy as well as unequal access have remained at the heart of global favourable discourses around AI governance in education.

3. AI-ENHANCED TEACHING AND THE REDEFINITION OF EDUCATOR ROLES (REDUCED & REFINED VERSION)

The integration of artificial intelligence in education has made significant changes in the way teachers design, deliver, and support education. Whereas teaching used to be concerned with transmission of content as its key focus, the new environment made possible because of AI requires educators to orchestrate dynamic learning experiences enabled by automation, adaptive analytics, and intelligent feedback (Holmes et al., 2022). AI now possesses the potential to perform such tasks as personalization of the instruction, generation, tracking student progress, and automation of administrative work, and free up teachers to focus more deeply on higher order pedagogical work. As a result, educators are being seen as increasingly more like architects of learning, guides of ethics, and mentors of data - a role which requires fluency in technology as well as pedagogical and ethical judgment. This section discusses the reconfiguration of the role of teachers including a focus on the design of AI-based environments, personalization of learning paths, integration of adaptive and generative tools, redesign of the curriculum with the help of AI-driven research, and co-design of learning materials with intelligent systems.

3.1 Section A: Educators As Learning Architects

Educators as learning architects are central in the design of the structure and flow of AI-enhanced learning ecosystems. Rather than merely providing deliverables, teachers have become strategic in the integration of artificial intelligence tools with the goal of personalizing instruction, supporting adaptive learning, and giving rise to meaningful human AI interaction (Chou & Chan, 2021).This role comes with an understanding of the role played by algorithms in using analysis of the learner's behaviour to make predictions and recommendations for resources. Teachers have a responsibility to find the right balance between the efficiencies that AI affords with the human-centric practices of making things contextually relevant and emotionally and culturally sensitive. As learning architects, educators build learning environments where the capacities of AI (i.e. real-time analytics, generative content, adaptive pathways, etc.) are used to amplify, not replace human decision-making. This shift has begun to emphasize teacher agency on the issue of shaping technology mediated learning experiences.

Figure 4. Educators as Learning Architects in AI-Supported Learning Environments

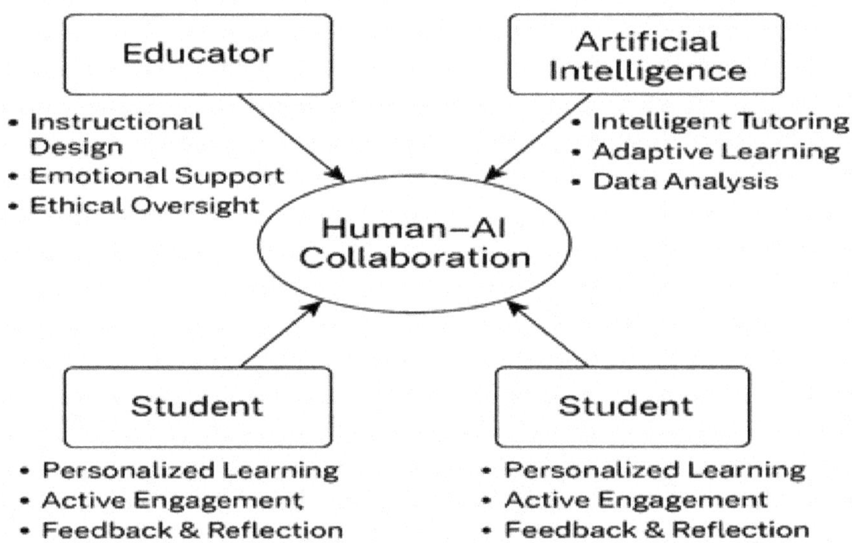

Table 1. Comparison of Traditional vs. AI-Enhanced Teaching Roles

Aspect	Traditional Teaching Role	AI-Enhanced Teaching Role
Instruction Delivery	Teacher-centered lectures	AI-assisted, personalized pathways
Content Creation	Manual lesson design	Generative AI content + teacher refinement
Feedback	Periodic, manual	Real-time AI feedback + teacher explanation
Student Support	Same-level support	Data-driven, individualized interventions
Curriculum Design	Static, uniform	Dynamic, analytics-informed revision
Teacher Focus	Content delivery	Learning architecture + mentoring

3.1.1 Designing AI-Supported Learning Environments

Designing AI-supported learning environments requires considering how to integrate intelligent learning tools to meet curricular objectives while preserving learner autonomy. Educators choose suitable features of AI, decide on student-AI interaction approaches and interpret data generated by the system for instructional improvement (Ifenthaler & Yau, 2020).

Effective environments make use of adaptive system, use the tutoring platforms / analytics dashboards to provide a real-time help and, on the one end, keep the opportunities open for critical thinking and a human connection. Teachers need to be aware of the benefits of AI - for example, pattern recognition, and quick feedback - and compensate for AI's shortfall of context, feeling and culture. This iterative design process is what is meant when we say that learning environments need to be inclusive, engaging and pedagogically purposeful.

3.1.2 Intelligent Learning Pathways And Personalization

AI based personalization can make learning paths adapted to the individual learner needs preferences and performance on a continuous basis. Adaptive systems are systems that are able to change the complexity, pacing and modality of contends in real-time; it is focused on providing more help to struggling learners and make the speed of learners who are advanced (Chassignol et al., 2018). Educators watch over these pathways, so it is fair, there is no algorithmic bias, and is in line with the curriculum standard and personalization. Teachers have not been eliminated but still do have power by validating AI recommendations and finding gaps where AI may not discover them and ensuring a personalized learning that is equitable and developmentally appropriate.

Figure 5. Ethical Responsibilities of Educators in AI-Driven Classrooms

3.1.3 AI Tools For Instructional Design

AI tools can be very useful in streamlining the process of instructional design that generates resources, analyse student performance, and make changes to instruction automatically. Adaptive platforms assist in prescribing the misconception while intelligent tutors give guidance in steps such as human tutoring (VanLehn, 2020). Generative AI technologies - such as ChatGPT, Gemini and DeepSeek - allow to quickly generate lesson plans and assessment and classroom activities (Chen et al., 2023). The benefit of these types of tools is a decrease in the workload of the teacher, but careful monitoring should occur from a pedagogical perspective, to ensure accuracy, eliminate bias, and ensure alignment with learning outcomes. Effective instructional designers combine their AI literacy with pedagogical expertise to develop their engaging and high-quality learning experiences.

3.1.4 Reimagining Curriculum Development With AI Insights

AI-generated analytics offer useful insights into student learning behaviours thus allowing educators to adjust curricula based on actual evidence and not just intuition. Data trends help to identify shared misconceptions, patterns of engagement and gaps in performance and drive changes to the depth and sequencing of content and level of scaffolding (Ifenthaler & Yau, 2020). Generative AI goes one step further and helps to make adaptive instructional materials that can be created to meet the varying needs of learners. While data is useful in guiding redesign, teachers must put data in context with cultural, emotional and developmental considerations so they don't make overly-mechanistic curriculum decisions.

3.1.5 Co-Creation Of Learning Content With AI

AI-enabled co-creation changes the nature of instructional design to be a collaborative process between teachers, students and Artificial Intelligence systems. Generative AI is helping educators create examples, explanations, multimedia content and problem scenarios to allow them to quickly adapt to learner needs (Luckin, 2021). Students also co-create with AI-powered writing tools, brainstorming tools, and simulations that help them to facilitate creativity and critical thinking. Educators look after AI generated content to make sure it is accurate, ethical, and respectful. As such, co-creation requires skills in prompt design, content evaluation, and ethical discernment - which shifts educators from solitary content creators to collaborative designers.

3.2 Section B: Educators As Ethical Guides

As AI gets woven into educational systems, educators are increasingly playing in the role of ethical guides that help learners navigate the issues of fairness, transparency, data privacy and the responsible use of technology. AI tools generative models to predictive analytics - pose complex ethical questions concerning how algorithms make decisions about student learning, whose data they are using, how they influence student learning trajectories (Williamson & Eynon 2020). Because students are interacting with AI without always being aware of its limitations or dangers, it's important that teachers act as critical mediators in the process, opening up new ethical literacy, critical thinking and reflective engagement with AI. In this expanded role, educators ensure academic integrity and foster informed choice-making and the consistency of using technology in line with human values and educational equity. Ethical matters in AI-boosted learning are especially important to those in lower income or marginal positions. Unequal access to in digital infrastructure, potential data bias training, and a failure of language skills in educational AI systems may actually increase existing educational inequalities if left unaddressed. Educators have a pivotal role to ensure equitable AI is used and this is important for contextualizing algorithmic outputs, promoting inclusive education practices and important for building a culture of critical AI literacy for all learners.

Table 2. Ethical Risks of AI in Classrooms and Mitigation Strategies

Ethical Issue	Description	Mitigation Strategy
Algorithmic Bias	AI favors certain groups based on training data	Bias audits, diverse datasets
Privacy Risks	Student data misuse or leakage	Strong data governance policies
Over-Reliance	Students depending blindly on AI	AI literacy training, boundaries for use
Misinformation	Wrong or fabricated AI outputs	Human verification + fact-checking
Transparency Gaps	AI decisions not clearly explained	Explainable AI (XAI) tools

3.2.1 Guiding Students In Responsible AI Use

Responsible AI use requires that students become aware of the capabilities and limitations of AI tools, especially as they come to rely on AI to assist them with writing, problem-solving and creative work. It is important that educators teach learners how to question AI generated content, check for accuracy, identify errors or bias and avoid academic misconduct (Holmes et al., 2022). This guidance involves helping students to understand data privacy - also what kind of information AI systems collect and how it can be used - and to encourage ethical decision-making in digital environments. By encouraging responsible use, teachers ensure that students do not grow up to be unreflectively dependent on the use of automated tools, but grow up to be critical AI literate citizens.

3.2.2 Teaching Digital Citizenship And Algorithmic Awareness

Digital citizenship and algorithmic awareness are now a necessary skill set because students are interacting with algorithmic-driven platforms on a regular basis. Educators must work to teach learners about the role of algorithms in the curation of information, online visibility, and influence on attitude or behaviour (Siemens, 2018). By becoming aware of the ways in which algorithms mirror human choices and have the potential to be biased, students are more engaged in a critical, informed way as digital participants. This is also an instruction in learning how to recognise misinformation, how to evaluate sources, and how to behave ethically online, and gives them a greater power to navigate the digital ecosystems in a responsible way.

3.2.3 Preventing Bias, Misinformation, And Over-Reliance On AI

AI systems can unintentionally perpetuate cultural or linguistic biases based on limitations of training data and generative AI can be used to create misinformation that is assumed to be credible. Educators have to be proactive and help students when they are looking at AI outputs to question their assumptions and understand when algorithms do not provide them with unbiased or accurate results (Chen et al., 2023). Preventing an over-reliance on AI is also important as over-reliance may undermine the critical thinking and creativity of the students. Teachers should set limitations to how AI should be used, encourage independent thinking, and create activity that require human judgment and thinking to ensure that AI is used as an aid - not a substitute! - for learning.

3.2.4 Ethical Dilemmas In AI-Assisted Assessment

AI assisted assessment raises ethical issues of fairness, transparency and student rights. Automated scoring tools may not be able to understand the nuances of language, or other forms of cultural expressions, and may not have the contextual awareness to score complex work (Lu et al., 2021). Educators need to make sure that pupils are aware of the way that the evaluations by AI take place and maintain human oversight to make sure that there are no errors or inequities in grading. Over-reliance of AI in assessment also holds in danger the relationships and motivation parts of feedback. Teachers have a major role to play in making sure that when AI assessment tools are used, they are used in a supplementary way where human judgement is the ultimate authority.

3.2.5 Supporting Students' Socio-Emotional Well-Being In Human–AI Interactions

As students begin to interact more and more with AI tutors, chatbots and adaptive systems, educators need to keep track of the socio-emotional impact of these interactions. AI may be able to pick up on emotional signals, but it is not able to bring the same level of empathy, authenticity, and relate-ability as a human teacher (D'Mello & Graesser, 2021). Some students may rely too much on the AI support and others may feel inadequate when AI beats them in a particular task. Educators need to help build emotional resiliency and encourage the balanced use of AI, and intercede when technology is a source of stress and low self-esteem. By putting the well-being of the students first, teachers can make sure that AI is being used to enhance learning and not to undermine the human connection and emotional growth of students.

4. CHALLENGES AND BARRIERS IN AI-ENHANCED TEACHING

Despite the transformative potential of artificial intelligence in education, there are still a number of challenges and barriers preventing the effective integration of artificial intelligence in education. These challenges have a technological, ethical, institutional and psychological dimension, which underlies the complexity of the integration of AI in different education contexts.

While the promise of AI tools includes efficiency, personalisation and analytics-driven insights, their adoption is associated with adequate infrastructure and policies and appropriate preparedness of teachers which are at various level across education systems around the world (UNESCO, 2023).

Concerns around algorithmic fairness, data privacy, transparency and disempowering teachers with the potential for teacher shortage are also issues which make the process of implementation a more difficult one. Furthermore, the speed of innovation in AI can be more than the school system can keep up, causing uncertainty and resistance in the education system. Understanding these challenges is extremely important in order to create sustainable, equitable and ethical ecosystems of AI-enhanced teaching processes.

4.1 Technical And Infrastructure Limitations

One of the biggest hurdles to AI-enhancing teaching is the existence of technical and infrastructure hurdles, especially in poor educational settings or in developing ones. Effective utilization of AI requires the availability of proper internet connectivity, high performance computing systems, updated hardware and secure data storage infrastructures - which many institutions do not have (Zawacki-Richter et al., 2019). Even in the technologically advanced setups, integration problems with the existing learning management systems, compatibility issues, or a system failure that can interrupt the learning processes can occur with the AI tools. Limited bandwidth can be a challenge faced by real-time analytics platforms and adaptive learning platforms whilst a lack of technical support prevents teachers from becoming comfortable implementing an AI solution. On top of the above, the cost of using AI tools, maintenance, software subscriptions and cybersecurity systems means financial constraints for institutions who have limited budgets to spend on them. These infrastructural inequalities contribute towards the digital divide which makes it impossible to give equitable access to AI enhanced learning opportunities. To overcome these barriers, there needs to be long-term investments in the digital infrastructure, capacity-building programmes and sustainable technological ecosystems within educational systems.

4.2 Bias, Transparency, And Explainability Issues In AI Tools

Bias, transparency and explainability are important issues in the adoption of AI technologies to support teaching and learning. AI systems are trained on large datasets which may have understated cultural, language or socio-economic biases which may result in inequitable consequences in content recommendations, assessments or predictive analytics (Chen et al., 2023). Lack of transparency in algorithmic processes - sometimes called "black-box" AI - makes it difficult for educators to know how decisions are made and, therefore, they may not be able to access fairness or accuracy. The problem of explainability killed trust as teachers and students won't be able to fully understand the reason behind AI's recommendations to follow certain learning paths for students, or the determination of who is "at-risk." Inaccurate or biased output will disproportionately affect marginalized or marginalized groups and contribute to system of inequalities rather than solving them. To overcome these risks, educators must leverage the opportunity to leverage artificial intelligence (AI) tools general AI that apply explainable AI (XAI) principles and focus on algorithmic accountability as well as enabling clear documentation of data sources and decision-making mechanisms. Ethical oversight and teacher training in algorithmic literacy is important in ensuring the use of AI is used to aid equitable learning.

4.3 Teacher Digital Literacy Gaps

Teacher digital literacy gaps are a significant barrier to the use of AI in education, as it takes more than simply knowing how to use technology effectively in the classroom to use AI effectively - including deeper skills of understanding data interpretation, knowing how algorithms work, and being able to use technology responsibly. Many educators feel that they are not well-equipped to incorporate AI tools into their teaching practices because they haven't been properly trained, have not been exposed to them, or are afraid of the technological complexity involved (Holmes et al., 2022). Some teachers are challenged with how to take AI-generated analytics and use it to customise adaptive learning platforms, or assess the accuracy and appropriateness of AI-generated content. Professional development initiatives often do not offer the kind of sustained hands-on training required to build confidence and expertise in AI literacy. As a result, AI adoption is uneven, with technologically proficient teachers adopting AI to a great extent, while others avoid it entirely. Teacher readiness is critical because educators are the mediators between AI systems and the students, without a certain level of digital literacy they are unable to guarantee meaningful, ethical and pedagogical integration. Bridging the gaps in digital literacy needs comprehensive training programs, ongoing support, and policies that focus on empowering teachers rather than mandating technological solutions.

4.4 Privacy, Ethics, And Security Concerns

Privacy, ethics and security issues are major challenges in AI enhanced teaching, as AI systems tend to gather large amounts of data that are related to student behaviour, performance, identity and interactions. The storage, processing and sharing of this sensitive data raises questions about student consent, ownership of data, and the potential misuse. (Williamson & Eynon, 2020) Security vulnerabilities - data breaches, unauthorized access, and cyberattacks are all dangerous for learners and institutions. Ethical concerns arise when AI tools use surveillance-like monitoring features which may be compromising student autonomy or may be psychologically discomforting. In addition, unclear policies with regard to data retention, third party access and commercial use of student data create confusion and risk to institutional decision-making. Educators have the responsibility to make sure that they are in line with the legal frameworks (GDPR, COPPA and national data protection laws) and teach tests how to safely and ethically deal with the use of AI tools. Building transparent data governance systems and measures are necessary, and implementing robust cybersecurity measures can be key to peace of mind in addressing these concerns and paving the way to also ensure AI is ethically trained with proper ethics education.

4.5 Institutional, Policy, And Regulatory Challenges

Institutional, policy and regulatory issues have a major impact on the rate and success of AI adoption within education. Many institutions have failed to create large scale AI strategies, which leads to conflicting AI implementation, and teacher responsibilities, ethics, data management, and expectations for instruction (Redecker, 2020). Policymakers find it difficult to keep pace with the pace of development of AI technologies, resulting in outdated or incomplete regulations which have failed to address new challenges such as misuse of generative AI technologies, automated decision making, and algorithmic accountability.

Institutional leadership may also find it difficult to find a balance between innovation and prudence as AI tools are often commercial and the policies around data and technical features may not find a congruence with the values of education. Resistance to change, fear of financial investment and bureaucratic processes to decide on the change are additional delays to innovation. In order to address these issues, institutions need to create clear AI governance frameworks, find a balance between the adoption of technology and pedagogical objectives, and create structures of accountability that will ensure that learners are protected while allow for meaningful innovation.

4.6 Psychological And Professional Concerns (Job Displacement Fears, Autonomy Loss)

Psychological and professional issues by the educational community, mostly fear of job replacement and loss of professional freedom, is their biggest hurdle when integrating AI.

As AI systems take over things like grading and generating content and providing feedback on analytics, some teachers have been concerned about the extent to which their job as educators will be reduced and even replaced by technology (Holstein et al., 2020). Although the existing research is consistent with the idea that it is more likely that AI will augment teachers than replace them, the way that the threat is perceived can lead to resistance, anxiety and scepticism. Loss of autonomy is another problem as educators are potentially pressured to carry out the algorithmic way of suggestions or standardized analytics frameworks that limit creative and context-sensitive teaching methodologies. Such limitations kill the agency of teachers and can lead to a reduction in job satisfaction.

In addition, there is issues psychological, with the fear of failure technology, fear of having their data monitored permanently and ignorance of the ethical considerations in environments mediated by AI. Addressing these concerns will require clear communication about the supportive role that AI plays, opportunity for educator participation in AI design processes, and institutional policies and actions that will promote the autonomy of the teacher, promote AI literacy and confidence. If AI-driven recommendations are blindly followed, there is a risk of limiting the ability of educators to exercise their pedagogical autonomy and this reminds us of the importance of preserving the role of human judgment as the ultimate arbitrator of instruction decisions.

5. PEDAGOGICAL FRAMEWORKS FOR AI-ENHANCED TEACHING

Pedagogical frameworks for A.I. enhanced teaching is a method to introduce artificial intelligence to learning environments in meaningful and ethical ways, in a way that makes pedagogical sense as well. As AI systems become a part of how teaching is done, how feedback is given and how learners are engaged, educators are in need of clear models to guide how technology can aide in the teaching process and not cannibalize it. These frameworks are a roadmap of connecting the AI capabilities with the already set pedagogical principles in such a way that innovation can be used to support human development and educational equity (Holmes et al., 2022). By citing roles and processes; and ethical considerations and competences, such frameworks prepare the teachers to deal with the complexities of AI enhanced learning ecosystem. This section describes five basic pedagogical models--AI augmented pedagogy, human-AI collaborative learning, data-informed teaching, ethical guidance for AI integration and competency development for AI era educators--that all represent different points of view on how teaching can change in light of technological transformation.

Table 3. AI-Enhanced Pedagogical Frameworks and Their Key Components

Framework	Core Elements	Teacher Responsibilities
AI-Augmented Pedagogy	Automation + personalization	Guide, interpret, refine AI outputs
Human–AI Collaboration	Shared human–AI tasks	Maintain oversight + emotional support
Data-Informed Cycle	Analytics-driven decisions	Interpret data, act, reflect
Ethical Guidance Model	Fairness, transparency, privacy	Teach AI ethics, ensure compliance
Competency Framework	AI literacy, data skills	Continuous professional development

5.1 AI-Augmented Pedagogy Model

The AI-augmented pedagogy model is focused to the use of artificial intelligence as a supportive tool that enhances instruction capabilities of educators and not as a substitute for a human expertise. In this model, for example, AI systems are used to carry out tasks such as providing personalized feedback to learners, analysing the engagement of learners, automating administrative tasks, and recommending instructional resources to the teacher, thereby allowing the teacher to focus on higher-level pedagogical roles such as creative lesson design, mentorship and relationship-building (Chen et al., 2023). AI augmentation is very similar to both constructivist and socio-cultural theories, owing to the way it offers learners personalized scaffolding and real-time support to improve autonomy and inquiry-based learning experiences. The model requires educators to evaluate the output of AI in a critical manner, contextualize algorithmic insights, and integrate AI support in a manner that is consistent with the learning objectives. Ultimately, AI-augmented pedagogy looks at AI as a complementary source that helps to improve the quality, efficiency, and personalization of instruction keeping teachers at the core of creating human-centered educational experiences.

5.2 Human–AI Collaborative Learning Framework

The human-AI collaborative learning framework represents a learning process as a cooperative interaction between learners, educators, and AI systems based on dynamic interactions between them. In this framework the role of AI tools is to assist students (e.g., providing adaptive feedback, generating examples, supporting inquiry, and facilitating practice), while the role of teachers is to provide emotional support, ethical judgment, understanding of the context and rich pedagogical insight (Holstein et al., 2020). Rather than as an AI replacing humans, the framework emphasizes what AI is best at, such as data processing and pattern recognition, and teachers are placed as important architects who lead the collaboration and ensure that it is impactful. Students, meanwhile, take an active part by engaging with human and non-human sources of knowledge in critical thinking and foster the hybrid set of competencies, including critical AI literacy, and collaborative problem-solving skills. The framework advocates for transparency, conversations and collaboration to make sure that AI systems are used with human oversight and support rather than make educational decisions without human oversight. Through nurturing the balanced relationship between human cognition and computational intelligence, human-AI collaborative learning framework encourages depth of understanding, creativity and ethical awareness.

5.3 Data-Informed Teaching Cycle

The data-informed teaching cycle is a structured model that has been introduced for the integration of the learning analytics in pedagogic decision making. This framework is a continuous process of data collection, interpretation, action, and reflection in order for teachers to be able to use real-time insights to make their teaching more effective (Slade & Prinsloo, 2019). In the first phase, Artificial Intelligence (AI) systems gather data, that is related to student engagement pattern and performance and behavioural pattern using the digital learning platforms. The second phase is the teacher interpretation of analytics dash boards to determine trends, gaps and opportunities for intervention. In the third phase, educators use precisely targeted instructional strategies to address the specific needs of a student based upon evidence of his or her interpretation of the data (e.g. differentiated instruction, adaptive assignments or supplemental scaffolding). The cycle is closed with the reflection in which the teachers think about the effect of these types of interventions, and they do the right modifications to their approaches. This iterative model is to make sure that data is used as a supportive tool for improving learning outcomes instead of using it as a prescriptive mechanism. The key to successful implementation is that teachers must have competence in data literacy, knowledge of algorithms, and ethical data utilization in order to ensure that educational data analytics are able to improve human judgement and differentiated instruction.

Figure 6. Data-Informed Teaching Cycle Using AI Analytics

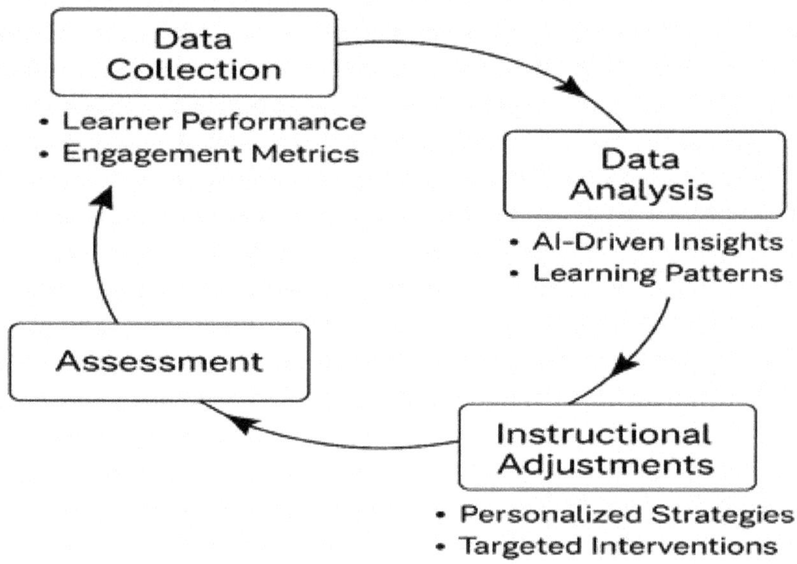

5.4 Ethical Guidance Model For AI Integration

The ethical guidance model for AI integration is a framework to ensure the use of AI technologies in a responsible, transparent and ethical way that promotes human and fairness. This model is founded on four key principles: Transparency, accountability, equity & student well-being (Williamson & Eynon, 2020). Transparency is a demand that educators should communicate effectively in terms of how AI tool's function, what data they are taking as well as how decisions are being made. Accountability helps to ensure that teachers keep watch and step in when the AI outputs are seen to be biased, misleading or harmful. Equity is about the importance of avoiding algorithmic discrimination and ensuring that AI tools are used by all learners irrespective of their socio-economic, cultural or linguistic background. The last principle - student well-being - suggests the importance of ensuring that AI is used to support rather than undermine learners in their emotional, cognitive and social development. Educators using this model are good stewards of ethics, they are guiding their students to be responsible in their engagement with AI, they are teaching algorithmic literacy and they are encouraging critical thinking. By considering ethical aspects of AI-enhanced instruction in the design and application of AI-enhanced instruction, the model helps to ensure that innovation is in line with educational values and societal expectations.

5.5 Competency Framework For AI-Era Teachers

Competency framework for teachers, for the artificial intelligence era: competency frameworks are narrow about what teachers need to know, be able to do, and be able to do about teaching in data-rich, artificial intelligence mediated environments. These competencies have been the understanding of AI literacy, ability to interpret data, understanding digital ethics, ability to design instruction that is adaptive to students and the ability to work with AI tools while maintaining the professional autonomy (Holmes et al, 2022). AI literacy helps teachers to be mindful of how algorithms work, how you assess AI generated content, and how to make informed decisions about the use of technology. Data interpretation skills allow educators to identify learning needs correctly and determine student progress and conduct evidence-based interventions. Ethical competencies are privacy of students & responsible AI usage to ensure that teachers are fair. Additionally, educators must be flexible, creative, and adaptable in their approach to teaching and learning, and to have the ability to adapt to the ever-changing technological landscape. As AI continues to develop, the role of teachers will increase as it will include teaching students how to be literate with AI, how to be a mentor in human-AI hybrid work and how to model ethical engagement with digital systems. This competency framework advises ongoing professional development and institutional support to ensure that educators are adequately prepared to face the challenges and opportunities that come with the AI-enhanced teaching approach.

Table 4. Essential Teacher Competencies for AI-Enhanced Education

Competency Area	Description	Examples of Required Skills
AI Literacy	Understanding how AI systems work and how to use them meaningfully in education.	Basic ML concepts, prompt design, evaluating AI outputs.
Data Literacy	Ability to interpret learning analytics and student data for pedagogical decisions.	Reading dashboards, identifying trends, ethical data use.
Pedagogical Design with AI	Integrating AI tools into instructional strategies effectively.	Designing AI-supported lessons, adaptive activities, blended AI-human learning tasks.
Ethical & Responsible AI Use	Ensuring fair, transparent, and safe AI use in the classroom.	Bias detection, privacy awareness, teaching AI ethics.

continued on following page

Table 4. Continued

Competency Area	Description	Examples of Required Skills
Human–AI Collaboration Skills	Working with AI as a co-teacher while maintaining human judgment and empathy.	Balancing automation with human oversight, socio-emotional support.
Digital Creativity & Innovation	Using generative AI and digital tools to create engaging learning materials.	Content creation, simulations, scenario design, multimedia integration.
Continuous Professional Development	Staying updated with evolving AI tools and pedagogical practices.	Attending AI workshops, learning new tools, reflective practice.

6. PROPOSED SOLUTIONS AND BEST PRACTICES

Doing so requires a whole set of solutions and good practice for pedagogy, targeted to educational preparedness, ethical design, policy congruence, and pedagogical innovation. As A.I tools are becoming more and more deeply entrenched within the classroom context, there is a growing need for strategic guidance that ensures that technology is used to complement and not disrupt teaching and learning processes. (Holmes et al., 2022). AI Implementation heavily relies on educators being enabled with AI literacy, transparent and accountable systems, educational policies securing and protecting learners and ensuring academic integrity/pedagogical strategies ensuring that the capabilities of AI are fused with the established learning theories. Global case studies show successful implementation of AI, showing how well thought implementation can promote personalization, accessibility, and engagement of learners. These solutions taken together will ensure that AI will contribute positively to the education and continue to keep human decision-making and ethical judgement at the heart of the education.

6.1 Capacity Building And AI Literacy For Educators

Capacity building and A.I. literacy are the building blocks that make it easier for the teachers to integrate A.I. in teaching practices. Educators need to not only have technical skills, but conceptual knowledge of how algorithms work, what sort of data is being processed and how data generated by AI should be interpreted and used. Professional development programs that deal with AI literacy with content on data analytics, generative AI, algorithmic bias and ethics are critical to enable educators to approach AI systems with confidence. (Chen et al., 2023). Workshops, certification courses, mentorship models, and hands-on training environments that provide meaningful opportunities for teachers to build-up of necessary expertise to offer a critical look and make informed decisions to use AI tools in the classroom environments. AI literacy also means encouraging reflective practices where educators are able to think critically about when or how best to use AI and any limitations and dangers to using AI. Capacity building helps to reduce anxiety as a teacher, increases the rate of adoption and ensures that educators are holding onto agency while using AI as a supportive tool. Ultimately, investment in the capacity of teachers is the best approach in terms of sustainable and responsible integration of AI.

6.2 Designing Ethical And Transparent AI Systems

Designing ethical and transparent AI systems is important when attempting to ensure fairness and accountability and create student trust in AI-enhanced learning environments. Ethical design implies that developers and educational institutions pay attention to factors such as explainability, data protection and parity of algorithmic behaviour when developing and deploying AI tools. Transparency refers to the clarity of the process of AI systems, of how they make their decisions, of what data is gathered and how their outputs are to be interpreted (Williamson & Eynon, 2020). Explainable AI (XAI) models are useful to the educator/student to understand why the recommendations and predictions and automated evaluations are made so that there is less uncertainty and a higher level of trust is built. Ethical AI design also involves continuous auditing for biases for any disproportionate effect that may exist with respect to groups of students, in order to ensure that these are detected and addressed. Furthermore, stakeholder engagement consisting of teachers, policymakers, parents and learners, is crucial in the development and implementation phases in order to ensure that solutions involving AI will reflect diversity of needs and values. Through open and ethical design practices, educational institutions can provide safe, equitable and accountable educational AI learning environments.

6.3 Policy Guidelines For Responsible Classroom AI

Effective policy guidelines are required to ensure a responsible use of AI in the classroom, establish boundaries, protect and establish expectations for both teachers and students. Policies need to address such core issues as data privacy, informed consent, algorithmic accountability, academic integrity and acceptable AI use in learning activities (UNESCO, 2023). Clear guidelines help educators to understand what they can integrate AI tools while adhering to ethical standards and legal frameworks of the system acknowledging both the misuse and safeguarding their students' rights.

Policies should detail the best practices for managing student data, controls around the use of generative AI in assessments and transparency in the use of AI-based assessments. Institutional AI policies should be in line with national data protection legislation and international ethical considerations to ensure compliance and protect the learners from undue technological risks. Regular updates to the policy are required to cope with fast-changing capabilities of AI. Well-defined guidelines help educators make informed decisions, ensure less ambiguity and facilitate safe, equitable AI deployment across educational settings.

6.4 Integrating AI With Bloom's Taxonomy And Constructivist Strategies

Assessment can be challenging - Assessment redesign has become one of the most pressing issues facing AI enhanced education not least because of the widespread adoption of generative AI tools; as well as concerns about authorship and academic integrity. Integrating AI with Bloom's Taxonomy and constructivist strategies, adding pedagogical richness by helping to synchronise the capabilities of AI with frameworks of learning well established. AI tools can be used to support lower order thinking skills such as remembering and understanding by automating retrieval practice, generating summaries, and providing immediate explanations. More importantly, AI can also support higher-order thinking skills (such as analysing, evaluating and creating) using activities related to simulation, problem-solving, scenario generation, and collaboration with generative AI models (Holmes et al., 2022). When used with the constructivist approaches, AI allows for learner autonomy by providing exploration, experimentation, and individual scaffolding. For instance, intelligent tutoring systems can facilitate learners to build knowledge through guided discovery, while generative AI makes it possible for learners to co-create artifacts to facilitate creative problem-solving. Educators have an important role to play in orchestrating these experiences to ensure that AI usage is aligned with learning goals and promotes deep and meaningful cognitive engagement. By combining AI and Bloom's and constructivist principles, it is possible for teachers to build dynamic and learner-centered environments that help to foster both foundational and advanced competencies.

6.5 Case Studies Of Effective AI-Enhanced Teaching (Global Examples)

The global case studies presented below are aimed at giving empirical grounding to the conceptual framework in this chapter and to provide evidence of the implementation of AI-enhanced teaching practices in practice in education. Global case studies show the success of teaching with the aid of AI, when done with well-thought-through design, suitable training and ethics. In Singapore, AI-enabled personalized learning platforms have been successfully introduced in secondary schools, which allows teachers to offer differentiated classes and timely interventions based on real-time analytics (Siemens, 2018). In the United States, universities like Arizona State University employ AI chatbots to help first-year students with academic guidance, thereby improving the retention rates and alleviating the bottlenecks while advising the students. China's investments in AI-driven tutoring and adaptive learning technologies that have been in place for years have led to massive-scale implementation of intelligent systems to improve mathematics and language learning outcomes (Chen et al., 2023). In Finland, teachers are collaborating with developers of AI to co-create curriculum-aligned generative AI tools, enhance the role of educators as co-designers rather than passive adopters. These are global examples, which point out that successful implementation of AI is a matter of contextual adaption, teacher training, ethical governance and human-centred design. When these things come together, the achievement of equity, engagement and learner achievement is boosted through AI enhanced teaching.

7. CASE STUDIES AND PRACTICAL IMPLEMENTATIONS

Case studies from a range of educational contexts across the globe provide valuable lessons concerning how AI technologies can be successfully implemented in order to enhance teaching and personalization and provide support for student success. These are real-life examples that prove just how successful AI adoption is in conjunction with pedagogical objectives, preparedness at an institutional level and teacher training and guidelines regarding ethics (Holmes et al, 2022).

By studying real-world implementations, educators can get an understanding of how AI tools work in real-world settings, as well as how students react to interactions with AI, as well as the challenges which need to be addressed in order to keep the integration going long-term.

This section focuses some of the practical case studies that are relevant to AI Personalization, Generative AI Classroom usage, Predictive analysis for Student Support, Ethical AI Teaching modules and Teacher Training innovations that encourage the pedagogy of AI.

Table 5. Global Examples of AI-Enhanced Teaching Practices

Country	AI Use Case	Educational Impact
Singapore	Adaptive learning systems	Improved personalization, mastery learning
USA (ASU)	AI chatbots for student advising	Increased retention, faster support
China	Intelligent tutoring systems	Higher test performance, math/language gains
Finland	Teacher–AI curriculum co-design	Stronger teacher agency, better alignment
India	Predictive analytics for at-risk students	Early intervention and improved outcomes

7.1 AI-Driven Personalization In Higher Education

AI driven personalization in higher education has shown great results in improving student engagement, retention and learning outcomes. One company stands out, in particular, the implementation of adaptive learning programs, ALEKS, and Cog Books by Arizona State University, which tailor instruction based on individual student performance and patterns of mastery (Siemens, 2018). These systems dynamically adjust the sequence and difficulty of learning tasks and allow students to progress through at their own pace and receive supports in areas of difficulty. In the United Kingdom, the Open University is using AI-powered analytics dashboards that can enable faculty to track learner behaviour, identify at-risk students, and step in to provide personalised academic guidance as soon as possible (Ifenthaler & Yau, 2020). Several Asian universities - including those in Singapore and South Korea - have adopted AI tutors to assist with mathematics and engineering courses to show a measurable improvement in conceptual understanding and exam performance. These case studies are example of how a personalized approach of AI promotes equity by providing personalized support that allows students with diverse backgrounds and abilities to succeed in higher education.

7.2 Classroom Applications Using Chatgpt, Gpt-4/5, Deepseek, Gemini, Etc.

Classroom applications utilizing generative AI tools like ChatGPT, GPT-4/5, DeepSeek, Gemini, and Claude have grown quickly and have changed the way students interact with content, finish assignments and develop academic skills. Teachers have employed ChatGPT in aiding brainstorming, writing scaffolds, automated feedback, vocabulary development and explanation of complex concepts in different disciplines (Chen et al., 2023). In the context of education of STEM students use GPT-based models to debug code, visualize mathematical concepts and generate simulations to enhance understanding. In language learning scenarios, AI chatbots act as conversational partners that offer instant corrections and adaptive dialogues that boost fluency and confidence. DeepSeek and Gemini models are embedded in inquiry-based learning activities, where students jointly develop research questions, analyse real-world data sets, or compare viewpoints across sources. Educators using generative AI focus on the importance of critical evaluation, where students should be required to check for accuracy in AI-generated materials, spot inaccuracies, and make corrections to AI-generated outputs to show that genuine learning has taken place. These uses are the educational value of generative AI and the importance of ethics and teacher management.

7.3 Use Of Predictive Analytics For Student Success

Predictive analytics has developed as a powerful tool to aid student achievement by supporting the early detection of academic issues and support the timely intervention of these issues. Institutions such as Georgia State University have taken the lead and are using predictive models to identify students who could potentially drop or fail a course by examining attendance, assignment submissions, LMS interactions and historical performance (Holstein et al., 2020). These systems generate warnings to encourage academic advisors and faculty to intervene in some way either through personalised contact outreach to students, followed by tutoring recommendations, or modifications of course design. Similar initiatives in Australia and Europe take scoring risk to the next level using AI to better retention rates and make decisions on student support services. In the education of K-12 students, predictive analytics platforms help educators monitor patterns of classroom participation, and also detect changes in behavior and personalize instruction based on data-driven insights. Although effective, these systems require careful implementation to ensure that they do not result in some form of bias that will disproportionately categorise learners who are from marginal groups. Effective application of predictive analytics is a powerful example of a way an AI solution can promote equity and support student outcomes if the solution is paired with human decision-making and the ethical consideration.

7.4 Ethical-AI Teaching Modules In University Programs

Universities across the world are starting to incorporate ethical-AI teaching modules onto their curriculum to ensure their students understand the societal, legal and ethical implications of AI technologies. We see that institutions like Stanford University, MIT and the University of Edinburgh, have launched interdisciplinary classes on algorithmic transparency, AI fairness, data privacy and responsible innovation (Williamson and Eynon, 2020). These modules encourage students to critically examine the biases that are built in to AI systems, examine case studies of how algorithms can cause harm, and suggest frameworks for the ethical design of these systems. In the case of India and Singapore, engineering and teacher education courses include ethics of AI in the foundation course to prepare the future professionals to make decisions mediated through technology. Courses often include a mix of both theoretical discussion and practical exercises where students go through the audit of the models of artificial intelligence or test for fairness or redesign algorithms to improve fairness. The use of ethical-AI modules helps to ensure that graduates enter the workforce with a high level of moral reasoning and a deep understanding of the responsibility of technology in addressing the increasing need for ethical literacy in fields that use AI.

7.5 Teacher Training Models For AI Pedagogy

Teacher training models for artificial intelligence pedagogy have become an integral part of educational reform practices providing educators with the knowledge and skills to effectively and responsibly incorporate AI into teaching practices. A number of countries - including Finland, Singapore and the United Arab Emirates - have developed national programs to educate teachers about AI literacy, algorithmic awareness, data interpretation and curriculum design augmented by AI tools (Holmes et al., 2022). These programs are normally designed to use combined blended learning formats of both online modules and practical workshops, professional learning communities and mentorship from AI experts. Universities that have teacher education programs continue to incorporate AI-based pedagogy courses that prepare future teachers to employ adaptive learning platforms, generative AI applications and analytics dashboards in their classrooms. Pilot studies indicate that teachers who are trained in AI report being more confident, more effective in their instruction, and more likely to engage in AI tools as a result of their AI training. These training models highlight the importance of continuous professional development aesthetics, ensuring that serving to teachers continue to be included in addition to being informative and empowered to relish within the ever-website of AI improvement.

8. FUTURE RESEARCH DIRECTIONS

Future research in AI in education will have to deal with the pedagogical, ethical, psychological, and systems knowledge to ensure artificial intelligence augments and not disrupt human-centred learning. As the capabilities of AI increase, particularly in the areas of generative modelling, cognitive simulation, predictive analytics and emotional sensing, researchers will need to ponder the ways in which these technologies (or generative intelligence) might be meaningfully and responsibly incorporated into instructional practices (Holmes et al., 2022). Key areas of inquiry include how AI can be used to support holistic learning, how emotion-aware and neuro-symbolic models of AI can be developed, what the long-term implications are of AI tutors, how governance frameworks can be strengthened, and how global teacher competency standards can be established. These directions are important for developing equitable, open, and effective educational ecosystems based on AI.

8.1 AI For Holistic Learning And Cognitive Modeling

AI for holistic learning and cognitive modelling is an up-and-coming frontier in which AI systems do not only measure academic performance, but support socio-emotional, creative, and metacognitive development. Current adaptive learning tools are mostly focused on cognitive tasks, like memory, problem-solving, and conceptual understanding, but it is possible that the next AI models incorporate affective data and motivational data to provide more complete learner profiles (D'Mello & Graesser, 2021).

Research is needed to examine how AI can support executive functioning, curiosity, resilience, creativity and collaboration all of which are important skills for success in the twenty-first century. Cognitive modelling provides opportunities to simulate how learners make sense of concepts, decisions, or mental models and educators can use this to design specific intervention strategies to support deeper learning. Future research should also focus on the way in which a combination of AI findings and human observations enhances accuracy and personalization without losing the learner's autonomy or privacy.

8.2 Emotion-Aware And Neuro-Symbolic AI In Teaching

Emotion-aware and neuro-symbolic AI are promising directions to pave the way for better teaching and learning via better, more interpretable, and human-aligned AI systems. Emotion-aware AI: The use of affective computing methods to analyse the emotional state of learners and respond accordingly, potentially making learning in digital environments more empathetic and supportive. However, there are ethical dangers of surveillance, emotional manipulation, and data privacy that need to be carefully investigated. Neuro-symbolic AI - which combine pattern recognition capabilities of neural networks with the symbolic aspect of reasoning - offers the potential of more transparent, explainable and pedagogical AI systems. Integrating these approaches into education may enable artificial intelligence (AI) models to better integrate student reasoning, provide guidance that is contextual, and avoid the "black box" problem that breeds distrust in generative and predictive artificial intelligence (AI) tools. Future research needs to address the practical, ethical and technical implications of the deployment of such models in actual classrooms by requiring them to augment rather than constrain teacher autonomy and student freedom.

8.3 AI Tutors Vs. Human Teachers: Long-Term Impacts

The comparison of AI tutors and human teachers raises some important questions about the future of teaching, classroom, and learner development. While AI tutors have demonstrated impressive abilities in providing personalized feedback, continuous assessment and adaptive instruction, they are deficient in emotional intelligence, ethical judgement and cultural responsiveness, all of which play a central role in human teaching (Holstein et al. 2020). Long-term studies are required to focus on the impact of dependency on the use of AI tutors on student motivation, creativity, empathy, and social skills. Questions also remain as to whether AI-supported learning enhances or reduces the capacity of learners to self-regulate, think critically and feel intrinsically motivated. Additionally, the changing roles of teachers in AI mediated environments need to be studied in the future to determine whether AI tools increase educator agency or contribute to deskilling educators or professional dependency. Comparative longitudinal studies would help identify the best models of hybridity where the AI tutors can support but not substitute human instruction to retain the essential human dimensions of education.

8.4 Policy, Governance, And Ethical Framework Evolution

As AI becomes increasingly entrenched in education systems around the world, it is important to have robust policies, governance and ethical frameworks in place in order to manage the risks, ensure fairness and guide responsible innovation. Current regulatory structures do not keep pace and there are new domains that require thorough consideration, such as algorithmic accountability, AI transparency, data governance and learner protection (Williamson & Eynon, 2020). Future research needs to consider the extent to which educational policies can develop in such a way that balances innovation and safety with supporting institutional autonomy and ethical commitments. Topics that need to be explored further include governance models for AI procurement, policies for generative AI use in work at the University and algorithmic auditing frameworks and protection of vulnerable learners from algorithmic harm. Comparative international studies may also identify best practices across countries from which globally relevant governance strategies may be developed. Ethical frameworks will have to change in line with technological developments, and ensure that AI will improve learning opportunities and not jeopardise student rights, privacy or well-being.

8.5 Global Standards For AI-Enhanced Teacher Competencies

Developing global standards of AI enhanced teacher competencies is very important as AI literacy is becoming an integral part of modern teaching. While several national education systems have launched AI training initiatives, there is little agreement on the types of competencies that educators need to use AI effectively, ethically and confidently (Holmes et al, 2022). Future research should work on developing universal frameworks to define competencies in areas such as an understanding of algorithms, data literacy, AI ethics, instructional design with AI tools, interpretive judgment and human-AI collaboration. These standards must be flexible in the cultural and institutional contexts, as they would be conducive to enabling an equal adoption of AI-enhanced pedagogy worldwide. Additionally, empirical studies are needed to assess the extent to which teacher preparation programs incorporate AI competencies, the learning and implementation of AI knowledge and skills by teachers, and the most suitable professional development models to support continuous learning. The development of global standards will help ensure that educators are at the heart of AI-enhanced education and empowered with the skills and values they need to help guide their students into an increasingly AI-driven world.

CONCLUSION

The explosive development of artificial intelligence has brought about the profound change in the educational landscape of the world as a whole and the role and professional identity of teachers has been redefined. Rather than replacing educators, AI augments teaching, with its two key capabilities: when it automated routine tasks, generated teaching content, analysed data in real-time and contributed towards a highly personalized learning experience. These capabilities imply that educators will need to assume new roles as learning architects who are responsible for the design of new environments integrated with AI, as ethical guides who are responsible for promoting the responsible use of technology, and as data-driven mentors who are responsible for interpretation analytics to be used to make instructional decisions. Such changing roles implies the new need for professional preparedness and ethical literacy and reflective judgement for AI mediated educational circumstances. Despite its promise, the integration of AI comes with a number of challenges like potential infrastructural gaps, algorithmic bias issues, transparency issues or data privacy issues, and teacher apprehension as it relates to autonomy and job security. To unpack these complexities, it's necessary to take action to coordinate efforts from policymakers, institutions and educators in line with ethical frameworks, instead of relying on under-structured governance frameworks, opacity of AI systems and continuous teacher training. Global case studies show that if implemented responsibly, AI can help increase student engagement, learning outcomes and instructional efficiency. Looking towards the future, future research should be focused around holistic learning, emotional intelligence, cognitive modelling and equitable access in order to ensure that AI will benefit all learners. However, the long-term success of AI-enhanced education will hinge on how well ethical governance considerations, teacher agency considerations, and addressing equity issues are built into success with AI. Without the above safeguards, AI stands to overexert arbitrary inequalities and not alter the learning in inclusive and meaningful ways. Ultimately, it is not about creating AI-driven classrooms, but AI-augmented ecosystems, in which humans increased potential and augmented the learning experience with technology. By embracing innovation and holding on to values of education, educators can serve as a force in identifying the transformation towards an inclusive, ethical and human-centred future of learning.

REFERENCES

Chassignol, M., Khoroshavina, A., Klimova, A., & Bilyatdinova, A. (2018). Artificial Intelligence trends in education. *Procedia Computer Science*, *136*, 16–24. DOI: 10.1016/j.procs.2018.08.233

Chen, X., Zou, D., & Xie, H. (2023). Implications of ChatGPT and generative AI for education. *Computers in Human Behavior*, *145*, 107730.

Chou, P. N., & Chan, T. W. (2021). Designing AI-enhanced learning environments. *Educational Technology Research and Development*, *69*(4), 1817–1838.

D'Mello, S. K., & Graesser, A. (2021). Automatic analysis of learners' emotions. *Annual Review of Psychology*, *72*, 589–618.

Downes, S. (2022). Connectivism in 2022: Extending learning networks. *Journal of Online Learning Research*, *8*(1), 33–48.

Holmes, W., Bialik, M., & Fadel, C. (2022). *Artificial intelligence in education: Promises and implications*. Center for Curriculum Redesign.

Holstein, K., McLaren, B. M., & Aleven, V. (2020). Human–AI collaborative teaching. *International Journal of Artificial Intelligence in Education*, *30*(2), 215–240.

Ifenthaler, D., & Yau, J. Y. K. (2020). Ethical and privacy considerations in learning analytics. *Educational Technology Research and Development*, *68*(1), 49–74.

Jonassen, D. (2018). Revisiting constructivist learning in digital environments. *Educational Technology Research and Development*, *66*(4), 785–801.

Koehler, M. J., & Mishra, P. (2020). TPACK and teacher knowledge in AI classrooms. *Journal of Digital Learning in Teacher Education*, *36*(2), 74–87.

Lu, X., Li, Y., & Li, X. (2021). Automatic scoring and assessment using AI. *Computers & Education*, *166*, 104–121.

Luckin, R. (2021). Machine learning and human intelligence. *British Journal of Educational Technology*, *52*(5), 1935–1955.

Means, B., Peters, V., & Zheng, Y. (2020). Learning online and the implications for teacher roles. *Review of Research in Education*, *44*(1), 99–127.

Redecker, C. (2020). AI and the future of teaching. *The Internet and Higher Education*, *47*, 100759.

Siemens, G. (2018). Learning in networks and AI-mediated systems. *Educational Technology*, *58*(5), 26–32.

Slade, S., & Prinsloo, P. (2019). Student data and analytics ethics. *British Journal of Educational Technology*, *50*(3), 1034–1048.

UNESCO. (2023). *Guidance for AI in Education: Policy and Ethics*. UNESCO.

VanLehn, K. (2020). Advances in intelligent tutoring systems. *International Journal of Artificial Intelligence in Education*, *30*(1), 19–43.

Williamson, B., & Eynon, R. (2020). Datafication, AI, and education: Critical concerns. *Learning, Media and Technology*, *45*(3), 202–216.

Zawacki-Richter, O., Marín, V. I., Bond, M., & Gouverneur, F. (2019). Systematic review of AI in higher education. *International Journal of Educational Technology in Higher Education*, *16*(1), 39–66. DOI: 10.1186/s41239-019-0171-0

Chapter 8
The Student as Prompt Engineer:
Culturing Precision, Intentionality, and Metacognition

Jagneet Kour
http://orcid.org/0009-0003-0341-3636
Akal University Talwandi Sabo, India

Sukhwinder Kaur
http://orcid.org/0009-0009-6288-0051
Eternal University, India

Raino Bhatia
http://orcid.org/0000-0002-5379-3003
Eternal University, India

ABSTRACT

Prompt engineering has emerged as a vital pedagogical practice in contemporary education, transforming how students interact with artificial intelligence–supported learning environments. This chapter positions the student as an active prompt engineer, emphasizing the development of precision, intentionality, and metacognitive awareness in shaping meaningful learning interactions. Prompt engineering is conceptualized not merely as a technical skill but as a reflective and cognitive process through which learners frame questions, guide inquiry, and critically evaluate generated responses. Drawing on an extensive review of existing literature, the chapter examines key components of effective prompt engineering, including content knowledge, clarity, critical thinking, creativity, collaboration, digital literacy, and

DOI: 10.4018/979-8-3373-8027-8.ch008

ethical judgment. It also addresses major challenges such as ambiguity, balancing specificity and flexibility, response reliability, accuracy concerns, ethical considerations, and student engagement.

INTRODUCTION

The emergence of Education 4.0 has introduced a flexible, learner-centered, and technologically integrated approach to teaching and learning, driven largely by advances in digital technologies and artificial intelligence (World Economic Forum, 2023). Within this evolving educational paradigm, the integration of artificial intelligence (AI) into learning systems has begun to fundamentally transform instructional practices, particularly in digital and online learning environments. AI technologies are increasingly recognized for their capacity to personalize learning pathways, automate instructional tasks, and adapt educational content to individual learner needs (Bonfield et al., 2020; Das, 2024). This transformation represents not merely a technological advancement but a broader pedagogical shift in lesson planning, instructional decision-making, and learner engagement (Kour et al., 2025). Recent research indicates a significant growth in studies examining the use of AI-driven tools to support learners across different stages of their academic journeys. Adaptive learning environments, personalized recommender systems, and Intelligent Tutoring Systems (ITS) are designed to tailor instruction according to learners' cognitive profiles, learning pace, and performance patterns (Gligorea et al., 2023; Mustfa & Ashiq, 2024; Bandara & Senanayaka, 2024; Saragih, 2024; Li et al., 2025). To enable such personalised learning experiences, a range of AI methodologies including machine learning (ML), deep learning (DL), and natural language processing (NLP) have been extensively explored from a technical and pedagogical perspective (Khampusaen, 2025; Rahamtalla et al., 2025). These approaches facilitate the identification of learning difficulties through interaction data, support the development of personalised study plans, and provide timely, context-sensitive feedback to learners (Kour & Bhatia, 2025). In online learning environments, AI-enabled systems are frequently integrated with learning analytics and educational data-mining tools, allowing for continuous data collection and analysis to enhance instructional effectiveness (Gligorea et al., 2023; Saragih, 2024). Empirical evidence supports the effectiveness of these technologies. For instance, An and Ngo (2025) reported statistically significant improvements in academic achievement and learner engagement among students using AI-supported learning platforms compared to those experiencing traditional instructional approaches.

Objectives of the Chapter

This chapter aims to conceptualize the role of learners in AI-enabled educational environments by positioning students as active prompt engineers rather than passive recipients of AI-generated outputs. In the context of Education 4.0 and the growing integration of generative artificial intelligence in teaching and learning, the chapter seeks to advance both theoretical understanding and pedagogical application of prompt engineering as a metacognitive learning capability.

Specifically, the objectives of this chapter are to:

1. Conceptualize prompt engineering as a metacognitive learning practice that supports precision, intentionality, critical thinking, and self-regulated learning in AI-mediated educational contexts.
2. Synthesize contemporary interdisciplinary literature on prompt engineering, artificial intelligence in education, learning sciences, and human–AI interaction to establish a coherent theoretical foundation for student-centred prompt design.
3. Examine pedagogical, ethical, and epistemic dimensions of prompt engineering, including issues of learner agency, cognitive responsibility, bias, hallucination, and academic integrity.
4. Analyse prompt engineering strategies as instructional scaffolds that support higher-order thinking, metacognitive awareness, and meaningful engagement across diverse disciplinary and professional learning contexts.
5. Identify practical implications for curriculum design, assessment, faculty development, and institutional policy, highlighting how prompt engineering can be systematically integrated into formal educational practice.

Through these objectives, the chapter aims to extend existing conceptual discussions by offering a learner-centered framework that aligns AI use with educational purpose, ethical responsibility, and sustainable learning outcomes.

SYNTHESIS OF PRIOR RESEARCH ON PROMPT ENGINEERING IN EDUCATION

The growing body of literature on prompt engineering reflects increasing scholarly attention to how human-AI interaction shapes learning processes, knowledge construction, and educational outcomes. While existing studies span diverse disciplinary domains, including education, healthcare, computer science, and human-AI interaction, a synthesis of prior research reveals four dominant thematic strands: (a) cognitive and metacognitive benefits, (b) instructional design and pedagogical integration, (c) ethical and epistemic challenges, and (d) gaps in empirical classroom validation.

Cognitive and Metacognitive Benefits

A substantial proportion of the literature conceptualizes prompt engineering as a cognitive and metacognitive activity that enhances learner engagement, reasoning quality, and self-regulation. Research grounded in learning sciences highlights that structured prompting supports higher-order cognitive processes such as analysis, evaluation, and synthesis by requiring learners to articulate intent, clarify assumptions, and monitor understanding. Studies linking prompt design to metacognitive regulation emphasize that learners who iteratively refine prompts demonstrate increased awareness of their thinking processes, improved precision in inquiry, and stronger control over learning strategies. This body of work positions prompt engineering as an extension of established theories of self-regulated learning, constructivism, and active engagement, suggesting its potential as a pedagogical scaffold rather than a purely technical skill.

Instructional Design and Pedagogical Integration

A second strand of literature focuses on prompt engineering as an instructional design strategy for AI-supported learning environments. Within this perspective, prompts are framed as pedagogical tools that guide learner–AI dialogue, structure inquiry, and align AI-generated outputs with curricular goals. Research highlights the effectiveness of instruction-based, example-based, and reasoning-oriented prompting techniques in improving the relevance and coherence of AI responses. However, much of this work remains conceptual or design-oriented, offering frameworks and typologies without systematic evaluation in authentic classroom settings. While these studies contribute valuable design principles, they often underemphasize issues of scalability, instructor workload, and alignment with formal assessment practices.

Ethical and Epistemic Challenges

A third body of scholarship critically examines the ethical, epistemic, and societal implications of prompt engineering. Concerns related to hallucinated information, algorithmic bias, data privacy, and learner over-reliance on AI are consistently highlighted. Researchers argue that without explicit scaffolding, prompt engineering may inadvertently reinforce surface learning, cognitive offloading, or uncritical acceptance of AI-generated content. In response, recent studies advocate for verification-oriented prompting, epistemic vigilance, and ethical literacy as integral components of prompt design. This literature emphasizes that prompt engineering must be situated within broader discussions of academic integrity, transparency, and responsible innovation, particularly in educational contexts.

Unresolved Tensions and Gaps in Empirical Validation

Despite the conceptual richness of existing research, a notable gap persists in empirical classroom-based validation of prompt engineering as a learning capability. Many studies rely on theoretical analysis, scoping reviews, or laboratory-based evaluations, with limited longitudinal or context-specific evidence from real educational settings. Additionally, tensions remain regarding the balance between learner autonomy and instructional guidance, the extent to which prompt engineering should be explicitly taught, and how learning outcomes associated with prompt quality can be reliably assessed. These unresolved questions highlight the need for pedagogically grounded frameworks that integrate theory, practice, and evaluation.

Positioning the Present Chapter

Building on these strands, the present chapter extends existing research by offering a learner-centred synthesis that positions prompt engineering as a metacognitive literacy rather than a technical optimisation practice. By integrating cognitive, pedagogical, and ethical perspectives, the chapter moves beyond descriptive reviews to propose a coherent educational framework that foregrounds learner agency, intentionality, and epistemic responsibility. In doing so, it addresses underexplored dimensions related to assessment, curriculum integration, and institutional readiness, thereby contributing a structured and educationally grounded perspective to the evolving scholarship on prompt engineering in education.

ETHICAL, PEDAGOGICAL, AND SOCIETAL CONCERNS OF AI-ENABLED LEARNING

Prompt engineering is increasingly positioned as a transferable digital skill, particularly relevant for educators, developers, and knowledge workers (Boonstra, 2025). Despite the demonstrated advantages of artificial intelligence in educational contexts, its integration into e-learning environments remains subject to critical scrutiny. A growing body of literature highlights the ethical, pedagogical, and societal challenges associated with AI-driven educational systems (Donatus et al., 2024; Han et al., 2024; Khampusaen, 2025; Rahamtalla et al., 2025). Central among these concerns are issues related to algorithmic opacity, automated decision-making, and the potential reinforcement of bias, all of which raise questions about transparency, accountability, and fairness in AI-supported learning environments. The extensive collection and analysis of learner data further intensify concerns regarding data privacy and security, particularly when such data are gathered without fully informed consent. Scholars caution that insufficient safeguards may expose students to risks of surveillance, data misuse, and loss of autonomy within AI-mediated learning systems (Khampusaen, 2025). In addition, several studies warn against the over-reliance on automation, which may inadvertently diminish learner agency and contribute to the gradual dehumanisation of the teaching-learning process (Gligorea et al., 2023; Bandara & Senanayaka, 2024; Donatus et al., 2024). These challenges have prompted an ongoing global discourse on how to achieve an appropriate balance between technological automation and human agency in education. While AI systems are effective in identifying learning patterns and generating pedagogical recommendations, they cannot replace the educator's role as a reflective practitioner, ethical guide, and facilitator of meaningful learning experiences. In response, international policy frameworks increasingly emphasise principles such as equity, inclusivity, transparency, and responsible innovation in the educational use of artificial intelligence (Boonstra, 2025). Learners' perceptions of AI-enabled instructional tools further reflect this complexity. Although students often acknowledge AI's capacity to personalise learning and improve academic efficiency, they simultaneously express apprehensions regarding surveillance, data exploitation, and diminished control over their learning trajectories (Khampusaen, 2025). Limited levels of AI literacy may further restrict students' ability to engage critically and responsibly with such technologies. Consequently, there is a pressing need to examine the AI techniques currently employed for personalised learning, evaluate their empirical effectiveness, and identify unresolved ethical and pedagogical risks. Despite rapid methodological advances, Schulhoff et al. (2024) highlight a lack of standardized evaluation frameworks and limited domain-specific validation, particularly in education and healthcare contexts (Patil et al., 2024). Recent scholarship positions prompt engineering as a structured, domain-sensitive, and literacy-dependent practice. Systematic and scoping reviews emphasize the need for paradigm-level clarity, standardized evaluation, and ethical safeguards, particularly in healthcare contexts (Patil et al., 2024; Zaghir et al., 2024). Expanding beyond text-only systems, multimodal prompt strategies for vision-language models demonstrate the growing complexity of prompt design (Gu et al., 2023). From an educational perspective, effective prompt engineering is increasingly linked to AI literacy, highlighting the role of metacognitive and critical competencies in human-AI interaction (Knoth et al., 2024). Industry-focused perspectives further frame prompt engineering as an operational skill that enhances efficiency and task performance (Lemeš, 2024).

Prompt Engineering: Conceptual Foundations

Prompt engineering refers to the strategic design and structuring of inputs provided to generative AI systems to elicit accurate, relevant, and context-sensitive outputs. Practical prompt design involves clarity of intent, contextual framing, and iterative refinement (Ekin, 2023). Rather than functioning as a purely technical skill, prompt engineering involves the thoughtful construction of prompts that encourage meaningful dialogue, critical reflection, and deeper engagement with learning material (Marvin et al., 2023). Well-designed prompts support students in generating insightful responses, receiving constructive feedback, and developing conceptual understanding through guided inquiry. At its core, prompt engineering is an iterative and reflective process involving continuous design, implementation, evaluation, and refinement. This dynamic cycle enables learners and educators to enhance the relevance, clarity, and instructional value of AI-generated outputs. As prompts are refined based on feedback and learning outcomes, the pedagogical effectiveness of AI-mediated interactions improves, reinforcing purposeful engagement rather than passive information retrieval. In professional disciplines such as healthcare education, where learners must integrate theoretical knowledge with complex real-world applications, effective prompt engineering plays a particularly critical role (Patil et al., 2024; Wang et al., 2025). Carefully structured prompts support critical thinking, applied reasoning, and clinical decision-making by encouraging learners to analyse scenarios, justify responses, and reflect on outcomes (Marvin et al., 2023). As a result, prompt engineering functions not only as a means of optimising AI responses but also as a pedagogical strategy that strengthens comprehension, retention, and applied learning.

The Importance of Prompt Engineering in Education

Prompt engineering plays a significant role in enhancing critical thinking, comprehension, retention, and learner engagement across educational contexts. It refers to the intentional and systematic design of instructions, queries, and task formulations that guide interactions between learners and artificial intelligence systems such as ChatGPT (Ekin, 2023; Schulhoff et al., 2024). When educators employ well-structured prompts, instructional time is used more effectively, as students are guided toward focused inquiry, reflective reasoning, and purposeful engagement with learning material. Empirical evidence further suggests that higher-quality prompt formulation is associated with improved quality of AI-generated outputs and more meaningful learner and AI interaction, particularly among students with higher levels of AI literacy (Knoth et al., 2024; Khampusaen, 2025). Similarly, when students interact with AI technologies such as ChatGPT or other generative systems through carefully designed prompts, they are more likely to receive responses that are accurate, relevant, and pedagogically meaningful (Walter, 2024).

Enhancing Conceptual Understanding

Well-crafted prompts assist learners in interpreting complex concepts by encouraging them to move beyond surface-level responses. By prompting learners to explain, justify, or apply concepts, prompt engineering fosters deeper understanding and strengthens the connection between theoretical knowledge and real-world application. This process supports meaningful learning by requiring students to actively construct knowledge rather than passively consume information (Chi & Wylie, 2014; Mayer, 2020).

Strengthening Retention

Prompt engineering also reinforces retention through active recall and elaborative rehearsal. When learners are repeatedly prompted to engage with content from multiple perspectives, they process information more deeply, increasing the likelihood of transferring knowledge from short-term to long-term memory. Research in learning sciences consistently indicates that structured questioning, retrieval-based learning, and elaborative engagement contribute to improved retention and long-term academic performance (Biggs & Tang, 2011; Dunlosky et al., 2013).

Promoting Critical Thinking

Well-designed prompts stimulate higher-order cognitive processes by encouraging learners to analyse, evaluate, and synthesise information. Prompts that require comparison, critique, or justification push learners to consider multiple viewpoints and assess the validity of arguments, aligning with higher levels of cognitive engagement described in established learning taxonomies (Bloom et al., 2001; Facione, 2015). In AI-supported learning environments, effective prompt engineering further enables the generation of diverse responses, allowing students to evaluate alternatives and develop nuanced understanding (Schulhoff et al., 2024).

Supporting Clinical and Applied Learning

In professional education contexts, particularly in medical and nursing education, prompt engineering supports the application of theoretical knowledge to authentic practice. Carefully structured prompts enable AI systems to generate realistic scenarios, case-based problems, and decision-making tasks that enhance clinical reasoning and problem-solving skills. Through scenario-based prompting, learners are encouraged to reflect on outcomes, evaluate choices, and strengthen applied competence, which is critical for professional judgement and transfer of learning (Zaghir et al., 2024; Patil et al., 2024).

Prompt Engineering as a Student Learning Capability

Prompt engineering has emerged not only as a strategy for optimising large language models (LLMs) but also as a cognitive and metacognitive learning capability within educational settings. From a pedagogical perspective, prompt engineering reflects a learner's ability to articulate intent, structure inquiry, monitor understanding, and iteratively refine thinking while engaging with AI systems. When viewed through this lens, prompt engineering functions as an instructional scaffold that promotes precision, intentionality, and metacognitive awareness (Vygotsky, 1978; Knoth et al., 2024). Rather than positioning students as passive users of AI-generated content, prompt engineering empowers them to actively shape learning outcomes through thoughtful inquiry. Students who engage in prompt engineering must consider how language choices, context specification, and task framing influence AI responses. This process reinforces academic skills such as clarity of expression, analytical reasoning, and reflective judgement, all of which are central to AI literacy and effective human-AI interaction (Knoth et al., 2024).

Foundational Prompting Strategies in Education

Prompt engineering has evolved into a structured and increasingly sophisticated methodological practice, with contemporary research systematically categorising techniques into instruction-based, demonstration-based (few-shot), reasoning-oriented, and optimization-driven approaches (Schulhoff et al., 2024). Instruction-based prompting relies on clearly articulated directives to guide model responses, whereas demonstration-based prompting provides exemplar inputs to shape output patterns. Reasoning-oriented strategies further advance this progression by encouraging stepwise reasoning, explanation, and justification, while optimization-driven approaches focus on iterative refinement and performance tuning to achieve more precise and contextually relevant outputs. This typological progression reflects the maturation of prompt engineering from a set of ad hoc interaction strategies to a coherent research domain grounded in methodological intentionality and theoretical framing (Schulhoff et al., 2024). The shift toward structured and reasoning-based prompts highlights an increased emphasis on transparency, interpretability, and cognitive alignment between human intent and model output. Importantly, empirical and practice-oriented literature consistently demonstrates that the quality, relevance, and reliability of AI-generated responses are highly sensitive to prompt formulation. Even minor variations in linguistic structure, contextual specification, or task framing can substantially alter model behaviour and output quality, underscoring the critical role of intentional prompt design in educational and research contexts (Ekin, 2023). Consequently, prompt engineering is no longer viewed merely as a technical adjustment but as a foundational interaction skill that mediates effective human-AI collaboration.

Zero-Shot Prompting: Cultivating Cognitive Clarity

Zero-shot prompting requires learners to issue instructions without providing examples. In educational contexts, this technique mirrors a student's ability to independently frame questions based on prior knowledge and conceptual understanding (Ekin, 2023; Schulhoff et al., 2024). Through zero-shot prompting, learners practise:

- Clear articulation of learning goals
- Concise expression of expectations
- Awareness of linguistic ambiguity

From a learning perspective, zero-shot prompting fosters disciplinary precision by encouraging students to reflect on how subtle variations in wording can significantly influence outcomes. This practice strengthens academic communication and conceptual clarity. Such practices align with constructivist views of learning, where meaning is actively generated through intentional cognitive engagement rather than passive reception (Chi & Wylie, 2014).

Few-Shot Prompting: Learning Through Exemplars

Few-shot prompting involves providing examples to guide AI responses and closely aligns with example-based learning and worked-example approaches in education. By selecting or constructing appropriate exemplars, students engage in purposeful scaffolding and demonstrate their ability to identify representative and pedagogically meaningful knowledge (Mayer, 2020; Biggs & Tang, 2011). This approach supports:

- Analogical reasoning
- Pattern recognition
- Transfer of learning across contexts

Well-planned exemplar-based prompting reinforces the principle that intentional design yields more effective learning outcomes than unstructured or ad hoc inquiry (Schulhoff et al., 2024).

STRUCTURED REASONING AND THE DEVELOPMENT OF METACOGNITION

Chain-of-Thought Prompting: Making Thinking Visible

Chain-of-Thought (CoT) prompting encourages sequential reasoning and aligns closely with metacognitive practices such as planning, monitoring, and evaluation. When learners request step-by-step reasoning from AI systems, they externalise cognitive processes, making thinking explicit and open to reflection (Wei et al., 2022; Knoth et al., 2024). This approach supports:

- Logical sequencing
- Error detection
- Transparent reasoning

By modelling structured thinking, CoT prompting strengthens students' problem-solving abilities and critical reflection skills (Zimmerman, 2002).

Advanced CoT Variants and Reflective Judgement

Variants such as self-consistency and logical chain-of-thought prompting enable learners to compare multiple reasoning paths and evaluate the validity of alternative conclusions. These techniques promote cognitive flexibility, reflective revision, and deeper engagement with knowledge. From an educational standpoint, such practices mirror expert learning behaviours, where conclusions are continually questioned and refined (Schulhoff et al., 2024; Facione, 2015).

NON-LINEAR REASONING AND ADVANCED PROMPTING STRATEGIES

Tree-, Graph-, and Thread-of-Thought Prompting

Advanced reasoning strategies such as *Tree-of-Thought (ToT), Graph-of-Thought (GoT), and Thread-of-Thought (ThoT)* prompting acknowledge the non-linear nature of human cognition. Unlike linear reasoning approaches, these methods encourage learners to explore multiple solution pathways, examine competing interpretations, and refine understanding through comparison and synthesis (Gu et al., 2023; Schulhoff et al., 2024).

When students employ non-linear prompting strategies, they actively engage in exploratory reasoning by generating alternative explanations and evaluating their relative strengths. This process supports deeper conceptual learning by allowing learners to identify assumptions, recognise gaps in reasoning, and integrate diverse perspectives. From a constructivist standpoint, such approaches align with learning theories that emphasise knowledge construction through exploration rather than passive reception (Vygotsky, 1978; Chi & Wylie, 2014).

Through non-linear prompting, learners are encouraged to contrast viewpoints, test hypotheses, and iteratively refine conclusions. As a result, these techniques cultivate cognitive flexibility and reinforce higher-order thinking skills essential for complex problem-solving in academic and professional contexts.

Reducing Hallucinations and Fostering Epistemic Responsibility

One of the most critical challenges in AI-supported learning environments is the risk of hallucinated or inaccurate information (Ji et al., 2023). Prompt engineering strategies such as Retrieval-Augmented Generation (RAG), ReAct prompting, Chain-of-Verification (CoVe), and Chain-of-Knowledge (CoK) can be reframed as pedagogical tools that promote epistemic responsibility among learners by explicitly embedding verification and evidence-grounding into inquiry processes (Lewis et al., 2020; Yao et al., 2023; Wang et al., 2023). Rather than accepting AI-generated outputs uncritically, students learn to engage in verification-oriented inquiry by cross-checking information, distinguishing between verified knowledge and speculative claims, and grounding conclusions in credible evidence. These practices align closely with principles of academic integrity and ethical scholarship, reinforcing responsible research behaviours (Donatus et al., 2024; Zaghir et al., 2024). By integrating verification-focused prompts into learning activities, educators can support the development of critical evaluation skills essential for AI-mediated knowledge environments, thereby transforming AI from a passive information source into a partner in disciplined academic inquiry.

Interactive and User-Centred Prompting: Adaptation and Learner Agency

Interactive prompting strategies, including Automatic Reasoning and Tool Use (ART), Automatic Prompt Engineering (APE), and Active Prompting, emphasise the learner's evolving role as an adaptive decision-maker rather than a passive user (Paranjape et al., 2023; Zhou et al., 2023). These methods enable learners to iteratively refine prompts based on feedback, reflect on response quality, and adjust inquiry strategies to align with learning objectives. Such approaches foster learner autonomy by reinforcing the principle that meaningful AI interaction depends on human judgement and reflective control rather than automation alone (Knoth et al., 2024). Through reflective modification and strategic selection of prompts, learners develop metacognitive awareness and control over their learning processes, a capability particularly valuable in complex tasks requiring ongoing revision and synthesis (Zimmerman, 2002).

Domain-Specific Learning Transfer through Prompt Engineering

Prompt engineering strategies vary across disciplinary contexts, reflecting the unique cognitive, epistemic, and procedural demands of different fields (Gu et al., 2023; Schulhoff et al., 2024). Techniques such as contrastive chain-of-thought prompting, emotion prompting, and code-based prompting illustrate how prompt design must be adapted to support domain-specific learning outcomes. In educational settings, these approaches facilitate learning transfer by encouraging learners to reflect on errors, apply procedural reasoning, and integrate affective awareness with cognitive processes (Mayer, 2020; Biggs & Tang, 2011). For instance, contrastive prompting supports conceptual differentiation, code-based prompting enhances computational thinking and algorithmic reasoning, and responsibly designed emotion prompting can foster engagement and empathy in reflective learning tasks (Lemeš, 2024). Recognising the context-sensitive nature of prompt engineering enables learners to align inquiry strategies with disciplinary norms and academic expectations.

Advanced Optimisation and Reflective Abstraction

Advanced prompting strategies such as Optimisation by Prompting (OPRO), Rephrase-and-Respond (RaR), and Step-Back Prompting support higher-level abstraction and reflective reasoning by encouraging learners to reconsider problem framing, identify underlying principles, and evaluate reasoning quality rather than focusing solely on outcomes (Zhou et al., 2023; Schulhoff et al., 2024). Through these strategies, learners move beyond surface-level inquiry and engage in deliberate knowledge construction. The emphasis on reframing and abstraction closely aligns with self-regulated learning principles, enabling learners to monitor understanding, revise strategies, and deepen conceptual insight (Zimmerman, 2002; Chi & Wylie, 2014).

Synthesis: Metacognitive Literacy through Prompt Engineering

When examined through an educational lens, prompt engineering functions not merely as a technical optimisation strategy but as a metacognitive learning framework. Collectively, prompt-engineering strategies cultivate intentionality, reflection, verification, and revision, and precision are core dimensions of metacognitive literacy (Flavell, 1979; Knoth et al., 2024). Through deliberate prompt design, learners gain awareness of cognitive processes and develop the capacity to regulate thinking in goal-directed ways. Intentionality aligns inquiry with learning objectives, metacognition is strengthened through reflection and revision, verification reinforces epistemic discipline, and precision ensures conceptual clarity and academic coherence. By positioning students as prompt engineers, AI is transformed from an answer-generation tool into an active cognitive partner, with learning quality contingent upon the learner's capacity to articulate intent, evaluate responses, and refine inquiry (Knoth et al., 2024).

ESSENTIAL ELEMENTS OF PROMPT ENGINEERING IN EDUCATION

Within educational contexts, prompt engineering extends beyond technical proficiency and enables learners to actively shape knowledge construction when interacting with large language models (LLMs). Acting as prompt engineers encourages students to think deliberately, communicate clearly, and make informed decisions regarding the creation and use of information. From this perspective, prompt engineering functions as a metacognitive practice that supports higher-order thinking, clarity, and intentional academic engagement.

Content Knowledge as Intentional Framing

Content knowledge plays a foundational role in effective prompt design, as learners must draw upon disciplinary understanding to frame contextually accurate and conceptually precise prompts (Biggs & Tang, 2011). Metacognitive prompting strengthens critical thinking by requiring explanation, evaluation, and synthesis, enhancing learners' ability to question reliability and validity in AI-generated content (Facione, 2015; Donatus et al., 2024). Iterative design positions learners as reflective practitioners who refine inquiry through cycles of testing and feedback, reinforcing metacognitive regulation and persistence (Zimmerman, 2002). Clarity and precision reduce ambiguity and cognitive load, improving interpretability and predictability of AI responses (Mayer, 2020). Intentional creativity supports engagement and transfer by encouraging novel inquiry without sacrificing academic rigour (Lemeš, 2024). Collaborative prompt construction fosters shared cognition, dialogue, and inclusive participation, mirroring real-world professional problem-solving (Vygotsky, 1978). Digital literacy and ethical judgement further ensure responsible engagement by promoting verification, accountability, and fairness in AI-mediated knowledge production (Ekin, 2023; Knoth et al., 2024).

Metacognitive Prompting and Critical Thinking

Critical thinking in prompt engineering involves intentionally crafting prompts that demand explanation, evaluation, and synthesis rather than surface-level responses. By incorporating directives such as compare, justify, analyse, or critique, learners encourage AI systems to generate outputs that reflect complex cognitive processes. This practice requires students to anticipate the depth and quality of responses they seek, thereby strengthening metacognitive awareness and control over inquiry (Bloom et al., 2001; Facione, 2015). Research further indicates that prompts designed to promote critical online reasoning enhance learners' ability to question the reliability, credibility, and validity of AI-generated content, which is essential in AI-mediated learning environments (Wineburg et al., 2016; Knoth et al., 2024).

Iterative Design as Reflective Improvement

Iterative design constitutes a central element of prompt engineering, positioning learners as reflective practitioners rather than passive users. Instead of viewing prompts as static inputs, students engage in cycles of testing, feedback, and refinement. Through this process, learners analyse AI responses, identify conceptual gaps or inaccuracies, and revise prompts to achieve improved outcomes. Such iterative engagement enhances metacognitive regulation by encouraging learners to evaluate their thinking, adjust strategies, and persist through refinement, which are core components of self-regulated learning (Zimmerman, 2002; Chi & Wylie, 2014). In educational settings, this reflective design practice contributes to instructional precision, deeper engagement, and sustained learning effort (Biggs & Tang, 2011).

Clarity and Accuracy in Learner-AI Interaction

Clarity and precision are essential for reducing ambiguity in AI-generated outputs. Effective prompts include well-defined expectations, explicit parameters, and structured guidance that enable AI systems to interpret learner intent accurately. From an educational perspective, clarity-focused prompting reduces extraneous cognitive load and improves response predictability, supporting more efficient learning (Mayer, 2020). When learners specify formats, constraints, or evaluation criteria, they demonstrate strategic communication skills that are foundational to academic writing, professional discourse, and disciplined inquiry (Biggs & Tang, 2011).

Intentional Creativity in Prompt Engineering

Creativity in prompt engineering enables learners to extend inquiry beyond basic information retrieval and apply knowledge in novel and meaningful ways. Intentional creative prompting encourages exploration of alternative perspectives, hypothetical scenarios, and role-based reasoning while remaining aligned with academic objectives. Rather than diminishing rigour, such creativity enhances engagement and deepens conceptual understanding when appropriately structured (Lemeš, 2024; Schulhoff et al., 2024). Creative prompts invite learners to reinterpret content by adopting different viewpoints, such as analysing a problem from the perspective of a historical figure, disciplinary expert, or real-world practitioner. These approaches stimulate imagination while reinforcing analytical reasoning and contextual awareness, supporting both cognitive flexibility and disciplinary thinking (Vygotsky, 1978; Chi & Wylie, 2014). Intentional creativity also supports long-term retention by promoting emotional engagement and curiosity, which strengthen motivation and problem-solving abilities across disciplines (Dunlosky et al., 2013).

COLLABORATIVE PROMPT CONSTRUCTION AND SHARED COGNITION

Collaborative prompt engineering emphasises shared cognitive responsibility and collective knowledge construction. In group-based learning activities, students co-create prompts for discussion, peer review, or problem-solving tasks, integrating diverse perspectives and negotiating meaning through dialogue. This collaborative process enhances communication skills, critical reasoning, and mutual accountability (Vygotsky, 1978; Johnson & Johnson, 2009).Through shared prompt construction, learners' articulate assumptions, justify choices, and refine inquiry collaboratively. Such practices mirror real-world professional contexts, where complex problems are addressed through teamwork and interdisciplinary collaboration. In educational environments, collaborative prompting fosters social learning and supports inclusive participation by valuing multiple viewpoints (Biggs & Tang, 2011).

Digital Literacy and Responsible Engagement

Digital literacy is a central component of prompt engineering in contemporary education. Learners must develop the ability to critically evaluate, ethically use, and responsibly generate digital content when interacting with AI systems. Prompts that require source evaluation, ethical citation, or credibility assessment encourage reflective engagement with AI-generated outputs and support epistemic vigilance (Wineburg et al., 2016; Donatus et al., 2024). By designing prompts that emphasise verification and reliability, learners strengthen their capacity to distinguish between credible information and unsupported claims. This critical engagement promotes responsible technology use and prepares students to navigate increasingly AI-mediated academic environments, contributing to informed decision-making and responsible digital citizenship (Knoth et al., 2024).

Ethical Judgement and Reflective Accountability

Ethical judgement in prompt engineering requires learners to consider the broader social and moral implications of AI use. Scenario-based prompts addressing issues such as bias, privacy, equity, and inclusivity encourage reflection on the consequences of technological integration in education and society (Zaghir et al., 2024). Ekin (2023) further emphasises responsible prompt design, cautioning against ambiguous or misleading instructions that may result in biased, incomplete, or unreliable outputs. Through ethical inquiry, learners develop moral reasoning and accountability in digital interactions. Reflective prompting practices enhance awareness of power dynamics, data sensitivity, and fairness, reinforcing ethical responsibility as a core dimension of metacognitive learning. As students engage in ethically informed prompt design, they strengthen their capacity for conscientious participation in digital knowledge systems (Knoth et al., 2024).

Integrating Metacognitive Elements in Prompt Engineering

A comprehensive framework for learner-centred prompt engineering emerges when content knowledge, critical thinking, iterative design, clarity, creativity, collaboration, digital literacy, and ethical judgement are integrated. Each element contributes uniquely to learning, and together they form a synergistic system that enhances cognitive engagement and knowledge construction (Chi & Wylie, 2014;

Biggs & Tang, 2011). Iterative design supports continuous improvement, content knowledge anchors inquiry, and creativity and collaboration enrich meaning-making, while digital literacy and ethical judgement ensure responsible engagement with AI technologies (Knoth et al., 2024; Donatus et al., 2024). This integrated approach aligns with constructivist learning principles, positioning learners as active agents in knowledge creation rather than passive recipients (Vygotsky, 1978; Hmelo-Silver et al., 2007).

PROMPT ENGINEERING DIFFICULTIES IN EDUCATION

While prompt engineering offers substantial pedagogical potential, positioning students as active constructors of AI-mediated inquiry introduces several cognitive, pedagogical, and ethical challenges. Effective prompt engineering requires precision, intentionality, and metacognitive awareness competencies that are still developing for many learners (Flavell, 1979; Zimmerman, 2002). Research on AI-supported learning environments highlights that without explicit scaffolding, students may struggle to regulate inquiry, evaluate outputs, and align AI interactions with learning goals (Knoth et al., 2024; Schulhoff et al., 2024).

Contextual Ambiguity and Misinterpretation

One of the most significant challenges in prompt engineering arises from the inherent ambiguity of natural language. When prompts lack clarity or contextual detail, AI systems may misinterpret intent and generate responses misaligned with learning objectives (Ekin, 2023; Ji et al., 2023). From a metacognitive perspective, learners must anticipate how missing context influences system responses. Teaching students to specify subject domain, conceptual scope, and expected depth strengthens planning, monitoring, and regulation of inquiry—core components of metacognitive control (Flavell, 1979; Zimmerman, 2002).

Balancing Specificity and Openness

Another persistent challenge involves balancing specificity and openness in prompt design. Overly broad prompts often yield superficial responses, while excessively constrained prompts can restrict exploration and suppress creative or critical thinking (Schulhoff et al., 2024). Achieving this balance requires reflective judgement and iterative refinement, enabling learners to evaluate whether prompts support meaningful inquiry while remaining aligned with curricular goals. Such adaptive reasoning is central to self-regulated and inquiry-based learning (Hmelo-Silver et al., 2007; Chi & Wylie, 2014).

Ensuring Consistency and Reliability of AI Responses

Inconsistency in AI-generated outputs presents an additional difficulty in educational contexts. Variations in depth, framing, or tone can disrupt cognitive continuity and undermine learner confidence (Ji et al., 2023). Research suggests that structured prompting—specifying format, reasoning steps, or perspective enhances response consistency and supports learners' ability to critically evaluate output quality (Schulhoff et al., 2024; Knoth et al., 2024).

Accuracy and the Risk of Misinformation

Ensuring the correctness of AI-generated content remains a critical concern. Large language models may produce fluent yet inaccurate responses, increasing the risk of internalising misinformation (Ji et al., 2023). This challenge highlights the need to cultivate learners as critical evaluators rather than passive recipients. Verification through credible sources, epistemic monitoring, and reflective judgement are essential practices for responsible AI-supported learning and academic integrity (Wineburg et al., 2016; Donatus et al., 2024).This challenge highlights the necessity of cultivating learners as critical evaluators rather than passive recipients of information. Verification through credible sources, reflective judgement, and epistemic monitoring are essential practices for responsible AI-supported learning.

Privacy and Ethical Considerations

Prompt engineering also raises ethical concerns related to privacy, data security, bias, and equity. Learners may unintentionally disclose sensitive information, while biased outputs may reinforce stereotypes if not critically examined (Zaghir et al., 2024). Addressing these risks requires ethically informed prompt design and explicit instruction in responsible digital practices, reinforcing ethical reasoning and digital citizenship (Floridi et al., 2018; Ekin, 2023).Addressing these concerns requires ethically informed prompt design and explicit instruction in responsible digital practices. Encouraging awareness of equity, inclusivity, and data protection supports ethical reasoning and responsible digital citizenship.

Sustaining Learner Engagement

Maintaining meaningful engagement through prompt-driven learning presents another challenge. Prompts misaligned with learners' prior knowledge or cognitive readiness may reduce motivation and encourage surface-level interaction (Biggs & Tang, 2011). Purposefully designed prompts that encourage exploration, reflection, and problem-solving support autonomy and sustained engagement, aligning with principles of self-determined and inquiry-based learning (Hmelo-Silver et al., 2007; Chi & Wylie, 2014).When implemented effectively, prompt engineering reinforces learner autonomy and affirms students' roles as active participants in knowledge construction.

Moving Toward Metacognitive Development through Prompt Engineering

These challenges demonstrate that effective prompt engineering extends beyond technical skill. By addressing ambiguity, refining specificity, verifying accuracy, and engaging with ethical considerations, learners develop precision, intentionality, and metacognitive control over learning processes (Flavell, 1979; Zimmerman, 2002). When integrated thoughtfully into instructional design, prompt engineering empowers students to become reflective designers of learning and cultivates adaptive, ethical, and critical competencies for academic and professional contexts (Knoth et al., 2024). Addressing these challenges requires collaborative efforts among educators, learners, and educational technologists. When thoughtfully integrated into instructional design, prompt engineering empowers students to become reflective designers of learning experiences and equips them with the critical, ethical, and adaptive competencies required for contemporary academic and professional environments.

THE ROLE OF CULTURAL PRECISION IN PROMPT ENGINEERING

Precision in learning is not merely a linguistic or technical attribute; it represents a cognitive and metacognitive discipline involving clarity of thought, depth of understanding, and intentional academic engagement. Within the *student as prompt engineer* paradigm, cultural precision refers to the deliberate cultivation of learners' capacity to articulate questions, intentions, and cognitive demands with accuracy and specificity. Through this process, precision becomes a core learning competency rather than a peripheral communication skill. Educational psychology consistently links conceptual clarity with higher-order thinking and organised knowledge structures (Biggs & Tang, 2011). In AI-mediated contexts, precision requires translating cognitive intent into structured prompts, engaging learners in metacognitive planning and regulation (Flavell, 1979). Learners who express questions precisely are better equipped to differentiate concepts, recognise relationships, and identify underlying assumptions. Research on cognitive processing suggests that precise articulation reflects well-organised knowledge structures, whereas ambiguous or poorly defined inquiries often signal fragmented understanding (Biggs & Tang, 2011). Consequently, cultivating precision contributes directly to deeper learning outcomes and stronger internal knowledge organisation. Inquiry research further indicates that the quality of learner-generated questions predicts engagement and achievement, positioning precision as a catalyst for meaningful inquiry (Chin & Osborne, 2008). Precisely framed prompts enable learners to progress from descriptive responses to analytical, evaluative, and creative thinking. Studies indicate that the quality of learner-generated questions strongly predicts academic achievement and engagement, underscoring the role of precision as a catalyst for meaningful inquiry (Chin & Osborne, 2008).

In AI-mediated learning environments, precision in prompt engineering requires learners to translate cognitive intent into structured inquiry. Learners must define scope, establish constraints, and specify desired levels of explanation, thereby engaging in metacognitive planning and regulation. The educational value of this process lies not solely in the AI-generated response but in the cognitive effort invested in refining the prompt itself.

Cultivating precision also enhances metacognitive awareness. As learners refine prompts, they are compelled to reflect on what they know, what they seek to understand, and how knowledge should be represented. According to Flavell's theory of metacognition, such awareness and control over cognitive processes are essential for effective learning (Flavell, 1979). Precision thus functions both as an outcome of learning and as a mechanism that stimulates metacognitive growth.

Intentionality in Educational Exchanges

Intentionality refers to purposeful, goal-directed engagement with learning tasks. Self-regulated learning theory emphasises that effective learners plan, monitor, and reflect on learning experiences (Zimmerman, 2002). Intentional prompt engineering aligns AI use with learning goals, supporting deep understanding rather than cognitive offloading. Inquiry-based learning research further shows that intentional questioning enhances conceptual understanding and knowledge transfer (Hmelo-Silver et al., 2007). In digitally mediated and AI-supported learning environments, intentionality plays a decisive role in determining whether learning remains superficial or evolves into deep, self-directed understanding. Intentionality is closely aligned with theories of self-regulated learning. Zimmerman (2002) emphasises that effective learners proactively plan, monitor, and reflect on their learning experiences. When students engage intentionally with prompt engineering, they design inquiries that align with specific learning objectives, thereby transforming AI interactions into structured cognitive engagements.

Purpose-driven questioning further reflects intentional engagement. Intentional learners ask questions not merely to obtain answers but to analyse arguments, explore relationships, and clarify concepts. Research on inquiry-based learning demonstrates that such intentional questioning enhances conceptual understanding and supports knowledge transfer (Hmelo-Silver et al., 2007). By understanding the *why* behind a task, learners sustain focus and integrate new information more effectively.

Intentionality also strengthens metacognitive regulation. Learners who engage intentionally are more likely to monitor comprehension, recognise misunderstandings, and adjust strategies accordingly. Flavell (1979) highlights that metacognitive control emerges through deliberate and reflective learning practices. In the context of prompt engineering, intentionality ensures that AI use supports intellectual autonomy rather than cognitive dependency.

A lack of intentionality in technology-mediated learning may result in surface learning and cognitive offloading, where learners rely excessively on AI-generated outputs without critical engagement. In contrast, intentional participation promotes ethical academic behaviour, critical thinking, and long-term retention. Pedagogically, intentionality can be fostered through explicit scaffolding, reflective questioning, and formative feedback that prioritises reasoning over correctness alone (Hattie & Timperley, 2007).

CLASSROOM APPLICATIONS OF PROMPT ENGINEERING

Case Vignette 1: Undergraduate Humanities Course (Critical Reading and Writing)

In an undergraduate humanities course focused on critical reading and academic writing, students were introduced to generative AI as a cognitive support tool rather than a content generator. The instructor explicitly framed students as *prompt engineers* responsible for shaping inquiry quality. Students were asked to design prompts that required the AI system to compare theoretical perspectives, identify underlying assumptions, and critique arguments rather than summarise texts.

Initially, many students used broad and ambiguous prompts, resulting in superficial or generic outputs. Through guided reflection and iterative refinement, students learned to specify context, analytical focus, and expected depth of reasoning. For example, prompts evolved from "Explain constructivism" to "Compare constructivist and behaviourist perspectives on learner agency, highlighting strengths, limitations, and implications for classroom practice." Students documented prompt revisions and reflected on how changes influenced response quality.

Observed outcomes included improved clarity in student writing, stronger argumentation, and greater awareness of their own thinking processes. The activity demonstrated that prompt engineering functioned as a metacognitive scaffold, supporting critical engagement, disciplinary precision, and reflective learning rather than cognitive offloading.

Case Vignette 2: Teacher Education Programme (Curriculum and Instruction)

In a teacher education programme, prompt engineering was embedded into a course on curriculum planning and instructional design. Pre-service teachers were tasked with designing lesson plans using AI-supported brainstorming, with the requirement that all AI interactions be guided by structured prompts aligned with learning objectives, assessment criteria, and student diversity considerations.

Students were instructed to construct prompts that specified learner age, curricular goals, pedagogical strategies, and inclusion considerations. They were also required to verify AI-generated suggestions against curriculum standards and reflect on ethical issues such as bias and equity. For example, prompts included directives to adapt lessons for multilingual classrooms and students with diverse learning needs.

Reflection journals revealed that students developed greater intentionality in instructional decision-making and increased confidence in evaluating AI-generated content. Rather than accepting outputs uncritically, they learned to question relevance, modify strategies, and justify pedagogical choices. This case illustrates how prompt engineering can support professional judgement, curriculum alignment, and ethical awareness in teacher preparation.

Case Vignette 3: Online Professional Course (Healthcare or Applied Sciences)

In an online professional development course for healthcare learners, prompt engineering was used to support clinical reasoning and decision-making. Learners interacted with AI systems through scenario-based prompts that required step-by-step reasoning, justification of choices, and reflection on potential risks. Prompts explicitly requested evidence-based reasoning and encouraged learners to identify uncertainties or alternative approaches.

Learners were guided to revise prompts when AI responses lacked clarity or clinical relevance. Structured reflection activities required participants to compare

AI-generated recommendations with established guidelines and peer-reviewed sources. This process reinforced verification practices and epistemic responsibility.

Participants reported improved confidence in clinical reasoning and greater awareness of the limitations of AI-generated information. Importantly, learners recognised that the quality of AI support depended on the quality of their prompts. This case highlights the role of prompt engineering in fostering reflective judgement, applied reasoning, and ethical responsibility in high-stakes professional learning contexts.

IMPLICATIONS OF THE FINDINGS

The synthesis of theoretical perspectives and contemporary research presented in this chapter yields several important implications for educational practice, curriculum design, assessment, faculty development, and institutional policy. By framing students as prompt engineers, the findings emphasize that the educational value of generative AI lies not in automated answer production but in the quality of learner inquiry, reflection, and metacognitive control.

Implications for Curriculum Design

Curricula in AI-enabled learning environments should explicitly incorporate prompt engineering as a learning competency rather than treating it as a peripheral technical skill. Embedding structured prompt design activities within subject disciplines can support deeper conceptual understanding, critical thinking, and intentional inquiry. Curriculum frameworks should emphasize precision, reasoning, verification, and reflective revision as core learning processes, ensuring alignment between AI use and educational objectives rather than content acceleration alone.

Implications for Assessment and Evaluation

Traditional assessment approaches that focus solely on final outputs are insufficient for evaluating learning in AI-mediated contexts. The findings suggest a need for assessment frameworks that foreground process-oriented indicators, such as the quality of prompts, evidence of iterative refinement, metacognitive reflection, and ethical evaluation of AI-generated responses. Rubrics assessing prompt clarity, reasoning depth, verification practices, and reflective judgement can more accurately capture learner engagement and cognitive growth.

Implications for Teaching Practice and Faculty Development

Educators play a critical role in modelling effective prompt engineering and scaffolding learners' metacognitive engagement with AI systems. Faculty development programmes should therefore include training in AI literacy, prompt design strategies, ethical AI use, and assessment practices aligned with metacognitive learning. Supporting educators in understanding both the capabilities and limitations of generative AI can reduce over-reliance on automation and reinforce the teacher's role as a reflective guide and ethical mediator.

Implications for Institutional Policy and Readiness

At the institutional level, the findings underscore the importance of clear policies that frame generative AI as a learning partner rather than a shortcut or threat to academic integrity. Institutions should develop guidelines addressing transparency, equity of access, data privacy, and responsible AI use, while also investing in infrastructure and professional learning that supports pedagogically sound integration. Attention to differential access, language diversity, and digital divides is essential to ensure that prompt engineering does not exacerbate existing educational inequalities.

Implications for Learner Agency and Ethical Responsibility

Positioning students as prompt engineers reinforces learner agency and epistemic responsibility. Students are encouraged to critically evaluate AI outputs, verify information, and reflect on ethical implications such as bias, accuracy, and fairness. This shift supports the development of responsible digital citizenship and prepares learners to navigate complex AI-mediated knowledge environments with intellectual autonomy and ethical awareness.

CONCLUSION

Reconceptualising students as prompt engineers marks a meaningful pedagogical shift in contemporary education—one that foregrounds learner agency, cognitive responsibility, and reflective participation in AI-mediated learning environments. Rather than positioning students as passive recipients of AI-generated outputs, this perspective reframes them as active designers of inquiry who shape learning through deliberate questioning, structured reasoning, and reflective engagement with knowledge. At the core of this framework are three interrelated dimensions: precision, intentionality, and metacognition. Precision enables learners to articulate cognitive intent with clarity, supporting deeper conceptual understanding and higher-order thinking. Intentionality anchors interactions with AI systems in purposeful academic goals, ensuring that technology serves learning rather than directing it. Metacognition integrates these dimensions by empowering learners to plan, monitor, and evaluate their thinking processes, thereby fostering self-regulated, adaptive, and reflective learning. From a pedagogical standpoint, viewing students as prompt engineers shifts instructional emphasis from the production of answers to the cultivation of thinking processes. Educators play a critical role in modelling reflective inquiry, scaffolding precise and purposeful questioning, and fostering ethically responsible engagement with AI technologies. Embedding prompt engineering within curriculum design, assessment practices, and teacher education can support the development of learners who are not only knowledgeable, but also critically aware, ethically grounded, and cognitively independent.

In sum, positioning the student as a prompt engineer offers a powerful lens for reimagining learning in AI-enhanced educational contexts. By intentionally embedding precision, intentionality, and metacognition into educational practice, this approach equips learners to navigate complexity with clarity, purpose, and intellectual integrity. Future research should empirically examine this framework across diverse educational settings to further validate its potential for fostering meaningful, equitable, and sustainable learning in an increasingly AI-mediated world.

REFERENCES

An, G. K., & Ngo, T. T. A. (2025). Unravelling success in AI-powered personalized learning in Vietnam: A study on the interplay of platform features and psychological responses. *Journal of Information Technology Education, 24*, 41. Advance online publication. DOI: 10.28945/5668

Bandara, W. M. H. K., & Senanayaka, S. G. M. S. D. (2024, April). Use of artificial intelligence in education: A systematic review. In *2024 International Research Conference on Smart Computing and Systems Engineering (SCSE)* (Vol. 7, pp. 1-5). IEEE. DOI: 10.1109/SCSE61872.2024.10550527

Biggs, J., & Tang, C. (2011). *Teaching for quality learning at university* (4th ed.). Open University Press.

Bloom, B. S., Krathwohl, D. R., & Anderson, L. W. (2001). *A taxonomy for learning, teaching, and assessing: A revision of Bloom's taxonomy of educational objectives*. Longman.

Bonfield, C. A., Salter, M., Longmuir, A., Benson, M., & Adachi, C. (2020). Transformation or evolution? Education 4.0, teaching and learning in the digital age. *Higher Education Pedagogies, 5*(1), 223–246. DOI: 10.1080/23752696.2020.1816847

Boonstra, L. (2025). Prompt engineering. Google. https://www.kaggle.com/whitepaper-prompt-engineering

Chi, M. T. H., & Wylie, R. (2014). The ICAP framework: Linking cognitive engagement to active learning outcomes. *Educational Psychologist, 49*(4), 219–243. DOI: 10.1080/00461520.2014.965823

Chin, C., & Osborne, J. (2008). Students' questions: A potential resource for teaching and learning science. *Studies in Science Education, 44*(1), 1–39. DOI: 10.1080/03057260701828101

Das, P. K. (2024). Artificial intelligence in higher education: Opportunities, challenges, and preventions. *Asian Journal of Management, 15*(3), 238–244. DOI: 10.52711/2321-5763.2024.00037

Dunlosky, J., Rawson, K. A., Marsh, E. J., Nathan, M. J., & Willingham, D. T. (2013). Improving students' learning with effective learning techniques. *Psychological Science in the Public Interest, 14*(1), 4–58. DOI: 10.1177/1529100612453266 PMID: 26173288

Ekin, S. (2023). Prompt engineering for ChatGPT: A quick guide to techniques, tips, and best practices. *Authorea Preprints*.

Facione, P. A. (2015). *Critical thinking: What it is and why it counts*. Insight Assessment.

Flavell, J. H. (1979). Metacognition and cognitive monitoring: A new area of cognitive–developmental inquiry. *The American Psychologist*, *34*(10), 906–911. DOI: 10.1037/0003-066X.34.10.906

Floridi, L., Cowls, J., Beltrametti, M., Chatila, R., Chazerand, P., Dignum, V., Luetge, C., Madelin, R., Pagallo, U., Rossi, F., Schafer, B., Valcke, P., & Vayena, E. (2018). AI4People—An ethical framework for a good AI society: Opportunities, risks, principles, and recommendations. *Minds and Machines*, *28*(4), 689–707. DOI: 10.1007/s11023-018-9482-5 PMID: 30930541

Gligorea, I., Cioca, M., Oancea, R., Gorski, A. T., Gorski, H., & Tudorache, P. (2023). Adaptive learning using artificial intelligence in e-learning: A literature review. *Education Sciences*, *13*(12), 1216. DOI: 10.3390/educsci13121216

Gu, J., Han, Z., Chen, S., Beirami, A., He, B., Zhang, G., . . . Torr, P. (2023). A systematic survey of prompt engineering on vision-language foundation models (arXiv preprint arXiv:2307.12980). https://arxiv.org/abs/2307.12980

Han, Z., Battaglia, F., & Terlecky, S. R. (2024). Transforming limitations of ChatGPT into opportunities for active learning and prompt engineering. *The Innovation*, *5*(2), 100065. DOI: 10.59717/j.xinn-med.2024.100065

Hattie, J., & Timperley, H. (2007). The power of feedback. *Review of Educational Research*, *77*(1), 81–112. DOI: 10.3102/003465430298487

Hmelo-Silver, C. E., Duncan, R. G., & Chinn, C. A. (2007). Scaffolding and achievement in problem-based and inquiry learning. *Educational Psychologist*, *42*(2), 99–107. DOI: 10.1080/00461520701263368

Ji, Z., Lee, N., Frieske, R., Yu, T., Su, D., Xu, Y., Ishii, E., Bang, Y. J., Madotto, A., & Fung, P. (2023). Survey of hallucination in natural language generation. *ACM Computing Surveys*, *55*(12), 1–38. DOI: 10.1145/3571730

Khampusaen, D. (2025). The Impact of ChatGPT on Academic Writing Skills and Knowledge: An Investigation of Its Use in Argumentative Essays. *LEARN Journal: Language Education and Acquisition Research Network*, *18*(1), 963–988. DOI: 10.70730/PGCQ9242

Knoth, N., Tolzin, A., Janson, A., & Leimeister, J. M. (2024). AI literacy and its implications for prompt engineering strategies. *Computers and Education: Artificial Intelligence*, *6*, 100225. DOI: 10.1016/j.caeai.2024.100225

Kour, J., & Bhatia, R. (2025). Artificial intelligence and human mental wellbeing: Striking a balance between innovation and productivity. In Efstratopoulou, M. (Eds.), *AI in mental health: Innovations, challenges, and collaborative pathways* (pp. 213–228). IGI Global Scientific Publishing. DOI: 10.4018/979-8-3373-5072-1.ch009

Kour, J., Bhatia, R., & Joshi, R. (2025). Artificial intelligence in education: Insights from gender- and locality-based perspectives. In Mobo, F. (Ed.), *Impacts of AI on students and teachers in Education 5.0* (pp. 193–210). IGI Global Scientific Publishing. DOI: 10.4018/979-8-3693-8191-5.ch007

Lemeš, S. (2024). Prompt Engineering. Artificial intelligence in industry, 4, 159-170.

Lewis, P., Perez, E., Piktus, A., Petroni, F., Karpukhin, V., Goyal, N., & Kiela, D. (2020). Retrieval-augmented generation for knowledge-intensive nlp tasks. *Advances in Neural Information Processing Systems*, *33*, 9459–9474.

Li, S., Zeng, C., Liu, H., Jia, J., Liang, M., Cha, Y., Lim, C. P., & Wu, X. (2025). A meta-analysis of AI-enabled personalized STEM education in schools. *International Journal of STEM Education*, *12*(1), 58. DOI: 10.1186/s40594-025-00566-y

Marvin, G., Hellen, N., Jjingo, D., & Nakatumba-Nabende, J. (2023, June). Prompt engineering in large language models. In International conference on data intelligence and cognitive informatics (pp. 387-402). Singapore: Springer Nature Singapore. DOI: 10.1007/978-981-99-7962-2_30

Mayer, R. E. (2020). *Multimedia learning* (3rd ed.). Cambridge University Press. DOI: 10.1017/9781316941355

Mustfa, M. J., & Ashiq, S. (2024). Harnessing the power of artificial intelligence for adaptive learning systems: A systematic review. *International Journal of Education and Management Engineering*, *14*(5), 12–22. DOI: 10.5815/ijeme.2024.05.02

Patil, R., Heston, T. F., & Bhuse, V. (2024). Prompt engineering in healthcare. *Electronics (Basel)*, *13*(15), 2961. DOI: 10.3390/electronics13152961

Rahamtalla, B. M., Medani, I. E., Abdelhag, M. E., Eltigani, S. A., Rajan, S. K., Falgy, E., Hassan, N. M., Fadailu, M. E., Khudhayr, H. A., & Abdalla, A. (2025). The AI-powered healthcare ecosystem: Bridging the chasm between technical validation and systemic integration—A systematic review. *Future Internet*, *17*(12), 550. DOI: 10.3390/fi17120550

Saragih, R. I. E. (2024). AI-powered education: Transforming learning through personalized and scalable solutions. *International Journal of Information System and Innovative Technology*, *3*(2), 1–9. DOI: 10.63322/qm9dk118

Schulhoff, S., Ilie, M., Balepur, N., Kahadze, K., Liu, A., Si, C., . . . Resnik, P. (2024). The prompt report: A systematic survey of prompt engineering techniques (arXiv preprint arXiv:2406.06608). https://arxiv.org/abs/2406.06608

Vygotsky, L. S. (1978). *Mind in society: The development of higher psychological processes*. Harvard University Press.

Walter, Y. (2024). Embracing the future of artificial intelligence in the classroom: AI literacy, prompt engineering, and critical thinking. *International Journal of Educational Technology in Higher Education*, *21*(1), 15. DOI: 10.1186/s41239-024-00448-3

Wang, J., Shi, E., Yu, S., Wu, Z., Hu, H., Ma, C., & Zhang, S. (2025). Prompt engineering for healthcare: Methodologies and applications. *Meta-Radiology*, *100190*. Advance online publication. DOI: 10.1016/j.metrad.2025.100190

Wei, J., Wang, X., Schuurmans, D., Bosma, M., Ichter, B., Xia, F., & Zhou, D. (2022). Chain-of-thought prompting elicits reasoning in large language models. *Advances in Neural Information Processing Systems*, *35*, 24824–24837.

Wineburg, S., McGrew, S., Breakstone, J., & Ortega, T. (2016). *Evaluating information online*. Stanford History Education Group.

World Economic Forum. (2023). *Education 4.0: Global framework for future-ready education*. https://www.weforum.org

Zaghir, J., Naguib, M., Bjelogrlic, M., Névéol, A., Tannier, X., & Lovis, C. (2024). Prompt engineering paradigms for medical applications: A scoping review. *Journal of Medical Internet Research*, *26*, e60501. DOI: 10.2196/60501 PMID: 39255030

Zimmerman, B. J. (2002). Becoming a self-regulated learner: An overview. *Theory into Practice*, *41*(2), 64–70. DOI: 10.1207/s15430421tip4102_2

Chapter 9
Reconfiguring Students' Role in the Age of Artificial Intelligence:
A Multi-Level Sociological Analysis of Identity, Inequality, and Learning

Neerav Sharma
http://orcid.org/0009-0004-7118-7930
Shoolini University, India

Supriya Srivastava
http://orcid.org/0000-0002-5440-4364
Shoolini University, India

Harish Chandan
http://orcid.org/0000-0003-1035-426X
Independent Researcher, USA

ABSTRACT

This chapter explores how artificial intelligence is reshaping the social role of students through a multi-level sociological perspective. Drawing on theories of Mead, Bourdieu, Parsons, Foucault, Beck, and Giddens, it examines transformations in identity formation, learning practices, inequality, institutional authority, and credentialing. The analysis highlights both opportunities and risks of AI-mediated education, particularly in relation to digital capital, hybrid cognition, and emerging inequalities in the Global South.

DOI: 10.4018/979-8-3373-8027-8.ch009

INTRODUCTION

For over a hundred years, students have been recognised as one of the primary components of modern educational systems. Schools have served as the main institution through which young people gain knowledge, learn acceptable or desired behaviours, and prepare for future work and citizenship (Parsons, 1959). There are many different forms and structures of educational systems around the world, but the role of the student, as an individual who learns based on effort, individual engagement, and measurable results, is historically consistent across societies. This well-established idea is being pushed back against by Artificial Intelligence (AI), through the rapid development of software that generates written product, summarises text, solves problems, and tutors learners (Selwyn, 2019). As a result, many of the typical ways in which students produce evidence of learning, and thus complete their designated tasks, are changing or becoming fully automated. In addition to making these tasks more efficient, the changes brought on by AI are also raising many questions about how we define the process of learning and how learning is viewed by others.

The discussion around the use of AI in education often centres on immediate and practical issues, such as cheating, plagiarism, classroom policies, and academic honesty. While these are all issues of importance, they only scratch the surface of a much larger sea change. AI is changing not only how students are able to complete their assignments, but also how institutions think about students and what institutions expect from their students. The introduction of intelligent systems that produce outputs of work in ways similar to human work complicates the logic used to evaluate, grant merit, and identify authorship of a given work (Williamson & Eynon, 2020; Srivastava, 2026). Historically, student work has represented a demonstration of the student's cognitive ability as measured independently from all other factors. AI complicates this relationship by creating the opportunity to share or enhance the student's cognitive output in ways that are not likely to be noticed or distinguished from other types of cognitive efforts.

The evolving nature of how students connect with knowledge also has changed drastically from past eras, in which knowledge was gained primarily by receiving information from instructors or textbooks, and where knowledge was limited by the availability of sources or materials. Under these past regimes, the student's job was to be able to recall the material they have learned (Parsons,1959). However, as AI becomes more and more capable of retrieving, processing, and reproducing information instantaneously, knowledge will become much easier to access, as well as much more plentiful, and thus, the role of a student will shift to choosing, interpreting, and managing the various types of information obtained through external sources (Srivastava, 2026). This shift does not diminish the impact of learning;

rather, it will alter how we as a society characterise learning. It suggests that the new requisite skill associated with the learning process will likely emphasise skills such as navigation, judgment, and collaboration with machines rather than memorisation and or reproduction.

The transformations brought about by AI also intersect with broader sociological questions about socialisation and inequality. In addition to skill development, schools provide opportunities for individuals to practice self-regulation, learn how to manage their time, learn responsibility, and compare themselves to other students (Bourdieu, & Passeron, 1977). Induction into these ways of thinking and behaving will help prepare people for new kinds of jobs and engagements that we will see in the future. AI can change how we express effort, share responsibility, and demonstrate mastery, while also potentially introducing new types of inequities among students and schools based on their access to digital tools and digital literacy (Bourdieu, 1984). Students with access to quality digital devices, reliable connectivity and support from family, friends and community members may become disproportionately successful compared to those who do not have access or support. The challenges outlined above are even more pronounced in the Global South due to existing structural inequalities between regions in terms of resource availability, ability to support language needs, and institutional capabilities with respect to the education system

This chapter argues that to understand these changes, by analyzing how students' social roles are evolving as a result of the impact of AI, rather than specifically concentrating on technology and classroom pedagogy (methods). As a means of accomplishing this goal, a sociological theoretical framework is employed with reference to the works of George Herbert Mead, Pierre Bourdieu, Talcott Parsons, Michel Foucault, Ivan Illich, Lev Vygotsky, and those of Ulrich Beck and Anthony Giddens. Each of these theorists provides an alternative vantage point from which to understand the issue of students' social role evolution, specifically through their respective discussions on the following concepts: (a) student identity (b) cultural capital (c) institutional socialisation, (d) discipline (e) informal learning (f) cognitive scaffolding and (g) risk. By combining these perspectives, the chapter examines how AI is reshaping the meaning, expectations, and experience of being a student in an age of artificial cognition. (Mead, 1934; Bourdieu, 1984; Parsons, 1959; Foucault, 1977; Illich, 1971; Vygotsky, 1978; Beck, 1992; Giddens, 1991, Zawacki-Richter et al., 2019).

TRADITIONAL CONCEPTIONS OF THE STUDENT ROLE

To understand how Artificial Intelligence is transforming the role of students, it is essential examine the historical construction of this role of students in the education system. Although educational practices vary significantly across countries and time periods, modern schooling has developed a surprisingly stable set of expectations regarding what it means to be a student (Zawacki-Richter, 2019). These expectations are not only pedagogical; they are deeply social. Schools do not simply transmit information. They shape identities, allocate individuals to future roles, and reproduce cultural norms (Parsons, 1959; Bourdieu & Passeron, 1977). Over the years, several sociological thinkers have tried to make sense of these functions. Their work provides a useful baseline for analysing what AI is now disrupting.

One part of the traditional student role is grounded in the idea of learning as cognitive labour. A student is defined as being involved in activities where they will read, write, solve problems, study material, and then show that they understand what they have learned by taking tests/essays, etc. By doing these activities, students require individual effort and self-discipline, which is also required of them when they are in a classroom, in the library, or studying for exams. In most modern systems, this form of cognitive labour must be visible or measurable in order to be recognised. Marks, feedback, and certification play this role by functioning as institutional signals that learning has taken place (Parsons, 1959).

Schools are also key settings of socialisation. Since the late nineteenth century, when mass education expanded alongside industrialisation and bureaucratic state-building, schools took on the task of preparing young people for participation in modern society. They taught punctuality, attention to instruction, respect for authority, cooperation with peers, and the ability to complete tasks under standardised conditions (Foucault,1977; Parsons, 1959).

The traditional student role is characterised by an expectation of originality and individual authorship. Students are presumed to create works that are distinctly theirs within most educational systems. Traditionally, teachers and textbooks function as the primary sources of legitimate knowledge. Students are expected to learn from those with recognised expertise. This arrangement creates a hierarchical epistemic order in which students occupy a subordinate position as knowledge receivers. Over time, students may move from passive reception to more active forms of inquiry, but the basic direction of knowledge flows from institutionally authorized sources to learners remains intact in most educational settings.

Both assessment and credentialing are equally important. Degrees, diplomas, and standardized examinations serve as formal markers of achievement. They allow schools to classify students by performance and allocate them to different educational or occupational pathways. From a sociological standpoint, these systems perform both integrative and selective functions. They help societies identify who is qualified for which roles and ensure that occupational tasks are filled by individuals deemed competent to perform them. At the same time, the credentialing process often reproduces social inequalities, because performance in schooling is influenced by family resources, cultural exposure, and linguistic capital (Bourdieu, 1984; Bourdieu & Paseron, 1977).

In addition to academic content and institutional sorting, the traditional role of the student has also been framed in moral and behavioural terms. Students are supposed to be diligent, curious, attentive, and willing to work hard. They are expected to practice delayed gratification by investing in long-term goals rather than immediate rewards. These expectations are reinforced through grades, praise, sanctions, and peer comparison (Foucault, 1977). The image of the ideal student is someone who puts in consistent effort, learns from mistakes, and strives for improvement. These moral expectations are so normalized that they often go unnoticed, yet they are fundamental to how societies conceive of education.

The conventional perception of a student is of a role that includes a separation between learning and doing. Learning is regarded as preparation for future involvement in work, civic engagement, and adulthood. The role of a student exists within an institutionally determined setting. Students are required to attend class regularly and to advance to the next grade according to predetermined, highly regulated criteria. Moreover, students move through standardized cohorts based on their age, must take the same courses as their peers, and are expected to complete a prescribed sequence of classes. This formalized system gives a student a degree of legal, bureaucratic, and societal authority. Additionally, being a student means that a student does not have thc option of determining whether or not they are a student; this is an ascribed social status with the accompanying rights, obligations, and expectations.

MICRO-LEVEL TRANSFORMATIONS: MEAD

Artificial Intelligence not only disrupts institutions or labour markets it also affects the ways through which students learn, form identities, interact with others, and make sense of themselves. Several studies increasingly come to the conclusion that generative AI systems are being used by students as writing guidance, supportive partners and blurring the boundaries between human cognition and machine support (Kasneci et al., 2023; Cotton et al., 2023). These are micro-level processes that unfold in everyday interactions and psychological experiences. According to sociologists and educational theorists, schools serve as a reflective outlet for their students. Through the eyes of their teachers, peers, and the structure of schooling itself, students develop a self-perception (Mead, 1934). The introduction of artificial intelligence into schools will bring about multiple changes to these environmental influences at the micro-level for the development of students as learners.

Two thinkers are especially useful for understanding these processes: George Herbert Mead, who examined how individuals develop a sense of self through social interaction, and Lev Vygotsky, who explored how learning is mediated through tools, language, and more capable peers (Mead, 1934; Vygotsky, 1978; Holmes et al., 2019). Their ideas allow us to explore how AI is affecting identity, interaction, and cognition at the level of the student's lived experience. While this is for supporting struggling learners, excessive reliance on automated assistance risks weakening (Kirschner & De Bruyckere, 2017; Selwyn, 2019), it also cause as productive struggle and deep internalisation.

Mead: Interaction, Role-Taking, and the Emergent Learning Self

For Mead, the self emerges not from introspection but from social interaction. Individuals learn who they are by taking the roles of others and by seeing themselves from the standpoint of the "generalized other" (Mead, 1934). This process is especially visible in schooling, where students learn to anticipate how teachers, classmates, and institutions evaluate their actions. When a student completes an assignment, raises a hand, participates in class, or submits an essay, they are participating in reciprocal role-taking that gradually builds a sense of identity as a learner.

Artificial Intelligence is changing how students interact with tutors, writers' workshops, and feedback. As these systems provide students with immediate feedback about their work, evaluate students based on their submitted assignments, and assist students in finding solutions to problems, they simulate aspects of what is traditionally viewed as Teacher-Student to some extent. Although the interaction takes place in a different way due to the lack of an acting intention on the part of the AI System, for a student, that does not affect the moral or psychological nature of their relationship in any way. The type of evaluative feedback provided by an AI system is similar to what teachers normally provided when the AI system indicates that a sentence is "unclear," suggests revision, or points out mistakes. Students may become accustomed to the way an AI system sees them and the way it expects them to behave or respond. Over time, a student's approach to learning tasks may begin to be shaped by their internalized expectation of what the AI system "sees" and expects of them (Mead, 1934). AI systems bring an added complexity to students' social interactions because they do not reside in the same stable social roles that peers and teachers occupy. On one hand, they lack human authority or status, but on another hand, AI systems hold technical status and authority, relative to the work students submit.

Mead noted that identity is formed through struggle and uncertainty. The process of trial and error in conjunction with evaluative feedback allows students to internalize norms of perseverance and self-correction. The use of AI Tools dramatically reduces or eliminates the amount of struggle students experience when receiving immediate responses, hints, and other generated solutions to lessons. Consequently, while accelerating the completion of work, they decrease or dilute the opportunities for students to experience the small frustrations that often lead to long-term learning and identity development.

AI as a New Type of Social Actor

Both Mead and Vygotsky demonstrate how AI introduces a new type of actor into environments where human learning takes place. This actor is neither a equal nor a superior in the traditional sense, but it is capable of teaching, judging, directing, and collaborating with others. It participates in feedback cycles, it alters learning trajectories, and impacts self perception. All these abilities make AI systems significant social actors even if they lack consciousness and free will.

Students may project human qualities onto AI systems, treating them as tutors, critics, assistants, or companions. This phenomenon is already visible in studies where young learners describe AI tutors as 'helpful,' 'smart,' or 'patient.' The attribution of social qualities to nonhuman actors is not new. Children have long 'anthropomorphized' objects and media, but AI intensifies these effects by responding interactively. From Mead's perspective, what matters is not whether AI is truly social, but whether students engage in role-taking with it. The evidence suggests they do, and this shifts how the learning self develops (Mead, 1934).

The Reconfiguration of Attention and Effort

Transformations at the micro-level also include the shift in how students distribute their time, attention and energy to learning. Students need to spend time focused and using directed thinking energy to learn. While AI tools may assist students in learning, they might also hinder it. The positive side of this effect is that, by providing structure for a student and reminding him/her when they must be focusing on his/her work, the student can better manage the load of cognitive processing (Lin & Chen, 2024). The downside of the effect of using AI is that when students have access to immediate answers to problems, they will be less likely to maintain their focus on a challenging problem and are more likely to take their time (Kirschner & De Bruyckere, 2017)

Finding the right balance between providing help to a student and enabling him/her to avoid putting forth the effort required to solve a difficult problem is tricky. If students often find ways to get out of putting forth the effort necessary to learn, even though they will finish their assignments more quickly and meet deadlines, they may actually diminish their overall capability of learning (Parsons, 1959). The issue of effort is significant because effort can be considered one of the hidden pillars of the student role. This absence of a relationship between performance and effort is harmful to the foundation on which schools establish both social order and academic accountability.

The Emergence of Hybrid Cognition

Micro-level changes also include the development of hybrid cognition, where human and machine cognition blend together (Clark, 2008). For instance, a learner may use AI to brainstorm ideas, organise an argument by hand, produce a draft with the help of a machine, and finally revise the draft by hand. In such a scenario, authorship is no longer localised but distributed among human and non-human agents (Adams & Thompson, 2023). Such distributed authorship defies conventional standards of academic integrity and originality (Vygotsky, 1978). More importantly, it changes the cognitive route that learners take when learning. Learners are no longer required to internalise whole processes but rather manage processes that involve human cognition and machine assistance.

Hybrid cognition does not necessarily reduce learning. It can, in fact, promote metacognitive abilities such as planning, judging, and managing tasks. It also obscures learning from teachers and institutions. Schools are set up to measure the output of human cognition. They are not yet ready to measure what learners have learned in a hybrid process (Vygotsky, 1978).

The micro-level, AI reshapes:

- identity formation (students see themselves differently)
- role-taking (students respond to new evaluators)
- cognitive scaffolding (assistance becomes constant and adaptive)
- effort and struggle (task difficulty is reduced or avoided)
- authorship and originality (work becomes collaborative with machines)
- attention and motivation (incentives shift from mastery to completion)

These changes may seem subtle when observed in isolation, but together they redefine the experience of learning. The traditional student role rested on a set of routines that involved listening, practising, struggling, and achieving. AI modifies each of these routines, sometimes gently and sometimes radically.

MESO-LEVEL TRANSFORMATIONS: BOURDIEU AND ILLICH

Whereas micro-level transformations are concerned with identity, cognition, and interaction, meso-level transformations are concerned with the ways in which AI transforms educational spaces, inequalities, norms, and the learning ecology. Schools are not merely places of individual development. They are also spaces where resources, recognition, and cultural capital are allocated. They are also institutions that have a monopoly over legitimate learning.

Digital inequality of scholars emphasises that access alone does not determine educational advantage; rather, it causes differences in skills, usage patterns, and institutional support that shape who takes advantage most from digital technologies or Artificial tools (van Dijk, 2020; Robinson et al., 2015). From Bourdieu's (1984) perspective, Artificial Intelligence introduces pressures that disrupt these functions by creating new forms of capital and by enabling learning beyond schools and universities (Bourdieu, 1984: Illich, 1971). Two theorists provide significant frameworks for understanding these changes. Pierre Bourdieu, who analysed how schooling reproduces inequality through cultural capital and field structures, and Ivan Illich, who proposed that learning could be liberated from schools through networks and informal institutions. AI makes both perspectives more relevant today.

Bourdieu: Capital, Habitus, and Educational Stratification

Bourdieu explains how educational systems function as both educational institutions and sorting mechanisms. For example, students come into school with differing amounts of cultural capital (e.g., linguistic ability, vernacular), which influence how well they can learn and follow the rules of academic life (Bourdieu, 1984; Bourdieu & Passeron, 1977). It is through the possession of certain forms of cultural capital that someone receives an advantage over others because schools reward them for having culturally valued expressions like proper vocabulary usage, discourse styles, interests, familiarity with abstract thought, comfort with institutional authority, etc. Schools reproduce social inequality under the guise of merit when they reward students for having these forms of cultural capital (Bourdieu, 1984).

AI interacts with the educational system in several ways. First, AI provides a form of digital cultural capital. This includes being able to effectively use and navigate AI tools, such as how to prompt, verify, adapt, and critically evaluate outputs of AI systems. Being able to ask better questions and improve upon AI system outputs allows students who have access to AI tools to create more sophisticated work than students who do not use AI tools. Although not yet codified in some curriculum or educational standards, it will soon be a major differentiator in education (Bourdieu, 1984). Access to superior AI tools is allowing many students to produce a higher quality essay, summary, translation or other types of technical solutions in less time than students who rely on traditional methods of producing academic work. For this reason, the advantages will be most pronounced in centrally determined objectives such as terminology, structure, and grammar, which Bourdieu observed reward individuals who have had prior cultural exposure to them.

Second, many students do not have access to the types of artificial intelligence resources available to others. Similar to private tutors, test prep, and extracurricular activities, many families can afford the high cost of AI systems, whereas others cannot. Therefore, students who rely strictly on institutional resources are likely to be at a disadvantage when compared to peers using paid AI systems or providing personalised plugins or other methods of utilising AI tools. In this sense, access to AI creates a new layer of educational stratification on top of existing economic, linguistic, and cultural disparities (Bourdieu & Passeron, 1977). The risk is not simply that some students will learn faster than others, but that some students will have access to and be able to use the resources made available through digital means, while others will not.

Third, AI will change what existing forms of capital are worth. For example, grammatical correctness and traditional writing style are used to convey excellence and cultural refinement and academic readiness. Consequently, with the advent of AI-generated content, such as automated grammatical correctness, this type of cultural capital has diminished in value. In addition, new forms of capital are developing as more students acquire computational literacy and digital critical thinking skills and become aware of algorithms. With the growing number of forms of capital that exist today, the previous forms of cultural capital required significant time investment or socialisation, while the new forms are going to become artificially abundant (Bourdieu, 1984).

Fourth, a Bourdieusian perspective on habitus describes students' habits, based on how they will navigate the social world. For example, students who have had access to digital technologies from an early age have developed a tendency to work with and through technology because of this ease of use. Conversely, students raised traditionally are likely to perceive digital technologies as unethical or inappropriate. Consequently, when these two views are combined in the classroom, there may be disagreements between students and teachers regarding how to utilise and view digital technology (Bourdieu, 1984).

Institutional Responses and the Recalibration of Merit

Schools and universities have begun to respond to the presence of AI with policies that restrict, regulate, or integrate these tools. In many cases, institutions attempt to preserve traditional definitions of merit by prohibiting automated writing, external assistance, or unsupervised cognitive outsourcing. These policies represent an institutional commitment to the belief that learning must be internalised and individualised. However, the enforcement of such policies is difficult, and students quickly learn to adapt to new technological contexts. In this way, educational institutions are faced with a legitimacy dilemma: on one hand, if they ban AI, they will appear to be antiquated and out of touch with the world outside the institution; on the other hand, if they adopt AI, they must then question how they can measure and verify learning in a way that maintains social trust.

The continued relevance of credentialing is also a key issue here. Most modern societies will utilise a degree or a diploma as the way in which they place people in jobs and position them in relation to other positions and social roles. The central feature of these credentials is their perceived ability to accurately measure the competency of an individual. If AI clouds the relationship between output and effort, then credentialing may become less credible. This creates a need for institutions to rethink how they assess learning, focusing on performance that is either embodied (such as oral exams or live demonstrations) or collaborative in new ways.

Illich: De-schooling and the Decentralisation of Learning

Where Bourdieu's work illuminates the impact of AI on reshaping inequality in schools, Illich's work provides insight into the impact of AI on reshaping the relationship between schools and society. Illich (1971) stated that schools are a monopoly of learning because they have the power to control access to knowledge, certification, and legitimacy. He had a vision of a world where learning would occur through open networks and communities, rather than through institutionalised learning..

AI makes aspects of this vision more plausible than ever. Students can now learn languages, programming, writing, and technical subjects through platforms that operate independently of schools. Intelligent tutors offer immediate feedback, adjust to individual pace, and often exceed the capacity of classroom instruction in personalisation. These developments weaken the monopoly schools once held over information (Illich, 1971). The teacher is no longer the exclusive transmitter of knowledge; nor is the textbook its exclusive source. Instead, knowledge flows through distributed networks that include corporate platforms, open-source communities, and AI systems.

Therefore, the challenge to schools' traditional justifications as the primary places for learning is obvious because schools still provide the authority to credential but do not have a monopoly on the resources for learning. In certain disciplines, particularly software development, employers have begun to place more emphasis on demonstrable skills than on formal credentials (degrees). The use of micro-credentials, portfolios and verified projects is replacing degrees/free form of credentials in providing evidence of competence in an increasing number of fields. The increased ability for people to develop skills independently and to demonstrate those skills publicly is being accelerated by the use of AI. Illich's criticisms of schooling also point to a distinction between learning and teaching. Illich believed that learning is a natural part of being human; on the other hand, the act of teaching is an institutional service that may not meet the individual needs of each learner. While many AI systems allow the individual to independently create and develop new forms of autonomous learning without institutional mediation, we can now rethink the line between learning and teaching. Students who do mathematics, write creatively or learn about history using AI are simply doing all of those things without the influence of traditional teaching (the teaching that would happen in an institutional setting). The institutional challenge is proving that any significant learning occurred without it ever being documented or assessed.

Informal Learning Ecosystems and the Erosion of Institutional Control

The emergence of AI-enhanced platforms has fundamentally affected the way in which students build their knowledge base. Whereas learning was traditionally done through one specific institution, more frequently, it is being developed through multiple different sources or ecosystems. Instead of working only at a school, a student might choose to watch an instructional video, use artificial intelligence as a tutor, chat in online discussion boards, and make use of augmented note-taking tools. All of these activities are completed without any of the normal oversight that traditionally would have been provided by a teacher or accredited service (Illich,1971). This pattern fits Illich's thesis that the plurality of learning networks can eventually accelerate and replace the school system as the centre of modern intellectual activity. These networks allow for open access to information, allow for shared feedback, and are developed through one's own interests rather than through a defined sequence of curriculum development.

In many cases, students are being motivated by their curiosity, vocational aspirations, or specific challenges. For instance, many young adults are opting to teach themselves coding and design skills by engaging with online networks (or communities) that support accelerated and real-world education rather than pursuing the conventional educational system. AI is supporting the growth of this process by making it easier to connect and access information beyond traditional channels.

Credentialing, Recognition, and the Value of Demonstration

Certification is a significant aspect of being a student. Students are not just learning for the sake of learning; they are acquiring credentials that demonstrate their competence to the world. AI makes this task more difficult by blurring the lines between what the students have produced and what the AI has produced. If students can produce essays, reports, coding exercises, and research projects with the help of AI, then their grades are no longer a measure of their competence. Institutions then face the problem of determining what counts as authentic learning (Parsons, 1959).

The recognition aspect of the recognition problem is also connected to labour markets, where employers primarily depend on credentials as a way of minimising uncertainty regarding who to hire. If credentials cease to convey meaningful information regarding competence, employers may turn to other methods of determining which candidate is capable of performing satisfactorily in that position, including asking for work-based samples of the candidate's work or providing evidence through certification exams, performance history of their competency (Parsons, 1959; Illich, 1971). Therefore, the emergence of AI impacts the connection between educational credentials and labour market position by providing examples of how students will need to work to establish proof of the knowledge and skills they have gained through their education. This reflects the vision expressed by Illich regarding a world where competence is established through practice rather than by merely meeting institutional requirements to maintain an enrolled status in a certain number of hours at an educational institution.

AI and the Shifting Boundaries of Institutional Authority

The problem of authority is another institution-wide concern. Historically, schools have determined what students need to learn, when they need to learn it and how they need to learn it. AI has challenged all three of these claims. Through AI, students can learn the same content earlier than the curriculum suggests, they can explore topics outside the course material, and they can develop skills that teachers do not possess. In some cases, this creates a reversal in the expertise of the student and the teacher. For example students use AI tools to learn about areas in which their teachers lack the necessary training to be effective instructors; this is not just an anecdotal example but is evident in many fields today (data science, software development and digital art, etc.) where students frequently find themselves relying on tutorials, forums and AI tools to augment or supplement what they are learning in school.

This shift creates additional complexity in the teacher-student relationship, as teachers now have to manage the learning trajectories of students who receive a portion of their education outside the confines of the institution. In some cases, teachers have chosen to limit students' access to these additional resources by discouraging or prohibiting the use of external resources, while in other cases, teachers have incorporated the use of additional resources into their classrooms. As such, the direction of these adaptations varies based on the individual institution, on the culture and policy environment of the community, and so forth; however, what is common to all of these institutions is the destabilisation of the traditional role of the teacher as the sole authority in relation to knowledge. As such, authority in education is becoming more broadly defined and can now be shared between human and nonhuman actors, leading to the need for all schools to reassess their place in this emerging network.

At the meso-level, AI transforms: the distribution of cultural and digital capital, how institutions confer merit and recognition, how students gain access to learning resources, the value and meaning of credentials, the economics of educational support, the legitimacy of school authority, the structure of learning ecosystems, and the reproduction of inequality through habitus

Bourdieusian concepts help in illuminating how these transformations create new winners and losers, while Illich's concepts highlight how they challenge the monopoly of schooling over learning. Together, these show that AI is not only disrupting classroom practices but is also reorganising the ecology through which learning takes place.

MACRO-LEVEL TRANSFORMATIONS: PARSONS, FOUCAULT, BECK, AND GIDDENS

While micro-level and meso-level changes involve identity, cognition, and institutional ecosystems at the macro level, educational institutions have other roles. Educators are not alone in their function, and many factors, including the political, economic, and cultural climate, create the context within which all educational institutions operate. Historically, in most of the 20th century, the education system has been used to assimilate individuals into an industrialised society, to classify talent into jobs, and to maintain the cultural identities of nations. In the current environment, artificial intelligence disrupts the functions previously performed by education (and thus by educators) at the macro level (Autor, 2015; Frey & Osborne, 2017, Seldon & Abidoye, 2018). In order to assess how these macro-level transformations are occurring, a theoretical framework provided by the various perspectives presented by both Thomas Parsons, Michael Foucault, and risk theory theorists, Ulrich Beck (1992) and Anthony Giddens (1991) can provide insight into the mechanics of integration between the individual and society.

.Parsons: Socialization, Achievement, and the Allocation of Roles

According to Parsons, the primary function of schooling is to provide a means of socializing people into the different roles that they will fulfil as adults within a complex society. As outlined in Parsons' model of education, schooling provides students with a guide to allowing them to function socially and successfully within the workplace. In addition to providing students with knowledge about universalistic norms such as ability and merit, schools also serve to classify individuals into tracks (i.e., lower, middle, and upper) and based on the type of education they received (i.e., vocational vs. academic). By sorting individuals into different categories based on their abilities, Parsons believes that schools serve the purpose of placing individuals into appropriate roles within society. (Parsons, 1959).

Artificial Intelligence complicates the process of socialisation and allocation. First, the foundation for the socialization of children is based on an assumption that the amount of effort put into a task will produce a reward; thus, there is an expectation that children will accept that they are performing according to those norms because their hard work will pay off. AI provides students with a way to produce high-quality work with much less effort than they would normally put forth (i.e., using AI as a tool to generate essays, analysis, or problem sets). Because machines produce products, it is difficult to determine how much effort was required to achieve that performance; therefore, this creates a question of how true the meritocracy that students' successes are founded on within our current education system. If successful students using AI generate the same level of success as if they had used their own effort (or personal labour), then it becomes very difficult for teachers and institutions to distinguish between what is competence versus what is delegated.

Second, AI makes allocation less stable by weakening the informational value of credentials. Employers use grades and degrees to judge how skilled someone is. If these signals can be inflated or distorted by AI, the allocation function loses reliability. This can lead to shifts in hiring practices. Employers may place greater emphasis on demonstrated skills, portfolios, or situational assessments rather than certifications. In this scenario, the linkage between higher education and labour markets becomes more tenuous, and alternative pathways to employment may proliferate.

Parsons also emphasised the importance of standardised evaluation. AI has a way to devalue the standardisation models of education because AI-based tutoring systems provide students with an opportunity to create their personalised learning path rather than adhering to a traditional chronological curriculum. As students interact with informal network resources or AI-assisted tutors, they may advance at different paces and in different orders than their peers, causing challenges to the use of age-based cohorts and grade level advancement. As a result, while student-centred approaches are supportive of the learning process, they also disrupt the administrative systems relied upon by many mass educational systems.

Foucault: Discipline, Surveillance, and the Datafication of Students

Foucault saw modern institutions, including schools, as disciplinary environments that shape individuals through surveillance, examination, and normalisation (Foucault, 1977). Schools monitor behaviour, enforce schedules, administer tests, and compare students against standardised norms. These mechanisms produce compliant subjects who internalise discipline. Artificial Intelligence extends and transforms these disciplinary practices.

One such change is the emergence of algorithmic surveillance. AI proctoring software relies on webcams, keystroke monitoring, body motion tracking, and eye-tracking software to detect cheating behaviour. Learning management systems track clickstream data, turn-in times, and reading activity. A predictive model tries to predict the likelihood of dropping out or performance on a task. These systems turn students into data subjects whose behaviour can be tracked, analysed, and interpreted at all times (Foucault, 1977; Williamson, 2017).

This datafication of education changes the power dynamic. Educators and institutions have new powers of surveillance and classification, and students have less power over how their behaviour is interpreted. The test, which Foucault described as the key mechanism of discipline, becomes a continuous process rather than an occasional one. Students are assessed on continuous data flows rather than discrete tests. This creates a condition of ambient discipline that is both invisible and ubiquitous.

AI is also providing opportunities for students to engage in self-monitoring. Tools that monitor focus, offer recommendations on how to improve focus, and provide a quantifiable measure of productivity are becoming popular with students. These types of technologies will enable students to self-regulate according to algorithmic norms. This supports Foucault's argument that power is productive and not simply repressive. The power of AI does not just restrict behaviour, but also shapes students' self-perception. There are many examples of self-tracking technologies that have emerged in other contexts (e.g., fitness trackers, sleep trackers, mood trackers), which have resulted in the internalisation of norm-based behaviours by individuals due to algorithmic power (Lupton, 2016). A similar trend is developing in education (e.g., study aids, writing aides, and cognitive enhancers).

Foucault's framework also exposes some tensions within AI and education. Historically, disciplinary power has been concentrated within institutions (such as schools and the state); however, with AI, the power is now more dispersed to private companies that develop platforms, control data, and develop algorithms (Foucault,

1977; Zuboff, 2019). Disciplinary power is now more dispersed and is no longer located in schools alone. Students are now subjects of corporate surveillance, even though they are declared to be engaged in schooling. This raises concerns around privacy, the autonomy of consent, and the commodification of student data.

Beck and Giddens: Risk, Reflexive Modernity, and the Uncertain Future of Skills

Beck and Giddens' studies to explore uncertainty, rapid change, and reflexivity characterise late modern society. Beck's risk society concept suggests that institutions are developing means to manage hazards emerging from technological and economic transformations, rather than from nature. Giddens points out that modernity becomes reflexive when social actors constantly reevaluate their use of institutions/practices based on new available information (Giddens, 1991). Education plays an integral role in both reflexive and risk societies as it helps prepare individuals for increasingly unpredictable futures (Beck, 1992; Giddens, 1991).

The dynamic of the risk society is further enhanced by the presence of Artificial Intelligence, which disrupts the conventional labour market and occupational structures, thus creating uncertainty about the value of certain skills at the point of graduation.

Institutions are also compelled to make reflexive decisions in order to prove the relevance of their curricula in terms of the continued relevance of knowledge. They are constantly required to modify their programs, accreditation, and teaching processes to keep abreast of the pace of technological innovation. Institutions that fail to do so risk losing their legitimacy. The pace of technological innovation makes it impossible to plan educational curricula over the long term; this is a source of tension between the need for stability in institutional reproduction and the need to adapt to innovation (Beck, 1992; Giddens, 1991).

AI further contributes to the risk society regarding the meaning attributed to culture; if the line between human cognition and machine cognition continues to dissolve, cultures must renegotiate notions of education and skill (Beck, 1992). If machines can perform the same functions as creative individuals, the value of creativity and originality will be questioned. Conversely, creativity and originality may become more valuable traits inasmuch as they are unable to be automated. This presents an ambiguity for all parties involved, thus spurring reflexive debate about the intent of education and the validity of various forms of knowledge.

INSTITUTIONAL AND POLICY IMPLICATIONS

The transformations mentioned in the previous sections of this report cannot help but trigger institutional reactions. Educational institutions do not function in a static context but adapt to new forces and re-establish their authority when it is threatened. Artificial Intelligence presents new challenges that force educational institutions to rethink the learning process. These reactions are still in progress, and in most instances, they are uneven, reactive, or experimental. However, some trends are emerging.

Redefining Assessment and Authorship

One of the most pressing institutional forces generated by AI technology is the issue of assessment. For over a century, essays, problem sets, and written exams have been the main evidence of student achievement. These were taken to be a reflection of individual minds. AI technology disrupts this by enabling the production of sophisticated work with little human input (Adams & Thompson, 2023). Institutions are now faced with the question of whether this work is to be regarded as valid, partially valid, or fraudulent (Rosenberg & Kumar, 2023).

The first reaction was to ban these technologies. Some institutions banned the use of AI-generated text, declared the use of such text to be plagiarism, or asked students to sign statements of authorship. But these bans proved difficult to enforce. Detection software was unreliable, and students were able to easily evade these bans. This caused some institutions to rethink the underlying model of education rather than simply trying to regulate behaviour. New models of assessment began to focus on oral defence, project-based learning, group work, and face-to-face performance. These approaches are less dependent on artefacts that can be outsourced and more on embodied demonstrations of competence (Parsons, 1959; Williamson & Eynon, 2020).

These changes are not only practical adjustments but also conceptual ones. They require institutions to clarify what they believe education is supposed to cultivate. If the goal of learning is internal understanding, then assessments must be designed to measure understanding rather than output. If the goal is the ability to orchestrate human-machine collaboration, then assessments must allow and evaluate such collaboration. For now, institutions are split between these philosophies, reflecting a transitional period in which the definition of learning is being renegotiated.

Teacher Roles and Professional Identity

Teachers have traditionally been a very important part of the education system, and many questions arise as to how the continued development of AI will change the roles of teachers in the future. Concerns have been raised that intelligent tutor systems, through the provision of highly personalized instruction to large numbers of students at once, could render teachers obsolete. The current evidence, however, shows a very different story: AI will not completely supplant the interpersonal, motivational, and relational roles that teachers provide; rather, it will simply change the nature of the work performed by teachers (Williamson & Eynon, 2020). For example, teachers will likely see many of the routine tasks associated with instructional delivery (e.g. grading, proofreading, and creating instructional materials) automated, allowing teachers to devote much more of their time to mentoring, facilitating discussions, and providing socio-emotional support to their students (Selwyn, 2019).

In this context, AI will support a larger pedagogical trend away from teachers being "transmitters of knowledge" and toward teachers being "orchestrators of the learning environment." However, the integration of AI into the classroom will create new pressures for many teachers, who may not feel adequately prepared to make use of AI in their instruction. Teachers' professional identities will also be in question, as some teachers will see AI as a tool that will enhance their effectiveness, while others will view it as undermining their authority and exposing their inadequacies. The success of teachers adapting to AI will depend a great deal on the quality of professional development and training they receive.

Institutional Authority and Legitimacy

Institutions' legitimacy is also impacted by Artificial Intelligence. Authority to issue a 'credential' or to train 'students' for employment has historically been one of the characteristics of a school/university; however as companies develop more 'automated' certification systems for learning through the use of AI, there is potential that the value of an educational credential could lessen and replace the authority of traditional higher education institutions (Parsons, 1959; Beck, 1992).

As universities are facing competition from the growth of online education delivery methods, such as MOOC's (massive open online course), boot camps for short-term skills training, and alternative process of credentialing called Micro Credentialing, the introduction of AI into teaching may create further competition through the ability to provide "self-paced" and "self-directed" education delivery systems (Illich, 1971; Beck, 1992; Williamson & Eynon, 2020).

Despite the increased competition from these new forms of education delivery, institutions maintain advantages that the decentralised nature of these types of learning does not allow to be easily replaced or replicated. Institutions' social environment, community of learners and faculty/students create a network of peers and professional mentors to encourage the development of identity as a learner/employee (Mead, 1934). Institutions issue graduates a state and industry-recognised 'accreditation' that provides the means to identify professionally qualified persons. The conflict between the legitimacy of traditional institutions and the technological disruption of education will continue to shape how educational institutions will operate in the next decade.

Economic and Labor Market Alignment

Governments and institutions must also take into consideration the alignment of the labour market. AI is changing the nature of skill demand, and the education system must adapt to this new reality. Skills in critical thinking, communication, teamwork, and human judgment could become more valuable as more and more cognitive tasks are automated (Autor, D. H. 2015). On the other hand, digital literacy, the ability to use computers, computational thinking, and data skills are necessary for functioning in an AI-mediated world. The policy talk is increasingly about future readiness, but what this actually means is still an area of debate.

Global South Perspective

The impact of Artificial Intelligence on education is not evenly distributed across the world. While many previous discussions about technology and learning assumed they were happening in wealthy places, the introduction of AI makes disparities more visible and, in some cases, more consequential. The Global South presents a set of economic, infrastructural, linguistic, and institutional that shape how AI enters educational systems and how it affects students. These conditions can magnify both the promises and the pitfalls of AI. In some regions, AI may serve as a tool for democratizing access to knowledge in others, it may deepen existing inequalities or create new ones (Tsing, 2005).

Uneven Access and the Digital Divide

The issue of inequitable device and connectivity access as well as the lack of digital literacy, has been extensively discussed throughout the Global South (Bangay & Nzimande, 2020). Most solar-powered devices are designed for use by individuals with access to a reliable internet connection, the most recent hardware, and knowledge of how to use a computer or tablet. However, this is not the reality for many parts of South Asia, Sub-Saharan Africa, Latin America, and Southeast Asia

(UNESCO, 2021). For example, students from rural areas may need to share devices with their siblings, experience difficulty accessing the internet, and/or reside in locations without a designated space for quiet study. Urban dwellers also experience inequality in terms of device access and the amount of income available to purchase them, which ultimately impacts the level of resources available to households, as well as the level of parental education (Bourdieu & Passeron, 1977).

These inequalities are more than simply technical issues; they also have significant social and pedagogical implications for education. As such, students with limited resources (e.g., devices, internet access) are unable to keep pace with students who are able to use the tools on a regular basis (World Bank, 2021). Consequently, the digital divide creates an academic divide for those students who do not have access to artificial intelligence (AI) tools and resources (Bond, 2020). While some schools may attempt to mitigate these inequities by providing technology (devices and computer labs), there are often greater gaps in infrastructure than can be overcome by schools alone. In addition, policymakers are now tasked with determining what new public investments, subsidies for families with low incomes, and regulatory measures must be established to ensure equitable access to AI-based education (Beck, 1992; UNESCO, 2021).

Language, Translation, and Cultural Representation

There is also a significant amount of disparities related to language. The vast majority of the entire commercial AI ecosystem has developed based mostly on English and few other major languages. In countries like India, where hundreds of languages exist at once and also differences in educational pathways from one linguistic region to another, the AI simulation tools created could favour the students who are already able to communicate proficiently in one of the global use languages. Although recent advances in the area of multilingual AI modelling provide some hope, there continues to be much difficulty for these types of models relating to upholding regional language idioms, terminology as it relates to education, and nuances associated with cultures. For many students who obtain their primary education in their native language or who do not have a high level of proficiency in English, the value of AI will likely be very severely limited.

At the same time, AI has the potential to reduce language barriers by offering translation, summarisation, and code-switching capabilities. Students who would otherwise struggle with English-language academic content can use AI to access explanations in vernacular languages. This opens possibilities for greater inclusion, particularly for first-generation learners who did not grow up in English-speaking environments. The net effect of AI on linguistic inequality may therefore depend on how quickly multilingual models are developed and how widely they are made available.

Teacher Shortages and Personalized Support

Artificial Intelligence in the Global South provides an opportunity to address teacher scarcity. Overcrowded classrooms, inconsistent teacher training, and a shortage of teachers qualified to teach certain subjects, such as Mathematics and Science, make instruction and achievement difficult for many students in many countries in the Global South (UNESCO, 2021). The use of AI Tutoring Systems enables the individualised evaluation and response of and for each student at any point in time, helping struggling learners access material initially missed in class. In regions where private tutoring is not available, AI could serve as an alternative for students who cannot otherwise access individualised instructional support.

The benefits of AI integration into teacher-led instruction are substantially greater than those of AI substitution. By positioning AI as a supplementary (additional) support to traditional instruction, teachers will be able to extend their reach to hundreds of additional students. However, for many students, particularly those who lack confidence in their academic abilities or have limited support from their families, the replacement of teachers with AI may detract from the relational and motivational bond between students and their teachers (Williamson & Eynon, 2020). There appears to be promising evidence that hybrid models (those that combine technology with teaching) offer greater potential for success in the Global South context.

CONCLUSION

Artificial Intelligence raises questions about many of the assumptions that have structured education for more than a century. The traditional role of the student has been based on expectations of individual cognitive labour, authorship, hard work, and socialization into norms of achievement. These have been based on pedagogical needs as well as social needs, such as sorting people into occupational roles, reproducing cultural norms, and certifying competence. AI challenges these in multiple ways, leading to conceptual and institutional challenges.

At the micro-level, AI changes the everyday activities through which students learn and through which they come to see themselves as learners. Feedback, tutoring, explanation, and problem-solving are no longer solely reliant upon teachers or peers but can now be obtained from algorithms. Hence, students are developing identities based not only on human expectations but also on those of algorithms. The concept of Scaffolding as proposed by Vygotsky, has also developed a new level of complexity because of the continuous support provided by AI, and the impact that this has on the rate of internalisation vs. externalisation. Similarly, the idea of the Learner as developing Self through interaction proposed by Mead evolves as AI becomes an additional form of interlocutor.

At the meso-level, there will be a re-ordering of resources, status, and cultural capital among all students due to how AI systems are leveraged within educational systems. Access to AI tools will provide advantages to some students and create barriers for others who do not have access to them. Bourdieu suggests that the impact of a digital gap will be clearly manifested via the educational system and indicate the disparity between the individuals capable of effectively using AI based on their cultural capital..

Illich's critique of institutions that monopolise learning becomes more relevant in this new world as more learning shifts to informal networks, online platforms, and private ecosystems that operate outside of the authority of schools. Therefore, the central role that schools play in all forms of legitimate learning is being challenged due to the decentralisation of education.

At the macro-level, AI disrupts the way schools function in terms of society. Parsons' theory of how people socialise and get jobs isn't really working anymore, because we don't know what effort will lead to what reward, and we don't know how much value a credential provides us with. Foucault's ways of controlling people through disciplining methods have also changed due to the fact that we are always under surveillance by AI algorithms. As Beck and Giddens explain, these two schools of thought on risk and reflexivity show the anxiety and uncertainty about the future of jobs and skills in an AI-based economy. Because of all these things, many schools feel nervous about finding ways to change without losing their credibility.

Notably, the Global South is affected by these changes in an unequal manner. While some students may be able to access opportunities that were not available before through AI, which will provide them with support in situations where there is a shortage of teachers. On the other hand, AI may widen the gap between students based on infrastructure, language, and socioeconomic factors. The role of the student in this situation is determined not only by technology but also by migration, labour market insecurity, and institutional capacity.

Cumulatively, these trends suggest an era of transition rather than closure. AI is not likely to render the role of students redundant, but will certainly transform what the role consists of. Students could transform into partners of AI, information curators, or managers of a complex educational environment. Conversely, they could transform into data subjects of algorithmic control or consumers in a learning market. The future of education will be shaped by the choices of institutions, governments, families, and students.

One thing that is certain is that the traditional view of the student as an isolated learner who solves problems using paper, books, and their own mind will become less representative of the future of education. We must learn to facilitate change rather than hinder it as we move forward. A balance between innovation and equity, personalisation and integrity, and efficiency and democratic values will all play a crucial role in our ability to shape the education of the future. The way in which each society weighs these factors will ultimately determine whether artificial intelligence will be a tool for facilitating human growth or if it will continue to perpetuate inequities.

REFERENCES

Adams, R., & Thompson, T. L. (2023). *Researching a posthuman world: Interviews with digital objects*. Palgrave Macmillan.

Autor, D. H. (2015). Why are there still so many jobs? The history and future of workplace automation. *The Journal of Economic Perspectives*, *29*(3), 3–30. DOI: 10.1257/jep.29.3.3

Bangay, C., & Nzimande, B. (2020). COVID-19 and educational disruption in the Global South. *Educational Research for Social Change*, *9*(1), 1–7.

Beck, U. (1992). Risk society: Towards a new modernity. *Sage (Atlanta, Ga.)*.

Bond, M. (2020). Schools and emergency remote education during the COVID-19 pandemic. *Educational Technology Research and Development*, *68*(6), 1–5. DOI: 10.1007/s11423-020-09816-3

Bourdieu, P. (1984). *Distinction: A social critique of the judgement of taste*. Harvard University Press.

Bourdieu, P., & Passeron, J.-C. (1977). Reproduction in education, society and culture. *Sage (Atlanta, Ga.)*.

Clark, A. (2008). *Supersizing the mind: Embodiment, action, and cognitive extension*. Oxford University Press. DOI: 10.1093/acprof:oso/9780195333213.001.0001

Cotton, D. R. E., Cotton, P. A., & Shipway, J. R. (2023). ChatGPT: A disruptive technology in higher education. *Innovations in Education and Teaching International*.

Foucault, M. (1977). *Discipline and punish: The birth of the prison*. Pantheon Books.

Frey, C. B., & Osborne, M. A. (2017). The future of employment. *Technological Forecasting and Social Change*, *114*, 254–280. DOI: 10.1016/j.techfore.2016.08.019

Giddens, A. (1991). *Modernity and self-identity: Self and society in the late modern age*. Stanford University Press.

Holmes, W., Bialik, M., & Fadel, C. (2019). *Artificial intelligence in education*. Center for Curriculum Redesign.

Illich, I. (1971). *Deschooling society*. Harper & Row.

Kasneci, E., Sessler, K., Küchemann, S., Bannert, M., Dementieva, D., Fischer, F., Gasser, U., Groh, G., Günnemann, S., Hüllermeier, E., Krusche, S., Kutyniok, G., Michaeli, T., Nerdel, C., Pfeffer, J., Poquet, O., Sailer, M., Schmidt, A., Seidel, T., & Kasneci, G. (2023). ChatGPT for good? On opportunities and challenges. *Learning and Individual Differences*, *103*, 102274. DOI: 10.1016/j.lindif.2023.102274

Kirschner, P. A., & De Bruyckere, P. (2017). The myths of the digital native and the multitasker. *Teaching and Teacher Education*, *67*, 135–142. DOI: 10.1016/j.tate.2017.06.001

Lin, Y., & Chen, N.-S. (2024). Artificial intelligence in personalized learning. *Computers & Education: Artificial Intelligence*, *5*, 100152. DOI: 10.1016/j.caeai.2023.100152

Lupton, D. (2016). *The quantified self.* Polity Press.

Mead, G. H. (1934). *Mind, self, and society*. University of Chicago Press.

Parsons, T. (1959). The school class as a social system. *Harvard Educational Review*, *29*(4), 297–318.

Robinson, L., Cotten, S. R., Ono, H., Quan-Haase, A., Mesch, G., Chen, W., Schulz, J., Hale, T. M., & Stern, M. J. (2015). Digital inequalities. *Information Communication and Society*, *18*(5), 569–582. DOI: 10.1080/1369118X.2015.1012532

Rosenberg, J. M., & Kumar, R. (2023). Artificial intelligence and academic integrity. *Journal of Educational Technology Systems*, *52*(1), 3–18. DOI: 10.1177/00472395231172970

Seldon, A., & Abidoye, O. (2018). *The fourth education revolution: Will artificial intelligence liberate or infantilise humanity?* University of Buckingham Press.

Srivastava, S. (2026). AI as a catalyst for transformation: Revolutionizing lifelong learning and professional development in human services for the digital age: AI and the imperative of lifelong learning in human services. In *Reimagining Business Education in the Age of Artificial Intelligence*, IGI Global Scientific Publishing. doi: 10.4018/979-8-3373-4377-8.ch012

Tsing, A. L. (2005). *Friction: An ethnography of global connection*. Princeton University Press.

UNESCO. (2021). *Reimagining our futures together: A new social contract for education*. UNESCO Publishing.

van Dijk, J. (2020). *The digital divide*. Polity Press.

Vygotsky, L. S. (1978). *Mind in society: The development of higher psychological processes*. Harvard University Press.

Williamson, B. (2017). Big data in education: The digital future of learning, policy and practice. *Sage (Atlanta, Ga.)*. Advance online publication. DOI: 10.4135/9781529714920

Williamson, B., & Eynon, R. (2020). Historical threads, missing links, and future directions in AI in education. *Learning, Media and Technology*, *45*(3), 223–235. DOI: 10.1080/17439884.2020.1798995

World Bank. (2021). Remote learning during [*Lessons from today, principles for tomorrow*. World Bank.]. *COVID*, •••, 19.

Zawacki-Richter, O. (2019). Artificial intelligence in education: A systematic review. *International Journal of Educational Technology in Higher Education*, *16*, 39. Advance online publication. DOI: 10.1186/s41239-019-0171-0

Zuboff, S. (2019). *The age of surveillance capitalism*. PublicAffairs.

Chapter 10
Teacher-Student Relationships in the AI Era:
Trust, Dialogue, and Human Bonding

Mohammed Umair
http://orcid.org/0009-0002-0476-5265
St. Joseph's University, India

ABSTRACT

The relationships between teachers and students are essential to quality education. As A.I. is more and more woven into educational practice, these relationships are being configured in ways that go beyond efficiency of instruction. Examine how AI-mediated educational environments influence the trust, dialogue, and human bonding targets of teacher-student relationships in the AI era. Through the lens of relational and ethical theories of education, AI is conceptualized as a sociotechnical mediator rather than a neutral/moral agent. The examination illustrates that algorithmic authority can destroy relational trust while the simulated interaction obscures the ethical grounding of pedagogical dialogue and over-automation threatens the loss of emotional presence and care. In response, the research forwards a human-centered relational framework that situates AI as an augmentative aid supporting rather than supplanting human judgment, dialogic engagement, and human bonding, and outlines implications for practice, teacher education, and policy.

DOI: 10.4018/979-8-3373-8027-8.ch010

1.0: INTRODUCTION

In all contexts and levels, an artificial intelligence (AI) is transforming the education sector by changing the design and implementation of teaching, learning, assessments and feedback. Artificial intelligence has already established itself as an integral aspect of educational practice, as a wide range of AI applications are being utilized for supporting education and learning. There has been much talk about AI in education and how it could improve efficiency, scalability, and personalization. Often, AI is looked at through this lens as a possible answer to age-old problems such as teacher workload, learner diversity, and instructional optimization. While these developments matter, they will need to ensure that the education debate does not focus on technical performance and instrumental outcomes. Education is essentially a relational, ethical, and humane process, not merely a technical enterprise. Learning and teaching take place in relationships based on trust, dialogue, care and moral responsibility. The relationship between teacher and student is essential for better academic outcomes, as well as for better motivation, identity, belonging and well-being. As AI fully integrated into teaching practice and relationship processes, its impact is felt beyond teaching effectiveness to the relational basis of education. Despite their relevance, the conceptualization and research of these relational dimensions remains insufficient.

A rising accumulation of vital studies has started to call into question the belief that artificial intelligence is a neutral or value-free educational tool. Rather, designers and policymakers are increasingly considering AI systems as sociotechnical actors, which encode assumptions concerning knowledge, learners, authority, success, and much more in their design, data practices, and operation. When artificial intelligence systems produce feedback, foresee performance, or imitate conversational engagement, they participate, either indirectly or directly, in influencing the formation of trust, the conduct of dialogue, and the perception of care. The above poses serious questions on how much authority should a teacher or algorithm have, how has this changed the agency of students, and the ethics of datafication and surveillance in learning.

In this context, teacher–student relationships are a crucial and underexamined site for the educational implications of AI. Many existing studies focus only on trust in technology, usability, or learning outcomes, overlooking how AI mediates relationships as integrated wholes. Trust is often thought of as confidence in systems rather than a relational achievement; conversation is confused with simulated speech; and care is seen as an emotional add-on not a moral action. As a result, the human aspects of education are at risk of being pushed aside or diluted under automation logic.

This chapter recognises these omissions and addresses them by prioritising trust, dialogue and human bonding as intertwined dimensions of teacher–student relationships in the AI era. Inspired by relational and human-centered educational theory, education within the research is construed as a practice sustained by relationship, ethical judgment and feeling. AI should not be treated as an autonomous pedagogic agent, but as a mediator that may augment or disrupt relational practices depending on the way it is designed, governed and enacted in classrooms. This framing allows for a critical examination of what AI can meaningfully contribute to education and, just as importantly, what it cannot do.

By using a relational lens, the study put to test dominant narratives about AI that privilege efficiency, scaling, and personalization. It does not only ask about how AI affects trust, but how it can actually reshape the conditions under which trust can be built, dialogue can be sustained, and human bonding can be preserved. Through this, the research develops a human-centred relational framework, thereby reemphasising the importance of teacher–student relationship and clarifying AI's role as an augmentative rather than moral agent in education

The chapter begins by theorising teacher–student relationships as relational practice and proceeds to a critical engagement with the ways in which AI reconfigures authority, agency and responsibility. The following sections explore trust under algorithmic mediation, the limited role of machines in dialogic pedagogy, and the non-replicability of human bonding and care. The essay subsequently synthesizes these insights into a coherent relational framework, discusses implications for practice, teacher education, and policy, and concludes with future research directions. With all these conversations, the goal is a more ethically informed and relationally aware perspective on AI use in education, which has human relationships at the core of educational development.

1.2: OBJECTIVE OF THE CHAPTER

This Chapter aims to critically evaluate how the incorporation of artificial intelligence in educational contexts reshapes teacher-student relationships, with particular emphasis on trust, dialogue and human bonding. With a theoretical perspective that is relational and human-centred, the aim of the study is to conceptualise education as something that is fundamentally relational and to investigate AI not as a neutral tool but as a sociotechnical mediator that reconfigures relations of authority, agency, responsibility and ethics. The study strives to add a framework which envisages how AI can assist rather than replace human relationships while protecting students' wellbeing, teachers' professional judgement, and the moral purpose of education by laying bare the relational dimensions often neglected in AI-in-education discourse.

1.3: CHAPTER OUTLINE

This chapter has been structured in such a way that the reader may build a relational understanding of AI concerning theory and critical analysis and implications. The author of the chapter offers a theoretical framing of teacher–student relationships as relational practice. Trust comes to the fore as a key dimension of meaningful education that incorporates the establishment of a human bond through dialogue. It elaborates on each construct in greater depth, employing educational theory to demonstrate their epistemic, ethical, and affective significance for learning and for student wellbeing. The chapter next studies AI in education as a mode of sociotechnical reconfiguration of teaching and learning. It outlines key pedagogically relevant AI applications. We conceptualize AI as an actor that can reshape authority, agency, and responsibility. Subclassifications of machine reaction follow, as do focused analytical parts on trust under algorithmic mediation, dialogue, and limits of machine interaction, and human bonding and emotional presence. They ask what is altered, threatened, or preserved when AI mediates relational practices. The chapter proceeds to outline a human-centered relational framework, integrating trust, dialogue, and bonding as a coherent conceptual contribution. These findings are juxtaposed against dominant narratives in AI-in-education that centre on efficiency and scalability. The chapter then describes the lesson of the study for educational practice, teacher education, policy, and governance.

The chapter ends with future research directions and a conclusion reiterating that education is inherently relational and ethical. AI has an augmentative role as a technology, and not as a moral agent. Therefore, it is advocated that AI must be integrated ethically, and more human-centred rather than technology-centred.

1.4: LITERATURE REVIEW

1. AI and relational change in education:

In the wake of the increasing use of AI in educational environments, several scholars began to pay attention to the relational aspect of teaching and learning, many years ago. In the early days of prominence of AIEd, papers that dealt with it were basically about cognitive outcome (e.g., student learning) and efficiency (e.g., Woolf, 2010). As research about the use of AI in education grew, they began to look at how it mediates teacher-student relationship and the impact it has on trust, dialogue, and lack of bonding (Luckin et al., 2016; Holmes, Bialik & Fadel, 2019). One of the reasons for this shift. AIEd literature often discusses the topic of trust. Mayer Davis and Schoorman's (1995) integrative model of trust, identifying ability benevolence and integrity as the three trustworthiness contributors, has been adapted by educational researchers to study trust in AI-supported learning environments.

2. Trust in teacher: student: AI interactions:

Recent research indicates that students' trust in AI tools depends on their perceptions of the tools' accuracy, transparency, and relatedness to teacher guidance (Pitts & Motamedi, 2025). In a similar context, teachers' trust in AI is dependent on explainability and perceived pedagogical control Feldman-Maggor et al. 2025. According to Kizil, when AI-generated suggestions or feedback is a "black-box", it reduces the professionalism of teachers and does not inspire confidence in them. Selwyn (2019) notes, "Trusting an Artificial Intelligence is not the same as trusting a man." Significantly, trust's distribution gets relationally redistributed. As students became more reliant on AI feedback, they started to trust their teachers less. Likewise

3. Dialogue, communication and social presence

As noted by Alexander (2008), dialogue is essential for teacher–student relationships. With the apparition of conversational agents, there research comparing a machine one-on-one dialogue and human pedagogic dialogue.

In a recent paper by Kim et al. (2021), participants reported significantly greater satisfaction and engagement when an AI instructor used relational forms of communication such as empathy, encouragement and adaptiveness than a transactional communication system. The study by Cheng et al. (2022) found that students often associate social presence with AI chatbots and consider them as learning partners or supporting characters.

Still, these scholars do have a concern and it is that the dialogue produced by the AI is a non-autonomous performance, that is, it is not performed deliberately by an agent which may be one or other human beings. This does not have real intention or 'moral' agency or reason-responsiveness behind a specific action (Friesen & Selwyn, 2022).

4. Human bonding, care and socio-emotional dimensions

A more modern and arguably broader definition of a genuine caring is one where the process of recognition and being attuned emotionally. Noddings (2013) defined human bonding in education as a process of caring, empathizing, recognizing and being attuned emotionally. Conversely, the AI systems are modelling affect and emotion but the literature.

Atchley et al. (2024) describes a second way in which AI helps humans come together. Through the use of AI to free up teacher time, this action allows for the returning of teachers to rich human interactions. We can lose sight of the fact that the idea of emotional intelligence can change in the not too distant future. It follows a similar principle to those suggested for AI-enhanced SEL, wherein AI should identify emotional patterns but must never independently intervene in students' emotional development (Zhai et al., 2020). Williamson and Eynon (2020), pointing to the problem with affect-detection systems, argue that such systems will eventually discipline learners through constant monitoring which is contradictory. Concerns about emotional surveillance, data privacy and cultural bias are the major concerns. The effectiveness of these methods are in question too.

5. Teacher professional identity and acceptance of AI

The professional identity and relational responsibility of teachers influence their acceptance of AI. According to Celik et al. (2025), using the Technology Acceptance Model (TAM), It is important to note that only perceived usefulness is not enough to predict adoption, other variables such as subjective norm, ethical concerns and threat to teacher's relational role also influences the adoption.

When AI systems seem to take the place of judgment, care or pedagogical discretion, teachers resist them. In contrast, the use of participatory design approaches results in far greater trust, ownership and alignment with relational pedagogies (Holstein et al., 2019

6. Ethical and socio-technical considerations

Up until October 2023, the literature on AI and teacher-student relations raises ethical issues. So, many research work talk about data privacy (Regan & Jesse, 2019), algorithmic bias (O'Neil, 2016. Human flourishing, relational dignity, and the broader values of education, should be placed at the centre of ethical AIEd design, we cannot look only for "optimization" (Holmes et al., 2019).

Some concerns are shared in a variety of policy documents.

1.5: SYNTHESIS AND RESEARCH GAPS

Research on artificial intelligence in education has previously concentrated on systems' effectiveness, learning performance and efficiency (Chen et al., 2020).

Looking at the literature, the teacher learner relationship for example is not addressed to quite the same extent. Many studies consider either single-agent trust in AI systems (Nguyen et al., 2020) or AI–student interaction (Hosny, 2020) as the unit of analysis, but both overlook how AI redefines interpersonal trust (e.g. teacher and student). Likewise, AI-for-dialogue primarily refers to studentAI communication, ignoring another important pedagogical dialogue, namely (Gweon et al., 2019; Tiquia et al., 2021).

Even with the identification of ethical issues such as privacy, surveillance and bias, the lived experience of teachers and students of relationships is rarely the focus. Many of the available studies are either survey-based or short-lived which gives no insight on the changing patterns. Research on teacher-student relationships that examines trust, dialogue and human bonding through AI is important. Notably, teacher-student relationships benefit human bonding. Human bonding involving care, empathy, and emotional connection is under-theorised in AIEd literature.

1.6: METHODOLOGICAL AND CONCEPTUAL POSITIONING

This study belongs to a conceptual framework that considers education as a human and relational practice. In this context, education is generally perceived as a practice that is constructed socially, dialogic and ethical. The relationship between a teacher and their student serves as the foundation for the formation of trust. This interpretation presents trust as a process that is relational, and can be negotiated and renegotiated through continuous interaction. Other analytical units of analysis include the concept of dialogue as a pedagogical practice in the co-construction of meaning and authority. In addition this includes a conception of human bonding as the emotional and moral dimensions of education which includes care, empathy, and mutual recognition. With the socio-technical perspective in mind, we reject the framing of AI as an independent or autonomous actor and reconceptualise AI as a mediating element embedded in existing educational relationships and institutional contexts. Perceptions and practices towards AI as a mediating element that shape. The research adopts an interpretivist qualitative methodology, which seeks to uncover the lived experiences and meaning-making processes of individuals engaged in a phenomenon. The study promotes a qualitative research design to capture the ongoing situation versus bound nature of trust, dialogue and bonding via interviews, observations and reflective accounts. Afterward, the thematic and interpretive data analysis is applied, highlighting relational processes rather than isolation at the level of individual variables. Accordingly, some congruence between concepts and qualitative research methodology enables how teacher–learner relations are found to be experienced, negotiated and sustained in AI-enabled education.

1.7: THEORETICAL FRAMEWORK: TEACHER–STUDENT RELATIONSHIPS AS RELATIONAL PRACTICE

Using a relationist approach to education, the contribution views teaching and learning as not just technical activities but lived practices emerging from social interaction, an ethical stance, and a sense of emotional involvement (Biesta, 2015; Noddings, 2013). Teacher-student relations do not sit on the edge of learning. Rather, they underpin teaching and learning. Learning is a relational achievement. This is through mutual trust, dialogue and human connection or bonding that shapes students' engagement, motivation and well-being (Palmer, 2007). As a lived practice, teacher-student relations are the theoretical framework of this contribution and, thus, a solid theoretical illustrative example to interrogate how AI education may mediate and enable or inhibit the practice of teacher-student relations.

1. Relational Trust in Education

Relational Trust has epistemic, affective, and moral dimensions (Mayer, Davis & Schoorman, 1995; Bryk & Schneider, 2002). The term epistemic trust means students consider teachers to be a truth to knowledge. Affective trust is trust in teachers as safe persons. The moral aspect of trust relates to students' beliefs that teachers have integrity, fairness, and interests committed to (the students).

More specifically, relational trust establishes the processes by which students can engage productively with the content of learning (Bryk and Schneider, 2002). Many studies have also found that trust is indispensable for students' learning.

There is bound to be a large degree of power asymmetry and vulnerability in pedagogy. Students assessment and evaluation power rests with the teachers. On the contrary learners rely on the acknowledgement of their teacher. Moreover, trust can act as a damping relational mechanism. Students and educators can experience vulnerability, which not only is not a threat but also presents a growth opportunity (Biesta, 2015) Without trust, students may tune out, conceal their lack of understanding and adopt a defensive mode of learning. Thus, trust acts as a precondition of learning, but is also a participant of learning. The presence of a well-trained teacher influences the students' psychological well-being and pedagogy.

2. Dialogue and Intersubjectivity

Dialogue refers to the relational and intersubjective process between teacher and students to co-construct meaning (Alexander, 2008) The reasoning of a teacher who applies dialogic pedagogy is that human beings learn by interacting through questioning and response, rather than one's transfer of knowledge to another. By talking to each other they can show their thinking, consider the views of others and deepen their own understanding (Mercer & Howe, 2012). Listening, responsiveness and recognition are key practices in dialogic relationships. For example, educators who heed and address students' inputs validate their roles as epistemic agents capable of effectively contributing to the knowledge creation process (Cook-Sather, 2014). In this way, dialogue is not just a pedagogical tool; it is also a pedagogical ethic based upon respect, mutual recognition and our shared humanity (Paulo Freire, 1970). In a similar vein, dialogic methods promote independent thought, freedom of choice, and feelings of acceptance which encourage learning and improve our well-being.

3. Human Bonding and Care Ethics

The grounding of education in human bonding elaborates in the presence of emotion, empathy, and moral responsibility. According to Noddings (2013), all of these are an important part of teaching ethics. The ethics-of-care perspectives argue education is sustained by relationships of attentiveness and responsiveness or caring for relationships. In addition, teachers actively recognize and respond to students' emotional and moral needs. The capacity to interact safely with others, having the right tools to bounce back, get involved, and stick with something. These are related with the academic performance significantly. Teaching is an exercise in relational labour (Hargreaves, 2001). This indicates that the work within the organisation and its stakeholders is emotional and often ethical. Education is a project that aims at the humanization of students as thinking, feeling and moral beings (Gert Biesta, 2015). Consequently, the quality of human bonding is an essential quality characteristic of education. Learning, wellbeing and ethical education is also a fundamental driver.

4. The reconfiguration of trust and pedagogical authority in the Indian context

In recent years, Indian scholarship on AI in education highlights its growing influence on teacher-student relationships. This can be seen in personalized learning platforms, automated assessment and learning analytics. As stated by studies, AI can help teachers reduce their administrative work and conduct focused pedagogical interventions that are expected to enhance teacher-student engagement (Sharma & Gupta, 2023; NITI Aayog, 2021). However, the researchers warn that the use of algorithmic systems might further depersonalise learning, weaken the autonomy of the teacher, and compromise the contextualisation of students' needs (Kumar, 2024; Bhatia & Jain, 2023). Concerns regarding privacy, surveillance, and algorithmic bias are particularly relevant in Indian classrooms with socio-economic and linguistic diversity (Sengupta & Mishra, 2022). A recent review of the literature on higher education suggests that trust can only be sustained if AI acts as a pedagogical aid and not as a decision-maker; teachers must retain interpretive and ethical control. (Rao & Pillai, 2024).

1.8: AI IN EDUCATION: SOCIOTECHNICAL RECONFIGURATION OF TEACHING AND LEARNING

Artificial intelligence is frequently discussed in popular media and the academic community as an emerging education technology. We now see all of these aspects coded in different educational applications where they can function as intelligent tutoring systems, learning analytics dashboards, automatic feedback, a type of adaptive assessment system and generative AI–based writing or tutoring assistants. While there is a wide range of physical instantiations, software architectures and computational processes, these applications are pedagogically relevant as they mediate communication activity components not only related to teaching, but also explanation, feedback, assessment, diagnosis or learner support. Researchers in education have shifted their attention from the technical architecture of AI applications to how their use reshapes learning environments through rearrangements of interactions, decisions, and pedagogical time. This means that the relevance of AI is not so much about its computational complexity, but about its ability to create an intervention into the social and relational ecology of teaching and learning.

The impact of AI on the management of relationships, authority, agency and responsibility in schools should educate us. We will treat AI as a sociotechnical actor, drawing on the sociotechnical and actor-network perspectives (Latour, 2005, Selwyn, 2019). AI refers to a system, a human concept whose impact can only be assessed with regards to its entanglement with human actors, institutional dominant logics and social structures. Furthermore, values are embedded in the design and implementation choices. Placing AI into the school system will change it as much as when computers were introduced into the blackboard based schooling system. It means understanding that what qualifies as knowledge, modalities of learning, and what counts as success are assumptions embedded in algorithms, which have pedagogical implications.

A key repositioning relates to teaching authority. Teachers use their authority in epistemic guidance and evaluation. Students, on the other hand, receive knowledge through relating to and engaging in dialogue (authority via relation). An AI system produces a recommendation, feedback or evaluative statement that is perceived as objective, independent, neutral, or authoritative. For example, a teacher could use live streaming while teaching to collect feedback from students or the AI can mark some video clips as being more engaging than others. Parents could receive reports that include the "engagement score" of the special needs child or may be part of the team sent a "warning" about the likelihood of exclusion or students may point out.

AI is also changing the agency in classroom relationships. While adaptive and personalized systems are promoted as empowering to learners, research shows agency is not 'given' but may be re-distributed unequally. Should the learning activities be algorithmically pre-structured, students can gain procedural autonomy but lose epistemic agency (Biesta, 2015). In this same vein, teachers may 'lose' agency by moving from being active agents making pedagogical decisions to passive agents overseeing algorithmic decision-processes in data-driven instruction. The engagement and motivation of the students is essential for learning the relation quality and well-being.

We recognize a strong link between agency and the reinvention of responsibility. One instance depicting the transformation of accountability in education with the help of AI is the conflicting and overlapping claims of accountability for learning outcomes, mistakes and harm raised by teachers, institutions and systems (Williamon et al., 2023). For instance, if a person is misled by the feedback or assessment generated through AI, if it causes harms by perpetuating a bias or misinformation, or if it undermines the trust. As per Williamon et al. (2023), this diffusion of responsibility can lead to a loss of moral clarity that underpins teacher–student relationships. Responsibility is being accountable for one's actions or omissions.

To this point, we argued that AI does not make sense as a purely technological actor or a purely human actor. AI is better viewed as a "sociomaterial configuration" to account for the many normative assumptions and materialities that it is imbued with and to go beyond dualisms. How is the topic related to the human institutions or other sociological components? Likewise, one might question how AI relates to educational institutions or the state. How AI interacts with students or educators, further. It should be noted that limited answers are available as the domain is still evolving.

Let us look at adaptive learning. The commercial triumvirate of Udacity, Coursera, and edX appeared with earlier proprietary adaptive software. A disconnect has arisen between real innovation and what is promoted. According to Wolf and Luckin's (2017) sharp critique of MOOC pedagogies, only some in higher education.

1.9: TRUST UNDER ALGORITHMIC MEDIATION

Artificial intelligence is no longer on the sidelines of education; it is increasingly mediating how teachers teach and how students are viewed. As algorithms influence feedback, assessment, and academic decisions, the foundation of the teacher-student relationship is being quietly reshaped. Traditionally, trust relied on human wisdom, attention, and situational awareness. The algorithmic systems tend to be opaque but authoritative, leading to a shift of trust towards a technical process that often appears objective. This proliferation of algorithmic systems, however, may obscure bias, simplify complexity, and curtail conversations. As students won't have any questions on which to judge a decision, they may not trust it. If teachers readily defer to it, they would risk losing their pedagogical authority. In the era of AI trust, things don't just happen, they need to be nurtured. It depends on transparency, ethical usage, and the teacher's willingness to contextualise, interpret, and, when needed, override algorithmic decisions. AI must work as a teaching assistant, not a substitute for human insight. In a classroom that employs AI, trust is socio-technical. The future of education will depend on whether teachers remain visible moral agents or algorithms quietly take over.

1. Algorithmic authority and teacher judgment

It is essential for teachers to enjoy trusted positioning for maximally productive teaching and learning. Nevertheless, at various education levels and in different countries, formal education is increasingly delegating responsibility to algorithms and reducing teacher judgment in formal education. AI-driven predictive analytics, recommendations, and automated feedback are touted as 'objective', 'data-driven' and, therefore, above criticism. Algorithms that hold this position obtain a certain authority that, for example, can eventually end up displacing or constraining teachers' judgement. In other words, trust may sometime be shifting away from relationally grounded credibility between teachers and students, to more technologically mediated forms of credibility.

2. Automation bias and epistemic displacement

One of the primary concerns in this respect is automation bias and epistemic displacement. Automation bias refers to the tendency of teachers or students to overly rely on a recommendation produced by an algorithm, for example, to opt for an algorithmic score of a student's paper rather than his or her own contextual knowledge or teaching skills and abilities. The end result of the epistemic displacement is that AI systems are getting relegated as the final authority on knowledge and teachers as facilitators, overseers or monitors rather than authoritative knowledge bearers. In this situation, by displacing the interpersonal processes of trust-maintenance, which include dialogue, explanation, and mutual recognition, relational trust is undermined. A student may trust an algorithm more than their teacher. Thus, trust is no longer relational. In this situation, a trust is formed.

3. Datafication and surveillance of students' learning behaviors

The datafication and monitoring of students' learning behaviour produce conditions of suspicion. Data is continuously collected from students by an AI system and required by it. Transformation of actions, feelings, and interactions of students into measurable indicators allows prediction and intervention (Williamson, 2017; Knox, 2020). The discourses of personalization, optimization, and efficiency normalize datafication and surveillance. Nonetheless, they present significant ethical concerns about privacy, consent and student agency (Regan and Jesse, 2019). According to research, surveillance encourages compliance and self-regulation among students, rather than fostering genuine engagement, curiosity, or risk-taking (Foucault, 1977; Selwyn, 2021). Surveillance jeopardizes trust as a relational condition.

4. Institutional trust and legitimacy

The institution's credibility is affected by algorithmic mediation or not. Trust in education extends beyond relationships with people. It likewise alludes to believing institutions to be ethical and responsible actors Tschannen-Moran & Hoy (2000). One example of this is where the AI system mediates an assessment, progression or disciplinary decision without transparency and with no meaningful human oversight. When transparency and understanding are lacking, responsibility becomes diffused across various actors and institutions. For example, a teacher might be blamed for an outcome that a hidden system will affect, but won't control. A student affected by a decision broadcasted by a complex and opaque system will presumably find it difficult to know who is in charge. Such institutional accountability dilemmas diminish legitimacy of powerful stakeholders and undermine students' sense of procedural fairness.

It is essential to understand that the algorithm is created not only by the humans but also by the data in fact, the algorithm is developed mainly by the data. Algorithm bias occurs when an inherent bias of a programmer is not taken care of or verified, and an algorithm is created based off their bias. Similarly, bias that is fed into the database for the algorithm which already exists, and propagates for training, which then helps in sanctioned decision-making based off the bias produced.

1.10: DIALOGUE IN AI-ENHANCED LEARNING CONTEXTS

Present-day AI systems have the ability to generate fluid and contextually relevant language (Levin and Hahn 2018). The significance of these developments – variously called 'simulated conversation', convincing 'machine talk', and dialogue in view from the machines' – is far-reaching (English and Welsh, 2015: 6). However, it is important not to confuse the former with the pedagogical idea of dialogue, as the latter is much more than a mere exchange of language. Current AI conversation is poor as dialogue which could be illustrated through the following example. Through a telematic art process, an international chat of multiple people and chat bots where it will be impossible to know who is who. Such a thing can be done technically and theoretically today. How about a live international telematic conversation with real people with psychosis, and an AI system–so indistinguishable from a person that we don't know who is who? That is probable.

The growing use of conversational AI in education brings a risk of dialogic outsourcing becoming prevalent in classrooms, a critical risk factor educators must watch out for. This occurs when someone's dialogic role is partly assigned to machines (Selwyn, 2019). An educator who probes, questions, provides feedback, and maintains inquiry is partially substituted by artificial intelligence, for instance. Outsourcing an activity or service will not raise any issues if it will result in greater efficiency or availability of timely feedback. (Friesen & Selwyn, 2022). Nonetheless, the emergence of dialogic outsourcing poses a risk when the act of decentering neglects to acknowledge the importance of dialogic learning. The objective of dialogic learning is to ensure students differ from each other through an interaction that develops. To combat these dangers, teaching methods need to shift back to human conversations and critique the outputs of the AI (Peters et al., 2023). For example, the crucial examination of responses means that students will question the output and assertions of an AI, as well as their accuracy, assumptions, omissions, and bias. Such practices do not yield epistemic authority to AI but rather transform it into an object of enquiry. AI output must be evaluated and verified, it is only a starting point. This relinquishing of epistemic authority develops a crucial epistemic vigilance and critical digital literacies (Peters et al., 2023).

Teaching involves addressing oneself by means of others. In other words, the teacher helps with the process through which the AI is introduced, interpreted and dialogised in class. The pivotal role of teachers will be to frame the AI output in relation to the curricula in use and the ethical imperative; and above all they will invite students to make sense together of what the AI output might mean and understand. Facilitated dialogue, as Alexander (2008) would say, has the features of the dialogue in teaching that meant a shared social activity of forming meanings (not a communication between a human and machine) Disagreement and reflection preserve the dialogue when teachers facilitate the discussion.

It is essential to preserve student voice and agency through AI-mediated spaces. Recognition of students as contributors who matter (not as objects or recipients) is imperative for pedagogical dialogue. Student voice is victim to algorithmic outputs which appear authentic if AI systems control our interaction. The use of purposeful dialogue tools facilitates student expression of understandings and interrogation of AI knowledge and their participation as knowledge creators. It fosters learning and well-being through agency, autonomy, and belonging.

To summarize, these observations explain why AI should be seen as a dialogic provocation and not as a partner. Artificial intelligence raises questions, offers alternative meanings and produces artefacts for classroom discussion, but not the other way around. The dimensions of dialogue that were missing from the pedagogical dialogue were ethical, relational and inter-subjective.

1.11: HUMAN BONDING, EMOTIONAL PRESENCE, AND THE LIMITS OF AI

1. Human Bonding

Human bonding lays the foundations of education on the basis of empathy, care, and moral judgment. These dispositions are not just affective but entail relational practices and solidarity. It is through "forms of presence, responsiveness, and moral responsibility" that they manifest and are enacted (Noddings, 2013, p. 2) and they carry with them political interpretations and contestations (Biesta, 2015). Although AI systems can perform sentiment analysis to simulate an affective response, identify emotional markers in their students, or analyse patterns of empathic language, they do not share in the lived experience or vulnerability of being human. Wishing, caring for or feeling for the other also imply moral judgment. Many researchers have previously proposed that empathy, care, and moral judgment cannot be replicated because it is uniquely human. Education is not about Empathy.

2. Morally addressable agents

Notably, this acknowledgment does not idealise or romanticise teaching's work. Teaching itself is not caring. There's nothing automatic about a positive supportive teacher–student relationship (A. Noddings, 2012). Teachers differ from AI systems in that they are morally addressable agents against whom one can make claims and hold to account (Biesta, 2015). The issue of a moral judgement in the pedagogical encounter is as follows: locating and delineating an instance - when to oppose or confront, when to facilitate or support, when to intervene. You cannot determine or stipulate any of this in advance, nor algorithmically.

3. Emotional labor and AI Bonding

The concept of emotional labor may provide further insights into the difficulty of AI bonding. According to Hargreaves (2001), teachers routinely do emotional labour when either managing their own feelings, responding to students' emotional needs or creating safe emotionally spaces for learning. The presence of digital and AI in education, this labour does not just go away, it enhances as teachers make up for less presence, fractured contact severed by episodes, and technology-mediated contact (Borup et al 2020). Experiencing students as being present, available and responsive is an achievement of the human, which calls for involvement and reflection of the deliberate and commitment of the ethically.

4. Risk of relational erosion

If we over-automate pedagogy, we might run into very serious risks of relational erosion. When feedback, evaluation, and student assistance are given over to computerised systems, it will thin, tran- sationalise and de-personalise further relations. It entails a higher distance, being less recognised, and being less responsive to students' life worlds (Selwyn, 2019).While students may get feedback quicker, and faster access to advisory staff, they can also be less seen as people (Selwyn, 2019). The weakening of relationships may cause disconnection and loss of belongingness. The erosion of relationality will most affect those that most depend on relationality. The experts assert that we must accept responsibility.

As digital mediation and augmented education solutions become more essential by the day, the invasive power of AI is becoming apparent. As the voluminous data collection and analysis are in place, the education system is moving towards anonymisation. It applies to policy-making, management and teaching and learning decisions involved. As a result, the use of algorithms in decision-making is giving rise to data racism. It can be formal or informal, clear or unspoken, a one-off or repeated. This is evident in the way people are treated when it comes to access, grades, behaviour, guidance, progression and so on.

1.12: DISCUSSION: TOWARD A HUMAN-CENTERED RELATIONAL FRAMEWORK

The personal connection between a teacher and their student is of utmost importance. As we use AI, the fundamental role of the teachers should always remain to facilitate interaction, collaboration and motivation. Consequently, it becomes essential for educators to impart teachable AI skills and digital life skills which help young people no matter whatever they choose in their life to be ready for the future.

1. Integrating Trust, Dialogue, and Human Bonding as Relational Practice

The idea we have of trust and dialogue and bonding must not be understood as additive or separate variables but rather as mutually constitutive dimensions of relational practice. The conditions for dialogue to happen are established by trust. Dialogue sustains and enhances trust by recognizing and responding. Ultimately, human connection provides an emotional and moral basis for these processes. The erosion of any of these three dimensions compromises the relational integrity of education. As a result, the study argues that educational implementation of AI has to be assessed not just for performance or personalisation alone but for their impact on this relational ecology.

Under algorithmic mediation, trust is the most fragile dimension. Through previous readings, it was discussed that trust in education has epistemic, affective, and moral dimensions, which can be diminished by the assumption of algorithmic authority or diffuse responsibility. When simulated interaction is false identified as a pedagogical dialogue between human and machine, reduced dialogue happen. When emotional presence and care are replaced or downgraded to a functional and affective simulation, human bonding is impacted. The proposed relational framework ultimately connects the two approaches mentioned above by viewing education as a relational achievement which needs human work to uphold and not just an accomplishment which can be designed through technical optimisation.

2. AI as Relational Mediator, Not Relational Replacement

AI serves as a mediator in relationships rather than a replacement in relationships. This makes a critical difference. If AI use replaces teachers' judgment, dialogue and care, it disposes of, rather than enhances, the relational capacity of teachers and students. AI that displaces rather than complements human activity, particularly relational activity, that undermines learning relationships. Conversely, artificial intelligence employed to promote interpersonal interactions, such as allowing more time for relational practices, revealing patterns to reflect upon, or provoking dialogue for deeper understanding.

According to Framework, AI must play a secondary role in interpretation, rather than the primary or authoritative one. This is not on its own feedback, suggestions and representations of data that are generated by artificial intelligence. Even so, this pedagogically actionable knowledge is a function of clerical mediation and relational context. Accordingly, educators continually examine the output of artificial intelligence (AI) for ethical positioning. This positioning defends the ethical and social responsability of educational practice which cannot be reduced, as well as its civic significance. To put it differently, entrusting the task of decision making to AI.

3. Challenging Dominant Narratives of Efficiency and Scalability

This chapter adds to the conversation by intentionally framing its findings in opposition to existing narratives in AI-in-education discourse, especially those which underscoring efficiency, scale and personalization. Although these objectives are often presented as self-evidently good, they risk narrowing the purposes of education to what can be automated, measured, or optimized. By using a relational approach the efficiency is not a neutral value and the gain in speed or scale may incur a cost in relational depth and dialogic richness and emotional presence.

Focusing on scalability is particularly challenging in terms of relational practices. The importance of trust, dialogue, bonding is so contextual, situated and not scalable (a condition to scaling). We are only able to regard certain students as we would any member of the community because they have particular histories and particular relatedness that we care about; likewise, we can only dialogue with certain people and trust them. As a result, trying to automate or "scale" these relational practices may produce "thin" imitations of care or dialogue without any moral content. According to this study, the belief that an educational practice works just because it works at scale is erroneous. After this, it argues for relational sufficiency to guide educational purposes meaning an educational technology must allow people to form 'good enough' relationships to develop trusting.

4. Trust Reconsidered: From Technological Confidence to Relational Achievement

The key theoretical shift proposed herein construes trust differently; much research on AI in education conceptualises trust as a psychological state that a technology must somehow engender. The more a user trusts an AI system, the more the user believes that it is accurate, reliable or helpful. Therefore, trustworthiness is a property of the AI system, while belief is an affective state. Our research redefines trust as a relational outcome sustained by transparency, accountability, and ethical responsibility. Trustworthiness cannot be generated by an AI artifact in and of itself. In the context of education, stakeholders must have confidence that the institution will act properly in the student's best interest. When professionals trust each other actually to do so and do so well, trust is there. In addition, the parties also trust the institution if they think it is ready to cure any breaches. With AI, however, trust becomes at risk as this professional activity becomes invisibly forced, one can say.

5. Dialogue Reclaimed as Human Meaning-Making

The discussion also reappropriates dialogue as a genuine human pedagogical ethic and not as a machine relationship. The intersubjective meaning-making of co-learners cannot be generated by conversational AI, although they may assist in learning through explanations or prompts. Dialogue, in the sense meant here is listening, responsiveness and mutual recognition. All of these capacities cannot be disentangled from being present in a human sense and taking responsibility.

Framing AI as a provocation for dialogue rather than a conversational partner opens up productive possibilities. AI outputs may initiate questioning, disagreement, and reflection, but the work of dialogue is human work. Teachers do this work by framing outputs of AI as provisional, contestable, and situated, thus reinforcing students' epistemic agency. This approach is geared towards critical pedagogy rather than a mechanical one and facilitates the cultivation of democracy and understanding.

6. Human Bonding and the Ethics of Presence

This framework's take on human bonding and emotional presence is perhaps most ethically significant. This paper argues, against some narratives claiming that artificial intelligences could eventually be made to care, or empathise, that these capacities are uncomputable because those capacities are ethical relations, not technical functions. Only human beings can meet the conditions of responsible behaviour, accountability and responsiveness that care entails.

This argument does not romantically view teaching. Teachers do not innately care and neither are relational practices automatically good. Despite institutional assumptions, we believe teachers are socially embedded agents with moral worth who can be held accountable for their actions. AI devices, on the other hand, operate without morals. It is significant to understand this as students' well-being in digitally-mediated situations would need to be intentionally constructed, not taken for granted.

7. Toward a Human-Centered Relational Framework: Guiding Principles

Findings synthesis, this study proposes a human-centered relational framework for AI in education, structured around the following guiding principles.

a. The teacher-student relationship is the most important aspect of education and therefore, AI must be assessed on trustworthiness, dialogue and bonding.
b. Responsibility of Teachers for consequences of decisions impacted by AI listens with Human Accountability.
c. Dialogic Mediation refers to the idea that AI outputs should cause humans to talk to each other, not to replace dialogue.
d. AI systems must be explainable and contestable in pedagogical relationships.
e. Educational value is assessed not in terms of how big it is but rather how deep its relationships are and how beneficial it is.

These principles present a conceptual model that can be utilized by empirical researchers and educational practitioners to assist the integration of AI with human purposes of education.

8. Implications for Research, Practice, and Policy

The framework urges researchers to adopt methodologies that track relational processes as they unfold over time, including qualitative and longitudinal methodologies. As for practitioners, the value of teacher mediation, dialogic design, and emotional presence in AI-mediated classrooms. Policymakers would require governance structures that protect relational integrity, teacher autonomy, and student dignity.

Ultimately, this articulation seeks to theoretically reframe AI in education – away from a discourse of enhancement and replacement toward one of mediation and relational enablement. By embedding trust, dialogue and human bonding into a coherent relational framework, the research reaffirms education as a fundamentally human practice. Accordingly, AI is not dismissed or celebrated in this context, but rather positioned as a significant sociotechnical force whose worth relies on how well it serves the relational underpinnings of teaching and learning.

1.13: IMPLICATIONS

The student-centered relational framework that we developed in this research fosters teacher education and education policy and practice development beyond conceptual contribution. The importance that emphasizes the use of AI in the Humanities implies that the integration of AI and education must enhance not only the possibilities of learning but also the opportunity for learning quality and student well-being.

1. Implications for Educational Practice

According to the findings, teacher mediation of AI is the most important thing for education. Artificial intelligence systems should not be seen as autonomous teaching authorities – essentially teachers – but rather as a pedagogical tool whose value depends on how teachers interpret, contextualize and implement them in relational practices. The effective framing of all AI outputs is essential. Teachers can skillfully reshape the assumptions underpinning AI output and question it. This mediation aids to maintain epistemic trust, mitigate automation bias and ensure human-centric and ethically grounded AI-assisted learning.

In addition, it calls for the intentional relational design of the learning environment. This means designing not just classroom practices and assessment strategies, but also digital environments that privilege dialogue, recognition and affective presence alongside cognitive learning goals. Don't use AI as a substitute for interaction, but to create space for richer human interaction. For example, if the AI can provide feedback, it liberates time for discussion, mentoring and collaborative inquiry. Intentional changes to organization design must increase efficiency, not at the expense of relational depth, student voice or well-being.

2. Implications for Teacher Education

The findings can help improve teacher education and professional development, especially regarding AI literacy. Essentially, AI literacy should go beyond technical skills to encompass knowledge of ethical, relational and pedagogical aspects. Educators must comprehend how AI systems work, but they must also grasp how these systems shape trust, authority, dialogue, and student identity. Teachers may not feel empowered or pressured into employing AI practices they may not agree with professionally without this broader grounding.

As a result, teacher education programmes must focus on reflective and critical pedagogical training to help future and practicing teachers interrogate rather than uncritically adopt AI tools. This involves forming capabilities to question whose values are embedded in AI systems, how data practices affect the dignity of students and how AI processes reshape relationships in classrooms.

By giving teachers tools that encourage reflection, they can further develop their personal agency, while also making ethical decisions that enable them to be mediated to teachers rather than simply implementers.

3. Policy and Governance Implications

The study discusses the need for safeguards that protect relational integrity on an institutional level in AI-mediated education. Policies on AI adoption should recognise relational risks, such as trust erosion; teacher authority erosion; and normalisation of surveillance. Clear lines of responsibility, meaningful oversight by teachers, and types of redress for affected students must be built in the implementation of AI systems in institutions.

Human dignity, relational trust, and student autonomy must take precedence over performance metrics in ethics and governance frameworks. This encompassed commitments to transparency, data minimization, informed consent, and the protection of emotional and relational data. It is significant to acknowledge that governance should not solely measure educational harm as learning loss, but also relational harm, such as loss of trust, belonging, or moral clarity. Embedding relational values into policy and governance will ensure that ai facilitates the education as an ethical and humanizing practice and does not undermine its foundational commitments.

Overall, these implications further confirm the main thesis of this research, namely, that AI in education must be governed, taught and practiced in ways that support rather than replace human relationships. If the applied educational practice, teacher education and policy is based on a relational framework then the potential of AI can be harnessed while safeguarding the trust, dialogue and human bonding that makes education meaningful and ethically legitimate.

1.14: FUTURE RESEARCH DIRECTIONS

Although the work provides a human-centered relational framework to understand AI in education, it also indicates key directions for future investigations which can strengthen empirical, contextual and longitudinal comprehension of AI-mediated educational relationships.

1. To begin with, a need clearly exists for empirical studies of relational trust in AI-rich classrooms. Going forward, those researching trust should not confine themselves to confidence over technology, but rather, look at the negotiation of trust between teachers, students and AI in everyday pedagogy. For instance, interviews and classroom observations as well as interactional analyses of qualitative and mixed-methods studies would help us understand how algorithmic feedback, automated assessment, and learning analytics shape students' willingness to engage, take risks, and trust the teacher's judgment. Comparing AI-

mediated and non-AI-mediated relational practices could reveal how different types of AI further contribute to trust development and learning processes.

2. Second, the perspectives of students from different cultural and education contexts have been given little attention. Many previous studies raised in Western' higher-income contexts make it hard for us to understand AI – students' experience. In particular how cultural norms, power relations, and educational traditions shape students' experiences of AI – mediated trust, dialogue, and care. Future research should prioritize student voice, especially from the Global South and marginalized contexts, to investigate how students understand AI authority, surveillance and personalization. Cross-cultural research that examines the most significant relational concerns raised in this study will help identify whether they are universal or context-specific and will serve to enhance the theoretical robustness and ethical relevance of scholarship on AI-in-education.
3. In future studies, the long term impact of AI on teacher identity, professional judgment, and emotional presence needs assessment. Short-term studies cannot sufficiently capture how continuous interaction with AI agents alters teachers' authority, responsibility, and relational labour over time. Studies are able to be longitudinal qualitative studies (e.g., narrative inquiry, ethnography) that tracked over a number of years teacher adaptation, resistance, reconfiguration, and so on regarding AI. It is important to undiscover whether AI is providing the support teachers need to remain as relational anchors or is systematically eroding their professional identity and emotional presence in subtle yet harmful ways.

The study of AI in education should not only be thought of as a technology but as a long-term relational intervention, say these research themes. In pushing this agenda along, multidisciplinary team work and methods that capture trust, dialogue and human bonding as evolving social practices rather than static variables will be needed.

1.15: CONCLUSION

This chapter has claimed that the stories of efficiency, scalability, or personalization alone do not capture the educational significance of artificial intelligence. Their influence must be assessed in light of the relational foundations of education: trust, dialogue and human relationship. Through investigating how AI mediates these relational dimensions, the study puts forward a human-centred view that reframes AI as a sociotechnical agent that alters the ways in which educational relationships are constructed and sustained, not a pedagogic solution. The main point here is that education is, fundamentally, relational; therefore, any meaningful use of AI has to be assessed on the basis of the effect on human relationships and not on the technical output.

As stated in the study, AI cannot have a moral standing like human beings. Trust must not be produced ONLY through algorithms; dialogue must not be understood ONLY as a simulation; and care must not be automated at the risk of its ethics. Human attendance, human judgment and human accountability are necessary for the use of these capacities. Refrain from presenting AI as a replacing or displacing agent as it would effectively violate the ethics of education and compromise students' dignity and well-being. If AI is allowed to take over our judgment and relational engagement, we may end up hollowing out what learning actually means.

The study therefore urges the need for ethical and human-centered use of AI in education. Teachers need to mediate for an extended period. Such approaches need design that is informed by relations. Such approaches need governance frameworks that emphasize trust, dialogue, and human bonding. Embedding the use of AI in any relations can keep educators, institutions and policy makers on the same page so that technological innovation affirms, rather than undermines, the human core of education. In essence, it is not what AI can do by itself that makes it promising. Rather it is how well AI will help the relational practices through which teaching and learning remain essentially human.

REFERENCES:

Alexander, R. (2008). *Towards dialogic teaching: Rethinking classroom talk* (4th ed.). Dialogos.

Biesta, G. (2015). *Good education in an age of measurement: Ethics, politics, democracy*. Routledge. DOI: 10.4324/9781315634319

Borup, J., West, R. E., & Graham, C. R. (2020). Improving online social presence through asynchronous video. *The Internet and Higher Education*, *47*, 100759. DOI: 10.1016/j.iheduc.2020.100759

Bryk, A. S., & Schneider, B. (2002). *Trust in schools: A core resource for improvement*. Russell Sage Foundation.

Chen, L., Chen, P., & Lin, Z. (2020). Artificial intelligence in education: A review. *IEEE Access : Practical Innovations, Open Solutions*, *8*, 75264–75278. DOI: 10.1109/ACCESS.2020.2988510

Cheng, Y., Chen, C.-H., & Huang, C.-Y. (2022). Students' perceptions of conversational agents in learning contexts. *Computers & Education*, *181*, 104461. DOI: 10.1016/j.compedu.2022.104461

Cook-Sather, A. (2014). Student-faculty partnership in explorations of pedagogical practice. *Teaching and Learning Together in Higher Education*, *1*(3), 1–8.

Feldman-Maggor, Y., Cukurova, M., Kent, C., & Alexandron, G. (2025).

Feldman-Maggor, Y., Cukurova, M., Kent, C., & Alexandron, G. (2025, December). The impact of explainable AI on teachers' trust and acceptance of AI EdTech recommendations: The power of domain-specific explanations. *International Journal of Artificial Intelligence in Education*, *35*(5), 2889–2922. DOI: 10.1007/s40593-025-00486-6

Foucault, M. (1977). *Discipline and punish: The birth of the prison* (Sheridan, A., Trans.). Pantheon Books.

Freire, P. (1970). Pedagogy of the oppressed. *Continuum : an Interdisciplinary Journal on Continuity of Care*.

Friesen, N., & Selwyn, N. (2022). Education and the limits of artificial intelligence. *British Journal of Educational Technology*, *53*(6), 1764–1777. DOI: 10.1111/bjct.13296

Hargreaves, A. (2001). Emotional geographies of teaching. *Teachers College Record, 103*(6), 1056–1080. DOI: 10.1111/0161-4681.00142

Holmes, W., Bialik, M., & Fadel, C. (2019). *Artificial intelligence in education: Promises and implications for teaching and learning*. Center for Curriculum Redesign.

Holstein, K., McLaren, B. M., & Aleven, V. (2019). Co-designing a real-time classroom orchestration tool. *Proceedings of the 2019 CHI Conference on Human Factors in Computing Systems*, 1–14. https://doi.org/DOI: 10.1145/3290605.3300768

Kim, Y., Song, H., & Lockee, B. (2021). "I like my relational machine teacher": The role of social presence. *Computers & Education*, *163*, 104079. DOI: 10.1016/j.compedu.2020.104079

Knox, J. (2020). Artificial intelligence and education in China. *Learning, Media and Technology*, *45*(3), 298–311. DOI: 10.1080/17439884.2020.1754236

Latour, B. (2005). *Reassembling the social: An introduction to actor-network-theory*. Oxford University Press. DOI: 10.1093/oso/9780199256044.001.0001

Luckin, R., Holmes, W., Griffiths, M., & Forcier, L. B. (2016). *Intelligence unleashed: An argument for AI in education*. Pearson.

Mayer, R. C., Davis, J. H., & Schoorman, F. D. (1995). An integrative model of organizational trust. *Academy of Management Review*, *20*(3), 709–734. DOI: 10.2307/258792

Mercer, N., & Howe, C. (2012). Explaining the dialogic processes. *Learning, Culture and Social Interaction*, *1*(1), 12–21. DOI: 10.1016/j.lcsi.2012.03.001

Noddings, N. (2013). *Caring: A relational approach to ethics and moral education* (2nd ed.). University of California Press.

O'Neil, C. (2016). *Weapons of math destruction*. Crown.

Peters, M. A., Jandrić, P., & Hayes, S. (2023). AI, education, and epistemic responsibility. *Educational Philosophy and Theory*, *55*(1), 1–15. DOI: 10.1080/00131857.2020.1867108

Pitts, G., & Motamedi, S. (2025). *Understanding human–AI trust in education*. *arXiv*. https://doi.org//arXiv.2506.09160DOI: 10.48550

Regan, P. M., & Jesse, J. (2019). Ethical challenges of edtech. *Educational Technology Research and Development*, *67*(6), 1671–1693. DOI: 10.1007/s11423-019-09666-0

Selwyn, N. (2019). *Should robots replace teachers? AI and the future of education*. Polity Press.

Selwyn, N. (2021). Ed-tech within limits. *Learning, Media and Technology, 46*(4), 347–350. DOI: 10.1080/17439884.2021.1952590

Tschannen-Moran, M., & Hoy, W. K. (2000). A multidisciplinary analysis of trust. *Review of Educational Research, 70*(4), 547–593. DOI: 10.3102/00346543070004547

Williamson, B. (2017). Big data in education. *Sage (Atlanta, Ga.).*

Williamson, B., & Eynon, R. (2020). Historical threads, missing links. *Learning, Media and Technology, 45*(3), 223–235. DOI: 10.1080/17439884.2020.1798995

Woolf, B. P. (2010). *Building intelligent interactive tutors: Student-centered strategies for revolutionizing e-learning*. Morgan Kaufmann.

Zhai, X., Liao, J., Li, Y., Wang, Y., & Zhang, Y. (2020). Artificial intelligence in education: A review. *IEEE Access : Practical Innovations, Open Solutions, 8*, 75264–75278. DOI: 10.1109/ACCESS.2020.2988510

ADDITIONAL READING

Aleven, V., McLaren, B. M., Roll, I., & Koedinger, K. R. (2016). Toward metacognitive tutoring. *International Journal of Artificial Intelligence in Education, 26*(1), 97–121. DOI: 10.1007/s40593-015-0057-0

Bayne, S., & Jandrić, P. (2017). From anthropocentrism to techno-materialism. *Educational Technology Research and Development, 65*(5), 1099–1109.

Buber, M. (1970). *I and Thou* (W. Kaufmann, Trans.). Scribner.

Deci, E. L., & Ryan, R. M. (2000). Intrinsic and extrinsic motivations. *Contemporary Educational Psychology, 25*(1), 54–67. DOI: 10.1006/ceps.1999.1020 PMID: 10620381

Dewey, J. (1938). *Experience and education*. Macmillan.

Eubanks, V. (2018). *Automating inequality*. St. Martin's Press.

Floridi, L., Cowls, J., Beltrametti, M., Chatila, R., Chazerand, P., Dignum, V., Luetge, C., Madelin, R., Pagallo, U., Rossi, F., Schafer, B., Valcke, P., & Vayena, E. (2018). AI4People—An ethical framework. *Minds and Machines, 28*(4), 689–707. DOI: 10.1007/s11023-018-9482-5 PMID: 30930541

Gadamer, H.-G. (2004). *Truth and method* (2nd rev. ed.). Continuum.

Gilligan, C. (1982). *In a different voice*. Harvard University Press.

Jobin, A., Ienca, M., & Vayena, E. (2019). Global landscape of AI ethics guidelines. *Nature Machine Intelligence*, *1*(9), 389–399. DOI: 10.1038/s42256-019-0088-2

Knox, J., Williamson, B., & Bayne, S. (2020). Machine behaviourism. *Learning, Media and Technology*, *45*(3), 297–300.

Kohn, A. (1999). *Punished by rewards*. Houghton Mifflin.

O'Connor, K. E. (2008). You choose to care. *Teaching and Teacher Education*, *24*(1), 117–126.

Perrotta, C., Gulson, K. N., Williamson, B., & Witzenberger, K. (2021). Automation, datafication and accountability. *Journal of Education Policy*, *36*(1), 1–20.

Rahwan, I., Cebrian, M., Obradovich, N., Bongard, J., Bonnefon, J.-F., Breazeal, C., Crandall, J. W., Christakis, N. A., Couzin, I. D., Jackson, M. O., Jennings, N. R., Kamar, E., Kloumann, I. M., Larochelle, H., Lazer, D., McElreath, R., Mislove, A., Parkes, D. C., Pentland, A. S., & Wellman, M. (2019). Machine behaviour. *Nature*, *568*(7753), 477–486. DOI: 10.1038/s41586-019-1138-y PMID: 31019318

Roeser, R. W., Eccles, J. S., & Sameroff, A. J. (2000). School as a context of early adolescence. *Development and Psychopathology*, *12*(3), 443–466. PMID: 11014747

Sewell, W. H.Jr. (1992). A theory of structure. *American Journal of Sociology*, *98*(1), 1–29. DOI: 10.1086/229967

Wegerif, R. (2011). Towards a dialogic theory of education. *Educational Philosophy and Theory*, *43*(2), 179–195.

Wentzel, K. R. (2010). Students' relationships with teachers. *Educational Psychology Review*, *22*(4), 399–418.

Yeung, K. (2018). Algorithmic regulation. *Regulation & Governance*, *12*(4), 505–523. DOI: 10.1111/rego.12158

Chapter 11
Ethical snd Privacy Concerns in AI-Mediated Education:
Toward a Human-Centered Pedagogy

Harun Çiftci
http://orcid.org/0000-0003-1444-641X
Independent Researcher, Turkey

ABSTRACT

Artificial intelligence (AI) has become an argumentative concern in educational contexts. This phenomenon offers personalization, adaptive tutoring, and real-time feedback for learners. However, its widespread use has triggered deep ethical and privacy concerns. This chapter reports these concerns by tracing how AI reshapes pedagogy, governance, and integrity in education. Taking the stance of community-wide ethical frameworks (Holmes et al., 2022) and bibliometric mappings of philosophical and practical principles of Yu & Yu (2023), it situates AI ethics within deontological, utilitarian, and virtue-ethical orientations that emphasize transparency, fairness, accountability, and non-maleficence. Particular attention is given to privacy as a pedagogical and policy issue. The datafication of learning, surveillance-based analytics, and the opacity of commercial EdTech infrastructures challenge both institutional trust and learners' autonomy (Ryan et al., 2021; Kousa & Niemi, 2023). In response, the chapter advances the notion of privacy literacy, the capacity of teachers and students to understand, question, and ethically manage data practices embedded in AI-mediated learning (Neff et al., 2024; Aljabr & Al-Ahdal, 2024). Parallel to privacy risks, the expansion of generative systems such as ChatGPT has destabilized conventional understandings of authorship and academic honesty.

DOI: 10.4018/979-8-3373-8027-8.ch011

Emerging concepts like AI-giarism expose new grey zones between assistance and misconduct (Cotton et al., 2023; Chan, 2025; Goddiksen et al., 2024). The chapter concludes by proposing an ethically resilient educational model that integrates critical AI literacy (Walter, 2024) and co-responsibility among teachers, students, and systems. Ethical resilience refers to the capacity of educational communities to adapt responsibly to technological change through privacy-by-design architectures, algorithmic explainability, and participatory policy-making. Finally, to safeguard integrity and privacy in AI-mediated education, stakeholders should seek regulatory oversight with the creation of transparent, equitable, and culturally responsive contexts. Thus, humans may not have devolved their positions to algorithms at the ethical core of digital learning.

1. INTRODUCTION

Garnering remarkable attention, artificial intelligence (AI) has become an indispensable colleague in every educational context throughout the world. This rapid infusion has promised new efficiencies in teaching, learning, and assessment. Intelligent tutoring systems, generative writing assistants, automated scoring tools, and adaptive analytics platforms now customize learning paths and make instructors' jobs easier by taking care of administrative tasks that used to be their responsibility (Wang et al., 2024; Zhai et al., 2021). Proponents describe this neology as the dawn of ''data-driven personalization,'' where algorithms assess learner needs and deliver tailored scaffolding at an unprecedented scale. AI is perceived as an egalitarian force that is capable of democratizing expertise, accelerating feedback loops, and improving access to quality instruction. This support is achieved across linguistic and cultural boundaries as a techno-optimist movement.

Despite its pedagogical benefits, the use of AI tools has aroused ethical, legal, and epistemic concerns in education. Systems trained on vast datasets reproduce the social biases and asymmetries embedded in those data. These large language models (LLMs) therefore exacerbate inequities while pretending to be neutral (Holmes et al., 2022). Predictive analytics, plagiarism detection software, and automated writing feedback tools gather and analyze detailed data on how learners behave. Without explicit consent, we frequently document clickstreams, keystrokes, drafts, and eye movements. This datafication of learning transforms educational experience into measurable tokens for commercial optimization by blurring the boundaries between pedagogy, surveillance, and corporate governance (Ryan et al., 2021; Kousa & Niemi, 2023). As AI mediates more aspects of instruction, educators should confront not only technical but also moral questions: Who owns learner data? What constitutes authorship or originality in a co-written human, AI text? How can fairness and accountability be ensured in algorithmic assessment?

Recently, researchers framed these tensions as the ethical part of productivity. Holmes et al. (2022) propose that ethical AI use in education rests on four community-wide principles. Transparency, fairness, accountability, and privacy are each easily proclaimed yet difficult to operationalize. Yu and Yu (2023) expand this foundation through a bibliometric and philosophical mapping that identifies three moral orientations underpinning current discourse: deontology (duty-based obligations), utilitarianism (maximizing collective benefit), and virtue ethics (cultivating moral character). According to them, these orientations coexist rather than compete, reminding educators that ethical decision-making in AI-mediated contexts is both rule-governed and value-laden. The intersection of these frameworks reveals a paradox. The same technologies are celebrated for enhancing precision and personalization that can simultaneously erode privacy, autonomy, and trust (Saeli et al., 2025).

Emerged as both a technical safeguard and a pedagogical imperative, privacy has been a concern within this ccontext. Data collection practices in learning management systems and generative AI interfaces often exceed users' awareness. This situation creates what Neff et al. (2024) calls for: ''ambient surveillance'' of learning. Dealing with such conditions requires more than regulatory compliance. It further necessitates the cultivation of privacy literacy, the capacity of instructors and learners to recognize, interpret, and ethically negotiate data practices embedded in their everyday tools (Aljabr & Al-Ahdal, 2024). Privacy literacy changes learners from passive data subjects to active guardians of their digital identities, aligning with the larger movement toward critical digital citizenship in higher education.

Parallel to concerns about data use, the proliferation of AI tools such as ChatGPT has unsettled long-standing conventions of academic integrity. Previous research documented institutional anxiety over ''cheating'' and ''contract writing'' in the wake of large-language-model (LLM) accessibility (Cotton et al., 2023). Recent studies, on the other hand, indicate that learners' moral reasoning regarding authorship and originality is changing, with many viewing it as a valid form of cognitive enhancement (Chan, 2025; Goddiksen et al., 2024). These shifting perceptions give rise to ambiguous areas of academic integrity, where detection metrics alone cannot define misconduct. Ethical teaching, therefore, includes assisting learners to discern the boundary between augmentation and abdication of intellectual responsibility.

The ethical challenges of AI are not distributed evenly. This paradigm interprets and enforces fairness and accountability based on institutional context, cultural values, and resource inequities. Vetter et al. (2024) argue for a local interrogation of AI ethics. This proposal is based on a contextualized approach that respects local ethical frameworks and disciplinary standards instead of trying to make everyone follow the same rules. In a similar vein, Ateeq et al. (2024) advocate for a comprehensive understanding of academic integrity that goes beyond punitive measures and instead cultivates communities of trust and moral agency. Across contexts, what remains constant is the need for ethical resilience, which is the collective capacity of educators and learners to adapt responsibly to technological change while safeguarding human dignity, autonomy, and justice.

This chapter is therefore based on two primary objectives. First, it synthesizes major theoretical and empirical contributions to the ethics of AI in education, emphasizing how principles such as transparency, fairness, privacy, and accountability intersect with practical issues of data governance and academic integrity. Second, it promotes a human-centered pedagogical framework based on ethical resilience. By linking macro-level policy discourse with micro-level classroom realities, the chapter demonstrates that the future of AI in education depends less on technical sophistication than on cultivating reflective, ethically literate communities capable of interrogating the technologies they use.

In the following sections, the argument proceeds through 5 interrelated lenses except the introduction. Section 2 focuses on the conceptual foundations of AI ethics in education by integrating philosophical and community-based frameworks. Section 3 proceeds with privacy as both a pedagogical and policy concern by proposing privacy literacy as a critical competency for twenty-first-century learners. Section 4 examines the transformation of academic integrity in the age of AI. What follows in section 5 is the ethical pedagogy for AI-mediated learning. Finally, section 6 concludes with a human-centered approach to adapt responsibly to algorithmic change through moral literacy, participatory governance, and privacy by design. Taken together, these six sections argue that the central task for contemporary education is not merely to adopt AI responsibly but to transform responsibility itself in the age of AI.

2. CONCEPTUAL FOUNDATIONS OF AI ETHICS IN EDUCATION

Research on AI in education has shifted from emphasizing efficiency and personalization to critically examining the ethical frameworks embedded within AI systems. As AI mediates learning, it inherently reflects social values and power structures. Therefore, ethical reflection is no longer just a way to follow the rules; it is now a requirement for real educational innovation. Two major trajectories in recent scholarship, one community-driven and the other philosophical, provide the conceptual grounding for this inquiry: Holmes et al.'s (2022) proposal for a community-wide ethical framework and Yu and Yu's (2023) meta-analysis identify the moral essences and guiding principles of AI ethics in education. Together, they illuminate the field's dual orientation: a pragmatic concern with policy and accountability and a normative concern with moral reasoning and human flourishing.

According to Holmes et al. (2022), ethical AI use in education should not only repose on technological fixes or institutional codes; it requires a participatory, community-wide effort involving developers, educators, learners, and policymakers. Their framework is structured around four interdependent principles, transparency, fairness, accountability, and privacy, each serving as both a technical design criterion and a pedagogical virtue. *Transparency* underpins that the operation, limitations, and decision rules of AI tools should be intelligible to non-experts. In educational contexts, transparency is closely tied to *explainability*. Thus, learners and instructors should understand how an algorithm generates feedback or grades in order to trust and meaningfully contest its judgments. Fairness requires that algorithms neither reproduce nor amplify historical inequities encoded in training data. Holmes et al. (2022) state that fairness should not be attenuated to statistical parity; however, it demands awareness of contextual and cultural differences in how merit, participation, and success are defined.

Accountability is about responsibility throughout the entire lifecycle of AI, from the moment it begins collecting data to pedagogical implementation. The stakeholders therefore share equal responsibility for the consequences of algorithmic decisions, including unintended harms. Finally, *privacy* anchors the framework by reminding stakeholders that learning data are the extensions of personal identity. Protecting those data upholds not only legal obligations but the moral dignity of learners as autonomous participants. Holmes et al.'s (2022) framework thus operationalizes ethics as a *relational practice* in which a dynamic negotiation exists among human agents rather than a static checklist. It also underscores a transformation: AI ethics in education should evolve through *co-design* with users. Thus, this case ensures that learners and instructors participate in shaping the norms included in their digital contexts. Furthermore, Ryan et al. (2021) have confirmed the need for this distributed accountability model by revealing the persistent gap between abstract ethical principles and their institutional realization.

While Holmes et al. (2022) provide a normative frame, Yu and Yu (2023) provide a panoramic view of how AI ethics in education have been theorized and practiced globally. Through bibliometric analysis of 880 publications using VOSviewer and CitNetExplorer, they identified three *ethical essences*. Deontology, utilitarianism, and virtue ethics were the three main principles that guided modern discussions. These principles included transparency, justice/fairness/equity, non-maleficence, responsibility, and privacy. Deontological reasoning derives moral legitimacy from adhering to duty and universal rules. Applied to Artificial Intelligence in Education (AIED), deontology emphasizes that regardless of efficiency gains, developers and educators are obliged to respect human rights, consent, and honesty (Yu & Yu,

2023). To illustrate, algorithmic grading should adhere to explicit and pre-agreed standards rather than opaque optimization functions.

Utilitarianism prioritizes outcomes by maximizing collective benefit while minimizing harm. From this view, ethical AI systems are those that demonstrably enhance learning outcomes, inclusion, and societal well-being. However, Yu and Yu (2023) remark that the utilitarian calculus might ignore marginalized individuals, masking their disadvantages with aggregate gains. Therefore, utilitarian reasoning ought to be adjusted by incorporating fairness metrics and human oversight. Derived from Aristotelian tenets, virtue ethics focuses on moral character and habituated excellence rather than rules or results. Within educational AI, virtue ethics provides reflection on how technologies cultivate or erode intellectual virtues such as honesty, curiosity, and empathy. It shifts focus from AI's benefits to its effects on learners' agency and dispositions.

Yu and Yu's (2023) framework effectively combines macro-level ethical theory with micro-level educational practices. Their integration of moral philosophy and bibliometric evidence shows that AI ethics in education is not monolithic. It is but pluralistic and shaped by intersecting philosophical traditions. This pluralism reflects the diversity of educational cultures. Western policy discourses frequently emphasize deontological accountability and transparency, while East Asian frameworks may prioritize virtue ethics derived from Confucian moral education (Tan, 2020). Recognizing these plural ethical genealogies helps practitioners prevent the use of a single cultural model of ''responsible AI.''

Juxtaposing Holmes et al. (2022) with Yu and Yu (2023) reveals the dialectic between *principles* and *essences*. Holmes emphasizes institutional and procedural safeguards; Yu and Yu expose the philosophical rationales that give those safeguards meaning. The convergence of these approaches produces a more complete framework in which ethics operates simultaneously at three levels:

1. *Philosophical orientation:* defining moral conduct (duties, consequences, virtues).
2. *Normative principles:* voicing general standards (fairness, transparency).
3. *Operational practices:* embedding these standards in design, pedagogy, and policy.

However, tensions emerge when these layers interact. First, transparency may conflict with privacy. Second, accountability mechanisms can produce surveillance. And lastly, utilitarian efficiency can undercut deontological rights. Such contradictions demand what Vetter et al. (2024) define as *local interrogation*. They contend that ethical reflection is rooted in disciplinary and cultural contexts rather than in abstract universality. For instance, one system may view a learning-analytics dashboard supporting data-driven differentiation as inclusive, while another may view it as intrusive. Ethical judgment thus becomes contextual reasoning rather than mechanical rule-following.

Both frameworks converge on a final insight: ethical governance alone is insufficient without *ethical literacy* among users. Instructors and learners should understand the principles guiding AI behaviour and be able to evaluate them critically. This requirement anticipates later discussions of *privacy literacy* and *critical AI literacy* (Walter, 2024), which extend moral reasoning into everyday classroom interactions. Ethical literacy transforms abstract codes into living practices of reflection, dialogue, and resistance to unethical automation. Furthermore, the cultivation of ethical literacy contributes to what Ateeq et al. (2024) describe as a holistic integrity culture. This is also a shift from rule enforcement to value formation. When learners comprehend the rationale behind fairness and accountability, they internalize these values as part of their scholarly identity. In this sense, ethics is not external regulation but an educational outcome in itself.

These perspectives result in an integrated conceptual model of AI ethics in education consisting of three concentric areas:

Moral Foundations (Why): deontological, utilitarian, and virtue-ethical orientations that define the purpose and justification of AI use.

Normative Principles (What): transparency, fairness/justice, non-maleficence, responsibility, and privacy as shared ethical key criteria.

Practical Implementation (How): community-based governance, participatory design, and ethical literacy.

This three-part structure underpins the framework for the rest of the chapter in which the moral reasoning of Yu and Yu (2023) and the procedural ethics of Holmes et al. (2022) are combined. This combination shows that responsible use of AI in education necessitates simultaneous attention to philosophical justification, normative guidance, and practical enactment. The framework also reads the later discussion of privacy and integrity by positioning them as expressions of these deeper moral logics.

Finally, the conceptual foundations of AI ethics in education demonstrate that the moral quality of technology stems from the relationships it fosters. Ethical AI is less about machines obeying codes than about communities that cultivate virtues of transparency, fairness, care, and critical awareness. Nowhere is this relational ethics more urgent than in the governance of educational data and the protection of learners' privacy, as is in the next section, in which the point where pedagogy, policy, and human dignity converge is discussed.

3. PRIVACY AS PEDAGOGICAL AND POLICY CONCERN

Educational systems are now entangled with what Williamson (2017) terms the *datafication of learning*. This model can be considered a transformation of learner behavior, cognition, and even emotion into quantifiable data points. Learning management systems keep track of attendance and participation. Adaptive platforms keep track of keystrokes and dwell time. And generative writing tools keep track of every prompt and revision. These data streams, when combined and processed by algorithms, promise personalized feedback and better efficiency in institutions. Still, they also expose new vulnerabilities. The erosion of learner privacy, the commodification of educational data, and the potential normalization of surveillance as pedagogy can be counted as the new threats (Williamson et al., 2020). Ryan et al. (2021) observed that ethical aspirations in AI often falter at the implementation stage, where institutional convenience overrides moral reflection. Their multi-case analysis revealed that data governance in educational organizations is frequently reactive, guided more by risk management than by human rights principles. When data collection is equated with accountability, the learner is redefined as a data subject, an object of analysis instead of an independent contributor to knowledge creation. This shift requires a rethinking of privacy not merely as protection from harm but as a pedagogical value integral to democratic education.

As a legal framework, the European Union's General Data Protection Regulation (GDPR) and UNESCO's Recommendation on the Ethics of Artificial Intelligence (2021) provide baseline conservation for data collection and algorithmic transparency. In education, privacy should be reframed as an ongoing ethical practice that functions as a way of cultivating respect for learners' autonomy, consent, and right to intellectual space. Kousa and Niemi (2023) emphasize this case from the EdTech industry's perspective. Their interviews with European technology firms reveal growing awareness of ethical obligations on the basis of limited capacity to operationalize them. Developers often rely on ''responsible AI'' statements that remain far beyond the classroom contexts. Without pedagogical translation, corporate privacy policies do not tell instructors or learners how their data moves between different platforms. Thus, the ethics of AI should not be outsourced to compliance officers; rather, it is to be embedded within teaching practices that make data relations visible and discussable.

The General Data Protection Regulation (GDPR) of the European Union and the Recommendation on the Ethics of Artificial Intelligence (2021) from UNESCO set minimum standards for data collection and algorithmic transparency. In education, privacy should be reframed as an *ongoing moral practice*—a way of cultivating respect for learners' autonomy, consent, and right to intellectual space. Kousa and Niemi (2023) highlight this tension from the EdTech industry's perspective. Their interviews with European technology firms reveal growing awareness of ethical obligations but limited capacity to operationalize them.

The concept of privacy literacy offers a bridge between technical governance and ethical pedagogy. Based on the broader framework of critical data literacy (Pangrazio & Selwyn, 2019) and digital citizenship (Mossberger et al., 2007), it refers to the capacity of individuals to understand how personal data are generated, processed, shared, and monetized. It is also a process that enables informed and ethical decisions about learners' participation in data ecosystems. Neff et al. (2024) found that although EFL learners and instructors expressed trust in AI-powered tools, they reported a lack of awareness of the scope of data retention by these tools. In a similar vein, Aljabr and Al-Ahdal (2024) reported that the instructors appreciated AI's capacity to deliver timely feedback; however, the data ownership and consent with learners remained vague. Both studies highlight the necessity of incorporating privacy literacy into instructor education and learner orientation programs.

At the institutional level, privacy literacy should be cultivated through transparency dialogues where structured discussions are held where learners and educators jointly explore how algorithms function and what data they require. Holmes et al.'s (2022) call for community-wide ethical responsibility aligns with such participatory approaches. They also align with Westin's (1967) longstanding definition of privacy's social function, which reconciles personal autonomy with communal trust. Teaching privacy, therefore, becomes an act of empowerment. This assists learners in reclaiming agency in digital environments that often obscure the conditions of their participation.

Inadequate privacy concerns extending beyond technical risk in educational contexts pose some pedagogical implications. When monitoring tools pervade learning spaces, learners may internalize a sense of constant observation. This *surveillance pedagogy* may suppress intellectual risk-taking and undermine the trust essential to authentic learning (Williamson et al., 2020). Recent research evidences this concern. Lower self-reported academic self-efficacy and increased performance anxiety were correlated with continuous analytics tracking in higher education (Jones et al., 2020). For language learners, whose progress depends on confidence and experimentation, such effects can be detrimental (Neff et al., 2024). As a result, privacy should be conceptualized both as a right to invisibility and as a condition for pedagogical openness, the freedom to make mistakes without algorithmic judgment.

Instructors thus face an ethical dilemma where they are obliged to balance their duty to ensure academic integrity with the obligation to protect learners' dignity. Cotton et al. (2023) and Chan (2025) both demonstrate how generative AI complicates this balance by blurring the boundaries between legitimate assistance and plagiarism. Excessive surveillance to detect AI use may inadvertently perpetuate mistrust. Thus, this case may push learners toward covert practices. A more constructive alternative is trust-based pedagogy. In this pedagogy, transparency and shared responsibility replace punitive monitoring.

Educational institutions should consider adopting a *privacy-by-design* ethos (Cavoukian, 2011). This means integrating privacy considerations at every stage of AI development and deployment, from data minimization to algorithmic explainability. Universities can set up ethics review boards for digital tools, similar to research ethics committees, to look at the risks before using them. Clear data-retention policies and opt-out mechanisms empower learners to make informed choices. Additionally, moving beyond abstract declarations towards applicable standards for educational AI is the responsibility of policymakers.

Holmes et al.'s (2022) community framework suggests human oversight, proportionality in data use, and algorithmic transparency. These ideas are based on the Council of Europe's 2022 Guidelines on AI and Data Protection in Education. However, Ateeq et al. (2024) state that the implementation of all these guidelines remains uneven across regions. This case is valid particularly in the regions where global technology vendors import digital infrastructures with varying privacy norms. Vetter et al. (2024) designate these asymmetries as local interrogation. They thus propose policies that are sensitive to cultural expectations and educational aims, rather than relying on uniform compliance.

Finally, privacy in education should not be reduced to secrecy or control; rather, it should be redesigned as a relational and developmental phenomenon. Protecting learner data is inseparable from nurturing ethical awareness. Through privacy literacy, instructors and instructors become *ethical mediators* who scaffold learners to negotiate the boundaries between openness and protection (Chan, 2025). Through privacy by design, institutions show respect for learners as moral agents rather than data sources. Last but not least, through participatory policy processes, educational contexts may construct the *ethical resilience* that is necessary to adapt to evolving technologies without sacrificing participant dignity (Fu & Weng, 2024).

4. ACADEMIC INTEGRITY AND THE RISE OF "AI-GIARISM"

The principle of authorship as moral ownership has long been the basis of academic integrity. Learners and scholars are expected to show independent thought, give credit where credit is due, and be honest about their work. However, generative artificial intelligence (GenAI) churns this concept by producing coherent, original-seeming text in seconds. According to Cotton et al. (2023), the use of ChatGPT by learners blurs the distinction between legitimate assistance and academic dishonesty. The issue is not simply the ease of copying but a transformation in what it means to write, think, and create in the digital age. When the ''other'' is an algorithm trained on billions of texts with no singular author, traditional definitions of plagiarism are no longer enough. As Chan (2025) showed, learners interpret AI output as *shared cognitive labor* rather than theft. This viewpoint is consistent with sociocultural theories of distributed cognition, which conceptualize learning as a collaborative endeavor facilitated by tools. Yet when applied to assessment regimes designed for human authorship, such reasoning produces ethical friction.

The term ''AI-giarism,'' recently introduced to characterize the unethical utilization of AI-generated content, reflects the increasing intricacy of academic misconduct in the era of machine collaboration (Chan, 2025). Cotton et al. (2023) revealed how university staff express both alarm and uncertainty about AI's role in learner cheating. Some people see generative models as new ways to cheat, while others see them as useful tools for writing, summarizing, or getting help with language. The resulting ambiguity creates what Goddiksen et al. (2024) call *grey zones of integrity*. In these zones, norms are negotiated rather than fixed. These grey zones are also shaped by context. In some courses, using AI to brainstorm or verify grammar may be encouraged; in others, it constitutes misconduct. Without explicit institutional guidelines, learners rely on intuitive or peer-shared norms. Chan (2025) discovered that learners' ethical reasoning frequently embodies pragmatism rather than deceit; they utilize AI to appear scholarly, surmount linguistic obstacles, or adhere to time limitations, rather than to engage in intentional cheating. This resonates with Neff et al.'s (2024) findings among EFL learners. They view AI writing tools as scaffolds for self-expression rather than substitutes for thinking.

Understanding AI-mediated authorship thus requires a transformation from rule enforcement to situated moral practice. Holmes et al. (2022) argue that accountability in AI use should be distributed across communities. It should not be imposed solely on individuals. In a similar vein, Ateeq et al. (2024) emphasizes a *holistic integrity culture* that includes education, empathy, and moral reasoning over punishment. Within this domain, misconduct is reframed as a failure of ethical understanding rather than a purely disciplinary infraction. Eaton (2021) characterizes academic integrity as a dynamic system upheld by collective values, including honesty, trust, fairness, respect, and responsibility. Generative AI tests each of these values. Honesty is considered conditional based on whether learners disclose their use of AI assistance and the manner in which they do so. Trust necessitates mutual transparency between instructors and learners about permissible use. Fairness includes consistent policies across classes and institutions to prevent inequities. Respect extends beyond peers to the ethical treatment of the data and labor underlying AI systems. Responsibility, finally, involves developing digital and ethical literacies that enable learners to evaluate AI outputs critically rather than accepting them unreflectively.

The principle of *fairness*, central to both Holmes et al.'s (2022) and Yu & Yu's (2023) frameworks, takes on new meaning in the integrity issue. Universities are concerned about AI's ability to make it easier for people to lie, but they often forget that algorithmic systems can be unfair on their own. As Vetter et al. (2024) argue, the tools used to detect misconduct or assess writing may embed linguistic or cultural bias. For instance, AI detectors negatively affect non-native writers who rely on AI tools. Such systems pose risks in reinforcing deficit narratives about linguistic competence while claiming to uphold integrity. Moreover, the digital divide amplifies inequities in AI access. Learners in resource-limited contexts may have restricted exposure to or instruction in the responsible use of AI tools. On the other hand, others utilize paid premium tools that improve fluency and coherence. Considering all learners to identical integrity standards without acknowledging such disparities undermines justice. Ethical AI governance must therefore balance the *fair use* of technology with equitable support structures.

Concerns about the nature of creativity and intellectual ownership have emerged beyond policy. Sotiri (2024) expresses that AI challenges the Romantic ideal of the solitary author by distributing creative agency across human-machine assemblages. In education, this necessitates distinguishing between *automation* and *augmentation*. Automation replaces cognitive effort; augmentation, on the other hand, extends it. Learning can be enhanced through using AI to explore ideas, visualize arguments, and clarify language on the condition that this learning is guided by reflection and disclosure (Çiftci, 2025). When learners use AI to bypass understanding, their learning collapses into mere mimicry. This distinction proposes virtue-ethical reasoning (Yu & Yu, 2023). Academic integrity thus arises from cultivating the virtues of honesty, diligence, and intellectual humility rather than strict rule adherence. So, teaching integrity in AI-mediated environments means encouraging the virtues of *responsible co-authorship*. Requiring learners to annotate their AI interactions, recording prompts, revisions, and personal reflections may make visible their reasoning process. Instructors might, for example, require learners to annotate their AI interactions, recording prompts, revisions, and personal reflections to make their reasoning process visible. Such transparency transforms AI use into an object of metacognitive learning rather than *AI-giarism*.

Higher educational institutions are commencing to develop policies that reflect this nuanced understanding. Dawson (2020) posits that surveillance alone cannot preserve integrity. Rather, it should be designed as an assessment. Authentic tasks requiring personal reflection, contextual knowledge, and multimodal expression are less vulnerable to generative automation. In a similar vein, Dwivedi et al., (2023) propose that integrating AI ethics modules into academic writing and research courses may assist learners in equipping themselves with critical awareness of bias, authorship, and intellectual property. In classroom contexts, instructors can model ethical reasoning by demonstrating transparent AI use. Such modeling aligns with Walter's (2024) concept of *critical AI literacy,* which encourages learners to question the algorithmic authority of AI tools. This concept transforms academic integrity from a barrier to innovation to its moral guide.

"AI-giarism" signifies a transitional moment in the moral evolution of academia. Integrity, once policed through detection and deterrence, should now be processed through dialogue and partnership. Ethical AI pedagogy acknowledges that misconduct frequently arises from confusion, pressure, or insufficient guidance rather than intentional wrongdoing. By engaging learners as co-researchers of AI ethics, educators may transform plagiarism into an opportunity for moral development. This shift embodies the ethical resilience introduced earlier, the ability of educational communities to adapt to technological change without abandoning humanistic values. The next section reviews the ethical pedagogy for AI-mediated learning in educational contexts, focusing on critical AI literacy, which is the ability to understand, question, and ethically engage with AI systems.

5. ETHICAL PEDAGOGY FOR AI-MEDIATED LEARNING

The ethical frameworks and institutional principles outlined in previous studies should be enacted in the everyday routines of teaching and learning. A framework that remains abstract, lodged in policy documents and institutional guidelines, risks being inert. Holmes et al. (2022) contend that ethics in AI-mediated education attains relevance solely when it is integrated as a pedagogical practice, reflected in curriculum design, instructor-learner interactions, and classroom culture. Instructors are required to incorporate AI tools and promote learners' critical engagement with them, thereby enhancing discernment, autonomy, and moral judgment. Ateeq et al. (2024) characterize the phenomenon as the rise of the "instructor as ethical architect," an educator who creates learning environments that balance technological efficiency with reflective responsibility. Such contexts rely on three intertwined principles. The first principle is critical AI literacy. What follows this principle are transparency and fairness audits. And the last principle is co-responsibility models that redefine the instructor-learner relationship in the age of intelligent machines.

Critical AI literacy refers to learners' and educators' ability to understand, question, and ethically engage with AI systems (Walter, 2024; Hagendorff & Hagendorff, 2020). It extends beyond technical know-how to include moral and epistemic awareness. Walter (2024) stresses that AI literacy includes three connected types of literacy: conceptual (knowing how generative and analytic systems work), critical (questioning biases, assumptions, and power structures), and ethical (acting responsibly in relation to AI's strengths and weaknesses). Developing such literacy in AI-mediated classrooms entails deciphering the complexities of the AI system. Educators should invite learners to investigate an AI tool's data flow. Thus, they may examine how prompts are interpreted, what training data underlie its "knowledge," and how output may reflect cultural or linguistic bias.

For instance, Neff et al. (2024) discovered that EFL learners frequently placed excessive trust in AI-generated corrections. They assumed grammatical authority without questioning stylistic bias toward Anglophone norms. A critical literacy approach would use such moments as teaching opportunities: asking learners to compare AI suggestions with their revisions, reflect on what constitutes "good writing," and discuss whose standards are being upheld. Inserting AI in the context of a larger digital ethics education is also part of critical AI literacy. For Neff et al. (2024), iterative reflection should assist moral reasoning in digital contexts. Instructors may also benefit from Socratic dialogue, peer feedback, and reflective journals whereby learners write about the choices they make while using AI tools. By externalizing their reasoning, learners begin to internalize ethical awareness, which becomes an outcome consonant with virtue-ethical pedagogy (Yu & Yu, 2023).

Classroom-level audits of fairness and bias may operationalize the principle of transparency. This case shapes the foundation of Holmes et al.'s (2022) ethical framework. These audits should not be disciplinary reviews. They should include participatory practices where learners and instructors collaboratively evaluate the ethical implications of the tools they use. Sepp (2025) suggest that analytics literacy may help people understand how algorithms work through the understanding of how data are collected and how they shape feedback. Instructors may design assignments where learners analyze the output of multiple AI writing assistants. Thus, they may compare the feedback each provides and discuss why differences emerge. This process transforms invisible algorithms into epistemic objects open to critique. Similarly, Zawacki-Richter et al. (2019) propose integrating ''AI explainability'' into educational technology curricula so that learners can comprehend how recommendations or grades are produced. Fairness audits extend this transparency to questions of justice. Learners may examine the treatment of gendered or cultural expressions by language models or the classification of learners as "at-risk" by predictive analytics. Such exercises develop empathy and ethical reasoning by linking algorithmic outcomes to human consequences. Instructors thereby reposition ethics not as prohibition but as inquiry, a continual questioning of how technologies distribute opportunity and recognition.

One of the major transformative implications of AI integration is the reconfiguration of responsibility in the learning process. Traditional classrooms center on a one-directional moral economy: instructors evaluate, and learners comply. AI disrupts this hierarchy by mediating feedback and generating content autonomously. To maintain ethical coherence, responsibility must be reallocated, transitioning to co-responsibility frameworks in which educators and learners jointly exercise moral agency in the context of AI utilization. Vetter et al. (2024) describe co-responsibility as a *situated partnership* grounded in dialogue. Instructors serve as ethical mediators who facilitate decision-making, whereas learners engage as reflective agents. In practice, this may entail AI usage contracts, collaboratively formulated agreements delineating permissible and impermissible uses, data limitations, and disclosure standards.

Such contracts encourage transparency and empower learners to articulate their values. Ateeq et al. (2024) show that when instructors model self-disclosure of AI use, acknowledging, for example, that an AI assistant assisted in generating quiz items or structuring feedback, learners are more prone to adopt similar honesty. Co-responsibility, therefore, promotes ethical equilibrium. Both parties therefore become accountable for the moral ecology of the classroom. This approach aligns with Ge's (2017) activity theory framework positing that learning emerges through mediated collaboration among human and nonhuman actors. In AI-mediated writing instruction, the instructor, learner, and AI tools form a triadic system. In this system, the outcomes depend on balanced interactions rather than unilateral control.

The ethical capacity of a classroom context depends on the instructor's readiness. Recent studies reveal that educators frequently perceive themselves as inadequately equipped to tackle AI ethics, considering it a technical rather than a pedagogical concern (Neff et al., 2024). Professional development should therefore emphasize ethical reasoning skills as much as digital competence. Workshops might integrate reflective practice, philosophical dialogue, and design-based activities where instructors prototype AI-mediated lessons and evaluate them through ethical lenses (Hagendorff & Hagendorff, 2020). Ateeq et al. (2024) and Kousa & Niemi (2023) stress institutional support. According to them, ethical pedagogy thrives when universities recognize it as professional labor, rewarding instructors for integrating ethics into instruction. Without such acknowledgement, ethical reflection risks remaining invisible work.

6. CONCLUSION

In this chapter, one significant point has emerged consistently. Technical fixes or regulatory compliance alone cannot solve the ethical and privacy concerns of AI in education. They require a reorientation of education itself. It also demands a recognition that technology is never value-neutral and that pedagogical relationships are the moral infrastructure upon which any digital system ultimately rests. The question is no longer whether AI should enter classrooms. It has already taken its place. However, education may retain its human core amid algorithmic mediation. AI has amplified both promise and peril. On one hand, it enables unprecedented personalization, formative feedback, and data-driven insight. On the other hand, it risks deepening inequities and eroding privacy by distorting the meaning of authorship and learning. The preceding sections have shown that ethics in AI education should be dynamic. Principles such as fairness, transparency, accountability, and privacy require ongoing interpretation across different institutional and pedagogical contexts. Ethical integrity is not a static condition (Holmes et al., 2022; Yu & Yu, 2023). It is rather a process of moral negotiation that includes relationships among humans, machines, and values.

The concept of *ethical resilience* concretizes this dynamic view. Drawing inspiration from resilience theory in psychology and systems ecology (Rutter, 1990), ethical resilience refers to the capacity of educational contexts to adapt responsibly to technological transformation while preserving moral coherence (Ateeq et al., 2024). It bridges the structural and the personal paradigms. Institutions cultivate cultures of trust and fairness. On the other hand, individuals develop moral literacy and critical judgment. Ethical resilience operates on three interconnected levels. On a personal level, it means being aware of and thinking critically about AI. At the *individual level*, it involves instructors and learners who are capable of interrogating algorithmic tools, rather than simply consuming them (Walter, 2024). At the *institutional level*, it covers embedding ethics in governance, assessment, and design processes. Thus, it ensures that the use of AI tools aligns with shared educational values (Vetter et al., 2024).

At the systemic level, it means that different voices should be heard and that everyone should be able to participate in the conversation about AI innovation (UNESCO, 2021). These layers reinforce one another: resilient individuals sustain ethical institutions, and ethical institutions nurture resilient individuals. Ethical resilience also means being ready emotionally and mentally for the unknown. In AI-mediated learning, outcomes are often unpredictable; algorithms evolve, and ethical norms lag behind. Instructors and learners must therefore cultivate what Neff et al. (2024) call moral adaptability, the ability to reassess decisions when contexts shift. This adaptability is not moral relativism; it is the practical acknowledgment that maintaining integrity in a dynamic environment necessitates both unwavering principles and adaptable reasoning. An ethically resilient community responds to disruption not with panic or cynicism but with critical curiosity and moral imagination.

Privacy has served as both a technical and moral anchor throughout this chapter. To sustain ethical resilience, privacy should be woven as a principle encapsulated in privacy-by-design into the very architecture of educational technologies (Cavoukian, 2011). This approach rejects reactive data protection measures in favor of proactive, anticipatory design that treats privacy as a foundational right rather than an optional feature. Privacy-by-design functions both pedagogically and technologically. At the institutional level, organizations should ensure that they collect minimal data. Additionally, consent mechanisms should be clear. Data sovereignty, on the other hand, should be local. In classroom contexts, instructors may operationalize privacy-by-design by embedding reflection on data use in everyday classroom contexts. To illustrate, learners might co-create data-sharing agreements as a part of digital citizenship curricula. Such practices transform abstract regulations into lived ethical literacy. Integrating privacy-by-design into instructors training and curriculum development programs therefore promotes ethical resilience institutionally. This inclusion also aligns with the United Nations' (2021) *Recommendation on the Ethics of AI*. This recommendation requires "human oversight and contestability" in AI systems to preserve agency and accountability.

REFERENCES

Aljabr, A., & Al-Ahdal, A. A. M. H. (2024). Ethical and pedagogical implications of AI in language education: An empirical study at Ha'il University. *Acta Psychologica, 251*, 1–8. DOI: 10.1016/j.actpsy.2024.104605 PMID: 39549599

Ateeq, M., Alnuaimi, S., & Al-Kuwari, H. (2024). Artificial intelligence in education: Implications for academic integrity and the shift toward holistic assessment. *Frontiers in Education, 9*, 1–11. DOI: 10.3389/feduc.2024.1470979

Cavoukian, A. (2011). Privacy by design. *In IGI Global eBooks* (pp. 170–208). DOI: 10.4018/978-1-61350-501-4.ch007

Chan, J. (2025). Students' perceptions of "AI-giarism": Investigating changes in understandings of academic misconduct. *Education and Information Technologies, 30*(6), 8087–8108. DOI: 10.1007/s10639-024-13151-7

Çiftci, H. (2025). Navigating ethics: EFL learners' awareness and use of AI tools in writing classes. *Focus on ELT Journal, 7*(2), 22–46. DOI: 10.14744/felt.7.2.2

Cotton, D. R. E., Cotton, P. A., & Shipway, J. R. (2023). Chatting and cheating: Ensuring academic integrity in the era of ChatGPT. *Innovations in Education and Teaching International, 61*(2), 228–239. DOI: 10.1080/14703297.2023.2190148

Dawson, P. (2020). *Defending assessment security in a digital world: Preventing E-Cheating and supporting academic integrity in higher education.* https://www.taylorfrancis.com/books/9780429324178

Dwivedi, Y. K., Kshetri, N., Hughes, L., Slade, E. L., Jeyaraj, A., Kar, A. K., Baabdullah, A. M., Koohang, A., Raghavan, V., Ahuja, M., Albanna, H., Albashrawi, M. A., Al-Busaidi, A. S., Balakrishnan, J., Barlette, Y., Basu, S., Bose, I., Brooks, L., Buhalis, D., & Wright, R. (2023). Opinion Paper: "So what if ChatGPT wrote it?" Multidisciplinary perspectives on opportunities, challenges and implications of generative conversational AI for research, practice and policy. *International Journal of Information Management, 71*, 1–63. DOI: 10.1016/j.ijinfomgt.2023.102642

Eaton, S. E. (2021). Plagiarism in higher education. *In ABC-CLIO eBooks.* DOI: 10.5040/9798400697142

Fu, Y., & Weng, Z. (2024). Navigating the ethical terrain of AI in education: A systematic review on framing responsible human-centered AI practices. *Computers and Education Artificial Intelligence, 7*, 1–20. DOI: 10.1016/j.caeai.2024.100306

Ge, W. (2017). Learning by expanding: An activity-theoretical approach to developmental research (2nd ed.). Yrj? Engestr?m. *Frontiers of Education in China, 12*(1), 130–132. DOI: 10.3868/s110-006-017-0011-8

Goddiksen, M., Willum Johansen, M., Armond, A. C., Centa, M., Clavien, C., Gefenas, E., Globokar, R., Hogan, L., Kovács, N., Merit, M. T., Olsson, I. A. S., Poškutė, M., Quinn, U., Borlido Santos, J., Santos, R., Schöpfer, C., Strahovnik, V., Varga, O., Wall, P. J., & Lund, T. B. (2024). Grey zones and good practice: A European survey of academic integrity among undergraduate students. *Ethics & Behavior*, *34*(3), 199–217. DOI: 10.1080/10508422.2023.2187804

Hagendorff, T., & Hagendorff, T. (2020). The Ethics of AI Ethics: An Evaluation of Guidelines. *Minds and Machines*, *30*(1), 99–120. DOI: 10.1007/s11023-020-09517-8

Holmes, W., Porayska-Pomsta, K., Holstein, K., Sutherland, E., Baker, T., Shum, S. B., Santos, O. C., Rodrigo, M. T., Cukurova, M., Bittencourt, I. I., & Koedinger, K. R. (2022). Ethics of AI in education: Towards a community-wide framework. *International Journal of Artificial Intelligence in Education, 32*(3), 504–526. DOI: 10.1007/s40593-021-00239-1

Jones, K. M. L., Asher, A., Goben, A., Perry, M. R., Salo, D., Briney, K. A., & Robertshaw, M. B. (2020). 'We're being tracked at all times': Student perspectives of their privacy in relation to learning analytics in higher education. *SSRN*, •••, 1–28. DOI: 10.2139/ssrn.3565553

Kousa, P., & Niemi, H. (2023). AI ethics and learning: EdTech companies' challenges and solutions. *Interactive Learning Environments*, *31*(10), 6735–6746. DOI: 10.1080/10494820.2022.2043908

Mossberger, K., Tolbert, C. J., & McNeal, R. S. (2007). *Digital Citizenship*. In The MIT Press eBooks. DOI: 10.7551/mitpress/7428.001.0001

Neff, J., Arciaga, K., & Burri, L. (2024). EFL students' and teachers' perceptions of the ethical uses of AI tools. *Technology in Language Teaching & Learning*, *6*(3), 1–19. DOI: 10.29140/tltl.v6n3.1714

Pangrazio, L., & Selwyn, N. (2019). "Personal data literacies": A critical literacies approach to enhancing understandings of personal digital data. *New Media & Society*, *21*(2), 419–437. DOI: 10.1177/1461444818799523

Rutter, M. (1990). Psychosocial resilience and protective mechanisms. In *Cambridge University Press eBooks* (pp. 181–214). DOI: 10.1017/CBO9780511752872.013

Ryan, M., Stahl, B. C., & Kinder-Kurlanda, K. (2021). Research and practice of AI ethics: A case study approach juxtaposing academic discourse with organizational reality. *Science and Engineering Ethics*, *27*(3), 1–29. DOI: 10.1007/s11948-021-00293-x PMID: 33686527

Saeli, H., Rahmati, P., Dalman, M., Shamsi, Y., & Koltovskaia, S. (2025). Embrace or resist? EFL teachers on adopting ChatGPT as a teaching and feedback tool. *Language Awareness*, •••, 1–21. DOI: 10.1080/09658416.2025.2577191

Sepp, S. (2025). Towards more transparency in learning analytics. *Journal of Learning Analytics*, *12*(3), 34–46. DOI: 10.18608/jla.2025.8713

Sotiri, E. (2024). The future of AI and authorship: The EU's legal framework for AI and copyright. *Pin Code, N° 19*(3), 1–10. .DOI: 10.3917/pinc.019.0001

Tan, C. (2020). Digital Confucius? Exploring the implications of artificial intelligence in spiritual education. *Connection Science*, *32*(3), 280–291. DOI: 10.1080/09540091.2019.1709045

UNESCO. (2021). *Recommendation on the Ethics of Artificial Intelligence*. UNESCO Publishing. https://unesdoc.unesco.org/ark:/48223/pf0000381137

Vetter, M. A., Lucia, B., Jiang, J., & Othman, M. (2024). Towards a framework for local interrogation of AI ethics: A case study on text generators, academic integrity, and composing with ChatGPT. *Computers & Composition. Computers and Composition*, *71*(6), 1–12. DOI: 10.1016/j.compcom.2024.102831

Walter, Y. (2024). Embracing the future of artificial intelligence in the classroom: The relevance of AI literacy, prompt engineering, and critical thinking in modern education. *International Journal of Educational Technology in Higher Education*, *21*(15), 1–29. DOI: 10.1186/s41239-024-00448-3

Wang, S., Wang, F., Zhu, Z., Wang, J., & Zhao, T. T. D. (2024). Artificial intelligence in education: A systematic literature review. *Expert Systems with Applications*, *252*(A), 1–19. .DOI: 10.1016/j.eswa.2024.124167

Westin, A. F. (1967). *Privacy and freedom*. Atheneum. https://scholarlycommons.law.wlu.edu/wlulr/vol25/iss1/20

Williamson, B. (2017). Big data in education: The digital future of learning, policy and practice. *Sage (Atlanta, Ga.)*. Advance online publication. DOI: 10.4135/9781529714920

Williamson, B., Bayne, S., & Shay, S. (2020). The datafication of teaching in Higher Education: Critical issues and perspectives. *Teaching in Higher Education*, *25*(4), 351–365. DOI: 10.1080/13562517.2020.1748811

Yu, L., & Yu, Z. (2023). Qualitative and quantitative analyses of artificial intelligence ethics in education using VOSviewer and CitNetExplorer. *Frontiers in Psychology*, *14*, 1–14. DOI: 10.3389/fpsyg.2023.1061778 PMID: 36968737

Zawacki-Richter, O., Marín, V. I., Bond, M., & Gouverneur, F. (2019). Systematic review of research on artificial intelligence applications in higher education – Where are the educators? *International Journal of Educational Technology in Higher Education*, *16*(39), 1–27. DOI: 10.1186/s41239-019-0171-0

Zhai, X., Chu, X., Chai, C. S., Jong, M. S. Y., Istenic, A., Spector, M., Liu, J.-B., Yuan, J., & Li, Y. (2021). A review of artificial intelligence (AI) in education from 2010 to 2020. *Complexity*, *2021*(1), 1–18. DOI: 10.1155/2021/8812542

Chapter 12
Ethical Integration of Artificial Intelligence in Education:
Opportunities, Risks, and Governance Frameworks

Rahul Singhal
http://orcid.org/0009-0002-8200-5632
Shoolini University, India

Supriya Srivastava
http://orcid.org/0000-0002-5440-4364
Shoolini University, India

Harish Chandan
http://orcid.org/0000-0003-1035-426X
Independent Researcher, USA

ABSTRACT

Artificial Intelligence (AI) is rapidly transforming educational systems by enhancing personalised learning, teaching efficiency, and institutional management. However, its integration raises significant ethical concerns related to data privacy, algorithmic bias, academic integrity, and human agency. This chapter examines the ethical foundations of AI in education, explores its pedagogical benefits, and analyses associated risks. It further highlights governance mechanisms and human-centred strategies necessary for responsible and equitable AI implementation in educational institutions.

DOI: 10.4018/979-8-3373-8027-8.ch012

1. ARTIFICIAL INTELLIGENCE AND THE EVOLUTION OF EDUCATIONAL TECHNOLOGY

Educational technologies had a difficult history of development until the early 20th century, when they were introduced as advancements in education, and technology progressively gained popularity. The integration of artificial intelligence into educational ecosystems represents not merely technological enhancement but a structural reconfiguration of lifelong learning and professional development systems (Srivastava, 2026).

1.1 Emergence of Artificial Intelligence in Educational Systems

Artificial intelligence is a tremendous improvement over previous learning technologies in its ability to autonomously process data, recognise patterns and perform predictive modelling. Artificial intelligence systems are starting to be integrated into multiple areas of education practice, such as teaching, evaluation, and administrative administration (Goldschmitt et al., 2025). An example of intelligent tutoring systems is instructional support simulated through personalised teaching by offering real-time feedback, scaffolding, and customised learning paths, depending on the responses of the students. These systems aim to recreate aspects of human tutoring, recognising misconceptions and adjusting the instructional strategies to these misconceptions.

In spite of these benefits, the mass adoption of AI systems has presented complicated deliberations over their influence on the pedagogical relations, professional roles, and decision-making. Incorporation of algorithmic systems into education is not a mere experiment anymore, but more normalised and thus requires a systemic study on the wider implications of its use.

1.2 Ethical Concerns in Early AI Adoption

The integration of AI technologies in the educational field has been rapidly increasing faster than the establishment of a set of ethical principles and governance frameworks. Schools often introduce AI-based solutions without considering the long-term implications of the use on both students and teachers, and the integrity of the institutions (Walter, 2024). Such an unequal relationship between technological innovation and regulatory readiness brings up the issue of responsible implementation.

The collection, storage, and analysis of large volumes of student data is one of the key aspects of ethical concern. Continuous data capture is a common feature of AI systems and it can consist of behavioural patterns, performance, and measures of engagement. In the absence of proper protection, these practices will undermine student privacy, autonomy, and informed consent. Furthermore, automatic decision-making algorithms can reproduce or even enhance the biases that are already inherent in training data, which can result in unequal access to education (Al-Zahrani, 2024).

There are also ethical issues in the context of learner-centred learning where artificial intelligence interferes with the preferences of the educators in terms of instructions. Using automated suggestions too often can decrease professional judgment and eliminate the possibility of subtle, context-driven instruction. As well, the emergence of generative AI technologies has brought about new issues pertaining to academic integrity, originality of student work, and validity of assessment.

Since education has a formative influence on personal growth and social advancement, ethical aspects of AI incorporation should be scrutinised with thorough and organised attention. These issues must be addressed to make sure that technological improvements are used to enhance fair, open, and sound educational practices, as opposed to compromising the best educational principles (Akgun & Greenhow, 2022).

2. THEORETICAL FOUNDATIONS OF ARTIFICIAL INTELLIGENCE IN EDUCATION

Artificial Intelligence (AI) is a concept that vaguely includes computational systems that do the work that is normally done by human thought processes, such as learning, reasoning, making decisions, and solving problems (Belenguer, 2022). In the educational environment, AI includes a set of technologies that may analyse high volumes of data, modify the content of the instruction, forecast the results of learning, and facilitate administrative processes. AI in education does not necessarily mean robotics or highly automated systems, but encompasses algorithmically driven systems installed on digital learning systems, assessment instruments, and institutional decision-making systems.

2.1 Types and Applications of AI in Education

One of the significant differences in AI discourse is that of narrow AI and general AI. The narrow AI, also known as the weak AI, is used to carry out certain, well-constrained activities in limited environments. The majority of the existing educational applications belong to this category. They are intelligent tutoring systems, automated grading systems, plagiarism detectors, and learning analytics dashboards. These systems are machine learning systems that are trained on past information to determine patterns and respond more optimally, but they cannot think independently of what they are programmed to think (Cajueiro & Celestino, 2026).

2.2 Philosophical Foundations of Ethical Decision-Making

Ethics, being a subdivision of philosophy, deals with the logical study of morals that shape human conduct and decisions. Ethical analysis is an educational and technological conceptual perspective that offers a model to analyse the implications, duty and worth of innovation. There are a number of classical theories of ethics that are especially applicable to the analysis of AI implementation in education. Ethical engagement with AI in education is also shaped by processes of attitude formation and value internalisation, which influence how educators and learners interpret technological authority and responsibility (Srivastava & Rojhe, 2021).

Deontological ethics is a type of ethics that is based on the reasoning of duties and highlights the need to follow the rules, obligations, and rights regardless of the outcomes. In the context of education, deontology encounters such concerns as the privacy of students, the presence of informed consent when using the data, and academic honesty. In this sense, AI systems need to be used with the predetermined professional ethical obligations in terms of fairness in testing and adherence to learner autonomy, although alternative solutions may provide an efficiency advantage (Bittle & El-Gayar, 2025).

Ethics based on consequences, especially utilitarianism, consider an action in its outcomes, giving importance to the decisions that have the maximum overall benefit. When applied to the field of AI in education, consequentialist reasoning would determine whether AI-based interventions enhance learning results, expand access, or make institutions more efficient (Darvishi et al., 2024). Nonetheless, the use of outcome-based arguments can only ignore the presence of unintended harms, including the exclusion of certain groups of students based on the algorithmic bias or the decrease in the possibility of engaging in meaningful teacher-student interactions.

A major overlap between AI Ethics and Educational Ethics lies in the intersection of the two disciplines, demonstrating that the former seeks to explain the latter, and the reverse is also true.

2.3 Intersection of Educational Ethics and AI Ethics

Educational Ethics and AI Ethics overlap a lot, exemplified by the fact that the former aims to explain the latter and vice versa. The intersection between educational ethics and AI ethics is a highly active area of concern since the two disciplines have common interests in terms of fairness, responsibility, and virtues of safeguarding human dignity. Nevertheless, AI poses new challenges that go beyond the conventional educational ethical issues. The process of algorithmic decision-making can be rather transparent; therefore, it can be hard to determine how educators and learners can determine the way in which recommendations or evaluations are produced. Without critical institutional reflection, algorithmic systems risk reproducing structural inequities embedded within broader socio-economic and gendered power relations (Srivastava, 2025).

Another major convergence point is equity and fairness. AI systems given historical biased data may reproduce systemic inequalities due to their disproportionate disadvantage of certain population groups. As an example, predictive analytics applications can identify students as at-risk based on patterns that are associated with socioeconomic or geographic factors, which might be reinforcing assumptions based on deficits. To achieve ethical educational practice, such systems are to be critically assessed on a regular basis to make sure that they do not promote inequitable results.

The AI integration also influences learner autonomy. Adaptive learning systems and algorithmic suggestions can steer the direction of instruction in a manner that constrains student agency or choice. Personalisation may help increase engagement, but too much automation may turn learners into people receiving decisions made by the system. Implementation ethics, hence, consists of striking a balance between technological efficiency and possibilities of critical reflection, independent learning, and mentorship by human beings.

The interplay of educational and AI ethics indicates the importance of interdisciplinary work between educators, technologists, and policymakers. The concept of ethical AI in education cannot be discussed only concerning technical design or pedagogical reform per se, but it should be organised in the framework of complex systems that take into account both technology affordances and educational values (Kamalov et al., 2023).

2.4 Core Ethical Principles Guiding AI Integration

Various fundamental ethical principles are used to inform the responsible adoption of AI in the education system and define the operational standards of both policy and practice. The key idea in making AI-driven processes transparent is to make the processes understandable and subject to analysis. Teachers and students must be provided with clear descriptions of the methods of data collection, how algorithms are used to make a recommendation, and how automated judgments affect assessment or teaching (Du Plooy et al., 2024). Open systems foster credibility and allow stakeholders to critically review the technological interventions.

Responsibility is also crucial in situations where the course of education depends on the work of the algorithmic system. Organisations need to put in place structures to delegate the decision-making process, which AI tools have produced or aided. This involves having supervisory mechanisms, regular audits of algorithm performance, and having human instructors as having final control over consequential processes, like grading or placement, or disciplinary measures. The mistakes or prejudices of automated systems can go unnoticed without definite accountability (Banker & Khetani, 2019).

The concept of beneficence and non-maleficence, usually linked with professional ethics, stresses maximising good and decreasing harm. In education AI implementation, beneficence entails using technology to increase the effectiveness, accessibility, and well-being of students. Non-maleficence implies the active detection and prevention of threats associated with the misuse of the data, biased results, or the weakening of pedagogic relationships. These principles imply constant surveillance on the effects of AI systems as opposed to a single consent on ethics.

3. OPPORTUNITIES AND PEDAGOGICAL BENEFITS OF AI IN EDUCATION

3.1 Personalised and Adaptive Learning

The ability of artificial intelligence (AI) to facilitate personalised and adaptive learning processes is one of the biggest contributions of this field to modern education. Conventional instructional designs tend to be based on standardised curricula and schedules, which may not sufficiently support the various requirements of learning, the level of prior knowledge, and the cognitive skills and capabilities of students. However, AI-powered solutions employ real-time data analysis to customise instructional information, feedback, and progression paths based on the profile of individual learners (Baek et al., 2025).

Another notable form of AI-powered personalisation is intelligent tutoring systems (ITS). These systems make use of features of one-to-one human tutoring to detect misconceptions of learners, track patterns of responses, and offer instructional assistance. ITS platforms adapt the complexity and sequencing of the learning materials and format to match the competence of the learner, through the use of iterative feedback loops. This personalised scaffolding will increase the level of engagement and can lead to the mastery of base concepts, especially in the areas of mathematics, science, and learning languages. Intelligent tutoring systems minimise the number of times that there is a delay between performance and correction by offering immediate feedback and adaptive remediation, which reinforces knowledge retention (Darling-Hammond et al., 2020).

Learning analytics goes a step further to expand the ability of AI to process large-scale educational data produced via digital platforms. Such analytics applications monitor such indicators as time-on-task, the frequency of engagement, the results of assessments, and patterns of interaction (Mazzullo et al., 2023). Through such points of data synthesis, AI systems create a comprehensive profile of students that aids in the decision-making process of instruction. Teachers can utilise this kind of information to help learners in need of further assistance, differentiate instruction and implement timely interventions. Early academic risk can also be identified using predictive models, and the institutions can then build focused retention policies.

As much as personalisation increases accuracy in instructional processes, it also changes the paradigms of education to competency-based development. The students can progress at a pace that suits them, repeating the difficult material or moving faster using known material. This allows flexibility, which encourages learner autonomy and motivation, coupled with minimised negative effects of uniform pacing structures (Nguyen et al., 2023). With the development of AI, adaptive learning settings have the potential to incorporate multimodal data (such as behaviours and performance indicators) to inform instructional advice.

3.2 Enhancing Teaching Effectiveness through AI

The AI technologies are also associated with the enhanced effectiveness of teaching, where the capacity of educators to handle the instructional-related tasks is augmented, as well as to make evidence-based decisions. Instead of substituting teachers, AI can only act as a decision-support system to simplify routine processes and deliver actionable insights that can be used to improve pedagogical plans. While AI may streamline instructional processes, technological intensification has been shown to reshape professional boundaries and contribute to work–life strain among educators (Gurung & Srivastava, 2021).

Automated assessment tools are a good example of this improvement as they simplify the time taken to grade objective and, to a growing extent, subjective student work. With high reliability, AI-based systems can effectively analyse multiple-choice questions, short answers, and structured problem-solving questions. With the development of natural language processing, automated scoring and feedback in an essay can now be done, providing students with formative assessment promptly. Feedback loops are especially useful when it comes to iterative learning because, through rapid feedback, students can address any errors and revise their knowledge without having to delay the process over a long period. Instructionally, automated grading saves time by decreasing the administrative workload, allowing the educators to focus their time on more instruction-related tasks, which include mentoring, discussion, and individualised instruction.

Besides assessment, AI technologies aid in planning the curriculum and instruction. Learning analytics based on data can be used to make decisions on content sequencing, pacing changes, and what was not covered. As an example, aggregate performance data can indicate trends of misconception within cohorts, leading to changes in curriculum or specific instructional intervention. The tools of content generation supported by AI could also be used to assist the educator in creating instructional content, quizzes, and learning materials in accordance with the identified learning outcomes (Nur Fitria, 2023).

All in all, the implementation of AI in the process of instruction is more efficient but does not decrease the primary role of educators as intermediaries in the learning process. Conducted appropriately, AI is a complementary resource that will increase the teaching capacity and facilitate data-driven pedagogical decision-making (Ahmad et al., 2022).

3.3 Administrative and Institutional Efficiency

In addition to being used in teaching, AI technologies can also have significant advantages in streamlining administrative and institutional processes. To manage operations, schools and other learning institutions produce a lot of data related to enrolment patterns, student development, use of resources and even management of infrastructures. Analytics systems based on AI have the capacity to analyse these databases, to streamline institutional planning and decision-making (Alfredo et al., 2024).

3.4 AI for Inclusion and Accessibility

AI technologies can also be used to achieve high potential in terms of inclusion and access in an educational setting. In the past, disabled learners, language diversity and learners of different socio-cultural backgrounds have faced challenges that restrain their fair access. Adaptive support that is offered to various needs using AI-enabled assistive technologies can address these challenges.

Examples of assistive AI applications are speech-to-text, text-to-speech applications, real-time captioning, automated translation, and adaptive interface design. These tools allow the visually, auditorily, and motor-impaired learners to access the learning materials in a better way. As an example, AI-based transcription services enable learners with hearing disabilities to follow the lectures, and text-to-speech systems can be used by students with reading challenges or dyslexia. Such technologies aim to facilitate universal design of learning to make instructional content accessible to a variety of modalities (Farhood et al., 2025) .

4. ETHICAL RISKS AND COMPLEXITIES IN AI-MEDIATED EDUCATION

4.1 Data Privacy, Surveillance and Consent

The combination of artificial intelligence with the work of the educational systems is based on the ongoing gathering, storage, and analysis of vast amounts of student data. As much as these data allow personalisation and predictive analytics, they also present serious ethical challenges to do with privacy, surveillance and ownership of data. Academic performance, measures of engagement, patterns of behaviours, and, in certain instances, biometric or location data are the types of information that educational technologies collect regularly (Brandao, 2025). The combination of these data sets forms somewhat detailed digital profiles that can be retained across institutional lines. Continuous digital surveillance and performance analytics may alter occupational stress patterns and institutional work cultures in subtle yet significant ways (Gurung et al., 2024). Ethical AI implementation requires structured risk assessment mechanisms that consider vulnerability, exposure, and cascading institutional impacts within interconnected systems.

This issue is about questions of data ownership. With most AI-driven systems, the data collected through interactions with students is being stored and processed by third-party vendors, in most instances under contractual deals, which are not exactly disclosed to the users. Students can lack knowledge of the ways their information is used, exchanged, and stored in the long term. This brings the question of commodification of educational information as well as the possibility of secondary use other than the instructional uses. Under ethical practice, there should be a clear understanding of who has access to student information, the duration of how long data is stored and whether students have the privilege to review or demand their records be deleted.

The principle of informed consent is also problematic in digitally mediated learning systems. The terms of service of an institution or platform are often taken by the students without getting a clear picture of the extent of data gathering. Consent can be nominal, as opposed to actually voluntary, in situations where attendance in AI-operated systems is a requirement to complete the course. This presents an ethical dilemma that has been raised between the efficiency of institutions and the autonomy of persons. Educational institutions should make sure that permission procedures are significant, understandable and they should have real alternatives when feasible.

Besides issues of privacy, AI-based surveillance systems have surveillance-related risks. Behavioural analytics platforms, engagement tracking dashboards and remote proctoring tools can be used to monitor the activity of students continuously. Although these kinds of systems are commonly defended as systems of preserving academic honesty or enhancing teaching and learning, over-monitoring may promote a lack of trust and generate psychologically invasive learning conditions. Surveillance as a matter of normal practice can also affect the behaviour of the students and make them more compliant instead of engaging in a genuine activity.

4.2 Algorithmic Bias and Discrimination

The example of algorithmic bias is one of the most popular ethical dilemmas related to AI integration in industries, including the educational industry (Giannakos et al., 2025). AI systems are trained with historical data, which might be biased with social, cultural or institutional aspects. In cases where such datasets are employed in the creation of predictive models, they are capable of reproducing or even increasing the number of inequities that already exist in the world. Biased algorithms can affect judgments regarding assessment, placement, intervention, or resource allocation in an educational context.

The lack of equal education opportunities can be observed when an impartial AI system is not properly put to the test, and it is used to make decisions. Recommendations on course placement, remediation or intervention strategies that are automated can influence such a learner trajectory in a manner that is hard to refute. The unintended result is that when the outputs of an algorithm are perceived as objective or authoritative, the educators will continue to perpetuate inequitable practices. The complexity of some machine learning models also makes this task more challenging, as the direction of decision-making is not readily explainable in such cases (Ben Zion et al., 2025).

To tackle the issue of algorithmic discrimination, it is necessary to perform constant audits, a variety of training data, and cross-disciplinary analysis. Ethical AI implementation should involve the possibilities to recognise uneven effects on groups of people and make sure that predictive models are provided to support the decisions and are not considered as an absolute determiner. The interpretation of algorithmic results in contexts of the wider education process is always under human supervision.

4.3 Academic Integrity and Misuse of Generative AI

New complexities regarding academic integrity have been brought on board by the growing access to AI-based tools that generate content. The generative AI systems have the ability to create essays, find complex solutions, create code, and synthesise information with little human input. Although these capabilities can be applied in a learning manner once applied effectively, they also provide avenues to abuse them, which puts traditional assessment systems to the test.

AI-assisted cheating is a trend that is increasing in the field of education. Learners can use the help of automated systems to generate papers that seem to be the original ones, but they are not based on personal knowledge and work. The fact that AI-generated content can be created with ease makes it hard to detect instances of academic misconduct, especially when the results are personalised and context-related. The standard forms of plagiarism detection techniques might not be capable of detecting AI-generated work, and this means that institutions will need to rethink their integrity policy and technological protection.

The existence of AI tools also raises more general issues on the matter of authorship and originality. Traditionally, assessment in education has been based on the premise that the work submitted reflects the cognitive processes of an individual with his/her course work. In the case when AI plays an important role in generating content, it is difficult to draw a line between the rightful support and the unethical replacement. Such ambiguity implies the need to give more specific recommendations about the use of AI in academic activities.

These developments have a special impact on authentic assessment practices. Written assignments that are standardised and assess the learning outcomes of students might no longer be a valid measure, assuming that the AI-generated responses can be used to simulate the expected performance. The educators are thus forced to consider other ways of assessment strategies that can focus on higher-order thinking, process-based assessment, and display of applied competence. These may be oral tests, project-based learning, reflective writing, and iterative feedback processes, which involve a long-term engagement.

4.4 Over-Reliance on Automation and Loss of Human Agency

Although AI is efficient and capable of decision support, overreliance on autonomous systems can result in reduced human agency in the education sector. The algorithmic suggestions that were incorporated in the instruction and administrative procedures can transform the professional roles and the powers of decision-making, unbeknownst to them.

Deskilling of teachers is one of the possible outcomes. When AI systems take on the task of evaluation, or instructional planning or monitoring of students, the teachers might slowly lose their involvement in analytic and evaluative activities that historically shaped their professional knowledge (Abdelaal et al., 2019; Akgun & Greenhow, 2022). In the long run, the reliance on automated feedback can decrease the possibility of pedagogical reflection and professional judgment. This movement poses a threat of converting teachers into passive structure engineers of preset technological trajectories. Persistent dependence on algorithmic systems may gradually influence professional identity formation and decision-making autonomy within educational environments (Gurung et al., 2024).

Excessive use of algorithmic suggestions also brings up the issue of decision-making independence. Recommendations can be based on predictive analytics concerning student placement, intervention strategies or performance evaluation. When institutional cultures consider these outputs as an objective or authoritative part of the world, then educators might experience the restriction of utilising contextual judgment. The belief in algorithmic determinism-the belief that predictions based on data are necessarily true-can mask the subtle awareness of individual learner situations (Wang et al., 2024) .

Adaptive learning systems may also reduce agency among students by determining the pace of instruction and the selection of learning content. Personalisation can make work more efficient, but too much automation can restrict the ability to explore and learn independently and think critically. Students can turn into inactive elements of the algorithmically mediated experiences instead of contributors to knowledge building (Abdelaal et al., 2019).

To ensure that human agency remains intact, focused design decisions are necessary that allow making AI more of an augmentative than a replacement technology (Zhai et al., 2024). The final control over the consequential decisions should remain in the hands of the educators, and the policies of the institutions should prioritise the human-in-the-loop models when the outputs of the algorithms are prone to interpretation by the professionals. Professional growth should also be ongoing, so that educators are aware of the skills and the weaknesses of the AI systems.

5. GOVERNANCE, POLICY AND REGULATORY FRAMEWORKS

5.1 Institutional Ethics and Governance Mechanisms

The governance of artificial intelligence (AI) in education should start on the institutional level, where policies should be used to help the selection, implementation, and monitoring of the AI-enabled systems in an appropriate manner. Institutions of higher education should also have formal codes of conduct that define expectations on ethical use of data, information about algorithmic decision-making, and preservation of student rights. These codes are operational documents that bring technological innovation broadly in line with institutional values (e.g. academic integrity, inclusivity, learning well-being). Sustainable AI adoption requires institutional resilience strategies capable of balancing innovation with ethical accountability and long-term organisational stability (Tomar & Srivastava, 2024).

The policies administered by the institutions must be clear on what AI can be utilised to teach, assess and administer, as well as specify the steps of testing the new technological tools before implementation. Vendor purchasing criteria may direct such vendors to reveal data handling information, algorithmic logic and security protection. Moreover, the contractual agreements by institutions must be characterised by the aspects concerning data ownership, retention, and user consent.

The institutional review mechanisms are very important in upholding ethical. Proposed AI implementations may be reviewed against pertinent ethical standards by committees or governance boards that are typically based on the same research ethics or technology oversight entities that they are suggested to implement. Such mechanisms could encompass the risk evaluation process, the pilot testing process, and the review of periodical performance reviews. Constant surveillance will keep AI systems in check with the institutional standards and will not lead to unwanted adverse long-term effects. Incorporating the ethical analysis into the organisational processes will help the institutions progress to active governance rather than reactive governance. Structured multi-criteria decision models, such as the Analytic Hierarchy Process (AHP), demonstrate how expert judgment and weighted evaluation frameworks can enhance transparency and rational prioritization in complex decision environments.

5.2 Transparency, Accountability and Explainability

Ethical AI governance also encompasses accountability and transparency as fundamental aspects, especially when the output of the algorithmic system affects the decisions made in education. Transparency means giving open yet easily available information on how AI systems are operated, the information they rely on and how they produce their outputs. In the absence of this clarity, the stakeholders may not be able to judge the reliability or fairness of algorithmic processes.

Explainable AI is one of the essential transparency-promoting mechanisms. Explainability is the ability of AI systems to give justifiable explanations as to why they make recommendations or decisions. In schools, this can include showing teachers reasons that are interpretable as to why a student has been identified as at risk or why a certain learning path has been suggested. To explain the results encourages professional judgment and minimises the potential of trusting automated results or output blindly.

Auditability also enhances accountability by providing an organised review of the algorithmic performance in the long run. The frequency of audits can determine whether the AI systems yield fair results between demographic groups, are correct, and comply with accepted ethical principles. Such assessments can involve in-house assessments that are done by institutional oversight committees or even by external assessments that are done by independent experts. Audit trails also provide a means of investigating mistakes or unintended consequences, which are documented.

The responsibility of AI-supported decisions should not be diffused, since clear lines of accountability should be set. The institutions are supposed to appoint control functions that would help in overseeing the performance of the systems, responses to the concerns of stakeholders, and the enactment of corrective measures where necessary. All the mechanisms of transparency and accountability help make the AI systems subservient to human authority instead of functioning as under-the-table decision-making machines.

6. STRATEGIES FOR ETHICAL IMPLEMENTATION

6.1 Human-Centred AI Design

Artificial intelligence (AI) in education should be performed ethically by adopting a human-centred approach of design, which prioritises the needs, values, and experiences of learners and educators. Instead of considering AI as an alternative to instructional skills, institutions must implement participatory design strategies that actively engage teachers, learners and academic administrators in developing and choosing AI-enabled tools. Involvement of end users in system design can increase the contextual relevance, usability and trust and reduce the chances of accidental negative consequences.

Collaboration between teacher and AI is an important principle of operation in human-centred design. The AI systems are supposed to play the role of decision-support mechanisms, which will complement instructional planning, feedback and monitoring the learners, but pedagogical decisions should remain in the hands of the educators (Alfiras et al., 2025). By means of such collaboration, teachers can decipher algorithmic advice using professional judgment knowledge and context to make sure that automated outputs are utilized properly in various learning settings.

6.2 Ethical Data Management Practices

Ethical data management practices will ensure responsible AI implementation by ensuring that the rights of students and institutional integrity are safeguarded. Whenever AI systems are collecting or analysing learner data, informed consent should become a central condition. Learning institutions ought to explain to their students what kind of information is gathered, how this information is utilized, who will access it, and the period of storage. The consent processes must be clear, understandable and where possible offer the learners meaningful choices on whether to participate or not.

Minimization of data also enhances the ethical considerations as it ensures that data that is directly related to instructional or administration goals is collected. Misuse and loss of privacy are more likely to occur especially when behavioural or performance data are collected excessively. The institutions are to introduce secure storage measures, where necessary, anonymization of data and set data retention policies that ensure sensitive information is not stored indefinitely. Informed consent and data minimization, together, assist in building trust and make AI-based analytics stay consistent with the real purpose of education (Zohuri & Behgounia, 2023).

6.3 AI Literacy and Professional Development

Professional growth among educators is necessary in the future to ensure positive and ethical application of AI technologies. The training programs must include both technical functionality and essential awareness of the restrictions of algorithms, possible biases, and ethical considerations. Providing a teacher with AI literacy will allow them to assess the work of the system and recognize anomalies and apply technological knowledge to practice that is pedagogically viable. Professional development programmes can be workshops, certification courses and group learning communities which promote ongoing skill development.

AI literacy is also significant to students. Schools and colleges also have a role to play in advancing the education of digital ethics that foster responsible technology usage, awareness of the academic standards of integrity, and the knowledge of how the outputs of AI can be interpreted. Through knowledgeable interaction with AI tools, the institutions in question will be able to curb the abuse and promote the emergence of key digital skills that will be instrumental in the modern learning setting (Oncioiu & Bularca, 2025).

6.4 Preserving Pedagogical Values in AI Integration

The AI should be ethically integrated so that it does not harm the fundamental pedagogical principles that include critical thinking, creativity, and learner autonomy. Excessive automation of the teaching process may unintentionally limit the possibilities of inquiry-based learning and reflective interaction. Teachers must thus come up with learning tasks that will ask the students to analyse, evaluate, and use knowledge (not only algorithmically generated responses).

Blended decision-making models offer a balanced strategy as they combine insights generated by the AI with the expertise of human beings. Within these models, algorithmic suggestions guide teaching practices but do not substitute the work of a professional (Huang et al., 2025). This balance will help to balance the efficiency of AI and retain the relational and interpretive aspects of education. By integrating AI in pedagogically informed practices, the institutions will be able to use technological innovation without compromising the anthropocentric roots of successful teaching and learning.

7. APPLIED ETHICAL ANALYSIS CASE STUDIES

7.1 Automated Assessment: Efficiency vs Equity

Assessment systems in AI have gained popularity to increase efficiency and consistency in assessing the performance of students. There are automated grading systems that are faster at evaluating objective answers, and more often, offer feedback on written work that is structured. These systems not only help to decrease administrative work on the part of the educator but also facilitate the timely feedback cycles, which are related to better learning outcomes. Also, AI-based marking has the potential to increase reliability and consistency among large samples and reduce the error of human subjectivity.

Nevertheless, the ethical issues are associated with fairness and validity. Automated essay grading models can be based on linguistic or style patterns, which give an advantage to some writing patterns, which can be unfavourable to students with other linguistic or cultural backgrounds. Transparency is also constrained by the opaqueness of certain algorithmic processes, where learners can hardly tell how their work was graded and also question perceived inaccuracies. Besides, overuse of automated grading threatens to reduce assessment habits to easily machine-scorable forms, and may omit sophisticated skills like critical thinking and innovation. Moral implementation, hence, necessitates human control, the verification of algorithmic scoring in reference to standard rubrics and the provision of channels of appeal or examination (*AI and the Future of Education*, 2025).

7.2 Intelligent Tutoring Systems and Learner Autonomy

Intelligent tutoring systems offer adaptive teaching aid by means of individual feedback and an adaptable sequence of content. Such systems have been found useful in enhancing conceptual knowledge, especially in areas that need progressive acquisition of skills. As the intelligent tutors diagnose the errors that learners make and provide remedial measures to them, they can recapitulate the individualised teaching aspect that is usually hard to come by in a large classroom setting.

Although these are considered to be beneficial, the issue of ethical considerations comes into play concerning learner autonomy and agency. Extremely modularised adaptive pathways could restrict exploration or self-directed learning, as students might never be allowed to discover or pursue individual student-directed learning pathways. Relying too heavily on an automated scaffold may decrease the ability to struggle productively, which also constitutes a key element of deep learning. Also, learners can grant the system-generated recommendations authority without doubting their validity.

In order to curb these risks, intelligent tutoring systems must also be structured in a way that allows learners to have the flexibility to make informed decisions concerning content flow. Teachers are also supposed to incorporate reflective tasks that would help the learners to challenge feedback, reason, and continue to actively participate in the learning process. Striking a balance between personalisation and autonomy means that AI-advocated teaching will adhere to the developmental and constructivist pedagogical theory ("AI in Education and for Education," 2025).

7.3 Predictive Analytics and Student Labelling

Predictive models are commonly used in learning analytics systems in higher education to determine students who are vulnerable to academic disengagement or drop out (Huang et al., 2025). These systems process historical data on performance, engagement, and demographics to produce early-warning signs. Predictive analytics, when applied properly, can make a difference in time interventions, targeted advising, and enhanced student retention results.

Nevertheless, the labelling, bias, and student agency ethical dilemmas are raised by the predictive quality of these systems. A label as being at risk can lead to either educator expectations or institutional reactions to act in a manner that unintentionally leads to the stigmatisation of learners. Predictive models can also be based on factors that are correlated with socioeconomic or geographic disadvantage, thus strengthening pre-existing inequities. Moreover, it is not clear to students that their data are utilised to create such classifications, and it brings up the issues of transparency and informed consent.

To be ethically responsible in using learning analytics, it is necessary to make sure that predictive outputs are not deterministic but advisory. The institutions should also have measures to protect against automated labelling to restrain the opportunities and should be given clear data regarding how their data helps in making a decision.

7.4 Lessons from Implementation Successes and Failures

The implementation of AI in education shows that technologies are highly associated with governance, transparency, and involvement of stakeholders. A successful implementation normally entails gradual adoption, constant review and active cooperation of teachers, technologists and administrators. These examples indicate that AI would be most effective when it is used as a supplement, which complements but does not substitute human judgment.

In contrast, the failure to implement AI in many cases is related to the introduction of these solutions into institutions without proper ethical consideration or training of their users. Poor transparency when it comes to the use of the data, a lack of control over the results of the algorithms, and too much reliance on automated decision-making may result in the opposition of stakeholders and loss of trust. These results indicate the need to ensure that technological innovation is matched to well-defined ethical standards.

All those case studies help to state that the responsible introduction of AI presupposes continual evaluation, human regulation, and participatory governance. The experiences gained both through success and challenges highlight that the implementation of ethics is not a single event but rather an ongoing process through which the effect of AI on educational equity, integrity, and the development of learners is evaluated.

8. EMERGING ETHICAL TRENDS AND RESPONSIBLE AI IMPLEMENTATION FRAMEWORK

The further development of artificial intelligence (AI) in the sphere of education is likely to present new ethical challenges, which are going to go beyond the existing regulations and implementation strategies. The rise of generative AI tools in the classroom is one of the most notable occurrences. Such technologies can create quality written content, solve complex tasks, create instructions, and imitate the tutoring conversation. Although these capabilities are considered to be of great pedagogical value, they break the established conceptions of authorship, originality, and authentic assessment. Institutions of learning need to re-evaluate the method of assessing learning outcomes in the case of students being exposed to systems that are able to execute activities that were, at one time, considered measures of learning. The integration of AI must also be interpreted within broader processes of intergenerational transition that reshape educational identities, authority structures, and social continuity (Srivastava, 2026). Artificial intelligence should therefore be conceptualised not merely as a technical instrument but as a transformative catalyst restructuring educational cultures, professional roles, and learning paradigms (Srivastava, 2026).

Generative AI also brings up the issue of epistemic reliability. The results of AI can look credible even though they are false or fabricated. With poor digital literacy, the student will not be in a position to critically assess generated responses. This requires pedagogical techniques that focus on verification, source assessment and metacognitive consciousness. Ethical issues are also presented in the areas of fair access, when unequal access (or institutional policy) can result in unequal benefits among learners.

Another kind of an emerging area of concern is AI-driven decision-making. It is becoming common to use predictive analytics systems to make admissions, academic advising, resource distribution, and performance evaluation decisions. Though such systems can increase efficiency and evidence-based planning, the use of algorithmic suggestions can hide assumptions or prejudices buried in the models. When such systems are regarded as ultimate sources of authority, there is the possibility that institutional decision-making mechanisms will not be as transparent or sensitive to the contextualities. Strategies to govern AI in the future need to ensure that the decisions made with the help of AI can be interpreted, challenged, and controlled by humans.

Educational institutions need detailed guidelines that will support the responsible use of AI to handle the emerging ethical issues. Sustainable integration entails the alignment of technological innovation to pedagogical goals, organisational strengths and institutional values over the long term. An organised approach to the implementation of AI responsibility must include aspects of transparency, accountability, inclusiveness, and constant review.

Lifecycle governance is one of the key elements that guarantee the implementation of ethical considerations at every step of the AI system development and implementation process, including procurement and design, deployment, monitoring, and eventual decommissioning. Institution impact assessment, which is carried out before adoption, should analyse possible risks associated with privacy, bias, and effectiveness of instruction. Empirical evidence about the performance of the system-level can be obtained through pilot testing in controlled settings prior to the massive application.

Models of human-in-the-loop constitute another important aspect of responsible integration. The models maintain educator power by making AI outputs advisory and not deterministic. Decision-support tools must be able to offer interpretable data that can be used by the educators and administrators to make professional judgments. Clearly defined policies of escalation in case of an algorithmic error or stakeholder grievance are another way to enhance governance frameworks.

Sustainability also involves investing in infrastructure, training and system evaluation. The institutions have to invest in technical upkeep, regular auditing and software upgrades to suit the changing regulatory needs. The models of ethical adoption must prioritise participatory governance, and it is important to have feedback, including teachers, learners and technical professionals, to make sure that AI products are in touch with the demands of instruction. Through the integration of constant checks and stakeholder interactions into their institutions, the education system will be able to sustain responsible innovation in the long term.

REFERENCES:

Abdelaal, E., Mills, J., & Walpita Gamage, S. (2019). Artificial intelligence is a tool for cheating academic integrity.

Ahmad, S. F., Alam, M. M., Rahmat, M. K., Mubarik, M. S., & Hyder, S. I. (2022). Academic and administrative role of artificial intelligence in education. *Sustainability (Basel), 14*(3), 1101. DOI: 10.3390/su14031101

Akgun, S., & Greenhow, C. (2022). Artificial intelligence in education: Addressing ethical challenges in K–12 settings. *AI and Ethics*, *2*(3), 431–440. DOI: 10.1007/s43681-021-00096-7 PMID: 34790956

Al-Zahrani, A. M. (2024). Unveiling the shadows: Beyond the hype of AI in education. *Heliyon, 10*(9), e30696. DOI: 10.1016/j.heliyon.2024.e30696 PMID: 38737255

Alfiras, M. I. I., Emran, A. Q., & Mohamed, A. M. (2025). Ethics and governance of generative AI in education: A systematic review on responsible adoption. *Discover Education*, *5*(1), 37. DOI: 10.1007/s44217-025-01051-y

Alfredo, R., Echeverria, V., Jin, Y., Yan, L., Swiecki, Z., Gašević, D., & Martinez-Maldonado, R. (2024). Human-centred learning analytics and AI in education: A systematic literature review. *Computers and Education: Artificial Intelligence*, *6*, 100215. DOI: 10.1016/j.caeai.2024.100215

Baek, E., Guo, Q., & Wilson, R. (2025). Transforming student support with AI-powered tutoring. In Wang, V. (Ed.), (pp. 335–370). Advances in Computational Intelligence and Robotics. IGI Global Scientific Publishing., DOI: 10.4018/979-8-3373-2397-8.ch012

Banker, S., & Khetani, S. (2019). Algorithm overdependence: How the use of algorithmic recommendation systems can increase risks to consumer well-being. *Journal of Public Policy & Marketing*, *38*(4), 500–515. DOI: 10.1177/0743915619858057

Belenguer, L. (2022). AI bias: Exploring discriminatory algorithmic decision-making models. *AI and Ethics*, *2*(4), 771–787. DOI: 10.1007/s43681-022-00138-8 PMID: 35194591

Ben Zion, Y., Yakov, S., Abramovitch, E., Balter, G., & Davidovitch, N. (2025). AI-based teaching evaluations: How well do they reflect student perceptions? *Computers and Education: Artificial Intelligence*, *9*, 100448. DOI: 10.1016/j.caeai.2025.100448

Bittle, K., & El-Gayar, O. (2025). Generative AI and academic integrity in higher education: A systematic review and research agenda. *Information (Basel)*, *16*(4), 296. DOI: 10.3390/info16040296

Brandao, P. R. (2025). The impact of artificial intelligence on modern society. *AI*, *6*(8), 190. DOI: 10.3390/ai6080190

Cajueiro, D. O., & Celestino, V. R. R. (2026). A comprehensive review of artificial intelligence regulation. *Journal of Economy and Technology*, *4*, 77–91. DOI: 10.1016/j.ject.2025.07.001

Darling-Hammond, L., Flook, L., Cook-Harvey, C., Barron, B., & Osher, D. (2020). Implications for educational practice of the science of learning and development. *Applied Developmental Science*, *24*(2), 97–140. DOI: 10.1080/10888691.2018.1537791

Darvishi, A., Khosravi, H., Sadiq, S., Gašević, D., & Siemens, G. (2024). Impact of AI assistance on student agency. *Computers & Education*, *210*, 104967. DOI: 10.1016/j.compedu.2023.104967

Du Plooy, E., Casteleijn, D., & Franzsen, D. (2024). Personalized adaptive learning in higher education: A scoping review. *Heliyon*, *10*(21), e39630. DOI: 10.1016/j.heliyon.2024.e39630 PMID: 39524879

Farhood, H., Nyden, M., Beheshti, A., & Muller, S. (2025). AI-based personalised learning in education. *Discover Artificial Intelligence*, *5*(1), 331. DOI: 10.1007/s44163-025-00598-x

Giannakos, M., Azevedo, R., Brusilovsky, P., Cukurova, M., Dimitriadis, Y., Hernandez-Leo, D., Järvelä, S., Mavrikis, M., & Rienties, B. (2025). The promise and challenges of generative AI in education. *Behaviour & Information Technology*, *44*(11), 2518–2544. DOI: 10.1080/0144929X.2024.2394886

Gurung, V., & Srivastava, S. (2021). Importance of work-life balance: A review from gender perspective. *Contemporary Issues in Social Sciences*, *YICCISS-2021*, 154–165.

Gurung, V., Srivastava, S., & Chhetri, S. D. (2024). Sociodemographic variables affecting the occupational stress of senior secondary school teachers in Himachal Pradesh. In N. Mansour & L. M. Bujosa Vadell (Eds.), *Finance and law in the metaverse world* (Contributions to Finance and Accounting). Springer Nature Switzerland. DOI: 10.1007/978-3-031-67547-8_37

Huang, D., Hash, N., Cummings, J. J., & Prena, K. (2025). Academic cheating with generative AI. *Computers and Education: Artificial Intelligence*, *8*, 100424. DOI: 10.1016/j.caeai.2025.100424

Kamalov, F., Santandreu Calonge, D., & Gurrib, I. (2023). New era of artificial intelligence in education. *Sustainability (Basel), 15*(16), 12451. DOI: 10.3390/su151612451

Mazzullo, E., Bulut, O., Wongvorachan, T., & Tan, B. (2023). Learning analytics in the era of large language models. *Analytics, 2*(4), 877–898. DOI: 10.3390/analytics2040046

Nguyen, A., Ngo, H. N., Hong, Y., Dang, B., & Nguyen, B.-P. T. (2023). Ethical principles for artificial intelligence in education. *Education and Information Technologies, 28*(4), 4221–4241. DOI: 10.1007/s10639-022-11316-w PMID: 36254344

Nur Fitria, T. (2023). The use of artificial intelligence in education (AIED): Can AI replace the teacher's role? *Epigram (e-Journal), 20*(2), 165–187. DOI: 10.32722/epi.v20i2.5711

Srivastava, S. (2025). *Women, work, and equity: A critical study of entrepreneurship challenges and opportunities in India*. IGI Global Scientific Publishing., DOI: 10.4018/979-8-3373-2903-1.ch004

Srivastava, S. (2026). AI as a catalyst for transformation: Revolutionizing lifelong learning and professional development in human services for the digital age. In *AI and the imperative of lifelong learning in human services*. IGI Global Scientific Publishing., DOI: 10.4018/979-8-3373-4377-8.ch012

Srivastava, S. (2026). *Artificial Intelligence and the Social Reordering of Insurance Risk, Trust, and Human- Technology Relations: Transformative Role of AI in the Insurance Sector* in AI-Driven Innovations in the Insurance Sector (Chapter 1). DOI: DOI: 10.4018/979-8-3373-2822-5.ch001

Srivastava, S. (2026). *Intergenerational solidarity and the social fabric: A sociological exploration of continuity and change*. IGI Global Scientific Publishing., DOI: 10.4018/979-8-3373-4367-9.ch005

Srivastava, S., & Rojhe, K. C. (2021). Attitude formation and attitude change: A social psychological perspective. In *Social Psychology*. IGI Global., DOI: 10.4018/978-1-7998-6960-3.ch001

Tomar, P., & Srivastava, S. (2024). Strengthening crisis response with organisational resilience strategies to achieve sustainability. In M. Tuba et al. (Eds.), *ICT systems and sustainability* (Lecture Notes in Networks and Systems, Vol. 1163, pp. 175–187). Springer Nature Singapore. DOI: 10.1007/978-981-97-8537-7_16

Walter, Y. (2024). Embracing the future of artificial intelligence in the classroom. *International Journal of Educational Technology in Higher Education*, *21*(1), 15. DOI: 10.1186/s41239-024-00448-3

Wang, S., Wang, F., Zhu, Z., Wang, J., Tran, T., & Du, Z. (2024). Artificial intelligence in education: A systematic literature review. *Expert Systems with Applications*, *252*, 124167. DOI: 10.1016/j.eswa.2024.124167

Zhai, C., Wibowo, S., & Li, L. D. (2024). The effects of over-reliance on AI dialogue systems. *Smart Learning Environments*, *11*(1), 28. DOI: 10.1186/s40561-024-00316-7

Chapter 13
Ethical and Privacy Concerns of Artificial Intelligence in Education

Ashish Kumar Yadav
http://orcid.org/0009-0000-3572-9553
Amity University, Greater Noida, India

Gourav Tomar
Amity University, Greater Noida, India

Durgesh Kumar Jha
http://orcid.org/0009-0004-9427-8210
Amity University, Greater Noida, India

ABSTRACT

Artificial Intelligence (AI) in the education sector is the application of computer-based technology that has capability to perform duties that were previously perform by human intelligence, including learning from experience, pattern recognition, natural language processing, and adaptive decision-making. At first, the role of educational technology was passive, involving the digitization and distribution of content. However, due to emergence of AI has changed the role of educational technology from passive to active, allowing data analysis, decision-making, personalization of learning experiences, and teaching, evaluation, and administrative assistance. The AI application in education sector has been fueled by the growth of e-learning platforms, learning management systems, the need to improve student performance, and the requirements of large educational institutions. In the Indian context, the Digital India campaign and the National Education Policy of 2020 have added to the development of AI-based educational technologies

DOI: 10.4018/979-8-3373-8027-8.ch013

1. INTRODUCTION

AI in education indicates the application of computer-based technology that can handle various duties that would be done by human intelligence. These tasks include learning from experience, pattern recognition, predicting and understanding languages, and adjusting responses as per the input provided by the operator. AI is a combination of technologies that are put together for various academic tasks like teaching, learning, testing, and administrative work. In education sector, the use of technology was mainly about putting content in digital forms. Application of computers, projectors, and education platforms was common for storing and circulating information. Hence the role of technology was passive only. After the introduction of Artificial Intelligence, it shifted the application of technology usage from passive to active systems that analyze data and make decisions. Now AI systems can create learning methods and even produce content for learning.

The integration process of AI in the education sector has been advancing for several reasons. It includes the emerging application of e-learning, Use of learning management systems, the need for improving student performance, and enhancing the output of large teaching institutions In India, initiatives like "Digital India" and "National Education Policy 2020" have further encouraged the use of digital technologies in the education system. AI has been seen as an effective means of enhancing accessibility, personalization, and the quality of education. Nonetheless, the issue of decision-making has been altered by AI within the education sector. Decisions were made only by the teacher or administrators. However, with the introduction of AI, the decision has to incorporate an algorithm. Therefore, it has implications related to ethics and privacy that need to be well recognized and established to ensure appropriate usage of AI within the education sector.

2. BACKGROUND

Key Characteristics of AI in Educational Contexts

AI-based educational systems also have some key attributes that mark them differently from other software applications in general.

One of the reasons is that AI is data driven. AI systems function through large amounts of data created by students or the institution. Such data includes learning performance, behavioral trends, levels of engagement, or online interactions. The type and representativeness of such data influence AI systems.

Second, AI systems are adaptive. Unlike static programs, in other words, AI tools continuously update their behavior on the basis of new data. Some adaptive learning systems, for instance, modify content difficulty and pacing based on student performance.

Third, AI systems are often predictive: they make predictions regarding student achievement, drop-out risk, or learning needs and thus provide a focus for institutional decisions and student support interventions.

Moreover, most AI systems work in an opaque way: It is difficult for the user to understand their internal logic, which raises serious questions about accountability and confidence in them. These features make AI powerful but also ethically sensitive, especially in education.

Adaptive Learning Systems

Adaptive learning systems are one of the most popular uses of AI technology in the field of education. Adaptive learning systems customize learning experiences according to the performance of the students. They make use of algorithms to understand the reaction of the students to questions, the time taken to accomplish a task, or identify the errors they make.

For example, in areas such as math, science, and language training, online learning tools can leverage technology to provide targeted training exercises that result in students receiving immediate feedback. This approach also allows students who are having difficulties in understanding some concepts to receive additional training while allowing other students to progress quickly if they are advanced learners in that subject matter.

Talking specifically about the Indian market, adaptive learning platforms find applications in online learning, preparing for competitive exams, and Edtech services. These platforms find relevance because they claim to fill the gaps that emerge when class sizes become huge, and many teachers cannot be appointed.

Nonetheless, adaptive learning systems rely significantly on data collection. Each activity completed by the student has been recorded and analyzed. The possibility exists that data obtained from early performances might categorize the student once and for all. This can cause adaptive systems to maintain or exacerbate, as opposed to diminish, inequalities.

Human oversight is thus imperative. The teacher will need to monitor the learning paths created by AI and make sure that the children are not put into overly narrow learning paths based on inadequate data.

Automated Evaluation and Grading Systems

Automated evaluation systems employ AI algorithms that can automatically rate students' work, such as quizzes, assignments, and essays. The use of these systems is usually common when teachers, especially in large classes, need a quick solution for workload reduction.

Objective tests, such as multiple-choice questions, are easier to automate. More difficult tasks, such as grading essays, involve Natural Language Processing, in which the structure, vocabulary, grammar, and coherence of language are analyzed. Although such technologies are able to recognize patterns, it is more difficult to assess creative thinking, critical thinking, or understanding in context.

It has been observed that automated grading systems can be harmful to students who use non-standard language forms, regional expressions, or creative writing styles. In a multilingual nation like India, where students tend to write English with the influence of local languages, it is a vital issue.

Automatic grading systems should thus be adopted for use alongside other tools rather than relying on them exclusively. Adopting ethical practices in this case involves transparency in the grading process and allowing for human oversight and editing.

Surveillance-Based Exam Proctoring Systems

AI proctors in examination environments rose to prominence during COVID-19 and related needs for online exams among students in different institutions. The system oversees students using webcams, microphones, and monitoring screens, among other methods, in some cases that involve facial recognition software.

The objective of proctoring technologies is to identify possible cheating activities like looking away at the screen, background chatter, and the presence of others. The reason given for their application is academic ethics preservation.

However, these methods have a serious privacy issue at this point. The students are under observation at home, which could disclose their personal living conditions. Biometric technology could not be precise regarding students with darker skin tones or various physical characteristics. There could be errors in internet connectivity that may result in false identification.

In Indian Scenario, students come from varying socio-economic backgrounds, which also increases these concerns. Effective application of proctoring system calls for reasons, clarity, options, or alternative approaches whenever possible, as well as strong data protection.

AI-Powered Administrative and Management Tools

In areas other than education, there are plenty of other applications of AI, as will be covered in this chapter. Artificial intelligence is also employed in the administration of education. This technology is employed in managing students' attendance. It is also employed in timetable preparation.

It can also be used as predictive analysis tool to use past data to pinpoint potential dropouts or underachievers among the students. This allows the institution the opportunity to offer support.

There can be negative implications when students are labelled according to predictions. They might receive different treatment according to the classification rather than their personal situations. There can be implications of a self-fulfilling prophecy as well.

The administrative use of AI must thus be closely regulated. Forecasts should guide support decisions and should not limit future possibilities and potential among students.

Predictive Analytics for Student Performance

The idea behind predictive analytics is that various data points about academic and behavior metrics are merged with clarity, and that forecasts about the future results of students will drive decision-making.

In theory, predictive analytics can help institutions efficiently allocate resources and focus interventions on students who need support. In practice, these systems reflect existing social and institutional biases represented in the historical data.

Predictive models would need to be employed cautiously in India, where disparities in quality of schooling, language proficiency, and technology access already are large. Ethical deployment requires periodic review, contextual interpretation, and human decision-making.

Generative AI in Teaching and Learning

Generative AI tools can support the creation of text, explanations, summaries, code, and educational material. Students are using them in study support, and teachers for lesson planning and content creation.

While Generative AI has empowered access to learning support, it has also raised concern about accuracy, over-dependency, and academic principles of AI. Artificial Intelligence may generate inaccurate as well as oversimplified content. Over-dependency on AI could weaken the skills of critical thinking.

Opportunities with generative AI require responsibility for guidance, clarity, and instruction on its limitations. These are tools to help in learning process but not to replace the entire effort and understanding.

Implications for Ethical and Privacy Concerns

It is essential to have an understanding of AI technologies used in education system when addressing the challenge of ethics and privacy. For every system, unique challenges arise in terms of data, bias, transparency, and accountability.

Artificial Intelligence is not an unbiased tool. It is a collection of human decisions, institutional choices, social conditions, etc. If not properly designed, AI may work against the educational parameters.

3. ETHICAL ISSUES IN AI-DRIVEN EDUCATION

The ethics in Artificial Intelligence within the field of education can be raised in consideration of the fact that AI systems are increasingly impacting learning, assessment, and opportunities in student's lives. Learning is not a technical function. In fact, learning is inextricably tied to the concept of human growth and dignity. If the use of AI systems in education is not accompanied by the adoption of ethics, damage can potentially be caused. In this section, we will explore the core ethical considerations surrounding the integration of AI within the educational setting and examine the areas of bias and discrimination, fairness and equity, transparency and explainability, human oversight, and academic integrity. Each of these considerations is, of course, interrelated and cannot—under any circumstances be considered independently.

Bias and Discrimination in Educational AI

Bias represents one of the biggest concerns associated with the application of AI in education. Bias refers to the situation where AI generates results that tend to favor one group of students over others based on parameters of language, gender, socio-economic status, geographical location, disability, or cultural identity.

AI models are trained on past data. The data obtained from education can reveal the current imbalances in schools, such as the level of the school, accessibility, language skills, and more. If an AI model is trained on the data, the imbalances can be perpetuated. These imbalances are not known to the AI model, which causes a problem.

For instance, in cases where historical data indicates that some students from particular geographic areas or types of schools underperform in standardized testing, predictive AI software could categorize students from similar backgrounds in the future as "high risk." These designations could then impact how educators, administrators, or schools interact with students, often by having lower expectations for them rather than remedying a problem that exists in some way.

The Indian scenario is further complicated by language, regional imbalances, caste, and socio-economic factors, making it difficult to deal with bias. AI Models that are mostly based on an urban, English-speaking, or private-school population could fail to capture the reality that faces students from other environments.

Bias in educational AI may relate to the grading process, admission filtering, awarding scholarships, or the prediction of performance. If such systems are considered objective or neutral, then the biased results will remain unchallenged, making it difficult to overcome the issue of discrimination.

Case Study 1: Bias in Automated English-Language Essay Grading

The use of automated essay scoring tools has been on the rise in learning institutions to manage large student data. However, empirical studies have shown that the tools reward standardized grammar and and penalize non-standard English, regional dialects, and culturally influenced writing styles. This has resulted in students from diverse linguistic backgrounds scoring lower even when they have strong conceptual understanding. These biases arise from training datasets and evaluation criteria that privilege dominant linguistic norms. This issue is particularly important in countries like India, where English is used alongside several regional languages, posing a threat to equity and validity in the use of AI tools in students grading system (Perelman, 2014;Wilson & Huang, 2024).

Sources of Bias in Educational AI Systems

Biases in AI systems within the educational sector are never caused by a single factor. Usually, they are the resultant outcomes of a multitude of factors.

One major source is data bias. The data gathered may have an imbalance where it favors some students and underrepresents others. These may include students from affluent schools and urban areas or students from the majority language backgrounds. When the AI is trained on such data, it may perform ineffectively on the underrepresented students.

Another source is that of algorithmic bias, which is generated through design principles set by developers. The selection and weight given to variables, and what constitutes success, might end up being discriminatory in unintended ways. For instance, students having language or cognitive differences, their response time varies, but if we give priority to response time, AI may end up providing biased results

But Biasness can also come from the institution. The policies in place can also affect how the data is used in an AI system. It might occur that if the institution already favors some standard test or performance grading, then the AI system will also provide similar results instead of opposing them.

Lastly, interaction bias emerges as students modify their responses to meet the AI grading system. Students may not give original or creative responses if their grades depend upon the pre-defined AI grading system as per the Institution standard. Thereby, learning might become boring and less innovative. Bias response can be solved through continuous observations and using different data sets.

Fairness and Equity in AI-Driven Education

Equity and Fairness may be considered as the most significant factors in the field of education. In this regard, AI tools offer an opportunity to address equity and fairness in education system by analyzing equity and issues related to equity. Issues related to equity are also an area where AI application may worsen.

'Digital divide' is one of the main issues in case of fairness and equity. Institutions having superior infrastructure can invest in better AI systems, leaving institutions having basic infrastructure struggling in digital race. In India, there has been huge gap between urban and rural institutions, private and government schools, and different regions.

When AI-enhanced learning system becomes accessible to only few institutions, there will be increase in educational inequalities. This will allow some students to get benefit from personalized assistance through AI technology, while others may be left behind even further.

Equity may also be impacted by Artificial Intelligence. AI tools which give prediction analytics can help students with low grades when put towards helping, they can be biased if the outcomes result in fewer opportunities or the 'track-and-follow' approach.

It is necessary to focus on the social framework and implications when applying ethics to AI systems. Technological systems should decrease the differences created by inequality; they should not provide ways through which inequality can be sustained.

Transparency and Explainability

Transparency is the capacity to define how an AI system works and how it comes to its decisions. Clarity is especially important in education field, as decisions made by AI algorithms effect grades, progression, and educational opportunities.

Students must have the right to know how their work will be assessed. Educators must be trained on AI tools for teaching applications. Without providing proper training, AI tools may behave like "black boxes," where there is less chance of improvement and counter questioning.

Sometimes, it is observed that many commercial AI tools do not offer proper explanations. In many cases, the code algorithms tend to be secret. It creates conflict of interest between the commercial and academic worlds.

In the context of higher education in India, where the assessment of the students is already opaque, the addition of opaque AI models makes the problem even worse. Trustworthy institutions should at least demand the question of explainer in the context of AI tools implementation.

Transparency helps encourage accountability. If information can be accounted for, then mistakes can be traced and remedied. If not, then accountability becomes questionable.

Case Study 2: Algorithmic Grading and Accountability in Public Examinations (UK, 2020)

In 2020, the United Kingdom's examination regulator used an algorithm to standardize the grading of students following the cancellation of public examinations due to the COVID-19 pandemic. The algorithm was highly dependent on the historical school performance data, leading to the systematically lowering of grades for students from public schools and those from disadvantaged socio-economic backgrounds. The lack of transparency in the grading process and failure of the appeal system led to public outcry and legal challenges, ultimately forcing authorities to discard the algorithmic results. This case highlights the ethical risks corelated with unclear algorithmic decision-making and the importance of accountability and human intervention in AI-driven educational assessment tools (Adams, 2020).

Human Oversight and the Role of Educators

Human supervision is an ethical necessity when it comes to AI applications in education. AI should aid educators, not replace them. Emotional intelligence, ethicality, and awareness on the part of educators, qualities which currently require human teachers, are beyond AI capability.

Too much dependence on AI could limit the autonomy of teachers. Some teachers could be compelled to act on the suggestions given by the AI, especially if they run contrary to the teachers' professional judgment.

The proper application of ethical principles in AI requires clear boundaries. Grades, judgments of assessment, or other decisions about student academic performance must remain in the hands of teachers and administrators. AI tool output should be advisory in this case, not final.

In the Indian context, where the teacher-student relation is very important in the learning process itself, the preservation of human judgment is highly necessary. AI should help the teacher in handling large numbers effectively and not damage the teaching profession.

Academic Integrity and Authentic Learning

The evolution of generative AI tools is threatening the traditional notion of Academic Integrity. Students can now produce essays, coding solutions, or projects effortlessly. Though these tools may assist in learning processes, they also provide a means to easily evade actual participation.

Conventional plagiarism detectors are ineffective in detecting AI-authored plagiarism. False Plagiarism accusations can negatively impact genuine student's work and go undetected for those who use AI tools for content generation without any actual work.

Instead, Institutions must focus on the proper use of these tools in AI technology. Students must be educated on the proper use of these AI tools, where they are used it as learning assistant, not as substitute for cognitive thinking.

Evaluation techniques may also have to change. More oral examinations, reflective writing, projects, and in-class assessments may encourage more meaningful learning while reducing wrongdoing.

Institutional Ethical Responsibility

The ethical use of AI is not solely the responsibility of developers or individual Educators therefore educational institutions have main role in shaping patterns of adoption and application.

Institutions need to decide what AI tools they use, who implement these tools and what effect these tools have on the students. These are all the main aspects of ethical responsibilities.

Grievance should be addressed if the students are affected by AI-powered decisions. Training should also be given to Educators to make aware them about ethics.

Absence of institutional integrity in applying ethical standards means that ethics itself is just a theory, and nothing

Summary of Ethical Issues

There are various issues related to ethics which may be linked to AI application in education sector. These may include bias, lack of fairness, transparency issues, limited human review, and integrity concerns.

To effectively handle this set of issues, a well-rounded approach is required that includes protection against technology, ethical knowledge, Institutes responsibility, and the responsibility of individuals involved, as well as active involvement by instructors and students. AI systems need to remain relevant with educational values without weakening them.

4. PRIVACY CONCERNS AND DATA PROTECTION IN AI-DRIVEN EDUCATION

Privacy forms one of the most sensitive and critical issues linked with the AI application in education. A significant amount of personal and sensitive information, including academic records, behavioral data, and sometimes biometric identifiers belonging to students, are managed by educational institutions. When AI comes into this setting, the volume, velocity, and depth that programs handle student data raise significantly. Therefore, serious questions have emerged on how student data is collected, used, stored, and shared.

Unlike most other sectors, education deals with children, adolescents, and young adults who cannot be expected to understand the implications of data collection and digital monitoring in the long run. Therefore, ethical responsibility for educational data practices needs to be more than in most commercial settings. This section looks at key privacy challenges related to AI in education: collection of data, consent, security of data, surveillance, retention of data, third-party involvement, and finally, the legal framework concerning AI in schools in India.

Nature and Scope of Data Collection in Educational AI

Educational systems aided by AI involve a continuous process of data collection. Conventional data in educational settings comprised elementary information about enrollment, attendance, and test performances. Educational systems aided by AI involve a vast amount of data relative to conventional data.

The learning management systems retain data on the frequency and duration spent logged in to the system by the students. The adaptive learning systems retain information on errors committed by the students, the time taken to respond to problems, the speed at which students learn, and the patterns in student progress.

The predictive analytics systems retain information on the academic background and often demographics.

AI-assisted proctoring systems gather very private information. Proctoring systems could be observing videos, audio, facial expressions, eye movements, keyboard inputs, or even room scanning before exams. In extreme situations, room scanning becomes a necessity before the exams start.

All these sets of data together form a comprehensive online profile of a student. These online profiles can reflect learning problems, emotional distress, language problems, socio-economic status, or personal circumstances of a student. Students are not aware of just how much information is being collected about them or for how long.

The ethics here are not just related to the volume of information gathered. It is also related to a lack of boundaries and guidelines. The data gathered for support services could end up being used for analysis for commercial or evaluation purposes without the student being fully informed.

Consent and Student Autonomy

Informed consent is a major tenet of ethics when it comes to information processing. However, when it comes to education institutions and information technology, informed consent is not a real possibility. It is a fact that students are compelled to use AI-powered tools as part of a mandatory curriculum or test.

The consent forms are lengthy, in legal language, which learners cannot really comprehend. Most learners sign without reading, especially where refusal of consent has implications for progressing in studies. For minors, consent is sought through parents/guardians, but learners might not fully appreciate anything.

Issues like that are especially pertinent in a place like India, which has varying levels of digital literacy. A student from a "rural or weaker section background" might not be aware of their rights regarding information or even know to query some of this.

For ethical applications of AI, it is essential that consent be:

- Clear and understandable
- Specific to particular data uses
- Freely given, without compulsion
- Revocable where possible

Students should be made aware of what is being collected, why it is being collected, and for what period. Alternatives should be made available where possible for the purposes of the collection of nonessential data.

Data Security and Cyber Risks

Educational institutions possess a substantial amount of confidential data making them prime targets for cyber-attacks. Data breaches have risen exponentially across the global education sector. Student information, identity, and even biometric identities have come to light due to breaches.

AI technology can potentially heighten security risks because it commonly relies on cloud technology and cloud suppliers. Poor passwords, outdated software, substandard encryption, and untrained Staffs are all potential security risk sources.

In India, many institutions especially government schools and colleges, faces shortage of resources to invest in cybersecurity. The risk of institutions continues as they choose AI systems without sufficient security infrastructure support and investment.

Result of data breach may be serious and far-reaching. Students could be at risk of identity theft, financial fraud, and damaged reputation. The effects of data breach on young students may last till their adulthood.

Institutions have a moral and legal obligation to safeguard student's data. This would include encrypting and controlling data access, conducting annual audits for security of data, and educating employees about this process.

Case Study 3: Student Data Breach in an Indian EdTech Platform

In 2022, a prominent Indian EdTech company suffered a massive data breach that revealed the personal details of millions of users, including the names, contact information, and education-related data of students It was found that the data breach was a result of poor cybersecurity measures and inadequate monitoring of vendors. The fact that many users were minors made this data breach a serious concern from an ethical and legal perspective. This example emphasizes the risks associated with the centralized management of education-related data and the need for proper governance structures and adherence to the Digital Personal Data Protection Act, 2023 (CERT-In, 2022).

Surveillance, Monitoring, and Student Dignity

AI-assisted surveillance is one of the most discussed topics in the domain of education technology. Technologies for surveillance are used to monitor attendance, engagement levels, behavior, and academic integrity. These technologies raise concerns about dignity and autonomy despite being used for efficiency and integrity purposes.

Online proctoring tools monitor students constantly using webcams and microphones. Students are therefore subjected to online observation from their homes also. What they do in their private lives would, therefore, come under observation. This would result in invading their privacy, especially in cases when their living conditions are crowded or when they come from poor family backgrounds.

Facial recognition technology in some monitoring software has been proven to be inconsistent in relation to various skin tones and face structures. Students with disabilities, illnesses, or poor internet connections may be labelled as suspicious.

Case Study 4: Ethical Challenges of AI-Based Exam Proctoring

During the COVID-19 pandemic, many institutions of higher learning adopted AI-based remote proctoring tools to ensure academic integrity during online exams. Students were often marked for suspicious activity based on eye movement, background noise, facial orientation, or unreliable internet connectivity. This was particularly true for students from rural backgrounds and the economically weaker segment of society, who did not have a private study space or adequate digital infrastructure. The popularity of AI-based proctoring tools also raised concerns about privacy violations, stress, digital divide, and loss of trust among students (Coghlan et al., 2021; Swauger, 2020).

Data Retention and Purpose Limitation

Another important aspect of privacy issues pertains to the period for which student information is retained or reused. Most AI applications retain the information for an indefinite period, even after the students have graduated.

Data collected for specific use, for example, for learning support, may later be used for a completely different purpose, such as research. The use of the learning information for research purposes would be considered a breach of the purpose limitation.

Institutions must set data retention policies. Student data should not be retained for longer periods than necessary. Once it ceases to be necessary, it should be deleted. This should not give the student any difficulty.

In fact, limiting the retention of data can help ensure that the data does not end up in the wrong hands.

Role of Third-Party Vendors and Commercial Interests

Most AI applications deployed in the education sector are developed, monitored, and conducted by private tech firms. Once the institution embraces the AI applications, the data is shared with a third party.

The vendors can process the data in various countries with different levels of legal safeguards. In addition, the vendors can use aggregated data for improving algorithms and developing or performing commercial analysis. In certain instances, the data could even be shared with partners and subcontractors.

However, institutions are still liable for student data. The contracts should define the issue of ownership as well as deletion. Institutions should not partner with institutions that do not show transparency.

Psychological and Social Impact of Datafication

Privacy is not a legal issue only. Constant data collection and surveillance may affect how Educators experience the learning process. If students feel that their every act is being recorded and monitored, they may feel that they are being just reduced to mere data.

Such an environment can impact the motivation and confidence of the learners. Furthermore, learners may change the way they conduct their operations to satisfy the algorithm. Hence, it can impact the creativity of the learners.

Ethical education requires a recognition of the fact that learning occurs in a human way that involves emotions, relationships, and development. Privacy protection becomes a key component in the process of maintaining a healthy learning context.

Indian Legal Framework: Digital Personal Data Protection Act, 2023

The Digital Personal Data Protection Act (DPDP Act of 2023) of India represents a critical component in the process of personal data protection.

Institutions of learning, which process student data, are categorized as data fiduciaries. They must process student data in a legal manner, ensure security of the processed data, as well as respect the rights of individuals.

This Act considers the data of students in a special manner. Although the DPDP Act is not an AI-specific legislation act, it impacts the use of AI systems in educational institutions.

Compliance with the law is necessary, but ethical accountability also demands that institutions exceed adherence to the law in actively ensuring student welfare.

Summary of Privacy Concerns

Privacy in case of AI-enhanced education is a complex phenomenon. The nature and extent of data mining, deficiencies in consent processes, surveillance, dangers to data security, and the use of data for commercial purposes seriously impact students.

These challenges require good governance methods, transparency processes, technology-based protection system, and the need for a student-focused model. Failure to address these challenges may result in the negative implications of AI dominating its positive aspects.

5. INTERNATIONAL POLICIES, GOVERNANCE FRAMEWORKS, AND INSTITUTIONAL RESPONSIBILITIES

These ethical and privacy issues in the application of the technology in the education sector cannot just be addressed within the classroom or the institution. In fact, the development of technology in the first place is in the hands of multinational technology firms with applications all over the world. In other words, the development of appropriate governance structures to govern the effective use of technology in the sector is critical.

This chapter will explore various international governance policies involving the ethicality of the technology and privacy policies. It will then conclude with the responsibilities of institutions in relation to the Indian regulatory policies.

Importance of Governance in Educational AI

Governance in relation to the adoption and monitoring of AI in institutions entails the establishment of policies, structures within which the adoption and monitoring of technology take place. In the education sector in particular, technology impacts decisions concerning assessing and enrollment of students.

Without clear guidelines governing the use of AI, the integration of AI may be induced only through efficiency and cost savings rather than through educational values. The responsibility for AI use may then diffuse through the school organization from administrators to teachers to technology companies.

Effective governance ensures that principles like ethics in decision-making, including fairness, transparency, accountability, and protection of privacy, become ingrained in institutions. It further ensures who is answerable for decision-making concerning AI and how rights are protected for students.

UNESCO's Recommendation on the Ethics of Artificial Intelligence

The UNESCO Recommendation Concerning the Ethics of Artificial Intelligence, adopted in 2021, is the first time in history that a global regulating framework has been available for ethics in AI. This recommendation suggests that AI systems should be human-focused and compatible with human rights and dignity.

In education context, the Recommendation highlighted a number of important factors:

- AI should be viewed as a tool for enhancing education equity.
- The privacy and security of the data of the learners should be ensured.
- Adequate human supervision should continue to be the focus of decision-making.
- Transparency and explainability are critical for trust.

UNESCO regards education as a "sensitive" area because, to a large extent, students tend to be vulnerable and have a dependent relationship with institutions of authority Such approach strengthens national policies and ethics that can be developed, especially regarding AI and education.

Although these Recommendation will not have to be legally binding in nature, it provides a good ethical foundation that forms different countries policies, including India.

OECD Principles on Artificial Intelligence

The Organization for Economic Co-operation and Development has launched the OECD Principles on Artificial Intelligence planned for the development and use of Trustworthy AI for Beneficial purposes. The principles are based on AI and human values.

In relation to educational institutions, the OECD guidelines should focus on:

- AI systems have to be reliable and safe.
- All critical decisions should remain in human hands.
- Discrimination and reinforcement of social inequalities must be avoided through AI.
- Corresponding institutions should be held accountable.

These guidelines are especially pertinent to higher educational institutions using AI for screening applications and/or talent forecasting. They call for the need to evaluate the effect of technologies, considering both their functional and ethical aspect.

GDPR and Its Relevance to Education

The General Data Protection Regulation is one of the most comprehensive data protection laws of the European Union. Though it is applicable directly to European citizens, its non-EU reach is global as well. This includes non-European educational institutions that manage European student data.

Key GDPR principles for educational institutions are:

- Data minimization: the principle of collecting only the necessary information
- Purpose limitation: Data will be applied for the stated purposes only.
- Informed consent and transparency
- Special protection for Student's data
- Rights to access, correction, and erasure

Furthermore, GDPR limits fully automatic decision-making that has a substantial effect on individuals. This is highly relevant in case of AI-based admissions and grading analysis. Students could have right to appeal decisions made automatically.

The GDPR has set a model in global data protection and has impacted policy formation in many countries worldwide, including India.

Indian Policy Context: NEP 2020 and Digital Education

In India, the National Education Policy (NEP) 2020 has a major impact on policy defining for the education technology. According to NEP 2020, the adoption and implementation of technologies in educational practices are encouraged. This refers to present technological advancements as well as technologies of the future.

In this regard, NEP 2020 also focuses on ethics, inclusiveness, and student-centric education. NEP 2020 realizes that technology is supposed to support Educators and students rather than functioning as a human replacement.

It highlights following requirements:

- Digital infrastructure development
- Teacher training in technology use
- Ethical and responsible adoption of educational technology

In educational institutions, AI tools implementation must meet the NEP 2020 objectives, focusing on overall development and social responsibility.

Digital Personal Data Protection Act, 2023 (India)

India's Digital Personal Data Protection Act, 2023 marks a remarkable achievement in supervising personal data processing across various sectors, including education. According to the DPDP Act, 2023, educational institutions that store and process students' data are considered as data depository.

This Act mainly focuses on:

- Consent-based data processing
- Purpose limitation
- Data security obligations
- Accountability for misuse or breach
- Special safeguards for Student's data

Although the DPDP Act does not specifically target AI, it has a direct impact on the use of AI in the educational sector. The institutions must follow the guidelines regarding consent for data processing, along with data security.

The Act requires that data be safeguarded by institutions regardless of whether it involves a third-party contractor.

Role of UGC, AICTE, and Other Regulatory Bodies

In the Indian scenario, bodies such as the University Grants Commission (UGC), All India Council for Technical Education (AICTE), and Central Board of Secondary Education (CBSE) play a significant role in influencing educational practices.

They increasingly work to facilitate digital learning projects, online platforms, and educational opportunities using technology. However, guidelines on ethical AI use are yet to be developed.

There is a growing need for regulators to:

- Issue AI-specific ethical guidelines
- Set standards for data protection in Institutions
- Monitor AI-based assessment system and proctoring tools
- Support capacity-building for institutions

There is a need for regulatory leadership to promote responsible AI adoption.

Institutional Responsibilities and Governance Structures

Although the responsibility for ethical AI use is set by national and international frameworks, the application of AI and its effect on students are the responsibility of the institutions and institutions alone.

Key institutional responsibilities include:

- Formulation of policies on AI and code of conduct
- Conducting ethical and privacy impact assessments
- Staff and faculty training on the ethical use of AI
- Establishing oversight committees or ethics boards
- Forming students' grievance handling system

Institutions also make sure that vendors should follow the data ethics and standards. Institutions need to focus on transparency and accountability in security rather than focusing on its cost.

Figure 1. illustrates a human-in-the-loop governance model, emphasizing that AI-generated outputs in educational contexts remain advisory and subject to human review and accountability.

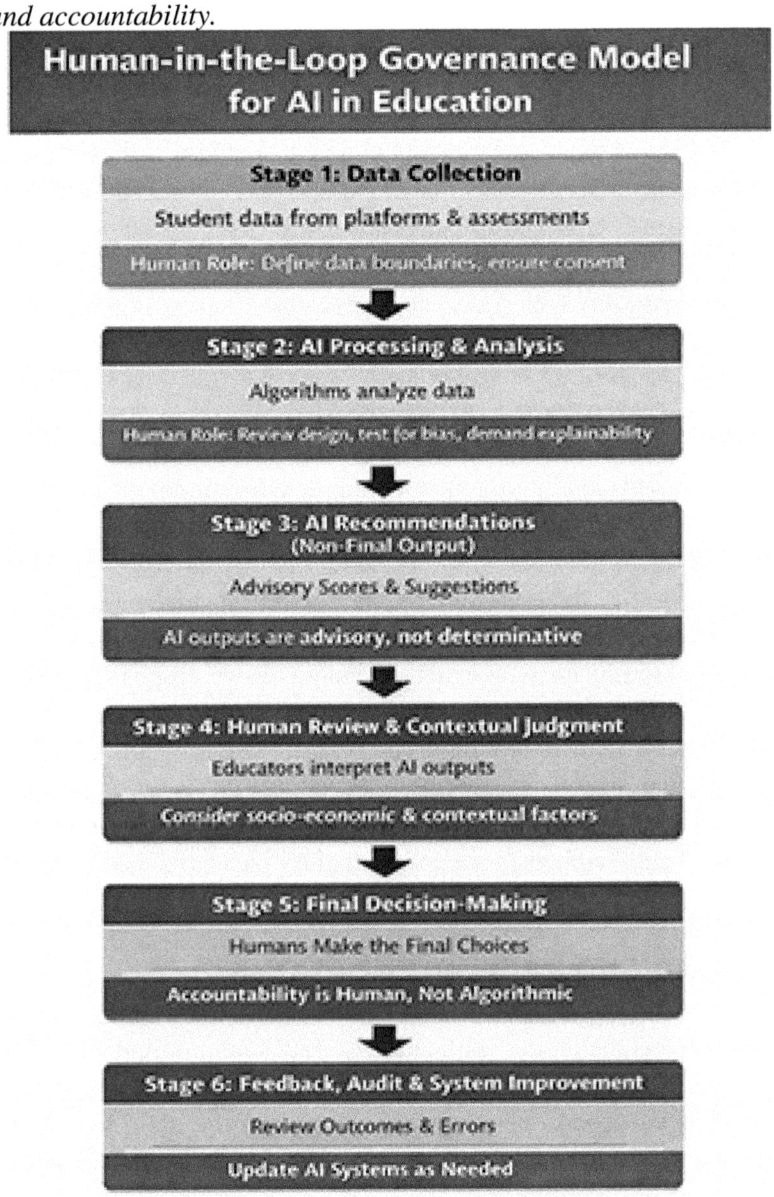

Challenges in Governance and Regulation

To address the issue of governance, regulation, and artificial intelligence, as well as data, it needs a comprehending strategy. Technological advancements that challenge the formulation of governance structures remain one of the issues that do not seem to go away soon. The evolving nature of artificial intelligence technology means that the centers that regulate it are unable to keep up with its progress pace.

Furthermore, the lack of subject matter experts of AI ethics and data governance at institutions also presents a significant obstacle to the AI regulation. This is because, without a certain level of knowledge and understanding of the ethical implications and challenges associated with AI systems, regulatory bodies might face difficulties formulating appropriate structures to address them.

Summary of Governance Frameworks

In the field of artificial intelligence within the educational setting, it is not only important to establish global and national regulations but also to ensure that they are implemented. If this is not done, the very benefit that AI is expected to bring to the educational setting may be threatened by the lack of trust and equity that it creates.

The role of governance structures in ensuring that the ethical applications of AI in the educational setting are well managed cannot be overemphasized. Governance structures provide the terms and conditions that are supposed to be followed in AI application. These structures are important in data regulation and decision-making procedure in AI applications, especially in the education sector. It must be that any unethical practice of AI tools should not happen within the education sector and in cases where such case happens, then accountability measures should be mandatory.

6. SOLUTIONS AND RECOMMENDATIONS

To make sure that the proper application of Artificial Intelligence (AI) in education, collaboration among the institution, educators, and the government has become essential. One of the approaches to ensure the correct use of AI technology in the college environment would be the establishment of clear protocols that define its responsibility and appropriate use.

In addition, regular evaluation of AI systems is essential to identify and address any ethical considerations that may emerge during the implementation process. It is important to ensure that AI systems are operating as intended without generating bias results. Moreover, educational institutions should work on the transparency regarding the application of AI tools in education (Luckin et al., 2016).

Development of Institutional Ethical AI Policies

One of the best methods to handle risks related to ethics is to formulate proper policies for use at the institutional level in the use of AI. This should indicate acceptable and unacceptable uses in teaching, assessment, administration, and monitoring of students.

AI policy in the institution ought to include the following aspects:

- AI systems must respect student dignity, privacy, and autonomy
- AI systems should not replace human judgment in critical decisions
- Bias and discrimination must be actively monitored and addressed
- Transparency and explainability are essential requirements

Such policies should be in tune with the national policies like the Digital Personal Data Protection Act, 2023, and the education policies set under NEP 2020. These policies should be periodically reviewed and updated based on the evolution of technologies.

Ethical Risk Matrix

Table 1. Ethical Risk Matrix for AI Applications in Education

AI Application Area	Key Ethical Risks	Level of Risk	Potential Impact	Required Safeguards
Adaptive Learning Systems	Data profiling, reinforcement of early performance bias	Medium	Unequal learning trajectories, reduced student autonomy	Human monitoring, periodic model review, diverse datasets
Automated Grading Systems	Linguistic bias, lack of transparency, unfair evaluation	High	Academic injustice, loss of trust in assessment	Human moderation, explainable models, appeal mechanisms
AI-Based Exam Proctoring	Privacy intrusion, surveillance stress, false positives	High	Psychological harm, exclusion of disadvantaged students	Optional use, clear consent, alternative assessment modes
Predictive Analytics	Student labeling, self-fulfilling prophecies	Medium–High	Reduced expectations, discrimination	Advisory-only use, human judgment, contextual interpretation
Administrative AI Tools	Over-reliance on predictions, opacity	Medium	Institutional bias in decision-making	Accountability frameworks, audit trails

continued on following page

Table 1. Continued

AI Application Area	Key Ethical Risks	Level of Risk	Potential Impact	Required Safeguards
Generative AI Tools	Academic integrity risks, over-dependence	Medium	Skill erosion, assessment validity issues	AI literacy, revised evaluation methods
EdTech Data Platforms	Data breaches, unauthorized data sharing	High	Privacy violations, legal consequences	Strong cybersecurity, vendor accountability, data minimization

Ethical Procurement and Vendor Accountability

Many ethical and privacy issues arise in connection with the acquisition of AI solutions, and many institutions end up using platforms without understanding how data is collected and processed on those platforms.

Before integrating any AI system within an institution, the following should be required by the institution from the vendors:

- Types of data being collected and purposes of use
- Location and duration of data storage
- Data Security and breach response protocols
- Use of data for secondary or commercial purposes
- Compliance with Indian data protection laws

The contracts must clearly define data ownership and prevent any unauthorized data transfer. Institutions should avoid partnering with those vendors who lack transparency or fail to meet ethical standards.

Privacy-by-Design and Data Minimization

Privacy-by-design represents a proactive approach that integrates privacy protection directly into AI systems. Instead of collecting the most possible data, the institution needs to follow the principle of data minimization.

This involves:

- Gathering data necessary for academic purposes
- Avoiding excessive monitoring or biometric data collection
- Limiting access to sensitive information of the students
- Using data-masking where possible

Adopting the privacy-by-design approach provides alignment with the ethical standards and the DPDP Act requirement.

Human-in-the-Loop Decision Making

Human-in-the-loop technology allows AI to support rather than replace human decision-making. In education, it allow educators and administrators to be responsible for decisions regarding grading and assessment.

AI systems may offer recommendations or predictions, but humans should:

- Examine AI outputs critically
- Consider contextual and personal factors
- Override algorithmic decisions when necessary
- Take responsibility for final outcomes

Having human Review system ensures students are protected from mistakes and uphold professional accountability.

Strengthening Data Security Measures

It is necessary to secure strong data for minimizing risks linked with privacy. Educational institutes should consider privacy a central mandate as opposed to a concern for the technical department.

Key factors regarding security measures include:

- Data Encryption during storage and transmission
- Role-based access control
- Regular cybersecurity audits
- Staff training on data protection
- Clear incident response plans

In case of India, where many institutions are grappling with resource challenges, government assistance and development in this area will play a major role in enabling cybersecurity in the education sector.

AI Literacy and Capacity Building

AI literacy plays an important role in effective risk management. All teachers and students need to learn about AI systems and their ethics.

AI literacy programs should help users in:

- Understanding basic AI concepts and decision-making processes
- Recognizing bias results and AI tools limitations
- Using AI system with critical understanding and responsibly
- Protecting personal data and privacy

AI literacy integration within educational courses for teachers and students supports NEP 2020's focus on critical thinking and digital literacy.

Continuous Monitoring and Ethical Auditing

Applying ethical principles to AI is an ongoing process that cannot be completed within a fixed timeframe. Organizations should review their artificial intelligence use each year to ensure their programs are fair, secure, and ethical.

Regular reviews should examine:

- Bias and discriminatory outcomes
- Compliance with data protection laws
- Transparency and explainability
- Impact on student well-being

Audit findings should inform policy updates and system improvements.

Summary of Risk Mitigation Strategies

Apart from the formulation of policies, the procurement process needs to be transparent and accountable in terms of choosing AI tools and systems. Educators, as well as educational institutions, need to be critical of the companies they deal with regarding their AI tools, ensuring that they meet privacy requirements as well as ethical principles. This needs to be accompanied by inquiries on the part of the educators or the educational institution regarding the handling of data, their compliance with global data protection policies, as well as how they deal with biases within their algorithms.

Another basic principle that should be followed is implementing "privacy by design." Privacy by design refers to an idea that encourages privacy champions to "bake" privacy into the development of new technologies, as opposed to trying to "bake it on after." Educational AI should be developed in such a way that it consumes as little data as necessary and defaults to anonymization methods wherever possible. Algorithms can be designed to learn from privacy protected and combined data sets, so that there is less risk of compromising students' private data.

7. FUTURE RESEARCH DIRECTIONS

Apart from the policy and technical approaches to achieve good AI practices, achieving sustainability in AI applications involves a major change in the approach taken by educational institutions towards innovation. The good AI culture must start with an approach of emphasis, awareness, and shared responsibility. This reform requires curricula revision, teaching methodology, and assessment to integrate the principles of good AI systematically.

Educational institutions must ensure that AI education includes courses that not only cover the technical sides of AI but also its impact on society. It would be important to develop programs that not only train AI students but also help them with critical thinking about how AI affects society. Another significant aspect that could help in this shift would be mentorship programs. It would be important to connect these students with industry experts who are interested in implementing their AI initiatives in an ethical way.

Promoting Ethical Awareness Among Students

Students should be informed about the AI implications in the classroom, as it directly impacts them. Orientation programs, workshops, or classroom discussions can be organized to make students aware of the moral implications of AI. The topics for such awareness programs can include the AI tools basics, their functioning, and the different uses. Once students understand AI capabilities, they will be able to recognize their benefits and drawbacks. For example, it can offer students personalized learning and carrying out administrative work, but there can still be biased results or inaccuracies.

Awareness is what encourages students to be curious, show concern, and motivated to participate in decision-making. This will help them to develop a critical viewpoint about the use of technology in their learning environment and personal life. Workshops may include topics like data privacy, the importance of ethical use of AI, and learning about how these tools can impact future work opportunities. Case studies highlight positive application of AI in learning environments as well as its misuse can open eyes to practical application. This is exactly what critical thinking can help us to see a balanced view of the world.

Encouraging Critical Engagement with AI

AI generated content should not be taken for granted. Students should be encouraged to verify such content using multiple sources. Critical engagement helps students to learn more effectively without depending on automated systems.

Responsible Digital Citizenship

A responsible digital citizen should value ethics, privacy, and social awareness. Education should help the students to use technology more responsibly both inside and outside the classroom. Ethical discussions about AI help students to develop stronger ethical thinking. A balanced curriculum should focus not only on technical details regarding the use of digital literacy but also highlights on the long-term effects of digital trail that the students tend to create through their activities online. Every activity involving the application of the internet, like posting contents on social media, blogging sites, and forums has big potential to affect the reputation and interpersonal relationships of the person involved.

Ethical discussions about AI help students develop moral reasoning and sense of responsibility. As AI increasingly influences many areas of life, from health and education to even the legal system, students need to understand the ethical structures behind these technologies. Topics such as algorithmic bias, privacy concerns, and consequences of machine learning should be part of the educational discussion. Using case studies in which AI systems has caused harm or injustice will help students to understand the complexity of these issues. For example, the investigation of events where biased result by AI has caused inequality can help students to develop a sense of responsibility to students as they may one day contribute to the development of these technologies.

Integrating Ethics Across the Curriculum

The study of AI ethics should not be limited to technical courses. It should also be included in courses like the humanities, social sciences and law. The impact of AI technologies is a global concern; therefore, people of different academic backgrounds should engage in the ethical issues related to this technological advancement. Including AI ethics in different academic courses helps a wider understanding of the complexity of the impact of technology on human lives. For instance, courses within the humanities can explore philosophical challenges of AI decision-making, such as agency, accountability, and personhood. In contrast, social sciences courses can examine how AI handles issues of bias and inequality.

Engaging with AI ethics in different academic fields, educators can raise a generation of people who are able to handle the complex relationship between technology and society. This approach can enable students to address the ethical environments surrounding their various professions such as law, business, medicine, or education. The initiative can encourage collaborations among different departments, leading to innovative discussions on the use of AI within respective fields. Examples of seminars involving students from different departments, such as computer science and law, would include sessions on AI and issues of data privacy or intellectual property.

Long-Term Institutional Governance

Sustainable and ethical AI practices need proper and permanent governance frameworks. The need for governance frameworks for ethical AI may be attributed to the fact that the rate of advancement of AI technologies is much faster than the prevailing ethics and regulations. There is, therefore, a need for organizations to be able to foresee the future and align their ethical policies and guidelines with the same. The committees made up of various stakeholders like ethicists, technologists, lawyers, and sociologists can provide an overall perspective to ethical issues related to AI.

The ethical use of AI technology should be working in long-term frameworks. There should be ethics committees, task forces, and reviewing processes designed by institutions. The significance of the role played by the ethics committee cannot be overemphasized since it is the body that has the mandate to supervise the establishment of AI initiatives in a way that takes into consideration human rights and the welfare of society. The ethics committee should be in constant communication with the internal community, as well as the external community, that has been impacted by the AI system.

Task forces consisting of interdisciplinarians should be assembled from time to time in order to deal with definite ethical questions that emerge in conjunction with AI. The task force would be able to investigate questions concerning bias in algorithms, data protection, and the overall effects of automation. It would help in the formation of key guiding principles in relation to the situation at hand. Moreover, it would help in the formation of refined ethics with the help of interdisciplinary research in the field of psychology, urban studies, and the environment.

8. CONCLUSION

Effective ethical governance must evolve alongside technological development while keeping a constant view on students' interests. This flexibility is essential in the rapidly changing educational landscape, shaped by rapid technological changes. Educational institutes have the ability to use innovation to promote creative learning; but it is equally important to understand how these innovations impact the core concepts of ethical governance. Engagement with these technologies, particularly AI, encourages educators and policymakers to reflect on their implication for equality, access, and student well-being.

Artificial intelligence has the potential to transform how education is delivered and enhanced, by improving access, personalized approaches, or efficiency. For example, AI-based platforms support learning opportunities according to the performance of individual students, allowing personalized learning trajectories that would meet the needs of different learning styles and abilities. Such innovations will help students who normally struggle within the standardized educational systems. However, despite these promises of potential benefits, one must acknowledge the challenges that accompany them head-on.

However, Use of artificial intelligence also raises important ethical and privacy concerns that must be addressed with great care. These include issues of discriminative practices, violation of privacy, issues of transparency, insufficient consent, and finally, accountability. Of these, discriminative practices are also a pressing problem, as there are discriminatory algorithms that, unintentionally, tend to favor some people over others. The violation of privacy, as well, raises important moral and ethical considerations, because there are moral implications associated with the storage and management of personal data of students. It is imperative for institutions of learning to take measures to ensure the moral and ethical management of data, not only from the perspective of laws, but also from a moral standpoint.

This chapter has listed the approach to the above-mentioned topics, the context in which India has experienced the above-mentioned matters, and the socio-economic setting that makes the discourse surrounding technology in education even more complex. The role that technology, specifically AI, plays in education should support and increase capabilities, not replace human judgment. The ethical manner in which technology is factored into the education sector demands a commitment to constant monitoring in order to ensure that the addition of AI in any manner furthers the purpose of education.

REFERENCES

Adams, R. (2020). Ofqual's algorithm and the problem of fairness in education. *The Guardian*.

All India Council for Technical Education. (2020). National [*Implementation guidelines for technical education*. Government of India.]. *Educational Policy*, •••, 2020.

Central Board of Secondary Education. (2022). *Guidelines on digital learning and online assessment*. Government of India.

Coghlan, S., Miller, T., & Paterson, J. (2021). Good proctor or "Big Brother"? Ethics of online exam supervision technologies. *Philosophy & Technology*, *34*(4), 1581–1606. DOI: 10.1007/s13347-021-00476-1 PMID: 34485025

Luckin, R., Holmes, W., Griffiths, M., & Forcier, L. B. (2016). *Intelligence unleashed: An argument for AI in education*. Pearson Education.

Organisation for Economic Co-operation and Development. (2019). *Principles on artificial intelligence*. OECD Publishing.

Organisation for Economic Co-operation and Development. (2023). *Artificial intelligence in education: Challenges and policy responses*. OECD Publishing.

Perelman, L. (2014). When "the state of the art" is counting words. *Assessing Writing*, *21*, 104–111. DOI: 10.1016/j.asw.2014.05.001

Swauger, S. (2020). *Our bodies encoded: Algorithmic test proctoring in higher education*. (Conference/Report). https://api.semanticscholar.org/CorpusID:229263801

UNESCO. (2021). *Recommendation on the ethics of artificial intelligence*. UNESCO.

UNESCO. (2023). *Guidance on generative AI in education and research*. UNESCO.

University Grants Commission. (2021). *Guidelines for online and digital education*. Government of India.

Wilson, J., & Huang, Y. (2024). Validity of automated essay scores for elementary-age English language learners: Evidence of bias? *Assessing Writing*, *60*, 100815. Advance online publication. DOI: 10.1016/j.asw.2024.100815

Chapter 14
Leveraging AI for Teaching and Learning

Bagas Yoas Sibagariang
http://orcid.org/0009-0009-1512-3429
Universitas Esa Unggul, Indonesia

Binastya Anggara Sekti
http://orcid.org/0000-0001-5489-4888
Universitas Esa Unggul, Indonesia

ABSTRACT

This chapter examines how artificial intelligence is reshaping teaching and learning by redefining the roles of educators and students within AI-supported educational environments. The purpose of this chapter is to provide a conceptual and practical foundation for understanding AI integration in education, with attention to pedagogical transformation, ethical considerations, and long-term implications. The chapter discusses the evolving role of AI as an educational actor, the changing responsibilities of teachers and learners, and the growing importance of critical thinking and AI literacy. It also explores the use of AI tools for instruction, assessment, and personalized learning, alongside the ethical and privacy challenges associated with AI-generated content. Practical applications and real world implementations are highlighted to bridge theory and practice. The chapter concludes by reflecting on lessons learned, institutional implications, and future directions for leveraging AI to enhance teaching and learning while preserving the human-centered values of education.

DOI: 10.4018/979-8-3373-8027-8.ch014

INTRODUCTION

The rapid advancement and widespread adoption of artificial intelligence have initiated a profound transformation in contemporary education systems. Across primary, secondary, and higher education contexts, AI technologies are increasingly embedded in instructional design, assessment practices, learning analytics, and academic support systems. From generative AI applications and intelligent tutoring systems to adaptive learning platforms and AI powered feedback mechanisms, these technologies are reshaping how knowledge is created, accessed, and evaluated. As a result, teaching and learning are no longer confined to traditional classroom structures but are becoming more personalized, data driven, and technologically mediated experiences (Govender et al., 2025; Guo et al., 2025).

The integration of AI into education extends beyond technical innovation and raises fundamental questions about pedagogy, agency, and the evolving roles of educators and students. While AI promises enhanced efficiency, scalability, and personalization, it simultaneously challenges long established educational practices and assumptions. Educators are no longer positioned solely as content transmitters but increasingly act as facilitators, designers of learning experiences, and ethical gatekeepers of AI mediated instruction. Students, in turn, are shifting from passive recipients of knowledge to active co constructors of learning, supported by AI driven tools that provide instant feedback, personalized pathways, and collaborative learning opportunities (Baťko et al., 2026; Ellis et al., 2025).

Generative AI, in particular, has accelerated debates regarding academic integrity, critical thinking, and the reliability of AI generated content. The ease with which learners can generate essays, solve problems, or simulate expert level responses has prompted concerns about superficial learning, over reliance on automation, and the erosion of essential cognitive skills. Studies have shown that students increasingly seek guidance on bypassing AI detection systems, highlighting the need for educational frameworks that emphasize ethical use, transparency, and critical engagement with AI outputs rather than prohibition alone (Foltýnek & Newton, 2026). These challenges underscore the importance of AI literacy, understood as the ability to critically, ethically, and effectively use AI systems, as a core educational competency.

At the same time, empirical evidence demonstrates that when thoughtfully integrated, AI can significantly enhance learning outcomes across disciplines. Research in mathematics, engineering, language learning, and health education indicates that AI supported instructional models can improve engagement, collaboration, and conceptual understanding by adapting content to learner needs and providing timely feedback (Gabriel et al., 2025; Hossain & Ayodele, 2025; Rädel-Ablass et al., 2025). Adaptive learning systems and AI powered teaching assistants have also been shown to support inclusive education by addressing diverse learning paces and styles, particularly in large or resource constrained educational settings (Filipović et al., 2026a; Rohanadeera & Hewagamage, 2026)

Despite these opportunities, the implementation of AI in education remains uneven and often lacks coherent pedagogical and ethical frameworks. Many institutions adopt AI tools in a fragmented manner, driven by technological availability rather than educational strategy. This has resulted in inconsistent learning experiences, limited professional development for teachers, and unresolved concerns regarding data privacy, algorithmic bias, and accountability (Sebihi et al., 2025; Yang et al., 2025). Consequently, there is a growing need for comprehensive approaches that align AI adoption with educational values, learning objectives, and long term institutional goals.

Addressing this need, this chapter is intended for academics, educational researchers, instructional designers, and higher-education leaders seeking a theoretically grounded yet practice-informed perspective on AI-enabled pedagogy. Rather than treating AI as a replacement for educators or an automated solution to complex educational problems, the chapter conceptualizes AI as a supportive and transformative tool that reshapes educational roles, practices, and relationships. Drawing on recent academic research and interdisciplinary perspectives, the chapter examines the implications of AI for teaching roles, student learning, critical thinking, ethical governance, and sustainable educational innovation (Taheri et al., 2026; Wang et al., 2026).

By situating AI within broader pedagogical, ethical, and institutional contexts, this chapter contributes to ongoing scholarly and practical discussions on the future of education in the AI era. Its contribution lies in synthesizing conceptual, ethical, and applied perspectives to clarify how AI can function as a collaborative educational partner rather than merely an instructional aid. Ultimately, the chapter argues that the meaningful integration of AI in education depends not on technological sophistication alone, but on informed, reflective, and ethically grounded educational practices that empower both educators and learners.

METHODOLOGICAL NOTE

This chapter adopts a structured narrative synthesis approach to examine the role of AI in teaching and learning. Relevant literature was identified through targeted searches in academic databases, including Scopus, Web of Science, and Google Scholar, focusing on publications from 2018 to 2025 to capture recent developments in generative AI and educational technologies.

Search terms included combinations of “artificial intelligence in education,” “virtual learning assistants,” “generative AI,” “AI literacy,” and “human–AI collaboration." Studies were selected based on their relevance to pedagogical applications, empirical insights, or conceptual contributions to AI-enabled learning environments. Priority was given to peer-reviewed journal articles, high-impact conference papers, and recent systematic reviews.

The synthesis distinguishes between descriptive reporting (e.g., tool capabilities, adoption trends) and evaluative claims (e.g., learning outcomes, ethical implications). Rather than conducting a formal meta-analysis, this chapter integrates findings to identify key themes, emerging patterns, and research gaps, particularly in the areas of AI literacy, pedagogical design, and human–AI interaction.

This approach ensures transparency in source selection while allowing flexibility to integrate interdisciplinary perspectives across education, computer science, and social sciences.

THE ROLE OF AI IN EDUCATION

Artificial intelligence has emerged as a pivotal force in redefining the structure and function of modern education systems. Its role extends beyond automation and efficiency, influencing how educational goals are conceptualized, how learning environments are designed, and how knowledge is constructed and assessed. AI operates at multiple levels of education, ranging from institutional decision making and curriculum design to classroom level instruction and individual learner support. As such, AI should be understood not merely as a technological tool but as a socio technical system that reshapes educational processes and relationships (Govender et al., 2025; Sebihi et al., 2025).

At the systemic level, AI supports data driven governance and strategic planning in education. Learning analytics and predictive models enable institutions to monitor student engagement, identify at risk learners, and optimize resource allocation. These capabilities offer opportunities to enhance retention, equity, and quality assurance when implemented transparently and responsibly. However, they also raise concerns regarding surveillance, data ownership, and algorithmic bias, reinforcing the need for clear ethical frameworks and human oversight in AI supported decision making (Sebihi et al., 2025; Yang et al., 2025).

Within teaching and learning environments, AI plays a transformative role by enabling personalization and adaptability at scale. Traditional one size fits all instructional models are increasingly challenged by AI driven systems that adjust content, pacing, and feedback according to individual learner needs. Adaptive learning platforms powered by large language models and machine learning algorithms can dynamically modify instructional materials based on learner performance and preferences, thereby supporting differentiated instruction and inclusive education practices (Filipović et al., 2026a, 2026b). These systems position AI as a mediator between curriculum intent and learner experience.

AI also contributes to the evolution of assessment practices by enabling formative, continuous, and authentic evaluation of learning. Automated feedback systems and AI based quiz generation tools provide learners with immediate insights into their progress, supporting self regulated learning and metacognitive development. Research indicates that AI powered assessment tools can enhance learning outcomes when aligned with pedagogical objectives and used to complement rather than replace human judgment (Qi et al., 2026; Vaghasiya et al., 2026) In this context, AI functions as an enabler of feedback rich learning environments rather than a purely evaluative authority.

Another significant role of AI in education lies in supporting innovation and creativity. Contrary to concerns that AI may standardize learning or reduce originality, studies demonstrate that AI can facilitate exploratory learning, creative problem solving, and collaborative knowledge construction when used intentionally. For example, AI supported role play simulations, virtual reality environments, and generative design tools allow learners to experiment with complex scenarios, reflect on multiple perspectives, and engage in higher order thinking tasks (Rädel-Ablass et al., 2025; Taheri et al., 2026). In such applications, AI acts as a cognitive partner that extends learners' creative capacities.

In addition to its functional role as an educational technology, AI increasingly occupies a conceptual position as a cognitive partner within learning ecosystems. Rather than merely automating instructional tasks, AI systems now participate in knowledge construction through adaptive feedback, intelligent scaffolding, and data-informed personalization. This shift redefines education as a human–AI collaborative process, where learning emerges from continuous interaction between learners, educators, and intelligent systems. Research highlights that AI-supported environments can enhance learner engagement and instructional responsiveness when aligned with sound pedagogical principles rather than technology-driven imperatives (Gabriel et al., 2025; Govender et al., 2025).

From a systems perspective, AI also functions as an infrastructural layer that connects curriculum design, assessment, learning analytics, and institutional decision-making. AI-driven platforms enable educators to interpret complex learning data, identify patterns of learner behavior, and intervene more effectively to support diverse learning needs. However, this expanded role necessitates a theoretical reorientation that situates AI within established educational paradigms such as constructivism, self-regulated learning, and formative assessment. Without such grounding, the use of AI risks reinforcing instrumental views of learning rather than fostering meaningful intellectual development (Filipović et al., 2026a; Sebihi et al., 2025).

Despite these advantages, the educational role of AI remains contested and context dependent. The effectiveness of AI integration is shaped by institutional readiness, teacher competencies, and pedagogical alignment. Educators' attitudes toward AI significantly influence how technologies are adopted and whether they are used to enhance or constrain learning. Evidence suggests that without adequate training and conceptual understanding, AI tools risk being applied superficially, reinforcing existing inequities or undermining meaningful learning experiences (Baťko et al., 2026; Ellis et al., 2025). This highlights the importance of viewing AI as part of a broader educational ecosystem rather than an isolated innovation.

Ultimately, the role of AI in education is not fixed but evolving. It is shaped by ongoing negotiations between technological possibilities, pedagogical values, and ethical considerations. Rather than positioning AI as an autonomous agent of change, this chapter conceptualizes AI as a supportive infrastructure that amplifies human expertise, supports learner agency, and enables more responsive educational systems. Understanding this role provides a critical foundation for examining how AI reshapes the responsibilities and identities of teachers and students, which is explored in the following section.

Figure 1. Conceptual Framework of AI in Education

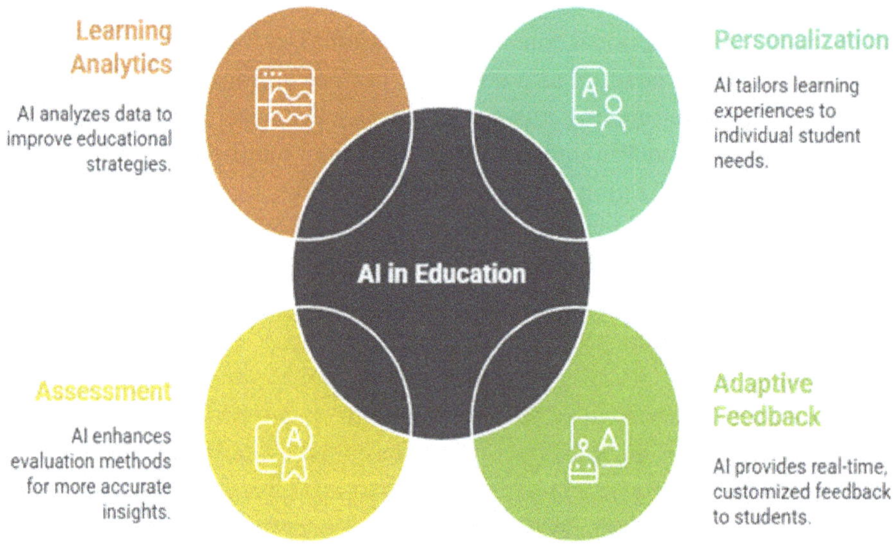

Figure 1 illustrates a conceptual framework positioning artificial intelligence as an integral component of contemporary educational ecosystems. It depicts the dynamic interactions among learners, educators, AI systems, and pedagogical processes, highlighting how AI supports personalization, adaptive feedback, assessment, and learning analytics. The framework emphasizes human–AI collaboration, where educators retain pedagogical authority as designers and facilitators, while students actively engage as self-regulated and critically aware learners. Overall, the figure establishes AI as an enabling infrastructure that enhances learning outcomes without replacing human agency in education (Gabriel et al., 2025; Govender et al., 2025; Sebihi et al., 2025).

CHANGING ROLES OF TEACHERS AND STUDENTS

The integration of artificial intelligence into educational contexts has fundamentally altered the traditional roles of both teachers and students. Historically, education has been structured around teacher-centered models in which instructors functioned primarily as knowledge transmitters and evaluators, while students assumed relatively passive roles as recipients of information. The emergence of AI-supported learning environments challenges this paradigm by redistributing cognitive, instructional, and evaluative responsibilities across human and technological actors. As a result, both teachers and students are required to renegotiate their roles, competencies, and identities within the learning process (Baťko et al., 2026; Ellis et al., 2025).

Figure 2. Changing Roles of Teachers and Students in AI-Supported Learning

Figure 2 presents a comparative model of the evolving roles of teachers and students in AI-supported learning environments. It contrasts traditional instructional roles with AI-enhanced roles, showing how teachers transition from content transmitters to learning designers, mentors, and ethical guides, while students shift from passive recipients to active, self-regulated learners and critical evaluators of AI-generated content. AI is represented as a cognitive partner that supports instruction through feedback, content generation, and personalized learning support. This transformation of educational roles is consistent with empirical findings that emphasize the need for pedagogical adaptation and professional readiness in AI-integrated educational contexts (Baťko et al., 2026; Ellis et al., 2025; Wang et al., 2026).

For teachers, AI introduces a shift from direct content delivery toward roles that emphasize facilitation, design, and ethical stewardship. AI-driven tools can automate routine tasks such as grading, content generation, and administrative reporting, enabling educators to allocate more time to higher-value pedagogical activities. These include mentoring, scaffolding complex learning tasks, fostering critical thinking, and supporting socio-emotional development. For example, in a university writing course, instructors may use generative AI to provide initial formative feedback on drafts, while class time is redirected toward discussion, revision strategies, and individualized mentoring. Research indicates that teachers who effectively integrate generative AI into their practice tend to adopt reflective and adaptive teaching strategies, positioning themselves as co-learners and learning designers rather than sole authorities (Ellis et al., 2025; Gabriel et al., 2025)

At the same time, the use of AI requires teachers to develop new forms of professional expertise. Beyond technical proficiency, educators must cultivate AI literacy, pedagogical judgment, and ethical awareness to evaluate the appropriateness and limitations of AI generated content. Pre service and in service teachers have expressed both optimism and concern regarding AI adoption, highlighting the need for structured professional development that addresses not only how to use AI tools, but why and when they should be used within specific instructional contexts (Baťko et al., 2026; Wang et al., 2026) This expanded role underscores the importance of teachers as critical mediators between AI systems and learners.

Students' roles are similarly transformed in AI supported learning environments. With access to AI powered tutors, adaptive learning platforms, and generative tools, students are increasingly expected to take greater responsibility for managing their own learning processes. AI enables learners to explore content independently, receive immediate feedback, and engage in personalized learning pathways that reflect their interests and abilities. This shift promotes learner autonomy and self regulated learning, but it also places greater demands on students' metacognitive and critical thinking skills (Filipović et al., 2026a; Qi et al., 2026).

However, the empowerment of students through AI is not without risks. The ease of generating high quality responses using generative AI can encourage surface learning and dependency if not accompanied by explicit guidance and reflective practices. Studies examining student interactions with AI generated content reveal a growing tendency to prioritize efficiency over understanding, particularly when academic performance is emphasized over learning processes (Foltýnek & Newton, 2026). Consequently, students must be supported in developing the capacity to critically evaluate AI outputs, question underlying assumptions, and integrate AI assistance into their learning in meaningful and ethical ways.

The changing roles of teachers and students also reshape the relational dynamics of education. AI mediated environments encourage more collaborative and dialogic forms of learning, in which teachers and students jointly engage with AI tools as shared resources. This collaborative orientation can reduce hierarchical boundaries and foster a culture of inquiry, experimentation, and mutual learning. Empirical evidence from collaborative learning and AI supported feedback systems suggests that such environments can enhance engagement and collective knowledge construction when supported by clear pedagogical intentions (Qi et al., 2026; Rädel-Ablass et al., 2025)

Ultimately, the redefinition of teacher and student roles in the AI era reflects a broader shift toward learner centered and ethically grounded education. Teachers remain indispensable as pedagogical leaders, ethical guardians, and designers of meaningful learning experiences, while students emerge as active participants who must navigate AI supported learning with agency and responsibility. Recognizing and supporting these evolving roles is essential for ensuring that AI enhances, rather than diminishes, the human dimensions of education.

AI TOOLS FOR TEACHERS AND STUDENTS

The rapid development of artificial intelligence has resulted in a diverse ecosystem of AI tools designed to support both teaching and learning activities. Rather than serving distinct and isolated user groups, many contemporary AI tools function as shared platforms that can be adapted to the needs of teachers and students alike. Their educational value depends not only on technical capabilities but also on how they are pedagogically framed, ethically governed, and integrated into learning environments. Understanding AI tools as part of a connected educational ecosystem is therefore essential for leveraging their potential effectively (Govender et al., 2025).

For teachers, AI tools primarily support instructional design, assessment, feedback, and learner support. Generative AI applications enable educators to create learning materials, examples, quizzes, and simulations more efficiently, allowing greater focus on pedagogical planning and learner engagement. AI based quiz generation and automated assessment tools can assist teachers in designing formative evaluations that provide timely feedback while reducing administrative workload. When aligned with learning objectives, such tools can enhance instructional coherence and responsiveness without diminishing the teacher's evaluative authority (Gabriel et al., 2025; Vaghasiya et al., 2026). Table 1 shows the AI Tools for Teaching and Learning.

Table 1. AI Tools for Teaching and Learning

Category	Tool Type	Function	Example Use in Classroom
Generative AI	Text generation (LLMs)	Idea generation, drafting, explanation	Students generate essay outlines and critique AI responses
Adaptive Learning Systems	Personalized learning platforms	Adjust content based on learner performance	Adaptive quizzes that adjust difficulty levels
NLP Tools	Text analysis and coding	Thematic analysis, summarization	Supporting qualitative coding exercises
Speech-to-Text	Transcription tools	Convert lectures or discussions into text	Recording and reviewing class discussions
Retrieval Systems (RAG)	Knowledge-grounded AI	Retrieve and synthesize academic sources	Assisting literature review with cited materials
Assessment Tools	AI-assisted grading	Feedback generation and rubric alignment	Providing formative feedback on assignments
Language Support Tools	Translation and grammar correction	Multilingual support and writing improvement	Supporting non-native speakers in academic writing

AI also supports teachers in managing complex and diverse classrooms through analytics driven insights. Learning analytics dashboards and AI powered feedback systems allow educators to monitor student progress, identify learning gaps, and tailor interventions accordingly. Research on AI powered feedback and collaborative learning systems suggests that these tools can strengthen teacher decision making and support differentiated instruction, particularly in large scale or blended learning contexts (Qi et al., 2026). In this capacity, AI functions as an instructional assistant that augments teachers' professional judgment rather than replacing it.

Students, meanwhile, increasingly interact with AI tools as learning companions and cognitive supports. Intelligent tutoring systems, AI powered teaching assistants, and adaptive learning platforms provide personalized guidance, explanations, and practice opportunities tailored to individual learner needs. Studies in higher education and professional training contexts demonstrate that AI driven tutoring systems can enhance learner engagement and conceptual understanding by offering on demand support and scaffolding complex tasks (Filipović et al., 2026a; Rohanadeera & Hewagamage, 2026). These tools enable students to learn at their own pace while maintaining continuity with curricular goals.

Generative AI tools also play a growing role in supporting creativity, exploration, and problem solving among students. When used responsibly, AI can assist learners in brainstorming ideas, simulating scenarios, and exploring alternative solutions, thereby fostering higher order thinking. Applications integrating AI with virtual and augmented learning environments further extend these possibilities by allowing students to engage with immersive and experiential learning tasks that would otherwise be difficult to implement (Rädel-Ablass et al., 2025; Taheri et al., 2026). In such contexts, AI acts as a catalyst for inquiry rather than a source of definitive answers.

Despite their benefits, AI tools for both teachers and students raise important pedagogical and ethical considerations. The accessibility and sophistication of generative AI can blur boundaries between assistance and substitution, making it difficult to distinguish between learner generated and AI generated work. Research highlights the growing prevalence of strategies aimed at bypassing AI detection tools, underscoring the need for clear guidelines, transparent assessment practices, and the cultivation of academic integrity (Foltýnek & Newton, 2026). These challenges emphasize that AI tools must be accompanied by explicit instruction on ethical use and critical evaluation.

Importantly, the effectiveness of AI tools depends on users' competencies and institutional support structures. Teachers require professional development to understand the affordances and limitations of AI tools, while students need guidance in developing AI literacy and self regulation skills. Without such support, AI tools risk reinforcing surface learning or exacerbating educational inequalities. Conversely, when embedded within coherent pedagogical frameworks, AI tools can enhance collaboration, inclusivity, and learning quality across educational contexts (Baťko et al., 2026; Sebihi et al., 2025).

In summary, AI tools for teachers and students should be viewed as complementary components of a shared educational infrastructure. Their value lies not in automation alone, but in their capacity to support meaningful teaching practices, empower learner agency, and foster innovative learning experiences. This perspective provides a foundation for critically examining AI generated content and its implications for learning, which is addressed in the following section. Table 1 shows the Examples of AI Tools for Teachers and Students. This table provides a comprehensive overview of how different AI technologies, ranging from generative tools to analytics systems, enhance educational functions by supporting both instructional delivery and personalized learning experiences. Table 2 shows the examples of AI Tools for Teachers and Students.

Table 2. Examples of AI Tools for Teachers and Students

Category of AI Tool	Primary Use for Teachers	Primary Use for Students	Educational Function
Generative AI Tools	Content creation, quiz design, feedback drafts	Idea generation, drafting, exploration	Supports creativity and formative learning
Intelligent Tutoring Systems	Monitoring learner progress	Personalized guidance and practice	Enhances conceptual understanding
Adaptive Learning Platforms	Curriculum alignment and differentiation	Self-paced personalized learning	Supports learner autonomy
Learning Analytics Systems	Identifying learning gaps and trends	Awareness of learning progress	Informs instructional decisions
AI-Powered Feedback Tools	Automated formative feedback	Immediate performance feedback	Improves learning responsiveness

CRITICAL AND ETHICAL EVALUATION OF AI GENERATED CONTENT

The increasing use of artificial intelligence in educational contexts has intensified the production and circulation of AI-generated content, including texts, problem solutions, feedback, simulations, and instructional materials. While such content offers efficiency and accessibility, it also raises critical and ethical concerns that must be carefully examined. The ability of generative AI systems to produce fluent and contextually appropriate outputs can obscure underlying inaccuracies, biases, or misalignments with learning objectives, making critical evaluation an essential competency for both educators and students (Ellis et al., 2025; Foltýnek & Newton, 2026).

One of the primary challenges associated with AI-generated content is its perceived authority. Learners often attribute a high level of credibility to AI outputs due to their coherence and apparent expertise, which can reduce critical scrutiny. Studies indicate that students may accept AI-generated explanations or solutions without questioning their validity, particularly when the content aligns with expected answers or assessment criteria. This tendency risks promoting surface learning and undermining epistemic curiosity if learners are not explicitly guided to interrogate AI outputs and compare them with authoritative sources (Filipović et al., 2026a; Qi et al., 2026).

From an academic integrity perspective, AI-generated content complicates traditional notions of authorship, originality, and responsibility for learning. The ease with which learners can generate essays, reports, or problem solutions using AI tools challenges existing assessment practices and raises concerns about misrepresentation of learning. Research examining student engagement with AI detection and avoidance strategies highlights a growing tension between technological enforcement and ethical education, suggesting that punitive approaches alone are insufficient to address these challenges (Foltýnek & Newton, 2026). Instead, ethical evaluation should be embedded within pedagogical practices that emphasize transparency, reflection, and accountability for learning processes.

Educators play a critical role in mediating the ethical and academic use of AI-generated content. Teachers must determine when and how AI assistance is appropriate, clearly communicate expectations to students, and design assessments that prioritize reasoning, process, and critical engagement rather than final outputs alone. Evidence from studies on teacher experiences with generative AI indicates that reflective and dialogic approaches enable more ethical integration of AI while preserving academic standards (Baťko et al., 2026; Ellis et al., 2025) This underscores the importance of professional judgment in evaluating AI-generated content within instructional contexts.

Bias and representation constitute additional ethical dimensions of AI generated content. AI systems are trained on large scale datasets that may reflect social, cultural, and linguistic biases, which can be reproduced or amplified in educational materials. Such biases can affect content accuracy, inclusivity, and relevance, particularly in diverse or underrepresented learning contexts. Critical evaluation therefore requires awareness of the limitations of AI training data and the potential implications for equity and fairness in education (Sebihi et al., 2025; Yang et al., 2025).

Beyond issues of accuracy and plagiarism, evaluating AI-generated content also involves assessing its pedagogical alignment. Content produced by AI may be technically correct yet pedagogically inappropriate, lacking coherence with learning outcomes, learner readiness, or curricular standards. Research on AI-supported instructional systems emphasizes the necessity of human oversight to ensure that AI-generated materials contribute to meaningful learning rather than fragmented knowledge acquisition (Filipović et al., 2026b; Gabriel et al., 2025). In this sense, critical evaluation is inseparable from pedagogical judgment.

In summary, the critical and ethical evaluation of AI generated content is a foundational requirement for responsible AI integration in education. It demands a shift from viewing AI as a neutral content provider to recognizing it as a socio technical system whose outputs must be actively interpreted, questioned, and contextualized. By fostering critical awareness, ethical reasoning, and reflective practice, educators and learners can engage with AI generated content in ways that support learning integrity and intellectual development. This focus on evaluation provides a necessary bridge to the development of critical thinking skills in AI supported learning, which is addressed in the next section.

DEVELOPING CRITICAL THINKING IN AI SUPPORTED LEARNING

The integration of artificial intelligence into learning environments has intensified the need to explicitly cultivate critical thinking skills among learners. As AI systems increasingly provide instant answers, explanations, and recommendations, students are confronted with information that appears authoritative yet may be incomplete, biased, or contextually inappropriate. In this landscape, critical thinking becomes a central educational objective, enabling learners to evaluate, interpret, and apply AI generated information thoughtfully rather than passively consuming it (Ellis et al., 2025; Wang et al., 2026).

AI supported learning environments present both opportunities and challenges for the development of critical thinking. On one hand, AI can scaffold higher order cognitive processes by offering prompts, feedback, and alternative perspectives that stimulate reflection and inquiry. Adaptive systems can adjust task complexity and encourage learners to revisit assumptions, compare solutions, and justify reasoning. Research on AI powered feedback and collaborative learning systems suggests that such scaffolding can enhance analytical reasoning and metacognitive awareness when learners are actively engaged in evaluating AI mediated feedback (Gabriel et al., 2025; Qi et al., 2026)

On the other hand, the convenience and efficiency of AI tools can inadvertently discourage deep cognitive engagement. When learners rely on AI generated solutions without examining underlying reasoning, critical thinking may be supplanted by procedural completion. Empirical studies indicate that students may prioritize task completion and performance outcomes over conceptual understanding, particularly in assessment driven contexts. This tendency highlights the importance of instructional designs that require learners to explain, critique, and extend AI generated outputs rather than simply reproduce them (Filipović et al., 2026a; Foltýnek & Newton, 2026)

Teachers play a pivotal role in fostering critical thinking within AI supported learning environments. By designing tasks that emphasize inquiry, argumentation, and reflection, educators can position AI as a stimulus for critical engagement rather than a shortcut to answers. Pedagogical strategies such as comparative analysis of AI and human generated responses, reflective journals on AI assisted learning processes, and collaborative critique of AI outputs encourage learners to question assumptions and evaluate evidence. Studies on teacher mediated AI integration demonstrate that such approaches support deeper learning and epistemic awareness (Baťko et al., 2026; Ellis et al., 2025).

Critical thinking in AI supported learning also involves developing AI literacy as a foundational competence. Learners must understand how AI systems generate outputs, including the probabilistic nature of large language models and the influence of training data. This knowledge enables students to contextualize AI responses, recognize limitations, and identify potential biases. Research emphasizes that AI literacy contributes to more informed and responsible use of AI tools, strengthening learners' ability to engage critically with technology mediated information (Govender et al., 2025; Sebihi et al., 2025).

Collaborative learning environments further enhance critical thinking by enabling learners to negotiate meaning and evaluate AI outputs collectively. AI powered collaborative platforms can facilitate peer discussion, feedback exchange, and joint problem solving, creating spaces for shared inquiry and reflection. Evidence suggests that when learners collaboratively analyze AI generated content, they are more likely to articulate reasoning, challenge assumptions, and construct deeper understanding than when working individually (Qi et al., 2026; Rädel-Ablass et al., 2025).

Within AI-supported learning environments, critical thinking must be intentionally cultivated rather than assumed as an automatic outcome of technology use. While AI tools can support analysis, synthesis, and reflection through adaptive prompts and feedback systems, they can also reduce cognitive effort if learners outsource reasoning processes to automated systems. Effective instructional design therefore positions AI as a catalyst for inquiry, encouraging learners to question outputs, compare multiple perspectives, and justify their own conclusions. Empirical evidence suggests that when AI is used to provoke reflection and dialogue rather than provide final answers, it can enhance higher-order thinking skills and metacognitive awareness (Qi et al., 2026; Sakthivel et al., 2026).

In summary, developing critical thinking in AI supported learning requires intentional pedagogical design that positions AI as an object of inquiry as well as a learning aid. By integrating reflective tasks, ethical discussions, and collaborative critique into AI mediated learning activities, educators can cultivate learners' capacity to think critically, evaluate information, and exercise informed judgment. These competencies are essential for navigating the ethical and privacy challenges associated with AI use in education, which are examined in the following section.

ETHICAL AND PRIVACY CONCERNS.

The integration of artificial intelligence into educational environments raises complex ethical and privacy concerns that extend beyond technical implementation. As AI systems increasingly rely on large volumes of learner data to personalize instruction, provide feedback, and support decision making, questions related to data ownership, consent, transparency, and accountability become central to responsible educational practice (Anwar, Rahaman, et al., 2025; Govender et al., 2025; Sebihi et al., 2025). Addressing these concerns is essential to ensure that AI enhances educational quality without compromising fundamental ethical principles or learner rights.

One of the most pressing ethical issues in AI supported education is data privacy. AI driven learning platforms collect extensive data on student behavior, performance, engagement patterns, and sometimes even biometric or affective indicators. While such data enable adaptive learning and early intervention, they also increase the risk of unauthorized access, misuse, or surveillance (Anwar, Sekti, et al., 2025; Sebihi et al., 2025; Yang et al., 2025). Learners may be unaware of how their data are collected, processed, and stored, raising concerns about informed consent and long term data security. Research emphasizes the importance of transparent data governance policies and clear communication with learners regarding the scope and purpose of data collection (Sebihi et al., 2025; Yang et al., 2025).

Closely related to privacy is the issue of algorithmic transparency and accountability. Many AI systems operate as black boxes, offering limited insight into how decisions or recommendations are generated. In educational contexts, opaque algorithms can affect assessment outcomes, learning pathways, and institutional decision making in ways that are difficult to scrutinize or contest. This lack of transparency poses ethical risks, particularly when AI outputs influence high stakes decisions such as grading, progression, or access to support services. Scholars argue that human oversight and explainable AI mechanisms are necessary to maintain trust and fairness in AI mediated education (Govender et al., 2025; Wang et al., 2026)

Bias and equity represent additional ethical challenges associated with AI in education. AI systems are trained on historical data that may reflect existing social, cultural, and linguistic inequalities. As a result, AI-generated content and recommendations can disadvantage certain learner groups or reinforce dominant perspectives. For example, automated feedback systems trained primarily on standard academic English may undervalue alternative linguistic expressions, potentially disadvantaging multilingual or non-native English-speaking students. In diverse educational settings, such biases may manifest in language use, examples, assessment criteria, or feedback patterns. Addressing these issues requires continuous evaluation of AI systems and deliberate efforts to ensure inclusivity and cultural responsiveness in AI-supported learning environments (Sebihi et al., 2025; Yang et al., 2025).

Ethical concerns also arise in relation to academic integrity and learner autonomy. The widespread availability of generative AI challenges traditional norms of authorship and originality, complicating the distinction between legitimate assistance and unethical substitution. Rather than relying solely on detection and enforcement mechanisms, ethical governance of AI in education should emphasize values based approaches that promote responsibility, honesty, and reflective use of AI tools. Studies suggest that fostering ethical awareness and shared norms among educators and learners is more effective than punitive strategies in sustaining academic integrity (Ellis et al., 2025; Foltýnek & Newton, 2026)

Educators and institutions bear significant responsibility in addressing ethical and privacy concerns associated with AI. Teachers must be equipped to guide students in ethical AI use, while institutions must establish policies that align AI adoption with legal frameworks, professional standards, and educational values. Professional development initiatives and institutional guidelines play a critical role in supporting ethical decision making and ensuring that AI systems are implemented in ways that respect learner dignity and autonomy (Baťko et al., 2026; Ellis et al., 2025).

In summary, ethical and privacy considerations are integral to the sustainable integration of AI in education. They require a holistic approach that combines technical safeguards, transparent governance, pedagogical responsibility, and ethical literacy. By addressing these concerns proactively, educational institutions can create AI supported learning environments that are not only innovative but also trustworthy and equitable. These ethical foundations are essential for the effective application of AI in teaching and learning, which is explored in the following section.

APPLYING AI IN TEACHING AND LEARNING

The application of artificial intelligence in teaching and learning represents a shift from experimental adoption toward systematic pedagogical integration. Rather than treating AI as an external add on, effective application requires aligning AI tools with instructional goals, curriculum design, assessment strategies, and learner support mechanisms. When applied thoughtfully, AI can enhance teaching effectiveness, improve learning outcomes, and support more inclusive and adaptive educational environments (Govender et al., 2025; Yang et al., 2025)

One of the primary applications of AI in teaching is instructional personalization. AI powered learning systems analyze learner data to tailor content difficulty, pacing, and feedback according to individual needs. This adaptive approach allows educators to address learner diversity more effectively than traditional one size fits all instruction. Research indicates that personalized learning environments supported by AI can increase learner engagement and motivation, particularly when combined with human guided instruction (Sebihi et al., 2025; Wang et al., 2026)

AI also plays an increasingly important role in assessment and feedback processes. Automated assessment tools can provide immediate feedback on quizzes, assignments, and formative tasks, enabling learners to identify gaps in understanding in real time. For educators, AI supported assessment reduces administrative workload and frees time for higher value pedagogical activities such as mentoring and curriculum refinement. However, scholars emphasize that AI generated assessment outcomes should complement, not replace, human judgment to preserve fairness and contextual understanding (Ellis et al., 2025; Foltýnek & Newton, 2026).

In teaching practice, AI can function as an instructional support system rather than an instructional authority. Educators use AI to generate lesson plans, learning materials, simulations, and examples that align with curriculum objectives. These applications support instructional creativity and efficiency while allowing teachers to maintain control over pedagogical decisions. Studies highlight that the most effective applications of AI occur when educators critically evaluate AI outputs and adapt them to specific learning contexts (Baťko et al., 2026; Yang et al., 2025)

Collaborative and inquiry based learning also benefit from AI supported applications. AI tools can facilitate group formation, recommend resources, and scaffold problem solving activities, enabling learners to engage in deeper exploration and knowledge construction. In such contexts, AI acts as a facilitator that enhances interaction rather than replacing peer collaboration or teacher guidance. This aligns with constructivist learning theories that emphasize active participation and social learning (Govender et al., 2025)

Despite its potential, applying AI in teaching and learning presents practical challenges. Educators require pedagogical and technical competence to integrate AI meaningfully, and institutions must ensure equitable access to AI tools and infrastructure. Without appropriate training and policy support, AI applications risk reinforcing surface level learning or overreliance on automated systems. Therefore, successful application depends on continuous professional development and institutional commitment to pedagogically grounded AI use (Ellis et al., 2025; Sebihi et al., 2025).

CASE VIGNETTE: AI AS A COGNITIVE PARTNER IN A UNIVERSITY WRITING COURSE

A practical illustration of AI as a cognitive partner can be observed in a first-year university academic writing course. In this setting, students were required to develop argumentative essays while interacting with a generative AI system as a structured "thinking partner." Rather than allowing unrestricted use, the instructor designed guided prompts that required students to (1) generate initial ideas, (2) critique AI-generated arguments, and (3) refine their own positions based on comparison.

The AI system was not used to produce final answers but to stimulate reflective thinking. Students were asked to explicitly document how AI suggestions influenced their reasoning, thereby creating a transparent audit trail of human–AI interaction. This approach enabled the instructor to assess not only the final output but also the cognitive process underlying the work.

The results indicated that students demonstrated improved argument structure and greater awareness of bias in automated outputs. However, the exercise also revealed risks of overreliance, particularly among students with lower confidence in writing. To address this, the instructor incorporated reflective checkpoints requiring students to justify when they accepted or rejected AI suggestions.

This example illustrates how AI can function as a cognitive partner rather than a replacement, supporting higher-order thinking while maintaining human interpretive control. It also highlights the importance of structured pedagogical design in ensuring that AI enhances, rather than diminishes, critical engagement.

In conclusion, applying AI in teaching and learning involves more than technological deployment. It requires intentional pedagogical design, critical oversight, and alignment with educational values. When applied responsibly, AI enhances personalization, assessment, instructional support, and collaborative learning while preserving the central role of educators and learners. These applications form the foundation for practical strategies to leverage AI effectively in real educational settings, which is addressed in the next section.

LEVERAGING AI FOR TEACHING AND LEARNING IN PRACTICE

Leveraging artificial intelligence for teaching and learning in practice requires moving beyond conceptual understanding toward concrete instructional strategies that can be implemented in real educational settings. This stage focuses on how educators and institutions operationalize AI tools to support teaching objectives, learner engagement, and academic development while maintaining pedagogical integrity. Practical implementation emphasizes contextual adaptation, iterative experimentation, and reflective evaluation rather than rigid technological adoption (Ellis et al., 2025; Govender et al., 2025).

In classroom practice, AI is often leveraged as a co-design tool that supports educators in planning and delivering instruction. Teachers use AI systems to generate lesson outlines, learning activities, and examples that align with course learning outcomes. These outputs are then reviewed, refined, and contextualized by educators to ensure relevance and academic rigor. For instance, in a large undergraduate course, an instructor may use generative AI to draft multiple versions of practice problems, then select and adapt them for in-class discussion while focusing instructional time on addressing misconceptions and facilitating peer interaction. Research shows that educators who approach AI as a collaborative assistant rather than an authoritative source demonstrate higher confidence and effectiveness in AI-supported teaching environments (Baťko et al., 2026; Wang et al., 2026)

AI driven learning platforms are also leveraged to support learner autonomy and self regulation. Through adaptive recommendations and personalized feedback, learners can monitor their progress, identify areas for improvement, and take greater responsibility for their learning. Such practices align with learner centered pedagogies and have been shown to improve persistence and academic performance, particularly in higher education contexts (Filipović et al., 2026a; Sebihi et al., 2025)

In practice based disciplines, AI is leveraged to simulate authentic learning experiences that are otherwise difficult to implement. AI enhanced simulations, role plays, and virtual environments enable learners to practice skills in safe and controlled settings. Studies in health and engineering education demonstrate that AI supported simulations improve skill acquisition and confidence when integrated with reflective activities and instructor feedback (Rädel-Ablass et al., 2025; Taheri et al., 2026)

Assessment practices also evolve when AI is leveraged effectively. Educators combine AI generated formative assessments with human evaluated summative assessments to balance efficiency and academic integrity. AI powered feedback systems can guide learners through complex problem solving processes while preserving transparency in grading criteria. Scholars emphasize that such hybrid assessment models are most effective when educators clearly communicate the role of AI and establish expectations for ethical use (Foltýnek & Newton, 2026; Qi et al., 2026)

Institutional practices play a critical role in leveraging AI at scale. Successful implementation requires policy frameworks that address data privacy, academic integrity, and equitable access, as well as attention to system security and sustainability. Research on AI enabled digital infrastructures highlights that responsible implementation depends on governance mechanisms that anticipate technological risks and embed ethical safeguards into large scale AI deployments, including those in educational contexts (Anwar, Sekti, et al., 2025; Govender et al., 2025; Sebihi et al., 2025) Professional development initiatives are essential to equip educators with the skills to evaluate, adapt, and innovate with AI tools. Without institutional support, AI adoption risks remaining fragmented and inconsistent across educational programs.

Overall, leveraging AI for teaching and learning in practice involves a continuous process of alignment between technology, pedagogy, and context. Effective practices are characterized by educator agency, learner empowerment, and ethical awareness. From a strategic perspective, research on AI technology management emphasizes that sustainable value creation emerges when AI adoption is guided by institutional strategy, human competencies, and governance structures rather than isolated experimentation (Govender et al., 2025; Sekti, 2025). By grounding AI use in reflective teaching practice and strategic management, institutions can maximize its benefits while mitigating potential risks. The insights gained from practical implementation inform broader lessons and long term implications, which are explored in the following section.

Figure 3. Integrated Model for Leveraging AI in Teaching and Learning

Figure 3: this figure depicts an integrated model for leveraging AI in teaching and learning by connecting theoretical foundations with practical implementation. It demonstrates how AI tools, pedagogical design, ethical and critical evaluation, learning activities, and assessment form a continuous and iterative process. The model highlights the importance of reflective practice, where insights from implementation inform ongoing improvement and long-term institutional strategies. By integrating technological, pedagogical, and ethical dimensions, the figure provides a holistic representation of sustainable AI adoption in educational practice.

LESSONS LEARNED AND LONG TERM IMPLICATIONS

The integration of artificial intelligence into teaching and learning has generated a number of critical lessons that inform its long term implications for education systems, educators, and learners. One of the most significant lessons is that AI adoption is not primarily a technological challenge but a pedagogical and organizational one. Institutions that focused solely on acquiring AI tools without aligning them with educational goals often encountered resistance, confusion, and uneven learning outcomes (Govender et al., 2025; Sebihi et al., 2025).

One key lesson emerging from current implementations of AI in education is that technological adoption alone does not guarantee pedagogical improvement. Sustainable integration requires alignment between institutional policies, educator competencies, and curricular goals. Institutions that invest solely in AI tools without parallel investment in professional development and governance frameworks often experience fragmented or superficial adoption. Long-term success depends on building organizational cultures that support experimentation, reflective practice, and evidence-informed decision-making regarding AI use (Baťko et al., 2026; Sebihi et al., 2025).

A key lesson learned concerns the evolving professional identity of educators. Rather than diminishing the role of teachers, sustained engagement with AI highlights the importance of pedagogical expertise, ethical judgment, and contextual decision making. Studies of teachers' experiences with generative AI show that educators who developed reflective and critical approaches to AI use were better able to integrate these tools meaningfully into their teaching practice (Baťko et al., 2026; Ellis et al., 2025). Over the long term, this suggests a shift toward teaching roles that emphasize learning design, facilitation, and critical mediation of knowledge.

From the learner perspective, long term implications center on the development of metacognitive and critical thinking skills. While AI systems can provide rapid feedback and personalized guidance, learners must be supported in understanding the limitations and assumptions embedded in AI generated outputs. Research indicates that students who are explicitly taught to question, verify, and refine AI assisted work demonstrate deeper conceptual understanding and stronger academic integrity (Foltýnek & Newton, 2026; Sakthivel et al., 2026). This underscores the need for curricula that embed AI literacy as a core academic competence.

Equity and access emerge as another crucial lesson. AI has the potential to reduce educational disparities by offering scalable personalized support, yet it can also exacerbate inequalities if access to tools, infrastructure, and training is uneven. Long term strategies must therefore prioritize inclusive design, open educational resources, and institutional policies that ensure all learners and educators can benefit from AI enhanced learning environments (Guo et al., 2025; Sebihi et al., 2025).

From a long-term perspective, AI has significant implications for the future of educational systems, particularly in relation to equity, access, and workforce preparation. While AI offers opportunities to personalize learning at scale, it also risks widening digital divides if access and digital literacy are unevenly distributed. Policymakers and educational leaders must therefore prioritize inclusive strategies that ensure AI-enhanced learning benefits diverse learner populations. Embedding ethical governance, continuous evaluation, and adaptability into institutional planning will be critical to ensuring that AI contributes to resilient and future-ready education systems rather than reinforcing existing inequalities (Govender et al., 2025; Yang et al., 2025).

Institutional governance represents a further area of long term impact. As AI becomes embedded in assessment, feedback, and learning analytics, universities and schools must develop robust frameworks for data governance, transparency, and accountability. Ethical guidelines and clear communication about how AI is used are essential to maintaining trust among stakeholders. Research highlights that institutions with proactive governance structures are better positioned to adapt to future developments in educational AI (Govender et al., 2025; Wang et al., 2026).

Finally, the long term implications of AI in education suggest an ongoing need for adaptability and continuous learning. AI technologies evolve rapidly, and educational practices must remain flexible to respond to emerging tools and challenges. Lessons learned from current implementations emphasize that sustainable AI integration depends on cultivating a culture of experimentation, reflection, and collaboration among educators, learners, and policymakers (Filipović et al., 2026a; Qi et al., 2026).

In summary, the lessons learned from early and ongoing applications of AI in education point toward a future in which technology supports, rather than replaces, human judgment and creativity. Long term implications include transformed teaching roles, enhanced learner agency, strengthened ethical awareness, and more resilient educational institutions. These insights provide a foundation for considering future directions in AI supported education, which will be addressed in the next section.

FUTURE DIRECTIONS

Future directions in leveraging artificial intelligence for teaching and learning are shaped by rapid technological innovation, evolving pedagogical paradigms, and increasing ethical awareness. Rather than focusing on isolated tools, future educational AI development is expected to emphasize integrated ecosystems that align learning analytics, adaptive content, assessment, and feedback within coherent pedagogical frameworks. This shift reflects a growing recognition that AI must be embedded within instructional design rather than appended as an auxiliary technology (Gabriel et al., 2025; Govender et al., 2025).

One major future direction involves the advancement of adaptive and personalized learning systems. Research on large language models and adaptive learning environments suggests that AI will increasingly support fine grained personalization based on learners' cognitive profiles, learning histories, and contextual needs. Such systems have the potential to move education away from standardized pathways toward more flexible and learner responsive trajectories, provided that transparency and explainability are maintained (Filipović et al., 2026a; Lin, 2026a, 2026b)

Another emerging direction is the integration of AI into collaborative and social learning contexts. AI powered feedback agents and learning companions are being designed to facilitate peer interaction, scaffold group problem solving, and support reflective dialogue. Studies indicate that when AI supports collaboration rather than individual automation, it can enhance collective knowledge construction and social engagement (Qi et al., 2026; Yang et al., 2025). This points toward future classrooms in which AI acts as a mediator of interaction rather than a substitute for human communication.

Teacher education and professional development will also be a critical area of future focus. As AI becomes more pervasive, pre service and in service teachers will require systematic training not only in tool usage but also in ethical reasoning, pedagogical integration, and critical evaluation of AI outputs. Research suggests that future teacher preparation programs will increasingly embed AI literacy as a core professional competence, ensuring educators can adapt to ongoing technological change (Baťko et al., 2026; Wang et al., 2026).

Ethical and regulatory considerations are likely to play an expanded role in shaping future directions. Issues related to data privacy, algorithmic bias, intellectual property, and academic integrity will require coordinated responses from institutions, policymakers, and technology developers. Future frameworks are expected to move beyond reactive regulation toward proactive ethical design and participatory governance models that involve educators and learners in decision making processes (Foltýnek & Newton, 2026; Sebihi et al., 2025).

Finally, future directions point toward interdisciplinary research and innovation. The intersection of AI with fields such as learning sciences, psychology, ethics, and human computer interaction will be essential for developing AI systems that genuinely enhance educational quality. Long term progress will depend on sustained collaboration between researchers, practitioners, and institutions to ensure that AI driven transformation remains pedagogically grounded and socially responsible (Hossain & Ayodele, 2025; Taheri et al., 2026).

CONCLUSION

The integration of artificial intelligence into teaching and learning represents not merely a technological shift, but a reconfiguration of educational practice and epistemic engagement. Rather than functioning as a replacement for human educators, AI systems operate most effectively as cognitive partners that augment, extend, and scaffold human thinking. This reframing is critical, as it positions educators and learners not as passive users of automated systems, but as active agents who guide, interpret, and critically evaluate AI-generated outputs. In this context, the value of AI lies not in efficiency alone, but in its capacity to support deeper inquiry, adaptive learning, and reflective knowledge construction.

At the same time, the adoption of AI in education introduces a set of interrelated challenges that cannot be addressed through technical solutions alone. Issues such as algorithmic bias, overreliance on automated outputs, and the erosion of academic integrity highlight the need for careful pedagogical design and institutional governance. Without explicit strategies to mitigate these risks, AI-supported learning environments may inadvertently reproduce inequalities, obscure epistemic accountability, and weaken critical thinking processes. Therefore, the successful integration of AI requires a balanced approach that combines technological innovation with ethical oversight and pedagogical intentionality.

The analysis presented in this chapter underscores the importance of aligning AI deployment with clearly defined educational objectives and contextual realities. Differences across educational levels, institutional capacities, and disciplinary practices must be acknowledged when implementing AI-supported systems. Equally important is the development of AI literacy among both educators and students, enabling them to engage with AI critically, responsibly, and effectively. By embedding human-in-the-loop approaches and transparent evaluation practices, educational institutions can ensure that AI remains a supportive component of learning rather than an unexamined authority.

Looking forward, the future of AI in education depends on the ability to sustain meaningful human–AI collaboration while preserving the core values of education, including equity, trust, and intellectual autonomy. Advancing this agenda requires not only continued research into the pedagogical and technical dimensions of AI, but also the development of robust governance frameworks and evidence-based implementation strategies. Ultimately, the goal is not to optimize learning through automation, but to enrich educational experiences through thoughtful integration of AI as a complementary and accountable partner in the learning process.

REFERENCES

Anwar, N., Rahaman, R., Widodo, A. M., Sekti, B. A., Erzed, N., Santiago Tangkudung, R. R., Muchlis, M., Yuhefizar, Y., & Budhisantosa, N. (2025). Sustainable cybersecurity in the AI era: Innovations in green computing and security. In *Sustainable Information Security in the Age of AI and Green Computing* (pp. 603–620). DOI: 10.4018/979-8-3693-8034-5.ch030

Anwar, N., Sekti, B. A., Widodo, A. M., Erzed, N., Gunawan, H., Tangkudung, R. R. S., Muchlis, M., & Budhisantosa, N. (2025). Emerging innovations in AI and green computing for cybersecurity. In *Sustainable Information Security in the Age of AI and Green Computing* (pp. 17–38). DOI: 10.4018/979-8-3693-8034-5.ch002

Baťko, J., Frolík, D., Rohlíková, L., Vejvodová, J., Visvizi, A., Voltrová, M., & Vrbová, V. (2026). AI and Pre-service Teachers: Attitudes to and the Prospect of Applying AI-Based Tools in Education. *Springer Proceedings in Complexity*, 271–283. DOI: 10.1007/978-3-031-78623-5_23

Ellis, R., Han, F., & Cook, H. (2025). Qualitatively different teacher experiences of teaching with generative artificial intelligence. *International Journal of Educational Technology in Higher Education, 22*(1), 33. Advance online publication. DOI: 10.1186/s41239-025-00532-2

Filipović, A. M., Fastić-Pajk, I., Puljiz, H., & Šabić, I. (2026a). AI-Driven Customization of Adaptive Learning Content: Lessons from Applying LLMs in Personalized Education. *Communications in Computer and Information Science, 2609 CCIS*, 67–81. DOI: 10.1007/978-3-032-02801-3_5

Filipović, A. M., Fastić-Pajk, I., Puljiz, H., & Šabić, I. (2026b). AI-Driven Customization of Adaptive Learning Content: Lessons from Applying LLMs in Personalized Education. *Communications in Computer and Information Science, 2609 CCIS*, 67–81. DOI: 10.1007/978-3-032-02801-3_5

Foltýnek, T., & Newton, P. M. (2026). What Does YouTube Advise Students About Bypassing AI-Text Detection Tools? A Pragmatic Analysis. *Journal of Academic Ethics, 24*(1), 8. Advance online publication. DOI: 10.1007/s10805-025-09675-3

Gabriel, F., Kennedy, J., Marrone, R., & Leonard, S. (2025). Pragmatic AI in education and its role in mathematics learning and teaching. *NPJ Science of Learning, 10*(1), 26. Advance online publication. DOI: 10.1038/s41539-025-00315-4 PMID: 40348764

Govender, R., Rzyankina, E., Bayaga, A., & Harun, I. (2025). Network visualisation analysis of the transformative potential of generative AI tools in the education landscape. *Discover Education*, *4*(1), 426. Advance online publication. DOI: 10.1007/s44217-025-00726-w

Guo, S., Halim, H. B. A., & Mohd Saad, M. R. B. M. (2025). Leveraging AI-enabled mobile learning platforms to enhance the effectiveness of English teaching in universities. *Scientific Reports*, *15*(1), 15873. Advance online publication. DOI: 10.1038/s41598-025-00801-0 PMID: 40335582

Hossain, S. K. S., & Ayodele, B. V. (2025). Revolutionizing Teaching and Learning of Material Science and Engineering in Chemical Engineering: The Impact of Generative AI. *Journal of Chemical Education*, *102*(12), 5160–5168. DOI: 10.1021/acs.jchemed.5c00539

Lin, H.-C. (2026a). A Generative AI-Supported Flipped Classroom Model for Personalized Skill Training in Engineering Woodworking Education. *Lecture Notes in Computer Science, 15914 LNCS*, 366–376. DOI: 10.1007/978-3-031-98197-5_39

Lin, H.-C. (2026b). A Generative AI-Supported Flipped Classroom Model for Personalized Skill Training in Engineering Woodworking Education. *Lecture Notes in Computer Science, 15914 LNCS*, 366–376. DOI: 10.1007/978-3-031-98197-5_39

Qi, X., Zhou, J., Dong, Y., & Chen, F. (2026). Enhancing collaborative learning through AI-powered feedback systems. *International Journal of Data Science and Analytics*, *21*(1), 20. Advance online publication. DOI: 10.1007/s41060-025-00882-0

Rädel-Ablass, K., Schliz, K., Schlick, C., Meindl, B., Pahr-Hosbach, S., Schwendemann, H., Rupp, S., Roddewig, M., & Miersch, C. (2025). Teaching opportunities for anamnesis interviews through AI based teaching role plays: A survey with online learning students from health study programs. *BMC Medical Education*, *25*(1), 259. Advance online publication. DOI: 10.1186/s12909-025-06756-0 PMID: 39966894

Rohanadeera, S. L., & Hewagamage, K. P. (2026). Generative-AI-Powered TA BOT for Enhanced Personalized Support in Software Engineering Education. *Communications in Computer and Information Science, 2380 CCIS*, 197–204. DOI: 10.1007/978-981-96-6291-3_16

Sakthivel, A., Swaroop, V. T. S., Malik, A., Meprathe, R., Suresh, S., & Shukla, A. (2026). Empowering Business Mathematics Learners: Leveraging Generative AI for Academic Excellence. *Lecture Notes in Networks and Systems, 1580 LNNS*, 281–291. DOI: 10.1007/978-981-95-0629-3_21

Sebihi, A., Schoelen, L., & Uwamwezi, B. (2025). Unveiling AI's impact in Rwandan higher education: Navigating trends, challenges, and imperatives at the University of Rwanda. *Discover Education*, *4*(1), 166. Advance online publication. DOI: 10.1007/s44217-025-00576-6

Sekti, B. A. (2025). AI Technology Management Concepts and Strategies. In *AI Technology Management and Value Creation* (pp. 1–32). DOI: 10.4018/979-8-3373-2497-5.ch001

Taheri, M., Tan, K., Flaten, O. E., & Cyma-Wejchenig, M. (2026). Enhancing Education Training with A Virtual Reality-Based Simulator Integrated Generative AI. *Lecture Notes in Computer Science, 15743 LNCS*, 394–406. DOI: 10.1007/978-3-031-97781-7_29

Vaghasiya, N., Zalavadia, K., & Vyas, A. (2026). AI-Based Quiz Generation Using ChatGPT. *Lecture Notes in Networks and Systems, 1533 LNNS*, 377–389. DOI: 10.1007/978-981-96-9196-8_25

Wang, T., Long, T., Mei, A., Li, J., & Zhi, Z. (2026). Fusing Six-Hat thinking with AI: How the Green Hat and ChatGPT Co-Regulate pre-service teachers' instructional design—insights from epistemic network analysis. *Thinking Skills and Creativity*, *59*, 102025. Advance online publication. DOI: 10.1016/j.tsc.2025.102025

Yang, W., Li, H., & Lee, J. C.-K. (2025). Tailoring AI agents for early learning: The Creative Project Approach. *Computers and Education: Artificial Intelligence*, *9*, 100473. Advance online publication. DOI: 10.1016/j.caeai.2025.100473

KEY TERMS AND DEFINITIONS

AI Literacy: AI literacy is the ability to critically, ethically, and effectively understand, evaluate, and use artificial intelligence tools in teaching and learning processes.

AI Supported Learning: AI supported learning describes educational environments in which artificial intelligence tools assist learners and educators through personalization, feedback, and adaptive instructional support.

Artificial Intelligence (AI): Artificial intelligence refers to computational systems designed to perform tasks that typically require human intelligence, such as reasoning, learning, problem solving, and language processing, within educational contexts.

Ethical Use of AI in Education: Ethical use of AI in education involves the responsible application of AI technologies with attention to academic integrity, data privacy, transparency, fairness, and human oversight.

Generative AI: Generative AI refers to AI systems capable of producing new content, such as text, images, or solutions, based on patterns learned from large scale datasets.

Compilation of References

Abarzosa, V. J., & Balaba, E. I. (2025). The Negative Effects of Over-Reliance on AI Tools in IT Student Learning. *Wisdom Journal of Humanities and Social Sciences, 2*(5 (May)), 20-29. https://so19.tci-thaijo.org/index.php/WJHS/article/view/1789

Abdelaal, E., Mills, J., & Walpita Gamage, S. (2019). Artificial intelligence is a tool for cheating academic integrity.

Adams, R. (2020). Ofqual's algorithm and the problem of fairness in education. *The Guardian*.

Adams, T. E., Jones, S. H., & Ellis, C. (2015). Autoethnography: Understanding qualitative research.

Adams, R., & Thompson, T. L. (2023). *Researching a posthuman world: Interviews with digital objects*. Palgrave Macmillan.

Adams, T. E., & Herrmann, A. F. (2020). Expanding our autoethnographic future. *Journal of Autoethnography, 1*(1), 1–8. DOI: 10.1525/joae.2020.1.1.1

Agboola, O. P., & Yassin, Y. N. H. M. (2025, July). AI applications in education: Enhancing human creativity through collaborative design. In *International Conference on Knowledge Management in Organizations* (pp. 45-69). Cham: Springer Nature Switzerland. DOI: 10.1007/978-3-031-95901-1_4

Aghaziarati, A., Nejatifar, S., & Abedi, A. (2023). Artificial intelligence in education: Investigating teacher attitudes. https://www.researchgate.net/profile/Sara-Nejatifar/publication/379042121_Artificial_Intelligence_in_Education_Investigating_Teacher_Attitudes/links/66c794bfc2eaa500230fbcc4/Artificial-Intelligence-in-Education-Investigating-Teacher-Attitudes.pdf

Ahmad, K., Iqbal, W., El-Hassan, A., Qadir, J., Benhaddou, D., Ayyash, M., & Al-Fuqaha, A. (2024). Data-Driven Artificial Intelligence in Education: A Comprehensive Review. *IEEE Transactions on Learning Technologies*, *17*, 12–31. DOI: 10.1109/TLT.2023.3314610

Ahmad, S. F., Alam, M. M., Rahmat, M. K., Mubarik, M. S., & Hyder, S. I. (2022). Academic and administrative role of artificial intelligence in education. *Sustainability (Basel)*, *14*(3), 1101. DOI: 10.3390/su14031101

Akgun, S., & Greenhow, C. (2022). Artificial intelligence in education: Addressing ethical challenges in K–12 settings. *AI and Ethics*, *2*(3), 431–440. DOI: 10.1007/s43681-021-00096-7 PMID: 34790956

Alam, A., & Mohanty, A. (2023). Educational technology: Exploring the convergence of technology and pedagogy through mobility, interactivity, AI, and learning tools. *Cogent Engineering*, *10*(2), 2283282. DOI: 10.1080/23311916.2023.2283282

Alam, S., Hameed, A., Madej, M., & Kobylarek, A. (2024). Perception and practice of using Artificial Intelligence in education: An opinion based study. *XLinguae*, *17*(1), 216–233. DOI: 10.18355/XL.2024.17.01.15

Alejandro, I. M. V., Sanchez, J. M. P., Sumalinog, G. G., Mananay, J. A., Goles, C. E., & Fernandez, C. B. (2024). Pre-service teachers' technology acceptance of artificial intelligence (AI) applications in education. *STEM Education*, *4*(4), 445–465. DOI: 10.3934/steme.2024024

Aleven, V., Baraniuk, R., Brunskill, E., Crossley, S., Demszky, D., Fancsali, S., & Xing, W. (2023, June). Towards the Future of AI-Augmented Human Tutoring in Math Learning. In International Conference on Artificial Intelligence in Education (pp. 26 – 31). Springer Nature Switzerland. https://link.springer.com/chapter/10.1007/978-3-031-36336-8_310.1007/978-3-031-36336-8_3

Aleven, V., Blankestijn, J., Lawrence, L., Nagashima, T., & Taatgen, N. (2022). A dashboard to support teachers during students' self-paced AI-supported problem-solving practice. In I. Hilliger, P. J. Muñoz-Merino, T. De Laet, A. Ortega-Arranz, & T. Farrell, *Educating for a New Future: Making Sense of Technology-Enhanced Learning Adoption Cham.* https://doi.org/10.1007/978-3-031-16290-9_2

Alexander, R. (2008). *Towards dialogic teaching: Rethinking classroom talk* (4th ed.). Dialogos.

Alfiras, M. I. I., Emran, A. Q., & Mohamed, A. M. (2025). Ethics and governance of generative AI in education: A systematic review on responsible adoption. *Discover Education*, *5*(1), 37. DOI: 10.1007/s44217-025-01051-y

Alfredo, R., Echeverria, V., Jin, Y., Yan, L., Swiecki, Z., Gašević, D., & Martinez-Maldonado, R. (2024). Human-centred learning analytics and AI in education: A systematic literature review. *Computers and Education: Artificial Intelligence*, *6*, 100215. DOI: 10.1016/j.caeai.2024.100215

Algerafi, M. A., Zhou, Y., Alfadda, H., & Wijaya, T. T. (2023). Understanding the factors influencing higher education students' intention to adopt artificial intelligence-based robots. *IEEE Access : Practical Innovations, Open Solutions*, *11*, 99752–99764. https://ieeexplore.ieee.org/abstract/document/10247529. DOI: 10.1109/ACCESS.2023.3314499

Aljabr, A., & Al-Ahdal, A. A. M. H. (2024). Ethical and pedagogical implications of AI in language education: An empirical study at Ha'il University. *Acta Psychologica*, *251*, 1–8. DOI: 10.1016/j.actpsy.2024.104605 PMID: 39549599

All India Council for Technical Education. (2020). National [*Implementation guidelines for technical education*. Government of India.]. *Educational Policy*, •••, 2020.

Álvarez Guayara, , D. LEspinosa Sarmiento, , D. M. (2025). Ambiente de aprendizaje híbrido para el fortalecimiento de las competencias investigativas de estudiantes de ingeniería. *Academia y Virtualidad, 18*(2), 117-133. DOI: 10.18359/ravi.7621

Al-Zahrani, A. M. (2024). Unveiling the shadows: Beyond the hype of AI in education. *Heliyon*, *10*(9), e30696. DOI: 10.1016/j.heliyon.2024.e30696 PMID: 38737255

Al-Zahrani, A. M., & Alasmari, T. M. (2024). Exploring the impact of artificial intelligence on higher education: The dynamics of ethical, social, and educational implications. *Humanities & Social Sciences Communications*, *11*(1), 1–12. DOI: 10.1057/s41599-024-03432-4

An, G. K., & Ngo, T. T. A. (2025). Unravelling success in AI-powered personalized learning in Vietnam: A study on the interplay of platform features and psychological responses. *Journal of Information Technology Education*, *24*, 41. Advance online publication. DOI: 10.28945/5668

Anwar, N., Rahaman, R., Widodo, A. M., Sekti, B. A., Erzed, N., Santiago Tangkudung, R. R., Muchlis, M., Yuhefizar, Y., & Budhisantosa, N. (2025). Sustainable cybersecurity in the AI era: Innovations in green computing and security. In *Sustainable Information Security in the Age of AI and Green Computing* (pp. 603–620). DOI: 10.4018/979-8-3693-8034-5.ch030

Anwar, N., Sekti, B. A., Widodo, A. M., Erzed, N., Gunawan, H., Tangkudung, R. R. S., Muchlis, M., & Budhisantosa, N. (2025). Emerging innovations in AI and green computing for cybersecurity. In *Sustainable Information Security in the Age of AI and Green Computing* (pp. 17–38). DOI: 10.4018/979-8-3693-8034-5.ch002

Ashoori Tootkaboni, A., & Maghsoudi, M. (2025). Exploring Pre-service EFL Teachers' Readiness to Integrate AI: A UTAUT2 Model Analysis. *Journal of Education, 00220574251379029*, 00220574251379029. Advance online publication. DOI: 10.1177/00220574251379029

Ateeq, M., Alnuaimi, S., & Al-Kuwari, H. (2024). Artificial intelligence in education: Implications for academic integrity and the shift toward holistic assessment. *Frontiers in Education*, *9*, 1–11. DOI: 10.3389/feduc.2024.1470979

Aust, A., & Caukin, N. (2024). AI and academic integrity: Guiding educators through the evolving challenge of student plagiarism. *International Journal of the Whole Child*, *9*(2), 73–78. https://libjournals.mtsu.edu/index.php/ijwc/article/view/2560/1518

Autor, D. H. (2015). Why are there still so many jobs? The history and future of workplace automation. *The Journal of Economic Perspectives*, *29*(3), 3–30. DOI: 10.1257/jep.29.3.3

Avci, H., Lunn, S. J., & Hazari, Z. (2025). Exploring STEM educators ' perspectives on the integration of AI-enabled technologies in teaching and learning. *Computers and Education Open*, *9*, 1–12. DOI: 10.1016/j.caeo.2025.100304

Avsheniuk, N., Seminikhyna, N., Ruban, L., & Sviatiuk, Y. (2025). Exploring overreliance on AI tools in English for specific purposes courses: challenges and implications for learning and academic integrity. https://papers.ssrn.com/sol3/papers.cfm?abstract_id=5238641

Baek, E., Guo, Q., & Wilson, R. (2025). Transforming student support with AI-powered tutoring. In Wang, V. (Ed.), (pp. 335–370). Advances in Computational Intelligence and Robotics. IGI Global Scientific Publishing., DOI: 10.4018/979-8-3373-2397-8.ch012

Bai, J. Y. H., Zawacki-Richter, O., & Muskens, W.BAI. (2024). RE-EXAMINING THE FUTURE PROSPECTS OF ARTIFICIAL INTELLIGENCE IN EDUCATION IN LIGHT OF THE GDPR AND ChatGPT. *Turkish Online Journal of Distance Education*, *25*(1), 20–32. DOI: 10.17718/tojde.1248901

Bandara, W. M. H. K., & Senanayaka, S. G. M. S. D. (2024, April). Use of artificial intelligence in education: A systematic review. In *2024 International Research Conference on Smart Computing and Systems Engineering (SCSE)* (Vol. 7, pp. 1-5). IEEE. DOI: 10.1109/SCSE61872.2024.10550527

Bangay, C., & Nzimande, B. (2020). COVID-19 and educational disruption in the Global South. *Educational Research for Social Change*, *9*(1), 1–7.

Banker, S., & Khetani, S. (2019). Algorithm overdependence: How the use of algorithmic recommendation systems can increase risks to consumer well-being. *Journal of Public Policy & Marketing*, *38*(4), 500–515. DOI: 10.1177/0743915619858057

Baťko, J., Frolík, D., Rohlíková, L., Vejvodová, J., Visvizi, A., Voltrová, M., & Vrbová, V. (2026). AI and Pre-service Teachers: Attitudes to and the Prospect of Applying AI-Based Tools in Education. *Springer Proceedings in Complexity*, 271–283. DOI: 10.1007/978-3-031-78623-5_23

Bautista, A., Estrada, C., Jaravata, A. M., Mangaser, L. M., Narag, F., Soquila, R., & Asuncion, R. J. (2024). Preservice Teachers' Readiness towards Integrating AI-Based Tools in Education: A TPACK Approach. *Educational Process: International Journal*, *13*(3), 40–68. DOI: 10.22521/edupij.2024.133.3

Beauchamp, C., & Thomas, L. (2009). Understanding teacher identity: An overview of issues in the literature and implications for teacher education. *Cambridge Journal of Education*, *39*(2), 175–189. DOI: 10.1080/03057640902902252

Beck, U. (1992). Risk society: Towards a new modernity. *Sage (Atlanta, Ga.)*.

Belenguer, L. (2022). AI bias: Exploring discriminatory algorithmic decision-making models. *AI and Ethics*, *2*(4), 771–787. DOI: 10.1007/s43681-022-00138-8 PMID: 35194591

Ben Zion, Y., Yakov, S., Abramovitch, E., Balter, G., & Davidovitch, N. (2025). AI-based teaching evaluations: How well do they reflect student perceptions? *Computers and Education: Artificial Intelligence*, *9*, 100448. DOI: 10.1016/j.caeai.2025.100448

Bender, E. M., Gebru, T., McMillan-Major, A., & Shmitchell, S. (2021). On the dangers of stochastic parrots: Can language models be too big? In Irani, L., Kannan, S., Mitchell, M., & Robinson, D. (Eds.), *Proceedings of the 2021 ACM conference on fairness, accountability, and transparency* (pp. 610–623). Association for Computing Machinery, New York, NY, United States. DOI: 10.1145/3442188.3445922

Biagini, G. (2025). Towards an AI-Literate Future: A systematic literature review exploring education, ethics, and applications. *International Journal of Artificial Intelligence in Education*, *35*(4), 1–51. DOI: 10.1007/s40593-025-00466-w

Biesta, G. (2015). *Good education in an age of measurement: Ethics, politics, democracy*. Routledge. DOI: 10.4324/9781315634319

Biggs, J., & Tang, C. (2011). *Teaching for quality learning at university* (4th ed.). Open University Press.

Bilbao-Eraña, A., & Arroyo-Sagasta, A. (2025). Fostering AI literacy in pre-service teachers: Impact of a training intervention on awareness, attitude and trust in AI. *Frontiers in Education*, *10*, 1668078. Advance online publication. DOI: 10.3389/feduc.2025.1668078

Bittle, K., & El-Gayar, O. (2025). Generative AI and academic integrity in higher education: A systematic review and research agenda. *Information (Basel)*, *16*(4), 296. DOI: 10.3390/info16040296

Bloom, B. S., Krathwohl, D. R., & Anderson, L. W. (2001). *A taxonomy for learning, teaching, and assessing: A revision of Bloom's taxonomy of educational objectives*. Longman.

Bond, M. (2020). Schools and emergency remote education during the COVID-19 pandemic. *Educational Technology Research and Development*, *68*(6), 1–5. DOI: 10.1007/s11423-020-09816-3

Bonfield, C. A., Salter, M., Longmuir, A., Benson, M., & Adachi, C. (2020). Transformation or evolution? Education 4.0, teaching and learning in the digital age. *Higher Education Pedagogies*, *5*(1), 223–246. DOI: 10.1080/23752696.2020.1816847

Boonstra, L. (2025). Prompt engineering. Google. https://www.kaggle.com/whitepaper-prompt-engineering

Borup, J., West, R. E., & Graham, C. R. (2020). Improving online social presence through asynchronous video. *The Internet and Higher Education*, *47*, 100759. DOI: 10.1016/j.iheduc.2020.100759

Boscardin, C. K., Gin, B., Golde, P. B., & Hauer, K. E. (2024). ChatGPT and Generative Artificial Intelligence for Medical Education: Potential Impact and Opportunity. *Academic Medicine*, *99*(1), 22–27. DOI: 10.1097/ACM.0000000000005439 PMID: 37651677

Bosch, N., Härkki, T., & Seitamaa-Hakkarainen, P. (2025). Teachers as reflective learning experience designers: Bringing design thinking into school-based design and maker education. *International Journal of Child-Computer Interaction*, *43*, 100695. Advance online publication. DOI: 10.1016/j.ijcci.2024.100695

Boulay, B. (2024). Pedagogy, Cognition, Human Rights, and Social Justice. *International Journal of Artificial Intelligence in Education, 34*(1), 116–121. DOI: 10.1007/s40593-023-00355-0

Bourdieu, P. (1984). *Distinction: A social critique of the judgement of taste.* Harvard University Press.

Bourdieu, P., & Passeron, J.-C. (1977). Reproduction in education, society and culture. *Sage (Atlanta, Ga.).*

Brandao, P. R. (2025). The impact of artificial intelligence on modern society. *AI, 6*(8), 190. DOI: 10.3390/ai6080190

Broussard, M. (2018). *Artificial unintelligence: How computers misunderstand the world.* Mit Press. DOI: 10.7551/mitpress/11022.001.0001

Brown, A., & Cariveau, T. (2024). A systematic review of simultaneous prompting and prompt delay procedures. *Journal of Behavioral Education, 33*(1), 1–22. DOI: 10.1007/s10864-022-09481-6

Bryk, A. S., & Schneider, B. (2002). *Trust in schools: A core resource for improvement.* Russell Sage Foundation.

Bulathwela, S., Pérez-Ortiz, M., Holloway, C., Cukurova, M., & Shawe-Taylor, J. (2024). Artificial Intelligence Alone Will Not Democratise Education: On Educational Inequality, Techno-Solutionism and Inclusive Tools. *Sustainability (Basel), 16*(2), 1–20. DOI: 10.3390/su16020781

Bulawan, A. A., Tilos, F. G., Bulawan, A., Samonte, J., Alejo, K., & Carasicas, M. (2023). The lived experiences of students in learning with technology in Noveleta senior high school: A descriptive phenomenological research study. *International Journal of Advanced Multidisciplinary Research and Studies, 3*(4), 438–441. https://www.multiresearchjournal.com/admin/uploads/archives/archive-1690182667.pdf

Buolamwini, J., & Gebru, T. (2018). Gender shades: Intersectional accuracy disparities in commercial gender classification. *Conference on fairness, accountability and transparency, 81*, 1–15. http://proceedings.mlr.press/v81/buolamwini18a.html

Cajueiro, D. O., & Celestino, V. R. R. (2026). A comprehensive review of artificial intelligence regulation. *Journal of Economy and Technology, 4*, 77–91. DOI: 10.1016/j.ject.2025.07.001

Carrillo, C., Flores, M. A., & Mena, J. (2025). Artificial intelligence in the context of teacher education: Emerging themes and critical issues. *European Journal of Teacher Education, 48*(5), 1143–1162. DOI: 10.1080/02619768.2025.2584283

Carr, N. (2010). *The shallows: How the internet is changing the way we think, read and remember*. Atlantic Books Ltd.

Castillo-Martínez, I. M., Flores-Bueno, D., Gómez-Puente, S. M., & Vite-León, V. O. (2024). AI in higher education: A systematic literature review. *Frontiers in Education, 9*, 1391485. Advance online publication. DOI: 10.3389/feduc.2024.1391485

Cavoukian, A. (2011). Privacy by design. *In IGI Global eBooks* (pp. 170–208). DOI: 10.4018/978-1-61350-501-4.ch007

Central Board of Secondary Education. (2022). *Guidelines on digital learning and online assessment*. Government of India.

Chan, C. K. Y. (2023). A comprehensive AI policy education framework for university teaching and learning. *International Journal of Educational Technology in Higher Education, 20*(1), 38. DOI: 10.1186/s41239-023-00408-3

Chang, D. H., Lin, M. P. C., Hajian, S., & Wang, Q. Q. (2023). Educational design principles of using AI chatbot that supports self-regulated learning in education: Goal setting, feedback, and personalization. *Sustainability (Basel), 15*(17), 12921. DOI: 10.3390/su151712921

Chan, J. (2025). Students' perceptions of "AI-giarism": Investigating changes in understandings of academic misconduct. *Education and Information Technologies, 30*(6), 8087–8108. DOI: 10.1007/s10639-024-13151-7

Charlton, P., Magoulas, G., & Laurillard, D. (2012). Enabling creative learning design through semantic technologies. *Technology, Pedagogy and Education, 21*(2), 231–253. DOI: 10.1080/1475939X.2012.698165

Chassignol, M., Khoroshavina, A., Klimova, A., & Bilyatdinova, A. (2018). Artificial Intelligence trends in education. *Procedia Computer Science, 136*, 16–24. DOI: 10.1016/j.procs.2018.08.233

Chen, S., & She, W. (2023) Values and Ethics- How artificial intelligence will better serve humanity. B. Majoul et al. (Eds.): ICLAHD 2022, ASSEHR 726, pp. 296 – 300, 2023. DOI: 10.2991/978-2-494069-97-8_37

Cheng, Y., Chen, C.-H., & Huang, C.-Y. (2022). Students' perceptions of conversational agents in learning contexts. *Computers & Education, 181*, 104461. DOI: 10.1016/j.compedu.2022.104461

Chen, L., Chen, P., & Lin, Z. (2020). Artificial intelligence in education: A review. *IEEE Access : Practical Innovations, Open Solutions, 8*, 75264–75278. DOI: 10.1109/ACCESS.2020.2988510

Chen, X., Zou, D., & Xie, H. (2023). Implications of ChatGPT and generative AI for education. *Computers in Human Behavior, 145*, 107730.

Chi, M. T. H., & Wylie, R. (2014). The ICAP framework: Linking cognitive engagement to active learning outcomes. *Educational Psychologist, 49*(4), 219–243. DOI: 10.1080/00461520.2014.965823

Chin, R. T. (2018). Education in the Artificial Intelligence Era - QS WOWNEWS. https://qswownews.com/education-in-the-artificial-intelligence-era/

Chin, C., & Osborne, J. (2008). Students' questions: A potential resource for teaching and learning science. *Studies in Science Education, 44*(1), 1–39. DOI: 10.1080/03057260701828101

Chiu, T. K., & Rospigliosi, P. A. (2025). Encouraging human-AI collaboration in interactive learning environments. *Interactive Learning Environments, 33*(2), 921–924. DOI: 10.1080/10494820.2025.2471199

Chou, P. N., & Chan, T. W. (2021). Designing AI-enhanced learning environments. *Educational Technology Research and Development, 69*(4), 1817–1838.

Chowdhury, A., Akter, S., Sultana, J., & Rahman, A. (2025). Computers and Education : Artificial Intelligence Can generative AI Be an effective Co-Teacher? An experiment. *Computers and Education: Artificial Intelligence, 8*(May), 1–15. DOI: 10.1016/j.caeai.2025.100418

Chowdhury, A., Bari, A., Sultana, J., Chowdhury, R., Meem, F., Islam, A., Mahmud, S., Jahan, I., & Sarkar, M. (2024). Computers and Education : Artificial Intelligence Why do students use ChatGPT? Answering through a triangulation approach. *Computers and Education: Artificial Intelligence, 6*(January), 1–13. DOI: 10.1016/j.caeai.2024.100208

Çiftci, H. (2025). Navigating ethics: EFL learners' awareness and use of AI tools in writing classes. *Focus on ELT Journal, 7*(2), 22–46. DOI: 10.14744/felt.7.2.2

Clark, A. (2008). *Supersizing the mind: Embodiment, action, and cognitive extension*. Oxford University Press. DOI: 10.1093/acprof:oso/9780195333213.001.0001

Clarke, V., & Braun, V. (2017). Thematic analysis. *The Journal of Positive Psychology, 12*(3), 297–298. DOI: 10.1080/17439760.2016.1262613

Coghlan, S., Miller, T., & Paterson, J. (2021). Good proctor or "Big Brother"? Ethics of online exam supervision technologies. *Philosophy & Technology, 34*(4), 1581–1606. DOI: 10.1007/s13347-021-00476-1 PMID: 34485025

Cook-Sather, A. (2014). Student-faculty partnership in explorations of pedagogical practice. *Teaching and Learning Together in Higher Education, 1*(3), 1–8.

Coşgun, G. E. (2025). Artificial intelligence literacy in assessment: Empowering pre-service teachers to design effective exam questions for language learning. *British Educational Research Journal, 51*(5), 2340–2357. Advance online publication. DOI: 10.1002/berj.4177

Cotton, D. R. E., Cotton, P. A., & Shipway, J. R. (2023). ChatGPT: A disruptive technology in higher education. *Innovations in Education and Teaching International.*

Cotton, D. R. E., Cotton, P. A., & Shipway, J. R. (2023). Chatting and cheating: Ensuring academic integrity in the era of ChatGPT. *Innovations in Education and Teaching International, 61*(2), 228–239. DOI: 10.1080/14703297.2023.2190148

Crawford, K. (2021). *The atlas of AI: Power, politics, and the planetary costs of artificial intelligence*. Yale University Press.

Creely, E., & Carabott, K. (2025). Teaching and learning with AI: An Integrated AI-Oriented Pedagogical Model. *Australian Educational Researcher, 52*(6), 4633–4654. DOI: 10.1007/s13384-025-00913-6

Creswell, J. W., & Poth, C. N. (2016). *Qualitative inquiry and research design: Choosing among five approaches*. Sage Publications. Sage Publications. https://www.sagepub.com/

Cuban, L. (2020). Reforming the grammar of schooling again and again. *American Journal of Education, 126*(4), 665–671. DOI: 10.1086/709959

Czerkawski, B., & Berti, M. (2021). Learning experience design for augmented reality. *Research in Learning Technology, 29*. Advance online publication. DOI: 10.25304/rlt.v29.2429

D'Mello, S. K., & Graesser, A. (2021). Automatic analysis of learners' emotions. *Annual Review of Psychology, 72*, 589–618.

Dadhich, A., Yadav, R., Yadav, M., Huzooree, G., & Dewasiri, N. J. (2025). Teacher-AI Collaboration and the Future of the Educator's Role. In *Transformative AI Practices for Personalized Learning Strategies* (pp. 355–378). IGI Global Scientific Publishing. DOI: 10.4018/979-8-3693-8744-3.ch013

Daher, R. (2025). Integrating AI literacy into teacher education: A critical perspective paper. *Discover Artificial Intelligence, 5*(1), 217. DOI: 10.1007/s44163-025-00475-7

Darling-Hammond, L., Flook, L., Cook-Harvey, C., Barron, B., & Osher, D. (2020). Implications for educational practice of the science of learning and development. *Applied Developmental Science, 24*(2), 97–140. DOI: 10.1080/10888691.2018.1537791

Darling-Hammond, L., Hyler, M. E., & Gardner, M. (2017). *Effective teacher professional development.* Learning Policy Institute. DOI: 10.54300/122.311

Darvishi, A., Khosravi, H., Sadiq, S., Gašević, D., & Siemens, G. (2024). Impact of AI assistance on student agency. *Computers & Education, 210*, 104967. DOI: 10.1016/j.compedu.2023.104967

Das, P. K. (2024). Artificial intelligence in higher education: Opportunities, challenges, and preventions. *Asian Journal of Management, 15*(3), 238–244. DOI: 10.52711/2321-5763.2024.00037

Davies, B. (1994). On the neglect of pedagogy in educational studies and its consequences. *Journal of In-service Education, 20*(1), 17–34. DOI: 10.1080/0305763940200103

Dawson, P. (2020). *Defending assessment security in a digital world: Preventing E-Cheating and supporting academic integrity in higher education.* https://www.taylorfrancis.com/books/9780429324178

Deriba, F. G., & Sanusi, I. T. (2025). Artificial intelligence in Ethiopian school curriculum: Educators' practices, challenges, and recommendations. *Computers and Education Open, 8*, 100251. DOI: 10.1016/j.caeo.2025.100251

Downes, S. (2022). Connectivism in 2022: Extending learning networks. *Journal of Online Learning Research, 8*(1), 33–48.

Du Plooy, E., Casteleijn, D., & Franzsen, D. (2024). Personalized adaptive learning in higher education: A scoping review. *Heliyon, 10*(21), e39630. DOI: 10.1016/j.heliyon.2024.e39630 PMID: 39524879

Dunlosky, J., Rawson, K. A., Marsh, E. J., Nathan, M. J., & Willingham, D. T. (2013). Improving students' learning with effective learning techniques. *Psychological Science in the Public Interest, 14*(1), 4–58. DOI: 10.1177/1529100612453266 PMID: 26173288

Dwivedi, Y. K., Kshetri, N., Hughes, L., Slade, E. L., Jeyaraj, A., Kar, A. K., Baabdullah, A. M., Koohang, A., Raghavan, V., Ahuja, M., Albanna, H., Albashrawi, M. A., Al-Busaidi, A. S., Balakrishnan, J., Barlette, Y., Basu, S., Bose, I., Brooks, L., Buhalis, D., & Wright, R. (2023). Opinion Paper: "So what if ChatGPT wrote it?" Multidisciplinary perspectives on opportunities, challenges and implications of generative conversational AI for research, practice and policy. *International Journal of Information Management, 71*, 1–63. DOI: 10.1016/j.ijinfomgt.2023.102642

Eaton, S. E. (2021). Plagiarism in higher education. *In ABC-CLIO eBooks*. DOI: 10.5040/9798400697142

Edeni, C. A., Adeleye, O. O., & Adeniyi, I. S.Chima Abimbola EdeniOlabisi Oluwakemi AdeleyeIdowu Sulaimon Adeniyi. (2024). The role of AI-enhanced tools in overcoming socioeconomic barriers in education: A conceptual analysis. *World Journal of Advanced Research and Reviews*, *21*(3), 944–951. DOI: 10.30574/wjarr.2024.21.3.0780

Edwards, J., Nguyen, A., Lämsä, J., Sobocinski, M., Whitehead, R., Dang, B., Roberts, A.-S., & Järvelä, S. (2025). Human-AI collaboration: Designing artificial agents to facilitate socially shared regulation among learners. *British Journal of Educational Technology*, *56*(2), 712–733. DOI: 10.1111/bjet.13534

Ekin, S. (2023). Prompt engineering for ChatGPT: A quick guide to techniques, tips, and best practices. *Authorea Preprints*.

Ellis, C., Adams, T. E., & Bochner, A. P. (2011). Autoethnography: An overview. *Historical social research. Historische Sozialforschung*, •••, 273–290. https://www.jstor.org/stable/23032294

Ellis, R., Han, F., & Cook, H. (2025). Qualitatively different teacher experiences of teaching with generative artificial intelligence. *International Journal of Educational Technology in Higher Education*, *22*(1), 33. Advance online publication. DOI: 10.1186/s41239-025-00532-2

Espino, C. (2025). Pre-service teachers' perspectives on generative AI: Insights, applications, and challenges in the classroom. *International Journal on Studies in Education*, *7*(3), 732–747. DOI: 10.46328/ijonse.1930

Essien, A., Bukoye, O. T., O'Dea, X., & Kremantzis, M. (2024). The influence of AI text generators on critical thinking skills in UK business schools. *Studies in Higher Education*, *49*(5), 865–882. DOI: 10.1080/03075079.2024.2316881

Facione, P. A. (2015). *Critical thinking: What it is and why it counts*. Insight Assessment.

Falebita, O. (2024). Evaluating Artificial Intelligence Anxiety Among Pre-Service Teachers in University Teacher Education Programs. Journal of Mathematics Instruction. *Social Research and Opinion*, *4*(1), 1–16. DOI: 10.58421/misro.v4i1.309

Farhood, H., Nyden, M., Beheshti, A., & Muller, S. (2025). AI-based personalised learning in education. *Discover Artificial Intelligence*, *5*(1), 331. DOI: 10.1007/s44163-025-00598-x

Feldman-Maggor, Y., Cukurova, M., Kent, C., & Alexandron, G. (2025).

Feldman-Maggor, Y., Cukurova, M., Kent, C., & Alexandron, G. (2025, December). The impact of explainable AI on teachers' trust and acceptance of AI EdTech recommendations: The power of domain-specific explanations. *International Journal of Artificial Intelligence in Education*, *35*(5), 2889–2922. DOI: 10.1007/s40593-025-00486-6

Feng, T., Xu, J., & Wu, K. (2025). Design of Multimedia Education and Teaching Management System based on Artificial Intelligence and Computational Technology. *Scalable Computing: Practice and Experience*, *26*(4), 1653–1670. DOI: 10.12694/scpe.v26i4.4531

Filipović, A. M., Fastić-Pajk, I., Puljiz, H., & Šabić, I. (2026a). AI-Driven Customization of Adaptive Learning Content: Lessons from Applying LLMs in Personalized Education. *Communications in Computer and Information Science, 2609 CCIS*, 67–81. DOI: 10.1007/978-3-032-02801-3_5

Fitria, T. N. (2021). Artificial intelligence (AI) in education: Using AI tools for teaching and learning process. In *Prosiding Seminar Nasional & Call for Paper STIE AAS* (pp. 134 - 147). https://www.researchgate.net/profile/Tira-Nur-Fitria/publication/357447234_Artificial_Intelligence_AI_In_Education_Using_AI_Tools_for_Teaching_and_Learning_Process/links/61ce7029e669ee0f5c76b2ba/Artificial-Intelligence-AI-In-Education-Using-AI-Tools-for-Teaching-and-Learning-Process.pdf

Flavell, J. H. (1979). Metacognition and cognitive monitoring: A new area of cognitive–developmental inquiry. *The American Psychologist*, *34*(10), 906–911. DOI: 10.1037/0003-066X.34.10.906

Flores, M. A., & Day, C. (2006). Contexts which shape and reshape new teachers' identities: A multi-perspective study. *Teaching and Teacher Education*, *22*(2), 219–232. DOI: 10.1016/j.tate.2005.09.002

Floridi, L. (2019). Translating principles into practices of digital ethics: Five risks of being unethical. *Philosophy & Technology*, *32*(2), 185–193. DOI: 10.1007/s13347-019-00354-x

Floridi, L., Cowls, J., Beltrametti, M., Chatila, R., Chazerand, P., Dignum, V., Luetge, C., Madelin, R., Pagallo, U., Rossi, F., Schafer, B., Valcke, P., & Vayena, E. (2018). AI4People—An ethical framework for a good AI society: Opportunities, risks, principles, and recommendations. *Minds and Machines*, *28*(4), 689–707. DOI: 10.1007/s11023-018-9482-5 PMID: 30930541

Foltýnek, T., & Newton, P. M. (2026). What Does YouTube Advise Students About Bypassing AI-Text Detection Tools? A Pragmatic Analysis. *Journal of Academic Ethics*, *24*(1), 8. Advance online publication. DOI: 10.1007/s10805-025-09675-3

Foucault, M. (1977). *Discipline and punish: The birth of the prison*. Pantheon Books.

Freire, P. (1970). Pedagogy of the oppressed. *Continuum : an Interdisciplinary Journal on Continuity of Care*.

Frey, C. B., & Osborne, M. A. (2017). The future of employment. *Technological Forecasting and Social Change*, *114*, 254–280. DOI: 10.1016/j.techfore.2016.08.019

Friesen, N., & Selwyn, N. (2022). Education and the limits of artificial intelligence. *British Journal of Educational Technology*, *53*(6), 1764–1777. DOI: 10.1111/bjet.13296

Fu, Y., & Weng, Z. (2024). Navigating the ethical terrain of AI in education: A systematic review on framing responsible human-centered AI practices. *Computers and Education Artificial Intelligence*, *7*, 1–20. DOI: 10.1016/j.caeai.2024.100306

Gabriel, F., Kennedy, J., Marrone, R., & Leonard, S. (2025). Pragmatic AI in education and its role in mathematics learning and teaching. *NPJ Science of Learning*, *10*(1), 26. Advance online publication. DOI: 10.1038/s41539-025-00315-4 PMID: 40348764

García-Vélez, R., Moreno, B. V., Ruiz-Ichazu, A., Rivera, D. M., & Rosero-Perez, E. (2021). Automating the Generation of Study Teams through Genetic Algorithms Based on Learning Styles in Higher Education. In *Advances in Intelligent Systems and Computing* (Vol. 1213). AISC., DOI: 10.1007/978-3-030-51328-3_38

Garg, A., Singh, A., & Yanan, J. (2024). Exploring the Impact of Digital Detoxification on Higher Education Students' Learning. In *Business drivers in promoting digital detoxification* (pp. 111-126). IGI Global Scientific Publishing.

Ge, W. (2017). Learning by expanding: An activity-theoretical approach to developmental research (2nd ed.). Yrj? Engestr?m. *Frontiers of Education in China, 12*(1), 130–132. DOI: 10.3868/s110-006-017-0011-8

George, A. S. (2023). Preparing students for an AI-driven world: Rethinking curriculum and pedagogy in the age of artificial intelligence. *Partners Universal Innovative Research Publication*, *1*(2), 112–136. DOI: 10.5281/zenodo.10245675

Giannakos, M., Azevedo, R., Brusilovsky, P., Cukurova, M., Dimitriadis, Y., Hernandez-Leo, D., Järvelä, S., Mavrikis, M., & Rienties, B. (2025). The promise and challenges of generative AI in education. *Behaviour & Information Technology*, *44*(11), 2518–2544. DOI: 10.1080/0144929X.2024.2394886

Giddens, A. (1991). *Modernity and self-identity: Self and society in the late modern age*. Stanford University Press.

Gligorea, I., Cioca, M., Oancea, R., Gorski, A. T., Gorski, H., & Tudorache, P. (2023). Adaptive learning using artificial intelligence in e-learning: A literature review. *Education Sciences*, *13*(12), 1216. DOI: 10.3390/educsci13121216

Goddiksen, M., Willum Johansen, M., Armond, A. C., Centa, M., Clavien, C., Gefenas, E., Globokar, R., Hogan, L., Kovács, N., Merit, M. T., Olsson, I. A. S., Poškutė, M., Quinn, U., Borlido Santos, J., Santos, R., Schöpfer, C., Strahovnik, V., Varga, O., Wall, P. J., & Lund, T. B. (2024). Grey zones and good practice: A European survey of academic integrity among undergraduate students. *Ethics & Behavior*, *34*(3), 199–217. DOI: 10.1080/10508422.2023.2187804

Gofman, M., & Jin, Z. (2024). Artificial Intelligence, Education, and Entrepreneurship. *The Journal of Finance*, *79*(1), 631–667. DOI: 10.1111/jofi.13302

Gómez-Chacón, I. M., & Marbán, J. M. (2024). Epistemic emotions and pre-service mathematics teachers' knowledge for teaching. *ZDM Mathematics Education*, *56*(6), 1223–1237. DOI: 10.1007/s11858-024-01624-5

Govender, R., Rzyankina, E., Bayaga, A., & Harun, I. (2025). Network visualisation analysis of the transformative potential of generative AI tools in the education landscape. *Discover Education*, *4*(1), 426. Advance online publication. DOI: 10.1007/s44217-025-00726-w

Gu, J., Han, Z., Chen, S., Beirami, A., He, B., Zhang, G., . . . Torr, P. (2023). A systematic survey of prompt engineering on vision-language foundation models (arXiv preprint arXiv:2307.12980). https://arxiv.org/abs/2307.12980

Guan, L., Zhang, Y., & Gu, M. M. (2025). Pre-service teachers preparedness for AI-integrated education: An investigation from perceptions, capabilities, and teachers' identity changes. *Computers and Education: Artificial Intelligence*, *8*, 100341. Advance online publication. DOI: 10.1016/j.caeai.2024.100341

Gümüş, M. M., Çakır, R., & Korkmaz, Ö. (2023). Investigation of pre-service teachers' sensitivity to cyberbullying, perceptions of digital ethics and awareness of digital data security. *Education and Information Technologies*, *28*(11), 14399–14421. DOI: 10.1007/s10639-023-11785-7

Gunder, A., Vito, M., Ramirez, M., & Arcolin, C. (2025). Bridging Borders: Global Faculty Learning Communities on AI for Transforming Teaching and Learning. *Ubiquity Proceedings*, *6*(1), 1–8. DOI: 10.5334/uproc.185

Guo, S., Halim, H. B. A., & Mohd Saad, M. R. B. M. (2025). Leveraging AI-enabled mobile learning platforms to enhance the effectiveness of English teaching in universities. *Scientific Reports*, *15*(1), 15873. Advance online publication. DOI: 10.1038/s41598-025-00801-0 PMID: 40335582

Gurung, V., Srivastava, S., & Chhetri, S. D. (2024). Sociodemographic variables affecting the occupational stress of senior secondary school teachers in Himachal Pradesh. In N. Mansour & L. M. Bujosa Vadell (Eds.), *Finance and law in the metaverse world* (Contributions to Finance and Accounting). Springer Nature Switzerland. DOI: 10.1007/978-3-031-67547-8_37

Gurung, V., & Srivastava, S. (2021). Importance of work-life balance: A review from gender perspective. *Contemporary Issues in Social Sciences*, *YICCISS-2021*, 154–165.

Gu, X., & Ericson, B. J. (2025). AI literacy in K–12 and higher education in the wake of generative AI: An integrative review [Preprint]. arXiv. https://arxiv.org/abs/2503.00079 DOI: 10.1145/3702652.3744217

Hagendorff, T., & Hagendorff, T. (2020). The Ethics of AI Ethics: An Evaluation of Guidelines. *Minds and Machines*, *30*(1), 99–120. DOI: 10.1007/s11023-020-09517-8

Hanifansyah, N. (2025). Reviving the Arabic Language Instinct: A Psycholinguistic and AI Synergy. *Al-Wazan: Journal of Arabic Education*, *3*(1), 32–47. DOI: 10.58223/al-wazan.v3i1.338

Han, Z., Battaglia, F., & Terlecky, S. R. (2024). Transforming limitations of ChatGPT into opportunities for active learning and prompt engineering. *The Innovation*, *5*(2), 100065. DOI: 10.59717/j.xinn-med.2024.100065

Hargreaves, A. (2001). Emotional geographies of teaching. *Teachers College Record*, *103*(6), 1056–1080. DOI: 10.1111/0161-4681.00142

Hattie, J., & Timperley, H. (2007). The power of feedback. *Review of Educational Research*, *77*(1), 81–112. DOI: 10.3102/003465430298487

Heffernan, N. T., & Heffernan, C. L. (2014). The ASSISTments ecosystem: Building a platform that brings scientists and teachers together for minimally invasive research on human learning and teaching. *International Journal of Artificial Intelligence in Education*, *24*(4), 470–497. DOI: 10.1007/s40593-014-0024-x

Hernández León, N., & Rodríguez-Conde, M.-J. (2024). Inteligencia artificial aplicada a la educación y la evaluación educativa en la Universidad: Introducción de sistemas de tutorización inteligentes, sistemas de reconocimiento y otras tendencias futuras. [RED]. *Revista de Educación a Distancia*, *24*(78). Advance online publication. DOI: 10.6018/red.594651

Herviana, A. (2025). Artificial intelligence in education: Opportunities and challenges of AI integration in Indonesian classrooms. *Journal of Smart Pedagogy and Education*, *1*(1), 33–45. DOI: 10.65101/spedu.v1i1.22

Hmelo-Silver, C. E., Duncan, R. G., & Chinn, C. A. (2007). Scaffolding and achievement in problem-based and inquiry learning. *Educational Psychologist*, *42*(2), 99–107. DOI: 10.1080/00461520701263368

Hok, C., Phin, K., Saroth, C., Sakhorn, S., Chheang, S., & Huot, S. (2026). Advancing ELT in Cambodia: Sustainability, digital inclusion, and culturally responsive pedagogy. *The Rubrics*, *8*(8), 79–99. DOI: 10.5281/zenodo.18149324

Holmes, W., Bialik, M., & Fadel, C. (2019). *Artificial intelligence in education promises and implications for teaching and learning*. Center for Curriculum Redesign. https://discovery.ucl.ac.uk/id/eprint/10139722

Holmes, W., Bialik, M., & Fadel, C. (2019). *Artificial intelligence in education promises and implications for teaching and learning*. Center for Curriculum Redesign.

Holmes, W., Bialik, M., & Fadel, C. (2019). *Artificial intelligence in education*. Center for Curriculum Redesign.

Holmes, W., Bialik, M., & Fadel, C. (2019). *Artificial intelligence in education: Promises and implications for teaching and learning*. Center for Curriculum Redesign.

Holmes, W., Bialik, M., & Fadel, C. (2022). *Artificial intelligence in education: Promises and implications*. Center for Curriculum Redesign.

Holmes, W., Porayska-Pomsta, K., Holstein, K., Sutherland, E., Baker, T., Shum, S. B., Santos, O. C., Rodrigo, M. T., Cukurova, M., Bittencourt, I. I., & Koedinger, K. R. (2022). Ethics of AI in education: Towards a community-wide framework. *International Journal of Artificial Intelligence in Education*, *32*(3), 504–526. DOI: 10.1007/s40593-021-00239-1

Holstein, K., McLaren, B. M., & Aleven, V. (2019). Co-designing a real-time classroom orchestration tool. *Proceedings of the 2019 CHI Conference on Human Factors in Computing Systems*, 1–14. https://doi.org/DOI: 10.1145/3290605.3300768

Holstein, K., McLaren, B. M., & Aleven, V. (2020). Human–AI collaborative teaching. *International Journal of Artificial Intelligence in Education, 30*(2), 215–240.

Hossain, S. K. S., & Ayodele, B. V. (2025). Revolutionizing Teaching and Learning of Material Science and Engineering in Chemical Engineering: The Impact of Generative AI. *Journal of Chemical Education, 102*(12), 5160–5168. DOI: 10.1021/acs.jchemed.5c00539

Hoya, F., Mah, D., Prilop, C. N., Jacobsen, L. J., & Weber, K. E. (2024). Pre-service teachers' AI usage: The effects of perceived usefulness, subjective norm, behavioral intention, and self-efficacy. DOI: 10.31219/osf.io/284gk

Hoyles, C., Kieran, C., Rojano, T., Sacristán, A. I., & Trigueros, M. (2020). Reflections on digital technologies in mathematics education across cultures. In *Mathematics Education Across Cultures: Proceedings of the 42nd meeting of PME-NA* (pp. 69-92). DOI: 10.51272/pmena.42.2020-1

Hoyles, C. (2010). *Mathematics education and technology: Rethinking the terrain* (Lagrange, J. B., Ed.). Springer., DOI: 10.1007/978-1-4419-0146-0

Hsu, H.-P., Mak, J., Werner, J., White-Taylor, J., Geiselhofer, M., Gorman, A., & Capurro, C. T. (2024). Preliminary Study on pre-service teachers' applications and perceptions of generative artificial intelligence for lesson planning. *Journal of Technology and Teacher Education, 32*(3), 409–437. DOI: 10.70725/869859beoezu

Huang, L. (2023). Ethics of artificial intelligence in education: Student privacy and data protection. Science insights education frontiers, 16(2), 2577-2587. DOI: 10.15354/sief.23.re202

Huang, D., Hash, N., Cummings, J. J., & Prena, K. (2025). Academic cheating with generative AI. *Computers and Education: Artificial Intelligence, 8*, 100424. DOI: 10.1016/j.caeai.2025.100424

Huot, S., & Em, S. (2025). Integrating English language teaching with environmental sustainability: A comprehensive review of pedagogical strategies and global impacts. [CJESS]. *Cambodian Journal of Educational and Social Sciences, 1*(2), 83–95. DOI: 10.69496/cjess.v2i2.68

Huot, S., & Loch, S. (2025). From rote to reflective: Integrating ChatGPT to transform learning outcomes in Cambodian education. *International Journal of Language and Literary Studies, 7*(4), 1–15. DOI: 10.36892/ijlls.v7i4.2188

Huot, S., Loch, S., Rin, R., Hok, C., Phin, K., Tep, P., Chay, C., Chheang, S., & Huot, S. (2026). Internationalization and competitive growth in Cambodian higher education: Pathways to positive developmental progress and global visibility. In Salendab, F. A. (Ed.), *Competition in higher education and the role of internationalization in university rankings* (pp. 381–412). IGI Global Scientific Publishing., DOI: 10.4018/979-8-3373-6856-6.ch014

Huot, S., Sam, R., & Nguon, T. (2024). Influencing factors in teaching career choices in Cambodia in teacher education colleges: A conceptual framework. *European Journal of Arts. Humanities and Social Sciences, 1*(6), 97–108. DOI: 10.59324/ejahss.2024.1(6).11

Huot, S., & Such, C. (2025). Leveraging social media for language learning: Opportunities and challenges. [JEILT]. *Journal of Education Innovation and Language Teaching, 1*(2), 10–29. DOI: 10.63381/jeilt.v1i2.56

Huot, S., & Tep, P. (2025). Advancing ChatGPT for pedagogical innovation in Cambodia: Insight from global evidence and local implications. *The Context: Journal of English Studies, 12*(4), 115–135. DOI: 10.5281/zenodo.15806972

Hurlburt, G., & Reisman, S. (2024). Intelligence in Education : First of Two Roundtables. *Computer, 57*(January), 21–26. DOI: 10.1109/MC.2023.3327648

Huynh, L., Le, T. H., Dang, B., An, B. T., Vu, C. T., & Nguyen, A. (2025). Mindset matters : Fostering teachers ' responsible AI use through professional development. *Journal of New Approaches in Educational Research, 14*(23), 1–24. DOI: 10.1007/s44322-025-00043-y

Ifenthaler, D., & Yau, J. Y. K. (2020). Ethical and privacy considerations in learning analytics. *Educational Technology Research and Development, 68*(1), 49–74.

Illich, I. (1971). *Deschooling society*. Harper & Row.

Inamdar, V., Jadhav, P., & Singh, S. (2024). SMART CLASSROOMS AND E-LEARNING : THE FUTURE OF BUSINESS EDUCATION. *ShodhKosh: Journal of Visual and Performing Arts, 5*(6), 2940–2950. DOI: 10.29121/shodhkosh.v5.i6.2024.6062

Ishizawa, T. (2025). Architectural informatics self-hackathon workshop — Reassessing professional essence through generic and generative artificial intelligence. *International Journal of Architectural Computing*, 14780771251335108. Advance online publication. DOI: 10.1177/14780771251335108

Jackaria, P. M., Hajan, B. H., Mastul, A. R. H., & Sali, F. Z. (2024). Generation AI in a reimagined classroom: challenges, opportunities and implications to education. *Exploring youth studies in the age of AI*, 181-192. DOI: 10.4018/979-8-3693-3350-1.ch009

Jackaria, P. M., Hajan, B. H., & Mastul, A. R. H. (2024). A Comparative Analysis of the Rating of College Students' Essays by ChatGPT versus Human Raters. International Journal of Learning. *Teaching and Educational Research*, *23*(2), 478–492. Advance online publication. DOI: 10.26803/ijlter.23.2.23

Jamshed, M., Fatimah Albedah, , & Sameena Banu, Mohd Sajid Ansari. (2025). Assessing the Efficacy of AI-Driven Corrective Feedback via WhatsApp Application to Improve ESL Learners' Writing Skills. [IJIM]. *International Journal of Interactive Mobile Technologies*, *19*(07), 190–205. DOI: 10.3991/ijim.v19i07.52709

Järvelä, S., Nguyen, A., & Hadwin, A. (2023). Human and artificial intelligence collaboration for socially shared regulation in learning. *British Journal of Educational Technology*, *54*(5), 1057–1076. DOI: 10.1111/bjet.13325

Jeon, J., & Lee, S. (2023). Large language models in education: A focus on the complementary relationship between human teachers and ChatGPT. *Education and Information Technologies*, *28*(12), 15873–15892. DOI: 10.1007/s10639-023-11834-1

Jeyakumaran, M., D., P. Saravanan, D., & K. Sundararajan, P. (. (2025). Revolutionizing Education: The Impact of Artificial Intelligence on Personalized Learning and Teacher Roles in India. [IJSMS]. *International Journal of Science and Management Studies*, *8*(1), 5–14. DOI: 10.51386/25815946/ijsms-v8i1p102

Ji, H., Han, I., & Ko, Y. (2023). A systematic review of conversational AI in language education: Focusing on the collaboration with human teachers. *Journal of Research on Technology in Education*, *55*(1), 48–63. DOI: 10.1080/15391523.2022.2142873

Ji, Z., Lee, N., Frieske, R., Yu, T., Su, D., Xu, Y., Ishii, E., Bang, Y. J., Madotto, A., & Fung, P. (2023). Survey of hallucination in natural language generation. *ACM Computing Surveys*, *55*(12), 1–38. DOI: 10.1145/3571730

Jonassen, D. (2018). Revisiting constructivist learning in digital environments. *Educational Technology Research and Development*, *66*(4), 785–801.

Jones, K. M. L., Asher, A., Goben, A., Perry, M. R., Salo, D., Briney, K. A., & Robertshaw, M. B. (2020). 'We're being tracked at all times': Student perspectives of their privacy in relation to learning analytics in higher education. *SSRN*, •••, 1–28. DOI: 10.2139/ssrn.3565553

Joyce, S., Umney, C., Whittaker, X., & Stuart, M. (2023). New social relations of digital technology and the future of work: Beyond technological determinism. *New Technology, Work and Employment*, *38*(2), 145–161. DOI: 10.1111/ntwe.12276

Kahne, J., & Bowyer, B. (2017). Educating for democracy in a partisan age: Confronting the challenges of motivated reasoning and misinformation. *American Educational Research Journal*, *54*(1), 3–34. DOI: 10.3102/0002831216679817

Kalniņa, D., Nīmante, D., & Baranova, S. (2024). Artificial intelligence for higher education: Benefits and challenges for pre-service teachers. *Frontiers in Education*, *9*, 1501819. Advance online publication. DOI: 10.3389/feduc.2024.1501819

Kamalov, F., Santandreu Calonge, D., & Gurrib, I. (2023). New era of artificial intelligence in education. *Sustainability (Basel)*, *15*(16), 12451. DOI: 10.3390/su151612451

Karataş, F., & Yüce, E. (2024). AI and the Future of Teaching: Preservice Teachers' Reflections on the Use of Artificial Intelligence in Open and Distributed Learning. *International Review of Research in Open and Distance Learning*, *25*(3), 304–325. DOI: 10.19173/irrodl.v25i3.7785

Kasneci, E., Seßler, K., Küchemann, S., Bannert, M., Dementieva, D., Fischer, F., Gasser, U., Groh, G., Günnemann, S., Hüllermeier, E., Krusche, S., Kutyniok, G., Michaeli, T., Nerdel, C., Pfeffer, J., Poquet, O., Sailer, M., Schmidt, A., Seidel, T., & Kasneci, G. (2023). ChatGPT for good? On opportunities and challenges of large language models for education. *Learning and Individual Differences*, *103*, 102274. DOI: 10.1016/j.lindif.2023.102274

Katsenou, R., Kotsidis, K., Papadopoulou, A., Anastasiadis, P., & Deliyannis, I. (2025). Beyond Assistance: Embracing AI as a Collaborative Co-Agent in Education. *Education Sciences*, *15*(8), 1006. DOI: 10.3390/educsci15081006

Kayyali, M. (2024). Future possibilities and challenges of AI in education. In *Transforming education with generative AI: Prompt engineering and synthetic content creation* (pp. 118–137). IGI Global Scientific Publishing. DOI: 10.4018/979-8-3693-1351-0.ch006

Kayyali, M. (2025). The Evolution of AI in Education From Concept to Classroom. In *Navigating Barriers to AI Implementation in the Classroom* (pp. 325–368). IGI Global Scientific Publishing. DOI: 10.4018/979-8-3373-1827-1.ch013

Khampusaen, D. (2025). The Impact of ChatGPT on Academic Writing Skills and Knowledge: An Investigation of Its Use in Argumentative Essays. *LEARN Journal: Language Education and Acquisition Research Network, 18*(1), 963–988. DOI: 10.70730/PGCQ9242

Kim, J. (2024). Leading teachers' perspective on teacher-AI collaboration in education. *Education and Information Technologies, 29*(7), 8693–8724. DOI: 10.1007/s10639-023-12109-5

Kim, J., Lee, H., & Cho, Y. H. (2022). Learning design to support student-AI collaboration: Perspectives of leading teachers for AI in education. *Education and Information Technologies, 27*(5), 6069–6104. DOI: 10.1007/s10639-021-10831-6

Kim, J., Yu, S., Detrick, R., Lin, X., & Li, N. (2025). Designing AI-powered learning: Adult learners' expectations for curriculum and human-AI interaction. *Educational Technology Research and Development, 73*(6), 1–25. DOI: 10.1007/s11423-025-10549-z

Kim, Y., Song, H., & Lockee, B. (2021). "I like my relational machine teacher": The role of social presence. *Computers & Education, 163*, 104079. DOI: 10.1016/j.compedu.2020.104079

Kirschner, P. A., & De Bruyckere, P. (2017). The myths of the digital native and the multitasker. *Teaching and Teacher Education, 67*, 135–142. DOI: 10.1016/j.tate.2017.06.001

Kirschner, P. A., & Van Merriënboer, J. J. (2013). Do learners really know best? Urban legends in education. *Educational Psychologist, 48*(3), 169–183. DOI: 10.1080/00461520.2013.804395

Kirsh, S. J. (2009). *Media and youth: A developmental perspective*. John Wiley & Sons. DOI: 10.1002/9781444317435

Klugman, C. M. (2021). Black boxes and bias in AI challenge autonomy. *The American Journal of Bioethics, 21*(7), 33–35. DOI: 10.1080/15265161.2021.1926587 PMID: 34152901

Knoth, N., Tolzin, A., Janson, A., & Leimeister, J. M. (2024). AI literacy and its implications for prompt engineering strategies. *Computers and Education: Artificial Intelligence, 6*, 100225. DOI: 10.1016/j.caeai.2024.100225

Knox, J. (2020). Artificial intelligence and education in China. *Learning, Media and Technology, 45*(3), 298–311. DOI: 10.1080/17439884.2020.1754236

Koehler, M. J., Mishra, P., & Cain, W. (2017). What is technological pedagogical content (TPACK)? In M. J. Koehler, P. Mishra, & W. Cain (Eds.), *Journal of Education: Pedagogical content knowledge* (Vol. 193, pp. 13–20). Boston University School of Education. https://www.researchgate.net/publication/260281100

Koehler, M. J., & Mishra, P. (2020). TPACK and teacher knowledge in AI classrooms. *Journal of Digital Learning in Teacher Education, 36*(2), 74–87.

Kohnke, L., Zou, D., & Xie, H. (2025). Microlearning and generative AI for pre-service teacher education: A qualitative case study. *Education and Information Technologies, 30*(15), 21221–21248. DOI: 10.1007/s10639-025-13606-5

Ko, U., Hartley, K., & Hayak, M. (2025). Exploring AI in education: Preservice teacher perspectives, usage, and considerations. *Journal of Information Technology Education, 24*, 21. Advance online publication. DOI: 10.28945/5592

Koukaras, C., Hatzikraniotis, E., Mitsiaki, M., Koukaras, P., Tjortjis, C., & Stavrinides, S. G. (2025). Revolutionising Educational Management with AI and Wireless Networks: A Framework for Smart Resource Allocation and Decision-Making. *Applied Sciences (Basel, Switzerland), 15*(10), 1–30. DOI: 10.3390/app15105293

Kour, J., & Bhatia, R. (2025). Artificial intelligence and human mental wellbeing: Striking a balance between innovation and productivity. In Efstratopoulou, M. (Eds.), *AI in mental health: Innovations, challenges, and collaborative pathways* (pp. 213–228). IGI Global Scientific Publishing. DOI: 10.4018/979-8-3373-5072-1.ch009

Kour, J., Bhatia, R., & Joshi, R. (2025). Artificial intelligence in education: Insights from gender- and locality-based perspectives. In Mobo, F. (Ed.), *Impacts of AI on students and teachers in Education 5.0* (pp. 193–210). IGI Global Scientific Publishing. DOI: 10.4018/979-8-3693-8191-5.ch007

Kousa, P., & Niemi, H. (2023). AI ethics and learning: EdTech companies' challenges and solutions. *Interactive Learning Environments, 31*(10), 6735–6746. DOI: 10.1080/10494820.2022.2043908

Kovari, A. (2025). A systematic review of AI-powered collaborative learning in higher education: Trends and outcomes from the last decade. *Social Sciences & Humanities Open, 11*, 101335. DOI: 10.1016/j.ssaho.2025.101335

Kuzu, S. (2025). Artificial intelligence in pre-service teacher education: Bibliometrics analysis. *Pedagogical Research, 10*(4), em0249. Advance online publication. DOI: 10.29333/pr/17402

Kyambade, M., Namatovu, A., & Male Ssentumbwe, A. (2025). Exploring the evolution of artificial intelligence in education: From AI-guided learning to learner-personalized paradigms. *Cogent Education*, *12*(1), 2505297. DOI: 10.1080/2331186X.2025.2505297

Lasky, S. (2005). A sociocultural approach to understanding teacher identity, agency and professional vulnerability in a context of secondary school reform. *Teaching and Teacher Education*, *21*(8), 899–916. DOI: 10.1016/j.tate.2005.06.003

Latour, B. (2005). *Reassembling the social: An introduction to actor-network-theory*. Oxford University Press. DOI: 10.1093/oso/9780199256044.001.0001

Lee, A. T., Ramasamy, R. K., & Subbarao, A. (2025, January). Understanding psychosocial barriers to healthcare technology adoption: a review of TAM technology acceptance model and unified theory of acceptance and use of technology and UTAUT frameworks. In *Healthcare* (Vol. 13, No. 3, p. 250). MDPI. DOI: 10.3390/healthcare13030250

Lemeš, S. (2024). Prompt Engineering. Artificial intelligence in industry, 4, 159-170.

Lewis, P., Perez, E., Piktus, A., Petroni, F., Karpukhin, V., Goyal, N., & Kiela, D. (2020). Retrieval-augmented generation for knowledge-intensive nlp tasks. *Advances in Neural Information Processing Systems*, *33*, 9459–9474.

Lim, S., & Keuk, C. N. (2017). A sociocultural analysis of Cambodian teachers' cognitions about cultural contents in an 'internationally imported' textbook in a tertiary English learning context. In Widodo, H. P., Perfecto, M. R., Canh, L. V., & Buripakdi, A. (Eds.), *Situating moral and cultural values in ELT materials: The Southeast Asian context* (pp. 87–110). Springer., DOI: 10.1007/978-3-319-63677-1_6

Lin, H.-C. (2026a). A Generative AI-Supported Flipped Classroom Model for Personalized Skill Training in Engineering Woodworking Education. *Lecture Notes in Computer Science, 15914 LNCS*, 366–376. DOI: 10.1007/978-3-031-98197-5_39

Lin, Y., & Chen, N.-S. (2024). Artificial intelligence in personalized learning. *Computers & Education: Artificial Intelligence*, *5*, 100152. DOI: 10.1016/j.caeai.2023.100152

Li, S., Zeng, C., Liu, H., Jia, J., Liang, M., Cha, Y., Lim, C. P., & Wu, X. (2025). A meta-analysis of AI-enabled personalized STEM education in schools. *International Journal of STEM Education*, *12*(1), 58. DOI: 10.1186/s40594-025-00566-y

Luckin, R. (2018). *Enhancing learning and teaching with technology: What the research says*. ERIC.

Luckin, R. (2021). Machine learning and human intelligence. *British Journal of Educational Technology*, *52*(5), 1935–1955.

Luckin, R. (2025). Nurturing human intelligence in the age of AI: Rethinking education for the future. *Development and Learning in Organizations*, *39*(1), 1–4. DOI: 10.1108/DLO-04-2024-0108

Luckin, R., Holmes, W., Griffiths, M., & Forcier, L. B. (2016). *Intelligence unleashed: An argument for AI in education*. Pearson.

Lumanlan, J., Ayson, M. R., Bautista, M. J., Dizon, J., & Ylarde, C. M. (2025). AI Literacy among Preservice Teachers: Inputs Towards a Relevant Teacher Education Curriculum. *International Journal of Multidisciplinary Educational Research and Innovation*, *3*(1), 242–253. https://philpapers.org/rec/LUMALA

Lupton, D. (2016). *The quantified self*. Polity Press.

Lu, X., Li, Y., & Li, X. (2021). Automatic scoring and assessment using AI. *Computers & Education*, *166*, 104–121.

Maggo, J., & Maggo, T. (2025). Disparities in educational opportunities between urban and rural regions across the globe and the potential of AI to bridge the divide. *International Journal of Business Analytics and Intelligence*, *13*(1), 44–54. https://www.proquest.com/docview/3233263880?pq-origsite=gscholar&fromopenview=true. DOI: 10.21863/ijbai/2025.13.1.005

Mahana, M., Johns, M., & Apte, A. (2012). Automated Essay Grading Using Machine Learning. Machine Learning Session Stanford University, 3–7. https://cs229.stanford.edu/proj2012/MahanaJohnsApte-AutomatedEssayGradingUsingMachineLearning.pdf

Marikyan, D., & Papagiannidis, S. (2024). Technology acceptance model: A review. *TheoryHub book*. https://eprints.ncl.ac.uk/302879

Mariyono, D., & Nur Alif Hd, A. (2025). AI's role in transforming learning environments: A review of collaborative approaches and innovations. *Quality Education for All*, *2*(1), 265–288. DOI: 10.1108/QEA-08-2024-0071

Marvin, G., Hellen, N., Jjingo, D., & Nakatumba-Nabende, J. (2023, June). Prompt engineering in large language models. In International conference on data intelligence and cognitive informatics (pp. 387-402). Singapore: Springer Nature Singapore. DOI: 10.1007/978-981-99-7962-2_30

Mayer, R. C., Davis, J. H., & Schoorman, F. D. (1995). An integrative model of organizational trust. *Academy of Management Review, 20*(3), 709–734. DOI: 10.2307/258792

Mayer, R. E. (2020). *Multimedia learning* (3rd ed.). Cambridge University Press. DOI: 10.1017/9781316941355

Mazzullo, E., Bulut, O., Wongvorachan, T., & Tan, B. (2023). Learning analytics in the era of large language models. *Analytics*, *2*(4), 877–898. DOI: 10.3390/analytics2040046

Mead, G. H. (1934). *Mind, self, and society*. University of Chicago Press.

Means, B., Peters, V., & Zheng, Y. (2020). Learning online and the implications for teacher roles. *Review of Research in Education*, *44*(1), 99–127.

Mehdaoui, A. (2024). Unveiling Barriers and Challenges of AI Technology Integration in Education: Assessing Teachers' Perceptions, Readiness and Anticipated Resistance. *Futurity Education*, *4*(4), 95–108. DOI: 10.57125/FED.2024.12.25.06

Melisa, R., Ashadi, A., Triastuti, A., Hidayati, S., Salido, A., Ero, P. E. L., . . . Al Fuad, Z. (2025). Critical Thinking in the Age of AI: A Systematic Review of AI's Effects on Higher Education. Educational Process: International Journal, 14. https://www.ceeol.com/search/article-detail?id=1338520

Memarian, B., & Doleck, T. (2024). Computers in Human Behavior : Artificial Humans Human-in-the-loop in artificial intelligence in education : A review and entity-relationship (ER) analysis. *Computers in Human Behavior: Artificial Humans*, *2*(1), 1–11. DOI: 10.1016/j.chbah.2024.100053

Mena-Guacas, A. F., Vázquez-Cano, E., Fernández-Márquez, E., & López-Meneses, E. (2024). Artificial intelligence and its scientific production in the area of education | La inteligencia artificial y su producción científica en el campo de la educación. *Formación Universitaria*, *17*(1), 155–164. DOI: 10.4067/S0718-50062024000100155

Menon, D., & Shilpa, K. (2023). "Chatting with ChatGPT": Analyzing the factors influencing users' intention to Use the Open AI's ChatGPT using the UTAUT model. *Heliyon*, *9*(11), e20962. Advance online publication. DOI: 10.1016/j.heliyon.2023.e20962 PMID: 37928033

Mercer, N., & Howe, C. (2012). Explaining the dialogic processes. *Learning, Culture and Social Interaction*, *1*(1), 12–21. DOI: 10.1016/j.lcsi.2012.03.001

Metzger, M. J., & Flanagin, A. J. (2013). Credibility and trust of information in online environments: The use of cognitive heuristics. *Journal of Pragmatics*, *59*, 210–220. DOI: 10.1016/j.pragma.2013.07.012

MoEYS. (2018). *Policy and strategy on information and communication technology in education*. Ministry of Education, Youth and Sport.

Mohebbi, A. (2025). Enabling learner independence and self-regulation in language education using AI tools: A systematic review. *Cogent Education*, *12*(1), 2433814. DOI: 10.1080/2331186X.2024.2433814

Molenaar, I. (2025). Human-AI Collaboration in Education: The Hybrid Future *Proceedings of the 30th ACM Conference on Innovation and Technology in Computer Science Education* V. 1, Nijmegen, Netherlands. DOI: 10.1145/3724363.3729083

Mossberger, K., Tolbert, C. J., & McNeal, R. S. (2007). *Digital Citizenship*. In The MIT Press eBooks. DOI: 10.7551/mitpress/7428.001.0001

Mpolomoka, D. L., Luchembe, M., Mushibwe, C., Muvombo, M., Changala, M., Sampa, R. L., & Banda, S. (2025). Artificial intelligence-related plagiarism in education: A systematic review. *European Journal of Education Studies*, *12*(4). Advance online publication. DOI: 10.46827/ejes.v12i4.6029

Murakami, Y., Sho, Y., & Inagaki, T. (2024). Improving Motivation in Learning AI for Undergraduate Students by Case Study. *Journal of Information Processing*, *32*(0), 175–181. DOI: 10.2197/ipsjjip.32.175

Mustfa, M. J., & Ashiq, S. (2024). Harnessing the power of artificial intelligence for adaptive learning systems: A systematic review. *International Journal of Education and Management Engineering*, *14*(5), 12–22. DOI: 10.5815/ijeme.2024.05.02

Muthukrishna, M., Dai, J., Panizo Madrid, D., Sabherwal, R., Vanoppen, K., & Yao, H. (2025). AI Can Revolutionise Education but Technology Is Not Enough: Human Development Meets Cultural Evolution. *Journal of Human Development and Capabilities*, *26*(3), 1–11. DOI: 10.1080/19452829.2025.2517740

Nagaraj, B. K., Kalaivani, A., Begum, S., Akila, S., & Sachdev, H. K. (2023). The emerging role of artificial intelligence in stem higher education: A critical review. *International Research Journal of Multidisciplinary Technovation*, *5*(5), 1–19. DOI: 10.54392/irjmt2351

Neff, J., Arciaga, K., & Burri, L. (2024). EFL students' and teachers' perceptions of the ethical uses of AI tools. *Technology in Language Teaching & Learning*, *6*(3), 1–19. DOI: 10.29140/tltl.v6n3.1714

Ng, D. T. K., Su, J., Leung, J. K. L., & Chu, S. K. W. (2023). Artificial intelligence (AI) literacy education in secondary schools: A review. *Interactive Learning Environments, 32*(10), 6204–6224. DOI: 10.1080/10494820.2023.2255228

Nguyen, T. N. T., Van Lai, N., & Nguyen, Q. T. (2024). Artificial Intelligence (AI) in Education: A Case Study on ChatGPT's Influence on Student Learning Behaviors. Educational Process: International Journal, 13(2), 105-121. https://www.ceeol.com/search/article-detail?id=1256337

Nguyen, A., Hong, Y., Dang, B., & Huang, X. (2024). Human-AI collaboration patterns in AI-assisted academic writing. *Studies in Higher Education, 49*(5), 847–864. DOI: 10.1080/03075079.2024.2323593

Nguyen, A., Ngo, H. N., Hong, Y., Dang, B., & Nguyen, B.-P. T. (2023). Ethical principles for artificial intelligence in education. *Education and Information Technologies, 28*(4), 4221–4241. DOI: 10.1007/s10639-022-11316-w PMID: 36254344

Ng, W. (2012). Can we teach digital natives digital literacy? *Computers & Education, 59*(3), 1065–1078. DOI: 10.1016/j.compedu.2012.04.016

Noddings, N. (2013). *Caring: A relational approach to ethics and moral education* (2nd ed.). University of California Press.

Nuong Deri, M., Singh, A., Zaazie, P., & Anandene, D. (2024). Leveraging Artificial Intelligence in Higher Educational Institutions: A Comprehensive Overview. *Education and Law Review*, (30). Advance online publication. DOI: 10.1344/REYD2024.30.45777

Nur Fitria, T. (2023). The use of artificial intelligence in education (AIED): Can AI replace the teacher's role? *Epigram (e-Journal), 20*(2), 165–187. DOI: 10.32722/epi.v20i2.5711

Nussbaum, M. C. (2011). *Creating capabilities: The human development approach*. Harvard University Press. DOI: 10.4159/harvard.9780674061200

O'Neil, C. (2016). *Weapons of math destruction*. Crown.

OECD. (2022). *Digital transformation and quality in higher education*. OECD Publishing., DOI: 10.1787/f622f257-

Ogunleye, B., Zakariyyah, K. I., Ajao, O., Olayinka, O., & Sharma, H. (2024). A systematic review of generative AI for teaching and learning practice [Preprint]. arXiv. https://arxiv.org/abs/2406.09520

Organisation for Economic Co-operation and Development. (2019). *Principles on artificial intelligence*. OECD Publishing.

Organisation for Economic Co-operation and Development. (2023). *Artificial intelligence in education: Challenges and policy responses*. OECD Publishing.

Ou, A. W., Stöhr, C., & Malmström, H. (2024). Academic communication with AI-powered language tools in higher education: From a post-humanist perspective. *System, 121*(January), 1–14. DOI: 10.1016/j.system.2024.103225

Ou, J., Nogueira, J., & Qin, C. (2025). Exploring the impact of AI-assisted practice applications on music learners' performance, self-efficacy, and self-regulated learning. *Frontiers in Psychology*, *16*(October), 1–15. DOI: 10.3389/fpsyg.2025.1675762 PMID: 41159183

P.T, S., Chacko, A. M., & Kumar, S. D. M. (2025). Beyond the One-Size-Fits-All: A Systematic Review of Personalized and Gamified e-Learning for Neurodivergent Learners. *Electronic Journal of E-Learning, 23*(3), 101-119. DOI: 10.34190/ejel.23.3.4051

Padovano, A., & Cardamone, M. (2024). Towards human-AI collaboration in the competency-based curriculum development process: The case of industrial engineering and management education. *Computers and Education: Artificial Intelligence*, *7*, 100256. DOI: 10.1016/j.caeai.2024.100256

Pahi, K., Hawlader, S., Hicks, E., Zaman, A., & Phan, V. (2024). Enhancing active learning through collaboration between human teachers and generative AI. *Computers and Education Open*, *6*, 100183. DOI: 10.1016/j.caeo.2024.100183

Pajares, F. (2006). Self-efficacy during childhood and adolescence. In Urdan, T., & Frank, P. (Eds.), *Self-efficacy beliefs of adolescents* (Vol. 5, pp. 339 367). IAP. DOI: 10.1108/978-1-60752-837-720251016

Pangrazio, L., & Selwyn, N. (2019). "Personal data literacies": A critical literacies approach to enhancing understandings of personal digital data. *New Media & Society*, *21*(2), 419–437. DOI: 10.1177/1461444818799523

Parsons, T. (1959). The school class as a social system. *Harvard Educational Review*, *29*(4), 297–318.

Patil, R., Heston, T. F., & Bhuse, V. (2024). Prompt engineering in healthcare. *Electronics (Basel)*, *13*(15), 2961. DOI: 10.3390/electronics13152961

Paul, R., & Elder, L. (2014). Critical thinking: Intellectual standards essential to reasoning well within every domain of human thought, Part 4. *Journal of Developmental Education*, *37*(3), 34–35. https://www.proquest.com/openview/534c73e3bddaeb5be21c4fbcd69596e4/1?cbl=47765&pq-origsite=gscholar

Perelman, L. (2014). When “the state of the art” is counting words. *Assessing Writing, 21*, 104–111. DOI: 10.1016/j.asw.2014.05.001

Peters, M. A., Jandrić, P., & Hayes, S. (2023). AI, education, and epistemic responsibility. *Educational Philosophy and Theory, 55*(1), 1–15. DOI: 10.1080/00131857.2020.1867108

Phommanee, W., Plangsorn, B., & Siripipattanakul, S. (2024). An exploratory study of current competency for learning experience designer: Job announcement analysis. *Journal of Computers in Education, 12*(2), 391–419. DOI: 10.1007/s40692-024-00315-0

Pitts, G., & Motamedi, S. (2025). *Understanding human–AI trust in education. arXiv*. https://doi.org//arXiv.2506.09160DOI: 10.48550

Pokrivcakova, S. (2019). Preparing teachers for the application of AI-powered technologies in foreign language education. *Journal of language and cultural education, 7* (3), 135 - 153. DOI: 10.2478/jolace-2019-0025

Popenici, S. A., & Kerr, S. (2017). Exploring the impact of artificial intelligence on teaching and learning in higher education. *Research and Practice in Technology Enhanced Learning, 12*(1), 1–13. DOI: 10.1186/s41039-017-0062-8 PMID: 30595727

Prestigiacomo, R., Hunter, J., Knight, S., Martinez-Maldonado, R., & Lockyer, L. (2020). Data in practice: A participatory approach to understanding pre-service teachers' perspectives. *Australasian Journal of Educational Technology, 36*(6), 107–119. DOI: 10.14742/ajet.6388

Puentedura, R. R. (2014). *SAMR and TPCK: A hands-on approach to classroom practice*. https://www.hippasus.com/rrpweblog/archives/2014/12/11/SAMRandTPCK_HandsOnApproachClassroomPractice.pdf

Qi, X., Zhou, J., Dong, Y., & Chen, F. (2026). Enhancing collaborative learning through AI-powered feedback systems. *International Journal of Data Science and Analytics, 21*(1), 20. Advance online publication. DOI: 10.1007/s41060-025-00882-0

Rädel-Ablass, K., Schliz, K., Schlick, C., Meindl, B., Pahr-Hosbach, S., Schwendemann, H., Rupp, S., Roddewig, M., & Miersch, C. (2025). Teaching opportunities for anamnesis interviews through AI based teaching role plays: A survey with online learning students from health study programs. *BMC Medical Education, 25*(1), 259. Advance online publication. DOI: 10.1186/s12909-025-06756-0 PMID: 39966894

Raes, A., Detienne, L., Windey, I., & Depaepe, F. (2019). A systematic literature review on synchronous hybrid learning: Gaps identified. *Learning Environments Research, 23*(3), 269–290. DOI: 10.1007/s10984-019-09303-z

Rahamtalla, B. M., Medani, I. E., Abdelhag, M. E., Eltigani, S. A., Rajan, S. K., Falgy, E., Hassan, N. M., Fadailu, M. E., Khudhayr, H. A., & Abdalla, A. (2025). The AI-powered healthcare ecosystem: Bridging the chasm between technical validation and systemic integration—A systematic review. *Future Internet*, *17*(12), 550. DOI: 10.3390/fi17120550

Rahiman, H. U., & Kodikal, R. (2024). Revolutionizing education : Artificial intelligence empowered learning in higher education Revolutionizing education : Artificial intelligence empowered learning in higher education. *Cogent Education*, *11*(1), 1–25. DOI: 10.1080/2331186X.2023.2293431

Ramnarain, U., Ogegbo, A. A., Penn, M., Ojetunde, S., & Mdlalose, N. (2024). Pre-service science teachers' intention to use generative artificial intelligence in inquiry-based teaching. *Journal of Science Education and Technology*, 1 - 14. DOI: 10.1007/s10956-024-10159-z

Rauf, A., Nadeem, S., & Tahir, L. (2024). Integrating artificial intelligence into curriculum design. Multidisciplinary Journal of Emerging Needs of Curriculum, 1(2), 10-19. https://researchcorridor.org/index.php/MJENC/article/view/17

Ravi, M. (2025). Using the TPACK Framework for Gen-AI Enabled Learning Activities: Design, Delivery and Evaluation. *Journal of Engineering Education Transformations, 38*(Special Issue 2), 175–181. DOI: 10.16920/jeet/2025/v38is2/25021

Reddig, J. M., Arora, A., & MacLellan, C. J. (2025). Generating In-Context, Personalized Feedback for Intelligent Tutors with Large Language Models. *International Journal of Artificial Intelligence in Education*, *35*(6), 3459–3500. Advance online publication. DOI: 10.1007/s40593-025-00505-6

Redecker, C. (2020). AI and the future of teaching. *The Internet and Higher Education*, *47*, 100759.

Regan, P. M., & Jesse, J. (2019). Ethical challenges of edtech. *Educational Technology Research and Development*, *67*(6), 1671–1693. DOI: 10.1007/s11423-019-09666-0

Robinson, L., Cotten, S. R., Ono, H., Quan-Haase, A., Mesch, G., Chen, W., Schulz, J., Hale, T. M., & Stern, M. J. (2015). Digital inequalities. *Information Communication and Society*, *18*(5), 569–582. DOI: 10.1080/1369118X.2015.1012532

Rohanadeera, S. L., & Hewagamage, K. P. (2026). Generative-AI-Powered TA BOT for Enhanced Personalized Support in Software Engineering Education. *Communications in Computer and Information Science*, *2380 CCIS*, 197–204. DOI: 10.1007/978-981-96-6291-3_16

Rosenberg, J. M., & Kumar, R. (2023). Artificial intelligence and academic integrity. *Journal of Educational Technology Systems*, *52*(1), 3–18. DOI: 10.1177/00472395231172970

Runge, I., Hebibi, F., & Lazarides, R. (2025). Acceptance of Pre-Service Teachers Towards Artificial Intelligence (AI): The Role of AI-Related Teacher Training Courses and AI-TPACK Within the Technology Acceptance Model. *Education Sciences*, *15*(2), 167. DOI: 10.3390/educsci15020167

Rutter, M. (1990). Psychosocial resilience and protective mechanisms. In *Cambridge University Press eBooks* (pp. 181–214). DOI: 10.1017/CBO9780511752872.013

Ryan, M., Stahl, B. C., & Kinder-Kurlanda, K. (2021). Research and practice of AI ethics: A case study approach juxtaposing academic discourse with organizational reality. *Science and Engineering Ethics*, *27*(3), 1–29. DOI: 10.1007/s11948-021-00293-x PMID: 33686527

Ryan, R. M., & Deci, E. L. (2000). Self-determination theory and the facilitation of intrinsic motivation, social development, and well-being. *The American Psychologist*, *55*(1), 68–78. DOI: 10.1037/0003-066X.55.1.68 PMID: 11392867

Saeli, H., Rahmati, P., Dalman, M., Shamsi, Y., & Koltovskaia, S. (2025). Embrace or resist? EFL teachers on adopting ChatGPT as a teaching and feedback tool. *Language Awareness*, •••, 1–21. DOI: 10.1080/09658416.2025.2577191

Sajja, R., Sermet, Y., Cikmaz, M., Cwiertny, D., & Demir, I. (2024). Artificial Intelligence-Enabled Intelligent Assistant for Personalized and Adaptive Learning in Higher Education. *Information (Basel)*, *15*(10), 596. Advance online publication. DOI: 10.3390/info15100596

Sakthivel, A., Swaroop, V. T. S., Malik, A., Meprathe, R., Suresh, S., & Shukla, A. (2026). Empowering Business Mathematics Learners: Leveraging Generative AI for Academic Excellence. *Lecture Notes in Networks and Systems, 1580 LNNS*, 281–291. DOI: 10.1007/978-981-95-0629-3_21

Saragih, R. I. E. (2024). AI-powered education: Transforming learning through personalized and scalable solutions. *International Journal of Information System and Innovative Technology*, *3*(2), 1–9. DOI: 10.63322/qm9dk118

Satapathy, D., Parida, D., & Pradhan, D. (2025). Pre-Service Teachers' Uses of AI Tools In Teaching-Learning Process. International Journal for Innovative Research In Multidisciplinary Field, 11. https://www.researchgate.net/profile/Deepak-Kumar-Pradhan-3/publication/393097124_Pre-Service_Teachers'_Uses_of_AI_Tools_In_Teaching-_Learning_Process/links/685ef76f39c35835120524c3/Pre-Service-Teachers-Uses-of-AI-Tools-In-Teaching-Learning-Process.pdf

Schulhoff, S., Ilie, M., Balepur, N., Kahadze, K., Liu, A., Si, C., . . . Resnik, P. (2024). The prompt report: A systematic survey of prompt engineering techniques (arXiv preprint arXiv:2406.06608). https://arxiv.org/abs/2406.06608

Sebihi, A., Schoelen, L., & Uwamwezi, B. (2025). Unveiling AI's impact in Rwandan higher education: Navigating trends, challenges, and imperatives at the University of Rwanda. *Discover Education*, *4*(1), 166. Advance online publication. DOI: 10.1007/s44217-025-00576-6

Sekti, B. A. (2025). AI Technology Management Concepts and Strategies. In *AI Technology Management and Value Creation* (pp. 1–32). DOI: 10.4018/979-8-3373-2497-5.ch001

Seldon, A., & Abidoye, O. (2018). *The fourth education revolution: Will artificial intelligence liberate or infantilise humanity?* University of Buckingham Press.

Selwyn, N. (2019). *Should robots replace teachers? AI and the future of education.* Polity Press.

Selwyn, N. (2019). *Should robots replace teachers?: AI and the future of education.* John Wiley & Sons.

Selwyn, N. (2021). Ed-tech within limits. *Learning, Media and Technology*, *46*(4), 347–350. DOI: 10.1080/17439884.2021.1952590

Selwyn, N., & Jandrić, P. (2020). Postdigital living in the age of Covid-19: Unsettling what we see as possible. *Postdigital Science and Education*, *2*(3), 989–1005. DOI: 10.1007/s42438-020-00166-9 PMID: 40477067

Sen, V. (2019). Hybrid governmentality: Higher education policymaking in post-conflict Cambodia. *Studies in Higher Education*, *44*(3), 513–525. DOI: 10.1080/03075079.2017.1379985

Sepp, S. (2025). Towards more transparency in learning analytics. *Journal of Learning Analytics*, *12*(3), 34–46. DOI: 10.18608/jla.2025.8713

Setiyawan, A., Soeharto, S., Wijaya, T. T., Korenova, L., & Lavicza, Z. (2025). Measuring Teachers' competencies for AI integration: Development and validation of the AI-TPACK in vocational education. *Computers and Education Open*, *9*, 100319. Advance online publication. DOI: 10.1016/j.caeo.2025.100319

Sharma, H., Soetan, T., Farinloye, T., Mogaji, E., & Noite, M. D. F. (2022). AI adoption in universities in emerging economies: Prospects, challenges and recommendations. In *Re-imagining educational futures in developing countries: Lessons from Global Health crises* (pp. 159–174). Springer International Publishing., DOI: 10.1007/978-3-030-88234-1_9

Shikun, S., Grigoryan, G., Huichun, N., & Harutyunyan, H. (2024). AI Chatbots: Developing English Language Proficiency in EFL Classroom. *Arab World English Journal*, *1*(1), 292–305. DOI: 10.24093/awej/ChatGPT.20

Shi, L., Ding, A. E., & Choi, I. (2024). Investigating Teachers' Use of an AI-Enabled System and Their Perceptions of AI Integration in Science Classrooms: A Case Study. *Education Sciences*, *14*(11), 1–19. DOI: 10.3390/educsci14111187

Shute, V. J., & Becker, B. J. (2010). *Innovative assessment for the 21st century*. Springer. DOI: 10.1007/978-1-4419-6530-1

Siemens, G. (2018). Learning in networks and AI-mediated systems. *Educational Technology*, *58*(5), 26–32.

Singh, A. (2022). Conceptual framework on Smart Learning Environment- An Indian perspective. *Education and Law Review*, (25). Advance online publication. DOI: 10.1344/REYD2022.25.36706

Sivasubramaniam, S. (2025). Deterring Academic Integrity Breaches: The Roles of Institutions, Academics, and Support Services. *Journal of Scholarly Publishing*, *56*(2), 240–268. DOI: 10.3138/jsp-2024-1115

Slade, S., & Prinsloo, P. (2019). Student data and analytics ethics. *British Journal of Educational Technology*, *50*(3), 1034–1048.

Soliha, I. A., & Fadila, Y. (2025). Implementation of an Interactive Chatbot System Using ChatGPT and Leonardo AI to Support Islamic Studies Teaching for MI Teachers. *GUYUB: Journal of Community Engagement*, *6*(2), 439–459. DOI: 10.33650/guyub.v6i2.10587

Somabut, A., Tuamsuk, K., Lowatcharin, G., Traiyarach, S., & Kwangmuang, P. (2025). Social Sciences & Humanities Open Preparing for the AI era : Science teachers ' readiness and professional development needs for generative AI integration in secondary education. *Social Sciences & Humanities Open, 12*(November), 1–14. DOI: 10.1016/j.ssaho.2025.102259

Sotiri, E. (2024). The future of AI and authorship: The EU's legal framework for AI and copyright. *Pin Code, N° 19*(3), 1–10. .DOI: 10.3917/pinc.019.0001

Sperling, K., Stenberg, C.-J., McGrath, C., Åkerfeldt, A., Heintz, F., & Stenliden, L. (2024). In search of artificial intelligence (AI) literacy in teacher education: A scoping review. *Computers and Education Open, 6*, 100169. Advance online publication. DOI: 10.1016/j.caeo.2024.100169

Srivastava, S. (2026). AI as a catalyst for transformation: Revolutionizing lifelong learning and professional development in human services for the digital age: AI and the imperative of lifelong learning in human services. In *Reimagining Business Education in the Age of Artificial Intelligence*, IGI Global Scientific Publishing. doi: 10.4018/979-8-3373-4377-8.ch012

Srivastava, S. (2026). *Artificial Intelligence and the Social Reordering of Insurance Risk, Trust, and Human- Technology Relations: Transformative Role of AI in the Insurance Sector* in AI-Driven Innovations in the Insurance Sector (Chapter 1). DOI: DOI: 10.4018/979-8-3373-2822-5.ch001

Srivastava, S. (2025). *Women, work, and equity: A critical study of entrepreneurship challenges and opportunities in India*. IGI Global Scientific Publishing., DOI: 10.4018/979-8-3373-2903-1.ch004

Srivastava, S. (2026). AI as a catalyst for transformation: Revolutionizing lifelong learning and professional development in human services for the digital age. In *AI and the imperative of lifelong learning in human services*. IGI Global Scientific Publishing., DOI: 10.4018/979-8-3373-4377-8.ch012

Srivastava, S. (2026). *Intergenerational solidarity and the social fabric: A sociological exploration of continuity and change*. IGI Global Scientific Publishing., DOI: 10.4018/979-8-3373-4367-9.ch005

Srivastava, S., & Rojhe, K. C. (2021). Attitude formation and attitude change: A social psychological perspective. In *Social Psychology*. IGI Global., DOI: 10.4018/978-1-7998-6960-3.ch001

Suhag, N., & Singh, A. (2026). Blended Learning in the Age of Artificial Intelligence: Transforming Education Through Innovation. In Ul Rehman, S. (Ed.), *Reshaping Blended Learning Environments With AI* (pp. 29–52). IGI Global Scientific Publishing., DOI: 10.4018/979-8-3373-3815-6.ch002

Su, J., Guo, K., Chen, X., & Chu, S. K. W. (2023). Teaching artificial intelligence in K–12 classrooms: A scoping review. *Interactive Learning Environments*. Advance online publication. DOI: 10.1080/10494820.2023.2212706

Su, J., & Yang, W. (2024). AI literacy curriculum and its relation to children's perceptions of robots and attitudes towards engineering and science: An intervention study in early childhood education. *Journal of Computer Assisted Learning*, *40*(1), 241–253. DOI: 10.1111/jcal.12867

Sukarno, A. A., Al-adzkhan, N. A., Bulkia, W. S. M., & Jackaria, P. M. (2026). Students Building Emotional Connections With AI: Insights Into the Future AI-Infused Classroom. In Generators, Bots, and Tutors: Creative Approaches to Human-AI Synergy in Classroom Instruction (pp. 161-184). IGI Global Scientific Publishing. DOI: 10.4018/979-8-3373-0847-0.ch006

Sun, N., & Sun, Y. (2025). Acta Psychologica The role of artificial intelligence (AI) tools in EFL teachers ' passion for self-directed professional development. *Acta Psychologica*, *260*(June), 1–7. DOI: 10.1016/j.actpsy.2025.105546 PMID: 40945144

Sutton, A., Clowes, M., Preston, L., & Booth, A. (2019). Meeting the review family: Exploring review types and associated information retrieval requirements. *Health Information and Libraries Journal*, *36*(3), 202–222. DOI: 10.1111/hir.12276 PMID: 31541534

Swauger, S. (2020). *Our bodies encoded: Algorithmic test proctoring in higher education.* (Conference/Report). https://api.semanticscholar.org/CorpusID:229263801

Taheri, M., Tan, K., Flaten, O. E., & Cyma-Wejchenig, M. (2026). Enhancing Education Training with A Virtual Reality-Based Simulator Integrated Generative AI. *Lecture Notes in Computer Science, 15743 LNCS*, 394–406. DOI: 10.1007/978-3-031-97781-7_29

Tan, X., Cheng, G., & Ling, M. H. (2025). Computers and Education : Artificial Intelligence Artificial intelligence in teaching and teacher professional development : A systematic review. *Computers and Education: Artificial Intelligence, 8*(October 2024), 1–19. DOI: 10.1016/j.caeai.2024.100355

Tan, C. (2020). Digital Confucius? Exploring the implications of artificial intelligence in spiritual education. *Connection Science*, *32*(3), 280–291. DOI: 10.1080/09540091.2019.1709045

Temitayo, I., Musa, S., & Ayanwale, A. (2024). Investigating the moderating effects of social good and confidence on teachers' intention to prepare school students for artificial intelligence education. *Education and Information Technologies*, *29*(1), 273–295. DOI: 10.1007/s10639-023-12250-1

Thomas, A. P. (2024). Balancing Innovation and Integrity: Addressing Concerns of AI in Classroom Environments. https://scholarworks.gvsu.edu/gradprojects/451/

Tomar, P., & Srivastava, S. (2024). Strengthening crisis response with organisational resilience strategies to achieve sustainability. In M. Tuba et al. (Eds.), *ICT systems and sustainability* (Lecture Notes in Networks and Systems, Vol. 1163, pp. 175–187). Springer Nature Singapore. DOI: 10.1007/978-981-97-8537-7_16

Tran, M. T. (2024). A systematic literature review on the human-AI partnership roles in higher education. *Enhancing and Predicting Digital Consumer Behavior with AI*, 28-38.

Tschannen-Moran, M., & Hoy, W. K. (2000). A multidisciplinary analysis of trust. *Review of Educational Research*, *70*(4), 547–593. DOI: 10.3102/00346543070004547

Tsing, A. L. (2005). *Friction: An ethnography of global connection*. Princeton University Press.

Tyson, M. M., & Sauers, N. J. (2021). School leaders' adoption and implementation of artificial intelligence. *Journal of Educational Administration*, *59*(3), 271–285. DOI: 10.1108/JEA-10-2020-0221

UNESCO. (2021). *Recommendation on the Ethics of Artificial Intelligence*. UNESCO Publishing. https://unesdoc.unesco.org/ark:/48223/pf0000381137

UNESCO. (2021). *Recommendation on the ethics of artificial intelligence*. UNESCO.

UNESCO. (2021). *Reimagining our futures together: A new social contract for education*. UNESCO Publishing.

UNESCO. (2023). *Guidance for AI in Education: Policy and Ethics*. UNESCO.

UNESCO. (2023). *Guidance for generative AI in education and research*. https://unesdoc.unesco.org/ark:/48223/pf0000386693

UNESCO. (2023). *Guidance on generative AI in education and research*. UNESCO.

UNESCO. (2023). *Technology integration of Cambodian higher education: Emerging changes since covid-19 and notable challenges*. Global Education Monitoring Report. https://www.unesco.org/gem-report/sites/default/files/medias/fichiers/2023/09/SopheakandPhyrom.pdf

UNESCO. (2024). *AI competency framework for teachers*. https://doi.org/10.54675/ZJTE2084

University Grants Commission. (2021). *Guidelines for online and digital education*. Government of India.

Un, L., & Sok, S. (2022). (Higher) Education policy and project intervention in Cambodia: Its development discourse. In McNamara, V., & Hayden, M. (Eds.), *Education in Cambodia: From year zero towards international standards* (pp. 215–239). Springer., DOI: 10.1007/978-981-16-8213-1_12

Uwosomah, E. E., & Dooly, M. (2025). It Is Not the Huge Enemy: Preservice Teachers' Evolving Perspectives on AI. *Education Sciences*, *15*(2), 152. DOI: 10.3390/educsci15020152

Vaghasiya, N., Zalavadia, K., & Vyas, A. (2026). AI-Based Quiz Generation Using ChatGPT. *Lecture Notes in Networks and Systems, 1533 LNNS*, 377–389. DOI: 10.1007/978-981-96-9196-8_25

van Dijk, J. (2020). *The digital divide*. Polity Press.

VanLehn, K. (2020). Advances in intelligent tutoring systems. *International Journal of Artificial Intelligence in Education*, *30*(1), 19–43.

Vartiainen, H., & Tedre, M. (2023). Using artificial intelligence in craft education: Crafting with text-to-image generative models. *Digital Creativity (Exeter)*, *34*(1), 1–21. DOI: 10.1080/14626268.2023.2174557

Vela, J. V., & Mursi, J. K. A. (2026). The Next Frontier: AI and Global Trends Shaping Higher Education-A Systematic Review. Consumer Decision-Making Processes in Higher Education, 279-316. DOI: 10.4018/979-8-3373-1499-0.ch011

Vetter, M. A., Lucia, B., Jiang, J., & Othman, M. (2024). Towards a framework for local interrogation of AI ethics: A case study on text generators, academic integrity, and composing with ChatGPT. *Computers & Composition. Computers and Composition*, *71*(6), 1–12. DOI: 10.1016/j.compcom.2024.102831

Vistorte, A. O. R., Deroncele-Acosta, A., Ayala, J. L. M., Barrasa, A., Lopez-Granero, C., & Marti-Gonzalez, M. (2024). Integrating artificial intelligence to assess emotions in learning environments: A systematic literature review. *Frontiers in Psychology*, *15*, 1387089. DOI: 10.3389/fpsyg.2024.1387089 PMID: 38966729

Voogt, J., & Knezek, G. (2016). Guest editorial: Technology enhanced quality education for all–outcomes from EDUsummIT 2015. *Journal of Educational Technology & Society*, *19*(3), 1–4. https://www.jstor.org/stable/10.2307/jeductechsoci.19.3.1

Vygotsky, L. S. (1978). *Mind in society: The development of higher psychological processes*. Harvard University Press.

Wafik, H. M. A., Mahbub, S., Arif, Z., Prince, S. K. A., & Huda, M. N. (2024). Academicians' Perspectives on AI Integration in Bangladesh's Education: Balancing Promise and Ethical Realities. *Cognizance Journal of Multidisciplinary Studies*, *4*(2), 139–158. DOI: 10.47760/cognizance.2024.v04i02.014

Wagner, C. J. (2024). Differentiating Children's Reading Materials with Artificial Intelligence: Exploring Possibilities for Personalized Learning. *The Reading Teacher*, *78*(3), 191–194. DOI: 10.1002/trtr.2361

Walter, Y. (2024). Embracing the future of artificial intelligence in the classroom: AI literacy, prompt engineering, and critical thinking. *International Journal of Educational Technology in Higher Education*, *21*(1), 15. DOI: 10.1186/s41239-024-00448-3

Wang, S., Wang, F., Zhu, Z., Wang, J., & Zhao, T. T. D. (2024). Artificial intelligence in education: A systematic literature review. *Expert Systems with Applications*, *252*(A), 1–19. .DOI: 10.1016/j.eswa.2024.124167

Wang, J., Shi, E., Yu, S., Wu, Z., Hu, H., Ma, C., & Zhang, S. (2025). Prompt engineering for healthcare: Methodologies and applications. *Meta-Radiology*, *100190*. Advance online publication. DOI: 10.1016/j.metrad.2025.100190

Wang, L., & Dai, J. (2025). Understanding Chinese EFL Teachers' Actual Experiences With AI-Mediated Instruction Through the Lens of Expectancy Value Theory. *European Journal of Education*, *60*(4), e70279. Advance online publication. DOI: 10.1111/ejed.70279

Wang, M.-T., Henry, D. A., & Degol, J. L. (2020). Chapter Four - A development-in-sociocultural-context perspective on the multiple pathways to youth's engagement in learning. In Elliot, A. J. (Ed.), Vol. 7, pp. 113–160). Advances in Motivation Science. Elsevier., https://doi.org/10.1016/bs.adms.2019.11.001

Wang, T., Long, T., Mei, A., Li, J., & Zhi, Z. (2026). Fusing Six-Hat thinking with AI: How the Green Hat and ChatGPT Co-Regulate pre-service teachers' instructional design—insights from epistemic network analysis. *Thinking Skills and Creativity*, *59*, 102025. Advance online publication. DOI: 10.1016/j.tsc.2025.102025

Warschauer, M., & Liaw, M.-L. (2011). Emerging technologies for autonomous language learning. *Studies in Self-Access Learning Journal*, *2*(3), 107–118. DOI: 10.37237/020302

Wei, J., Wang, X., Schuurmans, D., Bosma, M., Ichter, B., Xia, F., & Zhou, D. (2022). Chain-of-thought prompting elicits reasoning in large language models. *Advances in Neural Information Processing Systems*, *35*, 24824–24837.

Wei, L., Wang, F., & Wan, L. (2024). AI-Enabled Learning Engagement Assessment for Smart Classrooms : Applications, Trends and Opportunities. *Journal of Intelligence and Knowledge Engineering*, *2*(4), 64–73. http://www.stemmpress.com. DOI: 10.62517/jike.202404411

Westin, A. F. (1967). *Privacy and freedom.* Atheneum. https://scholarlycommons.law.wlu.edu/wlulr/vol25/iss1/20

Williams, J. J. (2014). Internationalizing legal education: A cooperative tool in a globalized world. *Indonesian Journal of International Law*, *12*, 457–473. https://heinonline.org/HOL/Page?handle=hein.journals/indjil12&id=496

Williamson, B. (2017). Big data in education. *Sage (Atlanta, Ga.).*

Williamson, B. (2017). *Big data in education: The digital future of learning, policy and practice.* SAGE Publications Ltd., DOI: 10.4135/9781529714920

Williamson, B., Bayne, S., & Shay, S. (2020). The datafication of teaching in Higher Education: Critical issues and perspectives. *Teaching in Higher Education*, *25*(4), 351–365. DOI: 10.1080/13562517.2020.1748811

Williamson, B., & Eynon, R. (2020). Datafication, AI, and education: Critical concerns. *Learning, Media and Technology*, *45*(3), 202–216.

Williamson, B., & Eynon, R. (2020). Historical threads, missing links, and future directions in AI in education. *Learning, Media and Technology*, *45*(3), 223–235. DOI: 10.1080/17439884.2020.1798995

Williamson, B., Komljenovic, J., & Gulson, K. N. (2023). Introduction: Digitalisation of education in the era of algorithms, automation and artificial intelligence. In Williamson, B., Komljenovic, J., & Gulson, K. N. (Eds.), *World yearbook of education 2024* (pp. 1–19). Routledge., DOI: 10.4324/9781003359722

Williamson, B., & Piattoeva, N. (2020). Objectivity as standardization in data-scientific education policy, technology and governance. In Jarke, J., & Breiter, A. (Eds.), *The Datafication of Education* (pp. 81–93). Routledge., DOI: 10.4324/9780429341359-7

Wilson, J., & Huang, Y. (2024). Validity of automated essay scores for elementary-age English language learners: Evidence of bias? *Assessing Writing*, *60*, 100815. Advance online publication. DOI: 10.1016/j.asw.2024.100815

Wilson, K., Cohen, J., & Erickson, S. (2025). Teacher Candidates' Perceptions of Mixed Reality Simulations: Variations by Task, Support, and Mode of Delivery. *AERA Open*, *11*, 23328584251375064. Advance online publication. DOI: 10.1177/23328584251375064

Wineburg, S., & McGrew, S. (2019). Lateral reading: Reading less and learning more when evaluating digital information. *Teachers College Record*, *121*(11), 1–56. DOI: 10.1177/016146811912101102

Wineburg, S., McGrew, S., Breakstone, J., & Ortega, T. (2016). *Evaluating information online*. Stanford History Education Group.

Winne, P. H., & Hadwin, A. F. (2013). Study: Tracing and supporting self-regulated learning in the Internet. In Azevedo, R., & Aleven, V. (Eds.), *International handbook of metacognition and learning technologies* (pp. 293–308). Springer., DOI: 10.1007/978-1-4419-5546-3_20

Wong, L. H., & Looi, C. K. (2024). Advancing the generative AI in education research agenda: Insights from the Asia-Pacific region. *Asia Pacific Journal of Education*, *44*(1), 1–7. DOI: 10.1080/02188791.2024.2315704

Woodruff, K., Hutson, J., & Arnone, K. (2023). Perceptions and barriers to adopting artificial intelligence in K-12 education: A survey of educators in fifty states. DOI: 10.5772/intechopen.1002741

Woolf, B. P. (2010). *Building intelligent interactive tutors: Student-centered strategies for revolutionizing e-learning*. Morgan Kaufmann.

World Bank. (2021). Remote learning during [*Lessons from today, principles for tomorrow*. World Bank.]. *COVID*, •••, 19.

World Economic Forum. (2023). *Education 4.0: Global framework for future-ready education*. https://www.weforum.org

Wu, J.-Y., Yang, C. C., Liao, C.-H., & Nian, M.-W. (2021). Analytics 2.0 for precision education. *Journal of Educational Technology & Society*, *24*(1), 267–279.

Xue, L., Rashid, A. M., & Ouyang, S. (2024). The Unified Theory of Acceptance and Use of Technology (UTAUT) in Higher Education: A Systematic Review. *SAGE Open*, *14*(1), 21582440241229570. Advance online publication. DOI: 10.1177/21582440241229570

Xu, Z. (2025). Patterns and purposes: A cross-journal analysis of AI tool usage in academic writing [Preprint]. arXiv. https://arxiv.org/abs/2502.00632

Yang, W., Li, H., & Lee, J. C.-K. (2025). Tailoring AI agents for early learning: The Creative Project Approach. *Computers and Education: Artificial Intelligence*, *9*, 100473. Advance online publication. DOI: 10.1016/j.caeai.2025.100473

Yu, L., & Yu, Z. (2023). Qualitative and quantitative analyses of artificial intelligence ethics in education using VOSviewer and CitNetExplorer. *Frontiers in Psychology*, *14*, 1–14. DOI: 10.3389/fpsyg.2023.1061778 PMID: 36968737

Zaghir, J., Naguib, M., Bjelogrlic, M., Névéol, A., Tannier, X., & Lovis, C. (2024). Prompt engineering paradigms for medical applications: A scoping review. *Journal of Medical Internet Research*, *26*, e60501. DOI: 10.2196/60501 PMID: 39255030

Zawacki-Richter, O., Marín, V. I., Bond, M., & Gouverneur, F. (2019). Systematic review of research on artificial intelligence applications in higher education–where are the educators? *International Journal of Educational Technology in Higher Education*, *16*(1), 1–27. DOI: 10.1186/s41239-019-0171-0

Zeide, E. (2019). Artificial intelligence in higher education: Applications, promise and perils, and ethical questions. *EDUCAUSE Review*, *54*(3), 1–11. https://ssrn.com/abstract=4320049

Zhai, C., Wibowo, S., & Li, L. D. (2024). The effects of over-reliance on AI dialogue systems on students' cognitive abilities: a systematic review. Smart learning environments, 11(1), 28. DOI: 10.1186/s40561-024-00316-7

Zhai, X., Chu, X., Chai, C. S., Jong, M. S. Y., Istenic, A., Spector, M., Liu, J.-B., Yuan, J., & Li, Y. (2021). A review of artificial intelligence (AI) in education from 2010 to 2020. *Complexity*, *2021*(1), 1–18. DOI: 10.1155/2021/8812542

Zhang, C., Liu, Z., Aravind, B. R., & Hariharasudan, A. (2024). Synergizing language learning: SmallTalk AI In industry 4.0 and Education 4.0. *PeerJ. Computer Science*, *10*, 1–26. DOI: 10.7717/peerj-cs.1843 PMID: 38435575

Zhang, C., Schießl, J., Plößl, L., Hofmann, F., & Gläser-Zikuda, M. (2023). Acceptance of artificial intelligence among pre-service teachers: A multigroup analysis. *International Journal of Educational Technology in Higher Education*, *20*(1), 49. DOI: 10.1186/s41239-023-00420-7 PMID: 36743849

Zhang, D., Landmark, L., Reber, A., Hsu, H., Kwok, O., & Benz, M. (2010). University faculty knowledge, beliefs, and practices in providing reasonable accommodations to students with disabilities. *Remedial and Special Education*, *31*(4), 276–286. DOI: 10.1177/0741932509338348

Zhang, J. J., Wang, Y. W., Ruan, Q., & Yang, Y. (2024). Digital tourism interpretation content quality: A comparison between AI-generated content and professional-generated content. *Tourism Management Perspectives*, *53*, 101279. Advance online publication. DOI: 10.1016/j.tmp.2024.101279

Zhang, J., & Zhang, Z. (2024). AI in teacher education: Unlocking new dimensions in teaching support, inclusive learning, and digital literacy. *Journal of Computer Assisted Learning*, *40*(4), 1871–1885. DOI: 10.1111/jcal.12988

Zhang, S., Ganapathy Prasad, P., & Schroeder, N. L. (2025). Learning About AI: A Systematic Review of Reviews on AI Literacy. *Journal of Educational Computing Research*, *63*(5), 1292–1322. DOI: 10.1177/07356331251342081

Zimmerman, B. J. (2002). Becoming a self-regulated learner: An overview. *Theory into Practice*, *41*(2), 64–70. DOI: 10.1207/s15430421tip4102_2

Zipf, S., Wu, C., & Petricini, T. (2025). Using the information inequity framework to study GenAI equity: analysis of educational perspectives. *Information Research an international electronic journal, 30*(iConf), 533-547. DOI: 10.47989/ir30iConf47284

Zouhaier, S. (2023). The impact of artificial intelligence on higher education: An empirical study. *European Journal of Educational Sciences*, *10*(1), 17–33. https://www.cccol.com/scarch/articlc-dctail?id=1111750

Zuboff, S. (2019). Surveillance capitalism and the challenge of collective action. *New Labor Forum*, *28*(1), 10–29. DOI: 10.1177/1095796018819461

Zuboff, S. (2019). *The age of surveillance capitalism*. PublicAffairs.

About the Contributors

Harish C. Chandan is an independent Researcher in Business. He retired from Argosy University as a Professor of Business at Argosy University, Atlanta. He was interim chair of the business program in 2011. He received the President's award for excellence in teaching in 2007, 2008 and 2009. His teaching philosophy is grounded in the learner needs and life-long learning. His research interests include research methods, leadership, marketing, organizational behavior and social psychology. He has edited 15 Business reference books, published 23 peer-reviewed articles in business journals and 25 chapters in business reference books. Dr. Chandan has presented conference papers at Academy of Management, International Academy of Business and Management, Southeast Association of Information Systems, and Academy of International Business. Prior to joining Argosy, Dr. Chandan managed Optical Fiber and Cable Product Qualification lab. for Lucent Technologies, Bell Laboratories.

Supriya Srivastava is currently serving as faculty in the department of Management Sciences and Liberal Arts at Shoolini University, Himachal Pradesh. She earned her Ph.D. from the University of Lucknow, India, and holds dual postgraduate degrees: an M.A. in Sociology from the University of Lucknow and an MBA in Human Resource Management from Punjab Technical University (PTU), Punjab. Prior to her postgraduate studies, she completed her undergraduate education in Economics and Sociology from Isabella Thoburn (IT) College, University of Lucknow. In addition to her formal degrees, Dr. Srivastava has pursued multiple postgraduate diplomas in Rural Development, Disaster Management, Corporate Social Responsibility, and Yoga Science, which underscore her commitment to interdisciplinary learning and application. With over fourteen years of academic and research experience, she has cultivated expertise at the intersection of Social Sciences and Management. Her research interests are wide-ranging and include social development, human resource management, inclusive development, disaster management, gender studies, religion, and spirituality. She has published extensively in reputed national and international journals, authored book chapters, and contributed to scholarly discourse through her academic writings and copyrighted works. Dr. Srivastava is also the author of two significant books: Women-led Development and Gender Budgeting: Indian Perspective and Gender Equality and Sustainable Development: Issues and Challenges, Serial Publications, New Delhi. These works reflect her deep engagement with contemporary debates in gender studies, policy frameworks, and sustainable development. Biodata(CV)_Supriya.docx

***

Rafiza Abdul Razak is the former Head of the Department of Curriculum and Instructional Technology, Faculty of Education, Universiti Malaya. She holds a Ph.D. in Instructional Technology from the International Islamic University Malaysia. Committed to educational innovation, she led the establishment of facilities such as the InTechPro Studio and collaborated with Microsoft to enhance teacher training. She has led multiple international research projects, registered 81 innovations (including patents and copyrights), published in WoS and Scopus journals, and received recognitions such as the Microsoft Master Trainer award. She was featured in Successful People in Malaysia. She can be reached via email at: rafiza@um.edu.my.

Hana An L. Alvarado is a pre-service mathematics teacher at Mindanao State University–Tawi-Tawi College of Technology and Oceanography (MSU-TCTO), Tawi-Tawi, Philippines, and an aspiring scholar in mathematics education. Her interests include ethnomathematics, STEM education, multilingual and culturally responsive pedagogy, and the integration of artificial intelligence in teaching and learning. She is committed to advancing innovative and inclusive practices that connect mathematics to culture, language, and real-life contexts, aiming to promote equitable and meaningful learning for diverse student populations.

Sovannaroth Chheang earned her bachelor's degree in English from Build Bright University, Phnom Penh, in 2016, where she built a solid foundation in language studies, communication, and pedagogy. She began her teaching career in 2013 as a Tutor at the Kindergarten Association, conducting both part-time and full-time English programs. Since 2018, she has served as a Teacher of English and General Assistant at Sovanna Elton Foreign Language School. Through these roles, she has developed broad expertise in classroom management, language instruction, curriculum design, and student engagement, supporting the school's mission of advancing foreign language learning. Ms. Chheang's academic interests center on pursuing a master's degree in English education or related fields within the humanities and social sciences. Passionate about integrating global research methodologies into her practice, she aims to enhance pedagogy, foster classroom innovation, and promote effective, research-informed teaching. Her commitment lies in bridging academic research with real-world practice to advance English education in Cambodia and beyond.

Nurul-Ainie S. Eldani is a licensed professional teacher and a graduate of Master of Education and is currently pursuing her second master's in Master of Science Education in General Science (MSciEd-General Science). She obtained her undergraduate degree, a Bachelor of Secondary Education major in Physical Science/ Physics, at Western Mindanao State University in 2011. She handled courses such as those in both professional education and science subjects at the said university.

Hok Chheangkhy is a lecturer at the Department of Khmer Literature, University of Heng Samrin Thbongkhmum. With a strong dedication to the study and preservation of Khmer language, literature, and culture, he has contributed to advancing literary education and research in Cambodia. His academic interests include classical and modern Khmer literature, linguistic analysis, and cultural studies. Mr. Chheangkhy is passionate about inspiring students to explore Cambodia's rich literary heritage and promoting the value of Khmer identity through education. In addition to teaching, he actively engages in academic writing and community cultural initiatives, aiming to strengthen the role of literature in contemporary Cambodian society.

Sovanna Huot is a scholar, currently pursuing a Ph.D. in Political Science at the University of Delhi, India, under a prestigious ICCR scholarship (2022). He serves as the Vice Principal of a government-recognized high school in Cambodia, where he actively leads academic innovation and institutional development. Sovanna's academic journey reflects a breadth of interdisciplinary expertise. He completed a two-year teacher training program (2010–2012) and holds bachelor's degrees in English and Educational Administration. His postgraduate achievements include master's degrees in law and TEFL, both earned through competitive scholarship programs, and a Master of Education in School Leadership with a specialization in Upper Secondary School Principalship from the National Institute of Education, Phnom Penh (2021). His research centers on educational reform, digital pedagogy, and the intersection of policy and practice in glonacal (global–national–local) contexts. With a growing portfolio of peer-reviewed publications, he contributes actively to the fields of political science and education. His scholarly work is indexed in Scopus (Author ID: 59316244400).

Sherlyn A. Iralan is a pre-service mathematics teacher and an undergraduate student pursuing a Bachelor of Secondary Education major in Mathematics at Mindanao State University–Tawi-Tawi College of Technology and Oceanography (MSU-TCTO), Philippines. Her research interests include mathematics education, and artificial intelligence in education.

Potchong M. Jackaria currently holds a rank of Associate Professor 3 under the Science and Mathematics Department of the College of Education, Mindanao State University Tawi-Tawi, College of Technology and Oceanography in Tawi-Tawi, Philippines. Prior to working at MSU, he had an extensive experience teaching in different public schools handling elementary level mathematics and later as school head. Asst. Prof. Jackaria obtained his master degree in Education in Administration and Supervision from MSU Tawi-Tawi College of Technology and Oceanography and a Master of Science Education Major in Mathematics from MSU-Iligan Institute of Technology. He was involved in teachers' training and is interested in research areas including mathematics teaching, technology in education, teachers professional development, and education policy.

Amirrudin Kamsin is an Associate Professor and the Head of the Department of Computer System and Technology, Faculty of Computer Science and Information Technology, Universiti Malaya. He holds a Ph.D. in Human-Computer Interaction from University College London. He has published over 120 research papers in SCI- and Scopus-indexed journals, with more than 10 of his articles cited over 100 times. He has secured research grants totaling over RM 2 million. His research interests include Human-Computer Interaction, Virtual Reality, Multimedia, Personal Task Management, and Personal Time Management. He can be reached via email at: amir@um.edu.my.

Sovanna Loch is a prominent figure at the Cambodian Monastery Rajgir, serving as a deputy in charge. He is also a PhD research scholar and ICCR Fellow in the Dept. of English at Nava Nalanda Mahavihara (Deemed University), an institution under the Ministry of Culture, Govt. of India. His academic background includes a bachelor's degree in Pāli and a master's in English, both obtained from NNM. His research primarily focuses on Cambodian classical and Buddhist English literature.

Kimyut Phin is a diligent and committed educator and emerging scholar. He is currently pursuing a Ph.D. in English at the University of Delhi, India. He holds bachelor's and master's degrees in English (TEFL and TESOL). He serves as the Director of the Institute of Foreign Languages of the University of Heng Samrin Thbongkhmum, Cambodia. He actively engages with academic management, leadership, innovation, institutional development, curriculum development, instructional design, assessment, projects, and research. He has involved in many Erasmus+ projects, such as the REACT, SICA, BALANCE, IND4.0, and UNICATION projects. He has also had teaching experiences in linguistics, applied linguistics, teaching methodology, second language acquisition, grammar for writing, academic writing skills, global studies, core English, and literature studies for years. Further, he has experience in lesson planning, classroom management, assessment and evaluation, and technology for teaching and learning. His research centers on teaching and learning approaches and methods, English language education, education quality, educational reform, digital pedagogy, literary theory and criticism, and learning motivation in Cambodia and beyond.

Monica Mae R. Pon is a college science instructor specializing in biology, and science education. She is currently pursuing a graduate degree in Genetics. Her interests include plant hybridization, molecular biology, conservation biology, and ecology. She is actively involved in research, instruction, and community engagement.

Jameel Qurashi pursued his Bachelors in Computer Applications from University of Kashmir in 2011 and Master in Computer Applications from University of Kashmir in year 2014. He was awarded with Ph.D. Degree in 2020 from Department of Computer and System Sciences, Jaipur National University, Jaipur. He is currently working as Assistant Professor in cluster University Srinagar. The Previous work organizations include Poornima University, Chandigarh University, JNU Jaipur, Kashmir University, RBL Bank and Dynacode. He was granted Quarterly Franklin Membership from London Journals United kingdoms in 2019 and awarded with Young Researcher award 2020 by INSC Bangalore. His Publications include various research papers in reputed international, national journals and conferences including IEEE. He has also contributed in writing book chapters published by CRC Press IN TAYLOR & FRANCIS, Rout and ledge and published 4 patents in IPR. The main research work focuses on Software Security, NFR Security, Hybrid Architectural security and Privacy, Algorithmic analysis, IoT and Computational Intelligence based education. He has guided Masters students and currently supervising 5 Ph.D. Candidates. Thereby concluding 8 years of Research Experience.

Binastya Anggara Sekti has been a lecturer at the Faculty of Computer Science, Esa Unggul University, Jakarta, since 2016. He is actively involved in the Artificial Intelligence and Information Security Study Group. He holds a Bachelor's degree in Informatics Engineering from the Bandung Institute of Technology and a Master's degree in Information Systems Management from Trisakti University, Jakarta. Prior to entering academia, he accumulated over 25 years of professional experience as an IT practitioner in various companies across Jakarta. His work focused on developing data centers for internet service providers and delivering IT solutions for the manufacturing and oil & gas sectors. His research interests include artificial intelligence, cybersecurity, and the development of IT infrastructure.

Bagas Yoas Sibagariang is an IT professional with an academic background in Information Systems from Esa Unggul University, Jakarta, Indonesia. His key interests include information technology, data analysis, and digital innovation. He has been actively involved in research and collaborative projects focusing on system development, data management, and the implementation of technology-driven solutions to support organizational efficiency. His work reflects strong analytical thinking, technical competence, and a commitment to continuous learning. Bagas is particularly interested in leveraging data analytics and information systems to enhance decision-making processes and business performance. He continues to develop his expertise in emerging technologies and contributes to research initiatives aimed at advancing digital transformation in both academic and professional environments.

Amrik Singh is working as Professor and HOD in the School of Hotel Management and Tourism at Lovely Professional University, Punjab, India. He obtained his Ph.D. degree in Hotel Management from Kurukshetra University, Haryana, India. He has published 115 Scopus-indexed publications. He has published 12 patents, and 01 patent has been granted in the inter-disciplinary domain. Dr. Amrik Singh participated and acted as a resource person in various national and international conferences, seminars, research workshops, and industry talks. He has published 20 books with IGI Global Publication, Emerald Publication, Bentham Publication, Nova Publication etc., on trending areas such as Food waste, Artificial Intelligence, Mountain Tourism, Virtual tourism, Healthcare Tourism, Guest behavior in tourism and hospitality. His area of research interest are Accommodation management, sustainability, Green practices, Human Resource Management in Hospitality, Artificial Intelligence, AR VR in hospitality, Hotel pricing, Employee Disability, Work life balance, women empowerment etc. He is currently guiding 8 Ph.D. scholars, and 5 Ph.D. scholars have been awarded Ph.D.

Mohammed Umair is a seasoned academic and corporate professional with over 16 years of teaching experience and 5 years in the corporate sector. Currently serving as a senior faculty member at the School of Business, St. Joseph's University, Bangalore, he specializes in Finance and Taxation for undergraduate, postgraduate, and MBA Executive programmes. Drawing from his professional background with leading MNCs, he seamlessly integrates industry insights into academia. Recognized for his student-centric approach, he has authored multiple textbooks, published research in journals, and presented at international conferences. He holds a Doctorate in Behavioural Finance. He has also contributed to academic leadership as Dean, Strategic Advisor, and member of key restructuring, recruitment, and admissions committees. He has also chaired curriculum committees, supported quality initiatives, served on statutory boards, and handled various student support an development roles.

Seema Yadav has academic qualifications of M. Sc. (Chemistry), M Ed (RIE), UGC-NET, and PhD in Education. Presently she is working as an Assistant Professor, in the Department of Education at The Bhopal School of Education, Bhopal. She has almost 18 years of teaching experience. Her areas of specialization are educational psychology, environmental education, digital learning, and curriculum development.

Longfa Yuan is a Ph.D. student at the Institute for Advanced Studies, Universiti Malaya (UM). He holds a bachelor's degree in E-Commerce and has an academic background in Computer Science, and a master's degree in Modern Educational Technology. His academic background and research focus lie at the intersection of Artificial Intelligence and Education. He has a strong interest in the application of AI in educational contexts and has published several papers in this area, offering unique insights and perspectives. His research interests include Educational Science, Artificial Intelligence in Education, and E-Commerce. He can be contacted via email at: 22104099@siswa.um.edu.my.

Index

A

C

D

E

G

H

I

L

M

P

R

S

T

www.ingramcontent.com/pod-product-compliance
Ingram Content Group UK Ltd.
Pitfield, Milton Keynes, MK11 3LW, UK
UKHW050843101026
15624UKWH00018B/483

9 798337 380278